# Elements of
# Language

## Third Course

**Lee Odell**

**Richard Vacca**

**Renée Hobbs**

Grammar, Usage, and Mechanics
Instructional Framework by

**John E. Warriner**

## HOLT, RINEHART AND WINSTON
### A Harcourt Education Company

**Austin** • Orlando • Chicago • New York • Toronto • London • San Diego

## STAFF CREDITS

### EDITORIAL

**Executive Editor**
Robert R. Hoyt

**Program Editor**
Kathryn Rogers

**Project Editors**
Randy Dickson
Eric Estlund
Ann Michelle Gibson

**Copyediting**
Michael Neibergall, *Copyediting Manager;* Mary Malone, *Copyediting Supervisor;* Elizabeth Dickson, *Senior Copyeditor;* Christine Altgelt, Emily Force, Julia Thomas Hu, *Copyeditors*

**Project Administration**
Marie Price, *Managing Editor;* Lori De La Garza, *Associate Managing Editor;* Christine Degollado, Janet Jenkins, *Editorial Coordinators*

### DESIGN

**Book Design**
Joe Melomo, *Design Director;* Candace Moore, *Senior Designer;* Rina May Ouellette, *Design Associate*

**Image Acquisitions**
Curtis Riker, *Director;* Jeannie Taylor, *Photo Research Supervisor;* Rick Benavides, *Photo Researcher;* Sam Dudgeon, *Senior Staff Photographer;* Victoria Smith, *Staff Photographer;* Lauren Eischen, *Photography Specialist*

**Media Design**
Richard Metzger, *Design Director*

**Cover Design**
Bill Smith Studio

### EDITORIAL PERMISSIONS
Susan Lowrance

### PRODUCTION
Carol Trammel, *Production Manager;* Belinda Barbosa Lopez, Michael Roche, *Senior Production Coordinators*

### MANUFACTURING
Shirley Cantrell, *Manufacturing Supervisor;* Mark McDonald, *Inventory Analyst;* Amy Borseth, *Manufacturing Coordinator*

**LEE ODELL** helped establish the pedagogical framework for the composition strand of *Elements of Language.* In addition, he guided the development of the scope and sequence and pedagogical design of the Writing Workshops. Dr. Odell is Professor of Composition Theory and Research and, since 1996, Director of the Writing Program at Rensselaer Polytechnic Institute. He began his career teaching English in middle and high schools. More recently he has worked with teachers in grades K–12 to establish a program that involves students from all disciplines in writing across the curriculum and for communities outside their classrooms. Dr. Odell's most recent book (with Charles R. Cooper) is *Evaluating Writing: The Role of Teachers' Knowledge about Text, Learning, and Culture* (1999). Dr. Odell is Past Chair of the Conference on College Composition and Communication and of the NCTE's Assembly for Research.

**RENÉE HOBBS** helped develop the theoretical framework for the viewing and representing strand of *Elements of Language.* She guided the development of the scope and sequence; served as the authority on terminology, definitions, and pedagogy; and directed the planning for the video series. Dr. Hobbs is Associate Professor of Communication at Babson College in Wellesley, Massachusetts, and Director of the Media Literacy Project. Active in the field of media education, Dr. Hobbs has served in the following capacities: Director of the Institute on Media Education, Harvard Graduate School of Education; Director of the "Know TV" Project, Discovery Networks and Time Warner Cable; and Board Member, The New York Times Newspaper in Education Program. She works actively in staff development in school districts nationwide. Dr. Hobbs has contributed articles and chapters on media, technology, and education to many publications.

**RICHARD VACCA** helped establish the conceptual basis for the reading strand of *Elements of Language.* In addition, he guided the development of the pedagogical design and the scope and sequence of skills in the Reading Workshops. Dr. Vacca is Professor of Education at Kent State University. He recently completed a term as the forty-second President of the International Reading Association. Originally a middle school and high school teacher, Dr. Vacca served as the project director of the Cleveland Writing Demonstration Project for several years. He is the co-author of *Content Area Reading; Reading and Learning to Read;* and articles and chapters related to adolescents' literacy development. In 1989, Dr. Vacca received the College Reading Association's A. B. Herr Award for Outstanding Contributions to Reading Education. Currently, he is co-chair of the IRA's Commission on Adolescent Literacy.

**JOHN E. WARRINER** was a high school English teacher when he developed the original organizational structure for his classic *English Grammar and Composition* series. The approach pioneered by Mr. Warriner was distinctive, and the editorial staff of Holt, Rinehart and Winston has worked diligently to retain the unique qualities of his pedagogy. For the same reason, HRW continues to credit Mr. Warriner as an author of *Elements of Language* in recognition of his groundbreaking work. John Warriner also co-authored the *English Workshop* series and was editor of *Short Stories: Characters in Conflict.* Throughout his career, however, teaching remained Mr. Warriner's major interest, and he taught for thirty-two years in junior and senior high schools and in college.

The following teachers and students worked with HRW's editorial staff to provide models of student writing for the book.

*Teachers*

**Priscilla Cheney**
Troy High School
Fullerton, California

**Kay Hannum**
Hobbs High School
Hobbs, New Mexico

**Steven Heffner**
Conrad Weiser High School
Robesonia, Pennsylvania

**Dianna Hubbard**
South Garland High School
Garland, Texas

**Vickie H. Smith**
William G. Enloe High School
Raleigh, North Carolina

*Students*

**Mayra Deloa**
South Garland High School
Garland, Texas

**Cheryl Flugan**
Belson High School
Winston, Florida

**Amy E. Hofmann**
Conrad Weiser High School
Robesonia, Pennsylvania

**Anthony King**
Morrison Christian Academy
Taichung, Taiwan

**Shanessa McClain**
Hobbs High School
Hobbs, New Mexico

**Amar Patel**
Troy High School
Fullerton, California

**Matthew Weber**
McNeil High School
Round Rock, Texas

**Blake Wynia**
William G. Enloe High School
Raleigh, North Carolina

The following teachers participated in the pre-publication field test or review of prototype materials for the *Elements of Language* series.

**Nadene Adams**
Robert Gray Middle School
Portland, Oregon

**Carol Alves**
Apopka High School
Apopka, Florida

**Susan Atkinson**
O. P. Norman Junior High School
Kaufman, Texas

**Sheryl L. Babione**
Fremont Ross High School
Fremont, Ohio

**Jane Baker**
Elkins High School
Missouri City, Texas

**Martha Barnard**
Scarborough High School
Houston, Texas

**Jennifer S. Barr**
James Bowie High School
Austin, Texas

**Leslie Benefield**
Reed Middle School
Duncanville, Texas

**Gina Birdsall**
Irving High School
Irving, Texas

**Sara J. Brennan**
Murchison Middle School
Austin, Texas

**Janelle Brinck**
Leander Middle School
Leander, Texas

**Geraldine K. Brooks**
William B. Travis High School
Austin, Texas

**Peter J. Caron**
Cumberland Middle School
Cumberland, Rhode Island

**Patty Cave**
O. P. Norman Junior High School
Kaufman, Texas

**Mary Cathyrne Coe**
Pocatello High School
Pocatello, Idaho

*Continued*

**Geri-Lee DeGennaro**
Tarpon Springs High School
Tarpon Springs, Florida

**Karen Dendy**
Stephen F. Austin Middle School
Irving, Texas

**Dianne Franz**
Tarpon Springs Middle School
Tarpon Springs, Florida

**Doris Frazier**
East Millbrook Magnet Middle
    School
Raleigh, North Carolina

**Shayne G. Goodrum**
C. E. Jordan High School
Durham, North Carolina

**Bonnie L. Hall**
St. Ann School
Lansing, Illinois

**Doris Ann Hall**
Forest Meadow Junior High
    School
Dallas, Texas

**James M. Harris**
Mayfield High School
Mayfield Village, Ohio

**Lynne Hoover**
Fremont Ross High School
Fremont, Ohio

**Patricia A. Humphreys**
James Bowie High School
Austin, Texas

**Jennifer L. Jones**
Oliver Wendell Holmes Middle
    School
Dallas, Texas

**Kathryn R. Jones**
Murchison Middle School
Austin, Texas

**Bonnie Just**
Narbonne High School
Harbor City, California

**Vincent Kimball**
Patterson High School #405
Baltimore, Maryland

**Nancy C. Long**
MacArthur High School
Houston, Texas

**Carol M. Mackey**
Ft. Lauderdale Christian School
Ft. Lauderdale, Florida

**Jan Jennings McCown**
Johnston High School
Austin, Texas

**Alice Kelly McCurdy**
Rusk Middle School
Dallas, Texas

**Elizabeth Morris**
Northshore High School
Slidell, Louisiana

**Victoria Reis**
Western High School
Ft. Lauderdale, Florida

**Dean Richardson**
MacArthur High School
Houston, Texas

**Susan M. Rogers**
Freedom High School
Morganton, North Carolina

**Sammy Rusk**
North Mesquite High School
Mesquite, Texas

**Carole B. San Miguel**
James Bowie High School
Austin, Texas

**Jane Saunders**
William B. Travis High School
Austin, Texas

**Gina Sawyer**
Reed Middle School
Duncanville, Texas

**Laura R. Schauermann**
MacArthur High School
Houston, Texas

**Stephen Shearer**
MacArthur High School
Houston, Texas

**Elizabeth Curry Smith**
Tarpon Springs High School
Tarpon Springs, Florida

**Jeannette M. Spain**
Stephen F. Austin High School
Sugar Land, Texas

**Carrie Speer**
Northshore High School
Slidell, Louisiana

**Trina Steffes**
MacArthur High School
Houston, Texas

**Andrea G. Freirich Stewart**
Freedom High School
Morganton, North Carolina

**Diana O. Torres**
Johnston High School
Austin, Texas

**Janice Voorhees**
Whitesboro High School
Marcy, New York

**Ann E. Walsh**
Bedichek Middle School
Austin, Texas

**Mary Jane Warden**
Onahan School
Chicago, Illinois

**Beth Westbrook**
Covington Middle School
Austin, Texas

**Char-Lene Reinhart Wilkins**
Morenci Area High School
Morenci, Michigan

# CONTENTS IN BRIEF

# CONTENTS

**CHAPTER**

**1**

# Creating a Word-Picture . . . . . 16

**Informational Text**

Narration/
Description

# CHAPTER 2

**Narration/
Description**

## Expressing Your Thoughts .... 50

# Exploring Similarities and Differences

# Reviewing Television ............ 282

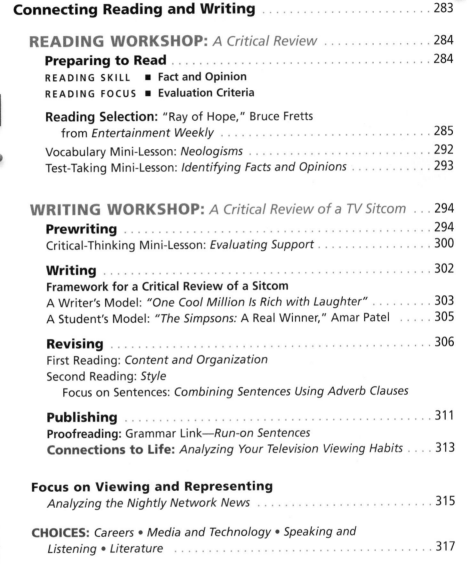

**Informational Text**

Persuasion

# The Parts of a Sentence
**CHAPTER**

*Subject, Predicate, Complement* . . . . . . . . . . . . . . . . . . . . **412**

13

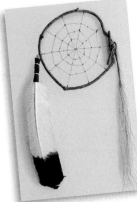

# The Phrase

# The Clause

# Agreement

**CHAPTER**

**16**

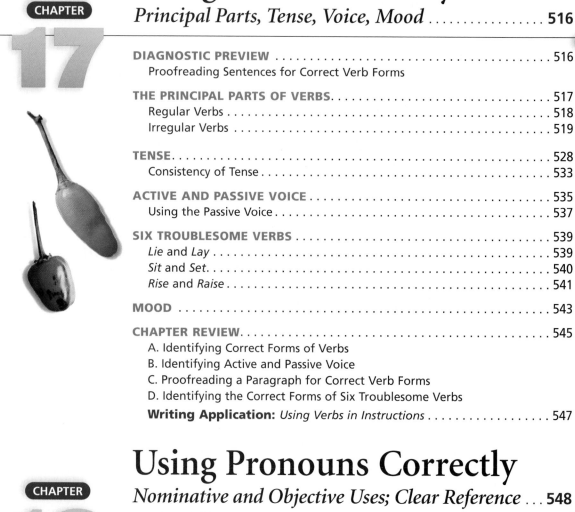

# Using Verbs Correctly

# Using Pronouns Correctly

# Using Modifiers Correctly
**CHAPTER**
## *Comparison and Placement* . . . . . . . . . . . . . . . . . . . . . . **570**

# A Glossary of Usage

# Capital Letters

# Punctuation

*End Marks, Abbreviations, and Commas* . . . . . . . . . . **636**

CHAPTER

**22**

The Granger Collection, New York.

# Punctuation

# Punctuation

# Punctuation

# Punctuation

# MODELS

# MODELS

- Jack London, **"To Build a Fire"**
- Martina Navratilova with George Vecsey, *Martina*
- Douglas Preston, **"The Granddaddy of the Nation's Trails Began in Mexico"**
- Donald and Lillian Stokes, *The Bird Feeder Book*
- Edwin Way Teale, **"The Death of a Tree"**

STUDENT MODELS →

- Mayra Deloa, **"The Use of Symbolism in Dorothy Parker's 'Solace'"**
- Cheryl Flugan, **"What Are the Effects of Running?"**
- Amy E. Hoffman, **"The Call of the Hornet"**
- Anthony King, **"Censored!"**
- Shanessa McClain, **"South Padre Island"**
- Amar Patel, **"The Simpsons: A Real Winner"**
- Matthew Weber, **"CDs and Cassettes, Not So Similar"**
- Blake Wynia, **"Carelessness"**

# STUDENT'S OVERVIEW

*Elements of Language* is divided into four major parts.

## PART 1  Communications

This section ties together the essential skills and strategies you use in all types of communication—reading, writing, listening, speaking, viewing, and representing.

**Reading Workshops**  In these workshops, you read an article, a story, an editorial—a real-life example of a type of writing you will later compose on your own. In addition, these workshops help you practice the reading process through

- a Reading Skill and Reading Focus specific to each type of writing,
- Vocabulary Mini-Lessons to help you understand unfamiliar words, and
- Test-Taking Mini-Lessons targeting common reading objectives

**Writing Workshops**  In these workshops, you brainstorm ideas and use the writing process to produce your own article, story, editorial—and more. These workshops also include

- Writing and Critical-Thinking Mini-Lessons to help you master important aspects of each type of writing
- an organizational framework and models to guide your writing
- evaluation charts with concrete steps for revising
- Connections to Literature and Connections to Life, activities that extend writing workshop skills and concepts to other areas of your life
- Test-Taking Mini-Lessons to help you respond to writing prompts for tests

**Focus on Speaking and Listening**
**Focus on Viewing and Representing**

This is your chance to sharpen your skills in presenting your ideas visually and orally and to learn how to take a more critical view of what you hear and see.

## PART 2   Sentences and Paragraphs

Learn to construct clear and effective sentences and paragraphs—what parts to include, how to organize ideas, and how to write these essential parts of compositions with style.

## PART 3   Grammar, Usage, and Mechanics

These are the basics that will help you make your writing correct and polished.

**Grammar**   Discover the structure of language—the words, phrases, and clauses that are the building blocks of sentences.

**Usage**   Learn the rules that govern how language is used in various social situations, including standard versus nonstandard and formal versus informal English.

**Mechanics**   Master the nuts and bolts of correct written English, including capitalization, punctuation, and spelling.

## PART 4   Quick Reference Handbook

Use this handy guide any time you need concise tips to help you communicate more effectively—whether you need to find information in a variety of media, make sense of what you read, prepare for tests, or present your ideas in a published document, a speech, or a visual.

### *Elements of Language* on the Internet

Put the communication strategies in *Elements of Language* to work by logging on to the Internet. At the *Elements of Language* Internet site, you can dissect the prose of professional writers, crack the codes of the advertising industry, and find out how your communication skills can help you in the real world.

As you move through *Elements of Language,* you will find the best online resources at **go.hrw.com.**

# The Reading and Writing Processes

D o these situations sound familiar? While reading, you suddenly realize you have read the same sentences several times without gaining any meaning from them. While writing, you stare at the single sentence you have written, unable to think of anything else to write. When you find yourself stuck, step back and look at the processes of reading and writing.

## Reading

The reading you do in school requires you to think critically about information and ideas. In order to get the most from a text, prepare your mind for the task before you read, use effective strategies while you read, and take time to process the information after you read.

**TIP** Reading and writing are both recursive processes—that is, you can return to earlier steps when needed. For example, you might make new predictions while you are reading a text or you might develop additional support for ideas when you are revising a piece of writing.

- **Before Reading** Get your mind in gear by considering your purpose for reading a particular piece of writing and by thinking about what you already know about the topic. Preview the text by skimming a bit and considering headings, graphics, and other features. Use this information to predict what the text will discuss and how challenging it will be to read.

- **While Reading** As you read, figure out the writer's point about the topic. Notice how the text is organized (by cause and effect or in order of importance, for example) to help you find support for that point. Connect the ideas to your own experiences when you can. If you get confused, slow down, re-read, or jot ideas in a graphic organizer.

- **After Reading** Confirm and extend your understanding of the text. Draw conclusions about the writer's point of view, and evaluate how well the writer communicated the message. Use ideas in the text to create a piece of art, to read more on a related topic, or to solve a problem.

## Writing

A perfect text seldom springs fully formed from your mind; instead, you must plan your text before you write and work to improve it after drafting.

- **Before Writing** First, choose a topic and a form of writing, such as a poem or an editorial. Decide who your readers will be and what you want the text to accomplish. Develop ideas based on your knowledge and on research. Organize the ideas, and jot down your main point.

- **While Writing** Grab attention and provide background information in an introduction. Elaborate your ideas to support your point, and organize them clearly. Then, wrap things up with a conclusion.

- **After Writing** To improve a draft, evaluate how clearly you expressed your ideas. Ask a peer to suggest areas that need work. Then, revise. Proofread to correct any mistakes. Share your finished work with others, and reflect on what you learned.

You may have noticed that the reading and writing processes involve similar strategies. The chart below summarizes these similarities.

## The Reading and Writing Processes

### Reading

### Writing

**— Before —**

| Reading | Writing |
|---|---|
| Determine your purpose for reading. | Identify your writing purpose and your audience. |
| Consider what you already know about the topic. | Draw upon what you know about the topic, and do research to find out more. |
| Preview the text to make predictions about what it will include. | Make notes or an outline to plan what the text will include. |

**— While —**

| Reading | Writing |
|---|---|
| Figure out the writer's main ideas. | Express your main ideas clearly. |
| Look for support for the main ideas. | Support them with details, facts, examples, or anecdotes. |
| Notice how the ideas in the text are organized. | Follow prewriting notes or an outline to organize your text so readers can easily follow your ideas. |

**— After —**

| Reading | Writing |
|---|---|
| Evaluate the text to decide how accurate it is and its overall quality. | Evaluate and revise your text. Use peer editors' comments to help improve your work. |
| Relate what you have read to the world around you by creating something, reading further, or applying ideas. | Relate your writing to the world around you by publishing it. |
| Reflect on what you have read. | Reflect on what you have written. |

The Reading and Writing Workshops in this book provide valuable practice for strategies that will help you effectively use these related processes.

# Communications

# Taking Tests: Strategies and Practice

# Taking Reading Tests

Every so often (maybe once a year), you'll face a national or statewide standardized test of reading and writing. A standardized reading test contains brief **reading passages** followed by several **multiple-choice questions** and sometimes an open-ended **essay question**. The testmakers are out to test every reading skill you are supposed to have learned by now.

## THINKING IT THROUGH     Reading Test Strategies

▶ **STEP 1** **Pace yourself.** Skim the test to see how many questions there are, and estimate how long you can spend on each question. Check every five or ten minutes to see if you need to work faster.

▶ **STEP 2** **Read carefully.** Read the directions and any introduction to the reading passage. Then, focus your complete attention on the passage. If you can mark the test booklet, underline key words.

▶ **STEP 3** **Make sure you understand the question.** Beware of words like *not* and *except,* which direct you to choose an answer that is false or opposite in some way. Watch out also for distracters— answers that are true but don't answer the question that's being asked. Never choose an answer until you've read *all* of the answers.

▶ **STEP 4** **Make educated guesses.** Eliminate answers you know are wrong. Then, make an inference, not a random guess. Remember that your answer must depend entirely on information in the reading passage—not on any prior knowledge you may have about the topic.

▶ **STEP 5** **Keep on going.** Don't get stuck on a difficult question. Skip questions that baffle you and return to them later if you have time.

▶ **STEP 6** **Watch your bubbles.** Make sure you neatly fill in the answer you intend. If you skip a question, don't lose your place.

▶ **STEP 7** **Check your work.** When you finish, try answering questions you skipped. Check your answers carefully, and erase any stray marks.

**TIP** Know how the test is scored. If no points are taken off for wrong answers, then answer every question. If wrong answers count against you, answer only the questions you know and those you can answer with an educated guess.

Read the following passages carefully. Then, choose the **best** answer to each question.

Will allowing humans to interact with these animals help or hurt this endangered species?

# Swimming with Manatees

by Monica Michael Willis

My first encounter with a manatee came during a school trip to a science-education center in Jupiter, Florida, when I was about 11 years old. After a lesson on marine biology, my classmates and I were allowed to take a dip in Jupiter Inlet, a narrow swatch of brackish[1] water that connects the Intracoastal Waterway with the Atlantic.

While I was swimming, something massive and scruffy suddenly brushed up against my leg. Thinking I was about to be attacked by a shark—the fear of all ocean-loving Florida kids who had seen the movie *Jaws*—I looked to my side and laid eyes on a huge, unfamiliar, gray creature. The next thing I knew, I was on the beach in a hysterical heap.

After my teacher assessed the situation, she informed me that I had come face-to-face with a manatee, possibly the least-ferocious animal on the planet—a blubbery behemoth[2] that would much rather nibble on sea grass than on my ankle.

Last winter, decades after that chance meeting, I had the opportunity to once again swim with manatees when I visited Florida's Citrus County, home to the biggest winter population of manatees in the world. According to Dr. Bruce Ackerman, a marine scientist who performs aerial surveys for the Florida Department of Environmental Protection, there are about 2,600 manatees in existence, of which he estimates approximately 15 percent winter in and around the Crystal River, a seven-mile waterway

---

**1. brackish:** a mixture of salt water and fresh water.

From "Swimming with Manatees" by Monica Michael Willis from *Country Living,* vol. 20, November 1, 1997. Copyright ©1997 by Country Living. Reproduced by permission of **The Hearst Corporation.**

---

**2. behemoth** (bə•hē′məth): an enormous, powerful animal.

that lies about 60 miles north of Tampa on the state's Gulf side.

In hopes of catching a glimpse of this endangered marine mammal, tourists from as far away as Asia and Europe now visit this largely rural area of central Florida, where swimming with manatees has become big business. Cameron Shaw, refuge manager at the Crystal River National Wildlife Refuge, a 45-acre preserve that encompasses Kings Bay (which is the headwaters of the Crystal River) and Kings Spring, one of the most popular spots among freshwater scuba divers, estimates that 60,000 visitors swam with these rare creatures in 1996. Since so many manatees congregate in the springs in the Crystal River and Kings Bay, guides and dive shops can virtually guarantee prospective clients that they'll encounter one or more of the animals while diving there. In Crystal River, Florida, the hub of much of the diving action, a half dozen or so dive shops operate excursions to spots along the shallow, spring-fed Crystal River and Kings Bay during the winter migration season, which runs from about December 1 to March 30.

The official marine mammal of the state of Florida, manatees are nearsighted, slow-moving herbivores that average about 10 feet in length and weigh in at roughly 1,200 pounds. Amazingly, considering their size, manatees are remarkably gentle. They are not territorial and they have no natural enemies and no known agenda—they pretty much just sleep and eat. (In Kings Bay and the Crystal River area, hungry manatees help to control hydrilla, an invasive—and prolific—aquatic plant that is clogging many Southern waterways.)

## Taking the Plunge

On the two days I went diving, I left my hotel at 6:00 A.M. to increase my chances of viewing the manatees as they congregate near the warm springs in the early morning. . . .

After we collected our snorkels, masks, and fins, we took a short boat ride to Three Sisters' Spring. Before we disembarked,[3] our guide reminded us that the exceptionally clear spring was not a petting zoo. A sign spelled out other rules: Divers should not pursue, ride, poke, or in any way harass the animals. In the event that we were approached by a manatee, we were told we could extend one open hand to it (placing two hands on an animal is considered riding and is against the law).

Moments after I entered the water, two massive manatees swam toward me. It was exhilarating as well as a little frightening to be in proximity to these enormous marine mammals. They appeared curious and sweet natured and perfectly content to be the center of my— and several other divers'—attention. One of the manatees even seemed to want its belly scratched.

"It's a unique experience for people to see a large aquatic mammal up close," says the Crystal River National Wildlife Refuge's Cameron Shaw. "Most people take away a memory of a lifetime."

## Manatee Mania?

Not everyone, however, is thrilled with the number of tourists coming to the area to swim with the manatees. . . .

Members of the Save the Manatee Club— cofounded in 1981 by musician Jimmy Buffett and former Florida governor Bob Graham— worry that the sheer number of people diving in the area will alter the endangered animals' natural behavior.

Patti Thompson, a biologist with the Maitland, Florida–based environmental group, refers to the animals that approached me near the spring as "ambassadors," manatees that she believes have become unnaturally accustomed

---

**3. disembarked:** left, got off.

to the presence of divers and that may have possibly been fed by humans in the past. "It's not natural behavior for a wild animal to swim up to you and roll over to have its belly scratched," she said. "Only a few exhibit this behavior." Although the Save the Manatee Club wishes tourists would go to a marine park or one of the state's manatee viewing areas to observe the animals from the surface, they acknowledge that many people would much rather swim with them. As a result, the club has begun promoting "passive observation," whereby divers watch manatees from the water but are instructed to refrain from touching the animals or interacting with them.

"Of all the endangered species the Fish and Wildlife Service is supposed to protect, the manatee is the only one they encourage people to interact with," says Thompson. "There is no other endangered species that they would condone such interaction with. It's because manatees are gentle and they know no one will be hurt. When the Fish and Wildlife Service extends the open-hand policy to grizzly bears, then I'll accept it for manatees."

## Fostering Advocacy

This apparent disparity[4] of policy may send a conflicting message to the public about endangered species, but many believe that divers who spend time with the manatees will be inclined to support programs that will safeguard this rare mammal and preserve its dwindling habitat. "We've found that swimming with manatees fosters a great advocacy for the species as well as for the whole ecosystem," says Shaw. . . .

---

4. **disparity:** inequality.

1. The article's main idea is that
   A. swimming with manatees is exciting
   B. experts have different opinions about swimming with manatees
   C. manatees naturally interact with humans
   D. tourism involving manatees is a big business in Florida
   E. manatees are an endangered species

2. The author's main purpose is to
   F. entertain the reader
   G. present new scientific research
   H. present both sides of a controversy
   J. describe the manatee's life cycle
   K. narrate a personal experience

3. When the author first swam with a manatee as an adult, she felt
   A. exhilarated
   B. terrified
   C. annoyed
   D. curious
   E. peaceful

4. *Condone* (second to last paragraph) means
   F. approve
   G. forbid
   H. question
   J. protect
   K. disapprove

5. In the last sentence, *advocacy* means
   A. interest in a controversial topic or issue
   B. love of the outdoors
   C. respect for the natural world
   D. support for a cause
   E. opposition to a proposal or idea

**6.** Biologist Patti Thompson compares manatees to grizzly bears because

   **F.** the Fish and Wildlife Service allows people to feed both animals

   **G.** both animals have severely injured people

   **H.** people should be allowed more contact with grizzly bears

   **J.** manatees are not protected as well as other endangered species

   **K.** both animals' habitats are in popular tourist areas

**7.** The writer describes her personal experiences with manatees in order to

   **A.** show how much she has changed

   **B.** add interest and information

   **C.** state her own opinion on the issue

   **D.** prove that she is an expert on manatees

   **E.** encourage readers to swim with manatees

**8.** Which of the following does *not* appear in the article?

   **F.** facts about manatees

   **G.** a personal anecdote

   **H.** a plan to protect manatees

   **J.** quotations from scientists

   **K.** quotations from politicians

**Write several paragraphs in response to *one* of the following questions:**

**9.** You are the editor of a general entertainment magazine for teenagers. Would you publish this article in your magazine or reject it? Give two or more reasons for your decision, and refer to the article to support your points.

**10.** If you had the chance, would you swim with manatees? Explain why or why not. Use details from the article to explain your decision.

# MAKING SENSE OF MANATEES

## by Doug Stewart

Among the habits of Florida manatees, one is particularly convenient for the biologists who try to keep tabs on these rare animals. "When the water temperature drops to about 68 degrees Fahrenheit, manatees start to move," says Jessica Koelsch, a biologist at Sarasota's Mote Marine Laboratory. "But they don't necessarily head south. Some actually go north to congregate in artificially warm water, such as the water around power plants." These winter-time reunions offer manatee-monitoring scientists a field day.

The hard part may be figuring out which way the animals will meander[1] once spring comes. "Because manatees disperse so widely, the nonwinter months are when it's most difficult to protect them," says Koelsch. In the summer of 1994, a headstrong Florida manatee dubbed Chessie was found swimming in the Chesapeake Bay and was airlifted home. The

From *"Making Sense of Manatees"* by Doug Stewart from *National Wildlife*, vol. 37, issue 3, April/May 1999. Copyright © 1999 by *Doug Stewart*. Reprinted by permission of the author.

---

**1. meander:** wander.

Scientists are just beginning to understand the complicated behavior of these engaging endangered mammals.

following summer, Chessie was spotted off Rhode Island. "We don't know what he is doing up here," confessed U.S. Geological Survey biologist Jim Reid at the time.

Figuring out why manatees do things like this is crucial to ensuring their long-term survival. Fewer than 3,000 of the creatures remain in and around Florida today, and their future is uncertain. Manatee behavior has been studied in depth only in recent years, as the plight of this small but charismatic[2] population—under pressure from habitat loss and frequent boat collisions—has garnered[3] widespread public attention. . . .

"Manatees are an endangered species," says Koelsch. "To protect them, we have to understand their behavior." Knowledge of what they eat when, which waters they prefer, and where they mate can help pinpoint, for example, where aquatic preserves might best be set up

for the animals. But before they can lobby for manatee-friendly sacrifices like new sanctuaries and slower boating speed limits, wildlife managers need to arm themselves with convincing data. . . .

A puzzling feature of sirenian[4] physiology[5] is a surprisingly small brain. In an adult manatee, it's about the size of a grapefruit—comparatively less than a quarter as big as the brain of most other large mammals, aquatic or terrestrial. If its brain is puny,[6] does that mean the manatee is less intelligent than other mammals? Roger Reep, a biologist at the University of Florida's College of Veterinary Medicine who, with Tom O'Shea, has studied the matter, suggests that is not the right question.

"Instead of saying manatees have small brains, you can look at them as having very large bodies," Reep says. The pressures of natural selection have probably made large, bulky bodies advantageous to manatees over time. "First, they're not chasing down prey," he adds, "and they aren't preyed upon to any degree, so they don't need elaborate behavioral repertoires[7] for pursuit or escape."

That does not mean a manatee leads a dull-witted life, just a relatively uncomplicated one. Second, the animal has a low metabolism.[8] Though this helps it avoid overheating in very warm surroundings, the creature still must burn enough energy to stay warm when conditions are cool. And living in water, it loses heat more easily to its surroundings than do, say, cows. "So you need a large body," Reep says. "If you're bigger, you have less surface area in proportion to your weight, so you lose heat less readily."

---

4. **sirenian** (sī•rē′nē•ən): of the order of mammals that includes manatees and dugongs.

5. **physiology:** the biological processes that account for the life functions of an organism.

6. **puny:** small.

7. **repertoires** (rep′ər•twärz′): techniques, special skills.

8. **metabolism:** the sum of all of the chemical and physical processes in an organism.

---

2. **charismatic** (kar′iz•mat′ik): charming, alluring.

3. **garnered:** gathered.

The manatee's unhurried lifestyle suits its low metabolic rate. Its normal cruising speed is a sedate two to six miles per hour. . . .

The manatee's lumbering pace is often blamed for its high mortality from boat collisions. The conventional wisdom is that the animal is too sluggish to get out of the way. Ed Gerstein, director of marine mammal research at Florida Atlantic University, is unconvinced. "A manatee is not all that slow," he says. "If frightened or excited, it can explode, moving 21 feet per second." . . .

A number of marine sanctuaries have been set aside on the Florida coasts to serve as manatee refuges. This gives agencies like the U.S. Fish and Wildlife Service and the Florida Department of Environmental Protection a chance to educate visitors about the manatee's plight. Federal guidelines allow divers and snorkelers to touch a manatee as long as the animal comes to them first and the swimmers touch it only with one open hand—an intimacy prohibited with other endangered species.

At least one researcher disapproves, however. "Manatees don't have claws and they don't have big teeth, which is unfortunate," says Patti Thompson, a biologist with Save the Manatee Club, a Florida advocacy group.

Manatees that solicit[9] handouts or that seem to pose for photos are behaving unnaturally, says Thompson, pointing out that nonhabituated[10] manatees are spooked by people standing on a beach. Gauntlets[11] of underwater tourists in some areas, she argues, could interfere with natural behavior such as reproduction and nursing.

"People say, 'Oh, manatees are so sweet and gentle,' but that's anthropomorphizing,"[12] observes Thompson. "Manatees' lack of predators has allowed them to evolve without the kinds of defenses that other animals have. They're not being sweet and gentle. They're being manatees."

---

9. **solicit:** seek.
10. **nonhabituated:** not accustomed to (people).
11. **gauntlets:** used here to mean a lot of people.
12. **anthropomorphizing** (anʹthrə•pōʹmôrʹfīzʹiŋ): giving an animal human qualities.

---

**11.** Scientists believe that manatees are gentle because manatees
   **A.** have a small brain and slow metabolism
   **B.** are large and slow-moving
   **C.** have no natural predators
   **D.** enjoy being petted and photographed
   **E.** live in warm tropical waters

**12.** What is the main reason scientists are studying manatee behavior?
   **F.** to teach people how to interact with them
   **G.** to learn why they have such small brains
   **H.** to find out where they go in the winter
   **J.** to compare them with other marine mammals
   **K.** to help an endangered species survive and recover

**13.** Unlike many people, Ed Gerstein believes that manatees
   **A.** can only swim very slowly
   **B.** can sometimes move quickly
   **C.** will be hurt by human contact
   **D.** should not be placed in sanctuaries
   **E.** are highly intelligent animals

**14.** During the summer months, manatees
- **F.** head south to warmer waters
- **G.** head north to colder waters
- **H.** stay in the warm water near power plants
- **J.** disperse widely
- **K.** search for tourists

**15.** In the sentence "The conventional wisdom is that the manatee is too <u>sluggish</u> to get out of the way," *sluggish* means
- **A.** stubborn
- **B.** ready to fight
- **C.** overweight
- **D.** slow-moving
- **E.** endangered

**16.** We can infer from this article that the greatest danger to manatees is
- **F.** collisions with boats
- **G.** severe storms
- **H.** diseases of marine mammals
- **J.** larger marine animals
- **K.** aquatic preserves

**17.** Patti Thompson suggests that as a result of not having any natural predators, manatees
- **A.** are slow-moving and fierce
- **B.** lack defenses most animals have

- **C.** live only in warm waters
- **D.** have multiplied in great numbers
- **E.** eat only marine plants

## Comparing the Passages

**18.** The second passage presents only facts about manatees, while the first one
- **F.** includes a first-person account of an experience with a manatee
- **G.** poses questions about manatees and then answers them
- **H.** presents problems and offers solutions
- **J.** tells the reader what to do to save manatees
- **K.** strongly encourages interaction with manatees

Write several paragraphs in response to *one* of the following questions:

**19.** What is each author's opinion of swimming with manatees, and how can you tell? Contrast the authors' points of view, using details and information from the passages to support your response.

**20.** Write a letter to the editor, arguing for or against allowing people to swim with manatees. Support your opinion with details and information from both passages.

# Taking Writing Tests

Writing tests come in two different formats:

- **On-demand writing prompts** ask you to write a narrative, expository, or persuasive essay in a limited time.
- **Multiple-choice questions** test your knowledge of sentence construction and revision, paragraph content and organization, and the conventions of standard English.

There you are, facing a writing prompt you've never seen before, perhaps with less than a hour to produce a coherent, well-written essay. Not to worry. Use the following strategies for writing all types of essays.

## THINKING IT THROUGH  Writing Test Strategies

> **STEP 1** **Analyze the writing prompt.** Read it carefully, and analyze what you're being asked to do. Look for key verbs (such as *analyze, argue, explain, summarize*) that define your task. (Before the test, review the chart of **key verbs that appear in essay questions,** page 866.) Consider all parts of the prompt. You'll lose points unless you cover the entire writing task. Identify your audience.

> **STEP 2** **Plan what you'll say.** If you have forty-five minutes to write the essay, take about ten minutes for prewriting. On scratch paper, brainstorm ideas, make a rough outline or graphic organizer, and think about organization. Before you start writing, decide on your main idea statement and how you'll support it.

> **STEP 3** **Draft your essay.** Allow about two thirds of your time to draft your essay, making sure you address all parts of the writing prompt. Include a strong opening paragraph and a definite closing. Strive to express your ideas as clearly as you can, and add relevant details to support and elaborate your main points.

> **STEP 4** **Edit and revise as you write, but leave some time to re-read your draft.** See if you can add transitions or combine sentences. If you add a word or sentence, insert it clearly and neatly.

> **STEP 5** **Proofread your essay.** Focus on correcting errors in grammar, usage, mechanics, and spelling. Your score depends in part on how well you follow the conventions of standard English.

**TIP** Don't skip this prewriting step. Using prewriting strategies will result in a stronger, more interesting essay.

**TIP** Quickly zero in on an incident—you do not have very much time to think. If you draw a blank with "courage," try thinking about a time when you felt frightened.

# Narrative Writing

**Sample Writing Prompt** *Think of an incident in your life that tested your courage. Describe the incident, and tell how you felt at the time. Then, looking back at your experience, tell how you feel and what you think about it now.*

What does the prompt ask you to cover in your autobiographical incident? Use a story map to plan your essay.

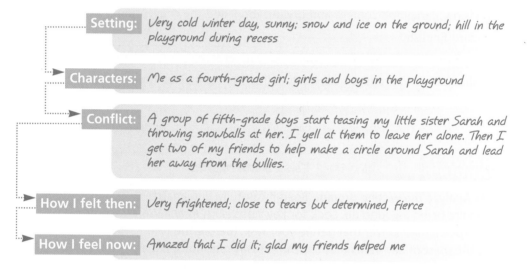

**Setting:** Very cold winter day, sunny; snow and ice on the ground; hill in the playground during recess

**Characters:** Me as a fourth-grade girl; girls and boys in the playground

**Conflict:** A group of fifth-grade boys start teasing my little sister Sarah and throwing snowballs at her. I yell at them to leave her alone. Then I get two of my friends to help make a circle around Sarah and lead her away from the bullies.

**How I felt then:** Very frightened; close to tears but determined, fierce

**How I feel now:** Amazed that I did it; glad my friends helped me

**Reference Note**

See **punctuating dialogue,** pages 686–690.

Give your autobiographical incident an interest-catching beginning and a definite end. Add some dialogue to make readers feel as if they're standing at your side, listening.

# Expository Writing

**Sample Writing Prompt** *Describe a change that you have observed in your school or neighborhood. It can be a small change or a big change. Discuss what you think are the causes or effects of that change.*

Find the two key verbs in this writing prompt. What are you being asked to do? Do you have to discuss both causes and effects? Choose a topic and brainstorm main points, specific details, and examples. Before you start drafting, express your main idea in a single sentence. Then, choose your strongest supporting points and arrange them in a logical order. In general, devote a paragraph to each main point, elaborating with specific details and examples. Create a strong introduction that includes your main idea statement and a conclusion that brings your essay to a definite end.

| Main Idea: In the last two years, Carver Middle School has grown by several hundred students. | |
| --- | --- |
| **Causes** | **Effects** |
| New housing developments; young families moving in | Larger classes; portable classrooms in athletic field |
| Became a magnet school for computer sciences | Better football team—more talent to choose from |
| Increase in city's population | I no longer know everyone in my class |

## Persuasive Writing

**Sample Writing Prompt** *The school board is considering requiring high school students to do 50 hours of community service during each school year. To graduate, a student must complete 200 hours. Consider the effects of such a policy, and decide whether you support it. In an essay, express your opinion and give at least three reasons supporting that point of view.*

Consider both sides of the issue—the pros and cons—to make up your mind. Here's a cluster diagram by a student who supports the policy and is trying to think of three good reasons.

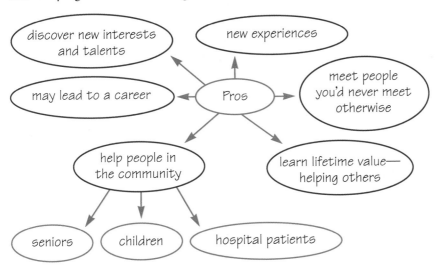

Draft an attention-getting introduction that ends with a clear opinion statement. Give each of your three best reasons, arranged in order of importance, a separate paragraph. You can use your own knowledge and experience to elaborate each reason with facts, examples, anecdotes, and other kinds of evidence. End with a strong concluding paragraph.

# Multiple-Choice Writing Questions

You may find a separate section of multiple-choice questions designed to test your understanding of sentences, paragraphs, and the conventions of standard English (grammar, usage, punctuation, capitalization, and spelling). Examples of some common types of multiple-choice writing questions are shown below.

**TIP** Review the strategies on page 3. They will also help you with multiple-choice writing questions.

**Read the following paragraph. Then, choose the best answer for each question.**

> (1) This week's unexpected heat wave across much of the Northeast and Midwest, coupled with recent reports about the surprisingly fast collapse of an Antarctic ice shelf the size of Rhode Island, has heightened fears of a long-term rise in temperatures brought about by global warming. (2) But this fear may be misguided. (3) In fact, paradoxically, global warming could actually bring colder temperatures to some highly populated areas like eastern North America and Western Europe.

*From* "The Heat Before the Cold" by Terrence Joyce from *The New York Times*, April 18, 2002. Copyright © 2002 by **The New York Times Company.** Reprinted by permission of the publisher.

1. To improve this paragraph, where would you place the sentence below?
   > Rhode Island, the smallest state in the United States, is one of the thirteen original colonies.

   A. before sentence 1
   B. after sentence 1
   C. after sentence 2
   D. after sentence 3
   E. nowhere; it destroys unity

2. This paragraph suggests that the rest of the article will follow which type of organization?
   F. cause and effect
   G. spatial order
   H. comparison and contrast
   J. chronological order
   K. pros and cons

3. What is the **best** way to elaborate the idea in sentence 3?
   A. a first-person anecdote about the heat wave
   B. a detailed description of the Antarctic ice shelf
   C. information about the size of Rhode Island
   D. details about how melting ice affects world temperatures
   E. the writer's opinion about global warming

4. In sentence 3, the word *temperatures* is the
   F. subject of the sentence
   G. direct object
   H. indirect object
   J. object of a preposition
   K. predicate nominative

**5.** Which transition can replace "In fact" in sentence 3 without changing the meaning?

   **A.** For example

   **B.** As a result

   **C.** However

   **D.** For instance

   **E.** None of the above

**6.** *Misguided* in sentence 2 means

   **F.** right

   **G.** wrong

   **H.** surprising

   **J.** serious

   **K.** essential

**7.** The word *paradoxically* in sentence 3 is

   **A.** a noun

   **B.** a pronoun

   **C.** an adverb

   **D.** an adjective

   **E.** a verb

**8.** How should the following sentence be corrected?

   Several factors is thought to contribute to global warming.

   **F.** change *factors* to *factor*

   **G.** add a comma after *factors*

   **H.** change *is* to *are*

   **J.** change *contribute* to *contributes*

   **K.** no change is needed

**9.** Maria is doing Internet research about the collapse of the Antarctic ice shelf. When she uses a search engine, which of the following keywords is likely to yield the **best** results?

   **A.** ice

   **B.** global warming

   **C.** heat wave

   **D.** Rhode Island

   **E.** melting Antarctic ice

**10.** Which is the **best** supporting sentence for the topic sentence below?

   The Gulf Stream current in the Atlantic Ocean warms winters in the northeastern U.S.

   **F.** In 1513, Ponce de León wrote about the Gulf Stream waters.

   **G.** Its warm waters raise air temperatures close to the eastern seaboard.

   **H.** Then it turns and heads toward the coasts of Spain and northwest Africa.

   **J.** It travels at a speed of four miles per hour.

   **K.** It flows from south to north and then turns east.

**Reference Note**

For more on preparing for reading and writing tests, see the **Test-taking Mini-Lessons** in each Part 1 chapter and **Studying and Test Taking** on pages 862–875.

# 1

# Creating a Word-Picture

## Reading Workshop

*Reading a Description of a Place*

## Writing Workshop

*Writing a Description of a Place*

## Viewing and Representing

*Creating a Video Postcard*

## Description

- An archaeologist writes about his discovery of the ruins of an ancient city. As he describes what life in the city might have been like, you imagine the city as it once was—filled with people and activity.

- A sportscaster describes a record-breaking home run over the radio. Baseball fans around the world listen and picture the moment.

One reason that descriptions like these are so vivid and powerful is that they come from **direct observations.** You feel as if you are seeing through the eyes of the writers, observing just what they observed.

Of course, vivid descriptions do not have to come only from direct observations. A writer might describe an imaginary world so well that it *seems* genuine to her readers. However, she might base parts of that world on places she has observed. The true power of any vivid written description—whether it is based more on direct observation or more on imagination—is that it makes the thing described become forever real in the mind of a reader.

> **Informational Text**
>
> Narration/ Description

### YOUR TURN 1  Observing and Describing

When you take time to observe carefully the places you see every day, you will quickly become aware that they are filled with things to describe. Take a careful look around the room you are in now, and then freewrite a short description of something that someone visiting the room for the first time might notice. After you have written your description, share it with a classmate.

internet **connect**

go. hrw .com

**GO TO:** go.hrw.com
**KEYWORD:** EOLang 9-1

# Reading a Description of a Place

**WHAT'S AHEAD?**

In this section, you will read an article and learn how to

- **identify an implied main idea and supporting details**
- **find and classify descriptive details**

**T**ry this: the next time you are at a school assembly or other gathering, observe with your eyes closed. Does that seem like a crazy idea? If it does, think about it a little more. Remember that you can observe with more than just your eyes. You can, for example, observe with your ears—using your sense of hearing. In fact, the following article, "The Sounds of the City," is a description based largely on the sense of hearing.

## Preparing to Read

**READING SKILL** ▶ **Implied Main Idea and Supporting Details** In descriptive writing, **main idea** refers to a quality or impression that a writer tries to convey. Sometimes, however, writers do not directly state that quality or feeling. Instead, they build a main idea by carefully selecting details that fit together like the pieces of a mosaic (a picture made of many small, colored pieces). The pieces may be beautiful by themselves, but they join with each other to form an even more beautiful, larger image. As you read "The Sounds of the City," pay careful attention to the writer's details and see if you can figure out the main idea.

**READING FOCUS** ▶ **Descriptive Details** Writers build a main idea in a description through the careful choice of specific details, including

- **sensory details**—details that appeal to the five senses: sight, hearing, smell, taste, and touch
- **figurative details**—details that use **figures of speech** (imaginative comparisons such as **metaphors** and **similes** or examples of **personification**)
- **factual details**—details that involve things like names, dates, and numbers

While reading "The Sounds of the City," see if you can recognize the different types of descriptive details the writer uses.

The following article offers some interesting observations of city life. As you read this article, write down your responses to the numbered active-reading questions.

*from* The New York Times

# THE SOUNDS OF THE CITY

## BY JAMES TUITE

New York is a city of sounds: muted sounds and shrill sounds; shattering sounds and soothing sounds; urgent sounds and aimless sounds. The cliff dwellers of Manhattan—who would be racked by the silence of the lonely woods—do not hear these sounds because they are constant and eternally urban.

The visitor to the city can hear them, though, just as some animals can hear a high-pitched whistle inaudible to humans. To the casual caller to Manhattan, lying restive and sleepless in a hotel twenty or thirty floors above the street, they tell a story as fascinating as life itself. And back of the sounds broods the silence . . .

### IMAGINATION TAKES FLIGHT

There are few sounds so exciting in Manhattan as those of fire apparatus dashing through the night. At the outset there is the tentative hint of the first-due company bullying its way through midtown traffic. Now a fire whistle from the opposite direction affirms that trouble is, indeed, afoot. In seconds, other sirens converging from other streets help the skytop listener focus on the scene of excitement.

But he can only hear and not see, and imagination takes flight. Are the flames and smoke gushing from windows not far away? Are victims trapped there, crying out for help? Is it a conflagration, or only a trash-basket fire? Or, perhaps, it is merely a false alarm.

The questions go unanswered and the urgency of the moment dissolves. Now the mind and the ear detect the snarling, arrogant bickering of automobile horns. People in a hurry. Taxicabs blaring, insisting on their checkered priority.

### SOUNDS OF THE NEW DAY

Even the taxi horns dwindle down to a precocious few

**1.** What do you predict the author will describe in the rest of the article?

**2.** What effect do the words *dashing* and *excitement* create?

**3.** Which words in this paragraph might be clues to the article's main idea?

The whistles of traffic policemen and hotel doormen chirp from all sides, like birds calling for their mates across a frenzied aviary. And all of these sounds are adult sounds, for childish laughter has no place in these canyons.

## FAREWELL TO THE DAY

Night falls again, the cycle is complete, but there is no surcease from sound. For the beautiful dreamers, perhaps, the "sounds of the rude world heard in the day, lulled by the moonlight have all passed away,"[2] but this is not so in the city.

Too many New Yorkers accept the sounds about them as bland parts of everyday existence. They seldom stop to listen to the sounds, to think about them, to be appalled or enchanted by them. In the big city, sounds are life.

in the gray and pink moments of dawn. Suddenly there is another sound, a morning sound that taunts the memory for recognition. The growl of a predatory monster? No, just garbage trucks that have begun a day of scavenging.

Trash cans rattle outside restaurants. Metallic jaws on sanitation trucks gulp and masticate the residue of daily living, then digest it with a satisfied groan of gears.

The sounds of the new day are businesslike. The growl of buses, so scattered and distant at night, becomes a demanding part of the traffic bedlam. An occasional jet or helicopter injects an exclamation point from an unexpected quarter. When the wind is right, the vibrant bellow of an ocean liner can be heard.

The sounds of the day are as jarring as the glare of a sun that outlines the canyons of midtown in drab relief. A pneumatic[1] drill frays countless nerves with its rat-a-tat-tat, for dig they must to perpetuate the city's dizzy motion. After each screech of brakes there is a moment of suspension, of waiting for the thud or crash that never seems to follow.

> **4.** What are two imaginative comparisons about the truck in this paragraph?

> **5.** What details in the last three paragraphs might contribute to the article's main idea?

---

1. **pneumatic** (no͞o•mat´ik) air-powered.

2. A line from the song "Beautiful Dreamer" by Stephen Foster (1826–1864)

## Implied Main Idea and Supporting Details

**Piecing It Together**   The writer of "The Sounds of the City" did not randomly select the details that make up his description. He chose the details very carefully to create the main idea he wanted to convey. A **main idea** is the most important point the writer wants to make. Like many writers of description, though, he never directly states this main idea—he expects his readers to piece it together from the details he provides in his article.

In some types of writing—especially in expository or persuasive writing—it is common for a writer to state the main idea in a **thesis statement** near the beginning. The writer then follows this **explicit** (directly stated) **main idea** with a number of supporting details. If you were to depict this thesis statement/supporting details pattern visually, it would look like the following diagram.

Explicit Main Idea Structure

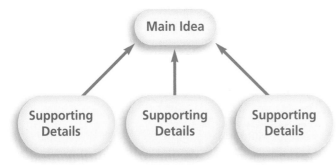

However, there are many pieces of writing—including most narrative and descriptive pieces—that do not follow this pattern. These pieces are said to have an **implied main idea** because they lack a thesis statement. The reader is left to determine the main idea by using the details of the piece to figure out the writer's focus. In a diagram showing the pattern for pieces like these, the main idea/supporting details structure is turned upside down. (The dotted line around the words *Main Idea* indicates that the main idea is implied by the supporting details instead of being directly stated.)

### Implied Main Idea Structure

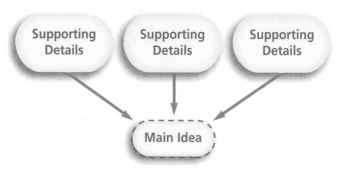

How exactly do you find a main idea when it is implied? The answer is that you need to look at each of the supporting details, because all of the supporting details in a text will often point to a single main idea. For example, look at the following diagram, which summarizes a description of a small country town. Then, read the Thinking It Through steps that follow to see how one student **inferred,** or figured out, the main idea of the description.

### Description of a Small Country Town

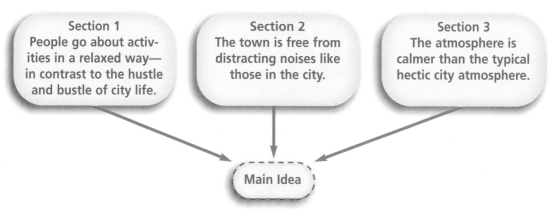

**Finding an Implied Main Idea**

To find an implied main idea of a piece of writing, use the following set of steps.

▶ **STEP 1 Read the whole piece carefully.** Ask yourself what the piece covers. That is its topic.

▶ **STEP 2 Write a summary of each major section of the piece.** To summarize, condense the information in each section into the smallest number of words that still give a complete picture of the section. For examples, see the three section summaries in the diagram on the previous page.

▶ **STEP 3 Look at your section summaries, and infer a main idea by writing an "umbrella" sentence that brings them all together.** This sentence will be the implied main idea. You can write this as an equation:

topic + main point = implied main idea.

Life in the town is calm, quiet, and relaxing—especially in contrast to life in the big city.

**TIP** Sometimes a passage or piece of writing begins with a question. The unwritten answer to that question is often the implied main idea.

**YOUR TURN 2 Identifying an Implied Main Idea**

First, look back at "The Sounds of the City" and use a graphic organizer like the one below to summarize the supporting details in each section of the article. Then, based on your summaries, write an umbrella sentence that reflects the main idea the writer is trying to convey. Write the main idea in the oval at the bottom of your graphic organizer.

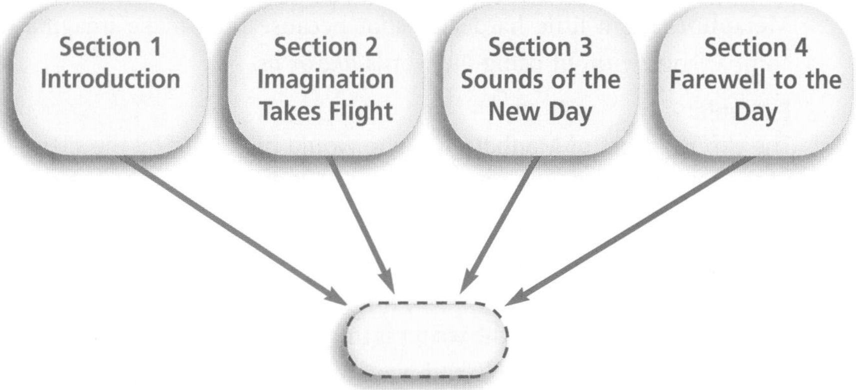

| Section 1 Introduction | Section 2 Imagination Takes Flight | Section 3 Sounds of the New Day | Section 4 Farewell to the Day |
|---|---|---|---|

# Descriptive Details

**Focusing In**   As you read the first paragraphs of "The Sounds of the City," you probably realized that most of the article's **sensory details** were based on just one sense: the sense of hearing. (For example, look back at the first sentence of the third paragraph: "There are few sounds so exciting in Manhattan as those of fire apparatus dashing through the night.")

The writer planned the article this way, of course. He didn't simply forget about the other four types of sensory details—details based on sight, smell, touch, and taste. He chose to focus on sound details to give his description greater **coherence** and **unity**—a clear connection between details so that the piece as a whole supports one main idea.

Sensory details are just one of three types of descriptive details that you will normally find in descriptive writing. The other two types— **figurative details** and **factual details**—may not be used as heavily, but they can also play a very important part in a well-written description.

**Reference Note**

For more on **unity** and **coherence,** see pages 355 and 359.

**Making Comparisons**   **Figurative details** use **figures of speech** to make imaginative comparisons—"special effects" language not meant to be taken literally. The most commonly used figures of speech in descriptive writing—or in almost any other kind of writing—are *similes, metaphors,* and *personification.*

- **Similes** are the easiest to spot, because they are comparisons that always use the words *like* or *as.*

  **Example:**
  The **sounds of the day** are *as* jarring *as* **the glare of a sun** that outlines the canyons of midtown in drab relief.

   As you can see, this simile clearly compares the sounds of the day to the glare of the sun, using the word *as.*

- **Metaphors** are a little harder to spot because they make imaginative comparisons without using the words *like* or *as.*

  **Example:**
  The **cliff dwellers of Manhattan**—who would be racked by the silence of the lonely woods—do not hear these sounds because they are constant and eternally urban.

   To recognize that this example is a metaphor, you first have to realize that there are not really any cliffs in Manhattan on which anyone could dwell. Instead, the writer is imaginatively comparing people who live in high-rise hotels and apartment buildings to people who live in cliff dwellings.

- **Personification,** though not quite as common as similes and metaphors, can also be used to create vivid images. Personification gives human qualities (or sometimes animal qualities) to nonhuman or inanimate things.

**Example:**

People in a hurry. **Taxicabs** blaring, **insisting** on their checkered priority.

Taxicabs are not really alive, of course. They cannot actually "insist" on anything, as people can. However, it is fun to imagine that the taxicabs' blaring horns are a sign that the cabs, like the hurrying people, are impatient with the city traffic.

**Facts and Figures**  Good descriptive writing may also include **factual details**: details that describe using names, dates, numbers, and other information that can be tested or checked for accuracy. Factual details are important in creating a precise image that no reader can misunderstand. To describe a certain neighborhood, a writer might provide factual details that tell his readers how many years old the neighborhood is or the number of city blocks the neighborhood covers, or he might list the names of some well-known people who grew up there.

**Connecting Details**  Did you notice that the simile from "The Sounds of the City" on the previous page—the one about the "glare of a sun," used as an example of a figurative detail—is actually a sensory detail also? As you read more descriptions, you will find that the categories of details often overlap. Some factual details, for example, may also be sensory details. This connection between the three categories of descriptive details can be illustrated by the following diagram. (The numbers in the diagram correspond to the example sentences on the following page.)

**TIP**  Although "The Sounds of the City" does not contain any factual details, do not let its lack of them lead you to think that they are not used in descriptive writing. Many descriptive writers actually depend quite heavily on factual details.

Sensory Details

The overlapping parts of the diagram represent descriptive details that fit into more than one category.

1  3
4
2

Figurative Details

Factual Details

| 1. Sensory/Figurative | The naturalist did not know the bird's name, but he said that its song was "like the sound of an Irish pennywhistle played by a dizzy hyena." |
|---|---|
| 2. Factual/Figurative | The great horned owl (*Bubo virginianus*), which ranges throughout North America, is a common symbol of wisdom—a kind of "philosopher bird." |
| 3. Factual/Sensory | Bobolinks (*Dolichonyx oryzivorus*) like to feed on rice, so rice fields are among the best places to hear the bird's bubbling, exuberant song. |
| 4. Sensory/Factual/Figurative | Emily Dickinson loved the jarring, whistling song of the orchard oriole (*Icterus spurius*); she once called the oriole "the Meteor of Birds." |

## YOUR TURN 3  Finding and Classifying Descriptive Details

To find and classify the descriptive details in "The Sounds of the City," first create a chart like the one below. Starting with the third paragraph of the article, fill in the chart by copying, from every paragraph, one phrase containing descriptive details. Then, label the type of detail (either *sensory, figurative,* or *sensory and figurative*) the phrase contains. Be careful to look for other figures of speech that relate to the "cliff dwellers" metaphor begun in the first paragraph.

### Descriptive Detail Log: "The Sounds of the City"

| Paragraph | Example of a Descriptive Detail | Type of Detail |
|---|---|---|
| 1 | "cliff dwellers of Manhattan" | figurative |
| 2 | "high-pitched whistle" | sensory |
| 3 | | |
| 4 | | |
| 5 | | |
| 6 | | |
| 7 | | |

## Figurative Language Context Clues

As you read "The Sounds of the City," you may have found unfamiliar words in a few of the **figures of speech.** You can predict the meanings of some unfamiliar words by looking for **context clues** in the figures of speech. These *figurative language context clues* can often help you infer, or make an educated guess about, the meaning of an unfamiliar word.

### THINKING IT THROUGH — Using Figurative Language Context Clues

When you find an unfamiliar word in a figure of speech, try using the steps below to infer the word's meaning. When you can, check your prediction in a dictionary.

**Example:**
"Metallic jaws on sanitation trucks gulp and *masticate* the residue of daily living, then digest it with a satisfied groan of gears."

| | |
|---|---|
| **STEP 1** List the words in the figure of speech that seem to be related in meaning. | Jaws, gulp, and digest seem to be related. |
| **STEP 2** Look for a pattern of meaning that connects the related words. | Jaws, gulp, and digest all have to do with eating. |
| **STEP 3** Predict the meaning of the unfamiliar word based on how it might relate to the pattern you found. | Masticate may be similar in meaning to chew because masticate seems to be done with jaws before digesting. |

### PRACTICE

Use the steps above to infer the meanings of the following italicized words. Write your answers on your own paper.

1. "The whistles of traffic policemen and hotel doormen chirp from all sides, like birds calling for their mates across a frenzied *aviary*."

2. The *vehement* whine of the fire trucks and police cars wailed through the night like war cries of attacking warriors.

3. Completely covering the streets in an over-whelming blanket of shadows, the *prodigious* buildings rose up from the sidewalks like large beings.

4. The calm of the morning was shattered by the *discordant* noise of empty trashcans angrily banging against one another in the back of a truck.

5. The first rays of the sunrise seemed to signal a rest for the *languid* stars, weary from a night spent lighting the darkness.

## Main Idea and Supporting Details

Reading tests often test your ability to find the main idea of a reading passage and to distinguish it from its supporting details.

Read the example reading passage that follows. Then, using the Thinking It Through steps below, find the best multiple-choice answer to the question that appears after the passage.

Noise pollution in cities results from a density of noise sources. For example, cities have many trucks, each capable of making ninety decibels of noise from fifty feet away. (One decibel is the smallest amount of sound an average human can hear.) One cross-town train can produce seventy-five decibels from fifty feet, and the outdoor part of one office air condi-

tioner can create sixty decibels from twenty feet. The commonness of such noise sources adds up to a heavy total amount of noise.

1. Which sentence is the best restatement of the main idea of the passage above?

   **A.** Heavy delivery trucks cause noise pollution in the city.

   **B.** One decibel is the smallest amount of sound an average human can hear.

   **C.** Because cities have many noise sources, they also have high levels of noise pollution.

   **D.** Cities would be much better without trucks, trains, and air conditioners.

**THINKING IT THROUGH**    **Finding a Main Idea and Supporting Details**

Use the following steps to find the main idea of a reading passage and to distinguish the main idea from its supporting details.

1. **Don't just choose the first answer that seems good.** It may be correct for only a part of the paragraph. Choice **A** above may look right, but it does not state the main idea of the *whole* paragraph.

2. **Don't choose an answer that states a supporting detail instead of the main idea.** Choice **B**, taken word-for-word from the passage, is a *detail* that supports the main idea—it is *not* the main idea.

3. **Look at the first and last sentences of the passage.** Either might be a topic sentence that **directly states** the main idea. In the example passage, both the first *and* the

last sentence seem to state the main idea.

4. **If you cannot find a topic sentence, try summarizing the passage.** Even without the first and last sentence, you could write: *City noise sources such as trucks, trains, and air conditioners make a large amount of noise.* That summary may *seem* like **D** at first, but it actually is much closer to **C**. The passage never suggests that cities would be "better" without noise sources—it simply states that the noise sources exist.

5. **Review the previous steps; then choose an answer.** The answer is **C**.

# Writing a Description of a Place

**WHAT'S AHEAD?**

In this workshop, you will write a description of a place. You will also learn how to

- gather, evaluate, and organize details
- decide on a dominant impression
- evaluate details for your description
- eliminate "dead-wood" adjectives
- select the correct case forms of personal pronouns

**P**ainters use oils and watercolors to create vivid pictures. Writers use descriptive words—words that make a scene seem to jump right off a page. A novelist, for example, might write a description that conveys the sights, sounds, and sensations of a baseball game where a big event in her novel occurs. A travel writer might write a description that helps you see, hear, and feel the raging surf of the North Shore of Oahu as he experienced it on a visit to the island. Each of these descriptions comes alive through the writer's word-pictures.

In this Writing Workshop, you will write a special kind of description: a description of a place. As you progress through the workshop, keep in mind that your goal is to make the place you describe seem as real to your readers as it does to you.

## Prewriting

### Choose a Place

**Snapshots** Most great photographers start out by taking snapshots of familiar subjects. As a developing writer, you should start by thinking about everyday subjects that you can describe within a few pages.

- **Look close to home.** Try sticking to places that you know well. There are probably many wonderful sights to describe right in your own neighborhood—or even right in your own backyard.
- **See the place with your own eyes.** It is easier to collect details when you observe a place as you write about it. Take a walk with a **learning log** in hand, and jot down notes about interesting sights along the way.

■ **Start small.** For example, instead of trying to describe a whole town, or even a single house, focus in on a single important room.

After you have made a list of a few places you could describe well, choose one place from the list that seems to stand out from the rest—the one you feel will be most interesting for you to write about and for others to read about.

## Consider Your Purpose, Audience, and Tone

KEY CONCEPT

**Facts or Feelings?**    In this workshop, you will be writing a subjective description. This means that **your purpose** (your reason for writing) **will be not only to describe a place, but also to share your thoughts and feelings about it with your audience.** (Sources that commonly contain subjective descriptions include journal entries, autobiographies, and personal letters.) Subjective descriptions are usually written from a *first-person point of view*, using such pronouns as *I, me, we,* and *us.*

When you are preparing any kind of description, you should always choose an **audience** *before* you write and keep that audience in mind at all times as you write. Once you have selected an audience, it should drive your choice of descriptive details. For example, if your intended audience is already familiar with the place you will be describing, you do not need to include the same kind of descriptive details that you would for an audience unfamiliar with the place.

Your purpose, occasion, and audience all help to determine your **tone**—the attitude with which you address your readers. If you are writing a subjective description for an audience that will expect more than just the facts, your tone should be friendly, informal, and conversational. Your **voice**—the unique style with which you express your ideas in writing—should also come through clearly in a subjective description.

> **TIP** A concept similar to purpose is **occasion,** which is the motivating force behind your writing.

> **TIP** If you write for an audience that wants you to stick to the facts, you should use **objective** description only. (Sources that contain objective descriptions include textbooks, science reports, and encyclopedia articles.)
>   Purely objective descriptions, which never include writers' personal feelings about the things they are describing, have very definite characteristics.
>
> ■ They are usually written from a *third-person point of view*, using such pronouns as *he, she,* and *they.*
>
> ■ Their tone is neutral, businesslike, and somewhat formal.
>
> ■ They emphasize the subject rather than the writer.

## Think about Details

**A Palette of Colors**   While creating a picture, painters work from a set of colors called a *palette*. As a descriptive writer, you also have a palette available—a palette that includes *sensory details*, *factual details*, and *figurative details*.

■ **Sensory details** are words and phrases that appeal to the five senses—sight, hearing, touch, smell, and taste. In your writing, you should try to include details from all the senses—not just sight details.

■ **Factual details** are things like names, dates, numbers, and quotations, as well as true statements. For example, in a description of a public park, a writer might say: "About a dozen seniors meet every morning to exercise near the fountain." That statement combines a number and a fact the writer has learned. Factual details are very important to objective descriptions, but they can also serve a purpose in a subjective description.

■ **Figurative details** include similes, metaphors, or examples of personification. They lose their effectiveness if they are overused. Think of them as spice to be sprinkled lightly on your description.

PEANUTS reprinted by permission of United Feature Syndicate, Inc.

## Gather Details

**Raw Material**   Where can you find details for your description? The raw material is all around you—just observe, recall, and research.

■ **Observe the place directly.** Go to the place you plan to describe, and spend at least five minutes observing. Then, take notes in a learning log. Use all of your senses. Consider how the place makes you feel.

■ **Recall details.** To describe a place from memory, first shut your eyes and concentrate. Create a complete mental picture—try to recall sounds, smells, tastes, and sensations along with images.

- **Do research.** You can even describe a place where you have never been. By reading about the place or by doing interviews with people who have been there, you can collect secondhand details.

As you observe, recall, and research, your goal should be to collect details that answer questions like the following ones.

- What **sensory details** will make it real to a reader?
- If I include **factual details**, what kinds should I use?
- Which **figures of speech** will spice up a description of the place?
- What are the place's **unique features?**
- What **thoughts and feelings** does the place bring to mind?

A writer planning to write a description of her family kitchen used her answers to the questions above to create the following chart. Notice the writer's use of first-person pronouns in her list of details.

> **TIP** To make your description seem real to your readers, you need to give them the same sensory information they would notice if they were at this place.

| | Descriptive Detail Log |
|---|---|
| **Sensory details** | • <u>Unique feature:</u> butcher-block table, its edges worn smooth, at the center of the room<br>• filled with the sounds of talking and laughter<br>• taste of fresh, warm bread<br>• heat from the oven radiating out into the room |
| **Factual details** | • There are 5 of us living in the house—my mother, father, grandmother, brother, and me.<br>• We have lived in the house for 10 years. |
| **Figurative details** | • Our kitchen is the heart of the house.<br>• <u>Thought/feeling:</u> It warms me like a big blanket on a cold morning. |

You can gather information about the place you have chosen to describe by making a chart like the one above and then filling it with descriptive details. Whenever possible, use details that *show* rather than *tell*. For example, you could tell your readers that a favorite quilt is old, or you could show its age by describing its mended tears, its frayed edges, its shiny smoothness from repeated washings, and its smell of cedar from years of storage. You will use the list of details in your chart to decide on the dominant impression to convey in your description.

# State Your Dominant Impression

**Reference Note**

For more on **implied main idea,** see page 356.

**Centerpiece**   Instead of directly stating their most important point, or **main idea,** in a thesis statement, writers of description often choose details that convey an **implied main idea** to the reader. **In descriptive writing, this implied main idea is known as a dominant impression**—a kind of centerpiece or central observation to which all of the descriptive details point. Just like a thesis statement, the dominant impression keeps the writer on track. (The word *dominant* means "controlling" or "ruling.") See the diagram below for a visual representation of the relationship between the details and the dominant impression.

**KEY CONCEPT**

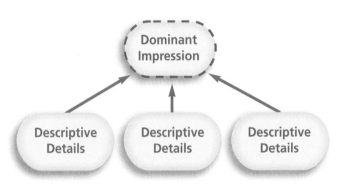

To decide on a dominant impression to convey in your description, follow the steps below. The student responses are based on the notes on page 32.

## THINKING IT THROUGH

### Deciding on a Dominant Impression

▷ **STEP 1** **Look at each of the details** you have collected, and ask yourself, "How is this detail related to other details on my list?"

▷ **STEP 2** **Use your answers to the questions in Step 1 to identify at least one descriptive thread** that runs through your list of details. I included several related details that all have to do with warmth: warm bread, heat from the oven, a big blanket on a cold morning.

▷ **STEP 3** **Write down a sentence that clearly states a dominant impression** in terms of one or more of the descriptive threads you have identified. If I had to describe what the kitchen means to me in one word, it would be the word warmth.

# MINI-LESSON CRITICAL THINKING

## Evaluating Details

Now that you have a list of details, you need to look at the list carefully, and then (with your **dominant impression** in mind) choose only the details you really want to include. To be able to choose the correct details, you need to practice the skill of **evaluating details**—judging which details will be most important to include in your description and which ones you can do without. Below are some standards, or criteria, that you can use to make your choices.

| Evaluating Details for a Description of a Place | |
|---|---|
| **Criteria** | **Example Sentence with Details** |
| **Are details included that will create a clear image of the place in the mind of a reader?** | The house looked like a fortress, with wrought-iron grillwork on the windows. |
| **Are details included that describe the location and size of the place?** | My neighborhood is on the south side and covers four square blocks. |
| **Are details included to show ways in which the place is unusual?** | The huge oak tree in my front yard is more than two hundred years old. |

### PRACTICE

Below is a list of details a writer made about his neighborhood basketball court. Using the criteria above, evaluate the details and cut the list down to a short list of the five most important details. (Remember that the details as a whole should support a **dominant impression**.) After you have made your short list, get together with two or three classmates and compare your results. You may not all agree on which details to include, so be prepared to explain your choices.

1. a comfortable place where I can have fun with my friends

2. sometimes gets repainted

3. maintained by the parks department

4. located halfway between my school and my family's apartment

5. two out of the six goals are missing nets, but no one minds too much—it's still fun

6. doesn't have a fence around it

7. asphalt is so hot in the summer that you could probably fry an egg on it

8. always alive with shouts: "I'm open—pass the ball! . . . Good game . . . . Look out!"

9. some people don't like to play basketball

10. the court is well-known in our city because an NBA player played pickup games here when he was in high school

11. sometimes used for volleyball

# Organize Your Details

**Space or Importance?**   Arrange your details in an order that makes sense to your audience—an order that supports the dominant impression you plan to convey and shows a **logical progression** of your ideas. For a description of a place, there are two common ways to arrange details.

- **Spatial order** (ordering details according to how they are arranged in space) is used mostly with sight details. One way to use spatial order is to begin by describing how a place looks from a distance, and then to zoom in to describe how it looks up close. You can plan a spatial ordering of your details by first drawing a map of the place you want to describe. Then, draw arrows at the places on the map where you plan to start and end your description.

- **Order of importance** works best when you have some details that are clearly more important than others. To arrange details by order of importance, you can start with your least important details first and then build up to your most important details. The opposite order (from most- to least-important) is sometimes used also. The "family kitchen" writer chose to use order of importance for her description, so she created the following chart to show her arrangement.

| Least Important Details | Body Paragraph 1: How the kitchen looks |
|---|---|
| More Important Details | Body Paragraph 2: How the kitchen looks to our family |
| Most Important Details | Body Paragraph 3: Why the kitchen is important to me |

## YOUR TURN 4  Planning Your Description

Before you begin writing your description, make sure that you have completed all of these prewriting steps:

- choose a place to describe
- consider your purpose, audience, and tone
- gather details, including details about your thoughts and feelings
- state the dominant impression you plan to convey
- arrange your details using either spatial order or order of importance

# Writing

## Description of a Place

**Framework**

**Directions and Explanations**

### Introduction

- Clearly identify the place you are describing.
- Include a statement that hints at a dominant impression.

### Body

- Use a variety of details (sensory, factual, and figurative).
- Include thoughts and feelings.
- Use either spatial order or order of importance.

### Conclusion

- End with a statement that wraps up your description.

**Prepare Your Readers**   Avoid opening with a dull introductory statement like "The place I will describe is . . ." Instead, get readers interested in learning more about the place by opening with a catchy sentence.

**Present a Dominant Impression**   Focusing on a dominant impression keeps your paper from being just a random collection of details. Help your readers get the picture by providing a statement that sets them up for the details that will follow.

**Pile on the Details**   Use a mix of sensory details, not just sight details. Also, remember *show*, don't tell. Instead of just saying that a room is old and run-down, show the room by describing its squeaky floor-boards and the cobwebs in its corners.

**Reflect**   Because this is a subjective description, you also need to reflect on your place by sharing your thoughts and feelings about it with your readers.

**Move Your Readers Along**   Guide your readers through the place you are describing. Provide your details in a clear spatial order or present them in a logically arranged order of importance.

**Close with a Flourish**   Restating your dominant impression is a good way to sum up your thoughts about the place you have described.

**YOUR TURN 5** **Writing a First Draft**

Read through the annotated Writer's Model on the next page to see how one writer used the framework to create a description of a place. Then, write the first draft of your paper, using the framework as a guide.

# A Writer's Model

**The following description of a place closely follows the framework on the previous page.**

work on the previous page.

### The Kitchen

Good food, sharing, and laughter are three things that come to mind right away when I think of my family's kitchen. It may seem strange to think of the kitchen as a special place, but for my family it is. We say goodbye there before school, and we say hello there when we get home. It is a place for food, of course, but it's also a place for sharing and for laughing. If I had to describe what the kitchen means to me in one word, it would be the word <u>warmth</u>.

A visitor seeing the kitchen for the first time might wonder why I chose that word. The kitchen looks quite ordinary, with the usual assortment of fixtures and appliances. It has wood-grain cabinets, a two-sided stainless-steel sink, a refrigerator/family bulletin board, and an old but sturdy stove. At the center of the room sits a butcher-block table, scuffed from years of use. That's where our family eats most meals. In short, almost any visitor would probably say it seemed like a plain, ordinary kitchen.

However, the five of us in my family see that room in a different way. We have lived in the house for ten years, and for us, the kitchen is a place that holds ten years of special sounds, smells, and memories. We enjoy the sound of my grandmother humming songs from her childhood as she cooks, and the smell of the fresh bread she bakes each week. We often sit in the kitchen talking while we wait for the bread to be ready. If it is cold outside, we might pull up our chairs around the stove, basking in its friendly heat as we talk.

Most importantly, though, our kitchen is the heart of our home. It may not seem like a special place to someone else, but when I am lonely or tired, it warms me—like a big blanket on a winter morning. It is just as important to everyone in my family. It is our place to come together and share our lives.

Most people probably would not think of a kitchen as an extraordinary place. However, for me and my family, our kitchen will always be a warm, wonderful place.

**TIP** Note that because a subjective description is less formal, the use of contractions is acceptable.

**INTRODUCTION**
Attention-getting statement

Hint of a dominant impression

**BODY**

Sensory details—sight

Factual detail

Sensory details— sound, smell, and touch

Word signaling order of importance

Figurative detail

Thoughts and feelings
**CONCLUSION**

Restatement of dominant impression

# A Student's Model

**Shanessa McClain, a student at Hobbs High School in Hobbs, New Mexico, wrote the following excerpt. It is a description of the beach activity at South Padre Island.**

## South Padre Island

Attention-getting statement

The sound of the waves crashing against the shore, the sight of the sea gulls swooping overhead, and the smell of sunscreen create an engaging place called South Padre Island. Located where one can relax and experience good times on the beach, South Padre Island offers an island-getaway adventure not soon to be forgotten. The sun, sand, and endless ocean make South Padre unlike any other place I have ever been. When I am on the beach at South Padre Island, I know I am in paradise.

Hint of a dominant impression

Figurative detail— personification

Sensory detail—touch

Perhaps the simplest delight of South Padre is the beach itself. This sparkling retreat embraces unbounded miles of sand. During the day the warmth of the sun beats down upon this sand, making beach goers spring as their feet hit the blistering sand. However, closer to the Gulf of Mexico, where the water moistens and cools the beach, children giggle as their sand castles are overtaken by a massive wave. Towels are no stranger to this sand. Sun worshippers spend hours lying upon them in an attempt to soak up even more blistering rays. The sand provides a soft cover as a teenager dives after the ball in the annual summer volleyball tournament, and it cushions two old men who swap stories as they wait for the hungry game fish that swim the waters of Padre Island. Looking across the beach, I see a rainbow of umbrellas and seashells of exquisite design and enchanting colors: a vision of paradise.

Sensory detail—sight

Thoughts and feelings

Sensory details

Another attraction of South Padre is the Gulf. The rushing waves both calm and provide amusement for many tourists. I could never truly understand complete tranquillity until I stood on the shoreline of Padre Island at night. The feel of the breeze, the smell of the salt-water, and the sight of the boat lights in the distance soothed my senses in a way that nothing else could. . . .

# Evaluate and Revise Your Draft

**Two Passes**   When you revise your writing, always make at least two reading passes: one for content and organization, and one for style. At each pass, **self-evaluate** your writing and consider **collaborating** or having a **writing conference** with a classmate.

▶ First Reading: **Content and Organization**   Start your evaluation by answering (or having a peer answer) the questions in the left-hand column below. For help with the questions, see the tips in the middle column. To revise, make the changes in the right-hand column.

## Description of a Place: Content and Organization Guidelines for Peer and Self-Evaluation

| Evaluation Questions | ▶ Tips | ▶ Revision Techniques |
|---|---|---|
| **❶** Does the introduction include a statement that hints at a dominant impression? | ▶ **Underline** the sentence in the introduction that seems to sum up the details in the paper. If you cannot find a sentence to underline, revise. | ▶ **Add** a sentence that hints at the dominant impression conveyed in the paper. |
| **❷** Does the description include a variety of details (sensory, factual, and figurative)? | ▶ **Put an S** above sensory words, an **N** above numbers, names, and dates, and an **F** above sentences that make imaginative comparisons—especially those that contain the words *like* or *as*. Revise if you do not see plenty of **S**'s with scattered **N**'s and **F**'s. | ▶ **Add** sensory details that appeal to several senses. **Add** significant dates, names, or numbers. **Add** figures of speech that support the dominant impression. **Replace** less-descriptive language with specific descriptive details. |
| **❸** Does the description include details about the writer's thoughts and feelings? | ▶ **Put an asterisk** next to every first-person pronoun (*I, me, we, us,* etc.). If you do not see at least one asterisk per paragraph, revise. | ▶ **Elaborate** by including first-person thoughts or feelings about the sensory, factual, and figurative details in the paper. |
| **❹** Is the paper clearly organized using either spatial order or order of importance? | ▶ **Number** the details. Then, draw a simple map of the place described and place the numbers on it. Revise if you cannot see a clear pattern to the numbers. | ▶ **Rearrange** details so that they fall into either a clear spatial order (far to near, top to bottom, and so on) or a clear order of importance (most to least or least to most). |
| **❺** Does the conclusion include a statement that wraps up your description? | ▶ **Bracket** the sentence that sums up your thoughts. If you cannot find a sentence to bracket, revise. | ▶ **Add** a sentence that summarizes your description or that restates your dominant impression. |

**ONE WRITER'S REVISIONS**  Here is how one writer used the content and organization guidelines to revise part of the description on page 37. Study the revisions, and then answer the questions that follow.

replace

Most importantly, though, our kitchen is ~~central to our lives.~~ *the heart of our home*

add

It may not seem like a special place to someone else, but *when I am lonely or tired,* it ~~really~~

replace

*warms me—like a big blanket on a winter morning.* ~~is to me.~~

## Analyzing the Revision Process

**1.** How does the writer's revision of the first sentence improve the paragraph?

**2.** What kinds of details does the writer add to the second sentence? Why do you think she added them?

**PEER REVIEW**

Ask a classmate to read your paper and answer the following questions.

1. Which details in the paper did you like best? Why?

2. What do you think this paper reveals about the writer who created it?

### YOUR TURN 6  Revising Content and Organization

Study the revisions shown above. Then, use the guidelines in the chart on the previous page to revise your paper's content and organization.

▷ **Second Reading: Style**  On your second pass through your paper, your goal is to improve your style. You have probably used a number of good descriptive adjectives—but have you also used unnecessarily repetitive adjectives like the ones in boldface type in the sentence below?

**Example:**
The **different, varied** colors of the grasses caught my eye.

*Different* and *varied* have almost the same meaning. Using both words adds length without adding any new ideas. The guidelines that follow will help you to get rid of these kinds of adjectives in your writing.

## Style Guidelines

| Evaluation Question | ▶ Tip | ▶ Revision Technique |
|---|---|---|
| Do some sentences contain unnecessarily repetitive adjectives? | ▶ **Circle** all pairs of adjectives (adjectives joined by a comma or by *and* or *but*). Revise any circled pair having almost the same meaning. | ▶ **Cut** one of the adjectives from a pair, or **replace** one with a contrasting adjective and change the connecting word *and* to *but*. |

# Deadwood Adjectives

Adjectives often work well in teams. In fact, carefully used pairs of adjectives can leave a powerful impression on readers. However, using two or more adjectives that pointlessly repeat the same meaning just adds useless deadwood to your writing. Like dead limbs on a tree, these words weigh your writing down and sap it of its strength. It is your job to cut out deadwood adjectives so that your writing stays strong. If you are unsure how similar your paired adjectives are, check their meanings in a dictionary or in a thesaurus.

**ONE WRITER'S REVISIONS**   Here is another example of some revisions made by the writer of the description on page 37. This time, the writer used the style guidelines on the previous page to evaluate and revise her paper.

**BEFORE**

It has wood-grain cabinets, a two-sided stainless-steel sink, a

refrigerator/family bulletin board, and an old, ancient stove.

At the center of the room sits a butcher-block table, scraped

and scuffed from years of use.

The circled words are pairs of adjectives having almost the same meaning.

**AFTER**

It has wood-grain cabinets, a two-sided stainless-steel sink, a refrigerator/family bulletin board, and an old but sturdy stove. At the center of the room sits a butcher-block table, scuffed from years of use.

changed to contrasting adjective

deleted repetitive adjective

## Analyzing the Revision Process

1. What change in meaning does the writer achieve by replacing the word *ancient* with *sturdy*?

2. If you wanted to describe the table using an adjective that contrasts with the word *scuffed*, what adjective would you add?

After studying the revisions on the previous page, revise the style of your paper using the directions in the Style Guidelines chart.

## Designing Your Writing

**COMPUTER TIP**

These are just a few of many considerations to keep in mind when you create Web pages. For more tips, do a search in a Web directory using the key-words *Web style* or *Web page creation.*

**Creating Usable Web Pages**   At some point, you may want to publish on the World Wide Web your description of a place. When you create a Web page, let the following tips guide some of the choices you make. All of these tips have to do with the concept of *usability*—the idea of designing something (in this case, a Web page) so that it works in the best possible way for the people (your readers) who will actually use it.

- **Loading time.** If your page uses graphics (including background images or scanned photographs), consider how long the graphics will take to load before readers can see them. If your graphics load too slowly, you run the risk of frustrating and annoying your readers.

- **Flipping pages *vs.* scrolling.** Printed documents have real pages that you can turn. Web pages have no page breaks. You read them by scrolling through them, in much the same way that readers did in ancient times with real scrolls. Design your pages in a way that will make scrolling through them easier for your readers. For example, avoid cluttered pages, summarize periodically, and use short blocks of text whenever possible.

- **Tall or wide.** Printed pages are usually taller than they are wide (think of an 8-1/2- x 11-inch page of typing paper). However, readers usually look at Web pages on computer monitors that are wider than they are tall (like an 8-1/2- x 11-inch page turned on its side). Therefore, it makes sense to design Web pages from side to side, rather than from top to bottom. This means that wide images usually work better in Web pages than tall images do.

- **Organization.** Put your most important information, such as the title and your main idea, near the top of the Web page so your readers know what to expect. Organize your information for quick scanning by using headlines that summarize and by using numbered or bul-leted lists. Create a standard footer for the bottom of each page with such information as the date of the last update, an e-mail address for feedback, and links to other pages.

- **Free of errors.** You do not want your readers to be distracted by mis-spelled words or grammatical errors. Therefore, proofread carefully and make any necessary corrections.

## Proofread Your Essay

**A Case for Correctness**  Your paper should be as error free as you can make it before you prepare a final copy. Check it thoroughly for grammar, usage, and mechanics errors, and fix them as you find them. Because it is common to have first-person pronouns in a subjective description, you will want to be especially careful to check that you have used correct pronoun forms throughout your paper.

**Reference Note**
For more on **proofreading guidelines,** see page 13.

## Grammar Link

## The Case Forms of Personal Pronouns

**Case** is the form that a noun or pronoun takes to show its relationship to other words in a sentence.

■ The subject of a verb should be in the nominative case. (*I, he, she, we, they*)

**Example:**
**She** wanted to describe a treehouse.

■ The direct object of a verb should be in the objective case. (*me, him, her, us, them*)

**Example:**
Mr. Lopez asked **me** to revise this essay.

■ When a sentence uses pronouns in a compound subject or a compound direct object, *all* the parts of the compound must still be in the correct case. For example, it would never be correct to write or say "she and me" or "her and I." To help you know whether the pronoun is correct, try each pronoun separately.

**Example:**
The **boys and (*they, them*)** helped **him and (*I, me*)** with the pamphlet. [*They* helped or *them* helped? *They* is correct. The boys and they helped *I* or helped *me*? The boys and they helped *me* is correct.]

The boys and **they** helped him and **me** with the pamphlet.

**PRACTICE**

Revise each incorrect pronoun in the sentences below. If a sentence is already correct, write C. Write your answers on your own paper.

**Example:**
1. Alberto and me made notes about our observations.

1. *Alberto and I made notes about our observations.*

1. This guidebook from our teacher, Mr. Halas, really helped Steve and I.

2. Marika found us later that same afternoon.

3. Rose and her discovered that this place is difficult to describe.

4. Our teacher took them to a library to get a few reference books.

5. The first group called Marika and they to help load the cameras.

For more information and practice on **pronoun case,** see page 549.

# Publish Your Essay

**Rewards**   You have worked hard to write and polish your description of a place. Now, you can reap the rewards of your hard work by sharing your description with readers. Try one or more of these publishing ideas.

■ If your description is of a place in your community, send a copy of the description to your local newspaper. Local newspapers often set aside space for community-related writing from their readers.

■ Self-publish your description as a Web page. Scan photographs of the place you described, and include them on the page. If your paper includes descriptions of sounds, record some of the sounds and create hyperlinks to sound files of the recordings. (Look back at the Designing Your Writing section on page 42 for more tips on turning your description of a place into a Web page.)

■ If any of your classmates have written descriptions that are related in some way to your description, bind all of your descriptions together as a booklet, give the booklet a title that summarizes the connection between the descriptions, and distribute copies of the booklet.

PORTFOLIO

# Reflect on Your Essay

**Decisions**   Look back at some of the decisions you made while writing this paper. You will see that in this workshop, you have practiced skills you can carry over into other writing assignments. To reflect on some of your decisions, write responses to the following questions.

■ What process did you go through to decide on a place to describe? How well did the process work?

■ From revising your description, what insights did you gain into your personal writing style?

   Make sure to attach your responses to your description of a place. Then, decide whether you want to include the paper in your portfolio.

## YOUR TURN 8   Proofreading, Publishing, and Reflecting

Make sure that you have completed all of the steps on this page and on the previous page. Remember to

■ proofread your work thoroughly before you prepare a final copy and publish it

■ reflect on the decisions you made while writing your paper, and think about the skills you have practiced

## Field Notes

You just wrote a *subjective* description of a place. Now is your chance to try an *objective* form of descriptive writing: *field notes*. **Field notes** are written records of firsthand observations made in the field (instead of in a lab or office, for example). Archaeologists, geologists, and naturalists all use field notes.

### Guidelines for Creating Field Notes

In different courses, such as science or social studies, you might be required to go outside of school and make precise observations of something. To record your observations, you will need to keep detailed field notes. Here are some guidelines to help you create field notes.

- **Start with a small, sturdy, bound notebook.** Don't use loose-leaf pages that can fall out and get lost. Choose something easy to carry—a notebook that fits into a pocket is best.

- **Write with a pencil, not a pen.** You may be making notes outdoors—not always in dry conditions. Unlike ink, pencil marks will not run or smear if they get wet.

- **Write down your first impressions quickly.** You can hold details in your short-term memory only very briefly. Don't count on remembering something long enough to write it down later. If you wait too long, you risk adding inaccurate or imagined details that don't reflect what you really observed.

- **Mark the date and location of your observations on each page.** You may need to look back later and check exactly when and where you made an observation.

- **Don't crowd notes onto your notebook pages.** You don't need to fill a page before you start a new one. Later, you may want to be able to find the specific details in your notes quickly—so don't bury all your details on overcrowded pages.

- **Never tear out pages, and avoid erasing anything.** Later, you may wish that you still had the page you tore out, or that you could still read the words you erased and wrote over. Instead, simply draw a line or an *X* through anything you are tempted to erase.

**YOUR TURN 9  Taking Field Notes**

To practice taking field notes, carefully observe something in the natural world, and make detailed notes describing it. Your subject might be a bird, an insect, a plant, a certain weather phenomenon, or anything else natural which you can observe firsthand.

# Creating a Video Postcard

**WHAT'S AHEAD?**

In this section, you will create a video postcard and learn how to

- **plan and tape a video**
- **use visual techniques to add interest to a video**

To make a word-picture come to life, a writer uses many descriptive devices, such as sensory and figurative details. Imagine creating a description using a videocamera instead of words. A **video postcard** is a special kind of description: a short (one minute or less) series of images, presented without sound, that are chosen to give a viewer a sense of what a place is like. Get ready for a filmmaking adventure: read the steps in this section carefully, arm yourself with a videocamera, give in to your imagination, and create your own video postcard.

## Why Make a Video Postcard?

A printed postcard is a visual souvenir from a place. People send postcards to one another as a way of saying, "I wish you were here with me to see this place, but since you are not, I am sending you this postcard to show you how it looks." A video postcard should have the same basic purpose: *It should be a visual memento of a visit to a certain place.* There are two good reasons for creating this kind of a visual memento.

- You can plan and film it so that it represents your personal view of a place—it will be as individual as you are.
- You can make use of a variety of visual techniques to make it a creative, unusual view of a place.

## Choosing a Place to Tape

The first step in creating a video postcard is to decide on a place to tape. Below are some points you should keep in mind as you consider places.

- **You do not have to travel.** The place you choose does not have to be a far-away, exotic place. It can be an interesting place close to home—a place you already know well.

- **Your focus can be small.** If you are creating a video postcard of a lake near your home, do not try to tape the entire lake—focus on the part of it that interests you the most.

- **You should observe before taping.** Before you decide on a place, observe it carefully and consider how you could make it look interesting on tape. Gather information by using all of your senses—by seeing, touching, tasting, smelling, and hearing. Think about the impression you want to make on your viewers. Some places will work better than others.

Of course, if you know that you will be traveling somewhere soon, you do not need to restrict yourself to filming a local place. You can bring a camera along and tape a place during your trip.

## Planning and Taping

The next step in creating a video postcard, creating a *storyboard,* is also an essential step whenever you are planning to tape or film anything. A **storyboard** is simply a set of rough sketches that you make before you begin taping or filming something. The storyboard shows the **sequence,** or order, of the scenes or shots you plan to use. In the case of a video postcard, a storyboard should show each of the major views of a place that you plan to include.

  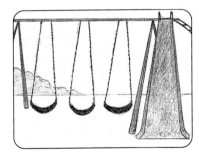

With your sequence of scenes decided and your storyboard in hand, you are ready to begin taping. Most professional directors don't actually film scenes in exactly the same sequence that they will be shown. However, to simplify your taping, you should tape in exactly the same sequence in which you plan for the tape to be shown, a technique called **in-camera editing.** It actually means that you don't do any editing at all after you have finished taping—you just show the original tape.

# Visual Techniques

While videotaping a place, try to use a variety of visual techniques to add interest and meaning to your final video postcard. Some of the visual techniques available to you will depend on the sophistication of the video-camera you use. However, you will want to cover the basics:

- **Use a combination of *close-ups* and *panoramic* (wide) shots.** Use wide shots to give viewers an impression of the grandness of a place; use close-ups to show small but important details.

- **Consider using some form of *time-lapse taping*.** You could set a video-camera on a tripod and tape just a few seconds of each hour—from dawn to dusk—and you would end up with a view of a complete day at that place, compressed into thirty seconds or so.

- **Vary the camera angles you use.** Don't film everything at eye level—try to get up above the place a little, and then shoot down to give a bird's-eye view. Also, think about getting down on the ground and filming up to portray a child's view of the place. Remember that shooting from a high angle makes the subject appear small, while shooting from a low angle makes the subject appear large and dominating.

Certainly, you will want to do a few practice runs *before* your actual taping session. Become comfortable with your camera; learn its parts and their specific functions. If necessary, study the instruction manual. The following terms should help you get started.

- The **iris ring** adjusts the brightness of the image.
- The **zoom ring** magnifies the image and can create a "zoom-in" effect.
- The **focus ring** makes your images sharper.

## YOUR TURN 10 Creating a Video Postcard

Get together with two or three classmates, and create a plan for making a one-minute silent video postcard. Remember to

- choose a place to tape
- create a storyboard showing the sequence of shots you will use
- tape the postcard using in-camera editing to save time and trouble
- use a variety of visual techniques to add interest and meaning

(If you do not have access to a videocamera, you may be able to do only the first two steps.) When you have finished your video postcard, screen it for the class and ask your classmates for feedback.

# Choices

**Choose one of the following activities to complete.**

## ▶ CAREERS

**1. Describing with Data**
Professionals in science careers often create written descriptions from data collected firsthand—measurements, for example. To practice describing with data, first find an object with characteristics you can measure, such as volume, temperature, dimensions, weight, age, and speed. Determine whether any special equipment is necessary for measuring. Then, make your measurements and use them to create a brief **written description** of the object.

## ▶ LITERATURE

**2. Imagined Places** Find a vivid description of a place in a novel or short story you have read recently, and analyze the writer's style. For example, does the writer use vivid verbs, series of adjectives, or a particular type of sentence structure? Then, create an **imagined description** of your own, using the short-story or novel description as a model. Be sure to choose a place you really want to describe. It might be a space station in the distant future or a city in the ancient past—just let your imagination guide you.

## ▶ VIEWING AND REPRESENTING

**3. Selling a Place** Create a **print ad** based on the description of a place you created in the Writing Workshop. Consider the information you should present to make this destination desirable. For example, explain the ease of traveling there, list its many activities, and praise its unique features. Keep in mind the **dominant impression** of the description, and use graphics and visual techniques to emphasize it.

## ▶ CROSSING THE CURRICULUM: WORLD LANGUAGES

**4. Translating Description**
To compare descriptive terms across languages, make a list of ten key descriptive words from the description of a place you wrote for this chapter. Then, use a bilingual dictionary to find the equivalents of the words in another language—a language you have studied or are now studying, or any other language in which you are interested. After you have made your list, create an **illustrated poster** showing the words and their equivalents.

PORTFOLIO

# Expressing Your Thoughts

## Reading Workshop

*Reading a Personal Narrative*

## Writing Workshop

*Writing a Personal Narrative*

## Speaking and Listening

*Presenting and Evaluating Oral Narratives*

M ichael Jordan's diary . . . Rita Dove's autobiography . . . your fifth-grade "My Last Vacation" essay. People writing about their own lives are creating personal narratives.

> Narration/ Description

"Write about what you know," someone wise once said. People write about what happens in their lives because they want to express themselves and their ideas about the world. People read to learn about the journeys others take to discover those ideas. Think of the possibilities: you may recount a moment of personal triumph when you first jumped off a rope swing, or you may read about the moment when a writer decided to become an astronaut. In any case, personal narratives offer a great opportunity to learn through your experiences or through the experiences of others.

### YOUR TURN 1 Keeping Personal Narratives in Mind

With a classmate or two, make a two-column chart. In the first column, make a list of people whose personal narratives you would like to read. In the second column, write what you would like to learn about the people from their personal narratives.

| People | What I would like to learn |
|--------|----------------------------|
| Maya Angelou | What working for Dr. Martin Luther King, Jr., was like |

**internetconnect**

**go. hrw .com**

**GO TO:** go.hrw.com
**KEYWORD:** EOLang 9-2

# Reading a Personal Narrative

**WHAT'S AHEAD?**

In this section, you will read a personal narrative and learn how to

- predict outcomes
- recognize elements of expressive style

**W**hat do you remember from your childhood? Remember the time your brother told you to watch your little sister and so you did—while your sister ate dirt? Writers use their memories and powers of description to re-create moments from their lives. We call this kind of re-creation **personal narrative,** which is a form of expressive writing. The selection you will read next is a personal narrative in which the author expresses feelings about memories both lost and found.

## Preparing to Read

READING SKILL

**Predicting Outcomes**   Do you have friends who always want to tell you what will happen next in a TV show? They like to make predictions. Before a game, do you ever talk about how many points your team will score? You are **predicting an outcome.** You take what you already know and apply it to something you are reading, listening to, watching, or experiencing. Then, you decide what you think will happen. As you read "Paper Airplanes" on the next page, try to make some predictions about what will happen next in the narrative or how a person will react.

READING FOCUS

**Expressive Style**   Style is the way writers express what they want to say. There are many different ways to write about an event or series of events. In **expressive forms** of writing, such as the personal narrative, writers use an **expressive style** to bring the reader into the writer's personal experience. Two easily recognizable elements of an expressive style are

- **first-person pronouns,** such as *I, me, we,* and *us,* used in order to connect more directly with the reader
- **personal thoughts and emotions** that would be out of place in other kinds of writing

When you read "Paper Airplanes," notice that the writer is neither objective nor removed from the subject: She tells us her unique, personal story.

Kyoko Mori was born in Japan and lived there the first twenty years of her life. She has spent another twenty years living, working, and writing in the United States. As you read Mori's personal narrative, write down your answers to the numbered active-reading questions.

*from* Polite Lies: On Being a Woman Caught Between Cultures

# Paper Airplanes
### by Kyoko Mori

**1. What do you think may happen in this personal narrative?**

What I miss most from not having a family close by is a sense that the past is an open and growing manuscript, expansive and forgiving. When we talk about the past with family, we often find that each of us remembers different aspects of the same experience. Though the difference in memory can sometimes lead to bickering, it's a relief to know that none of us has the sole responsibility for remembering—what we forget will be recalled by someone else. We occasionally learn details we didn't know because we were too young at the time or lived too far away. Family stories can shed a new light on the events we think we know. After the conversation, we add the new pieces to our memory. In this way, the past can expand rather than shrink. I look forward to seeing my mother's family on my short visits to Japan because that's one of the few times I can experience memory expanding.

The last time I saw my uncle, Kenichi, he had just finished reading my first novel, *Shizuko's Daughter*, in the Japanese translation. Many of the details in the novel's setting come from my grandparents' house in the country—the house where Kenichi had grown up. He was glad that I had included the child's wooden slide my grandfather built when my mother was born, the purple lantern flowers my grandmother used to grow, the cicadas that were always buzzing in the trees in the yard.

**2. How do you know the writer has fond memories of her grandparents' house?**

"I was amazed by how much you could remember," he said.

"Of course I remember a lot," I reassured him. His own kids, fifteen years younger than I, do not recall our grandparents in the same way—they were just babies when our grandfather died; by the time they were growing up, our grandmother was in her eighties and no longer able to take long walks with them or grow as many flowers in her garden as she used to. Kenichi was happy to have me remember and write about what his kids could not, so that the memories are kept alive.

**3.** How do you think Mori feels about her uncle? Why?

"There's one thing I felt really bad about," Kenichi confessed. "I thought about it the whole time I was reading your novel."

"What was that?" I asked him, leaning forward over the table where we were having dinner.

"Remember those diaries your mother kept when she was in high school?" he asked. "There were many of them, in those glossy, yellow notebooks."

"Yes," I said. "I have them." Shortly after I left for college, my grandmother had found them in the attic of her house and sent them to me.

"But you don't have all the volumes," Kenichi said. "Do you know why?"

I shook my head. There were a few months missing here and there, but I always assumed that one or two notebooks must have gotten misplaced.

**4.** Can you make a prediction about what has happened to the notebooks?

"When your mother finished high school and was in Kobe, working as a secretary, I was living in that house in the country with your grandparents and your Aunt Keiko. We were just kids." Kenichi paused.

I nodded, encouraging him to go on. Kenichi is sixteen years younger than my mother, who was the oldest of six children.

"Those diaries were already in the attic then. When I was in grade school, I found them there. The notebooks had such beautiful white paper—thick and glossy. I was only eight or nine, you have to remember. I tore the pages out and made paper airplanes. Every day, I would sit on top of the stairs, tear out page after page of your mother's diary, and fold paper airplanes. I watched them flying down the stairs. I got pretty good at folding planes. Some of them went quite a long way. That's how a couple of those notebooks got lost. When I read your novel, I remembered that and

**5.** Do you think the writer will be angry about the loss of the diaries? Why?

felt so bad." Kenichi made a face. "I can't believe how stupid I was as a kid," he concluded.

"Don't worry about it," I said, feeling suddenly so happy that I was laughing. I was imagining hundreds of white paper airplanes flying. "Your telling me about it now makes up for everything."

I'm not sure if Kenichi was convinced. I couldn't explain my feelings to him very well. But maybe it doesn't matter. In the book of my past, there is now an image of my uncle as a boy sitting on a stairway and flying paper airplanes, made of beautiful paper, with my mother's words in their precise creases. Kenichi might think that each plane deprived me of a page of my mother's writing, a page of memory, but the opposite is true. I see those planes floating down the stairway toward me, passed on from Kenichi to me because we share a past and we both loved my mother—because we belong to the same family. I cannot ask for more, except the impossible: that I had the eloquence[1] to tell my uncle, in his language, what I can only write in mine.

**6. How does Mori feel about the paper airplanes?**

---

**1. eloquence:** speech or writing that is vivid, forceful, fluent, and graceful.

| READING SKILL

## Predicting Outcomes

**Seeing into the Future**   You are reading a personal narrative about a week-long camping trip in the wilderness. The author says that he has never been camping before and has rarely left the big city where he was born. You think, "This kid is in for a shock. He'll be miserable and home-sick before the second day!" You keep reading to find out whether your prediction is accurate—or whether the author loves the adventure of the outdoors. When you read any well-written personal narrative, it is very likely that you are frequently asking yourself, "What will happen next?" Whenever you try to answer that question, you are **predicting outcomes.** If you are not predicting, then you may be missing what's going on in the personal narrative. Predicting outcomes helps you follow the narrative and keep from getting lost.

You already may be predicting outcomes—without even knowing it. You make predictions every time you

- read a sentence—and predict what will happen in the next sentence

- read the first paragraph—and think about what will happen at the end of the narrative

To predict, you take information and clues from what you are reading and combine them with what you already know to make an educated guess about what will happen next. Written as an equation, predicting outcomes might look like this:

**TIP**  The beauty of prediction is, you don't always have to be right—the importance of predicting is to be involved and active as you read.

The Prediction Equation

Information and clues in the reading + What you already know = Prediction

**Predicting Outcomes**

How do you solve the prediction equation? First, you need to sharpen your curiosity. Then, think through the mental steps below. (Here the steps are applied to an example sentence from "Paper Airplanes.")

**Example:**
"The last time I saw my uncle, Kenichi, he had just finished reading my first novel. . . ."

▷ **STEP 1** Compare what you have read with the catalog of events, behaviors, reactions, and people already in your mind.

He has read her novel. When I read a novel through, it means I really liked it. Maybe he liked the novel.

▷ **STEP 2** Ask yourself a question or two about the characters or events in the section you have read.

Will Kenichi say something about the novel? What will he say?

▷ **STEP 3** Answer your questions from Step 2. As you do, consider the clues in your reading.

- **Important events** and **ideas** might cause other events.

- The **sequence** in which things have happened could be a clue to what might happen next.

The first paragraph is about family sharing memories. Maybe the novel had something to do with the writer's memories of her family in Japan, and Kenichi will have something to say about that.

▷ **STEP 4** Predict an outcome by applying your experience to the clues from the text.

Kenichi probably liked the novel, and it's likely that he will tell her that he did. The writer and Kenichi will share a family memory.

As you continue reading and predicting, your comprehension of the narrative will become more complete and detailed. Better comprehension will help you make more accurate predictions. You will find that your predictions follow a spiral pattern like the one shown to the right. First, you predict. Then, you confirm or correct your predictions by comparing them with what you know. You then start the process all over again by making more predictions. This **prediction spiral** starts at the beginning of the narrative with general predictions and narrows to more specific and accurate predictions at the end.

predict → confirm
correct
compare what you know
predict → confirm
correct
compare what you know
predict → confirm
correct
compare what you know
the process continues

Although you have already read "Paper Airplanes" and know what happens, by practicing the steps in the Thinking It Through, you will be better able to apply them later to new material. Re-read the thirteenth paragraph in "Paper Airplanes," the one that begins with "Those diaries were already in the attic . . ." Then, work through the Thinking It Through steps to predict how the writer would react to Kenichi's confession about the diaries. On your own paper, copy the chart below and fill in the blanks.

| Steps | Responses |
|---|---|
| **1.** Write down how you think people in your experience would have reacted to Kenichi's tearing up the notebooks as a child. | |
| **2.** Write down questions about the writer's possible reactions to Kenichi's confession. | |
| **3.** Write down your answers to the questions you created in Step 2. | |
| **4.** Predict how the writer will respond to Kenichi. | |

READING FOCUS

# Expressive Style

**Reading Between the Lines**   In a personal narrative, writers use an expressive style to create a personal connection with their readers and to convey their thoughts and feelings. Writers of some forms of nonfiction use formal or neutral language in order to keep their feelings from showing through in their writing. In a personal narrative, however, emotion is an important part of the self-expression the writer is trying to achieve.

When writing personal narratives, writers generally use **first-person pronouns** such as *I, me, we,* and *us* to bring their readers into their world. In "Paper Airplanes," Kyoko Mori uses first person to tell you a story from her life. She wants her readers to know what she is thinking and feeling; her own thoughts and feelings are what make the story meaningful. For example, Mori writes about what she thought happened to her mother's missing diaries:

> I shook my head. There were a few months missing here and there, but I always assumed that one or two notebooks must have gotten misplaced.

Writers may insert **personal thoughts and feelings** into a personal narrative by using words such as *anxious, beloved,* or *triumphant* that **tell** directly how the writer or another person in a narrative feels. By carefully selecting words with certain shades of meaning, writers also use word choice to communicate thoughts and feelings in a less obvious way—to **show** you indirectly how they or other people in their narratives feel.

The two short passages below are about the same event. Notice, however, how the underlined parts of the second passage make it more personal by communicating thoughts and feelings.

> **Informative:** As a boy, Kenichi flew paper planes down a stairway. He shared the memory with his niece.
>
> **Expressive:** I see those planes <u>floating down</u> the stairway toward me, passed on from Kenichi to me because we share a past and <u>we both loved my mother</u>—because we belong to the same family.

While the first sentence contains information, it does not express any particular feeling. The second sentence **shows** and **tells** the thoughts and feelings the writer experienced. Notice how the writer's word choices give you clues about her feelings. By describing the planes with the gentle word *floating,* Mori **shows** that Kenichi's use of the diaries did not anger her. To **tell** her readers about a feeling she and her uncle shared, she uses the expressive word *loved*.

## YOUR TURN 3   Analyzing for Expressive Style

After reading the first and final paragraphs of "Paper Airplanes," complete the following steps.

1. Find and jot down several of the pronouns used. How would the narrative be different if Mori had used "she" instead of "I"?

2. Find and make a list of at least four key words that reveal the expressive style. Describe in your own words the thoughts and feelings you think those words express.

## Prefixes

Kyoko Mori's writing shows that she has mastered her second language. Her vocabulary is varied and includes words with prefixes that can help you determine their meanings. Studying these prefixes will help you to understand and use a wider variety of words. Here is a list of some words with common prefixes that appear in "Paper Airplanes."

| sample word | prefix | meaning |
|---|---|---|
| misplaced | *mis-* | wrong(ly), not |
| translation | *trans-* | across, through |
| expansive | *ex-* | out, from |
| remember | *re-* | back(ward), again |
| impossible | *in-* | not |

(Note: *In-* changes to *im-* before *m* and *p*.)

### THINKING IT THROUGH **Recognizing Prefixes**

Here is one way to become familiar with prefixes so that you can identify them and use them to understand new words.

1. Fold a sheet of paper in half. On the left-hand side, make a list of prefixes you want to learn. On the right-hand side, write the meanings of the prefixes.

2. Work to commit the prefixes and their meanings to memory. Quiz yourself on the prefixes by folding your paper to hide one of the two sides.

3. After memorizing the prefixes, find some words in your everyday reading that use them. Write down what you think each word means, given the meaning of the prefix. In these notes, underline the prefix and its meaning. For example,

misplaced     placed wrongly

4. Check your answers in a dictionary.

### PRACTICE

Use what you have learned about prefixes to choose the word that corresponds to each of the following definitions.

1. so fine in texture that one can see **through** to the other side
   (a) apparent (c) transparent
   (b) impart (d) obscure

2. **not** able to express oneself
   (a) transcendent (c) substantial
   (b) inarticulate (d) retroactive

3. to make someone sure **again**
   (a) ensure (c) assure
   (b) insure (d) reassure

4. to put away **wrongly**
   (a) delay (c) mislay
   (b) relay (d) inlay

5. to ship materials **out** of a place
   (a) purport (c) report
   (b) import (d) export

# Predicting Outcomes

Some reading tests contain questions that ask you to predict the **most likely** outcomes of events described in a reading passage. Since you will not be able to read about what happens next, you must be sure your prediction follows from the passage you have been given.

Read the example passage and answer the prediction question that follows.

If I took ballet, my mother decided, my awkward years would be less awkward. She was not right. Rather than a lesson in grace, my first ballet lesson was a lesson in humiliation. The teacher yanked my foot high as I attempted to lift my leg while sweeping my arm gracefully from one side to the other. However, my flawed leg lift was not the cause of the teacher's disgust; instead, the problem was the little bow on my slipper. No one had told me that you were supposed to tuck the bows into your shoes. This was just the first of many rules that I broke in my career of disgrace at Madame LaVec's School of Dance.

Based on the information in this passage, what is the narrator most likely to do?

**A.** go on to become a prima ballerina

**B.** dance in the school musical

**C.** be embarrassed again at dance lessons

**D.** quit taking dance lessons after the first one

## THINKING IT THROUGH — Answering Prediction Questions

Use the following steps to choose the correct answer.

▶ **STEP 1** Read the passage carefully. Everything you need to know is there. The correct answer must follow easily from the information in the passage—it should never depend on a change in a person or an unlikely turn of events.

▶ **STEP 2** Using the information in the passage, make a prediction about what will most likely happen next. Ask yourself what will result from the events in the passage.

▶ **STEP 3** For this kind of question, you will need to read all of the answers before you choose one. Eliminate answers by matching them against what you know from the passage and what you have predicted.

Answer **A** is the opposite of what would probably happen to the narrator; this answer would require an unlikely turn of events. Answer **B** does not follow easily from the description of the dance class given in the reading passage. If the writer is not a very good dancer, it is very unlikely she will dance in the school musical. Answer **C** makes sense because the person in the passage does something wrong and embarrassing. Also, the passage states that "this was just the first" event in a "career of disgrace." Answer **C** is clearly the correct answer. Answer **D** may seem likely at first, but the last sentence shows that the writer did *not* quit right away.

# Writing a Personal Narrative

## WHAT'S AHEAD?

In this workshop you will write a personal narrative. You will also learn how to

- **draw on your memory to find topics**
- **consider the significance of an experience**
- **include and organize vivid details**
- **improve your writing with strong verbs**
- **check for subject-verb agreement**

**W**hat experience could you tell about in a personal narrative? You might write about the time you overcame your fear of the dark and went into the basement, only to have a bird that seemed the size of a pterodactyl fly at you. You might recount a perfect afternoon and what it meant to you.

In this workshop, you will write a personal narrative that not only communicates experiences and the ideas that spring from them, but also adds to your own understanding of the experiences. Your personal narrative should include both an account of your experience and some reflections, or thoughts, about the meaning of that experience. You will rely on your memory and your powers of description to make the moment real to your readers. Your thoughtfulness will make the experience meaningful.

# Prewriting

## Search Your Memory for Topics

**Magic Moments** Because you will reflect on something personal for this paper, you will naturally think about your past. Jog your memory by taking one of the following suggestions.

- **Visit a place** you knew when you were younger to help you recall childhood memories. It could be a park, a school, or even a room. Notice how it may have changed. Think about one event you experienced there.

- **Pick a day** of the week or a certain special day and make a list of everything you did on that day. Was there something unusual about that day? If not, perhaps you would like to consider the ordinary workings of your everyday life.

- **Think about the first time** you did something—for example, the first time you rode a bike fast down a hill or went alone to the skating rink. Often in these "firsts" you can find a moment in which you learned about yourself or your world.

When you have thought of some memories that might make good topics, write a one-sentence description of each memory. Read over the sentences and choose two or three possibilities.

## Evaluate Your Potential Topics

**Do the Write Thing**   You must judge your topics to decide which one you want to pursue. To select one memory to write about, ask yourself the questions in the following chart. One writer used this chart to help her decide between two topics.

| Questions to Consider | Topic 1: I learn to build campfires. | Topic 2: I buy bread by myself for the first time. |
| --- | --- | --- |
| Is the experience important to me? Why? | 1. I trace my love of camping and the outdoors to this experience. 2. It shows my relationship with my dad. | 1. It was the first time I did such a grown-up thing. 2. It shows my mother's trust in me. |
| How well do I remember the experience? List details. | 1. We gathered sticks in the park and arranged them in the shapes of different campfires. 2. We were in New York City. | 1. I went to the corner market. I don't remember too many specifics. 2. Walking all alone felt strange. |
| Am I willing to share the experience? | Yes, it is not too private. | Yes, it is not embarrassing. |
| Will my experience be interesting to others? Why? | Yes, it is unusual to learn to build campfires in New York City. | Probably not. This experience might seem ordinary, not very lively. |

With this information, the writer can judge which topic would be the best to pursue. The writer of the chart on the previous page decided that although she would be willing to share either one, the campfire topic would be more interesting. The second one is a more common experience, and the details of it are less vivid in her mind.

## YOUR TURN 4 Choosing and Evaluating Topics

- Brainstorm a list of memories.
- Write a one-sentence description of each memory.
- Choose at least two topics to compare in a chart like the one on the previous page.
- Based on your chart, decide which topic is most appropriate.

## Define Your Purpose, Audience, and Tone

**Your Side of the Story**   In a personal narrative, your **purpose** is already decided: You will write to express yourself and to share your experience with your audience. Is the writer of the campfire narrative trying to tell her audience how to build campfires? No. She is writing about the love she has for her father, using campfires to show the bond between them.

**Reference Note**

For more on **expressive style,** see page 58.

Your **audience** is all the people who are going to read your personal narrative. It could be classmates, teachers, friends, or parents—any or all of them. Ask yourself some questions to get a feel for your audience.

- **Who is my intended audience?** If your audience only includes people who shared your experience, you might write differently than if you are writing for those who were not there.

- **What will the audience need to know to help them understand my experience?** Not everyone knows about campfires, so the writer may have to provide some background information.

- **How will I get my audience's attention?** You can ask a question or make a statement that makes people curious or creates suspense.

**KEY CONCEPT**

The **tone** of a personal narrative will always be—you guessed it—personal. You are telling your own true story. **Because you will write in your own voice, use first-person pronouns—*I, me,* and perhaps, *we, us,* and *our.*** Speak directly to your audience, creating an informal, even friendly, tone in your narrative. Use words that sound friendly. For example, you might use *say* or *show* instead of *express.*

# Gather Details

**Let Your Memory Be Your Guide**   Your memory will be your chief instrument for gathering details that will bring your readers into your experience. To search your memory for the little things that will make your story live, turn your attention to details about events, people, places, thoughts, and feelings. Remember to think of all five senses when you are gathering details. Often people use their visual memory. However, you must also ask yourself how a place smelled, how a person sounded, how a surface felt, or how a food tasted. You can chart your details, using questions to prompt specifics for your narrative. Below is a chart one writer created.

| Who or What | Trigger Questions | Details |
|---|---|---|
| Events | What is the main event in the experience? <br><br> What happened exactly? <br><br> What are some other events? | walking in the park, practicing building campfires, collecting twigs, laying them in patterns, camp contest, camping in the mountains |
| People | Who was in my experience? <br><br> What did they look like? <br><br> What did they say? | me—age five, tidy, wearing dress; dad—a young man, glasses, dressed for work, inventive |
| Places | Where did the experience happen? <br><br> How did the place look, sound, and smell? | a city park, summer, cool, early morning, big trees with full leaves, shady |
| Thoughts and Feelings | What did I think and feel as the events unfolded? | I loved time alone with my dad, felt happy skipping beside him, felt a bond we shared when camping |

**TIP**   Using **dialogue,** people's own words, will help your narrative come alive. Think about what the people in your experience said. Also, remember that not everyone sounds alike— your eight-year-old sister and your older neighbor use very different words and sentence structures. Try to make dialogue sound as natural and as real as possible.

# Organize Details

**Ducks in a Row**   Next, order your details. **Chronological order is most frequently used in narrative writing**—the event that happened first is at

KEY CONCEPT

**Reference Note**

For more on **time lines,** see page 818.

the beginning of the narrative, followed by the event that happened next, and so on. Guide readers through the sequence of events by including transitions such as *at first, to begin, then, later, after that, at last,* and *finally.* You might make a time line to organize the events in your narrative. Placing the events into a time line will help you accomplish three things: (1) to see which details connect to which events, (2) to order your details, and (3) to see which details are essential to your narrative.

## Reflect on Your Experience

**And So It Ends**   You chose a particular experience to write about because it was important to you in some way. You will want to convey this meaning to your readers, too. To reflect on the meaning of your personal narrative, ask yourself questions like these:

**TIP**   Personal narratives often do not have a thesis in the first paragraph. The writer will hint at the meaning of an experience but not reveal the meaning entirely until the final paragraph.

- How did I change from the beginning to the end of the experience?

- What did I learn about myself or the world or other people from the experience?

- What were my feelings at the beginning of, during, and at the end of the experience?

Write a simple sentence telling what the experience meant to you. Just remember that this meaning can change during the process of writing, as you reflect upon the experience. For the campfire topic, the writer developed this statement about its meaning:

> A simple lesson in building campfires shows the love my dad and I share.

When you read the Writer's Model (page 69), notice how this statement is expressed indirectly throughout the personal narrative.

**YOUR TURN 5**   **Plotting Details**

Use the prewriting instruction to plan your personal narrative.
- decide on your audience, tone, and purpose
- create a graphic organizer to help you search your memory for details
- arrange your details in chronological order
- reflect on the meaning of your experience

# Using Figurative Language

How can you help your readers to experience your personal story? Your language, as well as your subject matter, must draw your readers in. The details you include should show your readers something they have not seen before or make a familiar experience become more meaningful. One way to add this kind of life and power to your writing is to use **figurative language**—language that compares two unlike things. Figurative language takes readers by surprise and shows them a new way of seeing something. For example, in the sentence, "Damon looked up at the dishwater sky," the sky is compared to dishwater. The comparison makes you think about what the sky and dishwater have in common. You can probably remember days when the sky was dull and dirty looking, just like dishwater.

Examples of figurative language include **similes, metaphors,** and **personification.**

| | | |
|---|---|---|
| A **simile** compares two seemingly unlike things using the words *like, as, than,* or *resembles.* | Original:<br>Simile: | The clouds were heavy.<br>The clouds felt like an alien spaceship hovering ominously overhead. |
| A **metaphor** compares two seemingly unlike things without using *like, as, than,* or *resembles.* A metaphor says that something *is* something else. | Original:<br>Metaphor: | My dress blew around in the wind.<br>My dress was a sail billowing in a wind, making me feel as if I were about to keel over. |
| **Personification** gives human qualities to something that is not human, such as an animal, an object, or an idea. | Original:<br>Personification: | The spring rain fell.<br>Spring wept its bitter tears of rain. |

## PRACTICE

On a piece of paper, rewrite the following sentences using a metaphor, simile, or personification.

**Example:**

**1.** The mountain range rose out of the valley.

*1. The mountain range, like a man's craggy profile, rose out of the valley.*

1. The trees made shadows.
2. The building looked sleek and new.
3. I felt sad.
4. There were some scary noises.
5. The carpet was soft.
6. The dog was very smart.
7. The boat moved through the water.
8. She hit the tennis ball.
9. I hurried down the sidewalk.
10. The stream flowed quickly.

## Personal Narrative

| Framework | Directions and Explanations |

### Introduction

- Use an engaging opening.
- Supply background information.
- Hint at the meaning of the experience.

### Body

- Discuss first, second, third events and so on, including details.
- Use chronological order.

### Conclusion

- Express the meaning of the experience.

**Get Your Readers' Attention**   Draw your readers into your narrative by using a quotation, making an unusual statement, or posing a striking question.

**Build Background**   Give your readers some details they might need before reading your narrative.

**Hint at Your Meaning**   Though you will probably not want to reveal the meaning of the experience at the beginning, you should lay the groundwork for it in your introduction. Think of it as giving your readers clues about where you are going with the narrative.

**Work in the Details**   As the body of your narrative takes shape, think of the events as the skeleton and the details as the muscles that define the body and give it movement and life. When you add details, remember to include people, places, thoughts, and feelings, as well as dialogue, similes, and metaphors. Ordering your events chronologically is the simplest way to start.

**Reflect on Your Experience**   Referring to the groundwork you laid in your introduction, finish your narrative by reflecting on what you learned or how you changed. Show your readers the meaning you discovered in the experience.

**YOUR TURN 6** **Writing a First Draft**

Use the framework above to write a first draft of your personal narrative. The Writer's Model on the next page shows how one writer used the framework.

# A Writer's Model

This personal narrative follows the framework on the previous page. The notes in the margin highlight the elements in the framework that appear in this narrative.

## A Campfire Girl

Do people make campfires anymore? I suppose they do, but building campfires is prohibited in many places now. If campfires are not banned by rangers, there is still a common ecological agreement that picking the ground bare of wood and scarring the land with fire rings is a bad idea. Still, I am a campfire girl at heart. Even though I dutifully use camp stoves in the mountains and in the car camps, I still love a small blaze to warm my hands, to dry soggy socks, and to stare into on nights darkened by the distance from a city's glow.

It all began with a walk in a park in New York City. When I was a tidy little skirt-wearing five-year-old, my family lived in New York for a summer. My father and I would go out early, when it was still cool, to walk the dog. Dad would be dressed for work, his shoes treading the asphalt path as I happily did a quickstep along beside him.

One morning, as my father threw sticks for the dog, I started picking up sticks of my own. Always ready to play and teach, my dad crouched down to show me how to build a campfire. He took my sticks and helped me gather others, graduated in size from tiny twigs to hefty branches. Gently propping the twigs together, he started with a tepee shape. I watched his careful hands place sticks of the next size on top of the others. He warned me not to pack the sticks too tightly together, so the air could flow and feed the fire. (This was the theory at least; we did not light our fires there in the middle of the city.) While I worked on the tepee and other structures— the log cabin, the "A"—the sounds of the city faded away.

Several years later, at summer camp, we had a contest: who could make a campfire the fastest using just one match? I have no doubt that my lessons in the park in New York City laid the foundation for my championship fire building at camp. I used the "A" structure. I blew gently on my kindling, giving the flame just enough air to grow and light the larger sticks.

**INTRODUCTION**
Engaging opening
Background

Hint at meaning

**BODY**
First event

Details about people and places

Feeling
Second event

Details about event and people

Thought

Third event

Details about events and people

*(continued)*

(continued)

Fourth event
Feelings

Details about people, places

CONCLUSION

Meaning of the experience

Later, when I was no longer a tidy little girl, but a rugged teenager in jeans and work boots, I took special pleasure in collecting wood, placing each size in a separate pile. Then I would set the kindling and get it burning, making a small cook fire. Dad and I never built great big bonfires in rings with three- to four-foot diameters. We made campfires just big enough for the skillet we packed into the wilderness despite its weight. (It cooked so much better than the aluminum camp pans that came in mess kits.) We ate many meals over our fires—potatoes and onions and just-caught trout.

That day in the park, my dad could not have known of the backpacking trips he and I would share ten years later. Still, I see those little piles of sticks as my introduction to life outdoors. The thickly leafed trees of the park gave way to pines and aspen overhead, but the kinship I experienced with my dad stayed the same. I was his campfire girl, sharing in his love of the outdoors, sharing his skill with a fire. We were building something to warm us then and now.

# A Student's Model

**This is an excerpt from a personal narrative written by Blake Wynia, a student at William G. Enloe High School in Raleigh, North Carolina. The narrative recounts an incident that happened while the writer was clowning around at band camp and the lesson it taught him about carelessness.**

### Carelessness

. . . In a moment of carelessness, I started running towards the door with my hands stretched out in front of me. At this time I noticed the door had a three-by-four-foot rectangle of glass (with wires in it, of course) near the bottom of it, glaring at me villainously, almost mischievously. In front of the door, there was a black rubber mat, . . . slick with rain. I ran towards the door, the Mission: Impossible music blaring from my lungs. I was a speeding train off its tracks, about to crash. I stepped on the black mat, and my feet slid out from under me. I was sliding forward with my knees out, headed towards the ground. My knees hit the glass rectangle, and went through, shattering the glass like a hot air balloon bursting from intense air pressure. I immediately got up and saw the look on my friends' faces. They were all stunned, and they were all laughing, immaturely. I saw my own face in the reflection in the window, and it was sheer terror. My first thought was that I was going to get kicked out of the clinic for misbehavior . . . At this time, I felt a slight trickle down my leg. I looked down, and my right knee was bleeding from an inch wide gash. Later, . . . I was taken to the emergency room, where I got three stitches in my knee. Thankfully, I was not kicked out of the camp.

This experience taught me much on how to behave properly. The fear I had had of getting in trouble, combined with the disappointment of my mother in me, changed my attitude greatly. I now had learned how to restrain myself. I no longer do crazy things just to make my friends laugh. I am smart enough to think of safer ways to accomplish this feat.

**BODY**

**Event**

**Simile**

**Writer's thought**
**Sensory detail**

**CONCLUSION**

**Meaning of the experience**

# Revising

## Evaluate and Revise Your Draft

**Do Look Back**   To improve your draft, you must read it and read it again. Work collaboratively to concentrate first on content and organization and second on style. Looking twice will give you the necessary time to correct mistakes and also to make your writing more accurate and more powerful. Stronger writing will help you create an experience that will affect your readers.

➤ **First Reading: Content and Organization**   With a peer or on your own, use the guidelines below to evaluate your narrative and make improvements. The tips in the second column will help you locate any trouble spots.

### Personal Narrative: Content and Organization Guidelines for Peer and Self-Evaluation

| Evaluation Questions | ▶ Tips | ▶ Revision Techniques |
|---|---|---|
| ❶ Does the introduction include an attention grabber, some background information, and a hint at the meaning of the experience? | ▶ **Bracket** the attention grabber and background information. **Underline** the hint about the meaning of the experience. If there are no brackets or underlined sentences, revise. | ▶ **Add** background information or attention grabber. **Add** a sentence that suggests the meaning of the experience. |
| ❷ Do details of events, people, and places seem real? | ▶ **Circle** details. If you have fewer than three circles in each paragraph, revise. | ▶ **Add** details that answer *5W-How?* questions about people, places, or events in the paragraph. **Add** dialogue or draw on the five senses for additional details. |
| ❸ Are there details about thoughts and feelings? | ▶ **Highlight** sentences that contain thoughts or feelings. If the paper runs an entire paragraph without a highlighted sentence, revise. | ▶ **Elaborate** on details by answering the questions, "What did I think?" or "How did I feel?" |
| ❹ Is the order of events clear? | ▶ **Number** the events in chronological order. Revise if the numbers are not in sequence. | ▶ **Rearrange** events to show chronological order, or **add** transitional words and phrases to show how events are ordered. |
| ❺ Does the conclusion discuss the meaning of the experience? | ▶ **Underline** sentences in the conclusion that explain the meaning of the experience. If no sentences are underlined, revise. | ▶ **Add** a statement that shows what your experience means to you. |

**ONE WRITER'S REVISIONS** After looking at how one writer changed part of the personal narrative from page 69, answer the questions that follow.

It all began with a walk in a park in New York City. When I was ~~five~~ *a tidy little skirt-wearing five-year-old,* my family lived in New York for a summer. My

father and I would go out early, when it was still cool, to walk

the dog. Dad would be dressed for work. ~~He treaded~~ *his shoes treading* the asphalt

path as I did a *happily* quickstep along beside him.

add and elaborate

add and elaborate

add

## Analyzing the Revision Process

1. How did adding details improve the paragraph?

2. What does the word "happily" add to the last sentence?

PEER REVIEW

Ask a classmate to answer the following questions after he or she has read your paper.

1. What details helped you to imagine the writer's experience?

2. What details could the writer have included to make things more clear?

### YOUR TURN 7 **Focusing on Content and Organization**

Using the guidelines on the previous page, evaluate your personal narrative. Then, revise your paper so that it is clearer, more personal, and more interesting.

**Second Reading: Style** The first time you went over your paper, you revised your content and organization. Now, you need to refine style to suit your audience and your purpose. One way to shape your style is to use **precise verbs** to express what you mean. This allows your readers to live through the experience with you. In your second reading, use the following style guidelines to help you focus on making your verbs more precise.

## Style Guidelines

| Evaluation Question | ▶ Tip | ▶ Revision Technique |
|---|---|---|
| **Are your verbs precise?** | ▶ Pick four sentences in each paragraph. **Circle** only the verbs in them. Do the verbs hint at *how* or *in what way* something is done? If not, revise. | ▶ **Replace** at least two weak verbs per paragraph with precise ones. (Brainstorm for synonyms or use a thesaurus to find more precise verbs.) |

# Precise Verbs

Precise verbs often tell more than *what* was done. They tell *how* something was done—it's like having a built-in adverb. For example, if you have the word *run* in your narrative, think about more precise words that show **how** people run, such as *hurry, rush, dash,* or *flee.* In your quest for the right verb, choose the one that gives life to your writing. For example, if someone in your narrative is moving slowly in a carefree way, the verb *saunter* is a better choice than the verb *walk.* Writing with precision takes time: time to check the dictionary or thesaurus, and time to think about just the right word.

**ONE WRITER'S REVISIONS** Using the style guidelines on page 73, the writer of the model on page 69 revised for precise verbs in the following way. Study the revisions and answer the questions that follow.

**BEFORE REVISION**

I saw his careful hands place sticks of the next size on top of the others. He told me not to pack the sticks too tightly together. . . .

*Saw* is not very descriptive—how?
*Told* is fairly common—in what way?

**AFTER REVISION**

I watched his careful hands place sticks of the next size on top of the others. He warned me not to pack the sticks too tightly together. . . .

*Watched* better describes what she was doing.
*Warned* tells how he spoke.

## Analyzing the Revision Process

1. How does *watched* better describe what the girl is doing?

2. Why is the verb *warned* better than *told*? What other verbs could the writer use?

**TIP** Try using your word-processing program's thesaurus to find more precise replacements for imprecise verbs. Enter a tired, boring verb into the thesaurus, and explore the lists of possible replacements that the thesaurus gives. For example, for the word *make*, you will find *create, construct,* and *build.*

## YOUR TURN 8 Using Precise Verbs

Fine-tune the verbs in your narrative. Use the information on the previous pages to identify common or overused verbs and to replace them with precise ones.

## Designing Your Writing

**Using Illustrations** Make your paper inviting by illustrating it with a photograph or drawing. Choose an illustration that works well with the narrative. Whether you scan a photograph in on the computer or paste a drawing in manually, consider the following guidelines.

- The eye is drawn to images. Remember that readers will look at your illustration before they read your paper. Therefore, the illustration must truly complement your paper rather than distract from it. For the campfire story, a picture of a forest fire, a tent, or some wildlife—none of which are mentioned—might confuse the readers. A picture of a frying pan on a campfire would work better.

- Because you have written a personal narrative, you may wish to choose a photograph or drawing of yourself. You may even have a photograph of yourself taken at the time the events you have written about took place. For example, the campfire story could be illustrated with a photograph of the writer at five, or with one of her and her father around a campfire.

- You have used a lot of details to make your narrative vivid. Choose an illustration that will draw your readers in—one that gives them clues about key details in your narrative. A snapshot of the campfire girl among her friends or of her at her current age would give the wrong clues to her readers and would mislead them about the content of the paper.

- The placement of your illustration is important. If your illustration complements your paper as a whole, you may choose to place it at the beginning or the end. If your illustration relates to a particular detail, place the illustration near where that detail is mentioned in the text.

**TIP** If you are scanning a photograph onto the computer, you will need to decide on the resolution of the image. Resolution refers to the number of dpi (dots per inch) that will form the image. Generally, the higher the resolution (the more dots per inch), the sharper and more detailed the image will be. Keep in mind that your decisions about resolution affect the size of the file needed to store your image.

# Publishing

## Proofread Your Personal Narrative

**Reference Note**

For **proofreading guidelines,** see page 13.

**Error-Free Zone**  Proofread your paper before you prepare a clean copy for publishing. At this stage, you must rely on the **conventions of written English** to eliminate all grammar, punctuation, and spelling errors. One thing to pay special attention to is subject-verb agreement. While writing and revising, you may have added phrases between some of your subjects and verbs. If so, you might be confused about which form of a verb you need. Be sure your verbs agree with their subjects.

## Grammar Link

### Subject-Verb Agreement: Interrupting Prepostional Phrases

If you want your sentences to make sense to readers, it is important that your verbs agree in number with their subjects.

- **A singular subject should have a singular verb.**

**Example:**
That **cat climbs.**

- **A plural subject should have a plural verb.**

**Example:**
Those **cats climb.**

The number of a verb does not change even when a phrase comes between it and its subject. If a prepositional phrase following the subject contains a plural noun, you could be tempted to make the verb plural also. However, the verb should remain singular.

**Example:**
The **cat** as well as the dogs **wants** to chase birds and squirrels.

**Example:**
Those **cats** at the window **want** to chase birds and squirrels.

**Reference Note**

For more on **subject-verb agreement,** see page 493.

### PRACTICE

From each pair of verbs in parentheses, choose the form that agrees in number with the subject of each sentence.

**Example:**
1. The passengers on the crowded dock (*hurries, hurry*) to board.
1. The passengers on the crowded dock hurry to board.

1. The ship, along with four tugboats, (*come, comes*) slowly toward the dock.
2. The captain, on the lookout for dangers in the waters, (*bring, brings*) the ship to shore.
3. The passengers in the hold (*is, are*) seasick.
4. Their faces, by the porthole, (*lack, lacks*) any sign of hope or pleasure.
5. Observers of the scene (*note, notes*) that the ship has been at sea for just three hours.

# Publish Your Personal Narrative

**Writer Seeks Readers**  You have written your personal story. It is something to be proud of and to share with other people. Try some of the following ways to reach some readers besides your teacher and classmates.

- Send your paper in the mail or by e-mail to interested relatives or friends. If your narrative is about an event in their lives or about someone your readers know, they might be especially interested to read it. You might even consider giving your paper as a gift to someone for whom it would mean a lot.

- Check with your teacher or look for some magazines that have contests for this kind of personal essay. Well-written, authentic stories from students' lives are often welcomed in magazines for young people.

- Create a class book of personal narratives, dividing them thematically. For example, the themes for memories could be young childhood, school, jobs, and travel.

- If your personal narrative is about school life, you might consider submitting it to your school's yearbook committee.

# Reflect on Your Personal Narrative

 PORTFOLIO

**Count the Ways**  Use the following questions to look back at writing your personal narrative and to make a quick account of what you've learned. If you put this paper into your portfolio, include your responses with it.

- How did your writing this paper help you to understand this experience better or in a new way?

- Are you satisfied with how you conveyed the meaning of your experience? Why or why not? What would you do differently if you wrote another personal narrative?

## YOUR TURN 9  Proofreading, Publishing, and Reflecting

Using the suggestions and questions in the three previous sections of the workshop, take time to proofread your paper, publish it, and reflect on the steps you took to write it.

## Writing a Short Story

Many of the techniques that you used in writing your personal narrative can be applied to writing a short story. Like personal narratives, short stories thrive on details, put events in chronological order, and—often—involve more than one character.

When you write a short story, you can use first-person pronouns just as you used them in your personal narrative. However, if you decide to use first-person pronouns in a short story, remember that the narrator (the "I" in the story) does not necessarily have to be you—it can be any fictional character that you create.

**Stretch the Imagination**   In your personal narrative, the events actually happened to you. It is a true story—nonfiction. However, a short story is **fiction**; it comes from your imagination. You can write a short story about almost anything.

■ Are you interested in things past or in worlds of the future? Think of something you and your friends would like to read. Create a tale of seventeenth-century piracy or of life in a geodesic dome in the 2050s.

■ Even though a story comes from your imagination, you can still write about things you know. Is there something you know about that would serve as the basis for an exciting story? One student's quest to make the basketball team? A person's experience in a new town? Make a list of your ideas and then choose a few to explore when you begin to write.

**How to Begin**   There are four basic building blocks for any story: **plot, characters, point of view,** and **setting.** You will need to use all of them, but you can *start* by considering any one of them.

■ **Start with a plot.** What will happen in your story? Most stories have a **conflict**, or problem, that is the center of the action. Events lead up to the conflict and then, after a turning point, events unwind toward a **resolution** of the conflict. The conflict involves the main character and can be either internal (if a character is struggling with himself or herself) or **external** (if a character is struggling with outside forces). To begin, you can make a list of events that will unfold in your story.

■ **Start with a character.** Maybe you have a great idea for a character. Jot down what you know about your character, using lots of descriptive words—you know just what this character will look like and sound like, what the character will do, say, and think. Once you have your first character sketched out, you can create any others you will need.

■ **Start with a point of view.** Decide who will tell your story. Will one character be the narrator, telling the story from his or her point of view (**first-person point of view**)? Will the narrator be outside the story and able to recount everything that goes on in the mind of each character (**third-person omniscient point of view**)? Whatever point of view you choose, use it consistently throughout the story. Read the examples below to see the difference a choice between first-person point of view and third-person point of view can make.

**First Person:** I noticed Juana talking to Mark after school. I thought he looked nervous.

**Third-Person Omniscient:** When Juana spoke to Mark after school, he flushed with nervous excitement. Maybe, he thought to himself, she would go with him to the dance.

■ **Start with a setting.** Where and when does your story take place? What time of year is it? Setting can be as important to the story as character. In stories that show how a character struggles with natural elements, for example, setting is particularly important. Give your story atmosphere, a general mood or feeling to the place where everything happens.

**Setting an Example**  We do not know which of the elements Gwendolyn Brooks began with when she wrote the story below. Still, it is easy to see that she made good use of all the building blocks—plot, character, point of view, and setting. By reading the story and annotations, you may get some ideas about how you could tell your own story.

### Maud Martha Spares the Mouse
from *Maud Martha* by Gwendolyn Brooks

There. She had it at last. The weeks it had devoted to eluding her, the tricks, the clever hide-and-go-seeks, the routes it had in all sobriety[1] devised, together with the delicious moments it had, undoubtedly, laughed up its sleeve—all to no ultimate avail.[2] She had that mouse.

It shook its little self, as best it could, in the trap. Its bright black eyes contained no appeal—the little creature seemed to understand that there was no hope of mercy from the eternal enemy, no hope of reprieve[3] or postponement—but a fine small dignity. It waited. It looked at Maud Martha.

She wondered what else it was thinking. Perhaps that there was not enough food in its larder. Perhaps that little Betty, a puny child from the start, would not, now, be getting fed. Perhaps that, now, the family's

> Plot—The story starts with the capture of the mouse and flashes back to events and details of past weeks.

> Character—The mouse is a character.

> Setting—The author imagines how the mouse might perceive the world and elaborates, providing details that reveal setting.

---

1. **sobriety:** seriousness.
2. **avail:** help.
3. **reprieve:** temporary relief or escape from trouble or pain.

*(continued)*

**Point of View**—Readers see not only Maud Martha's point of view but the mouse's point of view through Martha's eyes and imagination.

**Conflict and Resolution**—Maud Martha must decide whether or not to set the mouse free. The resolution of the conflict comes when she imagines how the mouse might think and feel.

*(continued)*

seasonal house-cleaning, for lack of expert direction, would be left undone. It might be regretting that young Bobby's education was now at an end. It might be nursing personal regrets. No more the mysterious shadows of the kitchenette, the uncharted twists, the unguessed halls. No more the sweet delights of the chase, the charms of being unsuccessfully hounded, thrown at.

Maud Martha could not bear the little look.

"Go home to your children," she urged. "To your wife or husband." She opened the trap. The mouse vanished.

Suddenly, she was conscious of a new cleanness in her. A wide air walked in her. A life had blundered its way into her power and it had been hers to preserve or destroy. She had not destroyed. In the center of that simple restraint was—creation. She had created a piece of life. It was wonderful.

"Why," she thought, as her height doubled, "why, I'm good! I am *good*."

She ironed her aprons. Her back was straight. Her eyes were mild, and soft with a godlike loving-kindness.

**The Heart of the Matter**  In your personal narrative, you wrote about the meaning of your experience. In fiction, writers also convey a meaning, called **theme.** Gwendolyn Brooks has given her story a theme, or insight about life: By simply letting the mouse go, Maud Martha creates life. The meaning of the story is that creation can come from the most basic of acts—deciding not to do harm. Consider how you could use characters, plot, setting, and point of view to convey the theme, or meaning, of your own story.

**YOUR TURN 10  Writing Your Short Story**

Now, write your own short story. Use the building blocks—plot, character, setting, point of view—and be sure to choose a theme for your story. Fill your story with details, make sure the order of events is clear, and try to use precise verbs. After you have written a draft of your story, remember to revise, proofread, and publish it.

# Presenting and Evaluating Oral Narratives

Talk    Listen

**Y**ou have probably already told many personal narratives aloud—what happened when the family car broke down on vacation, what the new kitten did when you first brought it home, or how your team won the championship. When you tell a story aloud, you are giving an **oral narrative.** In this section you will learn how to tell a story aloud to your class or to an unfamiliar audience. You will plan, practice, and present this story, so the experience will be different from your everyday storytelling. Your story does not need to be true; it can be based on fact or imagination. You might tell a story you have heard from friends or relatives, or you might present the personal narrative you wrote for the Writer's Workshop. Just be sure to choose an interesting story that you can tell in a lively way.

## Remember Story Essentials

You are probably already familiar with the makings of a good narrative. As you are deciding on a narrative to tell, remember that a good story should

■ describe where and when the narrative took place

■ establish a point of view (let listeners know through whose eyes the events are being viewed)

■ include an interesting series of events and memorable personalities

■ provide details about events, places, people, thoughts, and feelings, including vivid images and sensory descriptions

■ have a meaning or theme

■ appeal to its intended audience (in this case, your listeners)

**TIP** Use your eyes to show emotion and to keep your audience with you. Making **eye contact** is a key part of any oral presentation. It helps the storyteller draw listeners into the narrative.

# Use Gestures to Tell Your Story

"Once upon a time . . ." Even the oldest stories can be made new and exciting with the right storytelling techniques. When you tell a story, you have the opportunity to enhance a narrative using **nonverbal** communication. To convey the meaning of your words, you must use your body, hands, and facial expressions in a **nonverbal** way. A gesture such as flapping your hand in one direction can signify a bird's flight or the escape of your hero. If someone in your narrative is surprised, then show an expression of surprise on your face to emphasize your words.

# Use Vocal Techniques to Tell Your Story

Perhaps even more important than gesture is your voice. In storytelling, you must use your voice like a musical instrument so that your listeners will eagerly follow your words. There are three principal ways you can use your voice to make your story more interesting.

- **Change the pitch of your voice** when different characters are speaking. Storytellers will often use a high pitch to represent a small character. Pitch can also create a mood or express feelings. A low, solemn voice, for example, might be appropriate at the beginning of a scary story.

- **Speak more loudly or softly,** depending on the number of people in your audience, and on what is happening in your story. A quieter voice, for example, would probably work better for a suspenseful story. Making your voice thunder can indicate not only a certain mood, but also a change in character.

- **Speak more quickly or more slowly.** To show excitement, speed up the pace of your speech. To show weariness, slow it down. These are just two ways to change your rate of speech to enliven your storytelling. Remember not to talk so fast that your audience cannot understand you or so slowly that your story drags.

## Practice, Practice, Practice

You may be able to tell a good story without rehearsing, but you probably cannot tell a great one without it. Take the time to practice in one of these ways.

- **Tell your story to a friend or relative,** and ask for feedback. Have your trial audience tell you whether you were expressive enough with both your voice and your gestures.

- **Use a tape recorder.** Although you may never get completely used to the sound of your own voice when it is played back to you, you still should be able to hear your **inflections,** the changes in the pitch or tone of your voice. If you do not hear many inflections, you should decide where you could vary your pitch, alter the pace, or change the volume of your voice.

- **Try your story out on video.** This is the best way to see and hear yourself as your audience will see and hear you. You can turn the sound off to see better what you are doing with your hands or your facial expressions. Make sure your gestures match the suspense or conflict in the story. You can also dim the picture and just listen to your voice. Evaluate both together to decide whether you are performing your story in the best possible way.

**TIP** You can use the feedback you get from your audience to evaluate the effectiveness of your presentation and **to set goals for future presentations.**

## Listening: Focus Your Body

If you are the storyteller, you must make a clear effort to interest and entertain your listeners. However, if you are the listener, you must take an active part in receiving the story so that you will understand and enjoy it. An active listener focuses attention on the story and becomes involved with what is being said. To be an active listener, here is what you should do *physically.*

- **Face the storyteller.** Use your body and the angle of your head to bring yourself to full attention. For example, your shoulders should be parallel to the storyteller's.

- **Look at the storyteller.** You will notice the nonverbal clues the storyteller gives you only if you see them. Keep your eyes on the speaker.

- **Make eye contact.** The storyteller is looking at you. To receive this communication and understand it better, look into the speaker's eyes.

- **Keep quiet.** This one is obvious. It is much harder to pay attention to a storyteller when you are talking as well.

**TIP** As you listen, try to monitor the speaker's message for clarity. At the end of the story, ask relevant questions to clarify your understanding.

- **Respond to the storyteller.** You can use nonverbal communication as you follow the story. Nod your head; smile at what you think is clever or funny.

## Listening: Focus Your Mind

**TIP** As you listen to narratives, try to identify and analyze the effect of **artistic elements** such as imagery, language, character development, and point of view.

Being an active listener involves more than what you do physically. Here is what you should do *mentally*.

- **Predict outcomes.** Just as you do when you are reading, ask yourself what will happen next in the story, and as you listen, confirm or correct your prediction.
- **Create images in your mind.** If you can picture what is going on in the story, you will enjoy it more. Listen for descriptions and flesh out your images of the story.
- **Remember your own experiences or stories.** Making connections with your own life and the things you know will make the story more clear and more enjoyable to you.

## Evaluating Oral Narratives

Whether you are listening to a classmate, a comedian on TV, or an actor in a one-person play, you will **evaluate,** or judge, the performance as you listen. To help you to evaluate, here are some questions you can ask yourself as you listen.

- Is the storyteller speaking loudly and clearly enough for you to understand?
- Do the storyteller's gestures highlight the narrative or do they distract listeners? In what way?
- Does the storyteller vary his or her pitch and pace?
- Does the storyteller use vivid details about events, places, and people? Does he or she include thoughts and feelings?

**YOUR TURN 11** **Storytelling Hour**

Choose a story to tell. Think about how you will present it: the gestures you will make, how you will use your voice to emphasize and bring meaning to the words. Practice your story and then present it to your class. When you are listening to your classmates' stories, use the guidelines above to help you to be an active and interested listener.

# *Choices*

## Choose one of the following activities to complete.

### ▶ CROSSING THE CURRICULUM: HISTORY

**1. Be Somebody**   Pretend you are a historical figure and write a **"personal" narrative** as that figure. You do not necessarily have to choose someone famous. You may wish to be anyone from an Anasazi artist or a nineteenth-century millworker, to a fighter pilot taking part in the Battle of Britain. Do some research to give historical accuracy to your personal narrative.

### ▶ CROSSING THE CURRICULUM: MUSIC

**2. Say It with Music**   Tell a story with music. Write **music** using the framework of a personal narrative (see page 68). Your musical piece should have an introduction with a melody (or theme). It should have events in the form of movements or sections, and a conclusion which sums up the whole musical narrative.

### ▶ CAREERS

**3. Job Story**   Visit someone at his or her place of work and write a **narrative** about your time there.

Use the framework on page 68 so that you are sure to have all the essential elements of a personal narrative. Ask yourself what you learned during your visit and use your answer as a reflection at the end of your narrative.

### ▶ LITERATURE

**4. Change Your Point of View**   Write a **short-story** version of your personal narrative. While in a personal narrative you must recount what really happened, in fiction you can use your imagination. You can fictionalize your personal narrative, inventing other events, characters, or details to make it a short story.

### ▶ SPEAKING AND LISTENING

**5. Personal History**   Learn, practice, and deliver a story from another generation. Does your father tell you about walking ten miles through the snow to get to school? Perhaps you have a relative or a neighbor who could share a good story from the time when he or she was your age. Give an **oral presentation** of the story using first-person point of view.

PORTFOLIO

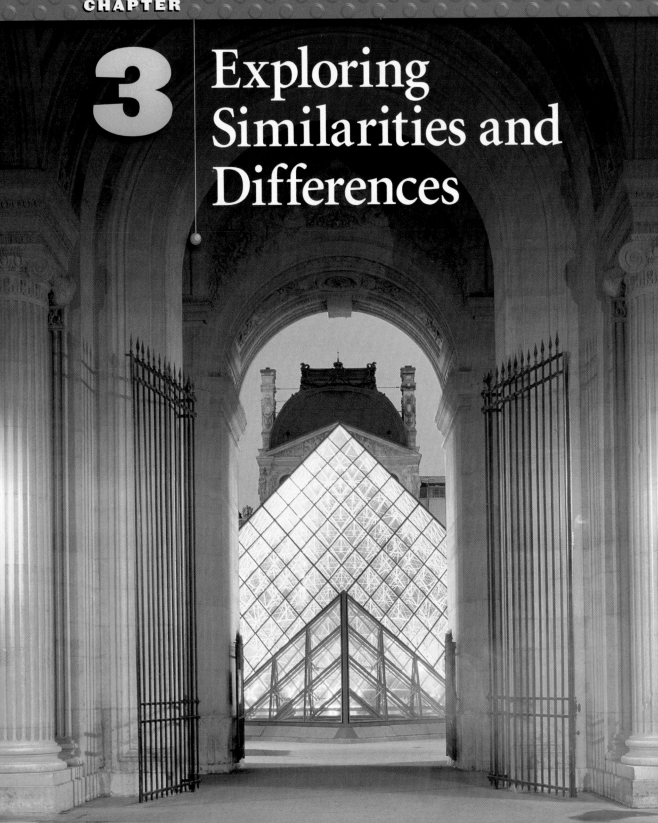

# 3

# Exploring Similarities and Differences

## Reading Workshop

*Reading a Comparison-Contrast Article*

## Writing Workshop

*Writing a Comparison-Contrast Essay*

## Viewing and Representing

*Comparing and Contrasting Media Coverage*

## Comparing and Contrasting

> **Informational Text**
>
> Exposition

- Two candidates are in the runoff for student-government elections. How will you decide which one gets your vote?

- After years of roller-skating, you decide to try ice-skating. Will your experience as a roller skater prepare you to ice-skate?

- How can you explain to a middle school friend what high school is like?

To respond to each of these questions, you would need to ask yourself two simple questions: *How are these things alike?* and *How are they different?* This type of questioning is called **comparison and contrast**. When you compare and contrast, you *classify* items by putting them into groups—a procedure that is particularly useful when you want to explain something new (like high school) by showing how it is similar to and different from something old and familiar (like middle school).

Although you might not be aware of it, you use comparison and contrast every time you make a decision or judgment and every time you weigh your options or compare products.

### YOUR TURN 1    Recognizing Comparison and Contrast

Brainstorm about times you have used or might use comparison and contrast. Think about when you have asked yourself how two things were alike or how they were different. Create a list of these times and be prepared to share it with a small group of your classmates.

internet**connect**

**go. hrw .com**

**GO TO:** go.hrw.com
**KEYWORD:** EOLang 9-3

# Reading a Comparison-Contrast Article

**WHAT'S AHEAD?**

In this section you will read an article and learn how to

■ identify explicit main ideas and supporting details

■ analyze point-by-point and block structure

**D**id you know Finland's national pastime is based on our national pastime? That's right, American baseball inspired the creation of a Finnish sport called *pesapallo.* Although the two sports are somewhat similar, the article on the next page, "Time Out! Is Baseball Finnished?" shows that the sports have many differences, too. Reading this article will help you think about the similarities and the differences between sports in the United States and sports in other countries.

## Preparing to Read

| READING SKILL

**Identifying an Explicit Main Idea and Supporting Details** All comparison-contrast articles have a **main idea**—a controlling idea for the piece that shows the writer's focus on differences or similarities. If the writer directly announces this idea, it is an **explicit** main idea. In this case, you will find a sentence that states the main idea near the beginning of the article. The **details,** then, are all the information and evidence that support and explain the main idea. As you read the following article, look for the main idea and the details that support it.

| READING FOCUS

**Comparison-Contrast Structure** To compare and contrast two subjects, writers organize their writing using the **block method** or the **point-by-point method.** For block, one block of text, usually a paragraph, gives *all* the points the writer wants to make about one subject. Then, a second block of text gives all of the comparable or contrasting points about a second subject. For point-by-point, each section presents a point about the first subject (A) *and* the same point about the second subject (B). Then, the writer uses *another* section to deal with a second point about both subjects, and so on. As you read the following article, look for ways the writer organizes his ideas.

How is baseball similar to or different from *pesapallo*? As you read the article below, write down answers to the numbered active-reading questions.

*from* THE MIAMI HERALD

# TIME OUT!

## Is Baseball Finnished?

BY BOB SECTER

Hancock, Mich.— There were lots of reasons why Jimmy Piersall was known as a flake back when he played major-league baseball; but one of the best came the day he hit a home run as a New York Met and ran the bases backward.

All of which has little to do with the subject of this story, except to illustrate the maxim that what may seem like buffoonery in one setting could make perfect sense in another. Had Piersall been playing in, say, Helsinki rather than New York, he might have fit right in.

Yes. Baseball has been Finlandized. The Finns call the game *pesapallo* and are so crazy about it that it is considered their national pastime. Of course they do it a little differently.

They don't actually back-pedal their way from base to base à la Piersall, but, looking at it from a chauvinist American perspective, they do take a backward route around the base paths. First base is where third base ought to be, second is sort of around where first should be and third is somewhere out in left field. . . .

The main selling point of *pesapallo*, devotees say, is action. There are no long pauses between pitches, the ball is almost constantly in play, and both fielders and

**1.** How does the writer grab your attention?

**2.** What is the main point the writer makes in this paragraph?

**3.** According to the writer, what do runners do differently in *pesapallo* and baseball?

**5.** Does the word *instead* indicate a similarity or a difference between the two sports?

runners are forever scampering all over the place.

"In American baseball, a runner on second is in scoring position but in our game, he's just tired," winked Jari Lemonen, who plays for the Repais. "Usually when we get out there, we pack a lunch."

The Abner Doubleday of Finland was Lauri Pihkala, a professor who apparently was mesmerized by baseball during early twentieth-century study tours in the United States. He combined the American game with some native ball-playing sports and *pesapallo* was born.

Both baseball and *pesapallo* feature four bases, three outs an inning, nine innings, nine players on a side, a hard ball, mitts, and a bat—although the Louisville Slugger of Finland is called a *Jarvinen Kanuuna*.

That's where the similarities end. The *pesapallo* pitcher, for instance, stands next to the plate and tosses the ball up in the air, varying his delivery not with curves or sliders but with the height the ball goes.

Instead of waiting in a dugout, teammates of the batter stand around what is roughly equivalent to the batter's box and scream out advice whether to swing or not at a pitch. The batter can hit as many as three fair balls before he has to run. And the route around the basepaths sort of zigzags first to the left, then to the right, then to the left again.

Confused? Try this. A three-base hit is a *kunnari*, or home run. The batter scores, even though he is allowed to stay on third and score again if somebody knocks him in. But getting a *kunnari* is not easy because a ball that's knocked out of the park— about 300 feet from home to the farthest point of the *pesapallo* outfield—is considered a *laiton* (foul).

When an outfielder catches a fly ball, that doesn't necessarily mean the batter is

out. He might just be *haava* (wounded), a sort of purgatory state for sluggers that requires them to forfeit the turn at bat but doesn't exactly count toward ending the inning. And when someone does make an out, he's not just out, he's *pallo* (killed). This is no game for wimps; that's for sure.

There's one other important difference. At the end of the game, American ballplayers hit the showers. "When we're done," said Thunder Bay shortstop Pavli Kaki, "we go off to the sauna."

**4.** This paragraph does not have much of a comparison. What other information is included? Why?

**6.** How does the writer use humor to conclude the article?

On your own paper, write answers to the following questions about "Time Out! Is Baseball Finnished?"

1. The article is mostly about the differences between baseball and *pesapallo.* In one paragraph, however, the writer does talk about *similarities.* What are those similarities?

2. Besides discussing *pesapallo* rules, what background information does the writer provide about the sport?

3. Why do you think the writer uses more space to discuss the rules and history of *pesapallo* than the rules and history of American baseball?

## Explicit Main Idea and Supporting Details

READING SKILL

**Primary Importance** "Time Out! Is Baseball Finnished?" contains an **explicit,** or stated, **main idea** and the details that support this main idea. In an article or essay, an explicit main idea, or **thesis statement,** is usually made up of a subject plus the point the author wants to make about that subject. This thesis drives the structure and focus of the piece. For example, an author's subject for an article might be *dogs,* but the author's main idea or thesis statement would be *Dogs make better pets than cats.* While the thesis statement usually appears in the introductory paragraph of an article, the remaining paragraphs develop and support the main idea or thesis. These paragraphs have their own stated main ideas called **topic sentences** and supporting details. Good types of supporting details are facts, statistics, or examples. A graphic depiction of main idea and supporting details might look like this.

**TIP** The explicit main idea for a single paragraph is called a topic sentence. The stated main idea for an *entire article* or *essay* is called the thesis statement.

```
                    Explicit main idea
                    (thesis statement)
                    /               \
    Explicit paragraph main      Explicit paragraph main
    idea (topic sentence)        idea (topic sentence)
        /         \                  /          \
  Supporting   Supporting      Supporting    Supporting
  details      details         details       details
```

How can you find a main idea? In many nonfiction pieces, the main idea is stated outright, neatly contained near the beginning of the writing. The main idea in a nonfiction piece might also be found, or alluded to, in the title of the piece. The example paragraph below is an introduction to an essay. It contains a main idea and supporting details for that main idea. Read the paragraph and use the Thinking It Through steps following it to practice identifying the main idea and supporting details.

### Two Famous Artists

The European Renaissance of the fourteenth, fifteenth, and sixteenth centuries produced many different artists and writers. However, some of the period's greatest artists were actually not all that different from each other. Leonardo da Vinci and Michelangelo were famous artists with a great deal in common. They were both extremely dedicated to art and often went days without sleeping or eating. Both artists were also masters of perspective and have continued to be famous throughout history.

### THINKING IT THROUGH

### Finding Explicit Main Idea and Supporting Details

Use the following steps to find a main idea and supporting details.

▶ **STEP 1** Read and determine the subject of the piece. Look at the title, and scan the piece for key words or phrases that repeat. Ask yourself who or what the piece is addressing.

*Leonardo da Vinci and Michelangelo are the subjects.*

▶ **STEP 2** Look for the **main idea**—one or more sentences that state the point the writer wants to make about the subject or subjects. It is often found in the introduction.

*Leonardo da Vinci and Michelangelo were famous artists with a great deal in common.*

▷ **STEP 3** Confirm the main idea by looking to see that other details in the piece support it.

*These details support the main idea: Both were extremely dedicated to art, both went days without sleeping or eating, both were masters of perspective, and both have continued to be famous throughout history.*

**YOUR TURN 2** **Finding Main Idea and Details**

Using the Thinking It Through steps on pages 92–93, find the main idea in "Time Out! Is Baseball Finnished?" (You may have to combine several directly stated ideas to figure out the explicit main idea.) Check your answer by making sure the details in the article support the main idea you find. On your own paper, write a sentence stating the main idea and three details that support it.

**TIP** If you have difficulty finding the main idea, you may want to start by drawing a graphic organizer like the one on page 91.

## Comparison-Contrast Structure

◀ **READING FOCUS**

**The Order of Your Points** Writers usually organize comparison-contrast essays so that readers can easily identify the points the writers are comparing about two or more subjects. Figuring out the structure of a comparison-contrast essay will make it easier for you to understand what the piece is about. Once you have determined the structure of a piece, you will be able to make predictions about the information to come. There are two main ways to structure comparison-contrast essays: the block method and the point-by-point method.

**Block method** Writers use the block method to address each subject in separate paragraphs—in different "blocks" of text. In one paragraph, the writer discusses all the relevant points about one subject; then, in a second paragraph, the writer discusses all the corresponding points about the second subject. In longer essays, a "block" may be several paragraphs.

**Point-by-point method** Writers use the point-by-point method when they want to focus on the points instead of the subjects. The point-by-point method allows writers to deal with both subjects in the same paragraph or section. The writer presents one point in each paragraph or section, discussing the point for the *first* subject and then for the *second* subject.

**TIP** To try out unusual ways of presenting their ideas, professional writers often vary the two common comparison-contrast methods of organization. When you read a professional piece, be on the lookout for hybrid, or mixed, forms of the block and point-by-point methods.

With either the block or the point-by-point method, writers try to present the information in a consistent order so their readers do not get confused. The chart below shows both methods of organization. The left-hand column shows how a writer would use the block method to compare and contrast ice-skating with roller-skating. The right-hand column shows how a writer would reorganize the same information using the point-by-point method.

| Block Method | Point-by-Point Method |
|---|---|
| *Subject 1: Roller-Skating*<br>    Point 1: Wooden rink<br>    Point 2: Boots with wheels<br>    Point 3: Jumps and spins | *Point 1: Type of arena* (contrast)<br>    Subject 1: Wooden rink for roller-skating<br>    Subject 2: Ice rink for ice-skating |
| *Subject 2: Ice-Skating*<br>    Point 1: Ice rink<br>    Point 2: Boots with blades<br>    Point 3: Jumps and spins | *Point 2: Footwear* (contrast)<br>    Subject 1: Boots with wheels for roller-skating<br>    Subject 2: Boots with blades for ice-skating |
| | *Point 3: Athletic moves* (comparison)<br>    Subject 1: Jumps and spins in roller-skating<br>    Subject 2: Jumps and spins also in ice-skating |

**TIP** Writers often use clue words to signal a transition from one subject to another. Contrast clue words include *however, still, yet, but, on the other hand,* and *although.* Comparison clue words include *similarly, like, as,* and *in the same way.* For example, *Roller-skating boots have wheels,* **but** *ice-skating boots have blades.* If you have trouble identifying the structure of a comparison-contrast article, try highlighting all the comparison and contrast clue words. Then, look for a pattern to the highlighting. Point-by-point structure should use more clue words because the writer has to switch subjects more often.

ARLO AND JANIS reprinted by permission of Newspaper Enterprise Association, Inc.

The organizational structure of "Time Out! Is Baseball Finnished?" is unusual. The writer examines two subjects, baseball and *pesapallo*. However, through most of the piece, he does not directly state his points about baseball. He assumes that his readers already know them. For example, in one paragraph, he gives the rules only about *pesapallo*. He expects his readers to fill in the rules of baseball for themselves.

YOUR TURN 3 ### Analyzing Comparison-Contrast Structure

To analyze the structure of "Time Out! Is Baseball Finnished?" fill in the content chart below with the missing points and the missing details about *pesapallo* and baseball. The items 1–8 below correspond to the main points of comparison between *pesapallo* and baseball in the order they appear in the article. Put your answers on your own paper.

| Points | Subjects<br>A. Pesapallo<br>B. Baseball (implied) |
|---|---|
| 1. direction to run bases | A. runners move clockwise<br>B. (runners move counterclockwise) |
| 2. pace of the game | A.<br>B. |
| 3. number of bases, outs, innings, and players on a side | A.<br>B. |
| 4. | A.<br>B. (on the pitcher's mound) |
| 5. | A.<br>B. |
| 6. rules for a home run | A.<br>B. (a ball hit out of the park) |
| 7. | A.<br>B. the batter is out |
| 8. | A.<br>B. |

**VOCABULARY**

## Comparison-Contrast Context Clues

Sometimes you can find the meaning of an unfamiliar word by examining **comparison-contrast context clues** near the unfamiliar word. A **comparison context clue** indicates that a synonym, or word with a similar meaning, is nearby. (It may also signal a nearby phrase with a similar meaning.) If you know the meaning of the synonym, then you are fairly close to knowing what the unfamiliar word (or phrase) means. Comparison context clue words include *like*, *as*, *in the same way*, and *similar to*. A **contrast clue word** indicates that an antonym, or word with the opposite meaning, is nearby. (It may also signal a nearby phrase with the opposite meaning.) If you know what the antonym means, then you can guess that the unfamiliar word (or phrase) has the opposite meaning. Contrast context clue words include *however*, *but*, *although*, *on the contrary*, and *on the other hand*.

**THINKING IT THROUGH**          **Using Comparison-Contrast Context Clues**

Take a look at the example below and the steps following it.

**Example:**
Louisa's comments about other cultures are *ethnocentric*; Ray's comments, on the other hand, show that he is not convinced that his culture is better than all other cultures.

1. **Look for a comparison or contrast context clue.** The phrase *on the other hand* signals that an antonym or a phrase with the opposite meaning may be nearby.

2. **Look for a synonym (for comparison clues) or an antonym (for contrast clues) of the unfamiliar word.** The phrase *is not convinced that his culture is better than all other cultures* may have the opposite meaning of *ethnocentric*.

3. **Make an informed guess about the meaning of the unfamiliar word.** *Ethnocentric* means something like "convinced that one's own culture is better than all other cultures."

**PRACTICE**

Use the steps above to find the meaning of the following italicized words. Put your answers on your own paper.

1. A *stereotype*, like any claim that many different people are alike, can be dangerous.

2. Joe did not think he could write without *prejudice*, but his article was open-minded.

3. Few cities are as *diverse* as New York. New York is a very multicultural city.

4. Some say the news story is *biased*, although others say the news story is neutral.

5. Ryan had *chauvinistic* views about his music. In the same way, Mia had an unreasoning devotion to her sports.

## Answering Analogy Questions

An **analogy** is a special kind of comparison—it points out how the relationship of two sets of words is similar. For example, *moon* and *earth* have the same relationship as *Saturn* and *sun*. In both cases, one orbits the other. **Analogy questions** measure your knowledge of individual words as well as your ability to identify relationships *between* words.

Look at the analogy question to the right. In analogy questions, the symbol *:* means *is to* and the symbol *::* means *as*. For example, the question to the right would read
*Scales is to fish as _____ is to _____.*

Examine the five answer choices to the right to determine which pair of words has the same relationship as that between *scales* and

*fish.* Follow the steps below to see how one student figured out the answer.

SCALES : FISH ::

**A.** perch : bass

**B.** eraser : pencil

**C.** tadpole : frog

**D.** sea gull : seashore

**E.** fur : mammal

**TIP** Don't be fooled by answers that are thematically related to the question. With analogy questions you should match *only the relationship* between the pairs of words. For example, perch and bass are kinds of fish, but **A** may not be the correct answer.

---

**THINKING IT THROUGH** **Answering Analogy Questions**

The following steps will help you answer analogy questions.

1. **Identify the relationship between the first pair of words.** Scales are a part of the larger whole of a fish.

2. **Express the relationship between the first pair of words in the form of a sentence.** The first word, scales, is part of the second word, fish. Scales cover a fish.

3. **Ask if each multiple-choice answer fits the order and relationship of the first pair.**

   A. Is a perch part of a bass? No, they are both kinds of fish.

   B. Is an eraser part of a pencil? Yes, it is.

   C. Is a tadpole part of a frog? No, it is an

   immature form of a frog.

   D. Is a sea gull part of a seashore? No, it lives at the seashore.

   E. Is fur part of a mammal? Yes, it is.

4. **Choose the answer that best completes the analogy.** Both **B** and **E** are examples of part-to-whole relationships. Which of these is even closer to the relationship of *scales* and *fish*? An eraser does not completely cover a pencil, but fur covers a mammal as scales cover fish. **E** is the *best* answer because it more closely matches the relationship between *scales* and *fish*.

# Writing a Comparison-Contrast Essay

## WHAT'S AHEAD?

In this workshop you will write a comparison-contrast essay. You will also learn how to

- **focus on similarities or differences**
- **eliminate irrelevant details**
- **organize support**
- **combine sentences using phrases**
- **correct misplaced modifiers**

**P**icture this: While you are away for the summer, you learn a great new game called fun ball. You are so excited that you write a letter to your friends back home about this new sport. The problem is they have never even heard of fun ball. How can you explain it to them in writing?

One way is to compare and contrast it with a sport they already know, like soccer. By writing about the *similarities* between the two sports, you help your friends make sense of the *differences*. In the following Writing Workshop you will have the opportunity to write an organized, informative essay that compares or contrasts any two subjects you choose.

# Prewriting

## Find Two Subjects

KEY CONCEPT

**"You Can't Compare Apples to Oranges."** *Comparison* points out the similarities between people, ideas, or things, while *contrast* points out the differences. However, the word *comparison* is often used to mean both comparing and contrasting. If your teacher assigns a comparison essay, make sure you understand the assignment. For this comparison-contrast essay, you will focus on either similarities or differences between two subjects, but not both.

The two subjects you write about should be similar enough to compare. Sure, apples and oranges are both kinds of fruit, but you will have a hard time finding other features they have in common. They may just be too different to compare.

Remember the following when choosing your subjects.

- **Good subjects have plenty of similar features.** Try comparing two types of apples, like Granny Smith apples and Golden Delicious apples. Some features you might choose to compare include their color, taste, texture, and size.

- **Good subjects are different enough to be interesting.** There is no point in comparing two identical apples. A good topic gives your readers new information.

With these guidelines in mind, brainstorm to find a topic to write about. Look around you for places that people make comparisons in everyday life. Here are a couple of suggestions to help you get started:

- **Do a little comparison shopping** before you buy. When you buy a pair of jeans, chances are you don't just pick the first pair off the rack—you compare several different brands or styles first.

- **Try something new.** Go for a walk down a different street. If you watch the news on TV, try reading the newspaper instead. Jot down a list of the differences you notice. In order to explain something that is new, you may want to compare it to something that is older or more familiar. For example, you might compare a movie and its sequel.

After brainstorming a list of topics, circle the one you find most interesting.

## Narrow Your Subjects

**Whittle It Down**   Examine your subjects. Are the subjects you want to compare too huge for one short essay? For example, comparing all of France to all of the United States may be too large a topic for one essay. It would be much more reasonable to compare one aspect of the two countries, such as their school systems, tourist attractions, or climate.

> **TIP** Try to make your comparison or contrast one that will bring a new subject to light or shed light on a familiar one.

## Think About Purpose, Audience, and Tone

**For Their Eyes Only**   The primary **purpose** of a comparison-contrast essay is to inform readers. A formal **tone** and voice work best for this purpose. When you provide readers with information about the subjects you are comparing or contrasting, you help them see the similarities or differences between people, places, objects, or ideas. For this reason, it is important to evaluate who your **audience** is and what your audience already knows about your subjects. Asking yourself the questions on the next page will help you direct your essay. Notice how the writer of an essay on body language in France and the United States answered each question.

- **Who are my readers?** My readers are American tourists traveling to France.
- **What do my readers already know about the subjects I am comparing or contrasting?** They know a lot about how Americans use body language to communicate.
- **What information might help my readers better understand the similarities or differences between my subjects?** They might need more information about how the French use body language to communicate.

## Gather Information About Your Subjects

**Collecting Data**   Before you write your comparison-contrast essay, you will need to gather plenty of information about your subjects to see whether you want to focus on similarities or on differences. Remember, though, that **for a comparison-contrast essay, you are not looking for just any kind of information—you are looking for *similarities and differences*.** One very good way to keep track of similarities and differences between your subjects is to create a Venn diagram like the one below.

**KEY CONCEPT**

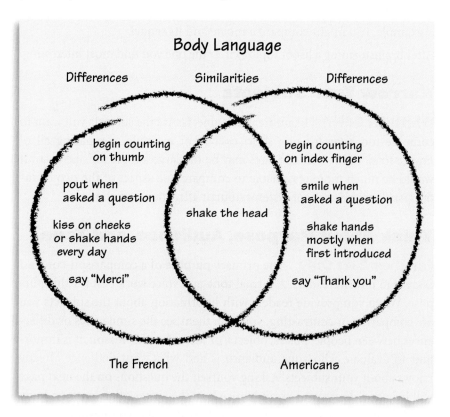

Body Language

Differences          Similarities          Differences

begin counting
on thumb

pout when
asked a question

kiss on cheeks
or shake hands
every day

say "Merci"

shake the head

begin counting
on index finger

smile when
asked a question

shake hands
mostly when
first introduced

say "Thank you"

The French          Americans

The writer who created the Venn diagram on the previous page wanted to inform her audience about the body language used by people in France and the body language used by people in the United States. Notice how she used the middle part—where the two circles of the Venn diagram overlap—to list the similarities she found. In the outer parts of the diagram, she listed differences.

When you create your Venn diagram, place the similarities you find in the middle part of the diagram, and place the differences in the outer parts. Label each circle with the names of the subjects you will be comparing or contrasting. If you are not familiar with your subjects, you may need to do some research—in the library, on the Internet, or through interviews or observation—before you create the diagram.

## Write Your Thesis

**What's the Big Idea?**   A thesis statement tells your audience what your essay will be about. It should identify what people, things, or ideas you are comparing or contrasting. Your **thesis statement** should also clearly state the main idea—whether you want to focus on the similarities or the differences between your subjects.

You can decide whether you want to focus your essay on similarities or on differences by looking at your Venn diagram. If, for example, you find that you have listed many similarities, but only a few differences, you will probably want to focus on similarities. After you have analyzed your information, write a thesis statement that states your subjects plus your focus on either similarities or differences.

For example, the writer who created the Venn diagram about French and American body language might decide that she wants to focus her essay on differences, because she listed more differences than similarities in the diagram. She might then write the following thesis statement.

**TIP**   If you have listed many differences, but only a few similarities, you will probably want to focus on differences.

> Most people know that residents of France and the United States speak different languages. However, few people know that body language in the two countries can be just as different.

**TIP**   Most thesis statements are one sentence long. Sometimes, however, a particularly complex thesis statement will be two sentences long. One way to get readers' attention in a comparison-contrast essay is to connect two opposite ideas in your thesis statement using a transitional word like *however, yet,* or *still.* For example, *Tamara and Lu came from opposite sides of the globe. Still, they had many of the same ideas, tastes, and friends in common.*

# Find Relevant Features

**To the Point**   When you choose subjects to compare and contrast, you must understand (1) *if* they have any features in common, and (2) *what* features they have in common. When you do this, you are actually using the critical thinking skill of **classifying:** grouping objects or ideas into categories that show their similarities.

When the writer of the Venn diagram on page 100 asked herself what the information in each circle had in common, she came up with the categories or features listed in the right-hand column below.

**TIP** Classifying ideas into categories takes time. Allow yourself the time to dwell on this important step. The features you come up with now will ultimately help you structure your final essay.

| The French | Americans | Feature |
|---|---|---|
| Begin counting on thumb | Begin counting on index finger | Hand signals |
| Pout when asked a question | Smile when asked a question | Facial expressions |
| Kiss on cheeks or shake hands every day | Shake hands mostly when first introduced | Greetings |
| ~~Say merci~~ | ~~Say thank you~~ | ~~Words to express thanks~~ |

To come up with names for these categories or features, the writer had to find similar pieces of information in each of the circles of the Venn diagram. Then she had to think of a word or phrase that described both pieces of information.

After classifying the information that you gather in your Venn diagram into categories or **features,** you should pick two to four **relevant features** to support your thesis. **Relevant features are the categories of support that relate to and develop your thesis statement.** For example, the writer who created the Venn diagram chose three relevant features of body language: hand signals, facial expressions, and greetings. All three features support the main idea in her thesis statement that body language in France can be quite different from body language in the United States. She eliminated the fourth feature she found, words to express thanks, because verbal expressions are not relevant to her topic of body language. When you write your essay, you may also need to eliminate irrelevant details or features that do not support your thesis statement.

| **KEY CONCEPT**

## MINI-LESSON CRITICAL THINKING

## Evaluating to Eliminate Irrelevant Details

When you write a comparison-contrast essay, you must make sure that all the supporting details you use are related to your main idea. Any irrelevant details will throw your reader off and weaken your essay. For example, a paper that compares or contrasts body language in France and the United States should use supporting details about body language in both countries. Different words, different foods, and different money in both countries would be interesting details to examine, but they are not **relevant** to the subject of body language. Instead, the writer should compare or contrast aspects of body language such as hand signals, greetings, and facial expressions.

If you were playing a game that required you to eliminate irrelevant details from a category, the questioner might ask you, "Which of these things do not belong together: algebra, history, stars, or physics?" The answer is *stars* because the other three items—*algebra*, *history*, and *physics*—are all school courses. *Stars* does not belong in the category of school courses.

### PRACTICE

Work with a partner to figure out which of the items in each list below does not belong. Write your answers on your own paper.

**Example**
**1.** red, orange, thirteen, green, purple
*1. Thirteen does not belong because it is not a color.*

1. Classical period, Middle Ages, Italy, Renaissance, Industrial Age, The Reformation

2. newspapers, videos, photographs, TV shows, movies, paintings, drawings, music

3. mumps, chickenpox, German measles, thermometer, pneumonia, flu, strep throat, tetanus

4. softball, bat, soccer, hockey, volleyball, football, basketball, baseball, lacrosse, tennis

5. balloon, oxygen, hydrogen, nitrogen, helium, neon, fluorine

6. Washington, D.C.; Mexico City, Mexico; Jupiter; Tokyo, Japan; London, England; Warsaw, Poland

7. Colorado, Himalayas, Alps, Rockies, Adirondacks, Cascades, Andes, Appalachians, Sierras

8. a poem, a painting, an opera, a canvas

9. democracy, monarchy, queen, dictatorship

10. a speech, a newspaper, a magazine, a radio program, a television show, a Web site

11. Manet, Monet, Renoir, Degas, Mozart, Gauguin, van Gogh, Matisse

12. Bolivia, South America, Asia, Africa, Australia, North America

13. sonnet, villanelle, sestina, meter, blank verse, free verse

14. Carnegie, Lincoln, Coolidge, Monroe, Washington, Eisenhower, Taft

15. jazz, rock, soul, country, blues, folk, swing, guitar, bluegrass

# Arrange Your Information

**Creating Order**  How will you organize your comparison-contrast essay? After you have chosen two to four relevant features, use a chart like the one below to help you organize your information. You can use either the point-by-point method or the block method to organize and arrange your information.

- In the **block method,** you discuss all the features about your first subject. Then you discuss all the features about your second subject. The block method works best for shorter pieces with fewer comparisons.

- In the **point-by-point method,** you present the first feature for *both* subjects. Then you use another sentence or group of sentences to present the second feature for both subjects, and so on. The point-by-point method works best for longer papers with more comparisons.

| Block Method | Point-by-Point Method |
|---|---|
| Subject 1: The French<br><br>Feature 1: Hand signals—count on their fingers starting with the thumb<br><br>Feature 2: Facial expressions—pout when asked a question<br><br>Feature 3: Greetings—greet each other by kissing on the cheeks or shaking hands every day | Feature 1: Hand signals<br><br>Subject 1: The French—count on their fingers starting with the thumb<br><br>Subject 2: Americans—count on their fingers starting with the index finger |
| Subject 2: Americans<br><br>Feature 1: Hand signals—count on their fingers starting with the index finger<br><br>Feature 2: Facial expressions—smile when asked a question<br><br>Feature 3: Greetings—shake hands when first introduced | Feature 2: Facial expressions<br><br>Subject 1: The French—pout when asked a question<br><br>Subject 2: Americans—smile when asked a question |
| | Feature 3: Greetings<br><br>Subject 1: The French—kiss on the cheeks or shake hands every day<br><br>Subject 2: Americans—shake hands when first introduced |

Remember to treat the relevant features in the same order for both subjects. The order of features is often most to least important, or least to most important. To figure out which features are the most important, start by examining how much information you have gathered about each feature. The feature you know the most about may very well be the one you want to discuss first. Another way to determine order of importance is to think about your audience's needs. Look back at the information you gathered about your audience on pages 99–100. Ask yourself what information your audience would like most to know about. If you first write about the feature that is most important to your audience, you are likely to grab your audience's attention and to convince your audience to keep reading the rest of your paper.

## YOUR TURN 4  Organizing Ideas

**COMPUTER TIP**

You can create tables within your word-processing program, and use them to organize your prewriting notes.

Go over each of the prewriting steps. Before you start writing your essay, remember to

- find two items that are similar enough to compare, but different enough to be interesting
- choose an appropriate audience and tone
- gather information that will support your comparisons or contrasts
- write a thesis statement that indicates whether you will be looking at similarities or differences
- select two to four relevant features to support your thesis statement
- organize your relevant features using the point-by-point method or the block method

HI & LOIS reprinted with special permission of King Features Syndicate, Inc.

 **Writing**

## Comparison-Contrast Essay

**Framework**

**Directions and Explanations**

### Introduction

- Capture your readers' attention.
- Provide background information.
- State your thesis.

**Hook Your Readers**   Begin with several details that are contrary to your thesis. Then, include your thesis statement, beginning with a transition to signal the switch to an opposite idea—like *however*, *yet*, or *still*. For example, begin with statements showing contrasts about the two things you plan to compare, or begin with statements showing similarities between the two things you plan to contrast. This will make your readers want to read more.

### Body

- Organize your information using either the block or point-by-point method.

**Explain the Context**   Provide relevant background information to help your readers understand the two subjects you will compare or contrast.

**State Your Thesis**   Tell your readers what to expect with a thesis that states what two items you will discuss and whether you will compare or contrast them.

**Organize Your Support**   To deal with each subject separately, use the block method. To deal with both subjects together, use the point-by-point method. Explain each of your subjects and provide supporting details for each feature you are comparing or contrasting.

### Conclusion

- Summarize how your support leads to your thesis.
- Bring your essay to a close.

**Sum It Up**   Restate your support and your thesis. You may also want to end with an evaluation—a final comment that judges the relative worth of the two subjects. For example, *Although brand A has a sleeker design, brand B really is more efficient.*

**YOUR TURN 5  Writing a First Draft**

Write the first draft of your essay using the framework and the directions and explanations above as a guide. The Writer's Model on the next page is a sample essay that closely matches the framework.

# A Writer's Model

**The following short essay uses the point-by-point method to contrast two cultures. Notice how it follows the framework.**

**TIP** Notice the highlighted contrast clue words signaling differences.

## Differences in Body Language

A pull on an eyelid, a pat on the wrist—either of these gestures could lead to confusion for an American in Paris. In fact, years of French language classes practicing *je, tu, il,* and *bonjour* may not be enough preparation for an American to communicate with a French person. Most people know that residents of France and the United States speak different languages. However, few people know that body language in the two countries can be just as different.

The difference in hand signals could lead to cultural misunderstandings between Americans and the French. For example, an American visiting France may be surprised when a waiter brings him three cups of coffee even though he thought he only ordered two. His problem? He held up his index finger and his middle finger to indicate the number *two*. Since the French start counting on the thumb, however, the waiter understood that hand gesture to mean *three*.

Hand signals are not the only difference in body language between Americans and the French. Facial expressions can also be different in the two countries. An American who asks a French person for her opinion may be surprised when she reacts by frowning. Americans tend to smile a lot, especially when responding to questions. The French, on the other hand, sometimes react by pouting the lips. This facial gesture shows that a French person is thinking.

The French also greet each other in a different way than Americans do. Every time they meet or say goodbye, French friends and family members kiss on the cheeks or shake hands. Americans, on the other hand, do not touch nearly as often when they greet each other.

A frustrated American with an extra cup of coffee and a pouting companion will probably find the unexpected surprise of a kiss or a handshake quite refreshing. However, an American visiting France may still need more than a dictionary to communicate with the French.

Attention-getting
INTRODUCTION

Thesis statement
(focuses on
differences)

BODY
Feature 1: Hand
signals

Americans

The French

Feature 2: Facial
expressions

Americans

The French

Feature 3: Greetings
The French

Americans

CONCLUSION that
sums up

# A Student's Model

**The following excerpt from a comparison-contrast essay was written by Matthew Weber, a student at McNeil High School in Round Rock, Texas.**

## CDs and Cassettes, Not So Similar

**INTRODUCTION**

From rap to rock and from country to classical, music is one of America's favorite pastimes. I have yet to find someone who has not heard a song from a cassette or CD. I have never been in a car that has not had either a cassette or CD player that was installed in it. When it comes to listening to music, CDs and cassettes are always right up there at the top of the list. **Thesis statement** Despite the many similarities of these two, though, there are many differences between cassettes and CDs.

**BODY**
**Feature 1: Price**

The first difference comes in the price. As most people know, the price varies in that cassettes are cheaper than CDs. The prices seem to depend upon things like how many tracks there are and if the songs are popular hits or are songs that have never been heard of. However, in the end, the results are the same. CDs are about five dollars more expensive than cassettes. Why then do people buy CDs when cassettes are cheaper? The reason is simple. Americans don't mind paying an extra buck for something that might be a little easier to run.

**Feature 2: Mechanics**

Another difference between the two is the way CD players and cassette recorders are run. For example, to skip tracks on a CD, people have to press one button, but they have to fast-forward the track on a cassette recorder, a process that usually means stopping every now and then just to see where they are in the song. It is a fairly tedious job just to get past one song.

**Feature 3: Sound quality**

Finally, there is a difference in sound quality between CDs and cassettes. CDs are made digitally by computers so that all the extra noise and unwanted sound can be taken out. Cassettes are not made digitally like the CD, so there still can be a static sound. For this reason, CDs are much better in sound quality compared to cassettes. . . .

# Evaluate and Revise Your Draft

**Smoothing Out the Bumps**   You should carefully read through your entire paper at least twice. During the first reading, work collaboratively to evaluate and to revise for **content** and **organization** using the guidelines below. When you do the second reading, use the guidelines on page 110 to evaluate and revise for **sentence style**.

▶ **First Reading: Content and Organization**   The chart below will help you evaluate and revise your writing. Working with a peer or on your own, start by answering the questions in the left-hand column. Then, if you need help, move on to the middle column of tips. If you need to revise, make the changes suggested in the right-hand column.

## Comparison-Contrast Essay: Content and Organization Guidelines for Peer and Self-Evaluation

| Evaluation Questions | Tips | Revision Techniques |
|---|---|---|
| ❶ Do the first one or two sentences grab the audience's attention? | **Put a check** above the interesting parts of the first two sentences. If you see no check marks, revise. | **Add** an interesting statement or example, or **replace** existing sentences with interesting statements or examples. |
| ❷ Does the introduction clearly identify both subjects and the thesis of the essay? | **Underline** the thesis statement and **draw a squiggly line** under each subject. Revise if you cannot identify a thesis and two subjects. | **Add** a sentence that clearly identifies both subjects. **Add** a sentence that states the main idea of the essay. |
| ❸ Is the body organized by the block method or the point-by-point method? | **Put a letter** *A* above each point about the first subject. **Use a letter** *B* for each point about the second subject. Block: The *A*'s should be in one block of text, and the letter *B*'s in another. Point-by-point: Each *A* should be closely followed by a *B*. | To fix the organization, **rearrange** sentences into either block order or point-by-point order. |
| ❹ Does the conclusion bring the essay to a definite close by summarizing or evaluating the subjects? | **Underline** sentences that summarize and evaluate. If there aren't any, revise. | **Delete** ineffective sentences. **Add** effective statements that summarize or evaluate. **Elaborate** on existing statements that summarize or evaluate. |

**ONE WRITER'S REVISIONS** Here is how one writer used the content and organization guidelines to revise part of the comparison-contrast essay on page 107. Look over the revisions and answer the questions following the sentences.

add

replace/add/replace

add

Most people know that residents of France *and the United States* speak *different* *s.* a language, However, few people know *that* about body language in the two countries *can be just as different.*

**PEER REVIEW**

Ask a few classmates to read your paper and to answer the following questions.

1. Which part of the essay confused you? How could it be made clearer?

2. What did you like best about the essay? Why?

## Analyzing the Revision Process

1. What type of information did the writer add?

2. How do these additions improve the thesis statement?

**YOUR TURN 6** **Revising for Content and Organization**

Using the sample revisions as a model, revise the content and organization of your essay. Be sure to refer to the content and organization guidelines on the previous page.

▶ Second Reading: **Style** When you wrote the first draft of your comparison-contrast essay, you may have found yourself using a series of short, choppy sentences. Using a few short sentences sprinkled throughout your paper can be an effective technique. If you use too many, however, your writing will sound very unnatural. To **vary sentence length** in your essay, use the following sentence-style guidelines.

## Style Guidelines

| Evaluation Question | ▶ Tip | ▶ Revision Technique |
| --- | --- | --- |
| Are sentence lengths varied in the essay? | ▶ **Highlight** each sentence with a colored marker so that you can compare sentence lengths. (Alternate between two different colors of marker to help your comparison.) If most sentences are the same length, revise. | ▶ **Combine** sentences by reducing some sentences to phrases and inserting them into other sentences. |

## Varying Sentence Length

When writing about how things are alike or different, as with all writing, it is important that your sentences have a smooth rhythm. To attain rhythm, you need to balance short sentences with longer, more detailed ones. **Sentence combining** helps you create this balance. You can combine closely related sentences by reducing one sentence to a phrase and inserting it into the other sentence. When inserted, the phrase gives additional information about an idea expressed in the sentence.

**TIP** To decide which sentences to combine, look for repeated words or phrases. They often signal the sentences that need to be reduced to phrases.

**ONE WRITER'S REVISIONS**   Here is how the writer of the model comparison-contrast essay on page 107 used the Style Guidelines to combine some sentences by using phrases.

**BEFORE REVISION**

Americans tend to smile a lot.  Americans especially respond like this to questions.  The French, on the other hand, react another way.  The French sometimes pout their lips.

All four sentences are about the same length.

**AFTER REVISION**
Americans tend to smile a lot, especially when responding to questions. The French, on the other hand, sometimes react by pouting the lips.

Reduce some sentences to phrases
Insert these phrases into other sentences

### Analyzing the Revision Process

1. What repetitive information did the writer delete? Why?
2. Why is the revised version better writing?

**YOUR TURN 7**   **Varying Sentence Length in Your Own Paper**

Use the guidelines on the previous page to evaluate your sentence length and to combine sentences if necessary.

**Reference Note**

For more on **varying sentence length,** see page 330.

# Publishing

## Proofread Your Essay

**Reference Note**

For **proofreading guidelines,** see page 13.

**Checking It Twice**  Read your essay at least two more times to make sure it is free of grammar, spelling, and punctuation errors. Be sure to correct any misplaced modifiers, words that modify the wrong word or word group. Just one misplaced modifier can confuse readers about the two items you are comparing. Once you have fixed the misplaced modifiers and any other errors, you will be ready to prepare a final copy of your essay.

## Grammar Link

### Correcting Misplaced Modifiers: Participial Phrases

When you are comparing and contrasting points about two drastically different subjects, a **misplaced modifier** can throw off your whole essay and confuse your audience. A misplaced modifier is a word, phrase, or clause that is confusing because it modifies the wrong word or group of words. Here, you will focus on misplaced modifiers that are participial phrases.

A participial phrase consists of a participle and its modifiers and complements. *Running through the sand, playing on the beach,* and *catching the beach ball* are examples of participial phrases. A participial phrase acts as an adjective, modifying either a noun or a pronoun. You have to be careful to place the phrase close to the word or words it modifies, or the sentence can take on an unintended meaning. A participial phrase that is in the wrong place is called a misplaced modifier.

**Misplaced**  Eating bamboo, the woman photographed the panda. [Was the woman eating bamboo or was the panda eating bamboo?]

**Improved**  The woman photographed the panda **eating bamboo.**

**Reference Note**

For more about **misplaced modifiers,** see page 587. For more on **using commas with introductory participial phrases,** see page 652.

#### PRACTICE

Revise each of the following sentences, correcting any misplaced modifiers. Note: You may have to add a comma if you move a participial phrase to the beginning of a sentence. Put your answers on your own paper.

1. Catalina saw a seashell diving into the water.

2. Pablo dreamed about beautiful sunsets sleeping on the blanket.

3. Hiding under a rock, Yumiko found a blue crab with four pairs of legs and two pincers.

4. Kareem hoped to prevent a sunburn adjusting the umbrella.

5. Biting his toes, he felt a little fish.

**Using Initial Letters**   One way you can keep readers interested in your comparison-contrast essay is to break up straight text by using **initial letters** and **dropped initial letters**. An initial letter, sometimes called an initial cap, is a large, raised first letter of an essay. The dropped initial letter, sometimes called a drop cap, is just like an initial letter, except that it is dropped into the body of the text. You can draw your initial letter or dropped initial letter by hand, or you can enlarge the size of a letter using a computer word-processing program. A point is a unit of measurement that is used to measure the height of printed letters.

**Example: Initial Letter**

Apull on an eyelid, a pat on the wrist—either of these gestures could lead to confusion for an American in Paris. In fact, years of French language classes practicing *je, tu, il,* and *bonjour* may not be enough preparation for an American to communicate. . . .

**Example: Dropped Initial Letter**

Apull on an eyelid, a pat on the wrist—either of these gestures could lead to confusion for an American in Paris. In fact, years of French language classes practicing *je, tu, il,* and *bonjour* may not be enough preparation for an American to communicate. . . .

Initial letters serve as a focal point, drawing the reader into the text. Consequently, your first initial letter should be for the first word of your essay. You can use one or two more initial letters at key points in your essay. For example, if you use the block method, you could use an initial letter to signal the beginning of each block. To avoid clutter, however, limit yourself to two or three initial letters in an essay. If you use the point-by-point method, do not add any extra initial letters.

If your teacher allows, experiment with different fonts for your initial letter until you find a font to fit the mood of your paper. (If you draw your initial letter, try experimenting with stencils or calligraphy pens.) To avoid confusing your reader, use only two fonts—one font and point size for your initial letters and a second, **legible** font for the rest of your paper. Examples of legible fonts include Times, Palatino, Garamond, and Helvetica.

**Reference Note**

For more on **document design,** see page 806 in the Quick Reference Handbook.

# Publish Your Essay

**Time to Shine**   You have worked hard revising, editing, and proofreading your comparison-contrast essay. Your finished paper is something to be proud of, so now is the time to share it. Here are some ways to share your comparison-contrast essay with an audience.

- If your essay compares consumer items, you could print a shoppers' guide and distribute it to friends in your class.
- If your essay compares middle school with high school, you could publish it in a guide for new high school students.
- You could make a Web page with links to information about each item you are comparing.
- If your essay compares two movies or books, you could submit the essay to the entertainment section of your school newspaper.

PORTFOLIO

# Reflect on Your Essay

**Learning from Experience**   One way to become a better writer is by reflecting on your writing. Write short responses to the following questions to see how this workshop has helped you improve your writing skills.

- Why did you use the method you chose to organize your essay? Do you think you made the most effective choice? Why or why not?
- What do you think is the best part of your essay? Why?
- What would you change about your essay? What might you do differently the next time you write a comparison-contrast essay?
- What did you learn by writing this paper that will come in handy with other types of papers?

    If you put your essay in your portfolio, be sure to include your responses to these questions.

## YOUR TURN 8 — Proofreading, Publishing, and Reflecting on Your Essay

Review each of the above steps. Before you hand in your comparison-contrast essay, remember to

- proofread it carefully, remembering to check closely for misplaced modifiers
- consider ways to design your writing effectively
- think through your publishing options
- answer the reflective questions about your writing process

## Vocabulary of the Mass Media

Did you know you spend half of your waking hours reading, viewing, and listening to mass media messages? From television to newspapers to the Internet, you are bombarded with hundreds of media messages each day. What do these messages have in common? How are they different? How does something like the news vary from medium to medium? You can use your comparison-contrast skills to answer these questions.

What are the similarities and differences among various news media? One aspect they all have in common is that they report the news every day. News happens constantly. Every day, journalists go out into the world, collect information, and craft it into news reports. They create complex media products such as newspaper articles, TV broadcasts, radio reports, or Web pages in a very short amount of time.

Have you ever wondered how journalists are able to pull off this feat? One answer is that news stories follow set formulas or patterns. Journalists save time by putting new information into old formulas. Another answer is that each medium, whether newspapers, TV, or the World Wide Web, also has its own set of unique features that are repeated over and over again. For example, every newspaper article has a **headline,** a title at the top of the page.

If you are going to be a savvy news consumer, you need to know the similarities and differences among the unique features and news formulas of each mass medium. To get you started, here are some media vocabulary terms for newspapers, television, and the Internet.

**Newspapers: On the Page**   You probably already know that a newspaper is a print product made up of articles, illustrations, and photographs. A newspaper article is made up of

- **the headline**—the title of the piece
- **the deck**—a subhead, or a smaller headline below the main headline
- **the byline**—a line that lists the author's name
- **the copy**—the text of the news story in column format

Newspaper articles may follow the **inverted pyramid pattern,** where the most important and interesting facts of the article are listed at the beginning, and the least important facts are at the very end. The beginning of an article is called the **lead.** It usually answers the questions *who, what, where, why, when,* and *how.* The reason for the inverted pyramid pattern is that if an article must be shortened for space, the last paragraphs can be deleted without losing any important information.

**Inverted Pyramid Pattern**

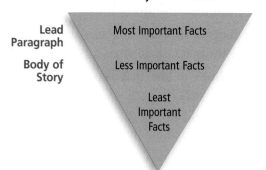

Lead Paragraph — Most Important Facts

Body of Story — Less Important Facts

Least Important Facts

An editor decides the **layout** or placement of articles, photographs, and **information graphics**—charts, graphs, maps, or other illustrations of data—in the newspaper. If a news article is important, it may have a **sidebar**—a second article on a closely related topic—next to it. Important articles are given a lot of **play,** or exposure, by being placed on the front page with large headlines and large photographs. Most photographs have **cutlines**—a few lines of explanatory text—directly underneath them.

## TV News: Coming to You Live

Among other things, a TV news report is different from a newspaper article because it contains video and audio pieces that are broadcast to you live. An **anchor,** the newscaster in the studio, usually does a **lead-in**—an introduction to a report from a reporter in the field. Then the camera **cuts**—makes a transition—to either a live segment with the reporter, or a report that was taped earlier in the day.

News reports begin with a **setup**—a few words to grab listeners' attention, and a **cover shot**—a long piece of video used to establish the location of the report. A news report uses a variety of **shots**—segments of video, including

- **close-up**—the camera shows just a person's face
- **medium shot**—the camera shows a person from the waist up
- **long shot**—the camera shows an entire person and the environment surrounding him or her

While these video shots play on your TV screen, audio segments play through your TV speakers. The main types of sound used in news reports are

- **sound bites**—short audio pieces of interviews
- **voice-overs**—the reporter's voice narrating the story over the video
- **natural sound**—birds chirping, cars rushing by, crowds roaring, or any other sounds that are part of the environment of the news report

At the end of a news report, the reporter usually does a **stand-up:** the reporter speaks directly into the camera and offers some finishing commentary to the report.

In contrast to a newspaper article, a TV news report is extremely brief. A typical TV news story is shorter than twenty sentences and runs for less than two minutes. Because of these time constraints, only a few important facts can be presented in a TV news story.

**Unlike the Inverted Pyramid Pattern, every fact in a TV news report must be important or interesting**

Most Important or Interesting Facts

### The Internet: Computer Connections

The Internet is different from newspapers and TV because it is a network of thousands of computers with which you interact. You can log on to this network any time to read the news. You can sign up for **listservs**—news-clipping services that send articles on specific subjects to your personal e-mail address. You can also become part of a **Usenet newsgroup** to read items posted on a bulletin board. **Bulletin boards** are public places where you can read messages that others have posted, or even post your own message. The **World Wide Web** is a system that uses hyperlinks to deliver the news. A **hyperlink** is an image or highlighted section of text that takes you to another Web page when you click on it. A **home page** is the first page of information in a Web document.

The Internet is evolving as a medium. It does not have any set news formulas, but two techniques communicators use to save time when creating news for the Internet are **threading** and **linking**. On bulletin boards, **threaded messages** are messages that are grouped together because they all contain the same subject line. This enables writers to follow and respond to postings on their topics and ignore irrelevant postings. On the Web, reporters do not always have to provide key items such as definitions of terms, or historical context for their news stories. Instead, they provide **links** to other people's Web sites that already contain the definitions or historical context.

**YOUR TURN 9 Practicing Your Mass-Media Vocabulary**

With a small group, look for examples of the inverted pyramid pattern, a headline, a byline, a deck, an informational graphic, a close-up shot, a medium shot, a sound bite, a voice-over, natural sound, a bulletin board, a home page, and a hyperlink. Have one person investigate newspapers, one person investigate TV news, and one person investigate the Web. When you have finished collecting your examples, prepare a formal, **workplace report** of your findings.

# Comparing and Contrasting Media Coverage

**WHAT'S AHEAD?**

In this section you will learn how to

- analyze and critique the way news stories are put together
- compare and contrast different media coverage of the same event

**H**ave you ever asked two friends to tell you about an event you did not attend, like a school play? Did they tell you exactly the same story, or did their stories vary a bit? Chances are that your friends' stories contained the same basic **facts** (such as the plot of the play) but focused on different **details.** Maybe one friend described the costumes, while the other friend focused on the acting. You might say that each friend put together his or her own *account,* or retelling, of the play.

## Examine Different Accounts of an Event

**The Way They See It**   Just as your friends create their own retellings of the same play, media sources put together different accounts of the same news event. For example, an account of a football game in your school's newspaper will look different from an account in the other team's newspaper. The newspaper writers will start with the same basic facts (who won and how many points were scored), but they will put together their own accounts of the game by focusing on different details. Use the chart below to compare and contrast the key features of two different accounts of a football game.

**TIP**   Both stories represent accurate accounts of the game. However, they are different because each newspaper focuses on different details.

|  | Winning School's Article | Losing School's Article |
| --- | --- | --- |
| **Headline** | *Victory!* | *Disappointing Loss* |
| **Photograph** | Team members jumping for joy | Star quarterback holding his head |

None of what you see and hear on TV and radio, in magazines and newspapers, or on the Internet comes to you "pure" or "unfiltered." This is because someone has to decide what will be included and what will be left out of a news story. Examples of these **editorial decisions** include what headlines, titles, sound bites, video clips, photographs, and informational graphics to use to retell news stories. You can compare and contrast the **editorial decisions** journalists and other media professionals make by examining the following aspects of news stories.

**Reference Note**

For more on **media terms,** see page 876.

- **The attention-getting techniques in news stories**   How are the images, words, and sounds arranged to get readers' and viewers' attention?

- **The point of view in each news story**   How is the main subject portrayed—negatively or positively?

- **The complexity of the news stories**   Does the story provide background information and multiple points of view or have these items been omitted?

- **The sequence of information in the news stories**   In what order does the story present information about its subject?

- **The emotional impact of the news stories**   What feeling or impression does the story create in readers or viewers?

## Looking at the News

**Two Sources/Two Views**   Think of all the news that comes out every day: political events, natural disasters, accidents, sporting events, community happenings. Important news stories are usually covered in a variety of media: on TV, in newsmagazines, in news sites on the Web, and in newspapers. However, all these media do not cover the same story in exactly the same way. For example, a TV report includes moving images and quick summaries of the story, while a newspaper article includes still photographs and in-depth details. By comparing how different media sources present the same story, you can see how different kinds of editorial decisions finally come across to readers or viewers. You can see how these editorial choices shape your view of the event.

One of the most important editorial choices news reporters make is about how to have an **emotional impact** upon the audience. A news story has emotional impact if it arouses the audience's feelings. High emotional impact can have powerful **effects** on audience members, causing them to act on feelings they get from a news story, rather than the accuracy of information in a news story.

**TIP**   As you look at the news, try to examine the effect of media on your own perception of reality.

News stories try to create an emotional impact by using anecdotes or examples from any of the following five categories:

- Love and Relationships
- Children
- The Unknown
- Death
- Animals

To compare and contrast the emotional impact of a story in a newspaper and on a TV news broadcast, count the number of times love, death, children, animals, or the unknown appear in the text, images, and sounds of each story. How are these categories used differently in each story? Look at the example below.

| News Story on a Major Flood | | |
| --- | --- | --- |
| | **TV News Report** | **Newspaper Article** |
| **Love and Relationships** | Video footage of a man holding a photo of his wife | Photo of a man with a photo of his wife |
| **Death** | Sound bite from the man saying his wife died | Quotation from an official saying that 25 people died |
| **Children** | Sounds of children crying | Sentence describing the sound of a child crying |
| **Animals** | Video footage of a horse struggling in deep water | Sentence saying many livestock died |
| **The Unknown** | Video footage of a flooded car whose owners are missing | Description of search for missing owners of car |

### YOUR TURN 10 · Comparing and Contrasting Media Coverage of an Event

With a small group, look for news coverage of an event in at least two different news media—the Internet, the newspaper, or TV. Make a chart like the one above to organize your relevant features. Then, present a brief oral report to your class, comparing and contrasting the emotional impact of each news story. In your report, answer these questions:

1. If you had seen only one of these stories, how would your impression of the event be different? Use evidence to support your answer, by examining each story separately.

2. How did each news story arouse the audience's emotions?

3. Did one story do a better job of covering your event, or was the coverage similar in both stories? Why do you think so?

# Choices

**Choose one of the following activities to complete.**

## ▶ CROSSING THE CURRICULUM: HISTORY

**1. The More Things Change . . .** Famous leaders have often copied the leadership style of earlier leaders. After all, if it works, why change it? Work with a partner to find two major historical leaders from different time periods who have something in common. If you are stuck, ask a history teacher for clues about where to look. Do some research in the library to investigate the leaders. Then, prepare a **report** that compares the two.

## ▶ LITERATURE

**2. They've Got Style** Over a lifetime an author can create many different works of literature. On close examination, however, you may discover that different works of literature by the same author actually have many aspects in common. Write a **literary essay** comparing two novels, poems, or short stories by your favorite author. Show how the author's unique thumbprint is present in each work. What distinctive features of the author's style can you find in both works?

## ▶ CAREERS

**3. Tough Decisions** Bosses often have to make decisions, but they do not always have the time to do their own research. That's where you come in. Assume your boss is about to make a purchase. Choose two office items to compare, such as two different pens, computers, or notebooks. Create a two-column chart that compares the advantages and disadvantages of each product. Then, write a **memo** to your boss that briefly summarizes your findings.

## ▶ SPEAKING AND LISTENING

**4. On the Other Hand** Choose an important issue that divides student opinion in your school. Think about issues like school uniforms, open lunch, or the student-government elections. You might even ask someone on the debate team what topics they are hashing out. Once you have found a topic, interview one student on each side of the issue. Then, prepare a brief **oral report** for your classmates that compares and contrasts both sides of the issue.

PORTFOLIO

# 4 Exploring Causes and Effects

## Reading Workshop

*Reading a Cause-and-Effect Article*

## Writing Workshop

*Writing a Cause-and-Effect Explanation*

## Speaking and Listening

*Giving an Informative Speech*

## Viewing and Representing

*Analyzing Stereotypes*

## Cause and Effect

- The school board has decided to close your school campus at lunch.

- Your mother's promotion will require your family to move.

- The state legislature has instituted a requirement that all high school students complete at least twenty hours of volunteer service each school year.

> **Informational Text**
>
> Exposition

Any of these scenarios would probably prompt you to ask the question *Why?* or *What are the effects?* In asking and answering these questions, you are examining causes and effects.

Of course you aren't the only one who wonders about causes and effects. Doctors and researchers look for the causes of diseases and the effects of exercise. Historians argue about the causes of the Civil War and the effects of space exploration on world politics. Scientists develop theories to explain the formation of the continents and the possible effects of a hurricane on a coastal city.

**YOUR TURN 1** **Brainstorming About Causes and Effects**

With two or three classmates, brainstorm instances where you have observed cause-and-effect relationships and areas in which people work to understand the causes and/or the effects of something. To get started, think about historians, detectives, and astronauts. Be prepared to share your responses with the class.

**internet connect**

**go. hrw .com**

**GO TO:** go.hrw.com
**KEYWORD:** EOLang 9-4

# Reading a Cause-and-Effect Article

**"Y**ou can't go to school without your coat. You'll get sick!" Is this expression just something adults say, or is it true that there is a connection between cold temperatures and getting sick? The article on the next page, "Hot Times in the Operating Room," can help you answer this question. In this article, the writer examines the cause-and-effect relationship between patient infection and the cold temperatures usually found in operating rooms.

## Preparing to Read

**READING SKILL**

**Implied Cause and Effect** The writer of the following article explores the cause-and-effect relationship between patient infection and cold temperatures in operating rooms. When you read about these causes and effects, you will learn how one event causes a later event. The first event is the **cause** of the next event, the **effect**. As you read, see if you can recognize the causes and the effects. Just remember that writers do not always signal causes and effects with clue words such as *if . . . then, because,* or *reasons why.* When signal words are missing, you will have to figure out the **implied** (suggested) **causes and effects**.

**READING FOCUS**

**Cause-and-Effect Organizational Patterns** When explaining causes and their effects, writers can organize their ideas in several ways; they can focus on the causes, on the effects, or on both in a causal chain. If you represented these patterns visually, they would look something like this.

As you read the following article, see if you can determine what organizational pattern the writer has chosen to use.

See if you can find out if cold temperatures have a connection with sickness. As you read, jot down answers to the numbered active-reading questions.

*from* **DISCOVER**

# HOT Times in the Operating Room

Working under bright lights and wearing heavy gowns can make surgery uncomfortably hot for doctors and nurses. Operating rooms, therefore, are traditionally kept quite cold. That makes the surgery patient quite cold, too—even slightly hypothermic. Body temperatures can drop by 4 degrees. Doctors used to think mild hypothermia was actually good for the patient because cold retards the growth of bacteria in the air. But according to a new study, the cold temperatures in operating rooms actually triple the risk of infection.

> **1. How does the writer immediately get your attention?**

> **2. What is the writer saying here about hypothermia and risk of infection?**

"What causes wound infection is not really bacteria floating around in the air but the patient's decreased resistance to bacteria on the skin or inside the body," says Daniel Sessler, an anesthesiologist at the University of California at San Francisco and the University of Vienna. To find out how operating-room temperatures affect that resistance, Sessler and his colleagues studied 200 patients undergoing surgery. In 104 patients, warmed intravenous fluid and forced-air blankets (which are like quilts with warm air blown through them) kept body temperature normal. The other 96 patients were not warmed during

> **3. Why does the writer tell us this story about Sessler's experiment?**

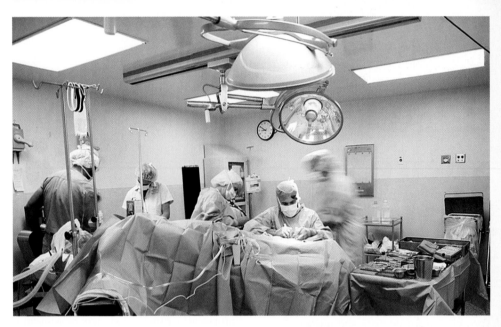

surgery, and their body temperatures dropped to an average of 94.5 degrees. Wound infections, Sessler found, occurred in 19 percent of the patients allowed to become hypothermic but in only 6 percent of the warmed patients. Unwarmed patients also stayed in the hospital nearly three days longer.

Hypothermia probably lowers the body's resistance in two ways, says Sessler. First, low body temperature reduces the flow of blood—and its oxygen cargo—to the wound. "Oxygen is essential to fighting infections," he says. The body's immune system breaks down molecular oxygen into highly reactive atomic oxygen. Immune cells release this oxygen near bacteria. "This is what kills them," says Sessler. Hypothermia also directly inhibits any functions of the immune system. "The cells and enzymes responsible for immunity simply don't work well when the body is cold."

"I think warming will become the standard of care in no time," says Sessler. "None of this is difficult, and none of it is expensive. Keeping people warm costs less than thirty dollars, which is nothing in the scheme of the operation. But it makes a big difference in terms of the outcome, is essentially risk free, and reduces costs. So it's sort of a no-brainer that you should keep people warm."

> **4. What causes low blood flow and low oxygen?**

> **5. What effect of hypothermia is mentioned here?**

> **6. In the conclusion, how does the writer bring the article to a close?**

## Implied Cause and Effect

READING SKILL

**Hidden Identity**   "Hot Times in the Operating Room," like all cause-and-effect articles, explains how one action or series of actions (the **cause**) causes something to happen (the **effect**). In many cause-and-effect articles, writers use **clue words** to help signal causes and effects for readers. These identity tags include words such as

| | | | |
|---|---|---|---|
| affect | because | determines | leads to |
| as a result | consequently | therefore | so that |
| reasons | if. . . then | in order | since |
| so | effect | why | thus |

**Example:**

           cause              clue word       effect

The use of iodine on the wound    affects    the recovery speed.

As you read about cause-and-effect relationships, however, you will see that whether something is a cause or an effect is not always obvious. After all, causes and effects don't always wear identity tags. So how can you determine causes and effects if there are no signal words? You have to infer the relationship—that is, use known facts and personal experience to determine whether it is a cause or effect. When causes and effects are not openly identified by the writer, they are known as **implied causes and effects**.

In the following sentence, there is a cause-and-effect relationship between low body temperature and slow blood circulation, even though the writer does not signal the cause or the effect with a clue word.

**Example:**

effect                                    cause

A person's blood circulation is slowed   by low body temperature.

## THINKING IT THROUGH — Implied Cause and Effect

Read the sentence below. Then, to figure out the cause or effect in this sentence, use these steps listed below.

A person's blood circulation is slowed by low body temperature.

▶ **STEP 1** Ask yourself, "What happened?" (What is the effect?)    Blood circulation is slowed down.

▶ **STEP 2** Ask yourself, "Why?" (What is the cause?)    Low body temperature.

▶ **STEP 3** What can you infer?    Low body temperature is the cause; slowed blood circulation is the effect.

## YOUR TURN 2 — Recognizing Causes and Effects

Using the three steps above, identify the causes and the effects in each of the following sentences from "Hot Times in the Operating Room." Put your answers on your own paper.

1. But according to a new study, the cold temperatures in operating rooms actually triple the risk of infection.

2. What causes wound infection is not really bacteria floating around in the air but the patient's decreased resistance to bacteria on the skin or inside the body.

3. Hypothermia probably lowers the body's resistance in two ways, says Sessler.

4. First, low body temperature reduces the flow of blood—and its oxygen cargo—to the wound.

5. Hypothermia also directly inhibits any functions of the immune system.

# Cause-and-Effect Organizational Patterns

**The Chicken or the Egg?**   Generally, every writer of a causal article tries to explain how causes and effects are related. However, not all cause-and-effect relationships are simple and straightforward. One cause can have several effects; one effect can result from several causes, and so forth.  There are so many different kinds of relationships that the **organization,** or **pattern,** of cause-and-effect writing can vary considerably. Each writer must choose a particular focus on causes, effects, or both. Then the writer can determine the most effective organization for the writing.

Knowing the organizational pattern, or structure, of a text can help you comprehend what you are reading. Specifically, cause-and-effect text structures can help you understand the causal relationship between ideas. Cause-and-effect text patterns, like any organizational pattern, are a kind of road map; they help you navigate unfamiliar text. When you learn these patterns, you will have a better idea of where to look to find the main idea and details in any cause-and-effect article. Examples of three common cause-and-effect text patterns follow.

**Three Types of Patterns**   Depending upon the focus of the writing—causes only, effects only, or both causes and effects—the organizational pattern may vary a great deal. As a reader, it is your task to figure out how the article is organized so that you can more easily identify causes and effects. Does this sound like a difficult task? It is not. In fact, most articles use one or more of three basic cause-and-effect patterns. Master these patterns, and you will have the key to understanding most cause-and-effect articles. The following examples are maps of the three common cause-and-effect patterns: a causal chain, focus on causes, and focus on effects.

▶ **Pattern 1: Causal Chain**   In a causal chain, an initial cause brings about an effect. Then that effect becomes a cause for another effect, and so on, until the final effect is reached.

cause ⟶ effect/cause ⟶ effect/cause ⟶ effect

**Example:**

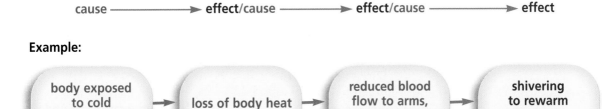

body exposed to cold temperatures → loss of body heat → reduced blood flow to arms, legs, and head → shivering to rewarm the body

> **Pattern 2: Focus on Causes**   In this pattern, the effect is stated in the thesis; then the causes are explained in the body paragraphs.

**Example:**

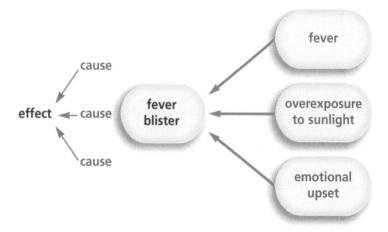

**TIP**   Notice that in Pattern 2, the writer starts by describing an effect and then jumps backward in time to describe the causes that brought about the effect. Writers tend to use this pattern when they want to emphasize *Why?* questions such as the question *Why do people get fever blisters?*

> **Pattern 3: Focus on Effects**   In this pattern, the cause is stated in the thesis; then the effects are explained in the body paragraphs.

**Example:**

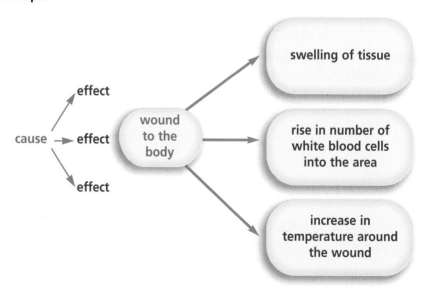

**TIP** Don't be surprised to find that a writer's organization does not exactly fit one of the three cause-and-effect patterns; most professional authors experiment with unusual ways to present their ideas.

For example, "Hot Times in the Operating Room" actually combines all three patterns. Also, the cause-and-effect chain for this article doesn't begin until the third paragraph; however, "decreased resistance" is mentioned in the second paragraph.

## YOUR TURN 3  Analyzing a Cause-and-Effect Pattern

To analyze the cause-and-effect pattern in "Hot Times in the Operating Room," complete the content map below. Put your answers on your own paper. (Remember, your answers to the active-reading questions and First Thoughts questions can help you analyze this pattern.)

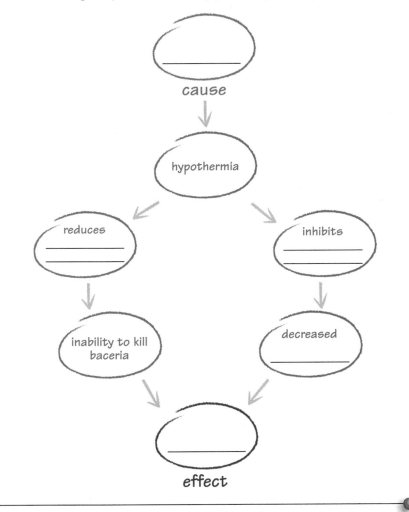

cause

↓

hypothermia

↙      ↘

reduces _____      inhibits _____

↓            ↓

inability to kill baceria      decreased _____

↘      ↙

_____

effect

## Cause-and-Effect Context Clues

Sometimes you can figure out the meaning of an unfamiliar word by examining its **context**: the words that surround the unfamiliar word and the way in which the word is used. One type of context clue, a **cause-and-effect clue,** indicates that something happens because of another event. If you know the likely cause or result of the action in the relationship, you can often use this information to determine the meaning of the unfamiliar word. Whenever possible, it is a good idea to check your guess in a dictionary.

**THINKING IT THROUGH**  **Using Cause-and-Effect Context Clues**

Take a look at the example below and the steps following it.

**Example:**
Because four patients had a natural **immunity** to the disease, the doctor did not give them medicine.

1. **Look for cause-and-effect clue words.** The word *because* tells why (cause) the doctor did not give the patients medicine.

2. **Ask a cause-and-effect question about the unfamiliar word.** *Why would an* **immunity** *cause the doctor not to give the patients medicine?*

3. **Answer your question.** *Patients who had a natural protection within their bodies against the disease would not need medicine. Therefore,* **immunity** *could mean "a natural protection against a disease."*

**PRACTICE**

Use the steps above to find the meaning of the italicized words in the following sentences. Put your answers on your own paper.

1. Because of *hypothermic* conditions, patients shivered during the operations, and many developed infections.

2. So that the brain is more alert in an emergency, hormones from the adrenal glands *induce* the heart to pump extra oxygen into the bloodstream.

3. Platelets *cleave* to the rough surfaces of a cut, a process that results in a protective blood clot at the wound site.

4. When viruses or bacteria enter your body, your immune system activates white blood cells that kill the *pathogens*. As a result, small-scale infections are usually repelled.

5. Partly due to an *impermeable* membrane, bacteria and viruses that bypass the protection of the skin do not penetrate vital internal organs.

## Implied Causes and Effects

Local, state, and national reading tests usually check your understanding of causes or effects that are implied, not directly stated. Since the reading passages often don't include any **clue words** like *because* or *since* to point out causes or effects, you have to figure out the answer.

Here is a typical **reading passage** and its cause-and-effect test question:

Solar-heating devices called *flat-plate collectors* have one or more covers made of clear plastic or glass. Beneath the covers is a black plate made of metal or plastic. The black plate gives off heat as it is warmed by sunlight, and this heat is contained by the clear covers.

A flat-plate collector can be very useful for heating household water. Air, water, or some other fluid is pumped through

tubes attached to the black plate of the flat-plate collector. Fluid inside the tubes passes through the collector and absorbs heat from the black plate. Another device called a *heat exchanger* is then used to transfer the heat from the fluid to a household hot-water system.

Heat can be trapped within a flat-plate collector because

**A.** tubes are attached to the black plate within the collector

**B.** the clear glass or plastic covers contain the heat inside the collector

**C.** all of the heat stays inside the black plate; the plate gives off no heat

**D.** heat energy is added to the collector by the fluid that flows over the black plate

---

**THINKING IT THROUGH**   **Answering Cause-and-Effect Questions**

Keep the following steps in mind as you work through the question:

1. Don't just skim the passage; read it carefully. Most of the time, these tests evaluate reading comprehension, not speed in answering the questions.

2. Look for important words in the test question that are the same as, or similar to, words in the passage. The test question above contains the words *heat* and *trapped*. The end of the last sentence of the first paragraph (. . . *and this heat is contained by the clear covers*) also includes the word *heat*, along with a word

similar to *trapped*: the word *contained*.

3. Now try asking yourself the cause-and-effect questions about the sentence:

   ■ What happened? (What is the effect?) *Heat was trapped within the collector*.

   ■ Why? (What is the cause?) *The glass covers contained (trapped) the heat*.

4. Select the answer choice that most closely matches your answers to the cause-and-effect questions. The answer is **B**.

# Writing a Cause-and-Effect Explanation

## WHAT'S AHEAD?

**In this workshop, you will write a cause-and-effect essay. You will also learn how to**

- **focus on causes or effects**
- **gather support for causes or effects**
- **recognize false cause and effect**
- **vary sentence beginnings**
- **correct inexact pronoun references**

Imagine this situation: The editor of your school newspaper wants you to write an article about the passage of a new rule requiring every student at your school to complete twenty hours of community service each year. Your first job as a reporter will be to decide what questions you want the article to answer. Many questions will come up, but two important ones might spring to mind right away: *Why did this happen?* and *What results will it have?*

If you wrote an article that answered those two questions, you would be writing about causes and effects—the same kind of writing you will be undertaking in this Writing Workshop. By completing the steps in the workshop, you can create an interesting, well-supported essay that explains any specific cause-and-effect topic that you choose.

# Prewriting

## Choose a Situation or Event

**A Wonder-full Topic**  A good topic for a cause-and-effect explanation is a situation or event that makes you wonder "Why?" or "What now?" To find such a situation or event, try a couple of these topic-generating ideas:

- **Keep a "wonder" journal** for a day. Make a note in it every time you find yourself asking "I wonder why . . . ?" or "What might happen if . . . ?" The things you wonder about during the day might make good topics for a cause-and-effect essay.

- **Read through a science magazine** for details on a scientific phenomenon with intriguing causes or effects. Look for interesting topics—the effects of tornadoes, for example, or the causes of black holes.

- **Browse the World Wide Web,** read a newspaper, or watch a TV news broadcast to find facts about an important current event. Look for an event with interesting causes—one with a fascinating "story behind the story"—or one with equally interesting effects.

When you have found a few situations or events that seem promising, list them and circle the one you really want to investigate.

## Narrow Your Topic

**Limit the Field**  Stop and take a second look at your topic; does it seem like too much to cover in a short essay? For example, if you try to write a two-page essay on the causes and effects of the American Revolution, you are bound to run into problems—that topic is just too large and complex for such a short paper. However, if you narrow the topic to two causes of the Boston Tea Party, you will have a much more manageable topic on your hands.

If you are looking for a topic that is more closely related to your own life, you could narrow your options by writing about the unexpected effects of getting a driver's license. With this specific focus on effects, you could discuss the topic in detail within a short composition.

> **TIP**  You may need to think about focusing on either the causes or the effects of your topic, not both.

## Consider Your Purpose and Audience

**Who's Reading?**   Your **purpose** in this essay is to inform your audience about causes and effects. However, do your readers know anything about the situation or event you are planning to write about? Do they care about your topic? **You need to line up your thinking with the needs of your audience.** Begin by analyzing your audience and its knowledge about your topic.

◀ KEY CONCEPT

## Analyzing Audience

To analyze the audience for your cause-and-effect essay, answer the questions below.

▶ **What do my readers already know about this situation or event?** If you were writing about the effects of getting a driver's license and you had students in mind as readers, you might decide that they already knew about one effect: the sense of freedom that comes with being allowed to drive. That does not mean you can't write about this effect—it just should not be the only one you discuss.

▶ **What might my readers want to know more about?** Your readers may not have thought about the greater responsibilities and lower grades that can sometimes result from being allowed to drive; those are two effects your readers will probably want to know about.

▶ **How can I get my readers to share my interest in the situation or event I am writing about?** When you have an audience in mind, think of a question or other "hook" that will draw them in—and plan to start your essay with this attention-grabber. If your writing is interesting, your audience will want to read on. For example, you might begin an essay on teenagers' getting a driver's license with the question "What privilege does the average teenager most want to have?"

> **TIP** Another aspect to consider as you make stylistic choices is the **occasion** for your writing. Your occasion is what prompts you to write on your particular topic.

## Write Your Thesis

**Bring It into Focus**   The focus that you choose for your essay determines what your thesis, or **main idea,** will be. Here is an example thesis for an essay that focuses on the **causes** of crash dieting. To support this thesis, each of the paragraphs in the body would discuss a different *cause.*

**Focus on Causes**

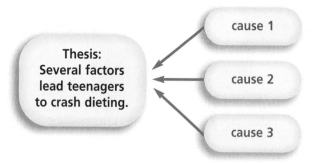

Thesis:
Several factors
lead teenagers
to crash dieting.

cause 1

cause 2

cause 3

The following example thesis clearly signals that the essay will focus on the **effects** of crash dieting. Each of the body paragraphs would present a different *effect*.

Focus on Effects

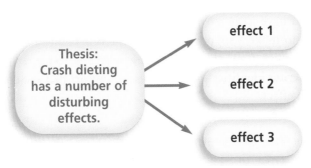

After you have thought about how you want to focus your essay, you will need to write a thesis that expresses the main idea you want to convey. Don't worry about making the thesis perfect right away; you can always refine it when you write, evaluate, and revise your first draft.

> **TIP** In **persuasive writing,** cause-and-effect relationships are often used to explain and support an opinion.

## Gather Support

**Support Yourself!** To make your explanation of causes and effects convincing, you need to include your support—examples, facts, and statistics. Otherwise, your readers might question your entire explanation. For example, an essay on the effects of crash dieting might include statistics on the percentage of dieters who become ill. As you look for sources from which to gather support, keep the following ideas in mind.

KEY CONCEPT

■ **Kinds of Sources** Choose the right kinds of sources. For example, if your topic deals with the effects of a current world event, choose timely, up-to-date sources such as current newspapers or magazines—not sources that are months or years out of date.

■ **Specialized Sources** Find specialized sources that relate specifically to your topic. For example, if you are preparing an essay about the effects of a particular battle during the Civil War, look for a book, magazine, or specialized encyclopedia devoted specifically to Civil War history.

■ **Web Searches**   If you look for information on your topic by using a World Wide Web search engine, you can narrow your list of search results by adding **cause-and-effect clue words** such as *causes*, *effects*, *reasons*, or *results* to your key word searches. For example, you could add the word *effects* to the search key words *Battle of Gettysburg*.

Once you have gathered your support, one of the best ways to keep track of it is to make a support chart like the one below. In the first column the writer lists three effects of getting a driver's license. In the second column the writer identifies specific types of support that she could use to back up each effect.

### SUPPORT CHART

| Effects of getting a driver's license | Support |
|---|---|
| A driver's license brings greater independence. | **Example:** My brother doesn't have to count on my parents or his friends for rides to school or events anymore. |
| A driver's license brings more responsibility. | **Fact:** State law requires drivers to maintain car insurance, to register cars, and to renew licenses yearly. |
| A driver's license can cause grades to drop. | **Statistic:** According to a survey at my school, fifty percent of students have a drop in grades after getting a driver's license. |

### YOUR TURN 4   Choosing a Topic and Organizing Ideas

Review each of the prewriting steps. Before you begin writing your essay, make sure to

■ choose a situation or event to write about, and narrow it down to a specific topic

■ think about what your audience will need to know

■ write a thesis that states your main idea

■ gather support for your cause-and-effect explanation

## False Cause and Effect

When you write about causes and effects, you need to avoid an error called **false cause and effect**—a mistake in logic that can make your cause-and-effect explanations less convincing. If your readers decide that some of your reasoning is faulty, they might be suspicious about the soundness of your entire essay.

Never ask your readers to assume that one event caused a second event just because the second event followed the first; you must show a real or logical connection between the two events. For instance, if you wash the family car and it rains the next day, you know that washing the car did not cause it to rain. The two events are not related.

False cause and effect often results from failing to consider more than one cause. For example, say that your school's football team plays a game in another town and loses. If you conclude that the team lost because they played

away from home, you are ignoring several other possible causes: that the team had been playing too many games and was tired, that the other team played better, or that two of your school's key players were out with the flu. Look at these further examples of false cause and effect.

**False Cause and Effect:**
I ate a mango for breakfast.
The next day, I felt ill.
The mango made me sick.

In this example, only coincidence relates the two events. The writer just assumes that eating the mango caused the sickness. Compare the example to the logical reasoning in the example below.

**Valid Cause and Effect:**
I felt ill, so I went to see a doctor.
She said I had the symptoms of a virus.
A virus may have caused me to feel ill.

**PRACTICE**

On a piece of paper, write an *F* for each of the following passages that contains a false cause-and-effect relationship. Write *OK* for any relationship that is valid. Be prepared to explain your choices.

1. After my brother installed a radio in his car, the car developed several engine problems. Of course, the radio caused all the problems.

2. In her chemistry class, my sister failed to get two solutions to react at room temperature. After she heated them, though, they reacted. She decided that heat is needed for them to react.

3. One day I saw my friend Tori having a serious conversation with her brother Luis. When I met her later in the day, she was in a bad mood. Something Luis said must have upset her.

4. The final game of the World Series had to be delayed because of rain. My favorite team ended up losing the game. The team is good, so they must have lost because of the rain delay.

5. I came to school with a cold yesterday and talked to my friend Andre in class. The next day, he was absent. He must have caught my cold and stayed home from school.

# Writing

## Cause-and-Effect Explanation

| Framework | Directions and Explanations |
|---|---|

### Introduction

- Get your readers interested right away.
- Give background information.
- Include a clear thesis.

**Grab Your Readers' Attention**   To draw in your readers, begin with an attention-getting statement or question that will make them want to read on.

**Provide Needed Background Information**   If your essay focuses on effects, you may need to give brief background details on causes. If your essay focuses on causes, you need to give background details on effects.

**State Your Thesis**   To prepare your readers for the explanations that will follow, clearly state the focus of your essay.

### Body

- Discuss first cause or effect and give support.
- Discuss second cause or effect and give support.
- Discuss further causes or effects and give support.

**Present Your Ideas**   You can organize your causes, effects, and support in two ways:

- chronologically (time order)
- by order of importance

As you write, you may discover that you have a cause-and-effect chain—a series of effects that become causes for other effects. Here is an example of a cause-and-effect chain taken from the Writer's Model on the next page:

car expenses ➤ more hours of work ➤ less study time ➤ drop in grades

### Conclusion

- Remind your readers about your thesis.

**Wrap It Up**   Restate the thesis—your main idea. If you think that your restatement may not be interesting enough, leave your readers with something further to think about by closing with an opinion statement or with a question.

**YOUR TURN 5   Writing a First Draft**

Using the framework above, write the first draft of your essay. The Writer's Model on the next page follows this framework.

# A Writer's Model

**The following short essay, which is a final draft, closely follows the framework on the previous page. Notice the highlighted cause-and-effect clue words the writer uses as linking devices.**

## Getting a Driver's License: The Effects

What one privilege does the average teenager most want? Many would probably say "the right to drive." To a teenager, a driver's license seems like a ticket to freedom: Teen drivers can go where they want when they want—up to a point. However, teenagers who put themselves in the driver's seat often end up facing effects and responsibilities that they may not have anticipated.

For a teenager, a driver's license is a big step toward independence. Teen drivers do not have to count on parents, friends, bus schedules, or good weather. They are not always asking favors, making last-minute arrangements, or following other people's schedules. They can accept jobs on the other side of town, and they will not miss parties because they are stranded at home without a ride.

However, a teen who no longer needs a chauffeur may unexpectedly become one. Many teen drivers find that they are now the ones asked to drive a sister to school or to go to the store for milk. Another effect is that carless friends—including some who never help with expenses—ask for rides.

Owning a car also costs money—in ways a passenger cannot appreciate. Gasoline is not free, insurance for teenagers is expensive, and maintenance (not to mention repairs) drains finances. To meet car expenses, teenagers often have to work more hours and thus have less free time. Unfortunately, some teenagers respond to that situation by studying less, which causes their grades to drop, which in turn may cause their parents to take away their car keys for several weeks.

The ultimate effect of getting a driver's license, then, is that it may help teenagers to grow up. Teen drivers find that they have to balance freedom with responsibility and learn how to afford their dream of driving without losing other things. Car keys can be the keys to a lot of fun and independence, but teenagers need to realize that a driver's license, like most things in life, comes at a price.

INTRODUCTION:
Attention-grabbing question

Thesis (focuses on effects)

BODY: Effect 1

Support for effect 1

Effect 2
Support for effect 2

Effect 3
Support for effect 3

CONCLUSION:
Restatement of thesis

# A Student's Model

**The following passages are from a cause-and-effect essay by Cheryl Flugan of Belson High School in Winston, Florida. Cause-and-effect clue words are highlighted.**

## What Are the Effects of Running?

**Attention-grabber**

I hovered in the doorway, waiting. Mari was crazy, I was sure. It was the end of our eighth-grade year, and Mari had decided to join the cross-country team. She asked me to do the same, but I said no. Me run three miles? Absurd. Now she was sealing her fate by speaking to the cross-country coach. Impatient to leave, I peered into the classroom. A piercing gaze captured my own.

"You running?" he inquired in a booming voice, his tone making the question seem more akin to a command. He pressed me for my answer while Mari looked on, amused. I squeaked out an "Um, yeah," being too afraid to answer no. The man looked satisfied. Mari looked shocked. I was certain I had signed myself up for five months of torture. Only recently have I realized that that day was a turning point for me, marking not only the birth of my athletic career, but also a major landmark in my growth as a person. I have benefited from the positive effects of running.

**Thesis (focus on effects)**

**Effect 1**
**Support for effect 1**

**Effect 2**
**Support for effect 2**

**Effect 3**

**Support for effect 3**

I was shy and unassertive coming out of the eighth grade, but running improved my self-confidence. Being part of a team forced me to meet new people. Through cross country I have formed many precious friendships. Running has also given me the confidence to be a leader and mentor for younger runners. Never before had I considered myself a role model, but now I am finding myself in that position. More than anything else, however, I think my improvement in self-confidence has resulted from learning to have the courage to succeed. Often I see girls who are reluctant to display their talents for fear of intimidating, and possibly losing, friends. A runner cannot think like that. I have learned not to apologize for being successful in running or in any other aspect of life.

# Evaluate and Revise Your Draft

**Fine-Tuning or Overhauling?** To refine your writing, you need to read through your whole paper carefully at least twice. The first time, you should evaluate and revise for content and organization, using the guidelines below. When you read through your paper a second time, you can use the guidelines on page 145 to evaluate and revise for sentence style.

▶ **First Reading: Content and Organization** Work collaboratively with another student in your class to revise the content and organization of your essay. You can use the following chart to guide your revisions. Respond to the questions in the first column. If you need help answering the questions, use the tips in the middle column and make the changes suggested in the last column.

## Cause-and-Effect Explanation: Content and Organization Guidelines for Peer and Self-Evaluation

| Evaluation Questions | ▶ Tips | ▶ Revision Techniques |
|---|---|---|
| ❶ Will the introduction quickly interest readers in the event or situation? | ▶ **Circle** the sentences in the introduction that you think will interest your readers. If you don't see any circles, revise. | ▶ **Add** information and details about the event or situation. **Delete or replace** repetitive words or phrases. |
| ❷ Can the readers identify a thesis that shows the focus of the essay—either causes or effects? | ▶ **Underline** the thesis statement twice. If you don't see a thesis statement, revise. | ▶ **Add** a thesis statement near the beginning of the paper. Be sure it focuses on either causes or effects. |
| ❸ Is the explanation of causes or effects supported with evidence? (Beware of false cause and effect.) | ▶ **Circle** each sentence that offers support. Revise if you don't see at least one circled sentence per cause or effect. | ▶ **Add** examples, facts, and statistics to support each cause and effect you have identified. **Elaborate** on existing support. |
| ❹ Is the information for each cause or effect organized in a clear, easy-to-follow way? | ▶ For chronological order, **number** causes and effects in sequence to see jumps. For order of importance, **underline** your most important cause or effect to be sure it is presented last. | ▶ **Rearrange** a chronological presentation to show the correct order. For order of importance, **rearrange** causes or effects to put the least important first and the most important at the end. |
| ❺ Does the conclusion include a sentence that restates the focus of the explanation? | ▶ **Circle** the sentence in the conclusion that restates the focus of your essay. Revise if the main idea is not restated. | ▶ **Add** a sentence that restates the focus of your explanation—either causes or effects. |

**ONE WRITER'S REVISIONS**  Here's how one writer used the content-and-organization guidelines to revise some sentences from the cause-and-effect essay on page 141. Study the revisions and answer the questions following the paragraph.

Owning a car also costs money—in ways a passenger can-

add  not appreciate. Gasoline is not free, *insurance for teenagers is expensive,* and maintenance (not to

mention repairs) drains finances. To meet car expenses,

teenagers often have to work more hours and thus have less free

time. Unfortunately, some teenagers respond to that situation by

rearrange  studying less, which *in turn* may cause their parents to take away their

add  car keys for several weeks. *which causes* If their grades *to* drop.

**PEER REVIEW**

Ask a classmate to read your paper and to answer the following questions. Use this feedback to prompt your revisions.

1. What did you like about the writer's paper?

2. Was the explanation of causes or effects clear? Why or why not?

## Analyzing the Revision Process

1. **What kind of information did the writer add to the second sentence? How does this information improve the sentence?**

2. **Why did the writer edit and move the last sentence?**

### YOUR TURN 6  Focusing on Content and Organization

Revise the content and organization of your essay using the guidelines on the previous page; use the example revisions shown above as a model.

▶ **Second Reading: Style**  In this reading, you need to look at the manner in which you have expressed your ideas—your sentence style. As you wrote your cause-and-effect explanation, you might have been tempted to begin each sentence the same way—with the cause or effect you are focusing on. However, this monotonous way of beginning sentences might cause your audience to stop reading altogether. So you won't fall into this rut, use the following sentence-style guidelines to help you **vary sentence beginnings.**

| Evaluation Question | ▶ Tip | ▶ Revision Technique |
|---|---|---|
| **Do many of the sentences begin the same way? Are some structures overused?** | ▶ **Put parentheses** around the first five words of each sentence. Do most subjects and verbs fall within the parentheses? If most do, revise. | ▶ **Reword** or **reorder** parts of some sentences for more variety. **Combine** sentences. **Add** transitions. |

## Varied Beginnings

**Focus on Sentences**

Have you ever read something that sounded monotonous? Sometimes writing seems boring because the writer begins each sentence the same way: a subject followed by a verb. Bored readers will be tempted not to finish reading your essay; varying your sentence beginnings is one way to keep your writing interesting and your readers interested.

**ONE WRITER'S REVISIONS**   Here is how the writer of the model cause-and-effect essay on page 141 used the guidelines above to revise some of her sentence beginnings.

**BEFORE REVISION**

(There is an unexpected part) of not needing a chauffeur. (It is that you can) become one. (Many teen drivers find that) they are the ones asked to drive a sister to school. (They're asked to go to) the store for milk. (They have carless friends who) ask for rides. (Some friends never help with) expenses.

In every sentence, the subject and verb fall within the parentheses.

**AFTER REVISION**

However, a teen who no longer needs a chauffeur may unexpectedly become one. Many teen drivers find that they are now the ones asked to drive a sister to school or to go to the store for milk. Another effect is that carless friends— including some who never help with expenses—ask for rides.

reword and combine

combine
reword and combine

## Analyzing the Revision Process

1. Why did the writer combine the first two sentences into one sentence?

2. How did the writer's revision of the last two sentences improve the paragraph?

**YOUR TURN 7** **Focusing on Sentence Beginnings**

Revise the style of your essay using the guidelines on the previous page. Use the example revisions shown on page 145 as a model.

## Designing Your Writing

**Cause-and-Effect Graphics**  You might want to strengthen your paper by including graphics to focus your explanations. In the example below, a writer has reinforced his explanation of the effects of pollution on the earth's ecosystems through the use of a chart. If you have graphics software at home or at school, use the software to create or edit diagrams, charts, photographs, or images that will support the cause-and-effect explanations in your essay. If not, create your own graphic as a way to summarize and clarify your work.

Remember that a graphic must be made a part of the text, not an ornament to it. Readers must be explicitly told what the graphic accomplishes, what they are to see in it, and why it is there.

### Example:

Too much pollution has affected ecosystems all over the world. As the following chart shows, in some European countries, water wells have been polluted, soil has been contaminated, and many forests are either damaged or dying. In the Czech Republic and Slovakia, many rivers no longer support fish or other aquatic life.

| Country | Effects of Pollution |
|---|---|
| Poland | 80% of water wells polluted 1/4 of soil contaminated |
| Bulgaria | 1/3 of forest damaged or dying |
| Czech Republic and Slovakia | 1/4 of rivers polluted |

## Proofread Your Essay

**Make No Mistake About It**   Before you prepare a final copy of your essay, make sure that it follows the **conventions of written language** and that it is free of grammar, spelling, and punctuation errors. You need to be especially careful to correct any inexact pronoun references your essay may contain; a perfectly good explanation of causes and effects can be weakened by one inexact pronoun.

> **Reference Note**
>
> For more information and practice on **clear pronoun reference**, see page 565.

### Grammar Link

## Inexact Pronoun Reference

The job of a **pronoun** is to stand in for a noun or phrase called the antecedent. *Antecedent* means "that which comes before." In other words, the pronoun refers to the noun or phrase that comes before it. What if two nouns or phrases come before a pronoun? Then your reader may be unsure which noun or phrase is the pronoun's antecedent. This problem is called **inexact pronoun reference.** Your pronoun references should be exact—each pronoun should clearly refer to one noun or phrase. Compare the *Inexact* and *Exact* sentences below to see one way an inexact reference can be fixed—by revising a sentence to completely eliminate the problem pronoun.

**Inexact**   My mother called my sister before she left for work. [Who left for work, the mother or the sister?]

**Exact**   Before leaving for work, my mother called my sister.

Other sentences can be fixed by keeping the problem pronoun, but revising so that it clearly refers to only one antecedent.

**Inexact**   Angel arrived before Cory, so he got a better seat. [Who got a better seat, Angel or Cory?]

**Exact**   Because he arrived before Cory, Angel got a better seat.

### PRACTICE

Revise each of the following sentences to correct any inexact pronoun references.

1. School clubs can give students valuable experiences if they are well organized.

2. After seeing my brother's latest painting and my friend's newest sketch at the art club's show, the judges gave him the grand prize.

3. When the drama club members performed a play for the new students, they were nervous and excited.

4. Joe asked his friend to join our writing club, so we asked to see his portfolio.

5. Clubs can make students more enthusiastic about school; they feel a part of the school community.

# Publish Your Essay

**Taking a Bow**   Here are some ways you might share your cause-and-effect explanation with your audience.

- If your topic is about the causes or effects of a current event, try submitting your essay to your school newspaper, which might publish the essay as a feature article.

- Find an Internet newsgroup related to your topic; then, post your essay to the group and ask for responses.

- If your topic deals with a scientific phenomenon and its causes or effects, share your essay with your science teacher and ask him or her to comment on it.

- If your topic is of interest to your peers, make a poster with a graphic showing the cause-and-effect relationships you discussed in your essay. Ask permission to display the poster at your school.

 PORTFOLIO

# Reflect on Your Essay

**Looking in the Mirror**   Writing short responses to the following questions will help you to reflect and to build on what you have learned from this workshop.

- How did you select the particular cause-and-effect topic about which you chose to write?

- How did you order the causes and effects in the body of your essay? What made you choose that order instead of the other types you might have used?

- Why did your revisions make your explanations more convincing?

   Use your responses to these questions to **set goals for future writing.** If you decide to include this essay in your portfolio, attach your responses to the essay.

 **Proofreading, Publishing, and Reflecting**

Review each of the steps discussed on this and the previous page. Before you turn in your essay, make sure to

- proofread it carefully
- consider publishing options
- reflect on your essay by answering specific questions about the steps you went through to create it

# Causes and Effects in Fiction

As you have seen, you can write an essay on cause-and-effect relationships in the real world—why something happened, what effects an event had. However, you will also find cause-and-effect relationships in the fiction you read, especially in works that show characters involved in conflicts—for example, short stories, novels, and dramas.

**Which Literary Work?** A cause-and-effect essay about a literary character should answer questions such as *What causes this character to change?* or *What effects do this character's actions have on the lives of other characters?* You could analyze the causes and effects of the actions of Doodle's brother in "The Scarlet Ibis" by James Hurst or those of Pip or Magwitch from Charles Dickens's *Great Expectations*. Romeo or Tybalt from *The Tragedy of Romeo and Juliet* by William Shakespeare would also make a good subject for a literary cause-and-effect essay.

**Causes and Effects with Characters**
To help you find a focus for your cause-and-effect essay, use the following questions as a trigger for brainstorming:

- What is the central conflict?
- What events cause each of the major characters to change?
- What actions on the part of the characters affect the lives of other characters? How?

**Get It Together!** Remember that all the support for your essay will come from the details in the literary work you select. The graphic organizers on the next page show how students gathered support for essays that focus on the effects of Romeo's rash actions in *The Tragedy of Romeo and Juliet* and on the effects of Pip's actions in *Great Expectations*. Your teacher may also want you to quote lines from the literary work you are writing about.

**Share and Share Alike** After you have written your essay, follow the Revising and Publishing steps given in the Writing Workshop. You may want to save your work in your portfolio.

## Causes and Effects in The Tragedy of Romeo and Juliet

**Thesis:** Romeo's rash actions have a tragic effect on three other characters in the play.

**Character One: Mercutio**
Mercutio does not know about Romeo's secret marriage to Juliet, so he fights Tybalt for Romeo's honor. This fight eventually leads to Mercutio's death.

**Character Two: Tybalt**
Romeo feels responsible for Mercutio's death and, without thinking of the consequences of his actions, kills Tybalt to avenge Mercutio.

**Character Three: Juliet**
Romeo, thinking that his beloved Juliet is dead, reacts by buying poison and then returning to Verona to see her in the tomb. When he sees her, he drinks the poison, killing himself. She then awakens to find Romeo dead and kills herself.

## Causes and Effects in Great Expectations

**Thesis:** The effects of Pip's growth into adulthood are reflected in his treatment of Joe Gargery.

**Beginning of the Novel**
Pip appreciates Joe's good nature, tenderness, and simplicity.

**Middle of the Novel**
After being in Miss Havisham's employ, Pip begins to see deficiencies in Joe. To Pip, Joe is ignorant, awkward, and common.

**End of the Novel**
At the end of the novel, Pip is reborn. Pip's ingratitude and false pride are gone. He is repentant and asks Joe's forgiveness for deserting him.

### YOUR TURN 9   Writing a Literary Cause-and-Effect Essay

Choose a literary work that interests you and write a cause-and-effect essay based on one of its characters. Remember that your thesis should focus on either causes or effects, not both.

# Giving an Informative Speech

**WHAT'S AHEAD?**

In this section, you will learn to

- plan and create an informative speech

- deliver your speech and use feedback

- evaluate an informative speech

**Y**our school is considering extending the passing period between classes. You have been chosen to present information to the faculty committee about the effects of extending the period. Are you up to the job? Giving **informative speeches** is a skill that you will need throughout your life. In this section you will learn how to plan and present an informative speech.

## Carefully Prepare the Speech

In an informative speech, your **purpose** is to give your **audience** facts and information. You will need to tailor the language and content of your speech so your audience will understand the facts and information you present. For example, for a general audience, you should use standard language and avoid using technical language. Your **task** and **occasion,** the context and reason behind the speech, are often assigned to you or are decided by circumstances. These two elements also drive your choice of details and the delivery of your speech.

When you have considered your purpose, audience, task, and occasion, you are ready to gather information. Use relevant information from books, periodicals, the Internet, CD-ROMs, and radio or television programs, as well as information you gather through interviews and surveys.

Turn your research results into a speech by organizing the information. Here are four ways to organize an informative speech.

- **Topical order** breaks a topic down into its parts and arranges the parts in an order determined by the speaker.

- **Chronological order** arranges details or events according to the order in which they occurred in time.

- **Order of importance** arranges details from most important to least important or from least important to most important.

**TIP** To make organizing easier, you may want to use note cards or an outline created on a word-processing program.

- **Cause-and-effect order** arranges information to show causes or conditions and the effects or results of those causes or conditions.

## Rehearse the Speech

The more thoroughly you rehearse your speech, the less nervous you will be. Try some of the following ideas to practice your delivery.

- Record yourself as you deliver the speech. Then, play the tape back and make notes about what you might want to change.
- Deliver your speech to friends or family, and ask for feedback.
- Deliver your speech in front of a mirror to judge the effects of your facial expressions and body language.

## Deliver the Speech and Solicit Feedback

Now it is time to deliver your speech. Remember to be enthusiastic, make eye contact with members of your audience, and speak clearly and audibly. After your speech, conduct a question-and-answer session to make sure your audience has understood your topic. To help you set **future goals as a speaker,** you might ask the audience to complete evaluation forms. See the evaluation questions below. These criteria can be adapted and used for evaluating informative presentations by speakers in your community or informative speeches on television or radio.

## Evaluate Informative Speeches

Use the following questions to make oral or written evaluations of informative speeches.

- Was the speaker's message clear? Was the speaker well-informed? (If possible, ask questions to clarify your understanding.)
- Was the information in the speech organized effectively?
- Did the speaker use effective verbal and nonverbal strategies such as pitch and tone of voice, posture, and eye contact?

**YOUR TURN 10** **Presenting an Informative Speech**

Use the steps described in this section to create, rehearse, deliver, and solicit feedback on an informative speech. Use the questions above to evaluate your classmates' speeches.

# *Analyzing Stereotypes*

**WHAT'S AHEAD?**

In this section, you will learn how to

- analyze television representations
- compare television representations to real-world experience

**D**o the images and words we see and hear on TV cause us to change the way we think; or does the media just *reflect* current trends in society? The answer to each of these questions is yes. Our view of the world is shaped by the media, and, in turn, the media mirrors the world around us. In this workshop, you will examine how television portrays people over the age of sixty-five, investigate whether this portrayal is accurate, and present your findings.

## TV Representations of Real Life

Each day TV brings you comedies about big-city life and dramas set in courtrooms and emergency rooms. Although these **representations** of real-life situations seem realistic, they are not always accurate portrayals of real life. For one thing, television's reality is often more structured and predictable than real life. Think about your favorite half-hour situation comedy. Every week, a conflict is introduced and resolved during a thirty-minute episode. Real life doesn't have that kind of regularity.

Television also creates and reinforces **stereotypes**—oversimplified ideas about groups of people. Stereotyped characters do not represent the complexity that real people have. Although stereotypical characters are more quickly understood than complex ones, they can be harmful. Unconsciously, we may begin to assume that real people are as simple as the ones on television and judge them based on their physical characteristics, occupation, race, or membership in a group, rather than on their individuality.

**TIP** The predictability of stereotypes makes them appealing to writers, who expect the viewer to recognize easily stereotypes such as the dumb jock, the ditzy blond, and the computer nerd.

## Analyze Media Representations

Think about how older people are represented on television dramas or sitcoms. Could TV's representations of older people affect how you view real people over the age of sixty-five and how you relate to them? Write down a description of one or two older characters you have seen on TV. To get started, look on the next page at the chart that one student created.

| | |
|---|---|
| *Name | Theodora Wilson |
| Television program name | "Hearts of Lafayette" |
| *Age and occupation | around sixty-five, retired |
| *Marital status | widow |
| Interactions with other characters | mostly calm, some arguments when children are unreasonable |
| *Role in family | gives advice and connection to history of family and community |
| *Where does he or she live? | her own house across the street from one of her daughters |
| Physical or mental disabilities/ troubles | seems fairly healthy, sometimes complains about "achy bones" |
| | sometimes she gets short-winded and dizzy (she says it's just part of "getting old") |
| *Clothing | casual, often she is out gardening in her jeans and T-shirt |
| *Hobbies | gardening, quilting, part of a seniors' bird-watching group |

## Investigate and Draw Conclusions

After examining how television portrays older people, find out for yourself what some older people are like. Using the starred questions from the chart above as a starting point, ask seniors about their attitudes, activities, and wants and needs in life. Try to interview at least four people over age sixty-five. You might talk to relatives, neighbors, and friends' relatives. Then, examine your findings and think about the ways television affects your perceptions of reality. Do you think your findings reinforce or challenge the representations of older people presented on television? Present your findings to the class.

**TIP** Include visual images as you report your findings. You might present a collage of photos, a collection of videoclips, or a chart illustrating statistics about older people.

### YOUR TURN 11 Analyzing Television

Follow the directions above to analyze and compare TV's portrayal of people over the age of sixty-five with your own experiences. After all reports have been given, use the following questions to discuss in small groups how television stereotypes might affect your perceptions of older people.

- What generalizations do you make about older people? Are any of these generalizations similar to the stereotypes you see on TV?
- If your findings challenged the representations of older people presented on television, were you surprised by these findings? If so, why?

# *Choices*

**Choose one of the following activities to complete.**

## ▶ CROSSING THE CURRICULUM: SCIENCE

**1. A Case from the "Y" Files**
Science careers often involve investigations of causes and effects. For example, if you were a working scientist, you might investigate the effects of acid rain or the possible causes of the extinction of the dinosaurs. To practice your investigative skills now, use library and community resources to research the causes and/or effects of a scientific phenomenon. Then, create a **multi-media presentation** explaining the phenomenon and summarizing its causes, its effects, or both.

## ▶ CAREERS

**2. Hypersolutions** Some Web designers create pages that use hypertext to explain complex issues. You, too, can exploit the potential of hypertext to "reveal" hidden causes and effects. Choose a social issue like teen smoking or dieting that has many causes and effects. Create a **Web page,** and use hyperlinks to connect causes and effects and text or images that explain or illustrate them.

## ▶ SPEAKING AND LISTENING

**3. The Way It Was** Apply your listening skills to a radio or TV program explaining a historical event. Make notes on the discussion of why something happened or what resulted from it; then, create a **visual summary** of the main points of the program to share with the class. Your summary might look something like the following.

## ▶ VIEWING AND REPRESENTING

**4. Rebel with a Cause**
Choose a movie or television miniseries in which causes or effects play a central role, and write a brief **analysis** of the cause-and-effect relationships. You might look at works that show character changes and their causes or that focus on the effects of some event on several characters.

PORTFOLIO

# 5 Analyzing a Poem

### Reading Workshop

*Reading an Analysis of a Poem*

### Writing Workshop

*Writing an Analysis of a Poem*

### Speaking and Listening

*Presenting and Responding to a Poetry Reading*

"Did you see the movie on channel five last night?" a friend asks. "Yes, I thought it was great," you answer. "Great? It was terrible," your friend responds. Then the debate begins. You point out which elements of the movie you think make it great. Your friend points out which elements she thinks make the movie terrible. Together, you dissect the movie: plot, characters, sequence of events, and special effects.

What are you and your friend really doing as you pick apart the elements of the movie? You are conducting an **analysis:** an examination of the parts, or elements, of the movie to figure out how they fit together as a whole. When you watch a movie, or when you read a story or a poem, you will react to it. When you begin to ask yourself why you respond to a particular work— whether a movie, a poem, or a play—you have taken the first step toward analyzing that work. The more you dissect the pieces of the work and examine your reactions to each piece, the more you gain an understanding of the work as a whole and the reasons for your response to it.

> **Informational Text**
>
> **Exposition**

## YOUR TURN 1 Thinking About Analysis

With a couple of classmates, think of four people whose professions involve analysis. Jot down a brief description of the way each professional uses analysis in his or her job. For example, a biologist analyzes when she dissects a specimen under a microscope. Be prepared to share your answers with the class.

**internetconnect**

**go.hrw.com**
**GO TO:** go.hrw.com
**KEYWORD:** EOLang 9-5

# Reading an Analysis of a Poem

**WHAT'S AHEAD?**

In this section you will read an analysis of a poem and learn how to

- **identify and make inferences**
- **analyze the use of literary text as support for main ideas**

**Y**our English teacher tells your class to read a certain poem on a certain page and to be prepared to discuss it. You read the poem, but it is absolutely meaningless to you. Then, your teacher discusses the poem with the class, point by point, and suddenly, it all starts to make sense. Why? Your teacher has led you and your classmates through an **analysis** of a poem, an understanding of its parts. The article on the next page is both a memoir and a literary analysis of a poem about change. In the first half of the article the writer recalls the changes that were happening in her life at the time the poem became her favorite; in the second half of the article she analyzes the elements of the poem that made it one of her favorites.

## Preparing to Read

**READING SKILL**

**Making Inferences**   Readers make **inferences** when they make educated guesses about ideas and details not directly stated in what they are reading. Good readers base their guesses on prior knowledge and experience and the information that is contained in a text. For example, you may guess, or infer, that a character in a story is a very young child, because the character acts or talks like children you have seen or read about. As you read the following article, try to spot places where the writer is expecting you to make educated guesses.

**READING FOCUS**

**Text as Support**   The subject of an **analysis** is usually a single work of literature—a single poem, for example. The most important support for the main idea in an analysis comes from the poem itself. In order to provide support for their main ideas, writers refer to characters, actions, or events, and quote the words, phrases, and lines of the work they are analyzing. As you read the article on the next page, notice how often the writer uses quotations from a poem and specific references to it.

The poem below is from Shakespeare's play *The Tempest*. The poem is actually a song that the character Ferdinand hears the spirit Ariel singing. In the analysis that follows, a writer examines the changes described in the poem and some changes in her own life. See if the writer clarifies the poem's meaning for you. As you read, jot down answers to the active-reading questions.

# Ding-Dong Bell: "Ariel's Song" from *The Tempest*

by NANCY WILLARD

### Ariel's Song
### by William Shakespeare

Full fathom five thy father lies,
　　Of his bones are coral made:
Those are pearls that were his eyes:
　　Nothing of him that doth fade,
But doth suffer a sea-change
Into something rich and strange.
Sea-nymphs hourly ring his knell:
　　*Burden* [*within*]. Ding-dong.[1]
Hark, now I hear them—ding-dong bell.

I grew up near the thumb of a lost mitten floating on the big waters of Lake Michigan and Lake Erie—lost, because only a single mitten remained, the left one. Until I was fifteen I lived my entire life between these two lakes. . . . When my father took a job in Los Alamos,[2] New Mexico, I felt as if we were moving to Mars. I had never seen the desert; the very word tasted like a dead planet. After school let out, my father

1. **Based on the details in this paragraph, what do you think is the writer's attitude toward moving?**

---

1. *Burden* [*within*]. **Ding-dong:** *Within* is a stage direction. The line means that the word *ding-dong* is sung as a *burden* (an obsolete word meaning *refrain*) by actors who are offstage.
2. **Los Alamos:** sometimes called the "atomic city," the site where the atomic bomb was developed.

packed the maps. My mother packed our clothes, sheets, blankets, pots and pans, and the radio. I packed my *Selected Poems of Emily Dickinson* and my *Poems and Songs from the Plays of William Shakespeare*. On the three-day drive from Ann Arbor to Los Alamos, I watched the familiar landscape of trees and cornfields disappear. The roads were so straight and the countryside so bare you could see to the naked rim of the earth.

We unpacked and settled in; my father went off to work every day—he worked in a high security area protected by an impressive fence—and I set myself the task of memorizing three poems a week from the books I'd brought. The first poet on my list was Shakespeare, and the first poem was a song from *The Tempest*, "Full fathom five thy father lies." I went over the poem before I left for my job teaching art to first graders in a summer Bible school. The regular teacher had read them the story of Noah's ark, and my assignment was to help the children produce an illustration for the story. On a long piece of shelf paper I painted the ark . . . and the children painted the water and the animals. Purple tigers roamed the sky, dinosaurs gamboled[3] in the bushes, butterflies as big as cows soared over Noah and his family. The teacher was not pleased; she reminded me that the animals had come in two by two, as if she'd personally witnessed the departure.

2. Why do you think the teacher was not pleased with the children's illustration?

There were no drowned people, no flooded homes, no deaths.

After supper I took out my Shakespeare and found that I had effortlessly memorized every word, as if the song had also been memorizing me. Now, many years later, I still marvel that it has stayed with me, perhaps for the very reason that it is a song, in which shape, sound, and image strike us deeper than the sense.

Sound is the very subject of the last lines:

*Sea-nymphs hourly ring his knell*

A knell, of course, is the sound of a bell rung slowly to announce a death. Though the word "ding-dong" is given only twice in "the burden" (or refrain), the nymphs must have gone on singing it during the remark that follows: "Hark, now I hear them." If the word "ding-dong" were not written out, the effect might be ominous;[4] the word *burden* derives from an old French word, *bourdon*, which can describe both a humming and the drone of a bagpipe.

3. What purpose do you think this line from the poem serves?

---

**3. gamboled:** jumped, frolicked.

**4. ominous:** threatening, sinister.

This bell is not rung by human hands, however; it is a sound that seems to come from the waves themselves. And the sea-nymphs ringing it do not feel the fear and sympathy that weigh on the minds of earthly mourners; as creatures of magic, they live outside of human mortality. The singer, Ariel, is a spirit of the air and a trickster. In *The Tempest*, Ferdinand, the son who hears the song, believes his father has drowned in the shipwreck that cast them both upon an enchanted island. Ariel knows that Ferdinand's father is not drowned. Does this make the song a lie? No. Father and son have lost something of their civilized selves and have indeed been changed by their encounter with the sea into "something rich and strange."

Because the sound of the bell is spelled out in syllables that echo Mother Goose ("Ding, dong, bell, / Kitty's in the well"), the listener knows this drowning is not the stuff of tragedy but of fairy tales, in which a transformation so often brings about the happy ending. Though the refrain is a death knell, the drowned man is as exquisite[5] as a temple god, newly wrought[6] in coral and set with pearls. He has crossed over into the kingdom of the spirits of air and water, who sing of human tragedies without participating in them.

I loved that song because it reminded me of water in a place where water was precious and of change in a time when I did not yet know what time would make of me. I have forgotten who I was at fifteen, but I have not forgotten the song. It still holds something of who I was, living in the atomic city where I first learned those words. Hark, now I hear them. Ding-dong, bell.

Sir John Everett Millais, *Ferdinand Lured by Ariel* (1849). Oil on panel (60.8 × 50.8 cm). The Makins Collection/Bridgeman Art Library, London/New York

**4.** **Why do you think the writer provides this background information about *The Tempest*?**

**5.** **Why do you think the writer ends with the words *Ding-dong, bell*?**

---

5. **exquisite:** beautiful.

6. **wrought:** fashioned, made of.

# Making Inferences

**Between the Lines**   To understand fully "Ding-Dong, Bell" you have to make **inferences**—educated guesses based on information a writer implies but does not directly state. For example, the writer never directly gives the reasons for her family's move. To figure out why they moved, you have to use evidence from the piece and your prior knowledge to make an educated guess.

Think of making inferences as the process of putting pieces of a puzzle together. Some of the pieces represent information, ideas, or other clues provided by the writer, and some represent what you, the reader, already know from your prior knowledge and experience. You make inferences by putting these pieces together until a picture that makes sense emerges.

**Question: Why did the writer's family move to Los Alamos?**

**Inference: The writer's father moved his family to Los Alamos because he got a job working with nuclear weapons.**

**Stated:** Writer says her family moved to Los Alamos when she was fifteen.

**Prior Knowledge:** Los Alamos was where a lot of secret and important work was done on nuclear weapons.

**Stated:** Writer's father worked in a "high security area."

**Prior Knowledge:** High security work is usually secret and important.

The following Thinking It Through provides steps that you can use to make inferences. Specifically, it shows how you can make an inference that answers the question "Why did the writer's family move to Los Alamos?"

## THINKING IT THROUGH — Making Correct Inferences

Follow the steps below to make inferences when you are reading.

▶ **STEP 1** Read and take note of relevant pieces of information in the text. These are the puzzle pieces the writer provides.

The writer moved to Los Alamos when she was fifteen.
Her father "worked in a high security area protected by an impressive fence."

▶ **STEP 2** Ask as many *5W-How?* questions—*Who? What? When? Where? Why? How?*—as you can about what the writer states.

**What** is significant or unusual about Los Alamos? **Why** was the writer's family moving there? **Why** was such high security necessary? **What** was her father's job?

▶ **STEP 3** Use your prior knowledge to answer as many of the *5W-How?* questions as you can. Your answers are the puzzle pieces you provide.

Los Alamos is famous for being the site where secret, important work was done on nuclear weapons. High security work, like the work the writer's father did, is usually secret and important.

▶ **STEP 4** To make an inference, put together the information the writer states and the answers you provide.

The family moved to Los Alamos for a high security (secret, important) job **+** Los Alamos is famous for secret, important work on nuclear weapons **=** **Inference:** The father moved his family to Los Alamos because he got a job working with nuclear weapons.

**TIP** Making inferences is a general skill that can be applied in many different instances while reading. For example, you make inferences when you identify the implied main idea of a reading and when you draw conclusions or make generalizations about what you have read.

Read each of the following passages from "Ding-Dong, Bell." Then, using the Thinking It Through steps on page 163, work collaboratively to choose the best inference from the list that follows each passage. Be prepared to explain how you made each inference.

1. "Purple tigers roamed the sky, dinosaurs gamboled in the bushes, butterflies as big as cows soared over Noah and his family. The teacher was not pleased; she reminded me that the animals had come in two by two, as if she'd personally witnessed the departure.
   There were no drowned people, no flooded homes, no deaths."

   It can be inferred from this passage that the teacher

   A. is afraid of tigers

   B. does not like purple paint

   C. thinks the story of Noah's ark should be depicted as it was described in the original text

   D. wants to see more butterflies in the illustration

   I inferred this from _____ .

2. "I loved that song because it reminded me of water in a place where water was precious. . . ."

   It can be inferred from this sentence that the location of the writer's new home is

   A. cold                C. wet

   B. dry                 D. humid

   I inferred this from _____ .

READING FOCUS

## Text as Support

**The Text and Nothing But**   As a critical reader, how can you judge Nancy Willard's analysis of "Ariel's Song"? Start by evaluating her use of **textual support**—**direct quotations** and **paraphrases** of the poem.

**Direct Quotations and Paraphrases**   Unlike other types of writing, a literary analysis goes straight to a **primary source**—the text of the poem itself—for support of main ideas. The strongest form of textual support in a literary analysis is a **direct quotation** from the text being analyzed.

As a reader, you can spot **direct quotations** fairly easily because they are set off in italics or quotation marks to indicate that the words are someone else's.

**Example:**

In her poem "the thirty eighth year," author Lucille Clifton says "the thirty eighth year / of my life, / plain as bread."

A **paraphrase** is a form of textual support that does not use the author's exact words. A paraphrase restates or rewords the author's words.

**Example:**

In her poem "the thirty eighth year," author Lucille Clifton explains that at age thirty-eight she feels like an ordinary woman.

**Elaboration** Textual support alone should not convince you of a writer's main idea. You also need to examine the writer's **elaboration,** or expanded commentary, on the textual support. In other words, in a poetry analysis you should expect to see solid elaboration that explains how the example from the work supports the writer's main idea.

The paragraph below is from a poetry analysis of "the thirty eighth year." Notice how the writer states the main idea about the poem, supports that main idea with quotations from the poem, and elaborates on that support.

> Poet Lucille Clifton carefully chooses figures of speech that support the image of a plain woman in her poem "the thirty eighth year." For example, the speaker uses two similes to compare herself to common foods. She says that she is "plain as bread" and "round as a cake" (lines 3 and 4). She also uses metaphors, saying she has "built" daughters who "blossom and promise fruit / like Afrikan trees" (lines 34 and 35). These metaphors show that the woman has also given the gift of life that promises to grow and develop.

Main idea

Direct quotations
Direct quotations

Elaboration

 **YOUR TURN 3** **Analyzing Textual Evidence as Support**

With a partner, find three examples of textual support from "Ding-Dong, Bell." Answer the following questions about each example:

1. Is the textual support a direct quotation or a paraphrase?

2. What idea does the quotation or paraphrase support?

3. Does the writer's elaboration make the support clear? Why or why not?

# MINI-LESSON VOCABULARY

## Denotation and Connotation

Poets often use the *connotations* of words to suggest meaning. The **denotations** of a word are its primary dictionary definitions. The **connotations** of a word are all the undertones—the ideas or emotional meanings—associated with the word. For example, *proud* and *arrogant* have similar denotations—"having a sense of self-importance"—but different connotations. "Proud" can mean having self-respect, but "arrogant"often means snobbish.

## THINKING IT THROUGH — Understanding Connotations

Use the steps below to determine how a word's denotations and connotations contribute to its meaning in a text.

> Whenever Richard Cory went down town,
> We people on the pavement looked at him:
> He was a gentleman from sole to crown,
> Clean favored, and imperially slim.

**STEP 1** Write down the word's denotation and any alternate definitions you find in the dictionary. It is possible one of these definitions could be a connotation.

"Crown" means "a garland or wreath worn on the head as a sign of honor." "Crown" also means "the position of monarch."

**STEP 2** Describe the undertones of the word. Look at the *context*—the other words surrounding the word—for clues.

"Crown" seems to have positive undertones. "Imperially" suggests Richard Cory has power. "Gentleman" suggests that Richard Cory is of high social standing. "Crown" in this context suggests power and nobility.

**STEP 3** Now re-read the poem, keeping these meanings in mind to determine what the connotations add to the lines.

The author said "sole to crown," instead of "head to toe." The lines seem to mean that Richard Cory is a man of high stature.

## PRACTICE

Using the steps above, describe the connotation of each underlined word below.

1. "I felt as if we were moving to Mars."

2. "Father and son have lost something of their civilized selves. . ."

3. "And the sea-nymphs ringing it do not feel the fear and sympathy that weigh on the minds of earthly mourners. . . ."

4. ". . . which can describe both a humming and the drone of a bagpipe."

## Inference Questions

To test your ability to infer, many reading tests include **inference questions.** These questions ask you to make inferences based on information provided in a reading passage. When you answer an inference question about a reading passage, you should be able to point to evidence in the passage that led you to your answer.

Below is a typical reading passage and an inference test question about it.

The young man was as dressed up as he had ever been—blue blazer, gray slacks, maroon tie, freshly polished shoes. He waited calmly offstage for his turn to make the first speech of his young life. Hearing his name announced, he marched onto the stage. Reaching the podium, he spread his note cards out carefully and adjusted the height of the microphone. Then he made direct eye contact with as many people as he could. As he gazed into the faces in the auditorium, the giggling and whispering faded into silence. He smiled and began to speak in a voice that reached the entire auditorium. He never glanced at the note cards.

1. A reasonable inference you can make from this passage is that the speaker is

   A. timid about speaking to people

   B. arrogant about his own importance

   C. nervous about how people view him

   D. confident about his public-speaking abilities

### THINKING IT THROUGH    **Answering Inference Questions**

Use the following steps to answer inference questions.

1. Read the passage slowly and carefully.

2. Pick out key words and phrases in the passage on which you might base your inferences.

   "Waited calmly," "marched," and "direct eye contact" are key words.

3. Consider every answer. You can usually eliminate one or two right away. Using the steps, you can make the following determinations about the multiple-choice answers provided for the example test question above.

   Answer **A** cannot be correct: a person who is timid would not look directly into the eyes of the people in an audience. The way the speaker "marched" onto the stage might show a touch of arrogance—but there is nothing else in the passage to support answer **B.** There are no indications of nervousness in the passage that would support answer **C.** Answer **D** is clearly the most reasonable inference; it is well supported by details in the passage: the speaker "waited calmly," he "marched" onto the stage, he made eye contact with the audience, he spoke in a loud, clear voice, and he never looked at his notes.

# Writing an Analysis of a Poem

**WHAT'S AHEAD?**

In this workshop, you will write an analysis of a poem. You will also learn how to

- analyze the elements of a poem, including sound elements
- gather support for a literary analysis
- remove or reduce unnecessary words and phrases
- use quotation marks

Imagine that you are sitting in class just before the bell rings. A friend walks by your desk, opens your notebook, and slips a piece of paper inside. You pull the paper out and begin to read a poem—about *you*. The vivid images and the humorous language describe all the things your friend thinks about you.

How might reading that poem make you feel? Would it make you laugh, or would it make you blush? Would it make you frown, or would it make you want to run and hide? One thing is certain: it would trigger some kind of response from you right away. Then, if you started to think about *why* you reacted to the poem as you did, you would be taking the first step in **analyzing** the poem.

This Writing Workshop will lead you through the process for writing an analysis of a poem. You will learn to analyze and respond to the different elements in a poem. Working through all the steps will allow you to create an essay in which you offer an interesting and authoritative insight into a poem.

# Prewriting

## Choose a Poem

**So Many Options**   When you begin your search for the right poem to analyze, you need to keep two things in mind. First, the poem cannot be so short and simple that it contains nothing worthwhile to analyze. Second, the poem should not be so long you cannot deal with it in detail in a short essay. A good rule of thumb for a paper of this type is to choose a ten- to fifteen-line poem. To find a good poem, try some of the following ideas.

- **Think of poems you have read before.** If you remember a few that you liked, find copies and re-read them.

- **Ask your teacher or librarian to help you** find a collection of poems that share a common theme—such as *conformity and rebellion* or *loss and acceptance*—that interests you.

- **Ask family members and friends** to recommend poems that they found especially memorable or moving.

  After you have found a few poems, look through them and choose the one you like best.

## Write Down Your First Thoughts

**From a Personal Point of View**   What does the poem you have chosen mean to you? Sometimes you know what a poem means to you, but you cannot easily express that knowledge in words. Here are some ideas that will help you turn your first thoughts and feelings about a poem into words on a page.

- **Write a response in your journal.** Start by writing a response to the **title** of the poem or to the line or **image** that you reacted to most strongly. Follow where your thoughts and feelings lead you.

- **Freewrite** about ideas that the poem brings to mind.

- **Copy words or lines** from the poem that you find especially meaningful, and jot down short comments next to them.

## Analyze Your Poem

**Reaching Deeper**   Your personal response to a poem is only the first step toward analyzing that poem. During the process of analyzing your poem, you will need to read and re-read it several times. The process of discovering what a poem means and how the poet communicates its meaning can take time. If you run into parts of your poem that do not make much sense to you right away, do not give up—try some of the following techniques to gain a better understanding of the poem.

- **Read by following the punctuation marks,** not the line breaks. Pause at the end of a line only if the line ends with a punctuation mark. Knowing when to pause and when not to pause will give you a much better understanding of the flow of meaning in the poem.

- **Copy down the entire poem** so that you can underline, circle, and annotate (make notes about) parts of it.

- **Break the poem into sections that express complete thoughts.** Keep in mind that periods, exclamation points, question marks, and semicolons usually mark the end of a complete thought—just as they do in other types of writing.

- **Seek out a second opinion.** Discuss your poem with other students in a response group. Your purpose is to share interpretations. Since this is a group discussion with your peers, choice of language and words will be informal but should still be appropriate for school. Be sure to pay attention to each speaker, to ask appropriate questions, and to respond appropriately to the group's questions.

> **TIP** Some **titles** of poems simply repeat all or part of the first line of the poem. Some titles, however, provide great hints about what a poem means.

## Find Examples of the Elements of Poetry

**Nuts and Bolts** Remember that when you analyze something, you examine each of its parts in order to understand how they work together as a whole. **In order to analyze a poem, you need to know the definitions of the elements, or parts, of a poem.** The chart on the next page contains the definitions of some important elements of poetry. To gain a better understanding of how the elements are used in the poem you have chosen, try answering the questions in the **Questions** column. For help, look at the information in the **Tips and Explanations** column. Take notes as you go. Keep in mind that not every element is important in every poem. If you cannot find a particular element or if an element does not seem to be important, do not worry about it. Go on with your analysis.

**KEY CONCEPT**

## The Elements of Poetry

| Element | Questions | Tips and Explanations |
|---|---|---|
| **Speaker:** the voice talking in a poem—the narrator of the poem (not necessarily the poet) | Who is speaking in the poem? Is the speaker the poet or a character created by the poet? | If the poem uses the pronouns *I* or *we*, the speaker (not necessarily the poet) is talking about himself or herself. If the poem uses *he, she,* or *they,* the speaker is talking about someone else. |
| **Diction:** the poet's word choice | What key words does the poet use? How does the poet use them? Look up all the definitions of key words from the poem in the dictionary. | If, for example, the word *wall* appears in the poem, ask yourself whether the poet means an ordinary wall in a house or a barrier keeping people apart. |
| **Figures of speech:** words or phrases that are not meant to be taken literally | Does the poet use metaphors or similes to make imaginative comparisons? | A **metaphor** is a comparison that equates two unlike things. *Adults are giddy children when they run* compares adults and children. A **simile** is a comparison using *like* or *as.* For example, *The cameras flashed like bursts of lightning.* |
| **Imagery:** words or phrases that appeal to the senses | What images are contained in the poem? How do they affect the poem's meaning? | Poets create **images** when they use language that appeals to your sense of sight, hearing, smell, taste, or touch. For example, the poet describes a *prickly* cactus. |
| **Rhyme:** the repetition of sounds in accented parts of words in a poem—especially in words that come at the ends of lines | Does the poem contain rhyme? If so, what is the pattern, and how does it affect the theme and tone of the poem? | A pattern of rhyming syllables with a long e sound, like *deep, sleep, creep, keep,* might have a mournful tone that goes with a sad theme. |
| **Rhythm:** the repetition of sound patterns organized as meter or as free verse | What sound pattern does the poet use to organize the poem? | Poetry written in **meter** has a regular pattern of stressed and unstressed syllables in each line. For example, the name Ĕlĕănŏr Roósĕvĕlt has a regular metric beat. Poetry written in **free verse** is free from strict patterns of stressed syllables and unstressed syllables. Free verse sounds very close to prose and to everyday spoken language. (See page 173 for more sound elements of poetry.) |
| **Theme:** the meaning, or main idea, that the poem reveals or suggests | Does the poem examine some common life experience or problem? Does it suggest solutions or answers? | A poem might comment on universal topics such as life, death, birth, love, or change. |
| **Tone:** the attitude the writer takes toward the audience, a subject, or a character | What is the speaker's attitude toward the subject of the poem? | A poem's speaker might, for example, seem angry or calm, sincere or sarcastic, or proud or ashamed. |

Below you will find the poem "Dream Deferred" by Langston Hughes and an analysis log that shows how one writer used the list of questions in the chart on the previous page to make notes about the poem. Notice how the writer made several guesses about the poem's theme as he filled out the analysis log.

ANALYSIS LOG

| Poem: "Dream Deferred" by Langston Hughes | Notes |
|---|---|
| What happens to a dream deferred?<br><br>Does it dry up<br>like a raisin in the sun?<br>Or fester like a sore—<br>And then run?<br>Does it stink like rotten meat?<br>Or crust and sugar over—<br>like a syrupy sweet?<br><br>Maybe it just sags<br>like a heavy load.<br><br>Or does it explode? | **Line 1** DICTION: "dream" = hope, aspiration for the future. "deferred" = delayed temporarily, to accept politely someone else's wishes. Possible THEME: This is a question about the topic in the title.<br><br>**Line 3** SIMILE and THEME: Deferred dream shrivels.<br><br>**Line 4** SIMILE: Deferred dream becomes diseased, infected.<br><br>**Line 6** SIMILE: Deferred dream stinks of decay.<br><br>**Line 8** SIMILE: Deferred dream is sickeningly sweet. RHYME: Meat and sweet.<br><br>**Line 9** Possible THEME: A guess about the topic, not the poet's question. SIMILE: Deferred dream is a burden; it makes the dreamer sag.<br><br>**Line 11** METAPHOR: Deferred dream is a bomb that explodes and destroys. Possible THEME: A dream deferred explodes. This is the answer to the poet's question. |

**YOUR TURN 4** | **Choosing, Responding to, and Analyzing a Poem**

Review each of the prewriting steps on the previous pages. Choose a poem and write down your first thoughts about it. Then, make an analysis log like the one above to collect your notes about the literary elements used in the poem. Copy down the poem in the left-hand column and write your analysis in the right-hand column.

## Sound Elements in Poetry

Poets often rely not just on the *meanings* of words, but on the *sounds* of words to reinforce a poem's mood or tone. For example, short *b* and *d* sounds—which interrupt the flow of text when you say them out loud—can show that someone or something in a poem is interrupting or annoying. On the other hand, a long *e* sound can indicate a slow, relaxed mood. Read a poem out loud and listen to its sounds to think about how the sounds contribute to the overall meaning of the poem.

Here are definitions and examples of three sound elements often used in poetry:

- **Alliteration** is the repetition of beginning consonant sounds. For example: *Samuel sang silly songs.*
- **Assonance** is the repetition of vowel sounds. For example: *Don't sit on the kitten or he'll nip your middle.*
- **Onomatopoeia** is the association of the sound of a word to the meaning of the word. For example: *Cling-clang went the bell.*

**PRACTICE**

For each item below, identify (a) each word that contains any of the sound elements described above, (b) the type of sound elements, and (c) how you think the sound element adds to the meaning of the passage. Since you only have a few lines of each poem, also examine *the title* of each poem for hints about meaning. Put your answers on your own paper.

1. Not answering the telephone is a way of
      rejecting life,
   That it is our business to be bothered, is
      our business
   To cherish bores or boredom, be polite
   To lies and love and many-faceted fuzziness.
   —Gwendolyn Brooks, "The *Chicago Defender* Sends a Man to Little Rock"

2. Acceleration is their need:
   A mania keeps them on the move
   Until the toughest nerves are frayed.
   They are the prisoners of speed
   Who flee in what their hands have made.
   —Theodore Roethke, "Highway: Michigan"

3. . . . Winter, you
   old clothes hamper, what mildew
   still molders inside you before March
   dribbles a bit, dries up, and is done for?
   —Kathleen Spivack, "March 1st"

4. He gives his harness bells a shake
   To ask if there is some mistake.
   The only other sound's the sweep
   Of easy wind and downy flake.
   —Robert Frost, "Stopping by Woods on a Snowy Evening"

5. The buzz saw snarled and rattled in the
      yard
   And made dust and dropped stove-length
      sticks of wood,
   Sweet-scented stuff when the breeze drew
      across it.
   —Robert Frost, "Out, Out—"

**Reference Note**

For more on **elements of poetry,** see page 171.

# Find the Focus of Your Analysis

**In Your Elements**   How will you choose the elements you want to focus on in your analysis? Look over your analysis log to find the literary elements emphasized in the poem you have chosen. Choose the one or two most important elements, and plan to make them the basis of your analysis. Remember that you cannot cover every literary element the poem contains and that different literary elements are more important in different poems. For example, imagery and figures of speech may be the most important elements in one poem, while diction and tone might be all-important in another. The writer who created the analysis log for "Dream Deferred" would probably want to focus on diction and figures of speech, since these are the elements that seem to be emphasized in the poem.

# Consider Your Purpose, Audience, and Tone

KEY CONCEPT

**Why, Who, How**   Do you have an **occasion** for writing an analysis of a poem? Perhaps your school's literary journal is focusing on analyses of poetry in the next issue, or perhaps your class will read aloud their analyses in a literary circle. **Your occasion will help to define your audience and the tone, the attitude or feeling, you use in your analysis.**

At the very least, you have two **audiences** for your essay—your classmates and your teacher. Your **purpose** is to provide your audience with some insights on how the poet created meaning in the poem. To achieve this purpose, relate the poem's meaning to a common, human experience. Your **tone** should be somewhat formal and academic, so you should use formal, standard language.

# Write Your Thesis

**The Key Point**   The thesis statement is the most important sentence in your essay—for both you and your audience—because it makes your task clear to you and your focus clear to your audience. To help you get started you can think of a thesis as a pattern. The pattern of a typical thesis for a poetry analysis can be written like this:

> In *title of poem*, *name of author* uses *key literary elements* to show (illustrate, make the point about) *the poem's theme.*

When you write your thesis statement, use the notes you made on your poem and follow the Thinking It Through steps on the next page. Keep in mind that you may need to revise your thesis statement as you write your analysis.

## Writing a Thesis

Use the following steps to develop your thesis statement.

▶ **STEP 1** Write the title of the poem.

"Dream Deferred"

▶ **STEP 2** Write the name of the poet.

Langston Hughes

▶ **STEP 3** Name the poetic element or elements on which your essay will focus.

diction and figures of speech

▶ **STEP 4** Write a statement of the poem's meaning or theme.

Keeping people from achieving their dreams can have destructive consequences.

▶ **STEP 5** Combine the results of steps 1 through 4 into your thesis statement.

In "Dream Deferred" Langston Hughes uses diction and figures of speech to make the point that keeping people from achieving their dreams can have destructive consequences.

## Gather Supporting Evidence

**The Poem as Witness**   Now that you have written your thesis statement, you need to gather details from the poem, either in your own words or as quotations, that will support it. Here is a strategy you might use.

- **Review your notes and the poem** again, looking for details and quotations you can use to support or illustrate your thesis.

- **Write down the details or quotations** and the line numbers of each in the order they appear in the poem. When quoting poetry, remember to use slashes to indicate where the lines break. For example, the student analyzing "Dream Deferred" could write "Does it dry up / like a raisin in the sun?" (lines 2–3) is an example of the poet's use of a figure of speech.

- **Elaborate—write explanations** of how the details and quotations you have found support your thesis. For example, the student analyzing "Dream Deferred" could explain that in the quotation above, the image created by the simile suggests that a deferred dream shrivels up as its juices evaporate.

The following chart shows how the student writing about "Dream Deferred" gathered details and quotations that support his thesis.

| Element | Detail or Quotation | Explanation |
|---|---|---|
| Diction | "dream", line 1<br>"deferred", line 1 | Two words together are the subject of the whole poem. "Dream" means hope for the future—something really important. "Deferred" means put off or postponed—suggests temporary. It also means that someone defers (gives in to) what someone else wants. |
| Simile | Four similes are questions:<br>Does a deferred dream<br>"dry up like a raisin" lines 2–3<br>"fester like a sore" line 4<br>"stink like rotten meat" line 6<br>"crust and sugar over like a syrupy sweet" lines 7–8<br>One simile is a guess: "sags like a heavy load" lines 9–10 | The similes seem to say that if a dream is postponed for a long time, it shrivels, gets infected, rots and stinks, or spoils and gets a nasty crust on it.<br><br>In the last simile it is as if, put off time after time, the dream becomes a heavy burden on the back of the dreamer. |
| Metaphor | "Or does it explode?" line 11 | A deferred dream is like a bomb. Finally, it explodes. The shift in figure of speech and to italics make this phrase look like the right answer to the poet's question. This idea fits the theme of destructive consequences. |

Make a chart like the one above, and fill it with details, quotations, and explanations that support your thesis.

## Organize Your Analysis

**Putting Things in Order**   The way you organize your ideas depends on the number of poetic elements you discuss. If, for example, you discuss diction and figures of speech, you might arrange your ideas and support by **order of importance**. If you intend to focus on a single element, you would probably want to stick to the order in which the elements appear in the poem. Regardless of the order you choose, you must make sure that the ideas in your analysis follow a **logical progression**.

The student analyzing "Dream Deferred" created the following organizational map of his thesis, his main supporting ideas, and some supporting details.

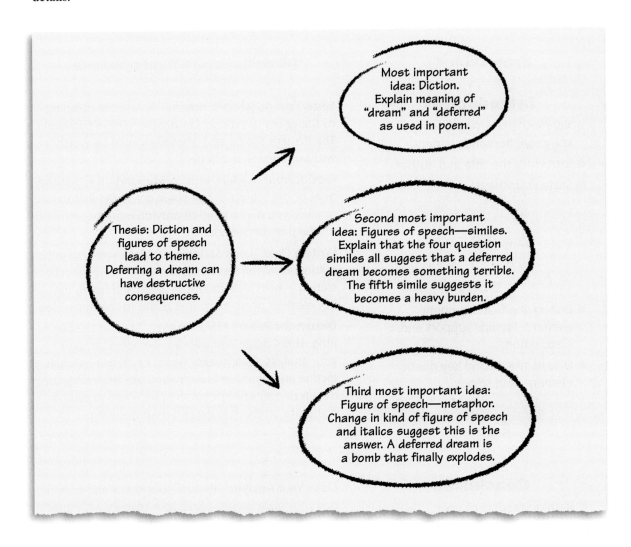

Most important idea: Diction. Explain meaning of "dream" and "deferred" as used in poem.

Thesis: Diction and figures of speech lead to theme. Deferring a dream can have destructive consequences.

Second most important idea: Figures of speech—similes. Explain that the four question similes all suggest that a deferred dream becomes something terrible. The fifth simile suggests it becomes a heavy burden.

Third most important idea: Figure of speech—metaphor. Change in kind of figure of speech and italics suggest this is the answer. A deferred dream is a bomb that finally explodes.

## YOUR TURN 5  Writing a Thesis, Gathering Support, and Organizing

Now it is your turn to write. Start by following the instructions for choosing a poem on page 168. Then, go over each of the prewriting steps on the previous pages. Make sure to write your thesis, gather and explain your supporting evidence, and organize your essay using a map like the one above.

# Writing

## Analysis of a Poem

| Framework | Directions and Explanations |
|---|---|

### Introduction

- Relate the poem's meaning to a common, human experience.
- Introduce the title and author.
- State your thesis.

**Seize Your Audience's Interest**   Relate the meaning of the poem to experiences people have in common. The Writer's Model asks what life would be worth without dreams and hope.

**Provide Your Readers with Background**   If either the poet or the subject of the poem are unfamiliar to readers, you might need to provide more background on the poet or the poem.

**Write a Clear Thesis Statement**   Make sure you tell readers what the rest of the essay will show them by stating a main idea about the poem and listing the key element or elements that relate to that main idea.

### Body

- Discuss the first key poetic element. Provide support and elaboration.
- Discuss the second key poetic element, and so on.

**Discuss the Poem's Key Elements**   Start at the beginning of the poem and walk your readers through your analysis. Clearly state which key terms—such as *diction* and *figure of speech*—you are analyzing. Use details or quotations from the poem and expand or elaborate on them to explain their meaning.

### Conclusion

- Remind readers of your thesis and summarize.

**Close Your Analysis**   Restate your thesis and summarize your main points. Leave your readers with something to think about by showing them how the poem relates to broader themes in life.

**YOUR TURN 6** **Writing a First Draft**

Using the framework and directions and explanations above, write the first draft of your analysis of a poem. Also, read the Writer's Model on the next page to see a sample analysis.

# A Writer's Model

**The following short essay is a final draft. It closely follows the framework on the previous page.**

Diction and Figures of Speech in "Dream Deferred"

What is life worth without dreams and the hope that those dreams can come true someday? What happens when the achievement of a dream is postponed—again and again? Langston Hughes answers these questions in a short poem called "Dream Deferred" by using diction and figures of speech to make the point that keeping people from achieving their dreams can have destructive consequences.

Hughes starts with a question to get his readers thinking about his message: "What happens to a dream deferred?"(line 1). His diction here is important. He uses the word "dream" to mean a hope for or vision of a better future. He chooses the word "defer" for its two meanings. It can mean "to put something off until some time in the future." Since most dreamers would not postpone their own dreams, someone else must have deferred the dream to which the speaker refers. "Defer" can also mean "to give in to what someone else wants." Hughes uses the word in both ways. The dream is postponed by someone else, but the dreamer gives in to the delay. The question then is, how long will the dreamer accept the postponement of his or her dream?

In the next part of the poem, Hughes answers the question about what happens to deferred dreams with a series of similes written as questions. The first of these asks if a deferred dream dries up "like a raisin in the sun" (line 3). The image of the dried and wrinkled raisin contrasts with the fat, sweet, and juicy grape the dream once was, before the dream dried up. The images created by the following three similes are worse. Does the deferred dream "fester like a sore— / And then run?" (lines 4–5) or "stink like rotten meat?" (line 6) or "crust and sugar over— / like a syrupy sweet?" (lines 7–8)? The images in these similes seem to say that if a dream is postponed, it rots or spoils or infects the dreamer. The last simile is not a question but a guess. "Maybe" a deferred dream "just sags / like a heavy load." (lines 9–10). This simile makes the

*(continued)*

INTRODUCTION

Author
Title
Thesis

BODY

First key poetic element: diction

Second key poetic element: similes

(continued)

deferred dream seem like a heavy burden the dreamer carries on his back, making him or her sag. All of these similes make it seem that a deferred dream becomes something terrible.

**Third key poetic element: metaphor**

In the last line, Hughes uses another figure of speech, a metaphor—"Or does it explode?" (line 11)—to address his message. He emphasizes the metaphor even more by using different print from the rest of the poem. He seems to be saying that this is exactly what happens: A deferred dream is a bomb that finally explodes. He might also mean that it is not the dream, but the dreamer that explodes—in anger.

**CONCLUSION**

Just what does happen when the achievement of a dream is postponed again and again? Hughes uses diction and figures of speech to tell his readers what might happen to a deferred dream. The word "deferred" hints that the dreamer might not always accept the postponement of his or her dream. The five similes seem to say that only the dreamer is hurt. In the final metaphor, the deferred dream is a bomb that will eventually explode and hurt a lot of people.

**Restatement of thesis**

ARLO AND JANIS, Newspaper Enterprise Association, Inc.

# A Student's Model

The following passages are excerpted from an analysis of a poem written by Mayra Deloa, a student at South Garland High School in Garland, Texas. Notice how the writer uses details, quotations, and elaboration to support her analysis of symbolism in the poem.

### The Use of Symbolism in Dorothy Parker's "Solace"

Author and title

"Solace," by Dorothy Parker, is a short poem about a person who encounters circumstances of a dreadful nature. This person witnesses three incidents in which a life is shattered, and in each case, is told that the loss is not so terrible because many more of those lives exist. With the author's specific use of diction, structure, parallelism, irony, and symbolism, this poem emerges into a metaphorical tale about the coldness and the negligence, rather than the sympathy and the consolation, that many people display during a great misfortune. . . .

Thesis

The wilting rose, the dying bird, and the abandoned girl all symbolize something that was once beautiful and full of life that dies in some sense. The poet's point is that fate is not fair, nor is it particular, whether a plant, an animal, or a human being. Another point the author makes with these symbols is that comfort and solace cannot be found in others. When the rose fades, "they" say, "What need to care . . .?" (line 4). After the girl's lover flees, "they" remark, "There's many another lad" (line 12). This is not the kind of compassion that the girl is seeking. When a life is lost or suffering, a person wants someone to offer condolences, not insensitivity. Aside from this, the narrator of the poem even turns an uncaring ear to the teller of the woe, stating "I did not answer them" (line 6). Does the narrator honestly not care about the deaths and the suffering, or does the narrator try to turn off feelings to keep from hurting, as so many people often do? When an event occurs that wounds to the core, people often hide their emotions to look strong and courageous. In this poem, however, the narrator looks away from the insensitivity that dismisses tragedy. . . .

Explanation of symbolism

# Revising

## Evaluate and Revise Your Draft

**Rework and Refine**   To make your literary analysis as clear, precise, and effective as it can be, you need to read your paper slowly and thoroughly at least two times. You should work collaboratively with your peers to read first for content and organization. During your second reading, you should be concerned with evaluating and revising style.

▷ First Reading: **Content and Organization**   The following chart will help you evaluate and revise your literary analysis. Answer the questions in the first column. If you do not know how to answer a particular question, look at the tips in the second column. If you need to make changes in your essay, look at the third column for suggestions.

### Analysis of a Poem: Content and Organization Guidelines for Peer and Self-Evaluation

| Evaluation Questions | ▷ Tips | ▷ Revision Techniques |
|---|---|---|
| ❶ Are the author and title named in the introduction? | ▷ **Highlight** the title and the author. If the title or author is not introduced, revise. | ▷ **Add** a sentence or phrase naming the author and the title. |
| ❷ Does the introduction have a clear thesis? Are key poetic elements introduced? | ▷ **Underline** the thesis statement. **Circle** the poetic elements introduced by the thesis. If you cannot find anything to circle, revise. | ▷ **Add** a sentence or a phrase introducing the key poetic elements. |
| ❸ Is the main idea of each body paragraph clear and does it support the thesis? | ▷ **Bracket** the key poetic element, such as *diction* or *figure of speech*, that is discussed in each body paragraph. If no key terms are present, revise. | ▷ **Revise** the body paragraphs so that each discusses a literary element using key terms. |
| ❹ Is the main idea of each body paragraph well supported with evidence and explanations? | ▷ **Draw a box** around each supporting quotation or detail and **a wavy line** under elaborations. If you don't find a box and one wavy line in each paragraph, revise. | ▷ **Add** details or quotations. **Elaborate** on each detail or quotation with commentary. |
| ❺ Does the conclusion effectively remind readers of the thesis and bring the essay to a close? | ▷ **Highlight** the sentence in the conclusion that restates the thesis. If there is none, revise. | ▷ **Add** a sentence restating the thesis. **Add** a sentence that relates the poem to human experience. |

**ONE WRITER'S REVISIONS** After looking at how one writer revised the introductory paragraph of the essay on page 179, answer the questions that follow.

> What happens when the achievement of a dream is post-
> poned—again and again? ~~These questions~~ <sub>Langston Hughes answers</sub> ~~are the subject of~~ ✓
> <sub>in a short</sub> ~~my poem.~~ <sub>called "Dream Deferred" by using diction and</sub>
> ~~The poem makes~~ the point that keeping people from <sub>figures of speech to make</sub>
> achieving their dreams can have destructive consequences.

add/delete

delete/add/delete/add

## Analyzing the Revision Process

1. What missing information did the writer add to the third sentence? How does this revision improve the introduction?

2. How did the writer improve the thesis statement?

**PEER REVIEW**

Ask a classmate to read your paper and answer the following questions.

1. What are the strong points of the essay? Explain why.

2. What is the most important sentence in the essay? Why?

**YOUR TURN 7** **Focusing on Content and Organization**

Revise the content and organization of your essay using the guidelines on the previous page and the example revisions shown above.

▷ **Second Reading: Style** You first concentrated on content and organization. In your second reading, pay attention to your style and its impact on your message. One style mistake many writers of literary analyses make is that they write sentences with more words than they need. Work collaboratively to use the following guidelines to revise wordy sentences.

## Style Guidelines

| Evaluation Question | ▶ Tip | ▶ Revision Technique |
|---|---|---|
| Do any of my sentences contain clauses that could be reduced to words or phrases? | **Highlight** clauses that begin with the following words: *which is, which are, that is, that are, who is, who are.* | **Reduce** half of these clauses to a participle or a participial phrase by **deleting** the pronouns *who, which,* or *that* and the *be* verb. If necessary, **rearrange** the remaining words. |

## Focus on Sentences

# Revising Wordy Sentences

Because you want to share your insights with your audience, be sure you are concise and clear. Wordiness can make readers want to quit. Writing that gets directly to the point, however, encourages readers to keep reading.

**ONE WRITER'S REVISIONS**   Here is how the writer of the model on page 179 used the Style Guidelines on page 183 to revise wordy sentences.

**BEFORE REVISION**

In the next part of the poem, Hughes answers the question about what happens to deferred dreams with a series of similes that are written as questions. The first of these asks if a dream that is deferred dries up "like a raisin in the sun."

*two clauses beginning with* that

**AFTER REVISION**

In the next part of the poem, Hughes answers the question about what happens to deferred dreams with a series of similes written as questions. The first of these asks if a deferred dream dries up "like a raisin in the sun."

*delete relative pronouns and* be *verbs*

*rearrange*

## Analyzing the Revision Process

1. Why do you think the writer cut *that are* from the first sentence?
2. What is the effect of moving the word *deferred?*

**Reference Note**

For more on **revising wordy sentences,** see page 341. For more on **participles** and **participial phrases,** see pages 449 and 451.

### YOUR TURN 8 — Revising Wordy Sentences in Your Own Paper

Use the guidelines above to examine your literary analysis for wordy sentences. Use the example above as a model, and revise any wordy sentences you find.

## Proofread Your Analysis

**The Final Touch**   You need to proofread or **edit** your paper carefully to spot and eliminate any errors in grammar, spelling, and punctuation that will weaken it. A couple of mistakes in punctuating quotations can be especially damaging to a literary analysis.

**Reference Note**
For **proofreading guidelines,** see page 13. For more on **using quotation marks,** see page 686.

---

# Grammar Link

## Using and Punctuating Quotations

Correctly punctuated quotations are an important part of every essay that analyzes a poem. First, remember that you use quotation marks when you quote the *exact words* of the author. Then, consult the following guidelines for using quotation marks with other punctuation marks.

- **Put quotation marks at the beginning and the end of the quotation.**

  **Example:**
  Anne Sexton begins, "They sit in a row."

- **Put periods and commas inside the closing quotation marks.**

  **Example:**
  Maya Angelou wrote the line "You're all that I can call my own."

- **Put question marks and exclamation marks inside the closing quotation marks** *if they are part of the quotation*. Colons and semicolons go outside the quotation marks.

  **Examples:**
  Emily Dickinson asked, "You may have met him—did you not?"
  Have you read Alice Walker's poem that begins "They were women then"?

- **When you quote more than one line of poetry, use a slash** ( / ) with a space before and after it to show where one line stops and the next starts.

  **Example:**
  Emily Dickinson wrote, "There is no frigate like a book / To take us lands away."

### PRACTICE

Rewrite each of the following sentences on your own paper. Add quotation marks and other punctuation marks where necessary.

1. He memorized the poem that begins, Shall I compare thee to a summer's day?

2. The first words of Elizabeth Barrett Browning's poem are How do I love thee?

3. Wherefore art thou, Romeo might be one of the most often misunderstood lines in Shakespeare.

4. My favorite two lines of poetry are these by Shakespeare: All the world's a stage, And all the men and women merely players.

5. The speaker in Frost's poem says, I took the one less traveled by, And that has made all the difference.

**Formatting Your Paper**   When you write a formal paper, such as an analysis of literature, it is important to choose a design that maximizes **legibility.** You want to make it easy for your readers to focus on the *ideas* in your paper, not the type. Illegible text will frustrate your readers and perhaps even make them quit reading. Below are some general guidelines to help you. Be sure to find out if your teacher has more specific formatting guidelines for you to follow.

**Reference Note**

For more on **document design,** see page 806 in the Quick Reference Handbook.

- **Line length and margins.** Text in a long, skinny column that extends to the edges of the paper is difficult to read. To avoid these problems, make sure the margins on your paper are about one inch wide.

- **Type size or letter size.** If you are writing your essay by hand, do not write too small or too large. If you are typing on a computer, choose a standard type size—anywhere from 10 to 12 points—and a legible font such as Times or Palatino.

- **Leading or spacing.** Leading (rhymes with *heading*) is the amount of white space *between* lines of text. The accepted standard for school papers is double-spaced text.

**COMPUTER TIP**

Storing your essay on disk makes it possible to submit it electronically for publishing.

# Publish Your Analysis

**Sharing Your Work**   Here are some suggestions on how you might share your literary analysis with a larger audience.

- Ask a writer to read and critique your essay.
- Submit your essay to your school's literary magazine.

**PORTFOLIO**

# Reflect on Your Analysis

**Relive the Experience**   Write brief responses to the following questions to reflect on what you have learned in this workshop.

- How did writing this paper change your feelings about the poem?
- What new techniques or ideas about writing did you learn?

    If you include your essay in a portfolio, attach your responses.

**YOUR TURN 9** **Proofreading, Publishing, and Reflecting**

Be sure to proofread your essay carefully, think about publishing options, and answer the reflective questions.

## Taking the Essay Part of a Writing Test

You have seen it before: the dreaded essay-writing portion of an English test. The reading passage of the test is the story of a boy who goes to great lengths to overcome his paralyzing fear of water. Once you finish reading the selection, you come to this prompt:

A wise person once said *Courage is a mastery of fear—not the absence of fear.* Write an essay explaining what you think this quotation means. You may use examples from the reading selection, real life, books, movies, music, or television to illustrate and support your ideas.

How do you even start your prewriting process? One method you can use to generate ideas for writing is to ask and answer the *5W-How?* **questions,** as shown in the Thinking It Through steps below.

**THINKING IT THROUGH** **Writing an Essay on an English Test**

Here is a prewriting strategy to generate ideas to answer the sample prompt.

▶ **STEP 1** Read and take note of important words in the prompt. Courage, mastery, and fear are important words in the question.

▶ **STEP 2** Restate the prompt in your own words by asking yourself *What am I being asked to explain or show?* I am being asked to explain the relationship between courage and fear.

▶ **STEP 3** Come up with your own interpretation of the quotation you are being asked to explain by asking yourself what you think the quotation means. The quotation means that all people have fears, but courageous people are the ones who face and work through their fears.

▶ **STEP 4** Come up with examples to support your interpretation by asking as many *5W-How?* questions—*Who? What? When? Where? Why? How?*—as you can about the important words in the prompt. Who is a courageous person I know? What are some examples I have seen of courage? When have I seen courage demonstrated? Where have I seen courageous people? Why did the wise person say "Courage is a mastery of fear"? How are courage and fear related?

▶ **STEP 5** Use your answers to the *5W-How?* questions as the first step in your prewriting process and as a springboard to writing your essay. After my sister was thrown off a horse, I watched her climb right back on. I saw a video documentary on people who overcome their fear of airplanes and learn how to fly. I guess courageous people really do have to master their fears.

# Writing a Poem

Here are a few guidelines to follow when writing a poem of your own. Keep in mind that poetry is the art of compact or compressed expression; try to pack as much meaning into as few words as possible. Do not simply *describe* a subject to readers; make readers *experience* the subject by using language that stirs their imaginations.

**Finding a Subject: Good Verse Hunting**  You can choose just about anything as the subject of a poem—a friend, a place, or an experience you remember vividly. The writer of the following poem chose *heat* as her subject.

| | |
|---|---|
| Title and subject | **Heat**<br>by H. D. |
| Image of wind | O wind, rend open the heat,<br>cut apart the heat,<br>rend it to tatters. |
| Image of fruit<br>Image of thick air | Fruit cannot drop<br>through this thick air—<br>fruit cannot fall into heat<br>that presses up and blunts |
| Alliteration | the points of pears<br>and rounds the grapes. |
| Image of wind as plow | Cut the heat—<br>plow through it,<br>turning it on either side<br>of your path. |

**Making Associations: Put Two and Two Together**  Now you need to decide what you want to say about the subject of your poem. One good way to generate ideas is to do some **free association.** Without stopping, freely write down any thoughts that come to mind when you think about your subject. The author of "Heat" associates the concept of heat with wind, fruit, and air.

**Creating Imagery: Put It in Sensurround**  The next step is to turn your free associations into images you can use in your poem. The images in your poem can be **literal**—*The warm rain soaks my hair.* The images can also be **figurative**—metaphors or similes, for example, as in *Spotted fawn, spring's youngest child.* Your images should connect to the five senses—how things look, taste, smell, feel, or sound.

The poem "Heat" captures the force of heat in images, such as the "thick air" that "presses up and blunts" to suggest the solidity and force of heat.

**Reference Note**

For more on **imagery** and **figurative language,** see page 171.

**Writing Your Poem: Make Like Shakespeare**  There are many different forms of poetry. "Heat" is a **free verse** poem— a poem without a regular metrical pattern. Whether or not you choose to write a free verse poem, you should draw on the same elements of poetry you used on page 171 to analyze a poem. You should carefully select elements of poetry which will enhance the subject of your poem. For example, "Heat" relies heavily on imagery.

As you begin to put together ideas, images, and other elements, you should experiment. Try arranging words, phrases, or whole ideas one way, and then try them another way. As you work and rework the elements of your poem, focus on the senses you want readers to use to experience the poem—sight, hearing, taste, touch, and smell.

### Polishing Your Poem: Make It Glow

Once you have written a first draft, you should revise your poem to make it more appealing to the imagination. To figure out where you need to revise, try reading your poem aloud to yourself or to friends. If, in reading, you trip across places that do not feel right, think of ways to revise. To the right are a few strategies for revision.

- **Change a descriptive word or phrase to a simile or a metaphor.** An *agonizingly slow pace* could become *like the pace of a slimy snail*, for example.
- **Add or improve images by using vivid words that appeal to the senses.** For example, the *smell of the dump* could become the *sickening stench of the dump.*
- **Change words within a line to create alliteration.** *The crooked road to my aching heart* could become *The winding way to my heavy heart.*

### Publishing a Poem: Share It with the World

Since a poem does not mean much without an audience to appreciate it, try sharing your poetry in one of the following ways.

- Post your poem to a poetry magazine on the Internet.
- Publish your poem in a literary journal.
- Organize a poetry swap with fellow poets. Pass around your poems, and read and discuss them as a group.

### YOUR TURN 10  Writing a Poem

Now it is your turn to write your very own poem. Remember to

- find a subject about which you have feelings
- make associations
- create imagery
- write a first draft
- revise, polish, and publish your poem

When you finish your poem, you may want to organize a poetry reading with your classmates to share your results.

**Talk** · **Listen**

**WHAT'S AHEAD?**

In this section you will learn to

- prepare and practice delivering a poetry reading
- respond to and evaluate a poetry reading

# Presenting and Responding to a Poetry Reading

**M**ost people experience poetry on pages in a book, but poetry was meant to be read aloud to an appreciative audience. Long before writing became a common means of communication, oral recitation was the main way that people shared poems and stories with one another. Today, the tradition of oral poetry continues at poetry readings in places like libraries and bookstores and at oral interpretation contests sponsored by schools. In this workshop you will have the chance to improve skills you would use as a speaker and listener at a poetry reading.

## Prepare for a Poetry Reading

**Getting Ready**  To prepare to recite a poem at a poetry reading, start by selecting a poem that you like. Whether the poem is the work of a famous author or one of your own, choose one that gives you the opportunity to be creative with your tone of voice and other presentation techniques. Remember also to pick a poem that fits the time limits you are given. Once you have picked a poem, work on preparing it for a reading by following the steps below.

- **Study the poem for its meaning.** Learn all you can about the **speaker** of the poem and the speaker's attitude toward himself or herself, toward the poem's subject, and toward the audience. Your study of the speaker will tell you what **tone** to take in your reading. Should it be happy or sad? serious or humorous? sincere or sarcastic?

- **Make a copy of the poem to help you prepare.** Mark the parts you need to emphasize, the places you need to pause, and the parts that need to be read slowly or quickly. Remember not to stop at the end of lines of poetry unless a punctuation mark stops you.

- **Decide what impression you want to leave with your audience.** Focus your presentation on the most important aspect of your poem—the one that you think will make the strongest impression.

## Practicing for a Poetry Reading

**Rehearsal Time**   Here are some ways you can make your presentation of a poem more enjoyable for yourself and your audience.

- **Get familiar with your poem.** You do not need to memorize your poem completely. You do, however, need to know it well enough that you can maintain eye contact with your audience while you are speaking. The better you understand your poem, the easier it will be to remember.

- **Practice reading your poem into a tape recorder and to a practice audience.** Play each reading back and critique yourself. At least once before you present your poem, have a dress rehearsal. Read it to one or more family members or friends and ask for ways you might improve your presentation. You can stand relatively still or you can move around, but you should not lose contact with the practice audience. You must make them feel you are speaking directly to them.

## Listening to a Poetry Reading

**All Ears**   When you listen to a poetry reading, your **purpose** is to listen in order to **enjoy** and **appreciate,** just as you listen to music or the dialogue in a movie. The first rule of good listening is, of course, to concentrate and listen carefully. Use the strategies below to listen effectively and appreciatively to poetry.

- **As you listen, try to picture what you are hearing.** Close your eyes if it helps you picture what the words you are hearing describe.

- **Note the rhyme, the rhythm and the sounds of the language.** Notice the rhythm, or motion, you feel when you hear the poem. For example, the rhythm of words in a poem about the ocean may be steady like waves lapping against the shore. Listen also for sounds in the poem. Do bees buzz? Does the snow sweep with repeated *s* sounds? The language of good poetry has both beauty and power. Listen for these qualities just as you do when you listen to music.

- **Pay attention to the reader's style—voice, movement, and contact with the audience.** Every poem has a speaker. The reader should become the speaker of the poem. Is the reader's style right for the poem? For example, if the speaker of the poem is a mouse, the reader might use a high-pitched, hurried tone of voice.

# Evaluating a Poetry Reading

**TIP** You can use the scale below to rate each item in the chart and to rate the overall average score.

**Making the Grade** Giving and receiving feedback to a poetry reading can help you sharpen your listening and presentation skills. Work with other students to evaluate poetry readings by filling out a chart like the one below. After all ratings have been given, add up the numbers and divide the total by six to find the average score.

**Scale:** 1—poor presentation  4—good
2—improvement needed  5—excellent
3—fair

**TIP** Use audience feedback to **evaluate** the effectiveness of your poetry reading and to **set goals** for future presentations.

| Criteria | Rating |
|---|---|
| The reader leaves the audience with an impression of the poem by emphasizing the effects of rhyme, imagery, and language. | |
| The reader's tone of voice matches the speaker's voice in the poem. | |
| The reader speaks at a speed that allows the audience to follow the words in the poem. | |
| The reader stresses appropriate words. | |
| The reader maintains eye contact with the entire audience. | |
| The reader is easy to hear and understand. | |
| TOTAL | |
| AVERAGE (Divide the TOTAL by six.) | |

**TIP** Try to attend a professional poetry reading. Public libraries often offer this type of presentation. As you listen to these professional readings, you can use these criteria to analyze, appreciate, and evaluate the performances.

**YOUR TURN 11** **Presenting and Responding to a Poetry Reading**

With a few classmates, take turns presenting your poems. After you finish your presentation, take notes on the feedback you receive. When you are part of the audience, take notes and fill out a rating chart, and calculate the speaker's average score. Be prepared to share and discuss your evaluation with your classmates.

*Choices*

**Choose one of the following activities to complete.**

▶ **MEDIA AND TECHNOLOGY**

**1. Start a Zine**   With several classmates, start your own **literary magazine** on the Web. Write, edit, and publish literary analyses, poetry, short stories, and essays. Ask for submissions from students all over the country for future issues of your magazine.

▶ **CAREERS**

**2. Will Write for Pay**   Do research to find out about careers in writing. Also, write to or interview people who make their living writing—professional poets, for example. Use the results of your research and interviews to compile a **report** on writing as a career. Present the report to your class.

▶ **SPEAKING AND LISTENING**

**3. Critic's Corner**   Plan and present an **oral response to literature.** Go beyond critical analysis to evaluate a short story, poem, or novel you've read. Tell your listeners whether you think the work is worthwhile, and support that conclusion with accurate and detailed references to the text. If you wish,

use presentation software to summarize important events, details, and ideas in the work.

▶ **VIEWING AND REPRESENTING**

**4. Win a Tony**   With two or three classmates, find a poem that has two or three characters and tells a story, such as Robert Frost's "The Death of the Hired Man." Transform the poem into a **script** for a play. Then, produce the **play** for the rest of the class, either as a live performance or on videotape.

▶ **CROSSING THE CURRICULUM: ART**

**5. Poetry on the Product** Work collaboratively with three classmates to choose a product such as tea or cereal. Next, design a **tea box,** a **cereal box,** or some other label to sell the product. The central selling point should be a few famous lines of poetry which describe the image you want to create for the product. See how many different images you can create simply by varying the lines of poetry you use. Present the three best pieces of poetry you find, and the designs you create with them, to the class.

PORTFOLIO

# Investigating a Research Question

## Reading Workshop

*Reading an Investigative Report*

## Writing Workshop

*Writing an I-Search Paper*

## Viewing and Representing

*Making a Video Documentary*

## Research

> **Informational Text**
>
> Exposition

■ A detective, unconvinced by a suspect's alibi, investigates the alibi and takes a dangerous criminal off the streets.

■ A doctor, puzzled by similar symptoms in several patients, investigates and discovers an outbreak of a rare disease.

■ A grandparent, interested in his family's roots, investigates and creates a detailed family tree.

In each of these scenarios, a curious person starts with questions, investigates by conducting research, and discovers answers. This process—investigating through research—requires patience and persistence. Researchers must be willing to ask many questions, to track down sources, and to draw conclusions, even if they do not like what they find. For researchers, investigating a question is much like traveling with an unfinished map. They may know their starting and ending points, but their research will probably take them places they never expected. Researchers write their investigations to share their discoveries with readers.

### YOUR TURN 1 — From Question to Investigation

Working in small groups, brainstorm a list of at least three famous discoveries. Then, for each discovery, ask what question the discoverer was trying to answer. For example, Columbus's question might have been "Can I find a trade route to the East by sailing west?"

internet**connect**

go.
hrw
.com
**GO TO:** go.hrw.com
**KEYWORD:** EOLang 9-6

# Reading an Investigative Report

## WHAT'S AHEAD?

In this section, you will read an investigative report and learn to

- summarize what you read
- identify and distinguish between primary and secondary sources

**P**eople are curious, and they like to have their curiosity satisfied—even if some investigative work is necessary to satisfy it. William Least Heat-Moon, the writer of the reading selection on the next page, "Regarding Fokker Niner-Niner-Easy," was curious about Chase County, Kansas, the geographic center of the United States. He wondered about the history and the importance of this core of the country. As you read, you will follow along with Heat-Moon as he recounts the steps in his search and the results of his discoveries.

## Preparing to Read

**READING SKILL**

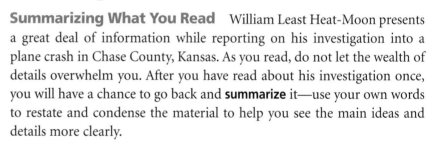

**Summarizing What You Read**   William Least Heat-Moon presents a great deal of information while reporting on his investigation into a plane crash in Chase County, Kansas. As you read, do not let the wealth of details overwhelm you. After you have read about his investigation once, you will have a chance to go back and **summarize** it—use your own words to restate and condense the material to help you see the main ideas and details more clearly.

**READING FOCUS**

**Primary and Secondary Sources**   The information that Heat-Moon presents in his investigation comes from many sources. In general, sources consulted in research fall into two categories: primary sources and secondary sources. A **primary source** consists of original, firsthand information—an eyewitness account of a devastating flood, for example. A **secondary source** contains secondhand or indirect information, for example, a magazine article about how government officials hope to prevent another flood. As you read, see if you can begin to recognize the kinds of sources Heat-Moon uses in his investigation.

On March 31, 1931, Knute Rockne (Noot RAHK-nee), a famous football coach and former college football star, died in a plane crash between the towns of Cottonwood and Bazaar, Kansas. As Capt. Robert Fry flew the plane in murky weather, co-pilot Jess Mathias received a radio call asking, "Do you think you'll make it? . . . Can you get through?" Mathias's reply, "Don't know yet, don't know yet!" was the last transmission from the plane. In the following excerpt, William Least Heat-Moon reports on his own investigation into the moments just before the plane crashed. As you read, jot down answers to the numbered active-reading questions.

# Regarding Fokker Niner-Niner-Easy

*from* PRAIRYERTH (A DEEP MAP)

BY WILLIAM LEAST HEAT-MOON

I went to the historical society in Cottonwood and looked at the relics: a large piece of the red fabric, a chunk of propeller, the pilot's Indian-head insignia pin, the cockpit nameplate, a piece of seat belt. I read the newspaper accounts; columnist "Peggy of the Flint Hills" wrote a week after the crash: *If Knute Rockne's pockets contained all the articles which local souvenir fans claim to have removed from them, it must have been that extra weight which brought down the plane.* An article four years later carried this headline: GOLD TOOTH IS FOUND ON SITE OF ROCKNE CRASH—VALUE $7. I read a 1942 story: MISSING ROCKNE PLANE TIRE TURNS UP AS SCRAP RUBBER. I talked with a half-dozen people who had been at the scene right after the accident and others who had visited it only years later; I saw in one home a wastebasket made from a piece of the Fokker rudder, and everywhere I heard as many tales as truths: *So-and-so carried off the coach's head in a basket,* and *They tied a rope around Rockne's waist to pull him from the ground with a team of horses,* and *What's-his-name years later found a human jawbone with two teeth out there. . . .*

In all my looking, I couldn't find what actually happened to Fokker 99E while it was struggling above old route 13, what had caused the wing to break off. Then

**1.** From what kinds of sources did the writer get the information for this paragraph?

**2.** What do you think the writer's use of italics signifies in this paragraph?

**3. What specific question does the writer seem to have set out to answer?**

one day I came across something called "Report on the Crash of Fokker F-10A Transport Near Bazaar, Kansas." It contained excerpts from records held at Wright-Patterson Field near Dayton, Ohio. At the top of page one in parentheses this: "Formerly Classified Secret." Within, hidden among all the official words, were things I hadn't heard or read anywhere else, bits and pieces scattered about like debris from the crash itself.

Fragment one: At ten-forty on the morning of the accident, the wife of E. S. Chartier, an Emporia weather observer for the government airmail service, recorded a rapid drop in atmospheric pressure, and she looked out to see in the southwest, toward Bazaar, a dark cloud with a short pendant nearly in a funnel shape; although the sun was shining elsewhere, the cloud appeared to be an isolated weather cell called an *upper-air tornado.*

**4. Why do you think the writer refers to the information from different sources in the report as "fragments"?**

Fragment two: A week after the disaster, the supervising aeronautical inspector for the Department of Commerce, Leonard Jurden, wrote a confidential letter to the federal director of air regulation, saying he had definite confirmation from pilots (most of whom insisted on anonymity) that the F-10 series planes, *particularly the long-winged job, do set up a decided flutter in the wing when the normal cruising speed is slightly increased and bumpy air encountered.* One pilot told the inspector the flutter was so rapid wing tips would move up and down as much as eight inches and keep increasing if not corrected by pulling the nose up and throttling back; he said all TWA pilots knew about the problem but never discussed it because they were afraid of being fired or blacklisted. After examining the wing of 99E, he said that it had broken at the very center of the flexing; soon afterward the same flier brought in a nonpilot who had also observed the flutter in a Fokker wing, and, on one occasion after a severe jolt from turbulence, saw the plywood skin on the underwing actually open up. Another TWA pilot told Jurden his instructor would never allow an F-10 to exceed the cruising speed, *being afraid of the roof coming off.* Several fliers said they didn't know a Fokker pilot who wasn't afraid of the ship. . . .

Fragment four: A few months before 99E went down, an aircraft inspector complained about the difficulty of periodically examining the internal structure of F-10 wings, sealed up as they were, but Gilbert Budwig, director of air regulation, told him he saw no need for worry as long as the plywood skin stayed glued to the internal trussing. . . .

**5. What is the relationship between the details in Fragment two and the information contained in Fragment four?**

Fragment seven: Jurden wrote in another letter, *The wing broke off upwards, under compression. Examination of these [wing] parts showed that in the upper*

and lower laminated portions of the box spars, some places the glued joints broke loose very clean, showing no cohesion of the pieces of wood. Other places showed that the glue-joints were satisfactory. Two pieces [revealed] definite compression breaks as well as poor gluing.

And this last fragment: federal inspectors, after stripping off the skin of one F-10 wing, discovered moisture accumulating in the interior had *caused deterioration of the glue, materially decreasing the strength of the wing, since this type construction is to a great extent dependent on glue.*

Now: Assembling the shards of what happened after those desperate last words, *Don't know yet, don't know yet!* Following Paul Johnson's mail plane, Captain Fry heads northwest, ninety degrees off course, in search of a way out of the murk and light rain icing the wings and beginning to shut down his instruments and radio, everything happening rapidly; the trimotor catches the tailings of

the cyclonic cloud, and the laden plywood wings begin to vibrate, the stress on the spar immense; the cabin fabric shudders terribly, and port-side passengers watch the wing tip flutter ever farther and faster until it appears to be flapping, and their terror—that fear of the novice air traveler of a wing falling off—is unspeakable: and then a loud, shattering report, and half the left wing is gone, severed as squarely as if this black mayhem of a cloud concealed massive shears: the plane turns over violently: cries of the helpless men, engines going silent, the hiss of the wind, the ship turning over again: upside down, the five-hundred-foot plunge begun, Niner-Niner-Easy falls into the prairie snow.

6. **Which details in the last paragraph come from the writer's investigation? Which come from his imagination?**

| READING SKILL

# Summarizing What You Read

**The Condensed Version**   A **summary** is a restatement of the important ideas in a text in a condensed form. To **summarize** a reading passage, you must analyze the passage to distinguish the most important points and supporting details from the least important. Analyzing a passage in order to make this distinction will help you to better understand the passage; then jotting down a summary based on your analysis will help you remember what you read. Summarizing skills will help you in class discussions, in taking notes for classes and for research, in preparing for tests, and in many other areas.

**What's the Difference?**   Below is a student's summary of part of the first paragraph of "Regarding Fokker Niner-Niner-Easy." How different is it from the original paragraph?

> In his investigation, William Least Heat-Moon looked at relics, read old newspaper clippings, and interviewed eyewitnesses. He discovered both tales and truths.

- **First, the main idea is stated in one short sentence.** ("He discovered both tales and truths.")

- **Second, the summary omits most of the supporting details,** such as the items William Least Heat-Moon saw in the historical society exhibit and the direct quotations.

- **Third, the summary condenses all the major supporting details** into one sentence ("In his investigation, William Least Heat-Moon looked at relics, read old newspaper clippings, and interviewed eyewitnesses.")

Keep the following points in mind as you prepare a summary of a reading passage. A summary

- condenses the main idea and important supporting details
- excludes nonessential information
- is much shorter than the original text

As a critical reader, you need to be on the lookout for the main idea and the most important supporting details of passages that you need to understand and remember. Taking the time to jot down a summary of what you read can prevent you from having to re-read an entire passage. Instead, you can re-read your summary to refresh your memory. Jotting down a summary is not a difficult task if you think of summarizing as a formula like the one below.

| Main Idea | + | Supporting Details | = | Summary |
|---|---|---|---|---|
| _____ | | 1. _____ | | _____ |
| _____ | | 2. _____ | | _____ |
| | | 3. _____ | | |

**THINKING IT THROUGH**  **Summarizing What You Read**

Remember that a good summary gives you a nutshell version—the absolute essentials—of a passage that you have read. To create a summary of a reading passage, use the steps that follow.

**STEP 1 Review the text and identify the main idea.** Often the main idea is stated in a topic sentence at the beginning or the end of a paragraph. If there is no topic sentence, the main idea is implied. You have to infer it by considering all of the details in the passage. Then, jot down a main idea statement.

**TIP** If you need to summarize a passage of several paragraphs, your summary should contain the main idea and most important support for each paragraph in the passage.

> **STEP 2 Re-read the passage and look for the key supporting details.**
> Be sure that the details you choose relate directly to the main idea.

> **STEP 3 Use the preceding formula to create a summary.** Check to see
> that the order of ideas in the summary is the same as in the original. If
> necessary, include transitions to ensure clarity.

> **STEP 4 Check your summary.** Does it provide a solid understanding of
> the original so that you will not have to re-read the original?

Here is how one student used the Thinking It Through and the formula
to summarize the first paragraph of "Regarding Fokker Niner-Niner-Easy."

| Condensed Main Idea | + | Important Supporting Details | = | Summary |
|---|---|---|---|---|
| William Least Heat-Moon discovered some tales and some truths. | | 1. He looked at relics. <br> 2. He read old newspaper clippings. <br> 3. He interviewed eyewitnesses. | | In his investigation, William Least Heat-Moon looked at relics, read old newspaper clippings, and interviewed eyewitnesses. From these, he discovered both tales and truths. |

**YOUR TURN 2  Summarizing What You Read**

Using the Thinking It Through above, summarize the second paragraph
of "Regarding Fokker Niner-Niner-Easy," on pages 197–199.

READING FOCUS

# Primary and Secondary Sources

**Consider the Sources**  Writers of articles and investigative reports
use research to enhance their knowledge and support their ideas. The
information researchers obtain comes from outside sources—sources
other than themselves. The two types of sources that these writers consult
in their research are **primary sources** and **secondary sources**.

**Primary Sources**   A primary source consists of original, firsthand information or raw data. It is unfiltered and unedited.

Even though William Least Heat-Moon consulted two primary sources—relics from the crash and people who arrived on the scene minutes after the crash—to find out what happened to Fokker Niner-Niner-Easy, neither source provided any useful information. Had Heat-Moon been searching days after the crash instead of more than fifty years later, he probably would have been able to find many useful primary sources.

One of Heat-Moon's sources, the government report on the crash of Fokker Niner-Niner-Easy, relied on information from Leonard Jurden, the supervising aeronautical inspector for the Department of Commerce. One primary source Jurden consulted in seeking the cause of the crash was a pilot experienced in flying the Fokker 10 aircraft. Jurden accepted what this pilot said about the flutter in the wing of the aircraft because other eyewitness accounts confirmed what the pilot told Jurden. In other words, Jurden consulted several primary sources who gave him the same information. As a critical reader, you can accept, as Jurden did, the **firsthand information** his primary sources provided.

**Secondary Sources**   Secondary sources provide indirect or secondhand information. When Heat-Moon found "Report on the Crash of Fokker F-10A Transport Near Bazaar, Kansas," a declassified government report, he had located an invaluable secondary source. It was invaluable because it was based, among other things, on firsthand information from pilots who had flown the same model Fokker aircraft as Fokker Niner-Niner-Easy. The reason these firsthand accounts were not primary sources for Heat-Moon is that they came to him through the author or authors of the government document.

As a critical reader, you must approach secondary source material with caution. Even well-established and respected secondary sources are guilty of getting their facts wrong or misinterpreting facts from time to time. The best way to check a writer's secondary sources is to check his or her facts against other secondary sources and against your own knowledge. If all the sources present the same set of facts, and these facts do not contradict what you know to be true, you can regard the information as reliable. From your point of view as a critical reader, an investigative report is only as reliable as the sources from which a writer gets his or her material.

The chart on the next page shows common primary sources on the left. On the right is a partial list of secondary sources that could be based on the corresponding primary sources.

**TIP**   As a critical reader, you should be aware that the conclusions a writer draws from raw data may or may not be valid. For example, to decide which of two completely different interpretations of raw polling data taken a week before an important election was correct, you would have to see the election results.

An interpretation of raw data is not easily and concretely confirmed. You must use prior knowledge and logic to arrive at your own interpretation.

| Primary Sources | Secondary Sources |
|---|---|
| testimonies of eyewitnesses to an event | an article on the event based partly on eyewitness testimony |
| letters, speeches, personal remembrances | a biography based on a person's letters, speeches, and personal remembrances |
| autobiographies and diaries | a magazine article profiling a person partly on the basis of that person's autobiography or diary |
| historical documents | a history book interpreting the meaning or significance of a historical document |
| interviews | a newspaper or magazine article based on information obtained from interviews |
| raw data from such sources as scientific experiments, surveys, and polls | a paper or report compiling and interpreting the data from experiments, surveys, polls, and so forth |
| works of literature | a critical analysis of a work of literature |
| objects of art | a critical review of an object of art |
| performances | a critic's article about or review of a performance |

 **Evaluating Primary and Secondary Sources**

Imagine that you are aeronautical inspector Leonard Jurden, whose letter provided Heat-Moon with his most valuable information. On your own paper, identify each source described below as primary or secondary. Then, label each source as reliable or unreliable, and explain why.

1. A report written by a witness to weather conditions in the area of the crash at the time of the crash.

2. A pilot experienced with the Fokker F-10 who reported a decided flutter in the wings of the Fokker F-10 series at slightly more than normal cruising speed.

3. A report by an aircraft inspector describing the difficulty of examining the internal structure of F-10 wings.

4. Raw data on weather conditions recorded from one hour before until one hour after the crash.

5. A manual written by Fokker designers and engineers describing the F-10's ability to fly in difficult weather conditions.

## Researching the Origins of Words

William Least Heat-Moon tried to research the story behind an airplane crash. Some people, called *etymologists*, research the stories behind words. Every word in the English language has a history; some have a short and simple past, while others have a long and complicated one. When you want to know the **etymology** of a word, you can look it up in a dictionary. By studying etymologies, you can better understand both the current usage of words and your language as a whole.

Here is the entry for a word from the reading selection as it appears in *Webster's New World Dictionary, Third College Edition.* The etymology is enclosed within double brackets—[[...]]. You can find a listing of abbreviations and symbols used in the dictionary inside the back cover of most dictionaries.

**ex•cerpt** (ek surpt´, ik–; *also, and for n., always,* ek´ surpt´ ) **vt.** [[< L *excerptus,* pp. of *excerpere,* to pick out, choose < *ex–,* out + *carpere,* to pick, pluck < IE * *kerp* < base *(s)ker–,* to cut, scrape > HARVEST]] to select, take out, or quote (passages from a book, etc.); extract—**n.** a passage selected or quoted from a book, article, etc.; extract—**ex•cerption n.**

Below is an explanation of how to decipher the symbols, abbreviations, and other information in the etymology of *excerpt.*

1. *Excerpt* is derived from (<) the Latin (L) word *excerptus,* which is the past participle (pp.) of *excerpere,* which means "to pick out or choose."

2. *Excerpere* is derived from (<) *ex–,* a prefix meaning "out," plus the verb *carpere,* which means "to pick or pluck."

3. *Carpere* is derived from (<) the Indo-European (IE) word * *kerp.*

4. *Kerp* is derived from (<) the base *(s)ker–,* which means "to cut or scrape."

5. The modern English word *harvest* is also derived from (>) the Indo-European base *(s)ker.*

An asterisk (*) is used before Indo-European words because Indo-European is a hypothetical language. Linguists have reconstructed Indo-European—a language spoken long before writing was invented—by studying the many languages derived from it.

### PRACTICE

Use the explanations above and a dictionary to trace the etymologies of the following words from "Regarding Fokker Niner-Niner-Easy." Put your answers on your own paper.

1. compression (see *compress*) (page 198)
2. debris (page 198)
3. fabric (page 197)
4. murk (page 199)
5. novice (page 199)
6. pendant (page 198)
7. problem (page 198)
8. relic (page 197)
9. trussing (see *truss*) (page 198)
10. weather (page 198)

## Answering Summary Questions

Standardized reading tests often ask you to identify the best summary of a reading passage. Read the passage and sample test question below. Then, use the steps in Thinking It Through to determine the best answer to the question.

> What happened to aircraft . . . regulations after the plummet of 99E would have happened sooner or later anyway, but the changes came about earlier because of a famous coach [Knute Rockne] going down near Bazaar, Kansas. . . . The government abandoned its policy of secret crash inquiries and records, and it received authority to investigate air accidents, hold formal hearings, subpoena witnesses, and require testimony; the unofficial removal of even the smallest fragment of a wrecked aircraft became a federal crime; and, by the next winter [1932], commercial planes carried a de-icing substance. In fact, a couple of years after the Rock fell, the only defeated proposal to improve airline safety was a law requiring a parachute for every passenger.

Which of the following statements is the best summary of the passage?

**A.** A law requiring a parachute for every person aboard an airliner was defeated.

**B.** An airline crash that takes the life of a famous person gets the public's attention very quickly.

**C.** It became a federal crime to remove fragments of a crashed aircraft.

**D.** The airplane crash that took the life of Knute Rockne hastened the creation of laws designed to improve airline safety.

---

**THINKING IT THROUGH**   **Answering Summary Questions**

Follow these steps to answer summary questions correctly on standardized tests.

▷ **STEP 1 Look for the main idea and the most important supporting details as you read the passage slowly and carefully.**

▷ **STEP 2 Consider every answer choice,** eliminating those that restate a single detail from the passage, make a general statement about the passage but include no important details, or have little or nothing to do with the passage.

▷ **STEP 3 Be sure that the answer you choose covers the *entire* passage by including the main idea and major supporting details.** A is true, but merely restates a single detail. B is also true, but it is a general statement that excludes details. C is true, but, like A, simply restates a detail. D is the best answer. It summarizes the main idea and the most important details of the entire passage.

# Writing an I-Search Paper

Chances are that the last time you were asked to write a research paper, you had a list of topics from which to choose. In this Writing Workshop, you will choose a topic that has immediate relevance to your life—a topic about which you have a genuine need or a real desire to know more. You will write a personal research paper, sometimes called an I-Search paper.

To write an I-Search paper, you pick a subject to which you have a personal connection, and write about it from a personal point of view. Your paper will consist of three major parts:

- **The story of your search**   This section tells readers what you knew about your subject before you began your research, what you wanted to know, and the research steps you went through to find out what you wanted to know—including both the steps that led to useful information and the steps that turned out to be dead ends.

- **What you learned**   In this section, you give readers the results of your search—both the answers you found and the answers you did not find.

- **Your reflections on the search**   You use this final section to tell readers what the experience has taught you about conducting and documenting a search.

**WHAT'S AHEAD?**

In this workshop, you will write an I-Search paper. You will also learn how to

- **form a research question**
- **start a search journal**
- **evaluate Web sources**
- **eliminate *there is* and *there are* sentence beginnings**
- **punctuate titles**

# Prewriting

## Select a Topic

**A Need to Know**   Even though an I-Search paper is usually less formal and more personal than a traditional research paper, its purpose is the same—to find information. The difference is that the topic for an I-Search comes from a personal need to know something—that is what the "I" in I-Search represents.

It is very important, then, for you to choose a topic that you truly want to investigate. Here are a few ways to generate ideas for a topic if you do not already have one in mind.

- **Use trigger phrases.** The phrases below are called "trigger" phrases because they prompt you to think about particular subjects. To use these phrases, write them down and fill in the blanks with whatever comes to your mind.

  I always wanted to know how to _____.

  I need help with _____.

- **Take an inventory of places to which you would like to travel.**

- **Make a list of priorities.** Include the factors that have the greatest impact on your life, including family, health, economics, education, law, and so forth.

Remember, your goal is to find a topic you want to know something about—one that is driven by a real desire or need in your life. For example, one student who discovered that he had asthma felt he needed to know everything he could about the disease and its possible effects on his life.

Brainstorm a list of several topics. Then, circle the one you want to research.

**TIP** When you select a topic, be sure that it is a suitable one. It should be not only interesting and informative, but also lend itself to research. In other words, you should be able to locate adequate information on your topic from a variety of outside sources. If the information on your topic comes only from your knowledge and experience, there is no need for a search.

## Form a Research Question

**In a Nutshell** To avoid gathering information that you cannot use in your I-Search paper, you must focus as tightly as you can on one key aspect  of your topic. **The best way to achieve a tight focus is to form a research question**—a question that asks exactly what you want to find out from your research.

Keep in mind that you should not be able to answer your research question with a single word. Ideally, it should be a question that gives rise to several more detailed questions. To get started, ask yourself the following questions. One writer's responses are shown as an example.

—**What is my topic?** My topic is asthma.

—**Why am I interested in this topic?** I have asthma, but I want to live an active, full life.

—**What do I hope to learn from my research?** Basically, I want to learn whether I can keep my asthma from interfering with my life. If I can, I need to know how.

—**Research Question:** Can I manage my asthma so that I can lead a full, active life?

Once he had developed a research question, the writer then divided his initial question into several more detailed questions, all having a direct bearing on how he could manage his asthma so that he could live normally.

—What can I do to keep playing sports and doing other physically demanding activities?

—Are there certain foods or plants I should avoid?

—How do different environmental conditions affect my asthma?

—What are the effects of pets on asthma?

—What kinds of medications are available for people suffering from asthma?

—Is there some kind of physical conditioning I could do to lessen the effects of asthma?

After forming his research question and subdividing it, this writer has a specific goal for his research. Focusing his question allows him to gather relevant information and dismiss any information that has nothing to do with his specific topic—managing asthma.

## Share Your Research Question

**Two (or More) Heads Are Better . . .** To get your search off to a good start, spend some time in small groups discussing each other's research questions. Your group can discuss ways to improve your research questions and to find information. One of your group members might know an expert in the very topic you have decided to research. Another might suggest a better way to focus your research question.

**TIP** Once you begin to search for answers to your research question, step back from the question every so often and ask yourself if you need to revise your question slightly or come up with a completely new one. Such changes are a natural part of the research process.

# Identify Your Purpose, Audience, and Tone

**Why Write?**   The **purpose** of your I-Search paper is to demonstrate to your readers that your search has had or will have an impact on your life.

**Who Will Read It?**   Your **audience** consists of your classmates, your teacher, and anyone else with whom you wish to share your experience. Because you want your readers to understand and appreciate your experience, you should ask yourself these questions:

1. Will I need to provide my readers with more information than I knew when I started my search?

2. How can I make my dead-end searches interesting for my readers?

3. How can I be sure that I give my readers complete answers to all aspects of my research question?

4. How can I let my readers know how exciting my search was without sounding insincere?

**What Tone of Voice?**   For an I-Search paper, you adopt a more informal **tone** than you would in some other types of research papers. However, you should not be so informal that you use slang and nonstandard English.

> **TIP** Remember: **Voice** is the sound and rhythm of a writer's language. You should allow your own **voice** to show through your words.

# Start a Search Journal

**Keeping the Record Straight**   It is important to keep a daily record of your research process so that you will have this information when you write the story of your search. To record your daily progress, start a **search journal** in a notebook. On the first page, list the following items:

- your research question
- feedback from your group discussion (see "Share Your Research Question," page 209)
- things you already know about your research topic and things you want to learn
- your preliminary research plan—how to tackle your research question

Write in your search journal every day, starting today. Include the day's date, a brief listing of that day's research results and findings (include both successes and setbacks), and a short daily reflection on your progress. Use a chart like the following one to record your information. A record of your research process will be invaluable when you begin to write your paper. A well-kept journal can provide everything you need for the story of your search, the first section of your paper.

| Date | Research Results and Findings | Thoughts on my progress |
|------|-------------------------------|-------------------------|
| 10/18 | I found a Web site about asthma and downloaded information about the causes of the illness. I also visited in a chat room with another teen who has asthma. | So far, so good. Getting information has been easy. I'm finding out a lot. |
| 10/23 | I wanted to interview Dr. Anders, my asthma specialist, but she is going to be out of town for a few days. | I think I waited too long to call Dr. Anders. Now I'm not sure if I will have time to interview her and still get the paper done. Next time, I'll start the interviews early! |
| 10/24 | A packet of information that I requested from one of the online groups came in today's mail. It has a lot of information about athletes who have asthma and still play sports. | This is great information! It answers some of my research questions. Best of all, I got some tips on how to play sports and not get too short of breath. |

### YOUR TURN 4  Planning Your I-Search Paper, Part One

Review this list of prewriting steps before you start to research for your I-Search paper. Make sure to

- select a topic
- form a research question
- share your research question
- identify your audience, purpose, and tone
- start your search journal

## Find Sources

**A Wealth of Information**  As you conduct your research, you will be looking at two basic sources of information—**primary** and **secondary. Primary sources include legal documents, letters, diaries, eyewitness accounts, and surveys. Secondary sources are interpretations of primary materials written by other authors.** For example, if a historian studied diaries, letters, official military records, and eyewitness accounts to write a biography of a famous general, he would be using primary sources. If that same historian consulted material from other biographies of the same

KEY CONCEPT

general or from history books that included material about the general, he would be using secondary sources.

The first place to begin your search is your school library, but you should also consider your community library and any college or university libraries in your area. Although your search might start at the library, it certainly should not end there. Check out community resources, including the World Wide Web, and do not forget the various government agencies—local, state, and national—that might be valuable sources. The charts below list resources that may be available in your area libraries and in your community, along with the sources or types of information they provide.

| Library Resources | |
| --- | --- |
| **Resource** | **Source or Information** |
| **Card catalog or online catalog** | books listed by title, author, and subject; in some libraries this catalog also lists audiovisual materials—videotapes, records, CDs, audiotapes, filmstrips, and films. |
| *Readers' Guide to Periodical Literature* | articles in magazines and journals |
| **Microfilm or microfiche or online databases** | indexes to major newspapers such as *The New York Times,* back issues of newspapers |
| **General and specialized reference books and CD-ROMs** | encyclopedias (electronic or print), biographical references, atlases, almanacs |
| **Videotapes and audiotapes** | movies, documentaries, instructional tapes, audiotapes of books |
| **Librarian/media specialist** | help in using reference materials and finding sources, including audiovisual materials |

| Community Resources | |
| --- | --- |
| **Resource** | **Source or Information** |
| **World Wide Web and online services** | articles, interviews, bibliographies, pictures, videos, sound recordings; access to the Library of Congress and other libraries |
| **Local government agencies** | facts and statistics on various subjects, policies, experts on local government |
| **Local offices of state and federal government officials** | voting records, recent or pending legislation, experts on state and federal government |
| **Local newspaper offices** | accounts of events of local interest, historical information on city or area |
| **Museums, historical societies, service groups** | historical events, scientific achievements, art and artists, special exhibits, and experts on these subjects |

| Schools and colleges | print and nonprint sources in libraries, experts on various subjects |
|---|---|
| Video stores | documentary and instructional videotapes and audiotapes |
| Hospitals, medical offices | brochures, pamphlets, doctors, and other medical experts |

# Evaluate Your Sources

**A Source to Trust?**   Just as members of a jury have to decide which witnesses are **credible,** or believable, and which are not, you have to determine the extent to which you can trust your sources of information. Here are some questions you can use to put your sources to the test.

1. **Is the information up-to-date?** Information is generated so quickly now that it is easy to find current material. If information on your topic is constantly changing, be sure that you are as up-to-date as possible. For example, a report on asthma medications from 1975 would not reflect current research and might be incorrect according to today's medical standards.

2. **Does the information seem factual?** Check the information against your own knowledge and against other sources. If you find an inconsistency between two sources, check a third source to determine which information is accurate.

3. **Does the source seem objective and logical?** Some sources may be biased, or slanted, toward one point of view. Others may use poor logic. You would not, for example, expect an objective assessment of one political party's platform from the leader of the opposing political party. However, it is a good idea to investigate all aspects of your topic, including various **points of view** on it.

**TIP**   You should always consider interviewing experts in the subject area you are researching. Experts can be valuable primary sources, and often they can direct you to other valuable sources. For more on **conducting interviews,** see page 854 in the Quick Reference Handbook.

# Prepare Source Cards

**Keeping Track of Everything**   Since you will use more than one source for your paper, you will need a way to keep track of all of your information. One method is to write each source on a 3- x 5-inch index card (sometimes called a bibliography card) and number the source. If you are keeping your sources on a computer, create a separate file or record for each. Choose the method that works best for you. If you use the guidelines given on the next page to record the information, you will have a head start on your final list of sources.

**Reference Note**

For more on **punctuating titles,** see page 234.

## Guidelines for Recording Source Information

1. **Book with One Author.** Write author's last name, then first name; book title (underlined); place of publication; name of publishing company; year of publication.

   Weinstein, Allan M., M.D. Asthma: The Complete Guide to Self-Management of Asthma and Allergies for Patients and Their Families. New York: McGraw-Hill, 1987.

2. **Book with More Than One Author.** Write first author, last name first. Other authors, first name first. Record other information as for a book with one author. (See source card #1 on page 215.)

3. **Magazine Article.** Write author's last name, then first name; article title; magazine name; day (if given), month, and year of publication; beginning and ending page numbers. If no author, start with the article title. (See source card #5 on page 215.)

4. **Newspaper Article.** Write author's last name, then first name; article title; newspaper name; day, month, and year of publication; section number (if there is one) and page number. If the newspaper has both morning and afternoon editions, write the edition and ed. before the page number. If no author is listed, start with the article title.

   Goode, Erica. "Can an Essay a Day Keep Asthma or Arthritis at Bay?" New York Times 14 April 1999. natl.ed.: A19.

5. **Encyclopedia Article.** Write author's last name, then first name; article title; encyclopedia name; edition number, followed by the abbreviation *ed.*; date of publication. If no author is listed, start with article title.

   Gallagher, Joan S. "Asthma." The World Book Encyclopedia. 1995 ed.

6. **Radio or Television Program.** Write episode or segment title (if any); program name, series title (if any); network name; local station call letters and city (if any); and day, month, and year of broadcast.

   "Stress and Kids' Asthma." Rpt. Michelle Trudeau. All Things Considered. National Public Radio. KUT-FM, Austin, Texas. 30 April 1997.

7. **Film or Video.** Write title; director or producer; medium (for video recordings); distributor; and year of release. (See source card #3 on page 215.)

8. **Personal or Telephone Interview.** Write interviewee's name; interview type (personal or telephone); and day, month, and year of interview. (See source card #4 on page 215.)

9. **Online Sources.** Write author's last name, then first name (if listed); title of document; underscored title of database or site; date of electronic publication; name of sponsoring institution; date information was accessed; <URL> [or] name of online service. (See source card #2 on page 215.)

10. **Portable Databases.** Write author's last name, then first name; title of document, article, or part of work; title of work; database title; edition, release, or version; publication medium (use the term *CD-ROM*, *Diskette*, or *Magnetic tape*); city of electronic publication, electronic publisher, and electronic publication date. (See source card #6 on page 215.)

In the following sample source cards, the writer used standard Modern Language Association (MLA) format. Notice that he gave each source a **source number,** which he wrote on the source card.

Source Number

Smolley, Laurence A. and Debra Fulghum Bruce.
Breathe Right Now: A Comprehensive Guide to
Understanding and Treating the Most Common
Breathing Disorders. New York: Norton, 1998.

Book with more than
one author

2

"Peak Flow Meters." American Lung Association
Web site. American Lung Association. 15 Apr. 1999.
<http://www.lungusa.org/asthma/astpeakflow.html>.

Online Source

3

Aerobics for Asthmatics. Videocassette. Allergy and
Asthma Network/Mothers of Asthmatics, Inc., 1993.

Video recording

4

Anders, Emma R. M.D. Personal Interview. 12 April 1999.

Personal interview

5

Berg, Susan. "Recently Diagnosed with Asthma?"
Asthma  Mar.–Apr. 1999: 22–24.

Magazine article

6

"85% of Americans Don't know the Air in Their Homes
May Be Hazardous to Their Health." The American Lung
Association Web site. 24 March 1999. American Lung
Association. 15 April 1999. <http://www.lungusa.org/
press/association/85percent.html>.

Portable database

# Take Notes from Your Sources

**The Researcher's Best Friend**   Unless you are one of those fortunate people who has a photographic memory, good notes are invaluable. If you take good notes, you will have a record of the important information you will need when it is time to sit down and draft your paper. When you take notes, you can **quote directly, summarize,** or **paraphrase.** Below are examples of each of these methods used to record notes on the same passage. Notice that each card has the number 1 written in the upper right-hand corner. This number matches the number on the source card identifying the source of the information in the note.

**TIP**   **Plagiarism** is presenting someone else's words or ideas as your own. Be sure to cite the sources of words and ideas you obtain from any outside sources. Distinguish your own ideas from those of others by using quotation marks if you repeat someone's exact words.

**Direct Quotation**   If the author of a source has a particularly effective or memorable way of saying something, you may want to quote him or her. Be sure to copy the passage you intend to quote exactly as it is in your source. To avoid accidental plagiarism, put clearly visible quotation marks at the beginning and end of quoted passages.

Allergens
"There are numerous substances and conditions that can trigger asthma. The largest category of triggers is allergens. Allergens are substances that produce an allergic reaction in people who are sensitive to them. They include pollen from trees, grasses, and weeds; mold and mildew; dust mites; and animal dander."

page 23

①

**Summary**   A **summary note** includes only the main idea and the most important supporting details of a passage. It allows you to save space because it is shorter than the original material. Write the note using your own words and sentence structure. Most of the notes you take will be summary notes. (For more information on summarizing, see page 864 in the Quick Reference Handbook.)

**Paraphrase**   A **paraphrase note** includes most of the author's ideas, not just the main ones. Like the summary note, it is written in your own words. You paraphrase to simplify the material you have read. (For more information on paraphrasing, see page 834 in the Quick Reference Handbook.)

1

Source number

Allergens
   Asthma can be triggered by allergens, the most common of which are pollen from plants; mold and mildew; dust mites; and animal dander.

                     page 23

Summary

1

Source number

Allergens
   Of the numerous substances that can trigger asthma, allergens are the largest category. These are substances that cause a reaction in people who are allergic to them. Allergens include pollens from plants; mold and mildew; animal dander; and dust mites.

                     page 23

Paraphrase

**THINKING IT THROUGH**     **Taking Notes from Sources**

To avoid getting lost in the information you gather, follow these steps for taking your notes and keeping them organized.

▶ **STEP 1 Record your notes on something easy to retrieve.** Use 3- x 5-inch cards, 8-1/2- x 11-inch paper folded in half, or computer files or individual records in a computer database.

▶ **STEP 2 Use a separate note card, computer file, or database record for each item of information and for each source.** Don't make a note of *every* piece of information. Note only facts or expert opinions that are **relevant** to your search.

▶ **STEP 3 Put a subject heading consisting of a key word or phrase in the upper left-hand corner above each note.**

▶ **STEP 4 Write the source number in the upper right-hand corner of each note;** write the number of the page on which the information was found at the bottom of the note.

▶ **STEP 5 Keep computer printouts in a folder.** Highlight key words and make notes in the margin.

**TIP** Take two kinds of notes:

**1.** Analyze and synthesize ideas from a variety of print and nonprint sources. Also, note any new questions you have based on what you learn.

**2.** Keep a daily record of your **research progress** in your search journal. Note your reactions and experiences as you do the research, including your failures as well as your successes. This record will be the basis for the story of your search and will also help you reflect on your experience.

# Write Your Thesis Statement

**The Bottom Line**   Your **thesis** is the main idea of your report. It is the answer to your research question. The writer who began with the research question *Can I manage my asthma so that I can lead a full, active life?* found through research that the answer to his question was "yes." He could lead a full and active life if he carefully managed certain factors that had a direct bearing on his asthma.

KEY CONCEPT   **To frame his thesis, he turned his research question into a statement and added the factors he would have to consider in order to manage his asthma.** By adding these factors, he developed a short summary of the results of his research.

> I can manage my asthma so that I can lead a full, active life by following my doctor's instructions on medication, by avoiding pets, by sticking to an exercise program, and by minimizing the effects of allergens that can trigger asthma episodes.

# Develop an Informal Outline

**TIP**   Your teacher may ask you to develop a **formal outline** for your I-Search paper. For more information about formal outlines, see page 895 in the Quick Reference Handbook.

**Make a Fluid Plan**   An outline for a writing project is like a map to a traveler. Good outlines and good maps give guidance and keep people going in the right direction but leave them free to change their plans. Outlines also guide the organization of your ideas. I-Search papers are organized into three basic divisions: the story of the search, the results of the search, and reflections on the search. Your search journal contains the information you need for the story of your search. Your research results—the answers to your research questions—are in the notecards you made from your sources. You can use your search journal and notecards to arrange the information you want in your paper in your informal outline. Here is how one writer organized an informal outline for his I-Search paper.

**1. The story of my search**
 Learning of my condition
 What I knew about asthma
 Questions running through my head
 Research question: *Can I manage my asthma so that I can lead a full, active life?*
 Searching online
 Interviewing my doctor
 Searching the library
 Thesis Statement

**2. The results of my search**

I can manage my asthma so that I can lead a full, active life if I
- Follow my doctor's instructions on medications—inhalers and allergy shots
- Avoid pets
- Stick to an exercise program for respiratory muscles
- Minimize environmental factors—dust, pollen, air pollution, weather

**3. In the end: Reflections on my search**

Made me a better planner and organizer
Helped me overcome shyness because I had to ask for help
Improved my writing skills
Improved my ability to draw conclusions
Gave me confidence that I can lead a full and active life

## YOUR TURN 5  Planning Your I-Search Paper, Part Two

Review the prewriting steps that follow Your Turn 4 on page 211. Then, find and evaluate sources, prepare source cards, and take notes. Next, write your thesis, and create an informal outline for your paper.

## Document Your Sources

**Where Credit Is Due**  In an I-Search paper, you use information and ideas that you obtained from outside sources. It is very important that you give credit to these sources by citing them in the body of your paper and by listing them at the end of your finished paper.

**Citing Sources in the Body**  When you are writing the body of your report, you must decide what to give credit for and how to give it.

- **What to Credit**  If the same information can be found in several sources, it is considered common knowledge. You do not have to document it. For example, it is common knowledge that Dr. Martin Luther King, Jr., gave his "I Have a Dream" speech in Washington, D. C. in 1963. However, any information that you obtain from outside sources that is not common knowledge must be documented.

- **How to Credit**  There are several ways to give credit. The two most widely used methods are **footnotes** (see the example footnote on the next page) and **parenthetical citations**. In this chapter you will see examples of the parenthetical citation format recommended by the **Modern Language Association of America (MLA)**.

> **TIP**  Your teacher might ask you to use a documentation format other than the MLA. The formats suggested by the **Chicago Manual of Style** and the **American Psychological Association (APA)** are two popular alternatives to MLA. Ask your teacher or librarian where to find them.

## Guidelines for Giving Credit Within the Paper

Place the source citation in parentheses at the end of the sentence in which you have used someone else's words or ideas. The following examples follow the **MLA** format.

1. **Source with One Author.** Last name of the author, followed by the page number(s) (if any) of the work being cited: (Berg 23)

2. **Source with No Author Given.** Title, or shortened form of it, followed by page number(s) (if any): ("Peak Flow Meters")

3. **Source with Two or More Authors.** All authors' last names, followed by the page number(s) (if any): (Smolley and Bruce 128)

4. **Author's Name Given in Paragraph.** Page number only. (23)

**TIP** If your teacher prefers a certain style of documenting sources—**footnotes** or **endnotes,** for example, follow that style exactly. Here is an example of one style of footnote for a magazine article with one author. The number 1 at the beginning of the footnote refers to a number in the report where there is information to document. The footnote gives the author's first and last names (in that order), the book's title, publication information, and a page reference.

> 1. Susan Berg, "Recently Diagnosed with Asthma?" Asthma March/April 1999:22.

**Include a *Works Cited* List** At the end of your I-Search paper, you need to include a *Works Cited* list that includes all the sources you have used in your paper. A *Works Cited* list may include both print and non-print sources, such as films or electronic materials. If you are using only print sources in your paper, you can entitle your list of sources *Bibliography.* You provide a *Works Cited* list or a *Bibliography* for readers who are interested in learning more about your topic.

## Guidelines for Preparing the List of Works Cited

1. Follow the format you used for your source cards. (See pages 214–215.)

2. List your sources in alphabetical order by the authors' last names (or, if no author is listed, by the title). Ignore *A, An,* and *The,* and use the first letter of the next word.

3. Begin each listing at the left margin. If the listing is longer than one line, indent the remaining lines five spaces. Double-space all entries.

4. Put your *Works Cited* list on a separate piece of paper at the end of your final I-Search paper. Center the words *Works Cited* at the top of the page.

## Evaluating Web Sources

One of the most important sources you can consult in researching for an I-Search paper is the World Wide Web, perhaps the richest source of information in the world. However, no system exists to ensure that what appears on the Web is accurate, reliable, and objective. You should evaluate every Web site you consider using for your paper, even those maintained by the government and educational institutions. You can evaluate Web sites by using the criteria and related questions explained below.

- **Coverage: How much information on a given topic is provided?** Is the information unique to this site, or is it available from some other source, like the library?

- **Accuracy: Is the information correct?** Remember that anyone can publish anything on the Web. Have you seen the same information in other sources? Do the authors of the Web page support their ideas with evidence?

- **Currency: What are the dates for creation, publication, and revision of the Web site?** These dates should appear at the bottom of the home page. Is the information up-to-date? When was the site last updated? Might the information have changed since then?

- **Authority: What are the qualifications of the creator and publisher of the Web site?** Sometimes authority is difficult to determine. Are the creator's qualifications shown on the Web page? If not, look for the creator's name in print bibliographies of works on the same subject as the Web page.

- **Objectivity: To what extent might the author's feelings about the topic affect the information he or she presents?** Does the Web site try to persuade you to adopt a particular point of view? Do the pages present both sides of an issue? Is the site affiliated with any major institutions or organizations?

### PRACTICE

Using the information above as a reference, answer the following questions about a Web site you used in researching for your I-Search paper.

1. Is the information from the Web site available from a more accessible source? If so, name the source. If not, explain why.

2. Could you confirm the accuracy of the information by finding the same information in another source? If so, name the source. If not, explain.

3. Explain why you do or do not believe that the Web site's information is up-to-date.

4. Explain why you do or do not believe the author of the Web site to be qualified to write on the topic.

5. Does the Web site present both sides of an issue? If the Web site does not deal with an issue, what is its purpose?

# Writing

## I-Search Paper

| Framework | Directions and Explanations |
|---|---|

### The Search Story

- Hook readers immediately.
- Explain what you already knew about your topic.
- Tell what you wanted to know about your topic.
- Include a thesis statement.
- Retrace your research steps.

**Grab Your Readers' Attention**   Begin with an attention-getting statement about your topic, and explain why it was important for you to find out more about it.

**Tell What You Knew**   Briefly mention the most important information and ideas you already knew about your topic.

**Tell What You Wanted To Learn and Why**   Let readers know what you wanted to find out about your topic and the reasons motivating your search.

**State Your Thesis**   Turn your research question into a statement and add the factors that complete the statement.

### The Search Results

- Describe important results of your research.
- Support your findings.

**Retrace Your Steps**   Describe the sources you began with and the ones you found later. Discuss successes and setbacks and any changes to your original research question.

**Discuss Your Results and Give Support**   Devote at least a paragraph to each important research result. Support your findings with direct quotations, paraphrases, and summaries of information from your sources.

### Search Reflections

- Describe the significance of your research experience.
- Restate your thesis.

**Reflect on Your Search**   Describe what you learned from your research experience. Discuss how your experience and your new knowledge might affect your future. Remind readers of your thesis statement.

 **YOUR TURN 6  Writing a First Draft**

Using the Framework above, write the first draft of your I-Search paper.

# A Writer's Model

**The I-Search paper below, which is a final draft, closely follows the framework on the previous page.**

Living with Asthma

The Story of My Search

"Well, Matt, it looks like you have asthma," the doctor told me. What a shock it was to hear those words. I thought I just had a stubborn cold. As I listened to the doctor explain my condition, questions started going through my head: Wasn't I too old to get asthma now? How could I stay on the basketball team? What about my camping trips?

I already knew that asthma is a chronic, or long-lasting, disease which affects the lungs and that certain medications help control the number and severity of asthma episodes (that's when the coughing and wheezing start). I did not know much more than that, though.

Since I am on the basketball team and also go on weekend camping trips with my Boy Scout troop, I wanted to find out more about the kinds of things that might trigger an asthma episode. Were there trees and plants I should avoid? Would I be able to keep up with my teammates on the basketball court? Would I still be able to get the dog my parents had finally agreed to let me have?

I made a list of all of the things I wanted to learn. From that list, I was able to form my research question: *Can I effectively manage my asthma?* Later, I was able to form an answer: I can manage my asthma and live a full, active life by following my doctor's instructions about medications, by avoiding pets, by sticking to an exercise program, and by minimizing the effects of environmental factors that can trigger asthma episodes.

My search took about three weeks, and it was a new experience for me. I started by doing an online search using the keywords *asthma* and *managing*. I was surprised at the amount of information I found. There were Web sites maintained by doctors, pharmaceutical companies, and support groups. I ordered some free print materials from one of the pharmaceutical companies; unfortunately, I had my first draft finished before they arrived. However, because it turned out to be good information, I went back and reworked part of the draft.

*Attention-grabbing statement*

*Background on known important facts*

*Brief overview of what the writer wants to learn*

*Thesis statement*

*Steps of the research process*

*(continued)*

The next thing I did was to call my allergy/asthma specialist, Dr. Anders. I forgot to take her busy schedule into account, and I did not know that she had planned a short vacation during the time I was doing my research. She graciously agreed to meet with me after her office hours one day. I am glad she did, because she gave me some very good advice. She also let me borrow a few videos about asthma.

During that same week I went to my school library. The librarian showed me the reference books and regular books. I went through the latest volumes of the *Readers' Guide to Periodical Literature* and found several magazine articles. By the end of the week, my head was swimming with a huge amount of information.

**Description of narrowing the research topic**

My original search question remained the same: *Can I manage my asthma?* However, I was able to define exactly what it was that I wanted to manage. I ended up narrowing my topic to four areas I had to deal with in order to manage my asthma: medications, pets, sports/exercise, and environmental factors.

The Results of My Search

**First major finding**

The first thing I found out was that certain substances can trigger an asthma attack of "coughing, wheezing, and shortness of breath" (Abramowicz). Allergens constitute the largest category of triggers. According to Susan Berg, "Allergens are

**Direct quotation**

substances that produce an allergic reaction in people who are

**Summary**

sensitive to them." Common allergens are pollens from plants, animal dander, dust mites, and mold and mildew (23). My doctor said she would test me for allergies right away. If I am allergic to certain things, allergy shots help by desensitizing me to them and make them less likely to trigger an episode (Anders).

**Second major finding**

If I find that I am allergic to certain pollens, I can reduce the chances of an asthma episode by staying indoors when those pollens are in the air. Indoors, I can reduce the risk of an episode by using the air conditioner to circulate air while keeping windows and doors closed to keep pollens out. Cleaning the air with an air cleaning device can reduce dust mites, mold spores, and other indoor allergens ("85% of Americans").

**Third major finding**

Several medications and devices help people with asthma. One device is called a peak flow meter. This is a tube about six inches long; its purpose is to measure your ability to push air out of your lungs. When you blow into it, you can find out if your lungs are working at their capacity. If they are not, you know it is time to take some medication ("Peak Flow Meters"). My doctor explained how the different medications work: an inhaler sends medication right into the lungs without a lot of side effects (Anders). She showed me another type of inhaler to use when my peak flow number is low, or if I get short of breath while I am exercising. This inhaler helps me get my breath back right away.

I also found out that certain anti-inflammatory drugs are used to keep air passages open and prevent asthma episodes. One type of these is called corticosteroids. I was glad to find that these are not the same kind of steroids that cause serious side effects in athletes who take them. The risk of side effects with corticosteroids is very small ("Asthma Medicines").

Physical exercise makes an asthmatic's condition worse, or so doctors believed twenty or thirty years ago. At that time doctors believed a quiet, restful life was best. Now new research is showing that "people with breathing disorders who can maintain a regular program of exercise and activity are able to experience maximum cardiovascular fitness along with greater symptom control, or an increased ability to exercise and do the activities of daily living. Exercise trains the respiratory muscles to work more efficiently" (Smolley and Bruce 127–128). I had been worried that I would have to drop off the basketball team and miss the next Boy Scout campout we had planned. These facts, however, make me confident that I can continue to play basketball and go on camping trips.

Nancy Hogshead, a former Olympic athlete, demonstrates some exercises for asthmatics on a video called *Aerobics for Asthmatics*. I tried some of the exercises, and they are great. Nancy is quite a role model. She and other Olympic athletes (including Rob Muzzio, Jim Ryun, Jackie Joyner-Kersee, and Amy Van Dyken) have had to deal with asthma, and many of these athletes still compete (Smolley and Bruce 128).

In fact, a recent study of Olympic athletes revealed that "more than 20 percent of the American athletes who participated in the 1996 Summer Olympic games may have had asthma" ("Olympians"). I am very encouraged by this fact.

**Fourth major finding**

**Fifth major finding**

**TIP** I-Search papers and their *Works Cited* lists are normally double-spaced. Because of limited space on these pages, A Writer's Model and A Student's Model are single-spaced. The *Elements of Language* Internet site provides a model of an I-Search paper in the double-spaced format. To see this interactive model, go to **go.hrw.com** and enter the keyword **EOLang 9-6.**

*(continued)*

(continued)

*Olympian Amy Van Dyken*          *Olympian Jackie Joyner-Kersee*

Answer to the
research question

After doing the research, I concluded that if I developed a plan for myself, I would be able to manage my asthma. This is my working plan:

1. Medical Treatment: Take allergy shots if it turns out I have allergies. Take my medications and monitor peak flow levels every day. Call the doctor as necessary. Go in for checkups every three months.

2. Environment: Give up going on hikes if the pollen count is very high. Avoid other allergens whenever possible.

3. Pets: Postpone a decision on pets until I find out whether I am allergic to them.

4. Sports/Exercise: Continue with all sports and activities. Use the peak flow meter before and after basketball games. Do warm-up breathing exercises. Keep an inhalator handy for emergency use.

Reflections on My Search

Significance of the
research experience

Doing the research took a lot more time than I thought it would. I have learned how to plan my time more efficiently and how to organize my thoughts better. I am getting better at organizing my paperwork, too. Since I am rather shy, it was good for me to be forced to ask the doctor and librarian for assistance. My writing skills also improved. Now I am able to write a paragraph and stick to one topic. I also learned how to evaluate sources of information I find on the World Wide Web. In addition to these academic benefits, I got a lot of information that will help me lead a full and active life—in spite of my asthma.

Restatement of thesis

## Works Cited

Abramowicz, Mark. "Asthma, Bronchial." <u>Microsoft Encarta 98 Encyclopedia</u>. CD-ROM. Microsoft Corp., 1993–97.

<u>Aerobics for Asthmatics</u>. Videocassette. Allergy and Asthma Network/Mothers of Asthmatics, Inc., 1993.

Anders, Emma R., M.D. Personal interview. 12 Apr. 1999.

"Asthma Medicines." <u>American Lung Association Web site</u>. American Lung Association. 15 Apr. 1999. <http://www.lungusa.org/asthma/astasmeds2.html>.

Berg, Susan. "Recently Diagnosed with Asthma?" <u>Asthma</u> Mar.–Apr. 1999: 22–24.

"85% of Americans Don't Know the Air in Their Homes May Be Hazardous to Their Health." <u>American Lung Association Web site</u>. 24 Mar. 1999. American Lung Association. 15 Apr. 1999. <http://www.lungusa.org/press/association/85percent.html>.

"Olympians Don't Let Asthma Hold Them Back." <u>Asthma</u> Mar.–Apr. 1999: 15.

"Peak Flow Meters." <u>American Lung Association Web site</u>. American Lung Association. 15 Apr. 1999. <http://www. lungusa.org/asthma/astpeakflow.html>.

Smolley, Laurence A. and Debra Fulghum Bruce. <u>Breathe Right Now: A Comprehensive Guide to Understanding and Treating the Most Common Breathing Disorders</u>. New York: Norton, 1998.

The following excerpted I-Search paper was written by Amy E. Hofmann, a student at Conrad Weiser High School in Robesonia, Pennsylvania. The *Works Cited* list is not included.

The Call of the Hornet

What I Knew

    I have always had a fascination with the Sportwagon Hornet, or "Punchbuggy" (whatever you choose to call it). They were cute cars with an odd design that put the engine in the back. I liked their unique shape and style. Hornets seemed to have their own personality and, I thought, would be fun to drive.

    I grew up on the lookout for Hornets, straining my eyes out of the school bus window searching for one. "Punchbuggy red (or blue, or black, or green) and no punch backs . . ." was a common phrase heard on the bus. The punches on the arm that followed were common, too. It was a fun way to pass the time.

    I grew to love the Hornets, and last year the idea came to me that I might own one of my very own. This prospect has led to my quest for the Hornet. I hope that in one to two years, I will be able to find a "Punchbuggy" that is perfect for me. For now, though, I must satisfy my curiosity and answer the call of the Hornet.

What I Wanted to Know

    I decided to base my search on one simple question (though it eventually turned out to be more complex than I thought). I wanted to know where I could find my dream, an affordable vintage Hornet in fairly good condition and fairly close to home. My search begins . . .

How I Searched

    I began with a single Web address: http://www.spwm.com, and a dream. I hardly knew where the combination would take me. Here I learned much about the new Hornet that will come out in the spring of 2004,

*Interesting opening*

*Reasons for the search*

*Thesis statement*

*The story of the search*

but that did not help me with what I wanted to know: Where can I find my dream Hornet?

From the Sportwagon Hornet Web site, I decided to try my luck with search engines. I tried only two and was swamped with all kinds of Web sites, ranging from Sportwagon restoration to shrines dedicated to Hornets to (at last!) Hornets for sale! Ha! The joke was on me, though. These Hornets, nice though they were, were all right-hand drive, British models, with their prices listed in pounds. If you are going to Europe, and would like to take a look at a few Hornets, scope it out (Euroauto).

It was really touch and go at times with the search engines. I had to read through many summaries before I came to the word "sale," and even then, I found very little of what I wanted.

The search engines finally led me to the Web site that provided the best information, a site that is basically a directory of advertisements from people all across the United States, with all kinds of cars for sale (Carsite). Being the inexperienced Internet surfer that I am, I began the hard way, searching in the "used cars" section, first by region, then by state, and then by model. If there were no Hornets, I would have to start the process over again. Then, one day, I happened to come across this little finder button, and lo and behold, I could search the entire United States of America for SW Hornets at one time! Here on Carsite, I found six. I printed out the descriptions of each and decided to make my search more personal, so I e-mailed three perfect strangers who shared at least one quality with me—a love for Hornets. . . .

My search for Hornets also led me to my local newspaper, but this, too, was discouraging. Only a small block of the "automobiles for sale" classifieds is dedicated to antique cars. I found this out after days spent poring over the entire classified section before I noticed the "antique" block. In the end, I discovered only one Hornet for sale.

I found the ad in a Friday newspaper. It read: "1966 SW Hornet—67,000 orig. mi., runs great, $1500"

*Thesis reiterated in the form of a research question*

*A setback in the search*

*Citation of online source with neither author nor title*

*A breakthrough in the search*

*A modification of the search*

*Citation of a classified ad in a newspaper*

*(continued)*

*(continued)*

("1966 SW Hornet"). On the following Monday I checked the paper again. The advertisement was gone. Needless to say, I was terribly disappointed.

What I Learned

Unless you really know what you are doing or exactly what you are looking for, trying to make your way around the Internet can be difficult. There seemed to be no easy way to find a site advertising only SW's for sale. There were many Web pages that were dedicated as shrines for personal Hornets or sites for restoration. . . .

For the most part, I learned that there are plenty of vintage Hornets around, as vintage Hornets have the highest percentage of vehicles from their era on the road. The catch is that they are already in the hands of restorers and SW fanatics. . . .

What My Search Told Me

What did my search tell me about finding a vintage Hornet that is close to home, affordable, and in good condition? It told me that the Internet is not the only way to search for things, but it is often more helpful than traditional sources. It told me that SW Hornets are hard to find. Even if you do find one, you need to inspect it to make sure it is in good condition.

What did my search tell me? It told me that if I am willing to do a little searching, I have a good chance of finding a Hornet in a year or two, a much better chance than I did before doing this paper. Now I know where to look. I know that all the Hornets will not disappear by then, despite the fact that my closest find was gone within days of discovery. They are out there, and there is a good possibility that mine is out there, just waiting for me to buy it. At least that is what I like to think. . . .

**Research results described in separate paragraphs**

**Reflections on the search**

**What the search means for future searches**

# Evaluate and Revise Your Draft

**Touch-Up or Major Overhaul?**   Did you know that many famous writers revise their works several times? Very few writers get it just right the first time. To refine your writing, read through your paper at least twice. First evaluate the content and organization, using the following guidelines. Then, use the guidelines on page 232 to revise for style.

First Reading: **Content and Organization**   If you are one of those writers who has difficulty evaluating and revising your own writing, the following chart should help you. Ask yourself the questions in the first column. If you need help answering the questions, use the tips in the second column. Then, make the changes suggested in the last column. You may want to collaborate with a peer to work through the chart.

## I-Search Paper: Content-and-Organization Guidelines for Peer and Self-Evaluation

| Evaluation Questions | Tips | Revision Techniques |
|---|---|---|
| **1** Does the thesis statement answer the research question completely? | **Underline** the thesis statement. **Box** the research results summarized in the thesis. If one or more results are missing, revise. | **Add** research results to the thesis statement until it is a complete answer to the research question. |
| **2** Is the story of the search in logical order? | **Number** each step of the search in the order it happened. If the numbers are out of order as you read through the paper, revise. | **Rearrange** the steps of the search so that they are in logical order. |
| **3** Are the results of the search adequately supported by information from outside sources? | **Circle** the major results of the search. **Underline** sentences containing information from an outside source. If you underline fewer than three sentences, revise. | **Add** information from outside sources. **Elaborate** on each major result with an interesting or surprising detail from an outside source. |
| **4** Are enough print and nonprint sources of information used? Are they recent, reliable and objective? | **Highlight** information taken from the note cards. Revise if both print and nonprint sources are not used or if some sources seem dated. | Consult a library's card or online catalog and the *Readers' Guide*. **Add** information from these sources to your report. |
| **5** Does the conclusion describe how the research experience affected the writer? | **Bracket** each sentence that describes the effects of the research experience on the writer. | **Add** statements that explain the effects of the research experience. |

**ONE WRITER'S REVISIONS**   Here is how one writer used the content-and-organization guidelines to revise some sentences from the I-Search paper on pages 223–227. Study the revisions and answer the questions following the paragraph.

> I made a list of all the things I wanted to learn. From that list,
>
> ~rearrange~ I was able to form my research question: Later, I was able to form
>
> an answer: I can manage my asthma and live a full, active life by
>
> *by avoiding pets,*
> ~add~ following my doctor's instructions about medications, by sticking
>
> to an exercise program, and by minimizing the effects of environ-
>
> ~delete~ mental factors that can trigger asthma episodes. ~The question~
>
> *Can I effectively manage my asthma?* ~was answered~.

**PEER REVIEW**

Ask a classmate to read your paper and answer the following questions.

1. Can you understand the writer's desire to research this topic? Why or why not?

2. About which aspect of the topic would you have liked the writer to tell you more? Why?

## Analyzing the Revision Process

1. Why does the writer rearrange the paragraph so that the research question comes in the second sentence?

2. Why is the information added to the paragraph important?

**YOUR TURN 7**   **Focusing on Content and Organization**

Using the guidelines on the previous page and the example revisions shown above as a model, revise your I-Search paper.

▶ Second Reading: **Style**   In your second reading, look at your sentence style. Avoid beginning sentences with *there is/are* or *there was/were*. The following style guidelines will help you vary your sentence beginnings.

### Style Guidelines

| Evaluation Question | ▶ Tip | ▶ Revision Technique |
| --- | --- | --- |
| Do sentences begin with the words *there is, there was, there are,* or *there were*? | ▶ **Highlight** each sentence that begins this way. Revise highlighted sentences that can be smoothly reworded. | ▶ **Rearrange** the sentence so that the subject comes first. Then, reword the sentence using a strong verb. |

## Eliminating "There is/There are" Sentence Beginnings

Starting sentences with phrases like *there is* makes your writing sound monotonous to readers. You can more effectively present ideas by putting the subject in the place of *there* and using a lively verb. For example, instead of writing *There was the girl (or boy) of my dreams,* write *The girl (or boy) of my dreams suddenly appeared in front of me.*

**ONE WRITER'S REVISIONS**   The writer of the model I-Search paper on pages 223–227 used the guidelines on the preceding page to revise sentence beginnings.

**BEFORE REVISION**

There is a video called *Aerobics for Asthmatics*, which features a former Olympic athlete named Nancy Hogshead doing aerobic exercises.

Sentence begins with *there is.*

**AFTER REVISION**

Nancy Hogshead, a former Olympic athlete, demonstrates some exercises for asthmatics on a video called *Aerobics for Asthmatics.*

Revise by putting subject first and using an active verb.

### Analyzing the Revision Process

1. What is better about using the verb *demonstrates*?
2. How does the focus of the sentence change?

**YOUR TURN 8   Focusing on Style**

Revise the style of your I-Search paper using the guidelines on page 232.

# Publishing

## Proofread Your Paper

**Reference Note**

For more information and practice on **punctuating titles,** see page 684 and page 692.

**A Fine-Toothed Comb** Before you prepare a final copy of your I-Search paper, make sure that it is free of grammar, spelling, and punctuation errors. Punctuating titles correctly is particularly important in an I-Search paper, where you must refer to sources with different types of titles.

## Grammar Link

### Punctuating Titles

You can use the following guidelines to punctuate any titles you include in your I-Search paper.

- **Use underlining for titles of books, plays, films, periodicals, works of art, and television programs.** (In print, underlining appears as *italic* type. If you are using a computer, you can use an italic font to indicate titles.)

Examples:
*The Red Badge of Courage* (book)
*Newsweek* (periodical)
*The Lion King* (film)
*Biography* (TV program)

- **Magazine articles, chapter headings, and titles of short poems, short stories, short musical compositions, and individual episodes of TV shows** should be placed in **quotation marks,** not italicized.

Examples:
"What You Need to Know about Vitamins" (magazine article)
"The Caged Bird" (poem)
Chapter 1, "Our Solar System" (book chapter)

- **Underline (or italicize) the title of a poem long enough to be published in a separate volume,** such as *The Rime of the Ancient Mariner*. Also, **italicize the titles of long musical compositions,** such as *1812 Overture* by Tchaikovsky.

The words *a, an,* and *the* before a title are italicized when they are part of the title. The article *the* before the title of a newspaper is italicized and capitalized only if it appears in the masthead of the publication.

Examples:
*The House on Mango Street*
*A Separate Peace*
the *San Francisco Examiner*

### PRACTICE

Copy the following sentences onto your own paper, correctly punctuating the titles in each sentence.

1. Have you read the novel The Dolphins of Pern by Anne McCaffrey?
2. Jane asked to borrow my Time magazine.
3. Yesterday's Philadelphia Inquirer newspaper had an article on asthmatic athletes.
4. The history book chapter titled The Renaissance has some magnificent pictures.
5. How to Make a Piñata was the best article.

# Publish Your Paper

**Share Your Experience**   Here are some ways you might share your I-Search paper with a larger audience.

- **Locate a group or organization that would have a special interest in your research.** For example, the writer of the Writer's Model on pages 223–226 could share his I-Search paper with a support group for people with asthma.

- **Submit your paper to a magazine—online or print—**that publishes either articles on your topic or articles by people your age.

- **Collect other I-Search papers from your class** for a special display at your school or in your classroom.

- **Send a copy of your paper to any professional** you might have interviewed. For example, the writer of the Writer's Model might mail a copy to the doctor he interviewed.

**TIP**   If you choose to write your paper by hand—either in print or cursive—be sure that your handwriting is **legible;** that is, neat and easy to read. Otherwise, use keyboarding skills to present your ideas in a professional-looking document.

**TIP**   If you have written your paper for a general audience and now wish to publish it for a more specific audience, you may need to refine it a bit, keeping in mind what that audience knows about your topic. You might also consider presenting your findings in a different format to appeal to a new audience.

PORTFOLIO

# Reflect on Your Paper

**Give It Some Thought**   Writing short responses to the following questions will help you build on what you have learned in this workshop.

- What difficulties did you encounter while writing this paper? What might you do to avoid them next time?

- What part of the paper was the easiest to write? Why?

- What part of the paper was the hardest to write? Why?

- What discoveries did you make about yourself as a writer while completing this workshop?

## YOUR TURN 9   Proofreading, Publishing, and Reflecting

Before you turn in your I-Search paper, be sure you
- proofread it carefully
- consider publishing options
- reflect on the effects of the I-Search experience

**Using Graphics Effectively** When you read a print document or a Web page, you usually see a combination of words and illustrations. These illustrations—photographs, line drawings, graphs, diagrams, maps, charts, and so on—are meant to increase the effectiveness of the text. Follow these guidelines if you use illustrations in your writing.

- **Think carefully about the information you want to convey to your readers.** Ask yourself which information would have a greater impact if it were presented pictorially. For example, if you are preparing a report on ethnic diversity in the United States, adding a pie chart showing the changes in ethnic distribution over a period of time might be much more effective than presenting such information using text only.

### Ethnic Diversity in the United States

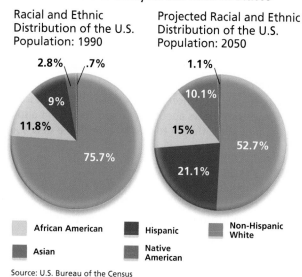

Racial and Ethnic Distribution of the U.S. Population: 1990

Projected Racial and Ethnic Distribution of the U.S. Population: 2050

Legend: African American, Asian, Hispanic, Native American, Non-Hispanic White

Source: U.S. Bureau of the Census

- **Provide drawings or illustrations of things with which your readers might be unfamiliar.** The writer of "Living with Asthma" describes a device called a peak flow meter. Most of his readers probably have never seen a peak flow meter, so an illustration would have helped his readers understand the use of the device.

- **Be sure the text and the art complement one another.** If your paper describes the great beauty of one of our country's national parks, actual photographs of the park would be much more appropriate than a line drawing or computer clip art. If, on the other hand, your I-Search paper is on the ups and downs of the stock market, a graph showing the actual rise and fall of stock prices would be more appropriate than a photograph of the stock exchange.

# Research for Fiction Writing

Although you might not have thought about it, research plays a part in fiction, especially **historical novels,** fictional works set in particular historical periods. Story characters can participate in historical events and move among actual historical figures, or they can be actual historical figures participating in fictionalized events. To make these fictional works seem real, writers must do the research necessary to lend a feeling of reality to their characters and details of place, time, and action.

Thorough research allows writers to assign their characters the appropriate dress, speech, hobbies, occupations, and so on. For example, a character in a story set in 1880 obviously could not work as a computer engineer—but what engineering work would such a character have been able to do in 1880? Research would answer this question.

**Research Tool Time** Like other researchers, fiction writers use both primary and secondary sources as tools. For example, to write a historical novel about the Vietnam War, an author might interview veterans of that war and also consult histories about the war.

**Keeping It Real** Imagine that you decided to write a short story about a famous unsolved crime that took place in your town during the Great Depression of the 1930s. What makes your story fictional is that your fictional hero will solve the crime.

Much of what you will need to research is obvious. You will need to learn all that you can about the people involved in the crime—victim, suspects, investigators—and the facts about the crime itself. However, you will need to research more if you want to make your story seem real. The following list of questions will give you an idea of the kinds of information you would need to make the story realistic.

■ What important events were going on locally, nationally, and internationally at the time of my story which would affect my story and its characters?

■ What did my town look like in the 1930s?

■ How did men and women dress in the 1930s?

■ What did people do for entertainment?

■ What did people do to earn a living?

## YOUR TURN 10 Researching for Fiction

Imagine that you and two classmates are collaborating on a story about three fifteen-year-olds growing up in a poor neighborhood in a city in the northeastern United States in 1900. Brainstorm at least five questions you would need to answer to give your story an air of reality. Then, list three or more sources you might consult to answer each question.

# Making a Video Documentary

In this section, you will create a three-minute video documentary. You will also learn how to

- create a script
- create storyboards
- edit and review your documentary
- show your documentary and get feedback

**M**ost of what you watch on television and in movie theaters—dramas, comedies, and so on—is fictional, or "made-up." Some of what you watch is not fictional. One important type of nonfiction is the **documentary**, a kind of television program or movie that deals with real people and events. Making a documentary requires research, just as writing a research paper does. However, while the research paper uses the printed page to convey its information, a movie or television documentary uses *spoken words*, *images*, *music*, and *action*.

## Planning a Video Documentary

**First Considerations First**   Before you do anything else, you have to make firm decisions about certain basics.

- **Topic**   You can choose a new topic for your documentary, but since you have already done research for your I-Search paper, you might consider using it as your topic and expanding your research as necessary.

- **Purpose**   Exactly what do you want your documentary to accomplish? Is your purpose to instruct, to inform, or to entertain? Is it a combination of all these purposes?

- **Audience**   Who will see your documentary? The content you choose for your documentary and the way you present it should differ according to your intended audience's age, gender, economic status, educational level, and so forth.

- **Length**   How long should your documentary be? In this case, three minutes is predetermined. Obviously, three minutes does not give you enough time to go into great detail in your documentary. The length of your documentary, then, determines the depth with which you can treat your subject.

Here are some decisions that one student producer made about the four items listed on the previous page.

| Topic | My topic is my search for the answer to an important question: Can I manage my asthma so that I can lead a full, active life? |
|---|---|
| Purpose | I want to show my audience part of my search for the answers to my question about asthma. I want my documentary to be both informative and engaging. |
| Audience | My audience will be made up of classmates. They will be male and female ninth-graders who can identify with my need to know how asthma will affect my life. |
| Length | Since I have only three minutes, I will have to hit the highlights, focusing on only the most important parts of my search. |

**Delivering the Message**   In the second phase of planning, you need to answer questions about three important issues that can make or break your documentary.

- **What is the controlling idea or message you want your documentary to deliver?** What, in other words, do you want your documentary as a whole to say to your audience?

- **How will you capture and hold your audience's attention?** You must engage your audience's emotions by allowing them to share in the emotional highs and lows of your experience. You want your audience to care about your subject.

- **What will you show your audience and what will you tell them?** What visual content and what audio content will you use in your documentary? In general, the best choices for **video content** are **action sequences, interviews, graphs,** and **still photos.** The **audio content**—the voices and music the audience will hear—provides explanations of what the audience is seeing and makes transitions, or bridges, between scenes.

Here is the way the student writing about asthma answered the above questions about his three-minute documentary.

**Message:** The fact that I have asthma does not mean that I cannot live a full and active life. The same is probably true of a lot of people who suffer from asthma if they would just go to the trouble to find out what they can do to keep asthma from ruling their lives.

**Audience:** I will engage my audience's emotions and make them care about my topic by showing them the fear and disappointment I felt when I first found out that I have asthma. Then, I will take them along on my search for an answer to the question of how much asthma might affect my life.

**Content:** With the help of a classmate camera operator, I will videotape partial re-enactments of my experience in the doctor's office when I learned that I have asthma and a complete re-enactment of my interview with Dr. Anders. I will have another classmate interview me on the results of my research. I will conclude my documentary with a videotape of me and several classmates demonstrating exercises for people with asthma. My classmate will do voice-over explanations of the exercises' benefits.

**Tricks of the Trade**  Professional video documentary makers employ many techniques to make their videos interesting and lively. Here are some basic techniques that student documentary makers can use.

| | |
|---|---|
| **Interviews** | • Change locations and speakers frequently to avoid losing the attention of the audience. |
| | • Divide interviews into short segments of five to ten seconds. |
| | • Ask one question at a time and do not interrupt the answer. |
| | • Increase interest and pace by showing **B-roll footage**. B-roll is video shown as background for an interview. It can be video of people, events, or objects being spoken of in the **A-roll**, the video of the interview. |
| **Narrator (Voice-over)** | • Create transitions between scenes, such as introducing the next scene by relating it to the scene just ending. |
| | • Avoid stating the obvious, like explaining something the video makes clear. |
| **Action Sequences** | • Alternate long shots of whole scenes with scenes showing people doing something and with close-ups of people's faces. |
| | • Hold the camera steady to follow the action. |
| **Transitions** | • Use a simple cut (stop taping when a scene is over) most of the time to end a scene and move on to the next. |
| | • Use the fade in/out (two- to three-second transition from a full signal to black in video and silence in audio) feature of your video camera for scene changes sparingly. Too much fade-in/out tends to make viewers feel seasick. |

**Learning the Shorthand** Every profession has its own shorthand—abbreviations and acronyms—to refer to important ideas, concepts, techniques, and so on. Videotaping a documentary (or anything else) has its own special shorthand, too. The following abbreviations are written into scripts so that people who operate the video cameras will know how to shoot (tape) a particular scene.

| Abbreviation | Meaning |
|---|---|
| EXT/INT | exterior or interior shot |
| SOT | sound on videotape audio track |
| VO | voice-over: narration heard over a video source and sometimes over music or sound |
| OSV | off-screen voice; speaker not visible |
| MIC | microphone other than a video camera's built-in microphone |
| POV | shot is taken from the point of view of a particular person |
| OS | over-the-shoulder shot that shows the back of a person's head and possibly one shoulder |
| SFX or FX | special effects; either *FX audio* or *FX video* for effects that are created during the production to alter reality. Special effects are not used very often in documentaries. |

**Put It in Writing** Next among planning tasks is to write a script for your documentary. As you go about scripting everything that your audience will see and hear, remember that both a too-slow and a too-fast pace can tire an audience. The norm for a scene is five to ten seconds. **Keep in mind that the most important parts are the beginning—where you want to seize your audience's attention—and the end—where you want to leave your audience with a good impression.** Here are some other guidelines you need to follow in writing your script.

KEY CONCEPT

- **Create a scene-by-scene outline of your documentary.**

- **Use short, concise sentences that get directly to the point.** Use only as many words as you need to make your point.

- **Use punctuation to help speakers correctly phrase their lines.** For example, commas indicate a short pause, dashes a longer pause, and periods a complete stop.

- **Make it clear who is speaking before he or she begins to speak.** Use a narrator in voice-overs to introduce the person speaking or have the speaker introduce himself or herself.

- **Do not overwhelm your audience with more information than they can process.** Give your audience time to absorb one point before moving to another.

**Outlining the Big Picture**   To create an outline of your script before you write it, you have to make several decisions.

- What scenes do I want to include in my documentary?

- In what order do I want to show these scenes?

- How much dialogue do I want to have, and who will say what?

- Do I want to use **voice-over**—dialogue spoken by a narrator who is not shown on camera?

Here is how one documentary maker outlined his script.

> ### My Search for a Way to Manage My Asthma
>
> **Scene 1:** a re-enactment of my family doctor telling me I have asthma
>
> **Scene 2:** a re-enactment of my interview with Dr. Anders, allergy and asthma specialist
>
> **Scene 3:** an interview with me in which I explain the results of my research
>
> **Scene 4:** videotape of me and several classmates doing exercises recommended for people with asthma, with voice-over explanation of the exercises' benefits

**TIP** Be sure you secure in advance the cooperation of those people you want to appear in your documentary. If at all possible, do a rehearsal of each scene before you film it so that you can make any necessary changes.

**Getting Down to Details**   Now that you have decided upon the scenes you want in your documentary and the order in which you want to show them, you can concentrate on the way you want to tape the scenes and the words you want the audience to hear. Here is how one student used a word processor to script parts of the first and third scenes of his documentary. Notice that the directions for the scene are in italic print. Special terms and abbreviations are in italic bold. Dialogue is in regular print. If you handwrite your script, use underlining for italics and all capital letters for bold.

**Scene 1:** *Int.* *I am sitting in front of the doctor's desk. The camera shows my face over the shoulder (**OS**) of the doctor. [A student plays the part of the doctor.] I look expectantly at the doctor.*

**Doctor:** *Sympathetic and concerned.* "Well, Matt, it looks like you have asthma."
*I look surprised, even a little shocked.*

**Scene 3:** *Int.* ***Close-up*** *of the interviewer as he introduces me and the subject of the interview.* ***Close-up*** *of me as I smile to acknowledge the introduction. Back to* ***Close-up*** *of interviewer.*

**Interviewer:** What was your mood when you started your research?

**Me:** ***Extreme close-up.*** Well, to tell the truth, I was very depressed. Dr. Anders did her best to reassure me, but in the back of my mind I had the awful feeling that my asthma was going to be a lot worse than she told me.

Only a part of the scene is scripted in the example above. A complete script would include directions for ending each scene.

**Now Picture This** The next step in the planning stage is to use your script to create a **storyboard**—visual plans of the tape footage you want your documentary to include. A storyboard does not have to be a work of art. All you need to do is sketch out what you want to tape and how you want to tape it. When you are finished, the storyboard will look something like a comic strip. You can arrange and rearrange the scenes until you are certain they are in the order you want them. You can also estimate the time you want each piece of footage to last, so that everything you want to include will fit within your three-minute time limit.

## Videotape Your Documentary

**Time to Shoot** Now that you have completed the planning of your documentary, it is time to videotape it. You will need to do at least two complete dry runs through the script with your cameraman. Then you can proceed to the actual scene-by-scene taping of your documentary.

Professional documentary-makers have entire crews of professionals working with them to create their documentaries. One of these professionals is the videotape **editor,** the person who electronically edits tape of scenes until exactly the right effect is achieved. Since you do not have an editor working for you, use **in-camera editing.** In-camera editing means videotaping exactly what you want your audience to see and hear. Tape one scene at a time. Review the tape immediately. Then, if there is a problem, retape the scene before going on to the next one.

**A Few Last Words of Wisdom**   Here are a few hints to keep in mind before you actually begin rolling the tape.

- **Make the bulk of your shots close-ups or medium close-ups** because television's relatively small screens need close-ups.
- **Make sure the people the camera focuses on are not wearing white clothes and are not being filmed against a light background.** Taping this way results in a videotape that has a washed-out look.
- **If possible, use an auxiliary microphone for interviews** instead of the video camera's built-in microphone to make sure that the voices on the tape are clear and steady.
- **If you use music as a background for a narrator's voice, make sure it is instrumental.** The audience cannot follow two voices at once.

**A Jury of Your Peers**   After taping your documentary, it is time to show it to an audience and get their reactions to it. The most efficient way of finding out what you want to know about your audience's reactions is with a questionnaire, or **feedback form,** that you have created in advance. The feedback you receive from your audience might convince you to revise your script and retape your documentary. Here are a few questions you might ask.

- What did you learn from this documentary?
- What was the strongest feature of this documentary? Why?
- What was the greatest weakness of this documentary? Why?
- If you could change one feature of this documentary, what would it be?

### YOUR TURN 11   Creating a Video Documentary

Follow the guidelines provided in this section to plan and to videotape your documentary. Then, show the completed documentary to your classmates. To find out your audience's reactions so that you can revise your documentary, ask them to answer the items in your questionnaire.

# Choices

## Choose one of the following activities to complete.

### ▶ CAREERS

**1. Inquiring Minds** If you enjoyed researching and writing your I-Search paper, you may want to consider a career as a researcher. Scientists, doctors, historians, and educators conduct research and write about the results. Choose an educator from a technical field (engineering, mathematics, the sciences) or from an academic field (social sciences, languages, arts) and interview him or her. Ask about research and the strategies he or she uses to write about research results. Write a short **report** of the interview and share it with the class.

### ▶ LITERATURE

**2. Dear Diary** Many famous authors and researchers keep journals or write memoirs. Wouldn't it be interesting to read Thomas Edison's notes about some of the trials, failures, and successes he experienced during his life of research and invention? Choose a famous researcher—inventor, scientist, explorer—who wrote a memoir or kept a journal. Read the memoir or journal. Then, prepare an **oral report** in which you describe the ups and downs of one of the author's searches.

### ▶ SPEAKING AND LISTENING

**3. Hear Ye, Hear Ye** One of the best ways to share your I-Search paper is through an informal **panel discussion.** Find other students who wrote on topics similar to yours, and form a panel of three to five students. Then, choose one student to be the moderator. You may want to videotape the discussion and play it for another class.

### ▶ VIEWING AND REPRESENTING

**4. Playing the Ad Game** Suppose that a major documentary producer decided that your I-Search paper should be made into a documentary for national television. The producer might decide to mount an ad campaign to attract the widest possible audience. You are responsibile for creating the campaign's **print ad**— an ad that will appear as a full page in several national magazines. Create the ad. Select images and words to make the topic of your I-Search paper as appealing as possible to a general audience.

PORTFOLIO

# 7 Supporting an Opinion

Take one teaspoon to **SAVE** natural resources

Every time a company makes a product, they also use energy and natural resources. Every time you make a purchase, you could save some of that energy and those resources. 'Cause when you buy durable and reusable products, there's less to throw away. And less to replace.

**BUY SMART.          WASTE LESS.          SAVE MORE.** SM

## Reading Workshop

*Reading an Opinion Piece*

## Writing Workshop

*Writing a Persuasive Paper*

## Speaking and Listening

*Making a Persuasive Speech*

## Persuasion

Sometimes it may seem that everyone is making decisions but you.

- Your teachers decide how much homework you should have.

- Your parent decides what your curfew is.

If you had a chance to change these decisions, how would you go about convincing people to accept your ideas? To be successful, you would have to use **persuasion**—the art of convincing others to change their minds or to take a certain action.

Even though you might not realize it, you see persuasion in advertisements, which attempt to convince you to buy certain brands of food, clothing, or other goods. You also hear persuasion in political speeches, in which the speaker tries to convince people to vote a certain way. You even find in many newspapers a section just for persuasion—the opinion page, or *Op-Ed* (*Opinion-Editorial*) section.

> **Informational Text**
>
> Persuasion

### YOUR TURN 1   Thinking About Opinions

Locate the opinion page in a newspaper or newsmagazine, and examine one of the letters or editorials. Then, analyze the editorial or letter using the following questions, and share your findings with the class.

- What is the writer's opinion? How does the writer attempt to convince you? Do you think the piece is convincing? Why or why not?

- What is your opinion on the subject discussed in the editorial or letter? What are your reasons for this opinion?

**internet connect**

**GO TO:** go.hrw.com
**KEYWORD:** EOLang 9-7

# Reading an Opinion Piece

**WHAT'S AHEAD**

In this section, you will read a newspaper editorial and learn how to

■ identify an author's purpose and point of view

■ distinguish emotional appeals from logical appeals

**N**ewspaper editorials—pieces written by the newspaper's editors about important issues—are the Paul Reveres of persuasion. These pieces urge us to take action or to accept a certain belief. No matter what the issue of the editorial, the writer's first job is to make the reader take the topic seriously. For example, you might laugh at a sensational Web page about asteroids that claims "The sky is falling! The sky is falling!" However, an editorial like the one on the next page might just convince you that you are not completely safe from incoming asteroids.

## Preparing to Read

**READING SKILL**

**Author's Purpose and Point of View**   The writer's **purpose** in the following editorial is to persuade his readers of something. Readers can assume an editorial writer's purpose is to persuade. However, if an article is not in an editorial section, readers may have to look for signs that the author is trying to persuade them. Along with a persuasive purpose, a writer of persuasion will have a distinct **point of view** that reflects the writer's opinions, attitudes, and beliefs about the topic of the article or essay. Consequently, readers must be able to determine a writer's point of view so that they can decide if they agree with what the writer is saying.

**READING FOCUS**

**Logical and Emotional Appeals**   Writers of persuasion know that they must appeal to their readers' minds by making **logical appeals—reasons and evidence—to support their opinions**. However, writers also know that readers react as much with their hearts as with their minds. Therefore, along with reasons and evidence, writers include **emotional appeals— words and examples that play upon the readers' feelings**. See if you can tell when the writer of the editorial on the next page is either appealing to your intelligence or tugging at your heartstrings.

In the following editorial, the writer refers to an asteroid that some scientists initially thought might strike the earth on October 26, 2028. The editorial was written after the announcement that the asteroid would not hit the earth, nor even come very close. Try to identify the author's point of view and the appeals used. As you read, write answers to the numbered active-reading questions.

*from* **THE BOSTON GLOBE**

# 2028 VISION

**1. What clues does the title give about the article?**

BOSTON, MASSACHUSETTS, MARCH 14, 1998

Earth got a scary astronomy lesson this week and shouldn't forget the message: The universe is a rough neighborhood, and scientists must watch it as diligently as municipal authorities keep track of city streets. Maybe more so.

The temptation is for the human race to emit a collective "whew" and dismiss the asteroid-that-could, which, with revised calculations, almost certainly won't hit earth with a 10,000-megaton punch on October 26, 2028.

The mile-wide space rock, called "1997 XF11" and discovered in December, is capable of blowing a 20-mile crater in the planet on a direct hit. So NASA calmed everybody down by announcing that it will probably pass by the earth with a comforting, 600,000-mile margin instead of being the celestial squeaker it would have been at 30,000 miles.

However, the rock has friends—at least an estimated 2,000 others as big or bigger, roaming earth's neighborhood with the potential for doing damage.

The International Astronomical Union has identified only 108 of them, which means that science and government have a lot more to do.

**2. What language does the writer use in the first paragraph to appeal to your emotions?**

**3. What reasons does the writer give to show that the topic is an important one?**

*Asteroid XF11*

**4.** What practical actions is the writer asking people to take?

**5.** Who is named in this paragraph? Why should the reader care what this person says?

**6.** To what does the writer compare the threat of an asteroid collision? How does this comparison make you feel?

The close call should inspire an international scientific effort to find, name, and track what's out there and to determine what may be on a collision course with earth. A plan should be in place for deflecting or nudging incoming asteroids out of their orbit. This might be done by firing rockets at them or by detonating nuclear weapons nearby them. Exploding an asteroid with a nuclear bomb would be a bad move, because the rock could splinter into hundreds of lethal pieces.

Richard Binzel, an astronomer at MIT, is also calling for an asteroid rating system, similar to the Richter scale, that would let the public know the danger. He also noted that people should understand that an asteroid must be tracked over time, and that includes "1997 XF11."

This week an asteroid provided the planet with the equivalent of a cosmic fire drill. Now people must make sure that they have enough smoke detectors and hoses—and that they work.

MIKE SHELTON reprinted with special permission of King Features Syndicate, Inc.

With a partner, discuss the following questions about the editorial "2028 Vision." Each of you should write the answers on your own sheet of paper.

1. Using your answers to active-reading questions 2 and 6, describe how the writer wants you to feel about the possibility of an asteroid striking the earth.

2. In the second, third, and fourth paragraphs, the author gives reasons for the reader to be concerned about the asteroid threat. Which affect you more strongly: the writer's reasons or the language the writer uses in describing the danger? Why?

3. The last three paragraphs of the editorial give the writer's opinion of what should be done about the threat of asteroid collisions. What specific actions does the writer suggest? Does he make a convincing case? Why or why not?

## Author's Purpose and Point of View

READING SKILL

**Read the Signs**   Writers of persuasive articles are not writing merely to inform their readers about something. They are trying to convince readers to think or act in a certain way. This is their **purpose** in writing.  If readers are not conscious of such efforts to persuade them, they could mistake a writer's position on an issue for the truth about that issue. How will you as a reader know if the purpose of an article or essay is persuasive? You can look for clues that writers often leave. The following chart gives explanations and examples of some of these common clues.

| Clues | Examples |
| --- | --- |
| ▪ words such as *could*, *should*, and *would* | Students *should* be required to complete seventy hours of community service before graduation. |
| ▪ statements in the future tense, especially when the rest of the article is in the present tense | Installing carpet in all classrooms *will raise* students' attention levels. |
| ▪ forceful words such as *must* or *need* | The school board *must* approve the purchase of new band uniforms. |

**What's the Angle?** After deciding that an author's purpose is to persuade, you need to identify that writer's **point of view**—his or her attitude, opinions, or beliefs about the topic. The author's point of view in a persuasive piece can show up in two ways:

- **directly** in a thesis statement
- **indirectly** through the writer's choice of examples and words

Any persuasive message has a point of view. Being *aware* of the point of view will help you follow the reasoning in the message. If you know the point of view, you can determine the position the writer is trying to persuade you to take. Also, knowing the point of view will help you to decide whether or not you agree with the writer's message.

To determine the point of view in the paragraph below, use the steps in the Thinking It Through on the next page.

### Spend at Home First

Our government has made the decision to spend millions of our tax dollars on the space program. We foolishly subsidized the space shuttle so that scientists could perform experiments on insects in outer space. We paid so that the Pathfinder could take pictures on Mars. We shelled out money twice for the Hubble Space Telescope—once to put it into orbit, once to fix it. Enough already! We could be spending our money to buy shelter and food for the homeless. Just think how grateful the hungry and cold children would be to have food and a place to live. We could also use those dollars to fund medical research programs. Which is more important: having lovely pictures of the Mars horizon or curing cancer? The choice seems obvious.

## Identifying an Author's Point of View

Use the steps below to help you figure out an author's point of view. The right-hand column applies the steps to the passage you have just read.

**STEP 1 Read the introductory paragraph or the title to determine the topic.** Then, check to see if the author reveals his or her point of view in a thesis statement or topic sentence.

*There does not seem to be a topic sentence in the paragraph, but the first sentence and the title focus on the topic of spending tax money on the space program.*

**STEP 2 Look for words and phrases about the topic that have positive or negative associations** if there is no topic sentence or thesis statement.

*Positive: "lovely"—but I don't think the writer used the word to mean "delightful."*
*Negative: "foolishly," "shelled out," and "Enough already!"*

**STEP 3 Determine if the words and phrases create mostly negative or positive associations.** What is the author's tone?

*Most of the words are negative; I think "lovely" is used jokingly.*

**STEP 4 Determine the author's point of view** by putting what you have found together: topic + word choice = point of view.

*The author has a negative point of view toward spending money on the space program.*

**TIP** Remember that **thesis statements** are frequently found in the last one or two sentences of an introductory paragraph. Also, authors of magazine and newspaper articles sometimes use a condensed form of a thesis statement as the title of an article.

    **Topic sentences** are usually the first one or two sentences of paragraphs, although a paragraph can have an implied topic sentence.

---

**YOUR TURN 2**   **Identifying an Author's Point of View**

Using the steps outlined in the Thinking It Through above, determine the author's point of view in "2028 Vision" on page 249.

---

## Logical and Emotional Appeals

◀ **READING FOCUS**

**Why and Wherefore**   People write persuasive articles because they want their readers to think or act in a certain way. However, just telling people to do something will not necessarily make them do it. People need convincing. For example, if a writer wants to convince readers that a new law should raise the age requirement for a driver's license, he or she must use **logical appeals** and might choose to include **emotional appeals** as well.

**Logical Appeals** Writers use the elements of a logical appeal, **reasons** and **evidence**, to target your ability to think. Recognizing reasons and evidence will help you understand a writer's position and decide whether or not you agree with it.

- **Reasons** tell readers why they should accept the writer's opinion.
- **Evidence** supplies support for the reasons. Evidence can be facts, examples, anecdotes, or expert opinions.

The following graphic organizer illustrates how opinions are supported by reasons and, in turn, how reasons are supported by evidence.

**TIP** The graphic to the right pictures only one of the writer's reasons. Keep in mind, however, that the writer of an editorial should be expected to include several reasons to support his or her opinion.

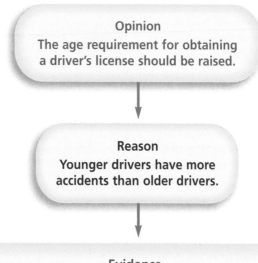

**Opinion**
The age requirement for obtaining a driver's license should be raised.

**Reason**
Younger drivers have more accidents than older drivers.

**Evidence**

**Fact:** Each year in our city, about two hundred accidents—or 40 percent of all accidents—involve drivers under the age of nineteen. **Expert Opinion:** Police Chief Caswell says "Our most accident-prone drivers are aged sixteen or seventeen. Many accidents have occurred on or near the high school campus."

**Emotional Appeals** By using emotional appeals, writers reach their readers' feelings. Think of an emotional appeal as the film footage that accompanies a news story on TV. For example, a reporter giving a story about a Midwest flood might cite statistics of homes lost or natural resources destroyed. However, the picture of one family standing in front of their flooded home is likely to have a greater impact on viewers than the facts alone would. Readers should look for two ways that writers appeal to their emotions: through **anecdotes** (brief stories) and through **word choice**.

- **Anecdotes** bring situations to life with real people and specific events with which readers can relate.

| Example | Explanation |
|---|---|
| Last week a young woman with two small children was seriously injured when a teenage driver ran a red light. The young mother is still in the hospital. | Many readers will feel strong sympathy for the young mother and for her children, who must live without her while she recuperates. |

**TIP** Often anecdotes appeal to both the reader's logic and emotions. The anecdote to the left, for example, works as evidence— it is a fact. It also carries an emotional appeal.

- **Word choice** is the palette an author, like an artist, uses to paint a picture for the reader. Writers use words' **connotations,** the associations or feelings that a word suggests, to appeal to the emotions. When words or phrases suggest very strong emotions, we call those words **loaded language.** Because loaded language appeals to strong emotions (for example, disgust or respect), it can bias people for or against something. Words like *victim, home, family,* and *freedom* are just a few of the many words that are loaded with strong connotations.

| Example | Explanation |
|---|---|
| Over ten thousand teenage drivers are **running loose** in our town and are **menacing** other drivers—these teenagers are **an accident waiting to happen.** | Rather than using more neutral terms, the writer uses words that appeal to the readers' fears to make teenage drivers sound uncontrolled and dangerous. |

**TIP** Readers should be suspicious of a writer whose persuasion relies heavily on loaded language. If a writer depends on outrageous terms to provoke strong emotion, the logical appeals could be weak.

## YOUR TURN 3 Recognizing Logical and Emotional Appeals

On your own paper, make a chart like the one below and fill it in with the logical and emotional appeals used in "2028 Vision" on page 249.

| Logical Appeals | Reasons:<br><br>Evidence: |
|---|---|
| Emotional Appeals | Ancedotes:<br><br>Word Choice: |

## Context Clues: Definition/Restatement

Asteroids and their behavior may not be part of your everyday conversation and vocabulary. If an unfamiliar word crops up in your reading, a good strategy to figure out its meaning is to look at the word's **context:** the words surrounding the unfamiliar word. One helpful context clue is a **definition,** which gives the meaning of the word directly or indirectly, usually in the same sentence.

Learning by *rote* involves heavy **reliance on repetition and memorization.**

Another kind of context clue, **restate-** **ment,** uses another word or phrase to repeat the meaning of the unfamiliar word.

Voters have grown dissatisfied with the mayor's *vacillation* on spending: **He is unable to make tough decisions.**

Often there are signals that indicate definition and restatement context clues.

- commas that set off or colons that begin the definition or restatement
- words or phrases such as *or, is, who is, which is, that is, in other words*

**Using Definition and Restatement Context Clues**

To use definition and restatement context clues, follow these steps. The student responses are based on the italicized word in the sentence from "2028 Vision."

"A plan should be in place for *deflecting* or nudging incoming asteroids out of their orbit."

1. **Look for definition or restatement signals** in the words surrounding the unfamiliar word. The word "or" might signal that "nudging" is a restatement context clue.

2. **Try replacing the unfamiliar word** with the word or phrase that you think is the

definition or restatement. "A plan should be in place for nudging incoming asteroids out of their orbit."

3. **See if your replacement works within the sentence.** The words "nudging . . . out of their orbit" seem to work.

Use definition and restatement context clues to determine the meanings of the italicized words in the following sentences.

1. We are *complacent,* content to believe that asteroids pose no threat.

2. Imagine the *barrage,* or pounding, the

earth would take if it passed through an asteroid belt.

3. Dr. Tate, the *doyen* of astronomers, is the senior member of the group.

4. Some people are *pessimistic;* they expect the worst to happen.

## Author's Purpose and Point of View

Standardized reading tests often have questions that ask you to identify an author's **purpose** and **point of view.** To answer, you will have to decide whether the author wants to inform, to entertain, or to persuade readers. Here is a typical reading passage and question about the author's purpose.

Now more than ever, it seems that creating news that sells is more important than creating news that is accurate and well analyzed. A prime example is the asteroid story of 1997, which predicted that a mile-wide asteroid would come within 30,000 miles of Earth. We had twenty-four hours of media mayhem, with reports squawking about collision and disaster. Then the story collapsed like a deflating balloon. The story was based on a scientist's initial calculation rather than on conclusive evidence. Using new data, scientists recalculated the asteroid's path and determined it would come no closer than 600,000 miles to Earth.

The author wrote this passage to

**A.** inform readers of new scientific findings

**B.** convince readers not to ignore the dangers of asteroids headed for Earth

**C.** describe how journalists fool people

**D.** convince people that the media should be more careful about accuracy

---

**THINKING IT THROUGH** **Identifying Purpose and Point of View**

Keep the following steps in mind as you answer a question about an author's purpose and point of view. The student responses are based on the sample passage and question above.

1. **Examine the passage for words with strong connotations.** Such language is a sure indicator of persuasive purpose. The words "mayhem," "squawking," and "irresponsible," are not neutral; therefore, the passage is probably persuasive.

2. **Check to see if the language is positive or negative.** [topic + word choice = point of view] The negative words "squawking," "story collapsed," and "irresponsible news story" indicate the writer's point of view.

3. **Look at the first few sentences to find the topic and to see if a topic sentence states the writer's point of view.** The first sentence suggests that the writer thinks news reporting should be more accurate.

4. **Look for the choice that best matches your analysis.** The answer that best matches is D.

# Writing a Persuasive Paper

**WHAT'S AHEAD**

In this workshop, you will write a persuasive paper. You will also learn how to

■ analyze your audience
■ provide support for your reasons
■ avoid circular reasoning
■ eliminate clichés from your writing
■ check for correct pronoun-antecedent agreement

**H**ave you ever wanted to change the world? For example, you might care deeply about an endangered species and want to change laws governing its habitat, or you might want to change the laws governing the educational testing in your state. It might seem that writing a persuasive paper has nothing in common with making these important changes, but the written word has been very powerful throughout history. For example, think of Supreme Court judgments, Martin Luther King, Jr.'s "I Have a Dream" speech, or the Declaration of Independence. These writings, all of which include elements of persuasion, have helped to change or create laws that affect the world we live in today.

Writing a persuasive paper is a way to take your own ideas and work to make them a reality. You can write an essay that communicates your own dream and persuades your readers not only to dream with you, but also to take action and help make it come true.

# Prewriting

## Choose an Issue

**Powerful Words from Powerful Beliefs**  The power of your persuasive writing will come from the strength of your beliefs about an issue. By definition, an **issue** is something about which people have opposing opinions or beliefs. If you do not believe in or feel strongly about one side of an issue, you will probably not convince anyone to agree with you. Therefore, as you search for an issue to write about, let your opinions and beliefs guide you. Choose something that matters to you. If you believe that wildlife protection is more important than urban growth, then you may have arrived at a suitable issue for your persuasive paper.

Use the following methods to find an issue for a persuasive paper:

- **Brainstorm about several issues** on which you have strong opinions. In as many ways as possible, complete the sentence: *If I could change anything in my community, I would ____.*

- **Read a local or national newspaper.** Pay special attention to the opinion and editorial pages. What issues are people concerned about? How do these issues concern you? What issue grabs your attention?

- **Browse high school newspaper Web pages** looking for editorials. Try to choose an issue that affects your own life and that is the subject of debate.

- **Watch television news shows or newsmagazines.** Are any of the issues discussed interesting or relevant to you?

- **Brainstorm collaboratively about issues that affect your school.** With a small group of classmates, discuss these issues, focusing on possible solutions.

When you have listed a number of issues about which you feel strongly, use the following checklist to choose one.

- Eliminate issues about which there cannot be differing opinions.

- Rate each remaining issue from 1 to 5, with 5 being the highest.

- Circle the issue that is most important to you—the one you rated 5.

- Check to be sure the issue you have chosen is an issue about which you feel comfortable sharing your feelings and thoughts.

## State Your Opinion

**Which Side Are You On?**   You have chosen an issue. Now make your **point of view,** your opinion and beliefs about the issue, as clear as possible to the reader. The best way to do this is to write an **opinion statement, one sentence that sums up the issue and your point of view on it**. This statement is the **thesis** of your paper.

**KEY CONCEPT**

**Issue:** State senators propose to create legal limits on volume levels for car stereo systems.

**Point of view:** I think the proposal is a bad idea.

**Opinion statement:** The state government should not create laws that limit the noise levels coming from car stereos.

Even though your thesis conveys what you believe or think, be careful not to include the words *I think* or *I believe* in your thesis. When you state your opinion your readers already know it is what you think or believe.

**TIP** Remember that while a **fact** is a statement that can be proven true, an **opinion** is a belief or judgment that cannot be proven. For example, if a school enrollment report shows that more students take art classes than take music classes, it is a *fact* that more students take art than music classes. However, it is an *opinion* that there should be a new art studio built at the school. When writing a persuasive paper, you can use facts to support the stand you are making, but your stand itself should be an opinion that you are trying to convince your readers to share.

## Consider Your Purpose, Audience, and Tone

**Rabble-rousing**  When you feel strongly about something, you have an **occasion** for writing, and your **purpose** for writing is clear. For example, you might believe it is wrong for the state government to regulate how loudly you can play music in your car. If so, you might feel compelled to write because you want to convince others to share your opinions. You might also want to encourage your readers to take action. However, to do either of these things, you first have to know who your readers are.

**THINKING IT THROUGH**    **Identifying Audience**

To identify your **audience**, think of the issue you have chosen and ask yourself the following questions.

▶ **Whom does this issue affect?** For example, if your issue is the closing of your school's campus during lunch, the issue probably does not affect a bachelor who lives across town. Your issue probably does affect, however, your fellow students and their parents, the teachers and administrators of your school, and the residents and business owners near your campus. These are all people who have a natural interest in your topic and will be a natural audience for your paper.

▶ **Whom do I need to convince?** Those who disagree with your opinion are the ones you must convince. For example, if school administrators have made the decision to close the campus during lunch hours, they may be your most important target audience. There may be some parents and students who also fit in this category.

▶ **Whom do I want to take action?** Identify other people who could help further your cause. For example, other students will probably agree with your position; you might call them to action. Also, those who are not sure where they stand on the issue may be swayed by your appeals and could make a difference for your cause.

Part of convincing your audience to accept your opinion or to take action comes with maintaining a respectful, thoughtful tone and voice. **Tone** is the attitude that you take toward your audience and topic. Your **voice** is how you sound as a writer—your unique way of using language. Imagine, for example, that you want to convince an audience that recycling makes a difference. Would you use the words "People who don't recycle are stupid"? Your readers would be much more likely to read on and be convinced if the tone were more formal, serious, and respectful.

The following chart shows notes one writer made about purpose, audience, and tone for a paper on recycling.

**Opinion statement:** Recycling is so important that it should be required of families in the community.

| | |
|---|---|
| Purpose | My purpose is to convince people that recycling should be a priority in our community. |
| Audience | Many people in my community understand the benefits of recycling. I should concentrate on people who still throw away a lot of material that could be recycled. |
| Tone | Some people might oppose my opinion at first. I need to be respectful toward them and use language that will help them see my point of view. |

**TIP** You can formulate questions about your issue by thinking about how it might affect your audience. Then you can clarify your ideas about your topic by deciding on a purpose for your essay.

## Support Your Opinion

**Building the Support Pyramid** It is not enough to state your opinion. You have to convince your audience that your opinion is logical (that it makes sense) and, perhaps, that action is needed. You do this by including **support** for your opinion. **Support includes reasons that tell *why* your opinion should be accepted and evidence to back up the reasons.** Support can also include stories, examples, details, and words that appeal to readers' hearts rather than their minds.

**KEY CONCEPT**

You can think of your persuasive paper as a pyramid. The top of the pyramid is your opinion statement. The base of the pyramid is made up of reasons and evidence that support your opinion. Without a base, the pyramid cannot stand. Consequently, if you cannot support your opinion statement with a solid base, then you will have to revise it.

**This Better Be Good**   Coming up with reasons is probably the toughest part of writing a persuasive paper. Use the following steps to develop strong reasons that support your opinion statement. Each reason can become the topic sentence of a paragraph in your paper.

**Reference Note**

For more about **generating reasons,** see **T.H.E.M.E.S. Strategy** on page 276.

**THINKING IT THROUGH**   **Generating Reasons**

**STEP 1** **Add two to three *because* clauses to your opinion statement.**

The state government should not create laws that limit the noise levels coming from car stereos.
1. because there are already laws about disturbing the peace that cover this situation
2. because such a law will only add to the burden of the already over-worked police

**STEP 2** **Delete the *because* from each clause and rewrite it as a sentence.** These will be your topic sentences for supporting paragraphs.

Laws already exist about disturbing the peace to cover this situation.

**STEP 3** **Add introductory or transitional words** (*one important reason, first, secondly, the most important reason*) **to each topic sentence, indicating its order in your paper.** *One reason for defeating the proposed law is that there are already laws about disturbing the peace that cover this situation.*

**Building the Foundation**   Support your reasons with evidence that appeals to both your readers' minds and their hearts—**logical appeals,** also called **logical arguments,** and **emotional appeals.** While you may use both kinds of support, your paper should rely more heavily on logical appeals.

**TIP**   In many school or test situations, persuasive writing must contain only logical appeals. This type of writing is called a **logical argument.**

**Logical Appeals**   Logical appeals speak to your readers' minds and are the foundation of your paper. Logical appeals consist of reasons supported by **evidence**—facts, statistics, expert opinions, anecdotes and examples.

- **Facts**—information that can be proven correct by testing or verification by reliable sources—show that there is concrete, reliable support for your opinion. For example, if you are writing about recycling, use **statistics** (facts that present numerical information) on the amount of waste material that could be recycled.

- **Expert opinions**—statements by people who are considered experts on the subject—show that the most knowledgeable people support you. For example, you might quote the city manager's opinion on recycling.

- **Anecdotes** and **examples** are illustrations of a general idea. While examples show specific instances, anecdotes are brief stories that are usually more personal in nature. To add an example to your evidence about the ease of recycling, you could write about someone who recycles regularly.

**TIP** Although it may be tempting, you should *never* make up evidence to support your opinion.

**Emotional Appeals**   Anecdotes and **examples** can appeal also to readers' emotions. Another way to appeal to your readers' hearts and complement your logical appeals is through **word choice**.

- **Anecdotes** and **examples** give a specific and often a human element to your paper. For example, when trying to persuade an audience that recycling is not difficult and heighten the emotional appeal, you might use an anecdote about a six-year-old who does the recycling for her family.

- **Word choice** can also enhance the emotional appeal of your paper by suggesting certain feelings that color the readers' understanding. For example, to describe a recycler with the words *avid* and *strong-willed* would give readers one sense of the person. The words *fanatical* and *stubborn* would give readers a less flattering sense of the person. Give clear definitions of any terms the reader might not understand.

**TIP**   Appeals are often logical *and* emotional. For example, both anecdotes and examples are factual and can therefore appeal to logic. However, they are also illustrations that provide human interest and therefore appeal to the emotions. Also, through word choice, facts can be made to appeal to emotions as well as to logic. For example, it is a fact that because some new paper is made of recycled paper, fewer trees are sacrificed to make that paper. Using the word *sacrifice* gives the fact an emotional appeal. As this diagram shows, emotional appeals and logical appeals can blend.

| emotional appeals | logical appeals |

**Pillars and Arches**   You can find logical appeals for your paper by researching your topic:

- by reading books, newspapers, and magazines at the library
- by searching the World Wide Web
- by interviewing local experts on your topic

You can gather material for emotional appeals from some of the same sources you use for logical appeals, such as articles and interviews. As you review these sources, keep an eye out for touching details and stories rather than just facts and statistics.

**TIP** Make sure that your evidence has the three R's. It should be

- *relevant*—tied closely to your issue
- *reliable*—from trustworthy sources
- *representative*—not all from one or two sources

Here is a support chart one writer created to make sure he had solid evidence for each reason supporting his position.

**Issue:** proposed law to ban large car stereo speakers and set legal volume levels

**Opinion Statement:** Playing a loud car stereo should not be a crime; this legislation must be defeated.

| Reasons | Evidence |
|---|---|
| 1. First, there are already laws about disturbing the peace that cover this situation. | **Expert opinion**—Sheriff Tharpe says that he just uses existing noise-pollution laws. (logical appeal) |
| 2. Another reason such a law should not exist is that it will only add to the burden of the already overworked police. | **Facts, example**—Use information from a newspaper article about overworked police forces. John's father, Deputy Marquez, had to work double shifts. (logical appeals) |
| 3. The most important reason is that singling out noise from car stereos is a form of discrimination. | **Example**—Most people make noise in public or participate in a noisy public event at some time, such as a football game, a concert, or a political rally. "Who would want to go to a quiet football game?" Use word "discrimination" to describe law. (emotional appeals) |

## YOUR TURN 4   Choosing an Issue and Developing Support

Use the examples, tips, and suggestions above to

■ choose an issue and write an opinion statement

■ organize your thoughts about your purpose, audience, and tone

■ gather support—logical appeals (reasons and evidence) and emotional appeals

## MINI-LESSON  CRITICAL THINKING

## Eliminating Circular Reasoning

As you have seen, solid support is important in a persuasive paper. Just stating your opinion in different words is not support; it is **circular reasoning**. Which of the following statements gives a valid reason by answering the question *Why?* instead of repeating itself?

1. Industrial pollution harms the ozone layer because it weakens the atmosphere.

2. Industrial pollution harms the ozone layer by releasing large amounts of carbon dioxide into the atmosphere.

If you decided that the first sentence merely restates the word *harms* as *weakens*, and that the second sentence gives a solid reason (pollution is harmful because it releases carbon dioxide), you were right.

When analyzed, circular reasoning ends up in a repetitive cycle, as shown in the diagram to the right. Valid reasoning, on the other hand, does not go in a circle. Instead, it leads the reader through a progression of thoughts. You can avoid circular reasoning by checking

that every statement in your paper is a valid reason and does not merely repeat what you have already stated. Ask the question *Why?* to make sure your statements are valid and progress toward building a reasonable case.

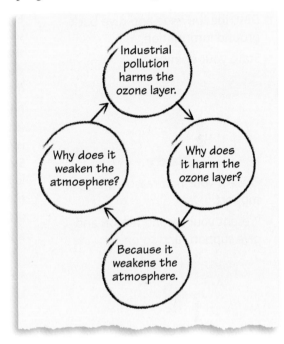

### PRACTICE

On a separate piece of paper, write *CR* for each of the following passages that contain circular reasoning. If the reasoning is valid, write *V*. Be prepared to explain your choices.

1. The United States should send its military to stop a foreign civil war because stopping the war would bring peace to the country.

2. Our school should allow restaurants to open food booths on campus because the booths would give students more choices.

3. Cigarettes are harmful to your health because smoking can cause many diseases, such as lung cancer and emphysema.

4. Soccer is more fun to watch than football because soccer is more interesting.

5. Teenagers should be encouraged to hold part-time jobs because jobs teach important lessons such as responsibility and the value of hard work.

# Writing

## Persuasive Paper

| Framework | Directions and Explanations |
|---|---|

### Introduction

- Grab your readers' attention.
- Describe the issue and give background information.
- State your opinion.

**Wave a Red Flag**   Begin with a startling statistic, a powerful quotation, or an anecdote.

**Explain the Issue**   Give brief background information so your readers will understand the issue; remember that you are leading your readers from a general statement in the first sentences to a specific statement of the issue in your thesis.

**Present Your Thesis**   Include a clear **opinion statement** (thesis) so your audience knows your position on the issue.

### Body

- Present your first reason and give support.
- Present your second reason and give support, and so on.

**Support Your Opinion**   Use the most convincing **logical** and **emotional appeals** from your prewriting notes. You may want to use the following strategy to organize your paper:

- Begin with your **second strongest reason** to make a strong appeal to your audience.
- Place your **least convincing reasons** in the middle.
- Save your **best reason** for last, to leave your audience with an impression of your strong reasoning.

### Conclusion

- Restate your opinion.
- Summarize reasons or include a call to action or both.

**Bring It Home**   **Restate,** but do not repeat, **your opinion.** You can **summarize your reasons,** give your audience a stirring **call to action,** or do both.

**YOUR TURN 5** **Writing Your Persuasive Paper**

Now it is your turn to draft a persuasive paper. As you write, clearly state your opinion and use the strongest reasons and evidence to provide support; establish your tone and appeal to your specific audience; and use the framework and the Writer's Model as a guide.

# A Writer's Model

### Music to Whose Ears?

Warm spring weather has arrived. A person gets in a car, rolls down the windows, pops a CD in the stereo, turns up the volume, and heads out for a lake. This is a recipe for a great feeling and harmless fun, right? Some state senators do not think so. To them, extremely loud car stereos are a public nuisance—even a dangerous one. They have proposed a law that bans car speakers above a certain size and sets legal volume levels. Playing a loud car stereo should not be a crime; this legislation must be defeated.

One reason for defeating the proposed law is that existing state laws already cover the problems the senators mention. According to Richard Tharpe, Hamilton County sheriff, "Right now we can arrest people for disturbing the peace, and state law even sets noise-pollution levels." In addition, if a stereo does cause a traffic accident—which Tharpe notes is uncommon and hard to prove—the driver can be charged. However, in the past five years only one such accident has been reported. To institute the proposed law, then, is just unnecessary repetition. It is obvious that legislators do not need to duplicate laws.

Another reason to stop this proposed legislation is that it will be extremely difficult to enforce. Our police force is already overburdened with enforcing the laws we have. A number of towns and cities in the state have admitted to staffing shortages. In fact, Deputy Marquez, my friend John's father, has had to work double shifts the last six months in order to ensure that all patrols are covered. According to Deputy Marquez, this shortage is due to the fact that officers must spend a large percentage of their time enforcing misdemeanor laws similar to the proposed ban on loud car stereos. Just because serious crime is no longer on the rise, the police should not have to add another misdemeanor to their beats.

*(continued)*

**INTRODUCTION**
Attention-grabbing anecdote—emotional appeal

Opinion statement

**BODY**
First reason
Evidence: Expert opinion and fact

Evidence: Fact

Second reason
Evidence: Fact

Evidence: Anecdote

Evidence: Fact

*(continued)*

Do they really have time to point decibel monitors at passing cars?

**Third Reason**

**Evidence: Fact and examples**

The most compelling reason to put a halt to this proposal is that singling out car stereos is a form of discrimination. After all, many other "public noises" are just as loud. Parades and rallies often use high-volume sound trucks. Radio stations broadcast live from stores and parking lots. Loudspeakers, bands, and cheering crowds at football games can be heard for blocks. For example, the cheering during last week's victorious game against the Tigers could be heard as far away as Main Street. Sound from any such event could be seen (or heard) as infringing on the public's right to peace. However, a law to eliminate these noises would be considered unfair and illogical. No one wants to go to a quiet football game. It would spoil the fun. Why should driving to the lake be different?

**Emotional appeal**

**CONCLUSION**
**Restatement of opinion**
**Call to action**

We all want our streets to be calm and safe, but the senators' approach is misguided. A law restricting the volume of car stereos is unnecessary and unfair, and each of us should write or call our legislators to say so.

ZITS reprinted with special permission of King Features Syndicate, Inc.

# A Student's Model

The following is an excerpt of a persuasive paper written by Anthony King, a student at Morrison Christian Academy in Taichung, Taiwan.

## Censored!

Is Internet censorship right? That is the question millions of people around the world are asking themselves—people like you and me who freely surf the Web every day reading the latest news or simply checking our e-mail. This freedom that we exercise daily is in danger of becoming another government regulated part of our lives. The Internet is a world of information which may be freely accessed by all; it should stay that way.

There are several arguments for and against the government's proposal for Internet regulations. There are many people who think the Internet should be censored because it gives underage surfers open access to undesirable material. The Internet can be freely accessed by anyone, including minors, and it is a place where people can freely exercise their constitutionally guaranteed freedom of speech. It is no secret that the Internet contains undesirable material, but whether or not an underage "netizen" has access to that type of information can be controlled by that child's parents or guardian. Programs such as NetNanny and Surf-Watch are two of many programs that provide protection against undesirable sites. There is no need for government intervention when the solution is so simple. The argument for Internet censorship based upon open access to this undesirable material is understandable, but since adults are capable of making the right decision to avoid such sites and protection is available for the underage surfer, access to unwanted material can be controlled without government regulations. However, those who do not feel satisfied with home control will be gratified to hear that there is a major Internet movement for private regulation.

INTRODUCTION

Position Statement

BODY

First Reason

Evidence: Facts

# Revising

## Evaluate and Revise Your Paper

**Give Your Paper the Once-Over, Twice**  As you evaluate and revise your draft, you should work collaboratively to do at least two readings. In the first reading, focus on the content and organization of your draft, using the guidelines below. In your second reading, concentrate on your sentence style, using the style guidelines on the next page.

➤ **First Reading: Content and Organization**  In your first reading, look at the paper as a whole and make sure all its elements are working together smoothly. Use the following chart to evaluate and revise your paper so that it is clear and effective.

### Persuasive Paper: Content and Organization Guidelines for Peer and Self-Evaluation

| Evaluation Questions | ▶ Tips | ▶ Revision Techniques |
|---|---|---|
| **❶** Does the introduction have an attention-grabbing opener and a clear opinion statement? | ▶ **Bracket** the one or two sentences that capture the reader's interest. **Underline** the opinion statement. Revise if there isn't an attention grabber or an opinion statement. | ▶ **Add** or **elaborate** on a sentence that engages the reader. **Add** an opinion statement that clearly states the position you have taken. |
| **❷** Does the paper include at least three valid reasons to support the opinion statement? | ▶ **Number** the reasons in the margins. Check each one for circular reasoning. If there is a problem, revise. | ▶ **Cut** any reasons that are circular. **Add** valid reasons that support your opinion statement. |
| **❸** Is each reason supported by at least one piece of evidence? If appropriate, are emotional appeals used? | ▶ **Circle** each piece of evidence (facts, examples, and so on). **Draw an arrow** from each item to the reason it supports. If you have any reasons without arrows pointing to them, revise. | ▶ **Add** facts, expert opinions, examples, or anecdotes to support your reasons. **Elaborate** on existing support by adding details or more evidence. |
| **❹** Are the reasons and evidence arranged in order of importance? | ▶ **Put a star** next to the strongest reason. If it is not the last one, revise. | ▶ **Reorder** the reasons so that they are in order of importance. |
| **❺** Does the conclusion restate the opinion and include a summary of reasons or a call to action? | ▶ **Underline** any sentence that restates the writer's opinion. **Put a check mark** next to any sentence that makes a call to action. If you lack underlining and/or check marks, revise. | ▶ **Add** a restatement of your opinion and a summary of reasons or a call to action. |

**ONE WRITER'S REVISIONS**    Here is how one writer used the content and organization guidelines to revise some sentences from the persuasive paper on page 267.

According to Richard Tharpe, Hamilton County Sheriff, "Right ~~The senators just want to restrict playing car stereos loudly~~ now we can arrest people for disturbing the peace, and state ~~because they think rock-and-roll is a lot of extreme noise pollu-~~ law even sets noise-pollution levels."              In addition, ~~tion. Their own law officers do not agree with them.~~ If a stereo                     Tharpe notes is uncommon and hard to prove does cause an accident—which hardly ~~ever happens anyway—~~

the driver can be charged.

Cut and replace

Add

Cut and replace

## Analyzing the Revision Process

1. Why do you think the writer replaced the first and second sentences?

2. Why is the added information important?

**YOUR TURN 6    Revising Content and Organization**

Revise the content and organization of your paper, using the guidelines on the previous page. Use the example revisions above as a model.

**PEER REVIEW**

Ask a few classmates to read your paper and to answer the following questions.

1. Does the paper convince you? Why or why not?

2. Do any reasons need supporting evidence? Why do you think so?

▶ **Second Reading: Style**    Persuasive writing requires that you use words that have an impact on your readers. After all, you are trying to get them to agree with you. Using **clichés,** or worn-out expressions, may lead your readers to assume that your thoughts are just as boring as your language. Use the following guidelines to find and eliminate clichés, such as *sharp as a tack, safe and sound,* and *rain on your parade,* from your writing.

## Style Guidelines

| Evaluation Question | ▶ Tip | ▶ Revision Technique |
|---|---|---|
| **Are there any clichés in the essay?** | ▶ Put an **X** through clichés—for example, *in a nutshell, rat race,* and *tough as nails.* | ▶ **Replace** each Xed-out phrase with a fresh, original expression. |

## Focus on

### Word Choice

## Eliminating Clichés

Have you ever watched a movie and thought to yourself, "Oh, I've seen this before." We have all seen the action hero who escapes certain death at the last possible second. Like this overused character, there are words and phrases that were once new and fresh but now are just boring and predictable. They are called **clichés** and include phrases like "few and far between," "as strong as an ox," and "last but not least."

**ONE WRITER'S REVISIONS** Here's how one writer used the evaluation and revision guidelines to eliminate clichés from the persuasive paper on page 267.

**BEFORE REVISION**

cliché

cliché

We all want our streets to be calm and safe, but the senators are ~~barking up the wrong tree~~. We need this law like we need a ~~hole in the head~~.

**AFTER REVISION**

reword

We all want our streets to be calm and safe, but the senators' approach is misguided. A law restricting the volume of car stereos is unnecessary. . . .

### Analyzing the Revision Process

1. How did replacing "barking up the wrong tree" with another phrase improve the first sentence above?

2. How else could you revise the cliché in the second sentence?

**YOUR TURN 7** **Eliminating Clichés**

Revise the style of your persuasive paper; remember to use the guidelines in this section to eliminate clichés.

## Proofread Your Essay

**Once More with Feeling**  You do not want to ruin the impact of your well-crafted words by letting little mistakes show up in your final draft. Review your paper to make sure it is free of grammar, spelling, and punctuation errors. If you find it hard to inspect your own paper for these mistakes, trade papers with a partner and examine each other's work closely. One of the things you should look for is correct pronoun-antecedent agreement.

**Reference Note**

For **proofreading guidelines,** see page 13. For more information and practice on **pronoun-antecedent agreement,** see page 507.

## Grammar Link

## Pronoun-Antecedent Agreement

When you are writing persuasively about an issue, be sure that your reasoning does not get lost in a pronoun mix-up. Check to see that each **pronoun** agrees with its **antecedent**—the word to which the pronoun refers. There are several rules that govern pronoun-antecedent agreement.

1. **Singular pronouns are used to refer to the following antecedents:** *each, either, neither, one, everyone, everybody, everything, no one, nobody, nothing, anything, anyone, anybody, something, someone,* and *somebody.*

| Incorrect | **One** of the horses closed **their** eyes. |
| Correct | **One** of the horses closed **its** eyes. |

Note: In conversation, plural pronouns are often used to refer to singular antecedents that are clearly plural in meaning: **Everyone** raised **their** hands and cheered. However, this usage is considered incorrect in formal writing.

2. **A singular pronoun is used to refer to two or more singular antecedents joined by** *or* **or** *nor.*

| Incorrect | **Katy or Val** has **their** grades. |
| Correct | **Katy or Val** has **her** grades. |

3. **Use a plural pronoun to refer to two or more antecedents joined by** *and.*

| Incorrect | **Dan and Maria** took **his and her** test. |
| Correct | **Dan and Maria** took **their** tests. |

## PRACTICE

Revise each of the following sentences, correcting errors in pronoun-antecedent agreement.

1. Each of the students should have to perform community service as part of their normal school curriculum.

2. We cannot assume that the school and the community can take care of itself.

3. Neither our teacher, Mrs. Gomez, nor Mia, the class president, has opposed the idea with their vote.

4. Everyone can create and manage a project of their own.

5. The plan will be implemented unless someone halts it with their veto.

# Publish Your Paper

**You Better Believe It**  You cannot persuade anyone if you are the only one who reads your paper. By publishing your paper you take the next step in making your opinion heard and making an impact on an issue. When determining how to publish your paper, think again of the audience you are trying to reach.

- A natural choice for publishing your paper would be the opinion page of your school or local newspaper. You should check the guidelines for letters to the editor in both publications to make sure your paper meets the necessary criteria.

- Send your paper to those who can make a difference on your issue. Whether your audience is the school board or your state representative, offer your opinion to those who can make changes.

- Publish your paper on the World Wide Web and ask other Web page publishers to create links to the paper. For example, if your paper is about an environmental issue, you can ask for a link on a Web page hosted by an organization that shares your views. Look for sites with similar topics, or post your work on your own personal Web page.

- Make a pamphlet from your persuasive paper. Passing out pamphlets at school is one way to get your words out to the public.

## Designing Your Writing

**Creating Pamphlets**  Fliers or pamphlets—those sheets of paper that show up clamped under your windshield wiper, tucked in your door, and posted on bulletin boards—have long been an outlet for persuasion. If you choose to create a pamphlet from your paper, you will need to change its format to make it more appealing and accessible to potential readers. Make folds in the paper, and break up the text to fit the folds. Move your text into columns or display your paragraphs in easy-to-read pieces with bold or catchy headings. Here are a few basic guidelines for creating pamphlets.

- **Use typefaces that are easy to read, and limit yourself to no more than two typefaces.** Your text can look too busy with lots of typefaces. Use one main typeface for body text and a second for headings to emphasize them.

- **Rework your paper.** You may have a lot to say, but if you make the print in your pamphlet too small, people will not read it. Rather than making the print tiny, you may need to shorten your paper. For example, you could take out your weakest reason.

- **Use a separate heading for each reason to make your position clear to your readers.** Headings are great tools to guide readers who may just be glancing at the pamphlet you hand to them. *Guide* is the important word here; be careful not to overwhelm your readers with headings that distract them.

- **Avoid using capital letters for emphasis;** they are harder to read than small letters, particularly if they go on for more than one line. If you want to emphasize your words, use italics or boldface.

- **Use drawings, graphs, charts, or tables to deliver your information, if applicable.** Per square inch of space, much more information can be conveyed through graphic presentations than in an explanation in the text. Use drawings to show objects, and include graphs, charts, and tables for presenting numerical data.

- **Be sure to follow these guidelines if you use graphics.**

  1. Create labels to identify important elements.

  2. Include a key if the graphic has shadings, colors, or other details that have special meanings.

  3. Title most graphics.

  4. Position graphics neatly and comfortably within your margins, leaving at least two blank lines above and below each graphic.

## Reflect on Your Essay

**PORTFOLIO**

**Take a Deep Breath**   Now that the hard work is over, think about your paper and the process you used to create it. Use your answers to the following questions to recognize your achievement and to identify ways you can improve your next effort. Include these answers with your essay if you put it in your portfolio.

1. What was the most convincing and powerful part of your paper? Which part was the weakest? Why do you think so?

2. What methods or techniques did you use that you could use when you write other papers?

**YOUR TURN 8   Proofreading, Publishing, and Reflecting**

Use the material on the last several pages to correct grammar, usage, and mechanics errors in your paper, and keep an eye out for pronoun-antecedent agreement; publish your paper to reach your audience; and reflect on your paper.

## T.H.E.M.E.S. Strategy

Local, state, and national writing tests often ask you to write a persuasive essay in response to a question on an issue. You are given a topic in a writing prompt, but you have to decide your opinion, or position, organize your response, write, and proofread—all in a limited amount of time. Thinking of what to say in support of an opinion can be the most difficult step on a writing test. Use the following strategy to think of supporting ideas quickly.

**THINKING IT THROUGH**    **Using T.H.E.M.E.S. Strategy on a Writing Test**

Each letter in T.H.E.M.E.S. stands for a subject category you could use to trigger ideas for reasons supporting your position. You may not be able to use every category, but at least some of them will probably apply.

| | | |
|---|---|---|
| T = Time | H = Health | E = Education |
| M = Money | E = Environment | S = Safety |

▶ **STEP 1** Memorize each letter and its category.

▶ **STEP 2** Using each letter, ask a question about the effect your opinion will have on time, health, education, and so on. These questions will then trigger ideas about reasons that support your position.

▶ **STEP 3** Answer each question to give you a reason that supports your opinion.

Below is an example of how one student used T.H.E.M.E.S. to generate reasons for a persuasive essay on banning smoking.

**Position: The city should ban smoking in all areas.**

**T** = Workers won't have to spend time cleaning ashtrays and picking up cigarette butts.

**H** = Banning smoking will reduce secondhand smoke inhalation and its health risks.

**E** = People will be more aware of the health problems associated with smoking.

**M** = Reduction in smoking might lower healthcare costs.

**E** = Public areas will have cleaner air, and the litter associated with smoking will be less widespread.

**S** = Banning smoking will reduce the risk of fire started by discarded cigarettes.

# Critically Viewing Persuasive Messages in the Media

Persuasion does not exist solely on newspaper editorial pages and in magazine articles. You are surrounded by persuasive messages every day, from your parents or teachers urging you to study to your friends telling you why you should listen to a certain new CD. You are also exposed to many different persuasive messages in the form of advertisements: on billboards, on TV, in films—seemingly everywhere. These advertisements try to persuade you to buy products or to adopt a certain point of view through their use of spoken words, music, writing, sound effects, and pictures.

It is important that you be aware of the persuasion used in media messages; otherwise, you might be convinced to do something that could be dangerous or contrary to your own beliefs. Use the following questions to help you analyze and evaluate the messages you receive daily.

- **Who created the message and why?** Think about an ad for a certain brand of pants. The creators of the ad's message are the owners of the brand and their employees. They create the message to convince people to buy this brand of pants.

- **How does the message make me feel?** There could be several reactions to the pants ad, but the advertisers certainly want to create a positive feeling. The people in the ad look happy; do you feel happy, too? If so, the ad's creators have transferred the ad's happy feeling to you.

- **Does the ad attempt to shape my attitudes** and perceptions about myself and the world around me? It is important to be aware that advertisers have **codes** and **conventions** (established techniques or practices) about the portrayal of women and men in ads.

1. **Voice-Over** Because men's voices are lower in pitch than women's, television commercials often have male narrators. Supposedly, a man's voice adds authority to the advertiser's message.

2. **Dismemberment** Another convention is to objectify women and men by showing only certain parts of bodies, such as the slim legs of women or the muscular chests of men.

3. **Foolishness** While men are usually seen as serious and reflective, women often are shown looking foolish.

4. **In Control** Women are often portrayed as subordinate to men, with men being in control of a situation.

5. **Approval** In many ads, women and men are judged as successful only if they are attractive.

The pants ad may subtly communicate attitudes you dislike.

- **What point of view are the creators trying to convince me to accept?** The point of view may be that wearing these pants will make you feel happy and have fun.

- **What techniques do the creators use to persuade me?** You may already know some of the techniques advertisers use and may be able to answer this question easily. If not, take a close look at the following chart, which gives definitions and examples of three popular persuasive techniques used in advertising. Recognizing these techniques will help you to analyze, or closely examine the details of, the various persuasive messages you encounter from the media.

| Technique | Definition | Examples |
|---|---|---|
| Glittering Generality | a word or phrase with positive connotations used to create good feelings about a product or opinion, regardless of any evidence | A brand uses the words *natural* or *organic* to appeal to people who want healthy, ecologically sound products. The word *gold* is often used to imply luxury. |
| Testimonial | a personal recommendation for a product or idea often offered by an expert or famous person who may not use or like the product or idea | A sports figure who has become a symbol of excellence and success recommends a particular restaurant. A smiling movie star recommends a certain brand of toothpaste. |
| Transfer | an attempt to connect a product, image, or idea with something respected, pleasing, or admired—even though that connection may not be logical | A TV star who played a trustworthy family man for many years describes a building company. A politician identifies herself with a beloved political figure of the past. |

To evaluate persuasive messages, you should also consider how visual techniques add to the meaning. Illustrators, graphic artists, and photographers may use the techniques below to give an ad extra impact.

- **Color** A grape juice ad might use a black-and-white image with bright purple juice to make the product look even more inviting to viewers.

- **Juxtaposition** Placing two images next to each other can create meaning. For example, an image of a person drinking juice followed by an image of a beautiful waterfall points out how refreshing the juice is.

- **Cropping** For images that are not staged by an ad producer, cropping can eliminate a product's negative points. For example, a photo of a taste test might be cropped to show only the face of a person enjoying juice in order to eliminate the giant purple stain the juice made on her shirt.

**YOUR TURN 9** **Critically Viewing a Persuasive Media Message**

Find a printed advertisement or a TV commercial that uses glittering generalities, a testimonial, or transfer, and analyze it in a short paragraph. Use the questions on page 277 as a guide. Present your analysis to a small group of students.

# Making a Persuasive Speech

**P**ersuasion is well suited to the spoken word. In fact, most of the persuasive messages you have been exposed to have been spoken ones. Now, you will have the **occasion** to give your own persuasive speech, to speak up—quite literally—for what you believe. You can use your topic from the Writing Workshop, or you can speak on a new topic. Because your purpose is to persuade, be certain that the issue you choose is something about which you feel strongly. You might want to discuss new topic ideas with another student to make sure you choose an appropriate topic for the speaking **task** with which you have been challenged.

## Prepare Your Case

After choosing an issue and identifying your position on the issue (or thesis), develop support for your opinion. Back up each reason with facts, statistics, expert opinions, or anecdotes. Use precise language to defend your point of view, and include both logical support (proofs) and emotional appeals. You might want to emphasize emotional appeals more in your speech than you would in a written piece, in order to keep your listeners interested and responsive to your cause. Your **audience** will probably be your classmates unless you have another audience in mind.

## Deliver Your Speech

Many speeches are outlined and rehearsed but not memorized. Such preparation is the best method for your persuasive speech. You will be much more persuasive if you make a relaxed presentation rather than giving a word-for-word memorized speech or reading from your paper.

You can adapt your speech from a persuasive essay or start from scratch with a complete outline. One of these options will be the blueprint for your speech, from which you will prepare note cards that list its main

**WHAT'S AHEAD?**

In this section, you will make a persuasive speech. You will also learn how to

■ present an opinion, or thesis, and reasons and evidence that support it

■ use verbal and non-verbal cues to present your speech

**TIP** In order to win people over to your cause or position, you may be tempted to distort the truth, exaggerate, or attack someone unjustly. Besides being unethical, these methods will cause your audience to lose trust in your words—and perhaps in your cause as well.

parts: the issue, your opinion statement (thesis), each reason with its support (logical and emotional appeals), and a summary of reasons or a call to action. Make a separate card for each item, and number the cards to help you keep them in order. Practice connecting the material on your note cards by rehearsing your speech with a friend.

**A Nod of the Head**   As you rehearse and deliver your speech, you will need to pay attention to **verbal** and **nonverbal strategies** as well as content.

Here are some essentials for improving your **spoken delivery.**

- **Speak at a reasonable rate and volume.** Practice speaking at a consistent rate, neither too fast nor too slowly, and make sure every member of the audience can hear you clearly.

- **Enunciate.** Do not slur your words or drop word endings. Avoid vocalized pauses such as *uh*, *um*, and *you know*.

- **Be enthusiastic.** Show that you believe in your material.

- **Use an effective pitch and tone of voice. Pitch** is the highness or lowness of your voice and can be used to convey and emphasize the meaning of your words. **Tone of voice** is the sound of your voice, and it should be appropriate to your subject matter.

Here are some methods for improving your **nonverbal behavior.**

- **Maintain eye contact** with your audience. Give everyone in your audience the feeling you are speaking directly to him or her.

- **Use appropriate gestures and facial expressions.** Try to relax and avoid overdoing gestures and facial expressions.

- **Use good posture.** Do not slouch or speak at the ground.

- **Breathe.** Remembering to breathe can help you feel less nervous.

## Rehearse Your Speech

To refine your speech, evaluate yourself in rehearsals or get pointers from others through collaborating or conferring. One rehearsal strategy is to deliver your speech to a friend or to your family, exactly as you plan to deliver it to your real audience. Ask your rehearsal audience for feedback on how to make your speech better, and use the feedback to set goals for future speeches.

**YOUR TURN 10   Making a Persuasive Speech**

Using the information above, prepare, practice, and present your persuasive speech.

**TIP**   As you listen to your classmates' speeches, use the bulleted items to the right to help analyze, evaluate, and critique their performances. In addition to these delivery points, you should also listen for clear major ideas and strong supporting evidence.

You can use the same criteria when you evaluate and critique public persuasive speeches and persuasive speeches given on television.

*Choices*

**Choose one of the following activities to complete.**

## ▶ LITERATURE

**1. "The Only Thing We Have to Fear"** Great speeches make great literature. Most speeches have an element of persuasion in them. Find a powerful persuasive speech in a book of speeches in the library, and memorize the speech. Locating the logical and emotional appeals in the speech will probably help you to remember it. Once you have committed it to memory, perform a **recitation** of the speech for your class.

## ▶ VIEWING AND REPRESENTING

**2. Creatures Great or Small** Have you ever noticed that some ads use animals to sell their products? Tigers sell breakfast cereal; koalas sell airlines. Design a **cereal box** or a **billboard,** using any animal you choose. Include text in your design, but focus on making your product visually appealing to a target audience. Then, present your design to a group of classmates as if you were an advertising executive pitching an ad campaign idea to the company whose product you are selling.

## ▶ SPEAKING AND LISTENING

**3. Putting Words in Their Mouths** Have you ever wondered what it would be like to be a speechwriter for a politician? Now is your chance to find out. Contact the office of a local political leader and ask to talk to his or her speechwriter. If possible, set up an interview. Then, ask the speechwriter about his or her writing strategies. Present your findings in the form of an **oral presentation.**

## ▶ CAREERS

**4. Pitching an Idea** Imagine that you have just invented or discovered something that will make a huge impact on industry. How can you convince your fellow workers that your discovery will work? Prepare a **media presentation** that introduces your idea and persuades your audience of its importance and benefits. Create visuals to help convince your audience. If you have access to a computer, you may want to take advantage of software designed to help you produce media presentations. Then, deliver your presentation to your fellow employees (that is, your fellow students).

**PORTFOLIO**

# 8 Reviewing Television

### Reading Workshop

*Reading a Critical Review*

### Writing Workshop

*Writing a Critical Review of a TV Sitcom*

### Viewing and Representing

*Analyzing the Nightly Network News*

**Informational Text**

Persuasion

How would you like to get paid to watch television, listen to music, or go to the movies? As a professional music, TV, or movie critic, you actually could make money doing these things—but you would also have to write persuasive **critical reviews.** Critical reviews, wherever they appear—in magazines, on the radio, on television—attempt to persuade people that the subject of the review is or is not worth their time and money.

You will find critical reviews almost everywhere you turn. They may be **informal reviews,** such as friends' recommendations of movies, music, and places to meet new people, or they may be **formal reviews** that appear in magazines and newspapers and on TV, radio, and the Internet. Reviews are so abundant because, with so many choices to make, people often find themselves asking questions like *Is that show I've heard about worth watching?* or *What are some good new books I might read?* In their reviews, critics help answer those kinds of questions by providing **informed opinions** on what they think is good or bad, worthwhile or not worthwhile.

**YOUR TURN 1**  **Turning Thumbs Up or Down**

Working in pairs, brainstorm a list of formal and informal reviews you have seen, read, or heard lately. Try to think of at least four examples of each kind of review. Then, for each item on your list, write down any reasons the reviewer gave for his or her opinion. Be prepared to share your results with the class.

*internet* **connect**

**go. hrw .com**

GO TO: go.hrw.com
KEYWORD: EOLang 9-8

# Reading a Critical Review

In this section, you will read a critical review of a television program. You will also learn how to

- identify facts and opinions
- analyze evaluation criteria

**W**ith so many shows on television, how do you decide what to watch? One way to find out if a certain show is worth watching is to watch it once and then decide if you like it enough to watch a second time. Another way is to read a **critical review** of the program.

The article on the next page, "Ray of Hope," is a critical review of a television sitcom (short for *situation comedy,* the most commonly seen type of comedy program on television). See if the writer is able to convince you that the show is worth thirty minutes of your time.

## Preparing to Read

**READING SKILL**

**Fact and Opinion**    The heart of any review is a critic's, or reviewer's, **opinion,** what he or she thinks of the program. However, **facts**—statements that can be proven true, such as the names of actors, the date and time a show is on, and what the show is about—also play a key role.

As you read "Ray of Hope," be on the lookout for statements of fact and statements of opinion.

**READING FOCUS**

**Evaluation Criteria**    Television critics and reviewers support their opinions about TV shows by explaining how well the shows measure up against specific **criteria**—standards they think good TV shows should meet. For example, most critics would list "must be funny" as a standard that a sitcom should meet, because a sitcom that is not funny is just not a good sitcom. While people do not always agree on what the criteria should be, or on which criteria are more important than others, there are common standards that most people would use to evaluate any type of TV show. As you read "Ray of Hope," try to determine what criteria the writer is using to evaluate the program.

The following review by television critic Bruce Fretts originally appeared in *Entertainment Weekly*. *Everybody Loves Raymond* was in its first year at the time of the review. As you read, jot down answers to the numbered active-reading questions.

from *Entertainment Weekly*

# Ray of Hope

by Bruce Fretts

A funny thing happened on the freshman sitcom *Everybody Loves Raymond* (CBS, Mondays, 8:30–9:00 P.M.) this year. It got better. No small feat, considering the fate of this season's other most promising pilots: *Spin City* stumbled badly and took several months to regain its footing, while *Millennium* immediately imploded. . . . Yet Ray Romano's family comedy didn't just grow funnier—it grew deeper.

What started as a likable and witty distillation of Romano's stand-up act—the travails of a dad with three kids under the age of six—transformed itself into a fascinatingly humane portrait of suburban dysfunction.[1] In fact, *Raymond* may now be the best sitcom on the air—its only real creative competition being *News Radio*. . . .

The series' setup is simple: Sportswriter Ray Barone (Romano) lives on Long Island with his stay-at-home wife (Patricia Heaton) and their three preschoolers (played by Madylin, Sullivan, and Sawyer Sweeten)—right across the street from his squabbling folks (Peter Boyle and Doris Roberts) and . . . cop brother, Robert (Brad Garrett). At first, this premise lent itself to predictable complications: The elder Barones always barged in unannounced, and Robert was constantly mooching. Yet, as the season progressed, *Raymond* became more about the struggle of a grown man trying to separate from his parents and establish his own family.

*Raymond* is the rarest of sitcoms—one with a genuinely original point of view. In the show's new and improved opening-

> **1. What important information does the writer include in the first sentence?**

> **2. Judging from the first two paragraphs, what would you say the writer thinks of the quality of the show?**

> **3. Why do you think the writer includes the information given in this paragraph?**

---

1. **dysfunction** (dis•fuŋk´ shən): used here to denote a family that cannot function normally.

credits sequence, Ray's family goes by on a conveyor belt, and, as his children pass, he assures viewers the show is "not really about the kids." Refresh-

**4. What good quality of the show does the writer seem to be discussing here?**

ingly, it's not. This is life seen through the eyes of one man as he attempts the near-impossible task of simultane- ously fulfilling the roles of husband, father, brother, and son.

It's a brilliantly realized vision, thanks to *Raymond's* remarkable cast. Like Garry Shandling and Jerry Seinfeld, Romano does such subtle work that it appears as if he's not even acting. His voice—a thick, nasal whine—initially sounds shticky,[2] yet he uses it like a finely tuned instrument, sliding from elation to frustration with only the slightest tonal[3] change.

As wife Debra, Heaton matches Romano beat for beat. She's taken the role's inherent thanklessness—the still

**5. What quality does he focus on in this paragraph?**

center around which Ray's crazy family revolves— and turned it into a virtue. Debra rails[4] against her status as "the normal one," recently launching into a tirade[5] that allowed Heaton to do dead-on impressions of the eccentric

Barones. And old pros Boyle and Roberts have created the most realisti- cally fractious[6] TV marriage since Archie and Edith Bunker's.

*Raymond's* secret weapon, though, is the towering Garrett. . . . As Ray's eternally unlucky sibling, he has devel- oped a wonderful chemistry with Romano. One charming episode, in which Ray gave his brother a stray bull- dog, expertly utilized Garrett's extra- large talents. Underneath that imposing[7] exterior beats the heart of a puppy. . . .

Raymond has skyrocketed in the ratings since CBS moved it to Mondays after Cosby. The network would be wise not only to renew it but to leave it where it is. With his winning mix of heart and humor, Romano seems the natural heir to Cosby's sitcom-dad throne.

**6. What recom- mendation comes through in the last two sentences?**

---

2. **shticky** (shtik´ ē): like an act intended to be funny.

3. **tonal** (tō´nəl): quality of tone.

4. **rails** (rālz): complains in a bitter way.

5. **tirade** (tī´rād; tī•rād´): a long and passionate speech.

6. **fractious** (frak´shəs): irritable; cross.

7. **imposing** (im•pō´ zin): impressive because of size or strength.

## Fact and Opinion

**Truths and Views**  To be a critical reader of persuasive writing—including critical reviews—you must be able to distinguish between facts and opinions. The writer of "Ray of Hope" provides you with **facts** when he gives you background information about *Everybody Loves Raymond*. For example, here is part of a sentence that provides key facts about the characters on the show and the actors who play them:

> Sportswriter Ray Barone (Romano) lives on Long Island with his stay-at-home wife (Patricia Heaton). . . .

You can confirm the facts in the sentence by watching the opening credits of the show and by observing the show itself.

"Ray of Hope" also includes a number of the writer's **opinions,** or personal views, about the show. Here is a part of a sentence from the second paragraph of the review that provides a key opinion:

> In fact, *Raymond* may now be the best sitcom on the air. . . .

This is a personal view that the writer has about the program, and it is debatable. If you were to watch *Everybody Loves Raymond*, you might not agree that it "may now be the best sitcom on the air."

Here is a good rule of thumb that can often help you to distinguish facts from opinions: Any statement, like the example above, that contains words like *best, worst, funniest,* and *saddest* is probably a statement of opinion, not a statement of fact. The chart on the next page lists more of the common signal words and phrases that are often found in opinion statements.

| Opinion Signal Words and Phrases |
|---|

- ugly/beautiful
- funny/boring
- love/hate
- happy/sad

- good/bad
- best/worst
- like/dislike
- terrible/great

- it is likely that
- in my opinion
- it is possible
- in my view

Be warned: Some writers will try to make their opinions sound more authoritative by presenting them as if they were facts.

**Example:**
Everyone knows that today's TV sitcoms are much less entertaining than sitcoms of past years.

The writer of this sentence used the phrase "everyone knows" to make it seem that the statement is not debatable—to make it look like a fact. However, no writer can reasonably claim to speak for everyone, so the statement is clearly *not* a fact. It remains a debatable opinion, despite the writer's attempt to disguise it.

Being able to tell the difference between facts and opinions is a vital reading skill. Without the skill, you run the risk of being persuaded too easily by weak reasoning or by opinions disguised as facts. With the skill, you become a discerning reader, able to see right into a writer's line of thought and recognize it for what it is.

### THINKING IT THROUGH — Identifying Facts and Opinions

Read the examples and the following steps to determine whether a statement is a fact or an opinion.

**Examples:**

**A.** If you like comedy, you will love *Fishing with John,* one of the funniest shows on television.

**B.** According to a study conducted by the American Academy of Pediatrics, by age eighteen the average American teenager will have spent more time watching television than in the classroom.

▶ STEP 1 **First, ask yourself, "Can this statement be proven true?"**
The answer for statement **A** is *no,* because it is possible that a person who loves comedy might not like *Fishing with John*—and many people may feel that the show is not funny at all. The answer for statement **B,** however, is *yes.*

▶ **STEP 2** **If your answer in step 1 is *yes*, the statement is probably a fact; consider sources where you might confirm it.** You could put statement **B** to the test by consulting a copy of the document in which the American Academy of Pediatrics reported the results of its study. Keep in mind, however, that most readers commonly accept the accuracy of factual statements that appear in sources they generally consider to be reliable—like established newspapers and magazines that have a history of accurately reporting facts.

▶ **STEP 3** **If the answer in step 1 is *no*, the statement is probably an opinion. One way to confirm this conclusion is to look for *opinion signal words* in the statement.** Statement **A** contains a strong opinion signal word: *funniest.* A statement containing this word will probably not be provable. For example, if you asked a group of your friends what the funniest show on television is, you would probably get several different answers.

**YOUR TURN 2** **Identifying Facts and Opinions**

To practice identifying facts and opinions, look back at "Ray of Hope" and follow the steps below. Write your answers on your own paper.

■ Identify two statements of fact and two statements of opinion.

■ Label each statement with either the word *fact* or the word *opinion.*

■ For a fact, tell how the fact could be proven or confirmed.

■ For an opinion, tell how you determined that the statement is an opinion. List any signal words the statement contains.

# Evaluation Criteria

**READING FOCUS**

**Backing Up Opinions**   Readers of "Ray of Hope" would not find the article very persuasive if the writer had not backed up his opinions about *Everybody Loves Raymond* with some kind of support. Critical readers do not simply accept what critics say. Instead, readers look to see whether the critics support their opinions by explaining how well their subjects measure up to certain standards, or **criteria.** Just as you must meet standards to qualify for your school's volleyball team or to receive an A in a course, a television program should measure up to certain standards to receive a good review from an able critic.

How do readers know whether critics are using commonly accepted criteria in evaluating a show? First, they have to look at the elements of the show on which the critics base their opinions. The elements critics consider will vary from one type of show to another. However, listed below are some common elements of sitcoms. If reviewers do not base their opinions on these elements, readers should have serious doubts about the quality of the reviews.

- **plot:** the sitcom's "story," including the conflicts and problems the characters experience
- **setting:** the location where the story unfolds
- **characters:** the fictional people in the sitcom
- **acting:** the portrayal of the characters by real people
- **writing:** the script (which includes **dialogue**) that the actors follow
- **theme:** the sitcom's "message"

"Okay," you say, "so a sitcom has these elements. How do critics decide what makes a particular plot or character good or bad?" One way they decide is to think back on good sitcoms of the past, and ask themselves what qualities of plot, character, acting, writing, and theme these shows had. The qualities they identify then become the criteria by which they evaluate current sitcoms.

As a critical reader, you must be aware that not every critic uses exactly the same set of criteria. However, there are common criteria that most of them use. The following checklist shows some of the common criteria that you should look for when you read a review of a sitcom.

| Sitcom Evaluation Checklist | |
| --- | --- |
| **Elements** | **Criteria** |
| **Plot** | <ul><li>keeps the viewer's interest</li><li>presents entertaining problems or conflicts for the characters to resolve</li></ul> |
| **Setting** | <ul><li>remains the same from week to week</li><li>represents a generalized geographic location</li></ul> |
| **Characters** | <ul><li>develop and grow over time</li><li>are entertaining people with whom the viewer can sympathize and identify</li><li>have interesting points of view</li><li>play off each other well</li></ul> |
| **Acting** | <ul><li>makes the characters believable and fun to watch</li></ul> |

| Writing | • creates humorous interactions between characters |
| | • provides natural-sounding dialogue that is funny and appropriate for the characters and plot |
| Theme | • is a message which the audience can recognize—one with which they can easily identify |

A reviewer will inform the reader about the evaluation criteria he or she uses to judge a show by the elements discussed in the review. The writer of "Ray of Hope," for example, makes (in the next-to-last paragraph) this statement about the actor who plays Ray's brother: "As Ray's eternally unlucky sibling, he has developed a wonderful chemistry with Romano." This remark tells the careful reader that one of the writer's criteria is that characters should have a "chemistry" with each other—that is, they should play off each other well.

## YOUR TURN 3 Recognizing Evaluation Criteria

Working with a partner, find five statements that reveal something about the criteria the writer of "Ray of Hope" uses to judge *Everybody Loves Raymond*. Refer to the chart above as often as necessary. Copy each statement onto your paper. Then, explain what each statement reveals about the criteria the writer uses to evaluate the program. Be prepared to share your results with the class.

# Neologisms

Changes occur so quickly in today's world that language has to change quickly, too. Writers and readers of all kinds of critical reviews—of movies, books, music, automobiles—have to keep up not only with innovations in their subject areas, but also with the new words that come into our language to describe or identify these innovations. These words are called **neologisms** (from *neo–*, meaning "new," and *logo*, meaning "word").

The four most common methods of creating neologisms are explained below.

- **Combining**   Some neologisms are created by putting two existing words together to create a new compound. For example, *free* and *way* were once combined to make *freeway*, a highway free of cross traffic and free of charge, too. A more recent example is *road rage*, a term created to refer to a driver's anger toward other drivers which can result in aggressive driving habits and sometimes violence.

- **Shortening**   Sometimes neologisms are created when an existing word is shortened. At one time, the word *phone* was a neologism created by simply shortening *telephone*. More recently, *nuke*, a shortened and slightly changed version of *nuclear*, was coined as a verb to describe what a person does to food by putting it into a microwave (a relatively new word created by combining the prefix *micro* and *wave*) oven.

- **Blending**   This method of creating new words consists of shortening and combining two existing words. *Emoticon*, for example, is a blend of *emotion* and *icon* that signifies the human expressions—such as :) —created with punctuation marks that often appear in e-mail (another blend). *Sitcom* is a blend created from *situation comedy*, a term describing a type of television program.

- **Shifting**   Sometimes a neologism is created by simply shifting a word's usage or meaning. At some point in the past, for example, the word *host*, a noun meaning "a person who entertains guests," was shifted so that it could also be used as a verb meaning "to entertain guests." A more recent neologism created by shifting is *chill*, a noun used as a verb meaning "to calm down or relax."

**YOUR TURN 4** **Creating Neologisms**

Working in groups of three or four, create at least five neologisms, using three of the methods explained above. To generate ideas, think about new technological advances, new fast foods, new courses in your high school curriculum, or new ideas, inventions, attitudes, or practices in any area.

## Identifying Facts and Opinions

Telling the difference between fact and opinion is important for more than reading reviews. Standardized reading tests often check your ability to distinguish facts from opinions. Here is a reading passage and a fact/opinion test question about it. A plan for answering the question follows in Thinking It Through.

Inside the Florida Museum of Natural History, an International Shark Attack File keeps track of how many sharks attack humans each year. According to the records in the file, an average of fifty to seventy-five shark attacks occur each year worldwide, with five to ten resulting in death. Statistically, this means that you are less likely to be killed by a shark than to die from a snakebite or a lightning strike.

Studies have proven that on those rare occasions when sharks *do* attack humans, they do so because they mistake the people for seals or other prey. To minimize the risk of attack, scientists advise swimmers to avoid excessive splashing, shiny jewelry, and bright-colored swimsuits, all of which make humans look like prey. Despite the rarity of attacks, sharks are undoubtedly the most terrifying creatures of the sea.

The author of the passage states an opinion when he says that

A. five to ten shark attacks result in death each year

B. sharks sometimes mistake people for prey

C. sharks are the most terrifying sea creatures

D. swimmers should avoid shiny jewelry

### THINKING IT THROUGH · Answering Fact-and-Opinion Questions

Use the following steps to answer a fact-and-opinion question like the one above.

▶ **STEP 1** Consider all the answer choices before marking your answer sheet.

▶ **STEP 2** Go through each answer choice, asking if the answer could be proven. Those that can be proven are facts. **A, B,** and **D** are facts supported by evidence presented in the passage.

▶ **STEP 3** The answers that are left are probably opinions. Look for opinion signal words that might help to confirm that they are opinions. **C** looks like an opinion. Not everyone would agree with the statement.

▶ **STEP 4** Be on the lookout for opinions disguised as facts. **C** is the correct answer. It is an opinion even though the word <u>undoubtedly</u> makes it sound like a fact.

# Writing a Critical Review of a TV Sitcom

**WHAT'S AHEAD?**

**In this workshop, you will write a critical review of a television sitcom. You will also learn how to**

- **analyze the audience for your critical review**
- **identify and use evaluation criteria**
- **evaluate support**
- **subordinate ideas to create complex sentences**
- **correct run-on sentences**

Imagine that your English class has been assigned a new project—to produce a magazine that reviews popular entertainment. You are given the specific task of writing a **critical review** of a current television program—a situation comedy.

You have no problem with your assigned topic. In fact, having watched a lot of **sitcoms,** you think of yourself as something of an expert on them. You could tell anyone who asks that sitcoms are thirty minutes long, that they feature the same characters in every episode, that these characters face and somehow solve new problems every week, and that the whole point is to make you laugh. You know all of these things about sitcoms, but you need to know more about critical reviews.

To get started, here is what you need to know: a **critical review** is a combination of analysis, evaluation, and persuasion. As a critical reviewer of a sitcom, you will analyze certain elements and evaluate how effectively the sitcom uses them. The purpose of the critical review you write in this Writing Workshop will be to evaluate the show, recommend or not recommend that people watch it, and then convince people to follow your recommendation.

# Prewriting

## Choose a Sitcom to Review

**Strong Opinions, Strong Reviews**   When you begin to look for a sitcom to review, keep this in mind: The stronger your opinion of the sitcom, the stronger the review you will be able to write. Here are some suggestions for finding the right sitcom for you.

- **Scan local TV listings** in a newspaper or magazine, or do a World Wide Web search (keywords: *television schedule*) to access listings. Scan the listings, noting titles that look interesting.

- **Read the entertainment or television section** of your newspaper to see which sitcoms seem to have caught the public's attention.

- **Watch one sitcom** recommended by a friend your age and another recommended by an adult, and choose the one that you prefer.

- **Think about reviewing one of your own favorites**—one on which you are an expert.

Make a list of three or four sitcoms, and then choose the sitcom that you would like to review. Unless you choose a sitcom with which you are already familiar, be prepared to watch a few episodes to become familiar with the program.

**TIP** Be sure to choose a show whose subject matter can be freely discussed in your classroom.

## Consider Your Purpose, Audience, Tone, and Voice

**Different Strokes For . . .** The **purpose** of any review of a television program is to persuade the audience for whom the review was written that the show is or is not worth watching. The **audiences** for reviews of television shows vary. Some reviews, for example, are written to tell parents how suitable a particular show is for children of various ages. Most reviews, however, are written for a general audience—the readers of newspapers or magazines, for example.

The **tone** of a review is the writer's attitude toward the subject of the review and the intended audience. Your **voice** is the personality you adopt to express the tone. For example, the tone you choose for an audience of peers may be more informal or friendly. (However, it should not be so casual that you lose the authority of your voice.) If, on the other hand, your audience consists of well-educated adults, your tone should be thoughtful and mature.

**TIP** As you consider the audience for your review, keep in mind whether or not those people will all have access to the show you select. For example, some shows can be watched only by viewers with cable television or satellite dishes.

**THINKING IT THROUGH**

### Considering Your Audience, Tone, and Voice

To analyze your audience and tone, write answers to each of the following questions.

▶ **STEP 1 Where do you plan to publish your review?** The answer to this question tells you who your readers or audience will be. It might be that you plan to publish your essay in class, or in the school magazine or newspaper, or in an online magazine for teens. In each of these cases, your readers will be your peers. If, on the other hand, you plan to publish your review in the local newspaper, your audience will include adults with a wide variety of interests and levels of education.

▶ **STEP 2 How much will your intended audience know about the sitcom you are reviewing?** This will determine how much background information your audience will need. If the show you choose to review is wildly popular with teenagers and you are writing to an audience of teenagers, you will need to provide little background. If, on the other hand, you are reviewing that show for an audience of adults, you will need to include a lot of background. The reverse will be true if you choose to review a show that is popular among adults.

▶ **STEP 3 What tone is appropriate for your review?** If your audience is composed of peers, you can use a more informal word choice and sentence structure to create a breezy, chatty tone—as if you were speaking to friends. For an audience of adults, you will want to write in a more sophisticated **style,** choosing words and sentence structure to create a mature and thoughtful tone. Remember, you want your readers to agree with you. If readers are turned off by your tone, they might tune out your review.

## Understand Evaluation Criteria

KEY CONCEPT

**The Critic's Criteria**   Your critical review will give your readers your opinion of a sitcom as a whole. **That opinion, however, is not worth much unless it is based on criteria: standards for evaluating the effectiveness of the individual elements of the sitcom.** For example, the author of the Writer's Model on page 303 bases her high opinion of a sitcom on criteria that address **plot, characters,** and **acting.** After reviewing the sitcom, she concludes that the plot is original, the main character as played by the lead actor is hilarious, and the supporting cast is excellent.

The chart on page 297 lists and defines the five important elements of sitcoms and some of the basic criteria used to evaluate them. The sitcom elements and evaluation criteria in the chart are not arranged by order of importance because the importance of each element is subjective, or based on personal preference. As you study the chart, think about how important the individual elements are for you.

> **TIP**   Critical reviewers rarely discuss all of the sitcom elements in a single review. They might focus on two or three elements important for a particular show. For example, some reviewers put more emphasis on character than on plot. Others are more interested in the quality of the acting than in anything else.

| Sitcom Element | Common Evaluation Criteria |
|---|---|
| **Plot:** a series of events that occurs as the result of conflicts between and within characters | The plot should be interesting, original, and funny. It should provide believable conflicts that the characters resolve realistically. Conflicts and problems should be creative and entertaining. Plot events may not match the predictions that you make, but they should follow logically from the situation. |
| **Setting:** the location where the story unfolds | The setting should be recognizable from week to week. It should give the impression of a general location, such as a newsroom, office building, home, or apartment. |
| **Characters:** the fictional people in the show who perform the actions and deliver the dialogue | The characters should be funny, realistic, and sympathetic. They should learn and grow as a result of their experiences. A show's characters should play off each other well. |
| **Acting:** the quality of the performances of the actors who play the characters | The acting should be consistent, believable, appealing, and fun to watch. |
| **Writing:** the script the actors follow in performing their actions and delivering their dialogue | The writing should provide funny and believable scenes. Dialogue should sound natural and fit the character. |
| **Theme:** the underlying message or messages communicated by an episode of a sitcom | The sitcom should develop themes which are relevant to the lives of viewers. |

## Review Your Sitcom

**Attention Focused, Pencil Poised**  Before you can write a critical review, you must actually watch your sitcom and evaluate it. If you have chosen to review a show that you don't already watch regularly, you may need to view a few episodes to get a good idea how the program handles the important sitcom elements. Reviewers often watch several weeks' worth of episodes before writing their reviews, although the examples they give to illustrate their ideas may come from a single episode.

Professional reviewers watch and rewatch the shows they review until they develop their opinions and the reasons for their opinions. You must do the same thing. It helps to use a log like the one on the next page, which shows how one writer reviewed a sitcom called *One Cool Million*. The show follows the adventures of a high school student as he tries to do his part-time job—deliver a million dollars from an anonymous benefactor to a different person every week. As she watched the program, this writer took notes by responding (in the right-hand column) to the questions listed in the middle column.

**TIP**  Another way to generate ideas about your choice of sitcom is to meet and discuss the show with other students who have also chosen this program. Just remember that in informal discussions like this one, you still have responsibilities as a speaker and a listener. For more on **group discussions,** see page 853 in the Quick Reference Handbook.

| Elements of a Sitcom | Questions Based on Evaluation Criteria | Reviewer Responses |
|---|---|---|
| Plot | Does the plot hold your attention? Is it entertaining? Is it original? Are conflicts believable? | plot—captivating, original, and funny; real-life conflicts lead to hilarious situations |
| Characters | Are the characters realistic? Funny? Sympathetic? Do they learn and change? Do they play off each other well? | lead and supporting characters realistic, funny, likable people |
| Acting | Are the actors believable and consistent? Are they fun to watch? | Lopez, Shoemaker, Crawford, Johnson—always very good |
| Writing | Are the scenes funny and believable? Is dialogue natural? | scenes are funny but sometimes hard to believe; natural dialogue |
| Theme | Are the themes relevant to viewers? | themes relevant; viewers easily identify |

## Critic's Checklist

Here is a list of supplies you will need to review the sitcom you have chosen.

- a VCR and a television set
- a videotaped copy of one or more episodes of your show
- pens, pencils, your copy of the reviewing log, and notebook paper
- a quiet place with sufficient light to watch and take notes

**YOUR TURN 5 Reviewing Your Sitcom**

Review and complete all the prewriting steps covered so far.
- Choose a sitcom to review.
- Consider your purpose, audience, tone, and voice.
- Use a Reviewing Log like the one above to record your evaluation of each of the sitcom elements.

# Identify Elements and Write Your Thesis

**TIP** Your thesis statement may be revised, if necessary, as you develop your essay.

Once you have reviewed the sitcom, you will have formed an initial opinion about whether or not you believe that the show is worth watching. Next, determine which elements most influenced your opinion. These will be the elements you include in your **thesis statement.** Your thesis statement includes your overall opinion of the sitcom and the reasons why the elements you have chosen do or do not measure up to the evaluation criteria. Take a look at the thesis statement from the review of *One Cool Million.*

> This show stands out from the pack for three reasons: a winning character played by a consistently hilarious Lopez, a captivating and original storyline, and an excellent supporting cast.

The first part of the sentence delivers the positive opinion of the show, and the second part states three reasons for the positive opinion.

## Gather Support

**Giving Weight to Opinions**   Writing a good review involves more than just stating your opinion. **If you want readers to accept your opinion, you must support it by telling them the reasons for your opinion.** Then, you must support your reasons with observations that explain how well or how poorly the elements you have chosen measure up to their evaluation criteria. Take a look at the notes the writer of the review of *One Cool Million* wrote to support her thesis statement.

**KEY CONCEPT**

### SUPPORT CHART

| Element | Reasons | Support |
|---|---|---|
| Main character and actor | good-natured character as played by Lopez | Lopez's gift for comedy as Hooper, his gangly frame and elastic face |
| Plot | captivating, original, funny; conflicts lead to hilarious situations | Hooper's job; mysterious boss; attitude of recipients of money; obstacles put in Hooper's way |
| Supporting characters and actors | excellent supporting cast | Shoemaker as sweet and unsuspecting mother; Johnson as loud, bossy best friend; Crawford as voice of Hooper's boss |

## Evaluating Support

All critical reviews are based on the reviewer's opinion of how well the thing being reviewed measures up to a set of standards. The most effective reviews are those that back up opinions with convincing support.

You say to a friend, "I'm thinking of buying a new computer."

"Don't even think of buying Brand X," your friend says. "They're terrible."

"Why do you think so?" you ask.

If your friend can give you no logical reason, you are not very likely to take his advice. If, on the other hand, your friend says, "I read a survey that said over half of Brand X owners reported serious problems with their computers," you will probably pay attention, because your friend has support for his opinion. The support you use in your critical review should consist of a reason based on **valid criteria** and backed up by **specific details** and **examples.** Look at the following examples of weak support and strong support.

**Weak support:**
*Whistling in the Graveyard* is great. It is much better than the other sitcoms.

In this example, the reviewer's opinion is supported only by a reason that is another opinion. The writer fails to mention any valid criteria and provides no details or examples to back up the idea that the show is better than other sitcoms.

**Strong support:**
*Chasing Cars* is a fascinating show. Its unique storyline features a teenager whose secret hobby is hanging out with a couple of car-chasing dogs.

In this example, the opinion is followed by a reason that is based on a valid criterion (plot, or storyline) and is backed by specific details. While other people might disagree with the reviewer's opinion of the show, no one can say that the opinion is not well supported.

**PRACTICE**

On your own paper, write your own evaluation of the support in each of the following items. Write *strong* if the item contains strong support, and *weak* if it contains weak support. Be prepared to explain your evaluations.

1. That is the worst car I have ever driven. It is so bad that I cringe every time I have to drive it anywhere.

2. Juanita's is a truly fine restaurant. It has great food, wonderful service, and a friendly atmosphere.

3. At the moment, the Rocky Rangers are the best team in the league. They lead in every important statistical category.

4. I do not understand why you recommended that book. The plot consists of one coincidence after another and the characters are colorless stereotypes.

5. The only good thing about the movie is the acting because everything else is terrible.

# Organize Your Paper

**Bring Forth Order**   Now you need to decide how you will organize your review. Some writers put the most important reason for their overall opinion first and the least important reason last. Take a look at the following map the reviewer of *One Cool Million* created. She started with the most important (1st) reason for her opinion, the main character and the performance of the actor playing him. Then, her second and third most important reasons followed.

**TIP**   To make your paper coherent, organize your ideas in a logical way. Provide support for each idea. (For more on **logical progression** of ideas, see page 361.)

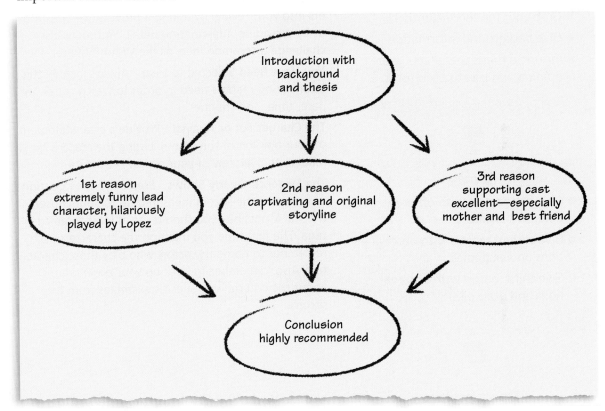

**YOUR TURN 6   Getting Ready to Write**

Before moving on to the writing stage, be sure you have

- identified the elements that shaped your opinion
- written a thesis that states your opinion and the basic reasons for it
- gathered support for your reasons
- planned the organization of your ideas

# Writing

## Critical Review of a Sitcom

| Framework | Directions and Explanations |

### Introduction

- Grab your readers' attention.
- Give background information.
- Include a thesis that states your opinion and lists reasons for it.

**Ladies and Gentlemen of the Jury** Draw your readers into your review by asking a provocative question or by providing a fascinating detail. You could also challenge a common idea, as the Writer's Model does.

**You Have Been Selected to Hear** Always include the information readers need in order to watch the show: date, time, and channel.

**The Charges For or Against** Provide a clear statement of your opinion of the sitcom. Listing the reasons gives readers an overview of your review's structure.

### Body

- Give first reason with observations and examples.
- Give second reason with observations and examples.
- Give third reason with observations and examples.

**The Evidence Clearly Shows** Present your evaluation of how well the sitcom measured up to your chosen criteria. If possible, you should use at least three criteria. The first time you mention the characters, remember to name the actors who play those characters. Also, remember to back up your observations about the criteria with specific examples from the sitcom.

### Conclusion

- Restate your opinion in the form of a recommendation.
- Bring review to a close.

**And the Verdict Is** As you bring your review to a close, restate your thesis—your overall opinion of the show—in the form of a recommendation that your audience watch, or not watch, the sitcom.

**YOUR TURN 7 Writing A First Draft**

Using the framework above and the Writer's Model on the next page as guides, write the first draft of your review.

# A Writer's Model

The following essay closely follows the framework on the previous page. Reviewers offer numerous details to back up their evaluation of a program. As you read this model, notice how many specifics the writer includes in order to convince you.

### *One Cool Million* Is Rich with Laughter

You think it would be easy to give away a million dollars, right? Well, that is what sixteen-year-old Harvey Hooper thought—until he landed the job of giving away a million a week on behalf of a mysterious and anonymous benefactor. As the focus of *One Cool Million* (Fridays at 9 P.M., ET, CBZ-TV), the latest addition to the highly successful "Fridaze" teen comedy lineup, Hooper (Jake Lopez) fills the screen with an active, loose comic energy. This show stands out from the pack for three reasons: a winning character played by a consistently hilarious Lopez, a captivating and original storyline, and an excellent supporting cast.

Those who know Lopez only from his dramatic roles will be utterly surprised by his gift for comedy. His portrayal of Harvey Hooper as a grinning, goofy, good-natured guy is a study in the art of physical comedy. Lopez uses his gangly six-foot frame and rubbery, expressive face to great advantage, often making the teenager he plays seem even younger and more awkward than his age would suggest.

Along with the winning character of Lopez, the unique storyline of *One Cool Million* provides lots of opportunities for laughs. Although much of the action takes place at a fictional high school, the main concern of many of the students, including Hooper, is their minimum-wage, part-time jobs after school. Hooper's job earns him quite a bit more than minimum wage, because his duties are much more challenging. Each week, Hooper is assigned to deliver the sum of one million dollars to a deserving, unsuspecting, and usually suspicious recipient. Hooper must navigate a series of obstacles put in his way by the show's talented writers. The lucky beneficiary's name and location, as well as the money, are supplied by Hooper's boss, a mysterious (and apparently very charitable) oil baroness.

*(continued)*

**INTRODUCTION**
Attention-grabbing opening

Background information

Thesis statement

**BODY**
First reason with support based on observations and examples

Second reason with support based on observations and examples

(continued)

**Third reason with support based on observations and examples**

Lopez is surrounded by an excellent supporting cast. The two standouts are Sarabeth Shoemaker as his sweetly unsuspecting mother (she still gives him a ten-dollar weekly allowance) and Chris Johnson as his loud, bossy best friend, Tony (the only person who knows what Hooper's job really entails). The presence of '80s film great Sybil Crawford might seem a bit out of place on a show about teenagers, but it works, adding another layer of interest to the proceedings. Though her famous face is never revealed (she is heard only through a speakerphone), her presence as Hooper's boss, "Mrs. B," is felt throughout each episode as she interrupts—predictably—at the most inopportune time. Her distinctive greeting, booming through the speaker phone, produces howls of laughter each time the audience hears her voice because she sets in motion Hooper's attempts to give away the money.

**CONCLUSION**

**Restatement of most of thesis as a recommendation**

Despite a few missteps (chalk them up to first-season jitters), *One Cool Million* is a hilarious romp through high school life in the year 2001, with enough uncommon twists to make it stand out from the pack. Crackling with comic dialogue, fast-paced scenes, and well-defined characters, *One Cool Million* is as generous with its laughs as Harvey Hooper's boss is with her dollars.

# A Student's Model

The following excerpt is from a review by Amar Patel of Troy High School in Fullerton, California.

## The Simpsons: A Real Winner

"Ay Caramba!" Everywhere you turn there are signs of "The Simpsons Fever," which has infected viewers throughout the United States. It is no wonder that The Simpsons, with its huge following and its creative scripts, was named "The Television Show of the [Twentieth] Century." The creation of executive producers James L. Brooks and Matt Groening, The Simpsons is a sitcom about the daily lives of Springfield's most outrageous and hilarious family. Filled with dozens of colorful characters and side-splitting comedic situations, it is one of the most innovative shows on television.

The show's great success is largely due to the charming and interesting identities given to its characters. The show is focused on the characters Bart, Homer, Lisa, Marge, and Maggie. The perennial favorite is Bart, the child who loves mischievous pranks. Bart is the clever, cunning youth who does everything the viewers would like to do, but cannot. Homer, Bart's father, is the town simpleton who always makes the stupid mistakes that are accompanied by his standard phrase of dismay, "DOOOOHHH!!!!" He may be a lazy couch-potato, but he is, nevertheless, a strong-willed, determined man, who is (believe it or not) good at heart. Marge is the cautious, protective parental figure in the show, the wife of Homer, and mother to his children. She is, in fact, the perfect mother: She loves both her children and husband. Although Marge may try to quell the adventure, hers is always the calm voice of reason. Lisa is the odd-one-out in the family, an extremely intelligent child, one who thinks independently and would persuade others to do the same. Despite their differences, though, the Simpsons are held together by love, a hallmark of this remarkable family. Perhaps it is this quality—not their faults—that makes them such a delightful family to watch. . . .

**Attention-getting opener**

**Background information**

**Thesis statement**

**First reason: colorful characters**

**Support based on examples and observations**

# Revising

## Evaluate and Revise Your Draft

**Refining Your Review**   Work collaboratively to make sure that your review is as good as it can be. You need to read your paper closely at least twice—once for the content and organization of your review, and a second time for style.

➤ First Reading: **Content and Organization**   If you have a hard time evaluating and revising your own writing, you will find the following chart very handy. The left column gives you some evaluation questions to ask about your review, the middle column gives tips on how to answer the questions, and the right column suggests ways to make changes.

| Critical Review: Content and Organization Guidelines for Peer and Self-Evaluation | | |
|---|---|---|
| **Evaluation Questions** | ▶ **Tips** | ▶ **Revision Techniques** |
| ❶ Does the introduction contain attention-grabbing sentences? | ▶ **Underline** any sentences in the introduction that draw attention. If you cannot underline one, revise. | ▶ **Add** a question or statement that will intrigue or challenge readers. |
| ❷ Does the introduction contain a sentence that states an opinion of the show with a brief list of reasons for that opinion? | ▶ **Highlight** the sentence that states the writer's opinion and reasons. | ▶ **Add** a sentence that clearly expresses the writer's opinion and lists the reasons for it. **Elaborate** on existing sentences. |
| ❸ Does each body paragraph present a reason based on criteria for evaluating sitcoms? | ▶ **Circle** key words (*plot, characters, dialogue*) in each paragraph that signal a reason based on criteria. | ▶ **Add** sentences that clearly state the reasons for the writer's opinion. |
| ❹ Does each body paragraph provide support for the evaluation in the form of observations and examples? | ▶ **Bracket** the supporting observations and examples from the sitcom. There should be at least three in each paragraph. | ▶ **Add** sentences containing observations and examples, or **elaborate** on existing sentences by adding observations and examples. |
| ❺ Does the review's organization contribute to its effectiveness? | ▶ **Number** the body paragraphs in the order of their importance as support for the thesis. | ▶ **Rearrange** the paragraphs so that the review begins or ends with the strongest support for the thesis. |
| ❻ Is the opinion restated as a recommendation in the conclusion? | **Put a checkmark** next to any sentence in the conclusion that restates the reviewer's opinion in the form of a recommendation. | **Add** a sentence that clearly and forcefully reinforces the reviewer's opinion of the sitcom and makes a recommendation. |

**ONE WRITER'S REVISIONS**   Take a look at how the author of the Writer's Model on page 303 used the content and organization guidelines to evaluate and improve the first body paragraph of her critical review. Then, answer the questions following the paragraph.

> Those who know Lopez only from his dramatic roles will be
> utterly surprised by his gift for comedy. His portrayal of Harvey
> *as a grinning, goofy, good-natured guy*
> Hooper is a study in the art of physical comedy. Lopez uses his gangly   add
>                   *and rubbery, expressive face*
> six-foot frame to great advantage, often making the teenager he plays   elaborate
> seem even younger and more awkward than his age would suggest.

## Analyzing the Revision Process

1. What does the writer achieve by inserting details into the second sentence?
2. What does the writer's elaboration of the third sentence contribute to your image of Lopez?

**YOUR TURN 8   Focusing on Content and Organization**

Evaluate and revise your review using the content and organization guidelines on the previous page.

**PEER REVIEW**

Choose a partner and read each other's review. Answer these questions and attach your remarks to your partner's review.

1. What did you find most convincing about the writer's opinion of the sitcom?
2. Would you watch the sitcom on the basis of this review? Explain.

**Second Reading: Style**   Your first reading dealt with content and organization. Now, you need to look at the way you express yourself. Your readers will not consider your opinion very carefully if they have to struggle through repetitive sounding sentences. To write sentences that flow smoothly, use the following sentence-style guidelines.

## Style Guidelines

| Evaluation Question | ▶ Tip | ▶ Revision Technique |
|---|---|---|
| **Does the review contain several simple sentences in a row?** | ▶ **Highlight** your sentences with alternating colors. If you see a pattern of simple sentences, revise. | ▶ Use adverb clauses to **combine** simple sentences that express closely related ideas. |

## Focus on Sentences

# Combining Sentences Using Adverb Clauses

Sentence patterns that are used over and over can make even an enthusiastic reader tune you out. One way you can make sure that your writing does not sound monotonous is to vary sentence structure.

A good way to vary structure is to use adverb clauses to combine simple sentences that are related in meaning. Adverb clauses begin with subordinating conjunctions, such as *after, although, as if, because, before, if, since, so that, than, unless, until, when, where, while.* You need to choose these conjunctions carefully, though, because besides joining sentences, they also indicate the relationship between the ideas in the adverb clause and the independent clause.

**Example 1: Two simple sentences**
1. You should see the new television show about photography.
2. The new television show about photography presents some incredible shots of the ocean.

**Example 2: One complex sentence with an adverb clause**
You should see the new television show about photography <u>because it presents some incredible shots of the ocean.</u>

For more on adverb clauses, see pages 337 and 476.

**ONE WRITER'S REVISIONS**   Here is how the writer of the model review on page 303 used the guidelines to combine simple sentences that express closely related ideas into complex sentences which make the relationships between ideas crystal clear.

**BEFORE REVISION**

all simple sentences

Much of the action takes place at a fictional high school. The main concern of many of the students, including Hooper, is their minimum-wage, part-time jobs after school. Hooper's job earns him quite a bit more than minimum wage. His duties are much more challenging.

**AFTER REVISION**

Although much of the action takes place at a fictional high school, the main concern of many of the students, including Hooper, is their minimum-wage, part-time jobs after school. Hooper's job earns him quite a bit more than minimum wage, because his duties are much more challenging.

*Combines using adverb clause*

*Combines using adverb clause*

## Analyzing the Revision Process

1. What relationship between the ideas in the adverb clause and the main clause is shown by the conjunction *although*?

2. Why do you think the writer chose *because* to combine the third and fourth sentences?

---

**YOUR TURN 9** **Focusing on Adverb Clauses**

Using the style guidelines, evaluate the style of the sentences in your review. Then, vary the structure of your sentences by using adverb clauses to combine closely related simple sentences into longer complex sentences.

---

## Designing Your Writing

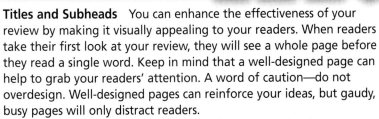

**Titles and Subheads** You can enhance the effectiveness of your review by making it visually appealing to your readers. When readers take their first look at your review, they will see a whole page before they read a single word. Keep in mind that a well-designed page can help to grab your readers' attention. A word of caution—do not overdesign. Well-designed pages can reinforce your ideas, but gaudy, busy pages will only distract readers.

One way to entice readers into reading your review is to create an attention-getting title and then to make it stand out from the text. The title of a critical review should hint at the review's contents and arouse the reader's curiosity. The title of the Writer's Model, "*One Cool Million* Is Rich with Laughter," is a good example. It makes the title of the sit-com the subject of a sentence that delivers—in brief—the writer's opinion of the show. In addition, the word *rich* in the title is a play on words: Every week *One Cool Million* makes a character rich with a gift of one million dollars. A title is always centered on the page, but the writer of the review of *One Cool Million* made her title stand out even more by making the print slightly larger than the print of the text.

In addition, consider providing **subheadings**—attention-getting phrases to hint at the main idea of the paragraph—for each of your main body paragraphs. Subheadings should be aligned with the left margin. You can also make the subheadings darker than the text.

Here is what part of the Writer's Model might have looked like had the writer chosen to use subheads. The subheadings here are like small signposts that help guide the reader through the review.

### A Gift for Comedy

Those who know Lopez only from his dramatic roles will be utterly surprised by his gift for comedy. His portrayal of Harvey Hooper as a grinning, goofy, good-natured guy is a study in the art of physical comedy. Lopez uses his gangly six-foot frame and rubbery, expressive face to great advantage, often making the teenager he plays seem even younger and more awkward than his age would suggest.

### A Fresh Idea

Along with the winning character of Lopez, the unique storyline of *One Cool Million* provides lots of opportunities for laughs. Although much of the action takes place at a fictional high school, the main concern of many of the students, including Hooper, is their minimum-wage, part-time jobs after school. . . .

**COMPUTER TIP**

If you create your essay on a computer, stick to two fonts—one for the text and another for titles and subheadings—and make sure that you select fonts that are easy to read.

If you decide to use larger sizes for titles and subheadings, be sure to make them only *slightly* larger. On a computer, titles should be no more than four points larger than the font size you use for the text, and subheads should be no more than two points larger. If, for example, you use 12-point type for the font, use no more than 16-point for your title and 14-point for your subheadings.

Both of these design features—titles and subheads—can be created in a handwritten essay as well as an essay typed into a word-processing program.

**TIP** Make sure to consult your teacher before doing anything that departs from standard formatting for writing assignments in your class.

## Proofread Your Review

**Increase Magnification** Just like professional reviewers, you need to make sure your review is completely error-free. If a serious error like a run-on sentence escapes your eyes, the entire review may be weakened.

**Reference Note**

For **proofreading guidelines,** see page 13.

**Grammar Link**

## Run-On Sentences

**Run-on sentences,** which consist of two or more sentences written as one sentence, can confuse a reader because they provide no markers to show where one idea ends and another begins. One type of run-on sentence, a **comma splice,** occurs when a writer separates two or more independent clauses—clauses that should be punctuated as sentences—with a comma and nothing else.

In television, *genre* means type of program, examples of television genres include drama, situation comedy, and nightly news.

Another type of run-on sentence, called a **fused sentence,** has nothing between two or more independent clauses to separate them.

In television, *genre* means type of program examples of television genres include drama, situation comedy, and nightly news.

To revise run-on sentences:

- Use a period to separate sentences.

  In television, *genre* means type of program. Examples of television genres include drama, situation comedy, and nightly news.

- Separate the clauses with a comma and a coordinating conjunction (*and, but, for, or, nor, so,* or *yet*).

In television, *genre* means type of program, and examples of television genres include drama, situation comedy, and nightly news.

- Separate the clauses with just a semicolon or with a semicolon and a conjunctive adverb (*for example, then, therefore, however,* and *meanwhile*).

In television, *genre* means type of program; for example, television genres include drama, situation comedy, and nightly news.

**PRACTICE**

Correct the following run-on sentences. Use each method described above.

1. Lucinda Perez is the star of *Nuevo Latino,* it is the only show broadcast in both Spanish and English on a major network.

2. The network at first provided a very small budget for *Nuevo Latino,* it is considered one of ZBC-TV's successes.

3. *Nuevo Latino* was first shown in Mexico in June of 2000 then, television stations in California and Texas began picking it up.

4. Ms. Perez has said that the key to her success is an ability to listen this is a skill she developed as a child.

## Publish Your Review

**Reaching Out to a Bigger Audience**   To reach a larger audience with your review, try publishing it in one of the following ways.

- Post your review to an Internet discussion group or mailing list. There are many TV-related groups and lists, including some that are devoted to discussions of specific programs.

- Submit your review to your school newspaper or your community newspaper for publication.

- Mail your review to the show's creators. You can find out who they are by watching the show's credits. You can also check to see if the show has a Web site. If it has one, it probably provides an e-mail address to which you can send your review.

- Publish a review magazine that includes all the reviews from your class.

PORTFOLIO

## Reflect on Your Review

**Reviewing the Reviewing Process**   To make what you learned in this workshop an experience you can build on, write responses to the following questions. (You can set goals as a writer based on your responses to the questions.)

- As you went through all the steps leading to your final draft, did your opinion of the sitcom you were reviewing change? If so, why?

- How did you decide which sitcom elements to discuss in your review?

- What other sitcoms would you include in a collection of reviews? Why?

- Which step in the revision process did you find most helpful? Why?

If you intend to put your review in a portfolio, attach your responses to it.

---

**YOUR TURN 10   Proofreading, Publishing, and Reflecting**

Before you turn your review in to your teacher, be sure you

- proofread it carefully, looking especially for run-on sentences
- consider ways to let others read your review
- reflect on your review by answering questions about the process you went through in writing it

---

# Connections to Life

## Analyzing Your Television Viewing Habits

You are probably used to hearing statements like this one: "Teenagers spend more time watching television than they do studying! It's no wonder that they know more about athletic shoes and chewing gum than they do about math and American history!" Have you ever wondered whether you are one of those teenagers who spend too much time in front of the TV? Keep track of how many hours you spend in front of the television set and what you spend your time watching. You might also ask, *Why am I watching?* and keep track of the many different answers to that question. You might be surprised by your findings.

**Diary of a Teenage TV Viewer**  Before you do anything else, estimate how much time per week you think you spend watching TV. Then, break down this total viewing time into an estimate of the time you think you spend watching different genres of shows. (The word *genre* is a literary term, adapted from French, meaning *type* or *kind.*) Examples of genres in television are **news, documentaries, talk shows, dramas, sitcoms, game shows, soap operas,** and **sports.** Television genres may also be divided into subcategories. For example, the genre of news programs can be divided into national news, local news, and documentaries. Then, subcategories are sometimes referred to as *news genres,* meaning types of news. Later, you can compare your estimates

| My Television Viewing Habits | |
|---|---|
| Day/Date | Mon. 10/5 |
| Time | 7–7:30 |
| Program Name | One Cool Million |
| Channel or Network | 24 |
| Genre (Type) | sitcom |

to the number of hours you end up actually watching.

To analyze your viewing habits, copy the preceding chart and keep it next to your television set. For a week, record the information required by the chart each time you watch all or most of a program. One entry has been made in the chart as an example.

**Totaling the Hours**  Once you have noted what you spent your time watching during the week, you need to tally the results. Only two rows of your chart—time and genre—need to be tallied. Add up all the time you spent watching shows from each genre. If, for example, the only news programming you watched for seven nights was a thirty-minute nightly news program, you would record three hours, thirty minutes for the genre. If you watched six different sitcoms during the week and each show lasted thirty minutes, you would record three hours for the genre. The following chart shows how your result totals might look.

**Sitcoms:** six hours

**News:** three hours, thirty minutes

**Dramas:** five hours

**Documentaries:** one hour

**Game shows:** five hours

**Sports:** four hours, thirty minutes

**Soap operas:** zero hours

**Talk shows:** four hours, thirty minutes

**The "Average" Teenager**   How do you think your own viewing habits compare with your classmates'? Once you have analyzed your personal viewing habits, get together with your classmates to compare notes. To get a class average, add the total viewing time for each genre,

then divide the total by the number of students in your class. Here are the findings of one class:

$$\overset{\text{5.6}}{\underset{\text{in class }30\,|\,168}{\text{students}}}\quad\begin{array}{l}\text{average hours per week}\\\text{watching sitcoms}\\\rule{4cm}{0.4pt}\\\text{total hours of sitcoms}\end{array}$$

Next, add the total viewing time for the week across all genres, then divide by the number of participants in your class to find the average number of *total* hours per week you and your classmates spent watching television. The example class came up with these findings:

$$\overset{\text{28}}{\underset{\text{in class }30\,|\,840}{\text{students}}}\quad\begin{array}{l}\text{average hours per week}\\\text{watching TV}\\\rule{4cm}{0.4pt}\\\text{total hours of all genres}\end{array}$$

**YOUR TURN 11   Reflecting on Your Viewing Habits**

Using your findings, consider your personal viewing habits and the average viewing habits for your class. On your own paper, write answers to the questions in the bulleted list below. Be prepared to share your answers with your class.

- Do you watch more or less TV than your classmates? Are you surprised by your findings?
- Which genres of shows do you like most? Why do you think this is so?
- Which genres of shows are most popular with your classmates? Why do you think these shows are popular with people your age?
- Now that you see how much time you and your peers spend watching television, do you plan to change your viewing habits? Why or why not?

# Analyzing the Nightly Network News

**W**ould it surprise you to learn that the people who produce the nightly news want to entertain you? While the primary purpose of a news program is to inform the viewer, it must also be as entertaining and attention-getting as possible to keep you watching. News programs, like other television programs, depend on ratings. Ratings translate into profits for television networks because ratings are based on the size of a program's audience. The bigger the audience, the more money advertisers are willing to spend to sponsor the program, and television networks are in business to make money.

# WHAT'S AHEAD?

In this section, you will analyze a network news program. You will also learn how to

- identify four techniques used to present the nightly news
- look behind presentation techniques for the importance of a news story

## Presentation Techniques

**Variety Is the Spice of News**   One way news programs keep you interested is to vary the way the news is presented. News programs manipulate the news by using four basic presentation techniques. The following chart describes the presentation techniques, provides examples of each, and explains the potential effects they can have on viewers.

| Presentation Techniques | Examples | Possible Effects |
| --- | --- | --- |
| **Personalizing the News:** concentrating on the people involved in an event rather than on the event itself | A story emphasizes the personality of a single member of a space shuttle crew while giving only brief mention of the shuttle's unique mission. | Viewers may miss out on information necessary for understanding the story. |
| **Dramatizing the News:** making engaging short stories out of news events—producers present the event using the language of drama and storytelling | A reporter says: "Our story begins in this tiny house in a small town." The accompanying video emphasizes the people involved and the events of the "plot." | Producers may omit important information. A viewer might think of a violent event reported on the news and a violent event depicted on a fictional police drama in the same way. |

*(continued)*

| Normalizing the News: reassuring viewers by presenting experts or officials to explain that things are under control and will soon return to normal | When a natural disaster occurs, government officials and experts reassure people that everything possible is being done to lessen the impact of the disaster. | After viewing such normalizing of the news, viewers who are not personally affected by the disaster tend to be left with a distorted view of the serious effects on the victims of the disaster. |
| --- | --- | --- |
| Fragmenting the News: presenting bite-sized pieces of information to viewers without explaining why the information is important | You hear on the nightly news that Congress has been unable to agree on a method of saving the Social Security and Medicare systems from financial ruin. Both systems will run out of money by the end of the year. | Viewers who are not dependent on these services might dismiss the story as unimportant because the impact of Congress's failure to agree is not explained. |

## Being a Critical Viewer

**TIP** Another way programmers keep your interest in a news program is by varying the number of personalities who present the news. Anchorpersons do not simply read the news reports as videotaped footage is shown. Instead, correspondents, commentators, and experts interact with them.

**You Be the Critic**   Viewing the news *critically* does not mean criticizing or finding fault with the news. Instead, it means questioning the news to determine, among other things, whether a news event has been shaped by one of the four techniques listed above. By becoming a critical viewer, you begin to recognize these techniques of manipulating the news and can make better sense of it. In short, the more *you* know about the way networks present news every night, the better you can judge the value of the news.

### YOUR TURN 12   Analyzing the Nightly Network News

Working in groups of four, watch a videotape of a recent nightly network news program. Use a chart like the one below to record the **subject** of each news item, **the length of time** devoted to it, and the **presentation technique** used to present the report. Briefly explain each technique you list. If an item does not conform to any of the four techniques, write *None* in the column. Be prepared to discuss your findings with the rest of the class.

| Subject of Report | Length of Report | Presentation Technique |
| --- | --- | --- |
| In spite of international aid, hunger is still widespread in Somalia. | 2 minutes | Dramatizing the News—Story focuses on people trying to prevent starvation rather than those who are starving |

# Choices

**Choose one of the following activities to complete.**

## ▶ CAREERS

**1. Consumer Reporter** Apply your analytical skills to plan and present an **oral review** of a real-world product. As part of your review, give a **demonstration** of how the product is used in order to point out its positive or negative qualities. Spell out for listeners what criteria you used and who you think should (or should not) buy and use the product.

## ▶ MEDIA AND TECHNOLOGY

**2. The Eyes Have It?** To compare how visual information affects the way we remember and learn, use a VCR to record an important news event reported on a nightly network news program. Use a tape recorder to record a radio news version of the same story. Play the television version for three classmates and the radio tape for three different classmates. Be sure neither group sees or hears the other group's tape. Have the members of each group record as much factual information as they can remember and a description of any memorable visual images or sounds from their news report. Write a **report** of the results and share them with the class.

## ▶ SPEAKING AND LISTENING

**3. A Voice from the Past** Watch a video of a historically significant speech—ask your teacher or librarian for recommendations—and evaluate what makes it memorable. Consider rhetorical devices such as repetition and analogy and other features of the speech's content or delivery. Use your criteria, supported with specific examples from the speech, to write a one- to two-paragraph **analysis.** After summing up your ideas, conclude your analysis by considering what impact you think the speech might have had on listeners at the time.

## ▶ LITERATURE

**4. The Rest of the Story** Rewrite one of your favorite narratives as a **news story** that will be reported on the nightly news over the course of five nights. Divide the plot of the narrative into segments that could be reported in the same short time most lead news stories are given—about three minutes. The last report should reveal the outcome of the story.

PORTFOLIO

# Sentences and Paragraphs

# Writing Complete Sentences

## Sentence Fragments

GO TO: go.hrw.com
KEYWORD: EOLang

A *sentence* is a word group that has a subject and a verb and expresses a complete thought. A *sentence fragment,* a word group that does not have all the basic parts of a complete sentence, does not express a complete thought. It is missing some important information.

Sentence fragments usually occur when you write in a hurry or become a little careless. You may leave out a word, or you may chop off part of a sentence by putting in a period too soon.

To find out whether you have a complete sentence or a sentence fragment, you can use a simple three-part test:

**1.** Does the group of words have a subject?
**2.** Does it have a verb?
**3.** Does it express a complete thought?

If you answer *no* to any of these questions, your word group is a fragment. It is missing at least one basic part.

FRAGMENT   Was the best sharpshooter in the United States. [The subject is missing. Who was the best sharpshooter in the United States?]

SENTENCE   Annie Oakley was the best sharpshooter in the United States.

FRAGMENT   Annie Oakley with Buffalo Bill Cody's Wild West show. [The verb is missing. What did she do with the Wild West show?]

| SENTENCE | Annie Oakley performed with Buffalo Bill Cody's Wild West show. |
|---|---|
| FRAGMENT | As it fell through the air ninety feet away. [This group of words has a subject (*it*) and a verb (*fell*), but it does not express a complete thought. What happened as something fell through the air?] |
| SENTENCE | Annie could shoot a playing card as it fell through the air ninety feet away. |

*Annie Oakley*

**NOTE** By itself, a fragment does not express a complete thought. However, fragments can make sense if they are clearly related to the sentences that come before or after them. These sentences give the fragments meaning because they help the reader fill in the missing parts.

The following passage is from an essay that describes the death and the cutting down of a great white oak on the writer's family homestead. The author's grandfather has carefully cut at the dead tree and is about to aim the final blows. See how the author uses fragments to describe the fall of the great tree.

> Then came the great moment. A few last, quick strokes. A slow, deliberate swaying. The crack of parting fibers. Then a long "swoo-sh!" that rose in pitch as the towering trunk arced downward at increasing speed.
>
> Edwin Way Teale, "The Death of a Tree"

Experienced writers like Teale sometimes use sentence fragments to achieve a certain effect. As a developing writer, however, you need to practice and master writing complete sentences before you begin to experiment with writing fragments.

**Exercise 1** **Identifying Sentence Fragments**

Some of the following items are sentence fragments. To find out which items are fragments and which are complete sentences, apply the three-part test on page 320. If the item is a complete sentence, write *C*. If a subject is missing, write *S*. If a verb is missing, write *V*. If the item has a subject and verb but does not express a complete thought, write *N*.

EXAMPLE    1. After he wrote "A Christmas Memory."

      *1. N*

1. Truman Capote was an American author.
2. Was born in New Orleans in 1924.
3. Grew up in Alabama.
4. Because he hated attending boarding schools.
5. A movie made from *Breakfast at Tiffany's*, probably his most famous novel.
6. When he moved to New York City.
7. Capote's short story "A Christmas Memory" was made into a television movie.
8. His characters lively and eccentric.
9. Is one of his most moving stories.
10. Spent six years researching the nonfiction book that he titled *In Cold Blood*.

┌ TIPS & TRICKS ┐

To find phrase fragments in your writing, read the sentences in your paragraphs from the last to the first. Reading this way helps you to listen for complete thoughts that make sense.

Reference Note

For more on **verbals** (participles, gerunds, and infinitives), see page 449.

# Phrase Fragments

A *phrase* is a group of words that does not have a subject and a verb and that is used as a single part of speech. There are three kinds of phrases that can easily be mistaken for complete sentences: *verbal phrases, appositive phrases,* and *prepositional phrases.*

## Verbal Phrases

*Verbals,* forms of verbs that are used as other parts of speech, sometimes fool us into thinking that a group of words has a verb when it really does not. Some verbals end in *–ing, –d,* or *–ed* and do not have helping verbs (such as *is, were,* or *have*) in front of them. Other verbals have the word *to* in front of the base form (*to go, to play*).

A *verbal phrase* is a phrase that contains a verbal. By itself, a verbal phrase is a fragment because it does not express a complete thought.

FRAGMENT    Learning about the Civil War.
SENTENCE    I enjoyed learning about the Civil War.

FRAGMENT    Gaining glory for itself and for all black soldiers.
SENTENCE    Gaining glory for itself and for all black soldiers, the 54th Massachusetts Regiment led the attack on Fort Wagner.

FRAGMENT    To become good soldiers.
SENTENCE    Black volunteers trained hard to become good soldiers.

FRAGMENT    Inspired by the 54th Massachusetts Regiment.
SENTENCE    Inspired by the 54th Massachusetts Regiment, other black soldiers fought bravely.

## Appositive Phrases

An **appositive** is a word that identifies or explains the noun or pronoun it follows. An **appositive phrase,** a phrase made up of an appositive and its modifiers, is a fragment. It does not contain the basic parts of a sentence.

FRAGMENT    A twenty-five-year-old soldier.

SENTENCE    The 54th Massachusetts Regiment was commanded by Colonel Shaw, a twenty-five-year-old soldier.

## Prepositional Phrases

A **prepositional phrase** is a group of words beginning with a preposition and ending with a noun or pronoun. A prepositional phrase cannot stand alone as a sentence because it does not express a complete thought.

FRAGMENT    With great courage on the battlefield.

SENTENCE    The 54th Massachusetts Regiment acted with great courage on the battlefield.

*The 54th Massachusetts Regiment*

> **NOTE** Usually a phrase needs to stay as close as possible to the word it modifies in a sentence. However, some phrases, such as the infinitive phrase "to become good soldiers," can make sense at the beginning or the end of a sentence.

**Reference Note**

For more on **placing phrases in sentences,** see pages 585 and 587.

### Exercise 2   Revising Phrase Fragments

Use your imagination to create sentences from the following phrases. You can either (1) attach the fragment to a complete sentence, or (2) develop the phrase into a complete sentence by adding a subject, a verb, or both.

EXAMPLE    1.  landing on the planet

　　　　　 1.  *Landing on the planet, the astronauts immediately began to explore.*

　　　　　　　　　　 or

　　　　　　 *The astronauts were landing on the planet.*

1. in a huge spaceship
2. setting foot on the planet
3. to explore the craters

**4.** walking around in a spacesuit

**5.** finding no sign of life

**6.** the astronauts' spaceship

**7.** checking the spaceship for damage

**8.** the planet's moon

**9.** to return to Earth

**10.** on a successful mission

# Subordinate Clause Fragments

A *clause* is a group of words that has a subject and a verb. One kind of clause, an *independent clause,* expresses a complete thought and can stand on its own as a sentence. For example, the group of words *I ate my lunch* is an independent clause. However, another kind of clause, a *subordinate clause,* does not express a complete thought and cannot stand by itself as a sentence.

| | |
|---|---|
| FRAGMENT | When Paris carried off the beautiful Helen of Troy. [What happened when Paris carried off Helen?] |
| SENTENCE | When Paris carried off the beautiful Helen of Troy, he started the Trojan War. |
| FRAGMENT | Who was a great hero of the Greeks. [Note that this would be a complete sentence if it ended with a question mark.] |
| SENTENCE | Odysseus, who was a great hero of the Greeks, took part in the Trojan War. |
| FRAGMENT | Because the wooden horse concealed Greek soldiers. [What was the result of the concealment?] |
| SENTENCE | Because the wooden horse concealed Greek soldiers, the Greeks finally won the Trojan War. |

**NOTE** A subordinate clause telling *why, where, when,* or *how* is called an *adverb clause.* Usually you can place an adverb clause either before or after the independent clause in a sentence.

EXAMPLE **After he started home from the Trojan War,** Odysseus had many more adventures.

*or*

Odysseus had many more adventures **after he started home from the Trojan War.**

If you put the subordinate clause first, use a comma to separate it from the independent clause. The comma makes the sentence easier for the reader to understand.

**Reference Note**

For more on **punctuating introductory adverb clauses,** see page 653.

### Exercise 3 · Revising Subordinate Clause Fragments

The following paragraph contains some subordinate clause fragments. First, find these clause fragments. Next, revise the paragraph, joining the subordinate clauses with independent clauses. (There may be more than one way to join them.) Change the punctuation and capitalization as necessary.

```
    People have been using cosmetics for
thousands of years. In Africa, the ancient
Egyptians used perfumes, hair dyes, and
makeup. That they made from plants and min-
erals. While they often used cosmetics to
be more attractive. They also used them to
protect their skin from the hot sun. Today,
cosmetics are made from over five thousand
different ingredients, including waxes,
oils, and dyes. The cosmetics business is a
huge industry. Advertisers are extremely
successful in selling cosmetics. Because
they appeal to our desire to be attractive.
They often hint. That their products will
make us beautiful, happy, and successful.
Although modern-day cosmetics ads look
different from the ads of eighty years ago.
They still appeal to our emotions.
```

### Exercise 4 · Using Subordinate Clauses in Sentences

Use each of the following subordinate clause fragments as part of a complete sentence. Add whatever words are necessary to make the meaning of the sentence complete. Add capitalization and punctuation as necessary.

**1.** as we watched the spaceship land
**2.** who approached the house in long leaps
**3.** which startled the dog
**4.** if we go outside the house
**5.** when they handed me a glowing sphere

**NOTE** A **series of items** is another kind of fragment that is easily mistaken for a sentence. Notice that, in the following example, the series of items in dark type is not a complete sentence.

FRAGMENT   I ate several things for lunch. **A sandwich, an apple, four pieces of celery, and some popcorn.**

To correct the fragment, you can

- make it into a complete sentence

*or*

- link it to the previous sentence with a colon

SENTENCE   I ate several things for lunch. I ate a sandwich, an apple, four pieces of celery, and some popcorn.

*or*

I ate several things for lunch: a sandwich, an apple, four pieces of celery, and some popcorn.

## Review A   Identifying and Revising Fragments

Some of the following groups of words are sentence fragments. Identify each fragment, and make it part of a complete sentence, adding commas where necessary. When you find a complete sentence, write *C.*

**Reference Note**

For more on **punctuating introductory phrases,** see page 653.

EXAMPLE   1. Originally raised to hunt badgers. Dachshunds are now popular as pets.

1. *Originally raised to hunt badgers, dachshunds are now popular as pets.*

1. Humans have kept dogs as pets and helpers. For perhaps ten thousand years.
2. Herding sheep and cattle and guarding property. Many dogs more than earn their keep.
3. Descended from wolves. Some dogs are still somewhat wolflike.
4. There are over one hundred breeds of dogs now.
5. If you have a Saint Bernard. You have one of the largest dogs.
6. Because Yorkshire terriers are very tiny and cute. Many people keep them as pets.
7. Since they are all born blind and unable to take care of themselves. Puppies need their mothers.
8. Most dogs are fully grown by the time they are one year old.

**9.** Dogs live an average of twelve years. Although many live to be nearly twenty.

**10.** If you like dogs. Consider having one for a pet.

# Run-on Sentences

A **run-on sentence** is two or more complete sentences run together as one. Because they do not show where one idea ends and another one begins, run-on sentences can confuse your reader. There are two kinds of run-ons. In the first kind, called a **fused sentence,** the sentences have no punctuation at all between them.

RUN-ON       Schools in the Middle Ages were different from ours students usually did not have books.

CORRECT     Schools in the Middle Ages were different from ours. Students usually did not have books.

In the other kind of run-on, the writer has linked together sentences with only a comma to separate them from one another. This kind of run-on is called a **comma splice.**

RUN-ON       Schools today have books for every student, many schools also have televisions and computers.

CORRECT     Schools today have books for every student. Many schools also have televisions and computers.

## Revising Run-on Sentences

There are several ways you can revise run-on sentences. As shown in the examples above, you can always make two separate sentences. However, if the two thoughts are equal to one another in importance, you may want to make a **compound sentence.**

RUN-ON       Canada has ten provinces each province has its own government. [fused]

                  Canada has ten provinces, each province has its own government. [comma splice]

**1.** You can make a compound sentence by using a comma and a coordinating conjunction (such as *and, but,* or *or*).

CORRECTED   Canada has ten provinces, **and** each province has its own government.

**COMPUTER TIP**

You can use a grammar-checking program to flag sentences in your writing that are longer than a certain number of words—sentences that have a higher chance of being run-ons. You can then use the information in this chapter to determine whether or not the flagged sentences are run-ons.

**TIPS & TRICKS**

To spot run-on sentences, read your writing aloud. Each point where you hear yourself making a pause as you read is a point where you should ask, *Do I need to create separate sentences here? Do I need to add a semicolon or period? Do I need a comma and a conjunction instead? Do I need additional punctuation here?*

**2.** You can make a compound sentence by using a semicolon.

CORRECTED    Canada has ten provinces; each province has its own government.

**3.** You can make a compound sentence by using a semicolon and a word such as *therefore, instead, meanwhile, still, also, nevertheless,* or *however.* These words are called **conjunctive adverbs.** Follow a conjunctive adverb with a comma.

CORRECTED    Canada has ten provinces; **also,** each province has its own government.

**Reference Note**

For more on **compound sentences,** see page 335.

NOTE    Before you join two sentences in a compound sentence, make sure that the ideas in the sentences are closely related to one another. If you link unrelated ideas, you may confuse your reader.

UNRELATED    Canada is almost four million square miles in size, and I hope to visit my relatives there someday.

RELATED    Canada is almost four million square miles in size, but most of its people live on a small strip of land along the southern border.

### Exercise 5  Revising Run-on Sentences

The following items are confusing because they are run-on sentences. Clear up the confusion by revising the run-ons to form clear, complete sentences. To revise, use the method given in parentheses after each sentence. (The examples on pages 327 and 328 will help you.)

EXAMPLE    **1.** Hollywood is still a center of American moviemaking fine films are made in other places, too. (Use a comma and a coordinating conjunction.)

    *1. Hollywood is still a center of American moviemaking, but fine films are made in other places, too.*

**1.** Movies entertain millions of people every day they are popular all over the world. (Make two sentences.)

**2.** Many films take years to make they require the skills of hundreds of workers. (Use a comma and a coordinating conjunction.)

*George Eastman and Thomas Edison*

3. The director of a movie has an important job the cast and crew all follow the director's instructions. (Use a semicolon.)

4. The director makes many decisions, the producers take care of the business end of moviemaking. (Use a semicolon and a conjunctive adverb.)

5. The first movie theaters opened in the early 1900s they were called nickelodeons. (Make two sentences.)

6. Thomas Edison was a pioneer in early moviemaking he invented the first commercial motion-picture machine. (Use a semicolon.)

7. The machine was called a kinetoscope, it was a cabinet that showed moving images through a peephole. (Make two sentences.)

8. Early movies were silent, sometimes offscreen actors at movie theaters would fill in the dialogue for the audience. (Use a comma and a coordinating conjunction.)

9. The first sound films were shown in the late 1920s they marked a milestone in moviemaking history. (Use a semicolon.)

10. Movies are great entertainment they are also an art form. (Use a semicolon and a conjunctive adverb.)

### Review B  Revising Fragments and Run-on Sentences

The following paragraph contains several sentence fragments and run-on sentences. First, identify all fragments or run-ons. Then, revise them, adding words and changing the punctuation and capitalization as necessary to make each sentence clear and complete.

During the Civil War. Women nurses showed remarkable heroism. They took care of sick and wounded soldiers, they risked their lives carrying supplies. To military hospitals. Sally L. Tompkins one such woman. She ran a military hospital in the South she was one of two women captains in the Confederate Army. Clara Barton was another heroic Civil War nurse, she worked tirelessly. Caring for sick and wounded soldiers in the North. In 1864, Barton superintendent of nurses for the Union Army. She later founded the American Red Cross Society. Served as president of the Red Cross. Until 1904.

*Clara Barton*

# Writing Effective Sentences

## Combining Sentences

Short sentences are often effective; however, a long, unbroken series of them can sound choppy. For example, notice how dull the following paragraph sounds.

> I have seen a lot of earthling-meets-alien movies. I have seen The Last Starfighter. I have seen all the Star Trek movies. I have noticed something about these movies. I have noticed that there are good humans in these movies. There are bad humans. There are good aliens. There are bad aliens. The humans and aliens are actually not so different from each other.

Notice how much more interesting the paragraph sounds when the short, choppy sentences are combined into longer, smoother sentences.

> I have seen a lot of earthling-meets-alien movies, including The Last Starfighter and all the Star Trek movies. I have noticed that there are good and bad humans in these movies, as well as good and bad aliens. The humans and aliens are actually not so different from each other.

# Inserting Words

You can combine short sentences by inserting a key word from one sentence into another. You usually need to eliminate some words in sentences that are combined. You may also need to change the form of the key word.

| Using the Same Form | |
| --- | --- |
| Original | Edgar Allan Poe led a short life. His life was tragic. |
| Combined | Edgar Allan Poe led a short, **tragic** life. |
| **Changing the Form** | |
| Original | Edgar Allan Poe wrote strange stories. He wrote horror stories. |
| Combined | Edgar Allan Poe wrote strange, **horrifying** stories. |

NOTE  Some verbs and nouns can be made into adjectives by adding *–ed* and *–ing,* and some adjectives can be made into adverbs by adding *–ly.*

### Exercise 1  Combining Sentences by Inserting Words

In the following sets of sentences, some words have been italicized. Combine each set of sentences by inserting the italicized word (or words) into the first sentence. The directions in parentheses will tell you how to change the word form if it is necessary to do so.

EXAMPLE
1. Edgar Allan Poe was a writer who wrote stories and poems. Edgar Allan Poe was an *American* writer.

1. *Edgar Allan Poe was an American writer who wrote stories and poems.*

1. The mother of Edgar Allan Poe died three years after he was born. She was *young.*
2. Poe was taken in by Mrs. John Allan and her husband. Their taking him in was *fortunate.* (Add *–ly* to *fortunate.*)
3. Poe created stories. He created *detective* stories.
4. Poe inspired the author of the Sherlock Holmes stories. The author had *talent.* (Add *–ed* to *talent.*)
5. Poe had theories about the writing of fiction. His theories were *original.*

In Exercise 1, the words you needed to insert were italicized. Now, try using your own judgment to combine sentences. There may be more than one way to combine each set; do what seems best to you. Add commas and change the forms of words when needed.

EXAMPLE  1. Luis Valdez is a talented and famous playwright. He is a Mexican American.

1. *Luis Valdez is a talented and famous Mexican American playwright.*

1. Valdez was born in Delano. Delano is in California.
2. He grew up in a family of farm workers. They were migrant workers.
3. As a child, Valdez began to work in the fields. He was six years old.
4. He champions the cause of underpaid migrant farm workers. He also champions the cause of migrant farm workers who suffer from overwork.
5. He organized the Farm Workers' Theater, a troupe of actors and musicians. The troupe travels.

# Inserting Phrases

You also can combine closely related sentences by taking a phrase from one sentence and inserting it into another sentence.

## Prepositional Phrases

A **prepositional phrase**, a preposition with its object and any modifiers of that object, can usually be inserted into another sentence with no changes. Just omit some of the words in one of the sentences.

ORIGINAL  Twelve million immigrants came to the shores of the United States. They came through Ellis Island.

REVISED  Twelve million immigrants came to the shores of the United States **through Ellis Island.**

**COMPUTER TIP**

You can use a word-processing program's cut and paste commands to find the best placement for a participial phrase within a sentence.

## Participial Phrases

A **participial phrase** contains a verb form that usually ends in *–ing* or *–ed*. The entire phrase acts as an adjective, modifying a noun or a pronoun. Sometimes, you can change the verb from one sentence into a participle by adding *–ing* or *–ed* or by dropping the helping verb if the main verb already ends in *–ing* or *–ed*. Then, you can combine the two sentences. Place the participial phrase close to the noun or pronoun it will modify to avoid confusing your reader.

ORIGINAL    Many immigrants faced long months of waiting at Ellis Island. They were weakened by their journeys.

REVISED    Many immigrants, **weakened by their journeys,** faced long months of waiting at Ellis Island.

## Appositive Phrases

An *appositive phrase* usually follows a noun or pronoun and helps to identify it. Sometimes you can combine sentences that have nouns or pronouns referring to the same thing by changing one of the sentences to an appositive phrase.

ORIGINAL    My grandfather was an immigrant. My grandfather brought with him photographs that are now souvenirs.

REVISED    My grandfather, **an immigrant,** brought with him photographs that are now souvenirs.

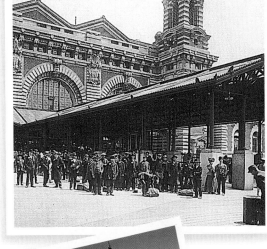

### Exercise 3   Combining Sentences by Inserting Phrases

Revise each of the following sets of sentences to create one sentence. There may be more than one way to combine the sentences. In numbers 1 through 5, the words you need to insert are italicized. In numbers 6 through 10, change the forms of words or omit words as indicated in parentheses, and add commas wherever they are needed.

**Reference Note**

For more information on **phrases,** see page 440.

EXAMPLE    1. Auguste Piccard was a Swiss physicist who studied the upper atmosphere. He studied it *by going up in balloons.*

    1. *Auguste Piccard was a Swiss physicist who studied the upper atmosphere by going up in balloons.*

1. Auguste Piccard was an inventor, scientist, and explorer. He was *from Switzerland.*
2. Piccard once spent sixteen hours in a balloon. He was *floating across Germany and France.*

3. Piccard attended the Swiss Institute of Technology. The institute is *in Zurich, Switzerland.*
4. Piccard was a young man when he became a professor. He became a professor *at the Swiss Institute.*
5. Piccard created an important invention. He invented *an airtight gondola.*
6. The gondola took Piccard ten miles into the air. The gondola was attached to a balloon. (Omit *The gondola was.*)
7. Piccard then made numerous balloon trips. He studied electricity. (Change *studied* to *studying.*)
8. Piccard turned his interest to the ocean depths. He designed a deep-sea diving ship. (Change *designed* to *designing.*)
9. Piccard and his son Jacques went two miles below the surface of the Adriatic Sea. They went in 1953. (Omit *They went.*)
10. Another deep-sea diving ship went almost ten miles below the surface of the ocean. It set the world's depth record in 1960. (Change *set* to *setting.*)

## Using Compound Subjects and Verbs

Another way to combine sentences is to make compound subjects and verbs. First, look for sentences that have the same subject or the same verb. Then, make the subject or verb compound by adding a coordinating conjunction such as *and, but, for, or, nor, so,* or *yet.*

| ORIGINAL | The Angles were fierce people. The Saxons were fierce people. [different subjects with same verb] |
| REVISED | The **Angles and the Saxons** were fierce people. [compound subject with same verb] |

| ORIGINAL | The Angles and Saxons invaded Britain. The Angles and Saxons conquered Britain. [different verbs with same subject] |
| REVISED | The Angles and Saxons **invaded and conquered** Britain. [compound verb with same subject] |

| ORIGINAL | The Angles conquered Britain. The Saxons also conquered Britain. They both pushed back the native Celts. [different subjects and different verbs] |
| REVISED | The **Angles and the Saxons conquered** Britain and **pushed back** the native Celts. [compound subject and compound verb] |

**NOTE** When you combine sentences by making compound subjects and compound verbs, make sure that your new subjects and verbs agree in number.

ORIGINAL   The dialect of the Angles is an ancestor of Modern English. The dialect of the Saxons is also an ancestor of Modern English.

REVISED   The **dialects** of the Angles and the Saxons **are** ancestors of Modern English. [The plural subject *dialects* takes the plural verb *are*.]

**Exercise 4**  **Creating Compound Subjects and Compound Verbs**

Here are five sets of short sentences. Combine each set into one sentence that has a compound subject, a compound verb, or a compound subject and a compound verb.

1. Bananas are a tropical fruit. Coconuts are also a tropical fruit.
2. Brazil produces bananas. India produces bananas. Both countries export bananas.
3. Some bananas are cooked as vegetables are. They are eaten as vegetables are.
4. By A.D. 600, the Egyptians were eating coconuts. Indians and Koreans were also eating coconuts.
5. Coconuts are not a major crop in the United States. Bananas are not a major crop in the United States, either.

# Creating a Compound Sentence

You can combine two sentences by creating a compound sentence. A *compound sentence* is two or more simple sentences linked by

- a comma and a coordinating conjunction

    *or*

- a semicolon

    *or*

- a semicolon and a conjunctive adverb

Before linking two thoughts in a compound sentence, make sure that the thoughts are clearly related and equal in importance. Be sure that you do not link two thoughts in a compound sentence when one thought is clearly more important than the other.

ORIGINAL    The cat knocked over a lamp. The dog chewed up my shoe.

REVISED    The cat knocked over a lamp, **and** the dog chewed up my shoe. [comma and coordinating conjunction]

The cat knocked over a lamp; the dog chewed up my shoe. [semicolon]

The cat knocked over a lamp; **meanwhile,** the dog chewed up my shoe. [semicolon and conjunctive adverb]

NOTE   You can use the coordinating conjunctions *and, but, nor, for, yet, or,* and *so* to form compound sentences. However, you should avoid overusing them. When you join two sentences with a coordinating conjunction, remember to use a comma before the conjunction.

### Exercise 5   Combining Simple Sentences to Create Compound Sentences

The sentences in the following pairs are closely related in meaning. Using the methods you have learned, combine each pair into a compound sentence. Add commas and semicolons where necessary.

1. Numbers from the United States 2000 census have been released. They show a country becoming more diverse.
2. For the first time, families could choose more than one racial group on the census form. We now have a better picture of the nation's complex ethnic and racial makeup.
3. Of all ethnic groups, Hispanics are the fastest growing. People of many racial backgrounds consider themselves Hispanic.
4. The number of Asians has also increased over the last ten years. Asians in the United States now number twelve million.
5. The vast majority of the people who live in the United States were born here. Of every ten residents, one is an immigrant.

## Creating a Complex Sentence

A *complex sentence* includes one independent clause—a clause that can stand alone as a sentence. It also has one or more *subordinate clauses*—clauses that cannot stand alone as sentences.

### Adjective Clauses

You can make a sentence into an *adjective clause* by inserting *who, which,* or *that* in place of the subject. Then you use the adjective clause to provide information about a preceding noun or pronoun.

| ORIGINAL | Many people are afraid of bats. They are usually harmless creatures. |
|----------|---------------------------------------------------------------------|
| REVISED | Many people are afraid of bats, **which are usually harmless creatures.** |

> NOTE  When you use adjective clauses to combine sentences, remember that *which* is not used to refer to a person, only to places and things. Use *who, whom, whose,* and *that* to refer to people.

## Adverb Clauses

You can turn one sentence into an ***adverb clause*** and combine it with another sentence. The adverb clause may modify a verb, an adjective, or another adverb in the sentence (the independent clause) to which it is attached.

Adverb clauses begin with subordinating conjunctions like *after, although, because, if, when,* and *where.* You have to choose these conjunctions carefully. They show the relationship between the ideas in the adverb clause and those in the independent clause. For example, *when* shows how the ideas are related in time, *where* shows how the ideas are related in space, and *although* shows under what conditions the ideas occurred. When you use an adverb clause at the beginning of a sentence, you need to separate it from the independent clause with a comma.

| ORIGINAL | Some people think bats are dangerous. They rarely attack humans. |
|----------|---------------------------------------------------------------------|
| REVISED | **Although some people think bats are dangerous,** they rarely attack humans. |

## Noun Clauses

You can make a sentence into a ***noun clause*** and insert it into another sentence just as you would an ordinary noun. You create a noun clause by inserting a word like *that, how, what, which,* or *who* at the beginning of the sentence. When you place the noun clause in the other sentence, you may have to change or remove some words.

| ORIGINAL | Dracula is such a frightening character. This does not help the bat's reputation. |
|----------|---------------------------------------------------------------------|
| REVISED | **That Dracula is such a frightening character** does not help the bat's reputation. [The word *that* introduces the noun clause, which becomes the subject of the verb *does help.*] |
| REVISED | **What does not help the bat's reputation** is that Dracula is such a frightening character. [The word *what* introduces the noun clause, which becomes the subject of the verb *is.*] |

┌ TIPS & TRICKS ┐

*This* in the original is an unclear (general) pronoun reference. General references can be corrected by creating a noun clause, as in the revised sentence. For more on **clear pronoun references,** see page 565.

## Exercise 6 — Combining Simple Sentences to Create Complex Sentences

Following are five sets of short, choppy sentences that need revision. Use subordinate clauses to combine each set of sentences into a single complex sentence. You may see different ways to combine some of the sets; choose the way that seems best to you. You may need to change or delete some words to make smooth combinations.

1. The shark is a member of a fish family. The family includes the largest and fiercest fish.
2. Most sharks have long bodies, wedge-shaped heads, and pointed back fins. The back fins sometimes stick out of the water.
3. Sharks live mostly in warm seas. Some sharks have been found in bodies of cold water.
4. The whale shark is harmless to people. It feeds on plankton.
5. However, many sharks are ruthless killers. They feed on flesh.

## Review A — Revising a Paragraph by Combining Sentences

Using all of the sentence-combining techniques you have learned, revise and rewrite the following short paragraph. Use your judgment about what sentences to combine and how to combine them. Work for clear, varied sentences that read smoothly; however, do not change the meaning of the original paragraph.

```
    Stonehenge is in southwestern England.
It is a series of stones. They are huge
stones. They weigh as much as fifty tons
each. Stonehenge was built about five thou-
sand years ago. The stones were moved to
their present site. They were moved by as
many as one thousand people. There are many
theories about the purpose of the stones.
One popular theory is that the stones
served as an observatory. The observatory
was astronomical. At one point in the sum-
mer, the sun rises over one of the stones.
It rises directly over that stone.
```

# Improving Sentence Style

In the first part of this chapter, you learned some techniques for making smooth sentence combinations. Now you will learn how to style your sentences by making them clear, balanced, and varied.

## Using Parallel Structure

When you combine several related ideas in one sentence, it is important to make sure that your combinations are balanced. You create balance in a sentence by using the same form or part of speech to express each idea. For example, you balance a noun with a noun, a phrase with a phrase, and a clause with a clause. This balance is called parallelism, or *parallel structure.*

| | |
|---|---|
| NOT PARALLEL | I am not much of an athlete, but I like softball, soccer, and playing hockey. [two nouns and a phrase] |
| PARALLEL | I am not much of an athlete, but I like **softball, soccer, and hockey.** [three nouns] |
| NOT PARALLEL | Dominic does not have enough time to play soccer, join the debating team, and band. [two phrases and a noun] |
| PARALLEL | Dominic does not have enough time **to play soccer, to join the debating team,** and **to participate in band.** [three phrases] |
| NOT PARALLEL | He said that he would meet you at the soccer field and not to be late. [clause and phrase] |
| PARALLEL | He said **that he would meet you at the soccer field** and **that you should not be late.** [two clauses] |

Bring balance to the following sentences by putting the ideas in parallel form. You may need to add or delete some words. If a sentence is already correct, write *C*.

1. Paris, the capital of France, is famous for its history, culture, and eating in excellent restaurants.
2. The Seine River runs through the city and supplies water to all Parisians.
3. Visiting the Notre Dame Cathedral, walking through the Louvre Museum, and the Eiffel Tower are all favorite pastimes of tourists.
4. It is interesting that Paris has always attracted artists and refugees have always been welcome.
5. Many famous Americans, including Ernest Hemingway, lived and were writing in Paris during the 1920s.

# Revising Stringy Sentences

Linking together related ideas is a good way to bring variety to your writing. If you overdo it, however, you may end up with a *stringy sentence.*

A **stringy sentence** just goes on and on. It usually has too many independent clauses strung together with coordinating conjunctions like *and* or *but.* Since all the ideas are treated equally, your reader may have trouble seeing how they are related.

There are three ways you can fix a stringy sentence. You can

- break the sentence into two or more sentences
- turn some of the independent clauses into subordinate clauses or phrases
- use a combination of the above strategies

STRINGY   The fire alarm bell rang, and everyone started to file out of school, but then our principal came down the hall, and he said the bell had been rung by mistake, and we went back to class.

BETTER   The fire alarm bell rang, and everyone started to file out of school. Then our principal came down the hall to say the bell had been rung by mistake. We went back to class.

BETTER   When the fire alarm bell rang, everyone started to file out of school. Then our principal came down the hall. He said the bell had been rung by mistake, and we went back to class.

Decide which of the following sentences are stringy and need revision. Then, revise the stringy sentences by (1) breaking each sentence into two or more sentences, (2) turning some independent clauses into subordinate clauses, or (3) turning some independent clauses into phrases. If you find a sentence that is effective and does not need to be improved, write *C*.

EXAMPLE

1. Alexandre Gustave Eiffel was a French engineer, and he designed the Eiffel Tower, and he designed the frame for the Statue of Liberty, but his greatest accomplishment may have been proving that metal was an important building material.

1. *Alexandre Gustave Eiffel was a French engineer who designed the Eiffel Tower and the frame for the Statue of Liberty. His greatest accomplishment may have been proving that metal was an important building material.*

1. Alexandre Gustave Eiffel was a famous Frenchman, and he was born in 1832, and he died in 1923.
2. Eiffel was an engineer, and he designed the Eiffel Tower, and it was built for the World's Fair of 1889.
3. Eiffel's chief interest was bridges, and the Eiffel Tower displays his bridge-designing skills, and so does another historical monument, and it is a monument that you know.
4. In 1885, Eiffel used his engineering knowledge to design part of a great American symbol, the Statue of Liberty in New York Harbor.
5. Toward the end of his life, Eiffel studied the effects of air on airplanes, and then in 1912, he built a wind tunnel and an aerodynamics laboratory, and later he conducted experiments from the Eiffel Tower, which is now a favorite tourist attraction.

# Revising Wordy Sentences

If someone says, "It would please me greatly if you would diminish the volume of your verbalizing during the time I am perusing this reading material," you might wonder what language is being spoken. How much easier and clearer to say "Please be quieter while I am reading." Here are three tips for creating sentences that are not too wordy.

- *Do not use more words than you need.*
- *Do not use fancy words where simple ones will do.*
- *Do not repeat yourself unless it is absolutely necessary.*

| WORDY | My friend Ken is a talented drummer who plays the drums with great skill. |
|---|---|
| IMPROVED | My friend Ken is a talented drummer. |

| WORDY | In the event that we are unable to go to the movie, we can play basketball at Alicia's house. |
|---|---|
| IMPROVED | If we cannot go to the movie, we can play basketball at Alicia's house. |

**Exercise 9** **Revising Wordy Sentences**

The writer of the following letter wants to make a complaint, but the wordiness of the letter gets in the way. Revise the letter, making it clearer and more effective. You may add details if you wish.

```
Dear Mr. and Mrs. Wilson,
    At this point in time, it is my unhappy
duty to inform you of the fact that I will
no longer be available to baby-sit Charles.
On the evening of July 13, I was hired by
you to perform the duties of baby sitter
for your three-year-old son. These duties
were performed by me to the best of my
ability. However, I do not feel that any
baby sitter should be in a position of hav-
ing to deal with the threat of harm to the
baby sitter's person. I feel that Charles's
hurling of objects at my person and his
action of locking me in the closet were
threats to my safety. The situation being
what it is, I feel I cannot safely perform
my duties, and I will no longer place
myself in danger by sitting with your son.
                   Sincerely,
                   Miguel Garza
```

# Varying Sentence Beginnings

Basic English sentences begin with a subject followed by a verb. However, beginning every sentence with a subject makes your writing dull. Notice how boring the following paragraph sounds.

```
    The theater was packed. Jan and I managed
to find our seats. The play began thirty min-
utes late. We were bored. We read the pro-
gram four times. Jan wanted to find out the
```

reason for the delay. She asked an usher.
The usher was amused. The usher said that
the star's costume had been damaged by her
dog. We laughed because the play was <u>Cats</u>.

Now, notice how much more interesting the same paragraph sounds with varied sentence beginnings. To create the varied beginnings, the writer has combined sentences. Some sentences became words, some became phrases, and others became subordinate clauses.

Although the theater was packed, Jan and
I managed to find our seats. The play began
thirty minutes late. Bored, we read the program four times. To find out the reason for
the delay, Jan asked an usher. Amused, the
usher said that the star's costume had been
damaged by her dog. We laughed because the
play was <u>Cats</u>.

---

### Varying Sentence Beginnings

**Single–Word Modifiers**

**Excitedly,** Marcia opened her presents. [adverb]
**Hungry,** the family stopped at the restaurant. [adjective]

**Phrases**

**With tears of joy,** Carla received her prize. [prepositional phrase]
**Smiling happily,** Tanya told us the good news. [participial phrase]
**To make good grades,** you must study. [infinitive phrase]

**Subordinate Clauses**

**Because the coach was angry,** the team ran ten laps. [adverb clause]

**When Tom found the kitten on his doorstep,** he decided to keep it. [adverb clause]

---

**TIPS & TRICKS**

To check your writing for varied sentence beginnings, put parentheses around the first five words of each of your sentences. If most of your subjects and verbs fall within the parentheses, you need to begin more of your sentences with single-word modifiers, phrases, or subordinate clauses.

**NOTE** If you use a prepositional phrase telling *when, where,* or *how* to vary your sentence beginnings, you can sometimes put the verb of the sentence before the subject. In the following example sentence, the subject is underlined once, the verb twice.

EXAMPLE    Down the street <u>rumbled</u> an old <u>cart</u>.

## Exercise 10 Varying Sentence Beginnings

The following sentences are all good, but they would make a boring paragraph. Here is your chance to practice varying sentence beginnings. The notes in parentheses tell you whether to start your revised sentence with a single-word modifier, a phrase, or a clause. In some cases, you may also want to add or delete a word to make the sentence sound better.

1. Animals are in danger of extinction in many different parts of the world. (phrase)
2. The aye-aye is a small animal related to the monkey, and it is one of the less well-known of the endangered animals. (phrase)
3. The aye-aye is endangered because the rain forest on its home island is being destroyed. (subordinate clause)
4. You must travel to the Pyrenees, Portugal, or the former Soviet Union to see the desman, a water-dwelling mammal. (phrase)
5. People are threatening the desman's survival by damming mountain streams. (phrase)
6. The giant otter of South America is protected, but poachers continue to threaten its survival. (subordinate clause)
7. Mountain lions are cautious and generally stay away from humans, who hunt them relentlessly. (single-word modifier)
8. The great peacock moth of Europe is in trouble because its home is being damaged by acid rain. (subordinate clause)
9. Wolves are expert hunters, and they prey on large animals. (phrase)
10. Gray wolves, sadly, are an endangered species. (single-word modifier)

## Exercise 11 Revising Sentences to Create Variety

Use what you have learned about varying sentence beginnings to revise the following paragraph. Reword some sentences so that they begin with single-word modifiers, phrases, or clauses. Some sentences may be reworded in several ways; choose the way that seems best to you. (Consult the chart on page 343 for help.)

Ocean animals unfortunately are often on endangered-species lists. Penguins are at risk in oceans of the Southern Hemisphere. Many penguin species have problems today because of oil pollution and commercial fishing. Turtles are endangered because they are slaughtered for food and for their beautiful, highly prized shells. Lobsters become threatened when people overfish. Mediterranean monk seals also are threatened by increased land development and tourism.

## Review B  Revising a Paragraph

The following paragraphs have many of the problems you have reviewed in this section. Show your writing style by rewriting and revising the paragraphs (1) to correct nonparallel structures, (2) to correct stringy and wordy sentences, and (3) to vary sentence beginnings. You may add or delete details as necessary.

One time in the recent past, we went on a picnic in Big Bend National Park in Texas. It had rained heavily all night north of the park. A friend of ours, Mrs. Brown, went with us. She had lived in that part of Texas for a large number of years. She knew all about what to expect if it rained. She told us that there could be a flash flood in the park and about how the park could be dangerous even if it did not rain there because the water could run across the dry desert sand.

Mrs. Brown made us turn our cars around to face in the other direction because she wanted us to be able to leave the low area quickly if a flood came. The sun was shining with great brightness, and everyone thought Mrs. Brown was crazy, and we started to eat our picnic.

A very high wall of water four feet high came toward us suddenly. We jumped into the cars and getting away just in time. We were glad to be alive, and we thanked Mrs. Brown.

# Understanding Paragraph Structure

## What Is a Paragraph?

A paragraph is made up of sentences grouped together for a reason—usually to present and support a single **main idea.** Like you, paragraphs are individuals—each has a purpose of its own. However, each of the paragraphs in a composition is also like a member of a team, working together with other paragraphs to develop ideas. You might think of a paragraph as a link in a chain—separating, yet connecting, ideas.

## Why Use a Paragraph?

Did you know that paragraphs have been around since the fourth century B.C.? The paragraph was used in ancient Greek texts to mark each place where a new topic was introduced. Today, paragraphs are used in much the same way—to divide an essay or article into blocks of separate thoughts or to divide a story into a series of events. Think for a moment how hard it would be to read a huge block of uninterrupted text. Where would your eyes rest? Wouldn't it be difficult to separate one complete thought from another?

In fact, even though we do not think much today about why we use paragraphs, they are very important tools. Paragraphs provide a visual sign to the reader that a new thought—or a new speaker—is coming. They also allow readers to take a little pause to digest what they've read so far. When you are writing, you might think of paragraphs as a way to lead your reader by the hand through your essay.

# What Are the Parts of a Body Paragraph?

Although some paragraphs—especially in narrative writing—do not have a central focus, most paragraphs do emphasize one **main idea.** Paragraphs like this, often called **body paragraphs,** usually have three major parts: a *topic sentence* (a statement of the paragraph's main idea); additional *supporting sentences* that elaborate on and support the topic sentence; and (often, but not always) a concluding, or *clincher sentence.*

## The Main Idea

Together, the sentences in the paragraph make its main idea clear. If the paragraph is part of a longer piece of writing, the surrounding paragraphs help you understand the main idea. Read the following paragraph, and try to determine what its main idea is.

> Those of us who live in the city should be grateful to our language, because the words that have to do with the city are usually flattering. We city-dwellers, at least in ancient days, were supposed to be more *civil* in our manners and more *civilized* in our ways than others, for both of these words, *civil* and *civilized,* are the eventual children of the Latin term *civis* which meant "one who lives in a city." All city folks, you see, were regarded as automatically cultured and well housebroken. And from ancient Latin we have borrowed the word *urbs* which also meant city, and we used it to create the word *urbane* which describes the smooth manners that were pre-sumed to be characteristic of *metropolitan* society. The
>
> *(continued)*

Copyright 1986 Watterson. Distributed by Universal Press Syndicate.

*(continued)*

Greek parts of the word *metropolitan* are *metro-,* "mother," and *polis,* "city," so a *metropolis* is the "mother city" or the chief or capital city of a country, and he who lives in a metropolis is supposed to inherit the sophisticated ideas and manners that go with such a center. And from the Greek *polis,* "city," we inherited our word *politic.* If you are *politic,* you are expedient, shrewd, discreet, and artful in your address and your procedure which sounds dangerously like a city slicker!

Wilfred Funk, *Word Origins and Their Romantic Stories*

The main idea of Funk's paragraph is stated in its first sentence, the topic sentence. All the other sentences give more specific information to support that idea; they give examples of what the writer calls "flattering" words that have to do with the city.

## The Topic Sentence

You will often express the main idea of a paragraph in a single sentence, called the **topic sentence.**

### Placement of a Topic Sentence

Although a topic sentence can be placed at any point in the paragraph, it often appears as the first or second sentence. In the passage on page 347, for example, the first sentence is a topic sentence.

A topic sentence at the beginning of a paragraph helps a reader know what to expect in the rest of the paragraph. The diagram below shows the typical three-part structure of a body paragraph that begins with a topic sentence.

S T Y L E    T I P

To create surprise or to summarize ideas, you may want to place a topic sentence at or near the end of the paragraph.

COMPUTER TIP

When you are revising a paragraph, try moving the topic sentence to various locations within the paragraph by using your word-processing program's Cut and Paste commands. You can then analyze which placement of the topic sentence is the most effective.

**Typical Body Paragraph Structure**

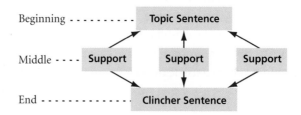

A topic sentence placed at the end of a paragraph can be quite effective. As you read the following paragraph, notice how the writer draws all the details together with a topic sentence at the very end.

> In the summer, hosts of big red-and-yellow grasshoppers, with heads shaped like horses, will descend and eat holes in all the softer leaves. Walking sticks fly like boomerangs. Shining brown leaf-shaped palmetto bugs scurry like cockroaches. Spiders like tiny crabs hang in stout webs. The birds snap at small moths and butterflies of every kind. A blue racer, the snake that moves across the cleared sand like a whiplash, will with one flick destroy the smooth, careful cup of the ant lion in the hot sand. The whole world of the pines and of the rocks hums and glistens and stings with life.
>
> Marjory Stoneman Douglas, *The Everglades: River of Grass*

## Importance of a Topic Sentence

Many paragraphs you read will not have a topic sentence. In fact, some of them, especially those that relate a sequence of events or actions, will not even seem to have a single main idea. However, that does not mean topic sentences are not useful. When you are reading, topic sentences at the beginning of a paragraph provide clues about what to expect in the rest of the paragraph. When you are writing, topic sentences help you focus the ideas in your paragraph. Also, whether you are writing a paragraph or reading one, the topic sentence can suggest the order of details in the paragraph—order by comparison and contrast or by cause and effect, for example.

NOTE If a paragraph is part of a composition, its topic sentence often contains key words or phrases to tie it to the paper's thesis.

STYLE TIP

Although it is possible to omit a topic sentence, you should get into the habit of including it in your own writing. The writing you do for school will benefit from the clarity and focus that a well-written topic sentence provides.

**Exercise 1** Identifying Main Ideas and Topic Sentences

Each of the paragraphs on the next page develops a main idea. State the main idea of each paragraph and, if there is a topic sentence, identify it. If there is no topic sentence, you may find it a little harder to determine what the main idea is.

1.   In my country, sports were one way to show national pride, one of the few safe ways. You could cheer for a Czech hockey team or soccer team, even against the Soviet Union. It was a tradition going back to the nineteenth century when people formed sports clubs like Sokol, to compete in gymnastics. It was the only way you could say to the Hapsburgs, "Look, we're still Czechs, even if we now belong to the Austro-Hungarian Empire."

Martina Navratilova with George Vecsey, *Martina*

Fabulous Jackalope

2.   Throughout the Western United States, you can buy postcards with a photograph of the fabulous jackalope. Stuffed specimens of this creature can sometimes be found on display, usually in bars. The jackalope is said to be a rare, nearly extinct antlered species of rabbit. Up close, the jackalope looks like a stuffed rabbit with a pair of horns or antlers stuck onto it. And, of course, that is exactly what it is.

Daniel Cohen, *The Encyclopedia of Monsters*

## Supporting Sentences: Elaboration

The topic sentence of a paragraph states a general idea. To make that idea clear and interesting to the reader, you have to **elaborate** on it, or develop it in greater detail. Other sentences in the paragraph give specific details or information to support the main idea of the paragraph. Depending on the subject you are writing about, you might support your main idea with sensory details, facts or statistics, or examples.

NOTE  With or without a topic sentence, a paragraph always needs specific bits of information to support the main idea. In fact, paragraphs without topic sentences are dependent on their details to reflect their main ideas.

## Sensory Details as Support

**Sensory details** are precise bits of information that you collect using any of your five senses—sight, hearing, smell, touch, taste. You might include a detail about the color of something, how it sounds when it moves, or what it feels like when you touch it.

The writer of the following paragraph uses details of sight, sound, and smell to elaborate on a description of what her childhood home was like in the morning.

| | |
|---|---|
| In the summer my mother got up just after sunrise, so that when she called Matthew and me for breakfast, the house was filled with sounds and | Sight |
| smells of her industrious mornings. Odors of frying scrapple or codfish cakes drifted up the back | Smell |
| stairs, mingling sometimes with the sharp scent of mustard greens she was cooking for dinner that | Smell |
| | Sight |
| night. Up the laundry chute from the cellar floated whiffs of steamy air and the churning sound of | Smell |
| the washing machine. From the dining room, | Sound |
| where she liked to sit ironing and chatting on the telephone, came the fragrance of hot clean clothes | Smell |
| and the sound of her voice: cheerful, resonant, | Sound |
| reverberating a little weirdly through the high-ceilinged rooms, as if she were sitting happily at the bottom of a well. | |

Andrea Lee, "Mother"

## Facts and Statistics as Support

Another way to support a main idea with specific information is to use facts or statistics. A *fact* is a statement that can be proven true, such as the statement "At the end of the Civil War, General Lee surrendered to General Grant in the front parlor of the Wilmer McLean house." A *statistic* is a fact that involves numbers; for example, "During the Civil War, the South lost about 260,000 soldiers, and the North lost about 360,000."

> **NOTE** If you use statistics in your writing, be sure that you choose them from reliable, unbiased sources. When you present statistics, do so in clear language.

In the following paragraph about movie theaters, facts and statistics support and prove the main idea that concession sales are big moneymakers. In case you are wondering about the word *Rialto,* it is a name that the writer uses to refer to movie theaters in general.

Statistic

Fact

Statistic

Statistic

Statistics

> Let's look at how concession sales affect the bottom line of the Rialto. In large cities, about 15–20 percent of all customers will stop at the concession stand (in smaller towns, even more customers eat), and the theater owner figures to gross about 75 cents for every customer who walks through the turnstile, meaning that the average purchase is over $3. The key to making money in the concession area is maintaining a high profit margin, and the items sold do a terrific job. The average profit margin on candy—77 percent; on popcorn—86 percent; on soft drinks—a whopping 90 percent. For every dollar spent at the concession counter, the theater operator nets over 85 cents.
>
> David Feldman, *Imponderables*

## Examples as Support

You can also use one or more examples to support a main idea. *Examples* are specific instances, or illustrations, of a general idea. A cow is an example of an animal. Your test score of 67 is an example of what can happen if you do not study. The line "The fog comes/on little cat feet," from Carl Sandburg's poem "Fog," is an example of **personification.** The following paragraph uses specific examples of bird behavior to show how bathing varies among birds.

Main Idea

Example 1

> Bathing behavior varies from species to species. Many birds stand in shallow water and, through a complex series of movements—rolling their head and body and fluttering their wings—get water trapped in featherless areas next to their body and then press the water out through their

feathers. Some aerial birds, like swallows, may dive into water and immediately fly up. Still others may jump into water and be briefly submerged before getting out. Some birds bathe in rain or drizzle, in dew on grass, or among wet leaves. Take time to watch bathing behavior; it is fascinating.

Donald and Lillian Stokes, *The Bird Feeder Book*

### Exercise 2  Collecting Supporting Details

Four general ideas you could write about are listed below. With each idea, a type of support—examples, facts and statistics, or sensory details—is suggested. Think of two details to support each main idea. You may have to do a little research (reading or talking to knowledgeable people) to find support, especially facts or statistics.

┌HELP─

If you have trouble thinking of ideas, use the *5W–How?* questions as trigger words to brainstorm details.

EXAMPLE  1. Because the audience loved puns, Shakespeare included several in *Romeo and Juliet*. (examples)

1. *When Mercutio is dying, he says, "Ask for / me tomorrow and you shall find me a grave / man." The pun is on the word* grave, *which means "serious" as well as "burial place." Romeo creates a pun with* soles *and* soul *in the following lines: "You have dancing shoes / With nimble soles; I have a soul of lead / So stakes me to the ground I cannot move."*

1. Physical education classes develop skills that people use throughout their lives. (examples)
2. Ponce de León, the Spanish explorer, led an expedition to what is now Florida. (facts and statistics)
3. On a rainy, cold afternoon, nothing could be better than going to see a movie. (sensory details)
4. Women's styles have often put appearance before comfort. (examples)

# The Clincher Sentence

You may want to end some paragraphs—especially long ones—with a sentence that restates or emphasizes the paragraph's topic sentence or main idea. This concluding sentence is called a ***clincher sentence*** because it pulls all the details together and signals that the end of the paragraph has come—often using a transitional word or phrase such as *therefore, thus, as a result,* and *consequently.* The clincher sentence in the following paragraph is underlined. Notice how the author uses the clincher sentence to emphasize his opinion of Michael Jordan as the "best player in basketball."

> Coming into New Jersey to play the Nets, the Bulls had won five games and lost only two since Jordan's return. Any doubts anyone might have had about his potential to reclaim his standing as the best player in basketball had been effectively removed three days after he hit the winning shot in Atlanta, when the Bulls traveled to New York to play the Knicks in Madison Square Garden. Jordan's performance that night—55 points, 21-for-37 shooting from the field, 10-of-11 free throws, all of this in only 38 minutes on the court—could not have taken place in a better setting for him (the New York and national media were on hand in force), and could not have come at a better time (the game was nationally telecast, to an audience that had been reading the stories about Jordan's struggles, had been seeing the TV coverage of his missed shots and missteps). Since that night he had scored 23 points in a win over the Boston Celtics, then only 12 points on 5-for-19 shooting against the Philadelphia 76ers. But the evening in New York had defined the possibilities inherent in his comeback; now the world was clamoring to watch every shot he took, and tickets to Bulls games, always extremely difficult to get, were just about impossible to buy at any price. <u>No one wanted to miss the next night when Jordan might explode.</u>
>
> Bob Greene, *Rebound*

**Exercise 3** **Writing a Clincher Sentence**

The paragraph on the next page does not have a clincher sentence. Read the paragraph and determine what its main idea is. Then, write a clincher sentence that (1) emphasizes the main idea and (2) signals that the end of the paragraph has come. (Try to include a transitional word or phrase.)

```
    Dr. Robert D. Ballard's book about the
discovery of the Titanic is fascinating. He
begins the book with an interesting account
of the search for the ship. A few chapters
later, he launches into the thrilling story
of the actual discovery. Then comes the cli-
max of the book: the section in which
Ballard describes the explorations of the
Titanic that he conducted using a submarine
and an underwater robot.
```

# What Makes a Good Paragraph?

A good paragraph has three major qualities:

- **Unity.** All the parts of the paragraph work together as a unit to express and support one main idea.
- **Coherence.** The ideas in the paragraph are arranged and connected in a way that will make sense to readers.
- **Elaboration.** The paragraph's main idea is developed or expanded using plenty of supporting details.

## Unity

A good paragraph has *unity*—all its sentences work together as a unit to express or to support one main idea. Sentences can work as a unit in one of three ways: (1) by supporting a main idea that is stated in a topic sentence, (2) by supporting a main idea that is implied (not directly expressed), or (3) by expressing a related series of actions.

### All Sentences Relate to the Topic Sentence

The topic sentence of the following paragraph expresses the paragraph's main idea—that whales are physical wonders. Notice how the supporting sentences all provide specific details about characteristics that make whales physically wonderful or unusual.

> Whales not only have fascinating behavior but are physical wonders as well. The Blue Whale is the largest animal that has ever graced our
>
> *(continued)*

Topic
Sentence

Detail

Detail   *(continued)*

Detail   planet. Such giant herbivorous dinosaurs as the brontosaurus weighed up to fifty tons. A Blue Whale weighs that much long before it reaches puberty; full grown they weigh a hundred and fifty

Detail   tons, as much as three brontosauri! Blue Whales grow to more than a hundred feet—longer than

Detail   any other animals. When such a whale is vertical in the water with its tail at the surface, its nose is deep enough to be subjected to the weight of three

Detail   atmospheres. It is possible that they dive deep enough, more than a mile, to be subjected to more than two hundred times the atmospheric pressure experienced by people on land at sea level.

Paul and Anne Ehrlich, *Extinction*

## All Sentences Relate to an Implied Main Idea

The following paragraph does not have a topic sentence. However, each sentence helps to support the implied main idea that the results of the battle between Nat and the birds are shocking and horrifying.

He took the blanket from his head and stared about him. The cold gray morning light exposed the room. Dawn and the open window had called the living birds; the dead lay on the floor. Nat gazed at the little corpses, shocked and horrified. They were all small birds, none of any size; there must have been fifty of them lying there upon the floor. There were robins, finches, sparrows, blue tits, larks, and bramblings, birds that by nature's law kept to their own flock and their own territory, and now, joining one with another in their urge for battle, had destroyed themselves against the bedroom walls or in the strife had been destroyed by him. Some had lost feathers in the fight; others had blood, his blood, upon their beaks.

Daphne du Maurier, "The Birds"

## All Sentences Relate to a Sequence of Events

The narrator of the following paragraph is trying to save a man named Harry, who fears that a deadly snake has slithered into his bed. The paragraph does not actually have a main idea. However, each action described in the paragraph is part of a sequence that begins when the narrator leaves the room and that ends as he stands beside the bed wondering what to do.

Like many narrative paragraphs, this paragraph is actually a cause-and-effect paragraph. What one character does (a cause) results in the next action (an effect).

> I went softly out of the room in my stocking feet and fetched a small sharp knife from the kitchen. I put it in my trouser pocket, ready to use instantly in case something went wrong while we were still thinking out a plan. If Harry coughed or moved or did something to frighten the krait and got bitten, I was going to be ready to cut the bitten place and try to suck the venom out. I came back to the bedroom and Harry was still lying there very quiet and sweating all over his face. His eyes followed me as I moved across the room to his bed, and I could see he was wondering what I'd been up to. I stood beside him, trying to think of the best thing to do.
>
> Roald Dahl, "Poison"

**NOTE** Even though a topic sentence is not usually used in a narrative paragraph, some narrative paragraphs begin with a topic sentence that either presents the writer's impression of the events or states the kind of event being presented.

### Exercise 4  Identifying Sentences That Destroy Unity

Find the sentences that destroy unity in the paragraphs on the next page. Remember: To have unity, all details in a paragraph must be related to the topic sentence (main idea) or the sequence of actions.

**1.**     A batter who steps up to the plate usually tries to hit the ball as fast and as far as he can. He takes a full swing, putting all of his strength behind the bat. Sometimes, however, he bunts the ball. He tries to tap it lightly so that it will land about halfway between the pitcher and the catcher. To bunt, the batter usually does not swing at the ball. Instead, he just holds out the bat so that the ball strikes it and falls to the ground. Bats are made of single pieces of hardwood or of aluminum. The player who bunts is almost sure to be thrown out at first base. On the other hand, while the opponents are occupied with his play, other runners on his team may be able to move on.

**2.**     The women's rights movement began at the Seneca Falls Convention in New York in 1848. At that time, Elizabeth Cady Stanton introduced a resolution demanding suffrage, or the right to vote, for women. In 1869, Stanton and Susan B. Anthony formed a national organization to seek voting rights for women. In 1872, Anthony was arrested for breaking the law by voting in a presidential election, but by 1896, four states had given women the right to vote. In 1912, women's suffrage at last became an issue in a presidential campaign. Two years later, a suffrage petition signed by 404,000 women was presented to Congress. President Woodrow Wilson, responding to pressure by women's groups, endorsed a new amendment. Black males were granted the right to vote after the Civil War by the Fourteenth and Fifteenth Amendments. Finally, in 1919, the Nineteenth Amendment, giving women the right to vote, was passed by Congress.

*Susan B. Anthony*

# Coherence

Along with unity, a good paragraph also has *coherence.* If you have ever read a paragraph that did not make any sense to you, it probably did not have coherence. In other words, it was not easy for you to see how all the ideas in the paragraph fit together—how they were arranged and connected. You can create coherence by paying attention to two things: (1) the **order,** or **organizational pattern,** in which you arrange your ideas, and (2) the **connections** you make between ideas.

## Order of Ideas

How you arrange, or order, ideas in your paragraph can help your readers to follow those ideas. Often, the subject you are writing about will suggest the order of ideas. Sometimes, however, you will have to pick among several organizational patterns that suit your topic. Here are four useful ways to organize your ideas:

- **chronological order,** used to relate events in the order they happened
- **spatial order,** used to describe things according to where they are located, in relation either to one another or to a viewer
- **order of importance,** used to show importance of details in relation to one another
- **logical order,** used to group related ideas

**Chronological Order**   What happened when Ebenezer Scrooge met the Ghost of Christmas Past? How did the Egyptians build the pyramids? What caused the American Revolution? To answer any of these questions, it makes sense to describe the actions or events as they occurred in time. In other words, you would use chronological order. In fact, the prefix *chrono–* means "time."

Chronological order is used to **explain a process, tell a story,** or **explain a cause-and-effect sequence.** In the following example, the writer explains a process: how to find a honey tree.

> To find a honey tree, first catch a bee. Catch a bee when its legs are heavy with pollen; then it is ready for home. It is simple enough to catch a bee on a flower: hold a cup or glass above the bee, and when it flies up, cap the cup with a piece of cardboard. Carry the bee to a nearby open spot—best an elevated one—release it,
>
> *(continued)*

**Reference Note**

For more on **telling a story,** see page 62. For more on **explaining cause and effect,** see page 134.

*(continued)*

and watch where it goes. Keep your eyes on it as long as you can see it, and hie you to that last known place. Wait there until you see another bee; catch it, release and watch. Bee after bee will lead toward the honey tree, until you see the final bee enter the tree.

Annie Dillard, *The Writing Life*

**Spatial Order** Look at this term closely and you will get a clue to its meaning. Spatial order is used to arrange details according to how they are spaced—nearest to farthest, left to right, or any other reasonable arrangement. Spatial order is especially useful in descriptions because it helps the reader picture how details fit together. In the following example, notice how the writer uses words such as *middle, left, right, east,* and *west* to organize his description into spatial order.

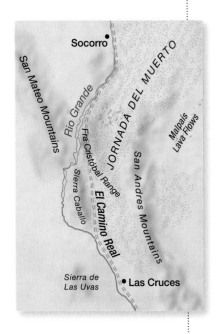

**View to the left**

**View to the right**

**View ahead (between left and right)**

My wife, Christine, and I are standing in the middle of the Jornada del Muerto, or journey of the Dead Man, a vast stretch of desert between Las Cruces and Socorro in south-central New Mexico. We are 40 miles from the nearest paved road, waiting for dawn. The austere Fra Cristóbal Mountains rise to our left, their barren summits flaring pink. To our right, a jagged line of broken basalt against the horizon marks the beginning of the *malpaís,* the badlands, an impassable area of immense lava flows. Between those lava flows in the east and the mountains in the west is a gap of only 500 yards. On geological survey maps it is called Lava Gate, and anyone traveling north or south in the Jornada del Muerto must pass through it.

Douglas Preston, "The Granddaddy of the Nation's Trails Began in Mexico"

**Order of Importance** You may find that one detail or piece of supporting information you want to use is more important than another. In this case, you may want to arrange your ideas by order of importance, keeping in mind that readers usually pay more attention to what they read first and to what they read last. The writer of the following paragraph about the effects of a long drought begins with the least serious problem—restrictions on watering lawns and washing cars. The paragraph ends with the most serious problem—the threat of fire.

> The two-year-long drought is causing serious problems in my hometown. For several months we have lived with severe limits on using water. We can water lawns or wash cars only from midnight to 4:00 A.M. Recently, restrictions have become even more severe. Our water use is regulated, so we must monitor how much water we use to wash laundry or dishes and bathe. Water quality has also become a problem. The water now has a sour odor, and most people do not feel safe drinking it. But the worst problem we are facing is the threat of serious fires. Three homes recently burned to the ground when a small grass fire grew out of control. Carelessness with fire, or lightning during a thunderstorm, could set our whole town ablaze.

**Logical Order**   For something to be logical, it has to make sense. In writing, logical order is created by grouping ideas together in a way that makes sense—that is, in a way that makes the relationships between the ideas clear. Logical order is especially important when you **compare and contrast subjects** or when you **define a subject.**

- **Comparing and Contrasting Subjects**   When you are dealing with two or more subjects, you will often find it useful to compare them (explain how they are alike), contrast them (explain how they are different), or both compare *and* contrast them.

- **Defining a Subject**   To define a subject, you first identify the large class or group to which it belongs. Then, you provide specific examples and details that distinguish the subject from other members of its group. The first sentence in the following paragraph defines the word *mummy,* and the other sentences give examples and details that show more specifically what mummies are and how they are preserved.

| Definition | A mummy is the preserved body of a human being or an animal, by any means, either deliberate or accidental. Mummies survive from many ancient cultures, some preserved in a wet state, |
| Specific example | others dry. The bog bodies of northern Europe, such as the 2,000-year-old Lindow Man, found in Cheshire, England, in 1984, belonged to people who had either fallen, or been thrown, into wet, |
| Details | marshy places. The exclusion of oxygen and acidity in the peat of the bog effectively preserved their |
| Details | bodies. Most mummies, though, were preserved by being dried, or desiccated. Many civilizations, |
| Details | including the Egyptian, Chinese and some South American cultures, tried to achieve this artificially. |

Christine El Mahdy, *Mummies, Myth, and Magic*

### Exercise 5  Choosing an Order of Ideas

Indicate which order (chronological order, spatial order, order of importance, or logical order) would work best for explaining each of the following topics. For some topics, you may indicate that more than one type of order would work well. Be prepared to explain your choices.

1. four characteristics of a good quarterback
2. choosing an after-school job
3. the perfect room for a teenager
4. middle school and high school
5. the right way to study for a test

### Review A  Identifying Order of Ideas

One of the following paragraphs is not well written; the sentences in it are not arranged in an order that is easy to follow. Read the paragraphs and identify the one that is not well written. Then, rewrite the paragraph, rearranging the sentences into an easy-to-follow order. Also indicate which order (chronological order, spatial order, order of importance, or logical order) is used in the other (well-written) paragraph.

1.   The naturalist Paul Rezendes has this advice for seeing nature and the great outdoors: Don't rush. Walk rather than drive a car or take a tour bus. Also try to spend some time alone. You notice new things when you aren't distracted by other people. Most important, he says, is to take your time. Take a pad and draw sketches or keep a journal, but don't take a camera. Rezendes says a camera makes you think you're capturing the place on film, when what you really need to do is to capture it in your mind.

2.   On the Fourth of July, we took the train into Boston. The second place we visited was the historic Old North Church. We first visited the *Constitution*, the famous American naval ship. We bought a takeout dinner at a little after five o'clock in the afternoon. We had a quick lunch at noon, and then we took a bus to see the aircraft carrier *John F. Kennedy*. At seven o'clock we ate our takeout dinner as we stretched out on a blanket beside the Charles River, waiting for the concert. By the time we finished our tour of the *John F. Kennedy,* it was almost five o'clock. After enjoying the concert, we made the long trip home.

## Connections Between Ideas

Along with putting ideas in an order that makes sense, you gain **coherence** in a paragraph by showing how the ideas are connected. You can show connections in two ways: by using **direct references** and by using **transitions**.

### Direct References

**Direct references** link ideas by referring to a noun or pronoun that you have used earlier in a paragraph. You can make a direct reference in three ways:

1. **Use a noun or pronoun that refers to a noun used earlier.**
2. **Repeat a word used earlier.**
3. **Use a word or phrase meaning the same as one used earlier.**

**STYLE TIP**

Direct references and transitional words and phrases can make connections between paragraphs as well as within paragraphs.

The following paragraph uses several direct references to make connections between ideas. Each reference is coded with the numbers above to show you what type of reference it is.

At the man's heels trotted a dog, a big native husky,[3] the proper wolf dog,[3] gray-coated and without any visible or temperamental difference from its[1] brother, the wild wolf.[2] The animal[3] was depressed by the tremendous cold. It[1] knew that it was no time for traveling. Its[1] instinct told it[1] a truer tale than was to be told to the man[2] by the man's[2] judgment. In reality, it was not merely colder than fifty below zero; it was colder than sixty below, than seventy below. It was seventy-five below zero.[2] Since the freezing point is thirty-two above zero,[2] it meant that one hundred and seven degrees of frost obtained. The dog[2] did not know anything about thermometers. Possibly in its[1] brain there was no sharp consciousness of a condition of very cold such as was in the man's[2] brain.[2] But the brute[3] had its[1] instinct. It[1] experienced a vague but menacing apprehension that subdued it[1] and made it[1] slink along at the man's[2] heels, and that made it[1] question eagerly every unwonted movement of the man,[2] as if expecting him[1] to go into camp or to seek shelter somewhere and build a fire. The dog[2] had learned fire,[2] and it[1] wanted fire,[2] or else to burrow under the snow and cuddle its[1] warmth away from the air.

Jack London, "To Build a Fire"

**Transitional Words and Phrases** The prefix *trans–* means "across" or "over." A transition in writing—whether it is a word, a phrase, or even a sentence—reaches *across* or *over* ideas, connecting one idea to another. When you use transitions, you not only connect ideas, but also show *how* they are connected—often by using phrases that include conjunctions and prepositions showing chronological or spatial order. The chart on the next page shows how certain transitions are related to certain types of writing.

| Transitional Words and Phrases | | | |
|---|---|---|---|
| **Comparing Ideas** | also | another | similarly |
| | and | moreover | too |
| **Contrasting Ideas** | still | in spite of | on the other hand |
| | but | instead | although |
| | yet | however | nevertheless |
| **Showing Cause and Effect** | for | so that | as a result |
| | since | because | therefore |
| | so | thus | consequently |
| **Showing Chronological Order** | after | eventually | at once |
| | then | finally | at last |
| | next | first | thereafter |
| | before | meanwhile | when |
| **Showing Spatial Order** | into | above | beyond |
| | next | across | down |
| | over | behind | around |
| | in | before | there |
| | here | inside | under |
| **Showing Order of Importance** | first | mainly | to begin with |
| | last | then | more important |

The following paragraph uses transitional words and phrases, which are underlined, to make connections in time and place.

> With nervous hands he lowered the piece of canvas which served as his door, <u>and</u> pegged it at the bottom. <u>Then</u> quickly <u>and</u> quietly, looking at the piece of canvas frequently, he slipped the records into the case, snapped the lid shut, <u>and</u> carried the phonograph to his couch. <u>There</u>, pausing often to stare at the canvas <u>and</u> listen, he dug earth from the wall and disclosed a piece of board. <u>Behind</u> this there was a deep hole in the wall, <u>into</u> which he put the phonograph. <u>After</u> a moment's consideration, he went <u>over</u> <u>and</u> reached <u>down</u> for his bundle of books and inserted it <u>also</u>. <u>Then</u>, guardedly, he
>
> *(continued)*

**STYLE TIP**

If you use transitional words and phrases (with the exceptions of *and* and *but*) in every sentence, your writing might sound artificial. Since direct references are more natural, feel free to use them frequently in your writing. Your readers will appreciate it.

*(continued)*

once more sealed up the hole with the board <u>and</u> the earth. He <u>also</u> changed his blankets, and the grass-stuffed sack which served as a pillow, <u>so that</u> he could lie facing the entrance. <u>After</u> carefully placing two more blocks of peat on the fire, he stood for a long time watching the stretched canvas, <u>but</u> it seemed to billow naturally with the first gusts of a lowering wind. <u>At last</u> he prayed, <u>and</u> got in <u>under</u> his blankets, <u>and</u> closed his smoke-smarting eyes. On the <u>inside</u> of the bed, <u>next</u> to the wall, he could feel with his hand, the comfortable piece of lead pipe.

Walter Van Tilburg Clark,
"The Portable Phonograph"

## Exercise 6 · Identifying Direct References and Transitions

The following paragraph uses both direct references and transitional words and phrases to connect ideas. Make two lists: one list of direct reference words and one list of transitions you find in the paragraph. (Hint: there are at least fourteen direct reference words and six transitions.)

EXAMPLE    My father started high school in Frederick, Maryland. When he was a junior, his family moved, and he finished high school in Baltimore.

| Direct References | Transitions |
|---|---|
| he | in |
| his | When |
| he | and |
| high school | in |

At Waterford Crystal in Ireland, each piece of crystal is still handmade. First, the glass-blowers dip long pipes into a 1,200-degree furnace. In the furnace, their pipes collect fiery lumps of molten crystal. Then they blow the hot lumps of crystal into "blank" cups, vases, and bowls of various sizes and shapes. Each piece must be thin and clear, yet thick enough to be engraved later. After the blank glass has cooled, the "masters" take over.

They use dime-sized diamond wheels to engrave the glass in one of Waterford's beautiful patterns. A typical Waterford glass takes about eight hours to make. To create a large, expensive piece, experienced engravers may take several weeks and go through a number of blank pieces of glass.

## Exercise 7 ) Using Transitions

The following paragraph is not completely clear. Revise it by adding transitions to make the connections it needs. Feel free to rewrite or combine sentences, too.

```
      Jason decided to hike across Glacier
National Park. He decided this at a young
age. He never actually did much hiking. On
his eighteenth birthday, he and a friend
made plans to explore Glacier National Park
on foot. Jason researched the history and
terrain of the park. He wrote to the park
service. He received a package full of
information and maps. He found out that
much of the park, which is in the northern
Rockies, is very rugged and isolated. He
bought clothing and packed provisions for
wilderness living. He arrived at the park
and talked to the park rangers. They told
Jason the best trails to follow. They gave
him safety tips.
```

## Elaboration

Along with unity and coherence, another quality of a good paragraph is **elaboration**. Remember that a good paragraph should contain **supporting sentences** that elaborate on the **main idea** presented in the paragraph's **topic sentence**. However, sometimes writers do not thoroughly develop, or elaborate on, a paragraph's main idea; these writers fail to provide enough supporting sensory details, facts and statistics, or examples. A paragraph with a poorly supported main idea is said to lack elaboration.

If you write a paragraph that lacks elaboration, you run the risk of confusing or misleading your readers—of not giving them enough information to understand the paragraph's main idea. The paragraph below lacks elaboration. Notice how something clearly seems to be missing from it.

> The youngest children in families often have a worse situation than their brothers or sisters. One reason they have it worse is that they are not taken seriously. The youngest children also live in the shadow of their siblings. Finally, the youngest children have parents who often are tired of teaching the same things they have taught so many times before.

The paragraph above cries out for more details. Do you wonder what the writer means when he writes that the youngest children "are not taken seriously"? What does the writer mean by the phrase "living in the shadow of their siblings"? What are the things the writer thinks that parents have "taught so many times before"? To see how the writer used elaboration to answer these questions, read the paragraph below.

| | |
|---|---|
| **Main Idea** | The youngest children in the family often have a worse situation than their siblings. One |
| **Reason 1** **Elaboration** | reason they have it worse is that they are not taken seriously. These children often have older brothers and sisters telling them that they are too little or too young or too weak to do something like set the table or program the VCR. |
| **Reason 2** **Elaboration** | The youngest children also live in the shadow of their siblings. It is not uncommon, for example, for the youngest child's achievements in school to be compared with the achievements of older brothers and sisters. Finally, the |
| **Reason 3** | youngest children have parents who often are tired of teaching the same things over and over. |
| **Elaboration** | Mother and Dad wonder how many times they will have to teach a child how to tie shoes and how to tell time. To sum up, with everything they must deal with, maybe the youngest children in the family do not deserve the "spoiled" label they are frequently given. |

The expanded details make the paragraph come alive and help the reader to understand more clearly the main idea the writer is trying to communicate.

**Exercise 8** **Elaborating with Details**

The following paragraph lacks elaboration. Add sensory details, facts and statistics, or examples to develop or expand on the ideas already present in the paragraph. To find facts and statistics, you will need to do some research. To find other details, you may want to work with a partner.

> Fantasy is often used in television commercials today. Commercials for household products frequently contain fantastic elements. Fantasy also frequently appears in fast-food commercials. Finally, commercials for pet food also sometimes use fantasy.

**STYLE TIP**

Elaboration is vital to writing strong paragraphs. Include at least two elaboration sentences for each of the major points in a paragraph.

# How Are Paragraphs Used in a Longer Piece of Writing?

So far, you have looked at the types of paragraphs that make up the bulk of a composition—body paragraphs. Be aware, though, that the beginning and the end of a composition are usually marked by two other types: an **introductory** paragraph and a **concluding** paragraph. You might think of the body paragraphs in a composition as the road between two destinations. The introductory paragraphs, then, are the points at which you check the map and set off; the concluding paragraphs are the points at which you look back on the journey and summarize it.

**Reference Note**

For strategies to use when **writing introductions and conclusions,** see page 905 of the Quick Reference Handbook.

## Dividing a Piece into Paragraphs

In the introduction to this chapter, you learned that paragraphs are used to mark a movement from one idea to another and to give a reader's eyes time to pause. When you write your own longer pieces, you will usually start a new paragraph for the following reasons:

- to discuss a different part of your subject or to explain another step in a process
- to show a jump forward or back in time

- to introduce another point of support for your opinion

- to indicate that the location of the action has changed

- to show (in a section of dialogue in a story) that a different person or character is speaking

**Exercise 9** **Dividing a Passage into Paragraphs**

The passage that follows was originally broken into three paragraphs. Discuss with some classmates where you think the paragraph breaks went—or should go. Be prepared to explain your choices.

> Both cattle and sheep ranches demanded hard work from everyone. As one Texan explained, the ranch owners "got right out with the boys on the trail" and did "just as much work." This description also applied to women, who played an integral part in ranch life. On most ranches, women did housework, cooked for all the cowboys, and helped with fence-mending, herding, or other chores. Many women organized their own ranch-related businesses. For example, Ella Bird accumulated her first herd of cattle by trading hand-sewn leather gloves and vests for yearlings. Ranch children often took on adult responsibilities at a young age. In addition to doing chores around the house, some boys and girls broke horses and herded cattle. The cowboy life offered children some interesting experiences, but the work was hard. John Norton, a young cowboy, said that he and his brother "leaped with joy" when the cattle they were herding were finally shipped for slaughter.
>
> from *The American Nation*

**Review B** **Writing a Paragraph**

Use elaboration to develop one of the skeleton paragraphs given on the next page. Be sure you use transitions and direct references to show how your ideas are connected.

**1.** Classrooms of the Ideal High School

The classrooms in the ideal high school are a dream come true for students. The desks are unbelievable. The technology is even better. The decorating contributes to a wonderful atmosphere.

**2.** Three Influential Areas

There are three areas of teenagers' lives that have a large influence on them. Early education and training affects them. Neighborhoods contribute to teens' lives. Friends are probably the most influential.

**3.** Fashion or Comfort?

People often seem to choose fashion over comfort. One area that reflects this idea is hair styles. Choices of clothing also show that comfort is secondary. Finally, make-up use definitely is not driven by comfort.

"Write me a sentence. Write me a paragraph. Write me a page. What are we? Her students or her pen pals?"

internet **connect**

GO TO: go.hrw.com
KEYWORD: EOLang

# Parts of Speech Overview
## The Work That Words Do

# Diagnostic Preview

### Identifying Parts of Speech

Write the part of speech (*noun, pronoun, adjective, verb, adverb, preposition, conjunction,* or *interjection*) of the italicized words in the paragraph below.

EXAMPLE   Pioneers [1] *learned* how to recognize danger.

   1. *verb*

The [1] *first* pioneers on the Great Plains [2] *encountered* many kinds [3] *of* dangerous animals. Grizzly bears and [4] *huge* herds of bison were menaces to [5] *early* settlers. One of the [6] *most* ferocious beasts of the plains [7] *was* a [8] *grizzly* protecting her cubs. However, [9] *neither* the bison *nor* the grizzly was the most feared animal [10] *on* the frontier. Not even the deadly [11] *rattlesnake*—nor [12] *any* of the other prairie creatures—was dreaded as much as the skunk. You may think, [13] "*Oh,* that is [14] *ridiculous.*" However, it is true. Skunks were not feared because [15] *they* smelled bad [16] *but,* instead, because they [17] *so* often carried [18] *rabies.* Since there was no vaccine for rabies in [19] *those* days, the bite of a rabid skunk spelled certain [20] *doom* for the unlucky victim.

# The Noun

**12a.** A *noun* is a word or word group that is used to name a person, a place, a thing, or an idea.

| Persons | Sharon, Major Brown, hairstylist, joggers |
|---------|-------------------------------------------|
| Places  | Iowa, districts, Mars, Antarctica, library |
| Things  | okra, Great Pyramid, toothpicks, merry-go-round |
| Ideas   | peace, truth, artistry, excellence, beauty |

## Common and Proper Nouns

A *proper noun* names a particular person, place, thing, or idea and is capitalized. A *common noun* names any one of a group of persons, places, things, or ideas and is generally not capitalized.

**Reference Note**

For more information on **capitalizing proper nouns,** see page 620.

| Common Nouns | Proper Nouns |
|--------------|--------------|
| scientist | Marie Curie, Charles Drew |
| woman | Coretta Scott King, Rita Moreno |
| city | Cairo, St. Louis, Paris |
| building | World Trade Center, Eiffel Tower |
| continent | North America, South America, Africa |
| day | Monday, Thursday, Labor Day |

### Exercise 1  Classifying Nouns

Identify each of the following nouns as a *common noun* or a *proper noun*. If the noun is proper, name a corresponding common noun.

EXAMPLE    **1.** Zora Neale Hurston

　　　　　*1. proper noun—writer*

1. man
2. month
3. Vietnam
4. singer
5. Athena
6. city
7. gumbo
8. self-esteem
9. Virginia
10. ocean
11. Mount Hood
12. Australia
13. Detroit
14. street
15. Amelia Earhart
16. mercy
17. cousin
18. automobile
19. blues
20. Christopher Columbus

BORN LOSER. reprinted by permission of Newspaper Enterprise Association, Inc.

# Concrete and Abstract Nouns

A *concrete noun* names a person, place, or thing that can be perceived by one or more of the senses (sight, hearing, taste, touch, and smell). An *abstract noun* names an idea, a feeling, a quality, or a characteristic.

| Concrete Nouns | cloud, poison ivy, thunder, silk, yogurt, Sarah |
|---|---|
| Abstract Nouns | freedom, well-being, beauty, kindness, Buddhism |

**Exercise 2** **Identifying and Classifying Nouns**

Write all the nouns that you find in each sentence. Then, circle the proper nouns.

EXAMPLE   1. English grows daily with the addition of new words.

1. (English,) addition, words

1. Some words come from other languages, such as Spanish and French.
2. Books, music, and movies often feature new words that are then added to everyday English.
3. Many useful and amusing words came into our language during World War II.
4. Now these words are familiar throughout the United States.
5. One of these words is *gremlin*.
6. Fliers were often troubled by mysterious mechanical problems.
7. Not knowing what caused these problems, they joked that gremlins—small, mischievous creatures—were in the aircraft.
8. According to Grandpa Leroy, these gremlins could be helpful as well as harmful.
9. Many fliers claimed that they had miraculously escaped danger only because the gremlins had come to their rescue.
10. Artists drew the imps as little men with beards and funny hats who played all over the planes.

# Compound Nouns

A *compound noun* consists of two or more words used together as a single noun. The parts of a compound noun may be written as one word, as separate words, or as a hyphenated word.

| One Word | firefighter, Iceland, newspaper |
|----------|--------------------------------|
| Separate Words | prime minister, Red River Dam, fire drill |
| Hyphenated Word | sister-in-law, Port-au-Prince, pull-up |

NOTE  If you are not sure how to write a compound noun, look in a dictionary. Some dictionaries may give more than one correct form for a word. For example, you may find the word vice-president written both with and without the hyphen. As a rule, use the form the dictionary lists first.

### Exercise 3  Identifying Compound Nouns

Each of the sentences below contains at least one compound noun. Write the compound noun(s) in each sentence.

EXAMPLE  1.  My cousin John is a political scientist.

1.  *political scientist*

1. I use a word processor or a typewriter in class.
2. We went swimming in the Gulf of Mexico.
3. My sister and my brother-in-law live in Council Bluffs, Iowa.
4. My Old English sheepdog is still a puppy.
5. Some almanacs give exact times for sunrises and sunsets.
6. We used to play hide-and-seek in the old barn.
7. Sitting Bull was the war chief who masterminded the Sioux victory at the Battle of the Little Bighorn.
8. Meet me at the bowling alley near the post office.
9. The fountain pen is not as popular as the ballpoint.
10. Luís Valdez is a playwright, actor, and director.

## Collective Nouns

A *collective noun* is a word that names a group.

| People | audience, chorus, committee, crew |
|--------|-----------------------------------|
| Animals | brood, flock, gaggle, herd |
| Things | assortment, batch, bundle, cluster |

**Reference Note**

For more on **collective nouns,** see page 501.

Identify the twenty-five nouns in the sentences below.

EXAMPLE    1. To enter the wildlife park, we walked through the mouth of a huge fake alligator.

1. *park, mouth, alligator*

1. Businesses sometimes use gigantic objects to advertise their products.
2. A stand that sells fruit might look like an enormous orange, complete with doors and windows.
3. A restaurant in Austin, Texas, has a delivery van shaped like a dinosaur.
4. Huge dogs, windmills, and figures of Paul Bunyan are formed with cement or fiberglass to help sell chain saws, trucks, and souvenirs.
5. An old hotel in New Jersey was even built to look like an elephant!

# The Pronoun

**12b.** A *pronoun* is a word that is used in place of one or more nouns or pronouns.

EXAMPLES    Stan bought a suit and an overcoat. **He** will wear **them** tomorrow. [The pronoun *He* stands for the noun *Stan*. The pronoun *them* stands for the nouns *suit* and *overcoat*.]

**Several** of the horses have gone into the stable because **they** are hungry. [The pronoun *Several* refers to the noun *horses*. The pronoun *they* stands for the pronoun *Several*.]

**Reference Note**

For more information about **antecedents,** see page 507.

The word that a pronoun stands for or refers to is called the *antecedent* of the pronoun. In the following examples, the arrows point from the pronouns to their antecedents.

EXAMPLES    The tour guide showed the **students** where **they** could see Mayan pottery.

Why did **Oscar** give **his** camera to the film school?

Darius scored a **field goal. It** was his first of the season.

Notice that a pronoun may appear in the same sentence as its antecedent or in a nearby sentence.

# Personal Pronouns

A **personal pronoun** refers to the one speaking (first person), the one spoken to (second person), or the one spoken about (third person).

| First Person | I, me, my, mine, we, us, our, ours |
|---|---|
| Second Person | you, your, yours |
| Third Person | he, him, his, she, her, hers, it, its, they, them, their, theirs |

EXAMPLES
**I** hope that **they** can find **your** apartment by following **our** directions.

**She** said that **we** could call **them** at home.

**He** asked **us** to help **him** clear away the fallen branches from **his** backyard.

**Their** dog obeyed **them** immediately and went to **its** bed.

**NOTE** In this book, the words *my*, *your*, *his*, *her*, *its* and *their* are called pronouns. Some authorities prefer to call these words adjectives. Follow your teacher's instructions on labeling these words.

Exercise 5  **Identifying Antecedents**

Give the antecedent for each italicized pronoun in the following paragraph.

EXAMPLE      In about A.D. 1150, a historian wrote down a strange tale English villagers had told **[1]** *him.*

1. him—historian

Since numerous people told the same story, the historian believed [1] *it.* Supposedly, a young boy and girl with bright green skin had been found wandering in the fields. [2] *They* spoke a foreign language and wore clothing made of an unknown material. At first, the two children would eat only green beans, but after [3] *they* learned to eat bread, [4] *their* skin gradually lost [5] *its* greenness. After learning English, the girl said [6] *she* and [7] *her* brother had come from a land called Saint Martin. The story sounds like science fiction, doesn't [8] *it*? Perhaps the villagers invented [9] *it* to amuse [10] *their* friends and fool historians.

## Reference Note

For information on **choosing pronouns that agree with their antecedents,** see page 507. For information on **clear pronoun reference,** see page 565.

S T Y L E        T I P

To keep your readers from getting confused, place pronouns near their antecedents—generally within the same sentence or in the next sentence.

CONFUSING
Please hand me the scissors. I also need some strapping tape. They are in the top drawer on the left. [Does *They* refer to the scissors or to both the scissors and the strapping tape?]

CLEAR
Please hand me the **scissors. They** are in the top drawer on the left. I also need some strapping tape. [Only the scissors are in the top drawer on the left.]

To find out if a pronoun is reflexive or intensive, leave it out of the sentence. If the meaning of the sentence stays the same without the pronoun, the pronoun is intensive.

EXAMPLES

Ron looked at himself in the mirror. [*Ron looked at in the mirror* doesn't mean the same thing. The pronoun is reflexive.]

Jenny painted the room herself. [*Jenny painted the room* means the same thing. The pronoun is intensive.]

Reference Note

For more information on **relative pronouns,** see page 473. For information on **subordinate clauses,** see page 471.

# Reflexive and Intensive Pronouns

A *reflexive pronoun* refers to the subject of a sentence and functions as a complement or as an object of a preposition. An *intensive pronoun* emphasizes its antecedent and has no grammatical function.

| First Person | myself, ourselves |
|---|---|
| Second Person | yourself, yourselves |
| Third Person | himself, herself, itself, themselves |

EXAMPLES    Elena treated **herself** to a snack. [reflexive]

               Albert **himself** organized the fund-raiser. [intensive]

# Demonstrative Pronouns

A *demonstrative pronoun* is used to point out a specific person, place, thing, or idea.

| this | that | these | those |
|---|---|---|---|

EXAMPLES    **That** is Soon-Hee's favorite restaurant in San Francisco.

               The tacos I made taste better than **those.**

# Interrogative Pronouns

An *interrogative pronoun* introduces a question.

| who | whom | which | what | whose |
|---|---|---|---|---|

EXAMPLES    **Which** of the songs is your favorite?

               **What** is your parakeet's name?

# Relative Pronouns

A *relative pronoun* introduces a subordinate clause.

| that | which | who | whom | whose |
|---|---|---|---|---|

EXAMPLES    The ship **that** you saw is sailing to Greece.

               Isabel is my friend **who** is training for the Boston marathon.

# Indefinite Pronouns

An *indefinite pronoun* refers to one or more persons, places, ideas, or things that may or may not be specifically named.

| | | | |
|---|---|---|---|
| all | each | most | one |
| another | either | much | other |
| any | everyone | neither | several |
| anybody | everything | nobody | some |
| anyone | few | none | somebody |
| anything | many | no one | something |
| both | more | nothing | such |

EXAMPLES    Angelo has **everything** he will need to go rock climbing.

                  Is **anyone** at home?

                  **Most** of the birds had already flown south for the winter.

┌─HELP───

Many of the pronouns you have studied so far may also be used as adjectives.

EXAMPLES

  **this** street
  **whose** puppy
  **many** acorns

Reference Note

For more about using **pronouns,** see Chapter 18.

### Exercise 6  Identifying Pronouns

Identify all the pronouns in the sentences below.

EXAMPLE    **[1]** My friend Hideko invited me to a Japanese tea ceremony at her house.

          *1. My, me, her*

**[1]** The tea ceremony at Hideko's house was more like some I have seen in movies than the traditional one shown in this picture. **[2]** "What happens during the tea ceremony, Hideko?" I asked as we entered the house. **[3]** According to Hideko, the purpose of the tea ceremony, a custom that dates back hundreds of years, is to create a peaceful mood. **[4]** In the ceremony, everyone sits quietly and watches the tea being made. **[5]** Before entering the room for the ceremony, I reminded myself to take off my shoes. **[6]** During the ceremony, each of us kneeled on a straw mat. **[7]** Hideko's mother was our tea hostess, the person who conducts the ceremony and prepares all of the tea. **[8]** She prepared the tea and served it in bowls that had been in the family for generations. **[9]** Then she served us sweet cakes called *kashi* (KAH-shee). **[10]** Afterward, Hideko herself gave me a box of tea leaves to take home with me.

GRAMMAR

# The Adjective

**12c.** An *adjective* is a word that is used to modify a noun or a pronoun.

## TIPS & TRICKS

The phrase *these five interesting books* can help you remember the questions an adjective can answer: Which books? These books. How many books? Five books. What kind of books? Interesting books.

To *modify* a word means to describe the word or to make its meaning more definite. An adjective modifies a noun or a pronoun by telling *what kind, which one,* or *how many.*

| What Kind? | **gray** skies | **Irish** lace |
| | **far-fetched** tale | **lowest** price |
| **Which One?** | **either** way | **those** girls |
| | **next** day | **last** chance |
| **How Many?** | **five** fingers | **fewer** hours |
| | **one** river | **some** problems |

## Demonstrative Adjectives

**Reference Note**

For more information about **demonstrative pronouns,** see page 380.

*Not being listed*

*This, that, these,* and *those* can be used both as adjectives and as pronouns. When they modify nouns or pronouns, they are called *demonstrative adjectives.* When they take the place of nouns or pronouns, they are called *demonstrative pronouns.*

| Demonstrative Adjectives | Did Jennifer draw **this** picture or **that** one? |
| | Let's take **these** sandwiches and **those** apples on our picnic. |
| Demonstrative Pronouns | **This** is mine and **that** is his. |
| | **These** are much more expensive than **those** are. |

## Pronoun or Adjective?

Some words may be used as either pronouns or adjectives. When used as pronouns, these words take the place of nouns or other pronouns. When used as adjectives, they modify nouns or pronouns.

| Pronoun | Adjective |
|---------|-----------|
| I like **that.** | I like **that** shirt. |
| **Either** will do. | **Either** car will do. |
| **Which** is yours? | **Which** one is yours? |
| **Whose** is it? | **Whose** hat is it? |

**NOTE** In this book, demonstrative, interrogative, and indefinite terms, such as those in boldface in the preceding chart, are called pronouns when they function as pronouns, and adjectives when they function as adjectives.

The words *my, your, his, her, its, our,* and *their* are called possessive pronouns throughout this book. Some authorities, however, prefer to call these words adjectives. Follow your teacher's instructions on labeling these words.

**HELP**

Possessive forms of nouns are also sometimes referred to as adjectives. Follow your teacher's instructions regarding these forms.

## Noun or Adjective?

Many words that can stand alone as nouns can also be used as adjectives modifying nouns or pronouns.

| Common Nouns | Adjectives |
|--------------|------------|
| cheese | **cheese** sandwich |
| snow | **snow** sculpture |
| winter | **winter** sale |
| weather | **weather** report |
| steel | **steel** girder |

Adjectives formed from proper nouns are called *proper adjectives.*

| Proper Nouns | Proper Adjectives |
|--------------|-------------------|
| Choctaw | **Choctaw** tradition |
| Texas | **Texas** coast |
| Picasso | **Picasso** painting |
| Dublin | **Dublin** streets |
| Roosevelt | **Roosevelt** administration |

**Reference Note**

For information about **capitalizing proper adjectives,** see page 620. See page 376 for more on **compound nouns.**

**NOTE** Sometimes a proper adjective and a noun are used together so frequently that they become a compound noun: *Brazil nut, French bread, Christmas tree, Swiss cheese.*

### Exercise 7  Identifying Nouns and Adjectives

Indicate whether each italicized word in the paragraph below is used as a *noun* or an *adjective*.

EXAMPLE     Do you want to see my new **[1]** *baseball* card?

1.  baseball—adjective

I love anything that has to do with [1] *baseball.* I save the [2] *money* I make mowing the golf course, and then I go to the [3] *card* [4] *store.* The [5] *store* owner sold me a terrific [6] *Don Mattingly* [7] *card* today. It came in its own [8] *plastic* case. I'll display my new card with my other favorites in a special [9] *glass* [10] *case* on the wall in my room.

## Articles

The most frequently used adjectives are *a, an,* and *the.* These words are usually called ***articles.***

*A* and *an* are called ***indefinite articles*** because they refer to any member of a general group. *A* is used before words beginning with a consonant sound. *An* is used before words beginning with a vowel sound.

EXAMPLES     **A** girl won.

They are having **a** one-day sale. [Even though *o* is a vowel, the term *one-day* begins with a consonant sound.]

**An** elephant escaped.

This is **an** honor. [Even though *h* is a consonant, the word *honor* begins with a vowel sound. The *h* is not pronounced.]

*The* is called the ***definite article*** because it refers to someone or something in particular.

EXAMPLES     **The** girl won.

**The** one-day sale is on Saturday.

Where is **the** elephant?

**The** honor goes to her.

# Adjectives in Sentences

An adjective usually comes before the noun or pronoun it modifies.

EXAMPLES   Ms. Farrell tells **all** students that **good** workers will be given **special** privileges.

A **sweating, exhausted** runner crossed the line.

In some cases, adjectives follow the word they modify.

EXAMPLE   A dog, **old** and **overweight,** snored in the sun.

Other words may separate an adjective from the noun or pronoun it modifies.

EXAMPLES   Beverly was **worried.** She felt **nervous** about the play.

**Cheered** by the crowd, the band played an encore.

NOTE   An adjective that is in the predicate and that modifies the subject of a clause or sentence is called a *predicate adjective*.

**Reference Note**

For more information about **predicate adjectives,** see page 573.

**Exercise 8   Revising Sentences by Using Appropriate Adjectives**

Add adjectives to make two entirely different sentences from each of the sentences below.

EXAMPLE   1. The waiter showed the woman to a table in the corner.

1. *The kindly waiter showed the shy woman to a pleasant table in the sunny corner.*

   *The haughty waiter showed the elegant woman to a private table in the shadowy corner.*

1. The blossoms on the trees filled the air with a scent.
2. As the clouds gathered in the sky, the captain spoke to the crew.
3. At the end of the hall were stairs that led to a room.
4. The car has a stereo and an air conditioner.
5. The singers and comedians gave a performance for the audience.
6. The birds flew to the birdhouse near the barn.
7. Theresa's interest in science began when she attended the class.
8. The house in the valley was constructed by builders.
9. The curtains on the windows added to the look of the room.
10. As the waves washed onto the shore, the children ran away.

**COMPUTER TIP**

Using a software program's thesaurus can help you choose appropriate adjectives. To make sure that an adjective has exactly the connotation you intend, look up the word in a dictionary.

## Review A  Identifying Nouns, Pronouns, and Adjectives

Indicate whether each of the italicized words in the following paragraph is used as a *noun,* a *pronoun,* or an *adjective.*

EXAMPLE  [1] Most high school *students* read at least *one* play by William Shakespeare.

1. *students*—noun; *one*—adjective

[1] *This* article tells about Shakespeare's *life.* [2] *Shakespeare,* perhaps the most *famous* playwright of all time, was born in Stratford-on-Avon in 1564. [3] He was baptized in the *small* church at Stratford shortly after *his* birth. [4] In 1616, *he* was buried in the *same* church. [5] If you visit his grave, you can find an *inscription* placing a curse on *anyone* who moves his bones. [6] Out of *respect* for his wish or because of fear of his curse, *nobody* has disturbed the grave. [7] As a result, his remains have never been moved to Westminster Abbey, where many *other* famous *English* writers are buried. [8] Visitors to *Stratford* can also see the house in *which* Shakespeare was born. [9] At *one* time tourists could visit the large house that Shakespeare bought for *himself* and his family. [10] *This* was where they lived when he retired from the London *theater.*

# The Verb

**12d. A *verb* is a word that is used to express action or a state of being.**

In this book verbs are classified in two ways—(1) as transitive or intransitive verbs and (2) as action, linking, or helping verbs.

## Transitive and Intransitive Verbs

A *transitive verb* is a verb that expresses an action directed toward a person, place, or thing. The action expressed by a transitive verb passes from the doer—the subject—to the receiver of the action. Words that receive the action of a transitive verb are called *objects.*

**Reference Note**

For more about **objects and their uses in sentences,** see page 431.

EXAMPLES  When **will** Neil **ring** the bell? [The action of the verb *will ring* is directed toward the object *bell.*]

Juanita **mailed** the package. [The action of the verb *mailed* is directed toward the object *package.*]

**Tell** the truth. [The action of the verb *Tell* is directed toward the object *truth.*]

An ***intransitive verb*** expresses action (or tells something about the subject) without the action passing to a receiver, or object.

EXAMPLES    Last Saturday we **stayed** inside. [The verb *stayed* does not pass the action to an object.]

After their long walk, the children **ate** quickly. [The verb *ate* does not pass the action to an object.]`

When she told her story, my, how we **laughed**! [The verb *laughed* does not pass the action to an object.]

A verb may be transitive in one sentence and intransitive in another.

EXAMPLES    Marcie **studied** her notes. [transitive]
Marcie **studied** very late. [intransitive]

The poet **wrote** a sonnet. [transitive]
The poet **wrote** carefully. [intransitive]

> **Exercise 9** **Using Transitive and Intransitive Verbs**\

Choose a verb from the following list for each blank in the paragraph below. Then, identify each verb as *transitive* or *intransitive*.

| | | | |
|---|---|---|---|
| drifted | landed | watched | experienced |
| floated | rode | met | admired |
| climbed | arrived | left | did |
| awaited | suggest | tried | drove |

EXAMPLE    Can you **[1]** _____ an activity for this weekend?
         *1. suggest—transitive*

Aunt Pam and I **[1]** _____ something really different last summer. We **[2]** _____ on inner tubes down a river in the wilderness. A guide **[3]** _____ our group with a truckful of giant tubes and picnic lunches and **[4]** _____ us about twenty miles upstream. Then everyone **[5]** _____ into a tube in the water. The guide **[6]** _____ in the truck for a picnic spot downstream, halfway back to the base. All morning, we **[7]** _____ lazily along in the sunshine and **[8]** _____ the wildlife along the shore. When we **[9]** _____ at the picnic spot, a delicious lunch **[10]** _____ us.

## Action Verbs

An ***action verb*** expresses either physical or mental action. Action verbs can be transitive or intransitive.

| Physical Action | write | sit | arise |
| | describe | receive | go |
| Mental Action | remember | think | believe |
| | consider | understand | know |

EXAMPLES   The audience **cheered** the lead actors. [transitive]

The audience **cheered**. [intransitive]

### Exercise 10  Writing Action Verbs

Write twenty action verbs, not including those previously listed. Include and underline at least five verbs that express mental action.

EXAMPLES   **1.** *soar*   **2.** *imagine*

## Linking Verbs

A *linking verb* connects the subject to a word or word group that identifies or describes the subject. The most commonly used linking verbs are forms of the verb *be*.

| | | |
| --- | --- | --- |
| be | shall be | should be |
| being | will be | would be |
| am | has been | can be |
| is | have been | could be |
| are | had been | should have been |
| was | shall have been | would have been |
| were | will have been | could have been |

Here are some other frequently used linking verbs.

| | | | |
| --- | --- | --- | --- |
| appear | grow | seem | stay |
| become | look | smell | taste |
| feel | remain | sound | turn |

**Reference Note**

For more about **intransitive verbs,** see page 386.

NOTE   Because they do not have objects (words that tell who or what receives the action of the verb), linking verbs are considered intransitive.

The noun, pronoun, or adjective that is connected to the subject by a linking verb completes the meaning of the verb and refers to the verb's subject.

EXAMPLES    The answer **is** "three." [The verb *is* links *answer* and "three."]

The answer **is** correct. [The verb *is* links *answer* and *correct.*]

The winners **are** they. [The verb links *winners* and *they.*]

The winners **are** happy. [The verb links *winners* and *happy.*]

Many linking verbs can be used as action verbs as well.

EXAMPLES    The wet dog **smelled** horrible. [The linking verb *smelled* links *dog* and *horrible.*]

The dog **smelled** the baked bread. [action verb]

The motor **sounded** harsh. [The linking verb *sounded* links *motor* and *harsh.*]

The engineer **sounded** the horn. [action verb]

The chef **tasted** the casserole. [action verb]

The casserole **tasted** strange. [The verb *tasted* links *casserole* and *strange.*]

Even *be* is not always a linking verb. Sometimes *be* expresses a state of being and is followed only by an adverb.

EXAMPLE    I **was** there. [*There* tells *where*. It does not identify or describe the subject *I.*]

To be a linking verb, the verb must be followed by a ***subject complement***—a noun or a pronoun that names the subject or an adjective that describes the subject.

**Exercise 11**  **Identifying Linking Verbs and the Words They Link**

Identify the linking verb in each of the sentences below. Then, give the words that are linked by the verb.

EXAMPLE    **1.** Dixie can be a very obedient dog.

*1. can be—Dixie, dog*

1. He felt foolish when his car ran out of gas.
2. Suddenly, it turned very dark, and the wind began to blow fiercely.
3. We had waited so long for dinner that anything would have tasted wonderful.

**Reference Note**
For a discussion of **adverbs,** see page 393.

**Reference Note**
For more on **subject complements,** see page 429.

**GRAMMAR**

4. The plot of that fantasy novel seems awfully childish to me now.
5. Kevin and I stayed best friends throughout middle school.
6. I am happy that you won the chess match.
7. If the coach had let me play, this game would have been my first one with the Tigers.
8. My father thinks that you should become a lawyer.
9. After practicing hard, Stef's band sounded great in the concert.
10. For a moment, Dr. Kostas thought the planet's rings appeared smaller.

### Exercise 12 Writing Appropriate Linking Verbs

Choose a linking verb for each blank. Try to use a different verb for each sentence.

EXAMPLE    **1.** The baby _____ sleepy after he was fed.

    *1. The baby grew sleepy after he was fed.*

1. That building _____ the new public library.
2. The car _____ funny.
3. The moose _____ huge.
4. I _____ very nervous about the driving test.
5. Her garden _____ dried and brown in the drought.
6. Let's hope the evening _____ cool.
7. We can eat the raspberries when they _____ red.
8. Burt _____ grouchy early in the morning.
9. The soup _____ too salty.
10. The puppy _____ healthy and playful.

### Exercise 13 Writing Sentences with Action Verbs and Linking Verbs

Choose five nouns from the numbered items below. For each noun, write two sentences, using the noun as the subject of each sentence. Use an action verb in one sentence and a linking verb in the other. Indicate which sentence contains the action verb and which contains the linking verb.

EXAMPLE    **1.** fireworks

    *1. The fireworks filled the night sky with bursts of color.—action verb*

    *The fireworks grew more colorful toward the end of the program.—linking verb*

1. pilot     4. skater     7. foghorn     9. movie

2. locomotive     5. football     8. Mrs. Wu     10. Lincoln

3. taco     6. coins

# Verb Phrases

A **verb phrase** consists of at least one main verb and one or more helping verbs. A **helping verb** (also called an **auxiliary verb**) helps the main verb express action or a state of being.

Besides all forms of the verb *be,* the following verbs can be used as helping verbs.

| | | | | |
|---|---|---|---|---|
| can | do | has | might | should |
| could | does | have | must | will |
| did | had | may | shall | would |

Notice how helping verbs work together with main verbs to form complete verb phrases.

EXAMPLES    **is** leaving      **may** become      **might have** remained

               **had** seemed      **should** move      **must have** thought

Sometimes the parts of a verb phrase are interrupted by other parts of speech.

EXAMPLES    She **had** always **been thinking** of her future.

               **Has** my sister **played** her new CD for you?

NOTE   The word *not* is an adverb. It is never part of a verb phrase, even when it is joined to a verb as the contraction *–n't.*

EXAMPLES    She **should** not **have borrowed** that necklace.

               She **should**n't **have borrowed** that necklace.

**Reference Note**

For information about **contractions,** see page 707.

## Exercise 14   Identifying Helping Verbs

Identify all the helping verbs in each of the following sentences.

EXAMPLE     **1.** How well did your brother recover from his back injury?

         *1. did*

1. Fortunately, he didn't need surgery.
2. His physical therapist has designed an exercise program for him.

3. Before exercising, he must spend at least five minutes warming up.
4. He will be using a back-extension machine.
5. Does he walk indoors on a treadmill or outdoors on a track?
6. At home, he will be exercising on a treadmill.
7. The doctor is always reminding my brother about proper techniques for lifting.
8. When lifting heavy objects, my brother must wear a back brace.
9. Should he try acupuncture or massage therapy?
10. Without physical therapy, he might not have healed as quickly and as completely.

### Exercise 15 Identifying Verbs and Verb Phrases

Identify all the verbs and verb phrases in the sentences below. Include all helping verbs, even if the parts of a verb phrase are separated by other words.

EXAMPLE    1. We will probably go to the movie if we can finish our assignment.

1. *will go, can finish*

1. Mr. Jensen always sweeps the floor first.
2. Then he washes the chalkboards.
3. He works slowly but steadily.
4. The weather forecaster had not predicted rain.
5. All morning the barometer was dropping rapidly.
6. The storm was slowly moving in.
7. Your dog will become fat if you feed it too much.
8. Dogs will usually eat everything you give them.
9. Generally, cats will stop when they have had enough.
10. After our team has had more practice, we will win.

### Exercise 16 Revising Dialogue Using Verbs

Using a variety of verbs can make dialogue more interesting. Rewrite the dialogue below. In six of the ten items, replace *said* with one of the verbs from the following list. In the other four items, choose your own verbs.

| | | | |
|---|---|---|---|
| wailed | bellowed | gloated | reported |
| responded | teased | soothed | confessed |
| exclaimed | replied | whined | accused |
| snapped | cried | muttered | called |
| howled | roared | pleaded | snapped |

EXAMPLE 1. "Mom, I'm home!" said Tony, sprinting in the door.

1. *"Mom, I'm home!" bellowed Tony, sprinting in the door.*

2. "I've got great news!" he said.

2. *"I've got great news!" he shouted.*

1. "Guess what? I won the spelling bee," he said.
2. "Honey, that's wonderful," said his mother.
3. "I spelled 'expeditious' when no one else could, not even Stephanie Greenblatt," said Tony.
4. "I'm so proud of you," said his mother.
5. "Who cares?" said his sister Amy.
6. "You're just jealous," said Tony.
7. "I am not!" Amy said, running out of the kitchen.
8. "Don't let her bother you," said his mother. "You should enjoy your success."
9. "I am enjoying it," said Tony, "but I wish I could share my happiness with Amy."
10. "She'll come around," his mother said. "Meanwhile, sit down and tell me all about it."

# The Adverb

**12e.** An *adverb* modifies a verb, an adjective, or another adverb.

An adverb tells *where, when, how,* or *to what extent* (*how long* or *how much*). Just as an adjective makes the meaning of a noun or a pronoun more definite, an adverb makes the meaning of a verb, an adjective, or another adverb more definite.

## Adverbs Modifying Verbs

In the following examples, each boldface adverb modifies a verb.

| Where? | When? |
|--------|-------|
| We lived **there**. | May we go **tomorrow**? |
| Please step **up**. | Water the plant **weekly**. |
| I have the ticket **here**. | We'll see you **later**. |
| Put that **down**. | He arrived **early**. |

**TIPS & TRICKS**

To identify a word as an adverb, ask yourself:

Does this word modify a verb, an adjective, or an adverb?

Does it tell *when, where, how,* or *to what extent*?

| How? | To What Extent? |
|---|---|
| She **quickly** agreed. | Fill the tank **completely.** |
| The rain fell **softly.** | He **hardly** moved. |
| Drive **carefully.** | Did she hesitate **slightly**? |
| He sang **beautifully.** | They **partly** completed the form. |

As you can see in the preceding examples, adverbs may come before or after the verbs they modify. Sometimes adverbs interrupt the parts of a verb phrase.

Adverbs may also introduce questions.

EXAMPLE    **Where** in the world did you ever find that pink-and-purple necktie? [The adverb *Where* introduces the question and modifies the verb phrase *did find.* The adverb *ever* interrupts the verb phrase and also modifies it.]

NOTE   Although many adverbs end in –*ly*, the –*ly* ending does not necessarily mean that a word is an adverb. Many adjectives also end in –*ly*: the *daily* newspaper, an *early* train, an *only* child, a *lonely* person. Also, some words, such as *now, then, far, already, somewhat, not*, and *right*, are often used as adverbs, yet they do not end in –*ly*.

## Exercise 17  Completing Sentences by Supplying Appropriate Adverbs

Complete each of the following sentences by supplying an appropriate adverb. The word or phrase in parentheses tells you what information the adverb should give about the action.

EXAMPLE   **1.**  He moved his hand (*how*).

**1.**  *gracefully*

**1.** The soldiers must travel (*how*).
**2.** You will probably sleep well (*when*).
**3.** They whispered (*how*) to Mr. Baldwin.
**4.** Tonya took a deep breath and dove (*where*).
**5.** Did you study (*to what extent*)?
**6.** Handle the ducklings (*how*).
**7.** My uncle Hans is (*when*) in a bad mood.
**8.** Your taxi should be (*where*) soon.
**9.** I could (*to what extent*) taste the tangy pizza.
**10.** (*When*), you should paste the pictures on the poster.

# Adverbs Modifying Adjectives

EXAMPLES   Beth did an **exceptionally** fine job. [The adverb *exceptionally* modifies the adjective *fine*, telling *to what extent*.]

**Slightly** cooler temperatures are forecast. [The adverb *slightly* modifies the adjective *cooler*, telling *to what extent*.]

Mr. Lomazzi is an **especially** talented chef. [The adverb *especially* modifies the adjective *talented*, telling *to what extent*.]

**GRAMMAR**

**Exercise 18** **Identifying Adverbs That Modify Adjectives**

Identify the adverbs that modify adjectives in the sentences below. For each adverb, give the adjective it modifies.

EXAMPLE   **1.** The compass I bought was incredibly cheap.

1. *incredibly—cheap*

1. If you are ever really lost in the woods at night, knowing how to find the North Star may be extremely important.
2. Here is one method that is quite useful.
3. First, find the Big Dipper, which is surprisingly easy to spot.
4. It consists of seven rather bright stars in the northern sky that are arranged in the shape of a large dipper.
5. Do not confuse it with the Little Dipper, which is somewhat smaller.
6. After you have found the Big Dipper, you must be very careful to sight along the two stars that form the front of the dipper bowl.
7. They are two points on an almost straight line to the North Star.
8. This method for getting your bearings is completely reliable—except when the clouds are so dense that you cannot see the stars.
9. It would be especially wise to check the weather forecast before going on a hike.
10. Remember to take a compass, water, and a fully stocked first-aid kit.

**Exercise 19** **Revising with Adverb Modifiers**

Make each of the phrases and sentences below more descriptive by adding one adverb that modifies each of the italicized adjectives. Use a different adverb in each item.

EXAMPLE    **1.** a *confusing* sentence

    *1.* an especially confusing sentence

1. a *sharp* turn
2. *playful* kittens
3. an *easy* question
4. a *swept* floor
5. Her little brother has a *bright* smile.
6. Terri felt *satisfied* that she had done her best.
7. The old mansion was *silent*.
8. Robert became *sick* and had to leave early.
9. Had Clara been *safe*?
10. Most of the questions on the test were *difficult*.

# Adverbs Modifying Other Adverbs

EXAMPLES    Calvin was **almost** never there. [The adverb *almost* modifies the adverb *never*, telling *to what extent*.]

    We'll meet **shortly** afterward. [The adverb *shortly* modifies the adverb *afterward*, telling *to what extent*.]

    She slept **too** late. [The adverb *too* modifies the adverb *late*, telling *to what extent*.]

**Reference Note**

For information about **compound sentences,** see page 481. For information on **adverb clauses,** see page 476.

NOTE    One kind of adverb—the **conjunctive adverb**—is an adverb used as a connecting word between independent clauses in a compound sentence.

EXAMPLE    We tried to be at the stadium by 6:30 P.M.; **however,** we arrived at the wrong time.

Another kind of adverb—the **relative adverb**—is often used to introduce adjective clauses.

EXAMPLES    Uncle Lionel told us about the time **when** he drove across the country.

    In 1815, Napoleon was sent into exile on the island of St. Helena, **where** he died in 1821.

# Noun or Adverb?

Some words that can be used as nouns can also be used as adverbs.

EXAMPLES  **Tomorrow** never seems to arrive. [*noun*]

We will leave **tomorrow**. [*Tomorrow* is used as an adverb telling *when*.]

Think of this place as your **home**. [*noun*]

He was eager to come **home**. [*Home* is used as an adverb telling *where*.]

When identifying parts of speech, remember: A word used to modify a verb, an adjective, or another adverb is called an adverb.

"I miss the good old days when all we had to worry about was nouns and verbs."

© 1984 by Sidney Harris–Punch.

**Exercise 20** **Identifying Adverbs That Modify Other Adverbs**

Identify all the adverbs that modify other adverbs in the sentences below. After each adverb, give the adverb it modifies.

EXAMPLE  **1.** Brian is so terribly shy that he blushes when people speak to him.

*1. so, terribly*

**1.** The cat leapt to the windowsill quite agilely.
**2.** The books were stacked rather haphazardly.
**3.** Corrie knew she'd have to get up incredibly early to watch the eclipse tomorrow.
**4.** The tornado almost completely destroyed the barn.
**5.** The famous diamond was more heavily guarded than any other exhibit at the museum.
**6.** My brother is nearly always finished with his paper route before I am finished with mine.
**7.** She registered too late to be eligible for the classes she wanted.
**8.** In the final four minutes of the game, Isiah Thomas shot extremely accurately.
**9.** Usually it seems that each month goes more rapidly than the month before.
**10.** They walked onto the stage most calmly, as if they felt completely relaxed.

## Exercise 21  Identifying Adverbs and the Words They Modify

Identify the adverb or adverbs in each of the following sentences. Then, give the word or expression that each adverb modifies. If a sentence does not contain an adverb, write *none*.

EXAMPLE
1. Have you ever thought about writing a movie script?

1. *ever—have thought*

1. Successful movie scripts, or screenplays, are written according to a very rigid formula.
2. The main character and the action of the story must grab an audience's interest quickly.
3. Almost exactly twenty-five minutes into the movie comes a "plot point."
4. A plot point is a surprising event that swings the story around in another direction.
5. Most of the action and conflict occurs in the next hour of the movie.
6. Then comes another plot point, about eighty-five minutes into the movie.
7. Finally, the audience learns what happens to the characters.
8. The last time I went to a movie I really liked, I checked my watch.
9. It was quite interesting to find that the movie's timing matched this formula.
10. Try this test yourself sometime.

## Exercise 22  Revising Sentences by Using Appropriate Adverbs

Revise each of the sentences below by adding at least one appropriate adverb. Try not to use the adverbs *too, so, really,* and *very.*

EXAMPLE
1. Dana, bring me the fire extinguisher!

1. *Dana, bring me the fire extinguisher now!*

1. Angelo promised me that he would try to meet the train.
2. My coat was torn during the long hike, so Barbara lent me her plastic poncho.
3. Engineering degrees are popular with students because job opportunities in engineering are good.
4. The Wallaces are settled into a new house, which they built by themselves.

5. When the baseball season begins, I will be attending games every day.
6. Ronald dribbled to his left and threw the ball into a crowd of defenders.
7. Visits to national monuments and parks remind us that our country has an exciting history.
8. We returned the book to Marcella, but she had planned her report without it.
9. Georgia O'Keeffe displayed her paintings and received the admiration of a large audience.
10. The recipe calls for two eggs, but I did not have time to buy any at the store.

**Review B** **Identifying Nouns, Pronouns, Adjectives, Verbs, and Adverbs**

Indicate whether the italicized words in the paragraph below are used as *nouns, pronouns, adjectives, verbs,* or *adverbs.*

EXAMPLE    **[1]** *You* may know that Brazil is the *largest* country in South America.

1. *You—pronoun; largest—adjective*

[1] My *best* friend's mother just *came* back from visiting her family in Brazil. [2] *She* showed us *some* pictures she took in Brasília, the capital, and told us about it. [3] It was amazing to learn that *this* area had been *jungle* until construction began in the 1950s. [4] At first, few people lived in Brasília because it was so *isolated.* [5] However, over the *years* hundreds of thousands of people *have* moved *there.* [6] Several other Brazilian cities *also* lie within one hundred *miles* of Brasília. [7] *A* number of *good* highways *connect* Brasília with other major cities. [8] Residents enjoy the wide streets and open spaces *that* are *shown* in this picture. [9] *One* of Brasília's *most* striking features is its bold architecture. [10] Aren't the government buildings at the *Plaza* of the Three Powers *fantastic?*

# The Preposition

**12f.** A *preposition* is a word that shows the relationship of a noun or a pronoun to another word.

By changing the prepositions in the following examples, you can change the relationship of *Saint Bernard* to *bed* and *Everything* to *beach*.

| | |
|---|---|
| The Saint Bernard slept **near** my bed. | Everything **about** the beach was wonderful. |
| The Saint Bernard slept **under** my bed. | Everything **except** the beach was wonderful. |
| The Saint Bernard slept **on** my bed. | Everything **from** the beach was wonderful. |
| The Saint Bernard slept **beside** by bed. | Everything **on** the beach was wonderful. |

The noun or pronoun that a preposition relates another word to is called the *object of the preposition.* In the examples above, *bed* and *beach* are the objects of the prepositions.

### Commonly Used Prepositions

| | | | |
|---|---|---|---|
| aboard | below | from | since |
| about | beneath | in | through |
| above | beside | inside | throughout |
| across | besides | into | till |
| after | between | like | to |
| against | beyond | near | toward |
| along | but (meaning *except*) | of | under |
| amid | | off | underneath |
| among | by | on | until |
| around | concerning | onto | up |
| as | down | out | upon |
| at | during | outside | with |
| before | except | over | within |
| behind | for | past | without |

**NOTE** Many words in the preceding list can also be used as adverbs. To be sure that a word is used as a preposition, ask whether the word relates a noun or a pronoun to another word. Compare the following sentences:

> Welcome **aboard.** [adverb]
> Welcome **aboard** our boat. [preposition]
>
> The runner fell **behind.** [adverb]
> The paper fell **behind** the cabinet. [preposition]

**STYLE** / **TIP**

In casual speech and informal writing, people often end sentences with prepositions. However, in formal speech and writing, it is best to avoid doing so.

Prepositions that consist of two or more words are called *compound prepositions*.

| Compound Prepositions | |
|---|---|
| according to | in place of |
| as of | in spite of |
| aside from | instead of |
| because of | next to |
| by means of | on account of |
| in addition to | out of |
| in front of | prior to |

**NOTE** As a rule, the object of the preposition follows the preposition.

EXAMPLE    Add a teaspoon of freshly ground **cinnamon.**
[*Cinnamon* is the object of the preposition *of.*]

Sometimes, however, the object of the preposition comes before the preposition.

EXAMPLE    He is a singer **whom** I've never heard of before.
[*Whom* is the object of the preposition *of.*]

Objects of prepositions may be compound.

EXAMPLES    Kyoko called **to Nancy** and **me.**
[Both *Nancy* and *me* are objects of the preposition *to.*]

The marbles were scattered **under** the **table** and **chairs.**
[Both *table* and *chairs* are objects of the preposition *under.*]

The preposition, its object, and any modifiers of the object together form a *prepositional phrase.* Notice in the following examples that modifiers of the object of the preposition can come before or after the object.

EXAMPLES    Joe went **to the nearest store.** [The noun *store* is the object of the preposition *to.* The adjectives *the* and *nearest* modify the noun *store.*]

Is she one **of those trailing behind**? [The pronoun *those* is the object of the preposition *of. Those* is modified by the participial phrase *trailing behind.*]

The kitten hopped **into the big paper bag that Anita brought.** [The noun *bag* is the object of the preposition *into. Bag* is modified by the adjectives *the, big,* and *paper* and by the subordinate clause *that Anita brought.*]

**Reference Note**

For more information about **prepositional phrases,** see page 442.

**Reference Note**

For more information about **infinitives,** see page 457.

NOTE   Be careful not to confuse a prepositional phrase that begins with *to* (*to town, to her club*) with an infinitive that begins with *to* (*to run, to be seen*). Remember: A prepositional phrase always has a noun or a pronoun as an object.

### Exercise 23   Identifying Prepositions and Their Objects

Identify each preposition and its object in the following sentences.

EXAMPLE    1. I've been studying Spanish in school for three years.

       1. *in—school; for—years*

┌HELP┐

Sentences in Exercise 23 may have a compound object of a preposition.

1. Last week, my Spanish class went on a field trip to Monterrey, Mexico, 140 miles southwest of Laredo, Texas, where we live.
2. Señora Ayala, our teacher, wanted us to practice speaking and reading Spanish outside the classroom.
3. Everyone was supposed to speak only Spanish during the trip.
4. We first went to the *Museo de la Historia Mexicana* and saw colorful displays of art and crafts and many other cultural exhibits.
5. J. D., Leo, Yolanda, and I looked around the museum and read the information about each exhibit.
6. Besides the museum, we visited the *Barrio Antiguo,* a beautiful district that dates from the seventeenth century.
7. Later, we decided to go to a restaurant near the *Gran Plaza,* the big square.
8. As Señora Ayala walked among our tables, she listened to us order our tacos, enchiladas, and frijoles in Spanish.

9. We walked around the *Gran Plaza* and then went into the cathedral, which was completed in the eighteenth century.
10. As we got ready to leave, we chatted in Spanish about all of the interesting things we had seen.

**Exercise 24** **Using Appropriate Prepositions**

Use appropriate prepositions to fill the blanks in the following sentences.

EXAMPLE  1. Tasty, fresh lobster is a treat, _____ many diners.
      1. *Tasty, fresh lobster is a treat, according to many diners.*

1. Lobsters are large, green or gray, bottom-dwelling shellfish that live _____ the sea.
2. The people who fish _____ these creatures are hardy and very determined folk.
3. Using small, specially built boats and a number _____ cratelike traps made _____ wood, they go to work.
4. Lobster fishing _____ the United States has been practiced only _____ the last century; before that time people thought lobster was not good to eat.
5. For centuries, farmers used the plentiful lobsters as fertilizer _____ their gardens.
6. To catch lobsters, the fishers first lower traps _____ chunks _____ bait _____ the sea.
7. Then the fishers mark the location _____ colorful floats that identify the owners.
8. If the fishers are lucky, the lobster enters the trap _____ the part called the *kitchen*, tries to escape _____ another opening called the *shark's mouth*, and then is trapped _____ the section called the *parlor*.
9. Fishers call a lobster _____ only one claw a *cull*; one _____ any claws is called a *pistol* or a *buffalo*.
10. By law, undersized lobsters must be returned _____ the sea.

# The Conjunction

**12g.** A *conjunction* is a word that joins words or word groups.

A *coordinating conjunction* joins words or word groups that are used in the same way.

## TIPS & TRICKS

You can remember the coordinating conjunctions as FANBOYS:

**F**or
**A**nd
**N**or
**B**ut
**O**r
**Y**et
**S**o

| Coordinating Conjunctions | | | |
|---|---|---|---|
| and | but | or | nor |
| for | yet | so | |

EXAMPLES    streets **and** sidewalks [two nouns]

on land **or** at sea [two prepositional phrases]

Judy wrote down the number, **but** she lost it.
[two independent clauses]

*Correlative conjunctions* are pairs of conjunctions that join words or word groups that are used in the same way.

| Correlative Conjunctions | |
|---|---|
| both . . . and | not only . . . but also |
| either . . . or | neither . . . nor |
| whether . . . or | |

**Reference Note**

A third kind of conjunction—the **subordinating conjunction**—is discussed on page 477.

EXAMPLES    **Both** Jim Thorpe **and** Roberto Clemente were outstanding athletes. [two proper nouns]

We want to go **not only** to Ontario **but also** to Quebec. [two prepositional phrases]

**Either** we will buy it now, **or** we will wait for the next sale. [two independent clauses]

**Neither** Mark Twain **nor** James Joyce won the Nobel Prize in literature. [two proper nouns]

We should decide **whether** to stay **or** to go.
[two infinitives]

## HELP

In the first example for Exercise 25, *and* is a coordinating conjunction, and *both . . . and* is a correlative conjunction. In the second example, *Neither . . . nor* is a correlative conjunction.

### Exercise 25   Identifying and Classifying Conjunctions

Identify all the coordinating and correlative conjunctions in the sentences below. Be prepared to tell which ones are *coordinating conjunctions* and which ones are *correlative conjunctions*.

EXAMPLES    1. For my family and me, moving is both an exciting and a dangerous experience.

     1. *and, both . . . and*

     2. Neither my father nor I have a sense of our limitations.

     2. *Neither . . . nor*

1. When we bought our new house, my mother wanted to hire movers, but my father and I said we could do the moving more efficiently by ourselves.
2. We said that doing the job ourselves would be not only much faster and easier but also far less expensive than having movers do it for us.
3. Neither my mom nor my brother was enthusiastic, but at last Dad and I convinced them.
4. Luckily, Uncle Waldo and my cousin Fred volunteered to help, for they thought it was a great idea.
5. Both Uncle Waldo and Fred lift weights, and they love to show off their muscles.
6. The rental truck we had reserved wasn't large enough, so we had to make several trips.
7. At the new house, we could get the sofa through neither the back door nor the front door, and Uncle Waldo strained his back trying to loosen the sofa from the door frame.
8. On the second load, either Fred or my father lost his grip, and the refrigerator fell on Dad's foot.
9. By the end of the day, all of us were tired and sore, but we had moved everything ourselves.
10. Whether we saved money or not after paying both Uncle Waldo's and Dad's medical bills and having the doorway widened is something we still joke about in our family.

# The Interjection

**12h.** An *interjection* is a word that expresses emotion. An interjection has no grammatical relation to the rest of the sentence.

| | | | |
|---|---|---|---|
| ah | hurrah | uh-oh | wow |
| aha | oh | well | yahoo |
| boy-oh-boy | oops | whew | yikes |
| hey | ouch | whoa | yippee |

Since an interjection is not grammatically related to other words in the sentence, it is set off from the rest of the sentence by an exclamation point or by a comma or commas.

Interjections are common in casual conversation. In writing, however, they are usually used only in informal notes and letters, in advertisements, and in dialogue. When you use an interjection, make sure the punctuation after it reflects the intensity of emotion you intend. Use an exclamation point to indicate strong emotion and a comma to indicate mild emotion.

EXAMPLES **Hey!** Be careful of that wire!

There's a skunk somewhere, **ugh!**

**Well,** I guess that's that.

I like that outfit, but, **wow,** it's really expensive.

**Oops!** The stoop is slippery.

Our team won the playoff! **Yippee!**

**Exercise 26** **Using Interjections**

In the following dialogue, Jason is telling his friend Michelle about a concert he attended. Use appropriate interjections to fill in the numbered blanks. Be sure you punctuate each interjection that you use.

EXAMPLES **[1]** "_____ You mean you actually got to go?" Michelle gasped.

1. *"Wow! You mean you actually got to go?" Michelle gasped.*

**[2]** "_____ I wish I could have gone!"

2. *"Boy-oh-boy! I wish I could have gone!"*

[1] "_____ how was the concert?" asked Michelle. "Tell me all about what happened."

Jason shook his head. "The opening act was terrible. [2] _____ It seemed as if they played forever!"

"How was the rest of the show, though? [3] _____ Give me some details, Jason!"

"The drummer was fantastic. [4] _____ He acted like a wild man. He was all over the drums! But the best part was Stevie's twenty-minute guitar solo. [5] _____ he really let loose. The crowd went crazy!"

# Determining Parts of Speech

**12i.** The way a word is used in a sentence determines what part of speech it is.

The same word may be used as different parts of speech. To figure out what part of speech *well* is in each of the sentences on the next page, read the entire sentence. What you are doing is studying the word's *context*—the way the word is used in the sentence.

EXAMPLES   At the bottom of the old **well** were more than five
thousand pennies. [noun]

Whenever the reunion was mentioned, tears of joy
would **well** in her eyes. [verb]

**Well,** you may be right. [interjection]

Do you really speak four languages **well**? [adverb]

Fortunately, the baby is quite **well** now. [adjective]

( Exercise 27 ) **Identifying Words as Different
Parts of Speech**

Read each of the sentences below. Then, identify the part of speech of
the italicized word. Be ready to justify your answer by telling how the
word is used in the sentence.

EXAMPLE   **1.** Aunt Shirley got a *raise.*

*1. noun*

**1.** Did Gander Pond *ice* over last year?
**2.** An *ice* storm struck.
**3.** *Many* of these items are on sale.
**4.** The light flashed *on* and we entered the garage.
**5.** We rode *on* the subway.
**6.** The radio is *on.*
**7.** They went to the *park.*
**8.** We can *park* the car here.
**9.** We waited, *oh,* about five minutes.
**10.** We are all here *but* Natalya.
**11.** I slipped, *but* I didn't fall, thank goodness.
**12.** *Off* the road they could see a light.
**13.** The shop was *off* the main street.
**14.** The deal was *off.*
**15.** "Can you climb *up* that tree?" asked Yolanda.
**16.** The sun was already *up* when they left for work.
**17.** Ernesto lives a few miles *up* the coast.
**18.** We had a long wait before the show started, but, *wow,* it was
worth it!
**19.** *Most* cats dislike taking baths.
**20.** Did they go all the way *through* the town?

HELP

Each missing
word in Exercise 28 is a
different part of speech.

## Exercise 28 Determining Parts of Speech

A soldier in the American Revolution brings his general this spy message
he found in a hollow tree. Unfortunately, termites have eaten holes in the
paper. For each hole, supply one word that makes sense, and give its part
of speech.

EXAMPLE     Please _____ this message to General Baxter immediately.
            *deliver—verb.*

*! The Redcoats are chasing me,     I expect them*
*to     me soon. They are camped     the river and*
*they are well rested. They will attack your     at*
*dawn's     light tomorrow. General,     must*
*prepare your troops to leave*
                        *Yours in haste, John Cadrain*

## Review C Writing Sentences Using the Same Words as Different Parts of Speech

Write forty sentences, using each of the words in the list below as two
different parts of speech. Underline the word and give its part of
speech in parentheses after each sentence.

HELP

Some words
may be used as more
than two parts of speech.
You need to give only
two uses for each word
in Review C.

EXAMPLE     1. up
            1. *We looked up. (adverb)*
               *We ran up the stairs. (preposition)*

| | | | |
|---|---|---|---|
| **1.** light | **6.** ride | **11.** help | **16.** that |
| **2.** run | **7.** in | **12.** drive | **17.** right |
| **3.** over | **8.** love | **13.** plant | **18.** signal |
| **4.** line | **9.** below | **14.** well | **19.** home |
| **5.** cook | **10.** picture | **15.** for | **20.** one |

# Chapter Review

## A. Identifying Parts of Speech

In each of the following sentences, identify the italicized word or word group as a *noun, pronoun, adjective, verb, adverb, conjunction, preposition,* or *interjection.*

1. Kofi Annan, who *became* secretary-general of the United Nations in 1997, is from Ghana.
2. *All* of the episodes of that show have been interesting.
3. I made *myself* a pimento cheese sandwich to take along.
4. This copy of the magazine is *hers.*
5. I wondered *whose* sculptures were on exhibit at the Dallas Museum of Art.
6. *That* is the third time Luisa has called me today.
7. "*Wow,* that was the fastest fly ball I've ever seen!" exclaimed Ernesto.
8. Rajiv *himself* was planning to show them around Kashmir.
9. Which of the liquids in the *smaller* beakers is clear?
10. Are those the bonsai trees *Mr. Yamamoto* told you about?
11. One of the oldest poems in the collection deals with the concept of *honor.*
12. The *cast* of the film includes many genuine descendants of Napoleon.
13. Erika and Mike *wrote* the screenplay together.
14. *Should* the alarm clock *have been set* to go off at 6:00 A.M.?
15. Those Italian clothes are well-made and *extremely* stylish.
16. *We* had been warned not to be late, yet by the time we arrived the show had already begun.
17. Warn Selena and him *about* the fire ants in the backyard before it's too late!
18. Marcel was coming down with a cold, *but* he felt obliged to keep his appointments.
19. Nancy enjoys reading about current affairs because it helps to broaden her general *knowledge.*
20. The gorilla admired *itself* in the mirror.

## B. Identifying Parts of Speech

In each of the following sentences, identify the italicized word or word group as a *noun, pronoun, adjective, verb, adverb, conjunction, preposition,* or *interjection.*

21. Football's most important contest *is* the annual Super Bowl game.
22. Thousands attend the game at the stadium, *and* millions watch it on television.
23. Professional football began with no system for *fairly* choosing a championship team.
24. Later, the *National Football League* was formed.
25. The two NFL teams *with* the best records play a championship game.
26. In the late 1950s the American Football League was formed, and *it* also held a championship game every year.
27. *Eventually,* the AFL and NFL championship teams played each other at the end of the season.
28. Ever since the *first* Super Bowl was played in Los Angeles in 1967, the competition has continued to improve.
29. Do *you* know any amazing records set by NFL players?
30. *Amazing!* Fran Tarkenton threw over three hundred touchdown passes in his professional football career.

## C. Identifying Parts of Speech

Identify the part of speech of each italicized word or word group in the following paragraph.

For **[31]** *me,* no **[32]** *spot* is **[33]** *better* than the beach. On **[34]** *hot,* sunny days, when the sand **[35]** *burns* my feet, I am always **[36]** *careful* **[37]** *about* putting on **[38]** *sunscreen.* I like to run **[39]** *through* the foaming surf and later relax under a beach umbrella. Most of the time, I **[40]** *enjoy* **[41]** *both* being with friends *and* being by **[42]** *myself.* With only **[43]** *strangers* around me, I **[44]** *feel* free to think my **[45]** *own* thoughts. I wander **[46]** *slowly* along the waterline, looking at all the interesting things that the sea **[47]** *has* washed up. Once I accidentally stepped on a **[48]** *jellyfish* and couldn't help but yell **[49]** "*ouch*!" when it stung my foot. Since then, I've learned to be **[50]** *more* careful about where I step.

# Writing Application

## Writing a Descriptive Paragraph

**Using Specific Adjectives**    Your class visited a wildlife park, but one of your friends was sick and could not go. Write a paragraph telling your friend about the field trip. Use specific adjectives to help your friend picture what he or she missed.

**Prewriting**    Make a list of the animals and the scenes that will interest your friend. Beside each item on your list, write one or two specific adjectives.

**Writing**    You may want to look at pictures of wildlife in magazines or books to help you think of exact descriptions as you write your first draft. Use a thesaurus to find adjectives that will help your reader visualize the animals you are describing.

**Revising**    Have a friend or classmate read your paragraph to see if you have created clear images. Revise your paragraph by adding specific adjectives if any descriptions are unclear or too general.

**Publishing**    Check your paragraph for errors in spelling and punctuation. Be sure that you have capitalized any proper adjectives. You and your classmates may want to create a wildlife-park bulletin board or multimedia presentation.

**Reference Note**

For more about **proper adjectives,** see page 620.

# 13

*(handwritten annotations in left margin:)*
subject-who or what is doing the verb (before)
1. Find verb-identify-L or A
linking verbs "seems to be" s= complement
2. verb what? who?
complement { a. p. N
{ b. p. A

# The Parts of a Sentence

## Subject, Predicate, Complement

## Diagnostic Preview

### A. Identifying the Parts of a Sentence

In the following paragraphs, identify each of the numbered italicized words, using these abbreviations:

| | | | |
|---|---|---|---|
| **s.** | subject | **p.a.** | predicate adjective |
| **v.** | verb | **d.o.** | direct object |
| **p.n.** | predicate nominative | **i.o.** | indirect object |

EXAMPLE     Are you a mystery **[1]** *fan*?

     1. p.n.

*(handwritten: p.n. I.O)*

Sir Arthur Conan Doyle certainly gave **[1]** *readers* a wonderful **[2]** *gift* when he **[3]** *created* the character of Sherlock Holmes. **[4]** *Holmes* is a **[5]** *master* of the science of deduction. He **[6]** *observes* seemingly insignificant **[7]** *clues,* applies logical reasoning, and reaches simple yet astounding conclusions. The Hound of the Baskervilles is an excellent **[8]** *example* of how Holmes solves a baffling **[9]** *mystery*. The **[10]** *residents* of a rural area are afraid of a supernatural dog that **[11]** *kills* people at night. Helpless against this beast, they seek the **[12]** *services* of Sherlock Holmes. Using logic, he solves the mystery and relieves the people's **[13]** *fear*. This story is **[14]** *one* of Conan Doyle's best because it is both **[15]** *eerie* and mystifying.

Link to Literature

*(handwritten: seems to be?)*

## B. Identifying and Punctuating the Kinds of Sentences

Copy the last word of each of the following sentences. Then, punctuate each with the correct end mark. Classify each sentence as *imperative*, *declarative*, *interrogative*, or *exclamatory*.

EXAMPLE    **1.** Sherlock Holmes has many dedicated fans

         *1. fans. —declarative*

**16.** How clever Sherlock Holmes is
**17.** Sir Arthur Conan Doyle wrote four novels and fifty-six short stories about Holmes
**18.** Have you read any of these stories
**19.** I particularly like the stories in which Holmes confronts the evil Professor Moriarty
**20.** Read just one of these stories, and see why millions of mystery fans love Sherlock Holmes

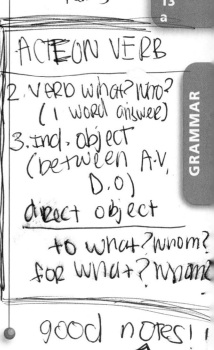

# The Sentence

In casual conversation, people often leave out parts of sentences. In writing, however, it is better to use complete sentences most of the time. They help to make meaning clear to the reader.

**13a.** **A *sentence* is a word or word group that contains a subject and a verb and that expresses a complete thought.**

A *sentence fragment* is a word or word group that is capitalized and punctuated as a sentence but that does not contain both a subject and a verb or does not express a complete thought.

FRAGMENT   Was waiting by the door. [no subject]
 SENTENCE   The clerk was waiting by the door.

FRAGMENT   The room with the high ceiling. [no verb]
 SENTENCE   The room with the high ceiling glowed in the sunset.

FRAGMENT   After you have finished the test. [not a complete thought]
 SENTENCE   Exit quietly after you have finished the test.

Some sentences contain an understood subject (*you*).

EXAMPLES   [You] **Stop!**

         [You] **Pass the asparagus, please.**

**Reference Note**

For information on **how to correct sentence fragments,** see Chapter 9. For information on **punctuating sentences,** see page 637.

**COMPUTER TIP**

Many style-checking software programs can help you identify sentence fragments. If you have access to such a program, use it to help you evaluate your writing.

**Reference Note**

For more about **understood subjects,** see page 423.

The Sentence   **413**

## Exercise 1  Identifying Sentences and Revising Fragments

Decide whether each of the following word groups is a sentence or a sentence fragment. If the word group is a sentence, correct its capitalization and punctuation. If the word group is a sentence fragment, revise it to make a complete sentence. Be sure to use correct capitalization and punctuation.

EXAMPLES  1. here are your glasses

1. *Here are your glasses.*

2. before going out

2. *Before going out, I always turn off the lights.*

1. on Monday or later this week
2. patiently waiting for the mail carrier
3. will you be there tomorrow
4. four people in a small car
5. just yesterday I discovered
6. two strikes and no one on base
7. it runs smoothly
8. leaning far over the railing
9. give me a hand
10. while waiting in line at the theater
11. on the way to the science fair
12. stand up
13. learning English
14. when is the marathon
15. it is time
16. to the left of the spiral staircase
17. romping along the shore this morning
18. it is theirs
19. you surprised me, Ellen
20. how you are

# Subject and Predicate

Sentences consist of two basic parts: *subjects* and *predicates*.

**13b.** The *subject* tells whom or what the sentence is about, and the *predicate* says something about the subject.

In the following examples, the subjects are separated from the predicates by blue vertical lines. Notice that the subject and the predicate may be only one word each, or they may be more than one word.

> Coyotes | were howling in the distance.

> The telephone in the lobby | rang.

> The woman wearing the red blouse | is my aunt.

In these three examples, the words that appear to the left of the vertical line make up the *complete subject.* The words to the right of the vertical line make up the *complete predicate.*

The subject may appear anywhere in the sentence—at the beginning, in the middle, or at the end.

EXAMPLES    In the dim light, **the eager scientist** examined the cave.

Does **Brian's car** have a CD player?

On the table stood **a silver vase.**

### Exercise 2   Identifying the Complete Subject

Identify the complete subject of each of the following sentences.

EXAMPLE    1. The art of quilting has been popular in America for a long time.

     1. *The art of quilting*

1. Ever since colonial times, Americans have made quilts.
2. Traditional designs, with names like Honeycomb, Tumbling Blocks, and Double Diamond, have been handed down from generation to generation.
3. The designs on this page are quilt blocks from a modern quilt.
4. They certainly don't look like Great-grandmother's quilts!
5. However, quilting techniques have stayed basically the same for well over a hundred years.
6. Small scraps of bright cloth are still painstakingly stitched together to create each block.
7. As in many antique quilts, each quilt block shown here was designed and sewn by a different person.
8. Some of the designs are simple.
9. In others, colorful details bring circus scenes to life.
10. A dark background is sometimes chosen to set off the brilliant colors of a quilt.

## Exercise 3 — Writing Complete Predicates

Rewrite each of the following items, adding a complete predicate to make a complete sentence. Be sure to use correct capitalization and punctuation.

EXAMPLE   1. that famous painting

1. *That famous painting sold for three million dollars.*

1. justice
2. some commercials
3. the store on the corner
4. the woman next door
5. one way to study
6. these guitars
7. the bicycle on the porch
8. the family reunion
9. a band
10. the best route

# The Subject

**13c.** The main word or word group that tells whom or what the sentence is about is called the *simple subject.*

The *complete subject* consists of the simple subject and any words, phrases, or clauses that modify the simple subject.

**Reference Note**

A compound noun, such as *Gloria Estefan,* is considered one noun. For more about **compound nouns,** see page 376.

EXAMPLES   A triumphant Gloria Estefan stepped up to the microphone.

| | |
|---|---|
| *complete subject* | A triumphant Gloria Estefan |
| *simple subject* | Gloria Estefan |

Out of the beaker rose a foul-smelling foam.

| | |
|---|---|
| *complete subject* | a foul-smelling foam |
| *simple subject* | foam |

Did you make the grits, Travis?

| | |
|---|---|
| *complete subject* | you |
| *simple subject* | you |

**NOTE**  In this book, the term *subject* generally refers to the simple subject unless otherwise indicated.

## Exercise 4 — Writing Complete Sentences

Make each of the following fragments a sentence by adding a complete subject. Underline each simple subject.

EXAMPLE   1. Did _____ watch the Super Bowl?

1. *Did your little <u>brother</u> watch the Super Bowl?*

1. _____ was baying at the moon.
2. _____ can make the pizza.
3. _____ is needed for this recipe.
4. Was _____ the person who won the match?
5. _____ rose and soared out over the sea.
6. _____ stood on the stage singing.
7. _____ were late for their classes.
8. Over in the next town is _____.
9. Buzzing around the room was _____.
10. In the middle of the yard grew _____.

## The Predicate

**13d.** The *simple predicate,* or *verb,* is the main word or word group that tells something about the subject.

The *complete predicate* consists of a verb and all the words that describe the verb and complete its meaning.

EXAMPLES   The ambulance raced out of the hospital driveway and down the street.

| | |
|---|---|
| *complete predicate* | raced out of the hospital driveway and down the street |
| *simple predicate* | raced |

Diego may have borrowed my book.

| | |
|---|---|
| *complete predicate* | may have borrowed my book |
| *simple predicate* | may have borrowed |

Are you following Mr. Fayed's advice?

| | |
|---|---|
| *complete predicate* | Are following Mr. Fayed's advice |
| *simple predicate* | Are following |

Notice that the simple predicate may be a single verb or a *verb phrase* (a verb with one or more helping verbs).

13
c, d

TIPS & TRICKS

When you are identifying the simple predicate in a sentence, be sure to include all parts of a verb phrase.

EXAMPLE
**Should** Marshal Ney **have used** the infantry at Waterloo? [The simple predicate is the verb phrase *Should have used.* The complete predicate is *Should have used the infantry at Waterloo.*]

### Commonly Used Helping Verbs

| | | | | |
|---|---|---|---|---|
| am | did | has | might | was |
| are | do | have | must | were |
| can | does | is | shall | will |
| could | had | may | should | would |

**NOTE** In this book, the word *verb* refers to the simple predicate unless otherwise indicated.

**Exercise 5** **Identifying the Complete Predicate and Verb**

For each of the following sentences, write the complete predicate. Then, underline the verb or verb phrase in each complete predicate.

EXAMPLE 1. Surfing and snow skiing are different in many ways.

     1. <u>are</u> *different in many ways*

1. The warm-weather sport of surfing uses the force of incoming waves.
2. The wintertime activity of snow skiing relies on gravity.
3. Surfers can pursue their sport with only a surfboard, a flotation vest, a swimsuit, and a safety line.
4. A skier's equipment includes ski boots, skis with bindings, safety cables, ski poles, warm clothing, and goggles.
5. Under their own power, surfers paddle out to their starting places, far from shore.
6. Must a skier buy a ticket for a ski-lift ride to the top of the mountain?
7. Oddly enough, some important similarities exist between surfing and skiing.
8. Both depend on the cooperation of nature for pleasant weather and good waves or good snow.
9. Do both surfing and snow skiing require coordination and balance more than strength?
10. In fact, each of these sports would probably make an excellent cross-training activity during the other's off-season.

**Exercise 6** **Writing Complete Sentences**

Make each of the following sentence fragments a complete sentence by adding a subject, a predicate, or both. Be sure to add correct capitalization and punctuation.

EXAMPLE 1. the barking dog

     1. *We were kept awake by the barking dog.*

1. the trouble with my class schedule
2. the legs of the table
3. appeared deserted
4. my billionaire aunt from Detroit
5. thousands of screaming fans

6. my grandparents in Oaxaca
7. thought quickly
8. after the intermission
9. until sunset
10. the science fair

**Review A** **Distinguishing Between Sentence Fragments and Sentences; Identifying Subjects and Predicates**

Identify each word group as a sentence (*S*) or a sentence fragment (*F*). Then, for each sentence, write the simple subject, underlining it once, and the simple predicate (verb), underlining it twice.

EXAMPLE    1. The talented musicians played well together.

1. *S—<u>musicians</u>—<u>played</u>*

1. Jazz music filled the room.
2. Supporting the other instruments, the piano carried the melody.
3. The saxophonist, with lazy, lingering notes.
4. Beside him, the bass player added depth to the band.
5. A female vocalist with a deep, rich voice.
6. Charmed the audience with her delivery.
7. The band's star performer was the drummer.
8. For most of the evening, she stayed in the background.
9. Until the last half-hour.
10. Then she dazzled everyone with her brilliant, high-speed technique.

# Finding the Subject

To find the subject of a sentence, find the verb first. Then, ask "Who?" or "What?" before the verb.

EXAMPLES    **Here you can swim year-round.** [The verb is *can swim.* Who can swim? *You* can swim. *You* is the subject.]

**There is Aunt Ivory's new truck.** [What is there? *Truck* is. *Truck* is the subject.]

**Into the pond jumped the frog.** [What jumped? *Frog* jumped. *Frog* is the subject.]

**Please close the window.** [Who is to close the window? *You* are—that is, the person spoken to. *You* is the understood subject.]

**Reference Note**

For information on the **understood subject,** see page 423.

## Exercise 7 Identifying Subjects and Verbs

Identify the verb and its subject in each of the following sentences. Be sure to include all parts of a verb phrase.

EXAMPLE
1. Long before the equal rights movement of the 1960s, women in the United States were excelling in their professions.

1. *were excelling—verb; women—subject*

1. Anne Bissell ran a carpet sweeper business in the late 1800s.
2. For a time, she served as corporation president.
3. Under her direction, the company sold millions of sweepers.
4. In the late nineteenth century, a journalist named Nellie Bly reported on social injustice.
5. On assignments, she would often wear disguises.
6. Ida Wells-Barnett became editor and part owner of the *Memphis Free Speech* in 1892.
7. By the early 1930s, she had been crusading for forty years against racial injustice and for suffrage.
8. At the end of her fourth term as general of the Salvation Army, Evangeline Booth retired in 1939.
9. Booth's efforts helped to make the Salvation Army a financially stable organization.
10. She also improved many Salvation Army services.

**13e. The subject of a verb is never in a prepositional phrase.**

EXAMPLES   **Most** of the women voted. [Who voted? *Most* voted. *Women* is the object in the prepositional phrase *of the women.*]

**One** of the parakeets in the pet shop looks like ours. [What looks? *One* looks. *Parakeets* and *pet shop* are each part of a prepositional phrase.]

Are **two** of the books missing? [What are missing? *Two* are missing. *Books* is the object in the prepositional phrase *of the books.*]

**Reference Note**

For more information about **prepositional phrases,** see page 442.

A *prepositional phrase* includes a preposition, the object of the preposition, and any modifiers of that object.

EXAMPLES

| | | |
|---|---|---|
| next to Jorge | by the open door | on the floor |
| of a good book | at intermission | after class |
| in the photograph | for all of them | instead of this |

Prepositional phrases can be especially misleading when the subject follows the verb.

EXAMPLE    Around the corner from our house is a **store.** [What is? *Store* is. Neither *corner* nor *house* can be the subject because each is part of a prepositional phrase.]

**Exercise 8**    **Identifying Verbs and Subjects**

Identify the verb and the subject in each of the following sentences.

EXAMPLE    1.  Most of the students in our class have enjoyed discussing our town's folklore.

      1.  *have enjoyed—verb; Most—subject*

1. Many regions of the United States have local legends.
2. One pine-forested area in New Jersey is supposedly inhabited by the Jersey Devil.
3. This fearsome monster reportedly chases campers and wayward travelers through the woods.
4. In contrast, Oregon is haunted by numerous legends of the less aggressive Bigfoot.
5. This humanlike creature supposedly hides in heavily forested areas.
6. Its shaggy coat of hair looks like a bear's fur.
7. According to legend, Bigfoot is gentle and shy by nature, avoiding contact with strangers.
8. Stories from the Lake Champlain area tell about a monster resembling a sea serpent in the depths of the lake.
9. Many sightings of this beast have been reported to authorities.
10. No one, however, has ever taken a convincing photograph of the monster.

## Sentences That Ask Questions

Questions often begin with a verb, a helping verb, or a word such as *what*, *when*, *where*, *how*, or *why*. The subject of a question usually follows the verb or helping verb.

EXAMPLES    How is the **movie** different from the book?

           Where is the **CD** I gave you?

           Does **she** have a ride home?

In questions that begin with a helping verb, like the third example above, the subject comes between the helping verb and the main verb.

---

**TIPS & TRICKS**

In many sentences, you can find the subject and the verb more easily if you cross out any prepositional phrases.

EXAMPLE
Several of the puzzle pieces are under the sofa.

SUBJECT
Several

VERB
are

You can find the subject by turning the question into a statement and then finding the verb and asking "Who?" or "What?" before it.

EXAMPLES    **Was the train late?** becomes **The train was late.** [What was late? The *train* was.]

               **Has she answered the letter?** becomes **She has answered the letter.** [Who has answered? *She* has.]

## Sentences Beginning with *There* or *Here*

The word *there* or *here* is almost never the subject of a sentence. Both *there* and *here* may be used as adverbs telling *where.* To find the subject in a sentence beginning with *there* or *here*, ask "Who?" or "What?" before the verb and the adverb.

EXAMPLES    **There are my cousins.** [Who are there? *Cousins* are.]

               **Here is your backpack.** [What is here? *Backpack* is.]

**NOTE**   Sometimes *there* starts a sentence but does not tell where. In this use, *there* is not an adverb but an expletive. An **expletive** is a word that fills out a sentence's structure but does not add to its meaning.

                          V       S

EXAMPLES    **There is a drawbridge over the river.** [*There* adds no information to the sentence, which could be rewritten as *A drawbridge is over the river.*]

                          V      S

               **There are insects in our garden.** [The sentence could be rewritten as *Insects are in our garden.*]

To find the subject in such a sentence, omit *there* and ask "Who?" or "What?" before the verb.

EXAMPLE    **There was a clerk at the counter.** [Who was? A *clerk* was.]

**Exercise 9**   **Identifying Subjects and Verbs**

Identify the subjects and the verbs in the following sentences.

EXAMPLE    **1.** Will you help me study for my history test?

          *1. you—subject; will help—verb*

**1.** There are many questions on American history in my book.
**2.** Naturally, there are answers, too.
**3.** Under whose flag did Columbus sail?
**4.** Here is Plymouth Rock, Anita.
**5.** How much do you know about the Lost Colony?

**6.** What does *squatter's rights* mean?

**7.** In what area did most of the early Dutch colonists settle?

**8.** Was there disagreement among settlers in Massachusetts?

**9.** What kinds of schools did the colonists' children attend?

**10.** How did people travel in colonial America?

## The Understood Subject

In a request or a command, the subject of a sentence is usually not stated. In such sentences, *you* is the **understood subject.**

| | |
|---|---|
| REQUEST | **Please answer the phone.** [Who is to answer? *You* are—that is, the person spoken to.] |
| COMMAND | **Listen carefully to his question.** [Who is to listen? *You*—the person spoken to—are.] |

Sometimes a request or a command includes a name.

| | |
|---|---|
| EXAMPLES | **Amber, please send us your new address.** |
| | **Line up, class.** |

*Amber* and *class* are not subjects in the sentences above. These words are called **nouns of direct address.** They identify the person spoken to or addressed. *You* is the understood subject of each sentence.

| | |
|---|---|
| EXAMPLES | **Amber, [you] please send us your new address.** |
| | **[You] line up, class.** |

---

**Exercise 10** **Writing Requests or Commands**

Using the following five situations, write sentences that are requests or commands. In two of your sentences, use a noun of direct address.

| | *Setting* | *Person Speaking* | *Person Addressed* |
|---|---|---|---|
| EXAMPLES | | | |
| **1.** | castle | queen | wizard |
| **2.** | kitchen | parent | teenager |

*1. Wizard, make this straw into gold.*

*2. Please don't drink out of the carton.*

| *Setting* | *Person Speaking* | *Person Addressed* |
|---|---|---|
| **1.** desert oasis | Aladdin | genie |
| **2.** courtroom | judge | defense attorney |
| **3.** child's room | child | baby sitter |
| **4.** spaceship | alien invader | crew member |
| **5.** forest | Big Bad Wolf | Little Red Riding Hood |

# Compound Subjects

**Reference Note**

For more information about **conjunctions**, see page 403. For more about using **commas between words in a series**, see page 644.

**13f.** A *compound subject* consists of two or more subjects that are joined by a conjunction and that have the same verb.

The conjunctions most commonly used to connect the words of a compound subject are *and* and *or*.

EXAMPLE   **Antony** and **Mae** baked the bread. [Who baked the bread? Antony baked it. Mae baked it. *Antony* and *Mae* form the compound subject.]

When more than two words are included in the compound subject, the conjunction is generally used only between the last two words. Also, the words are separated by commas.

EXAMPLE   Antony**,** Mae**, and** Pamela baked the bread. [compound subject: *Antony, Mae, Pamela*]

Correlative conjunctions, such as *neither . . . nor* and *not only . . . but also*, may be used with compound subjects.

EXAMPLE   **Either** Antony **or** Mae baked the bread. [compound subject: *Antony, Mae*]

### Exercise 11 Identifying Compound Subjects and Their Verbs

Identify the compound subjects and their verbs in the following sentences.

EXAMPLE   1. Roast turkey and cranberry sauce are often served at Thanksgiving.

1. *turkey, sauce—compound subject; are served—verb*

1. Gerbils and goldfish make good, low-maintenance pets.
2. April, May, and June provide the best opportunity for studying wildflowers in Texas and Oklahoma.
3. Kettles of soup and trays of sandwiches sat on the counter.
4. Both you and I should go downtown or to the movies.
5. Either *Macbeth* or *Othello* features witches in its plot.
6. In that drawer lay her scissors, ruler, and markers.
7. Star-nosed moles and eastern moles live in the United States.
8. There are many good jokes and riddles in that book.
9. Where will you and your family go on vacation this year?
10. There were eggs and milk in the refrigerator.

# Compound Verbs

**13g.** A *compound verb* consists of two or more verbs that are joined by a conjunction and that have the same subject.

EXAMPLES    Jim Thorpe **entered** and **won** several events in the 1912 Olympics.

               The committee **met, voted** on the issue, and **adjourned.**

               My sister **will buy** or **lease** a car.

    Both the subject and the verb may be compound.

EXAMPLES    The **students** and **teachers wrote** the play and **produced** it.

               Either **Jan** or **Beverly will write** the story and **send** it to the paper.

**NOTE**  There are other cases in which a sentence may contain more than one subject and verb.

EXAMPLES    The **defeat** of the Germans at Verdun in 1916 **was** a victory for France, but the **battle cost** each side nearly half a million casualties. [This kind of sentence is called a *compound sentence.*]

               Because **crocodiles are** descended from dinosaurs, **they are** the nearest living relatives of birds. [This kind of sentence is called a *complex sentence.*]

               Before the **movie started, Siva offered** to buy popcorn; **Melissa said** that **she would save** his seat. [This kind of sentence is called a *compound-complex sentence.*]

### Exercise 12  Identifying Subjects and Compound Verbs

Identify the compound verbs and the subjects in the following sentences. Be sure to include helping verbs. If a sentence contains an understood subject, write *(You).*

EXAMPLE    1.  Should I buy this pair of jeans now or wait for a sale?

            1.  *compound verb—should buy, wait; subject—I*

1. Tony rewound the cassette and then pressed the playback button.
2. Toshiro sings, acts, and dances in the show.
3. At the fair, Dan ran faster than the other boys and won the prize of twenty-five dollars.

**STYLE TIP**

The helping verb may or may not be repeated before the second part of a compound verb if the helping verb is the same for both parts of the verb.

EXAMPLES
My sister **will buy** or **will lease** a car.

My sister **will buy** or **lease** a car.

**Reference Note**

For more about **compound, complex, and compound-complex sentences,** see page 481.

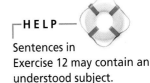

**HELP**

Sentences in Exercise 12 may contain an understood subject.

**4.** Will you walk home or wait for the four o'clock bus?

**5.** This kitchen appliance will slice, dice, and chop.

**6.** Velma will not only bring the salad but also bake bread for the party.

**7.** Please pick your socks up and put them either in the hamper or downstairs by the washing machine.

**8.** The marching band practiced hard and won the state competition.

**9.** Visit, rest, and relax.

**10.** The newborn calf rose to its feet with a wobble and stood.

### Exercise 13 Identifying Subjects and Predicates

Write each of the following sentences, underlining the complete subject once and the complete predicate twice. Be sure to include all parts of compound subjects and compound verbs.

EXAMPLE **1.** Gary Soto and Amy Tan are my favorite authors.

**1.** *Gary Soto and Amy Tan* are my favorite authors.

Link to Literature

**1.** Soto's poetry and short stories often are about his life.

**2.** Will he read from his works and sign books here tonight?

**3.** Carlos, Ted, and I will find front-row seats.

**4.** Where is your copy of *Too Many Tamales*?

**5.** Here is Gary Soto's latest collection of poetry.

**6.** His realistic way of presenting life appeals to me.

**7.** This particular poem brings back childhood memories.

**8.** Something similar happened to me in the first grade.

**9.** There are Sandra Cisneros and Rudolfo Anaya, other successful Hispanic American authors.

**10.** Their stories reflect a rich cultural heritage.

### Review B Finding Subjects and Verbs

Copy each of the sentences in the following paragraph. Then, complete steps A through D to find the subject and the verb in each sentence.

┌HELP┐
Not all steps apply to every sentence in Review B.

**A.** Cross out all prepositional phrases to help you isolate the verb and the subject.

**B.** Cross out *Here* or *There* at the beginning of a sentence to eliminate these words as possible subjects.

**C.** Underline all verbs twice, including all helping verbs and all parts of any compound verbs.

**D.** Underline all subjects once, including all parts of any compound subjects. If a sentence contains an understood subject, write and underline *you.*

EXAMPLE    **[1]** Quicksand can be dangerous to a hiker.

      1.  *Quicksand <u>can be</u> dangerous* <s>to a hiker.</s>

[**1**] In quicksand, you must remain calm. [**2**] Violent movement, such as kicking your legs, will only worsen the situation. [**3**] There are several steps to escaping from quicksand. [**4**] First, discard your backpack or any other burden. [**5**] Next, gently fall onto your back and spread your arms. [**6**] In this position, you will be able to float. [**7**] Only then should you slowly bring your feet to the surface. [**8**] Perhaps a companion or someone else nearby can reach you with a pole or a rope. [**9**] Are you alone? [**10**] Then you should look for the shortest distance to solid ground and paddle slowly toward safety.

# Complements

**13h.** A *complement* is a word or word group that completes the meaning of a verb.

Some groups of words need more than a subject and a verb to express a complete thought. Notice how the following sentences need the boldfaced words to complete their meaning. These boldfaced words are called *complements.*

EXAMPLES    It is a good **car** even though it is **old.**

            Who gave **Mr. Garcia** the **present**?

A complement may be compound.

EXAMPLES    Aunt Edna looks **happy** and **relaxed** today.

            My cats enjoy **eating** and **napping.**

A complement may be a noun, a pronoun, or an adjective.

              S       V         C

EXAMPLES    Marcella might become a **chemist.**

                 S     V    C

            The raccoon watched **us** gardening in the backyard.

               S          V   C

            The clerks at that store are **helpful.**

**Reference Note**

For information on **adverbs,** see page 393.

**Reference Note**

For information on **prepositional phrases,** see page 442.

**Reference Note**

For information on **independent and subordinate clauses,** see Chapter 15.

An adverb is not a complement.

EXAMPLES    Where did we go wrong? [*Wrong* is used as an adverb, not a complement.]

That answer is not **wrong.** [*Wrong*, an adjective, is a complement in this sentence.]

Sentence complements are never in prepositional phrases.

EXAMPLES    She watched the **cardinals.** [*Cardinals* is the complement.]

She watched **all** of the cardinals. [*Cardinals* is part of the prepositional phrase *of the cardinals.*]

**NOTE**    Both independent and subordinate clauses contain subjects and verbs and may contain complements.

           S    V     C    S     V           C

EXAMPLES    This **kitten is** the **one that climbed** the **curtains.**

           S    V       C    S     V       C

Before **Eli rides** his **bicycle, he checks** his **tires.**

**Exercise 14**   Identifying Subjects, Verbs, and Complements

Identify the subject, verb, and complement in each of the following sentences.

EXAMPLE    1. Many modern slang expressions sound okay to my great-grandfather.

     1. *expressions—subject; sound—verb; okay—complement*

1. Like every generation, my great-grandfather's generation had its own slang.
2. He still uses it all the time, particularly in stories about his youth.
3. Great-grandpa played the trombone in a jazz band in the 1930s.
4. He and other musicians developed many slang expressions.
5. Their language became *jive talk.*
6. Many of Great-grandpa's expressions are sayings of the entertainer Cab Calloway.
7. Great-grandpa uses phrases such as Calloway's *beat to my socks* (tired) and *out of this world* (perfect).
8. Great-grandpa's speech is full of words like *hepcat* (a lover of jazz music) and *hip* (wise) and *groovy* (wonderful).
9. Such language became popular all over the United States.
10. My great-grandfather, at least, still uses it.

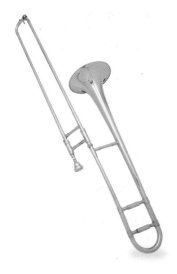

**Exercise 15  Writing Sentence Complements**

Write ten sentences by adding a complement to each of the following word groups. Be sure to punctuate each sentence correctly.

EXAMPLE       1.  The puppy is
              1.  *The puppy is playful.*

1. Jesse usually seems
2. Tomorrow the class will hear
3. That broiled fish looks
4. Last week our class visited
5. Do you have
6. Coretta finished the
7. The winners felt
8. Saturday the museum will sell
9. Fruits and vegetables filled the
10. How do you like

# The Subject Complement

**13i. A *subject complement* is a word or word group in the predicate that describes or identifies the subject.**

EXAMPLES       The surface felt **sticky.** [*Sticky* describes *surface.*]

               Mark Twain's real name was **Samuel Clemens.**
               [*Samuel Clemens* identifies *name.*]

Subject complements may be compound.

EXAMPLES       That winter seemed especially **mild** and **sunny.**

               The prizewinners are **Jennifer, Marcus,** and **Raul.**

Subject complements sometimes precede the subject of a sentence or a clause.

EXAMPLES       How **kind** he is! [*Kind* is a predicate adjective describing *he.*]

               I know what a **treat** this is for her. [*Treat* is a predicate nominative identifying *this.*]

NOTE  Subject complements always complete the meaning of linking verbs. A word that completes the meaning of an action verb is not a subject complement.

## TIPS & TRICKS

To find the subject complement in an interrogative sentence, rearrange the sentence to make a statement.

EXAMPLE
Is Darnell the treasurer?
Darnell is the **treasurer.**

To find the subject complement in an imperative sentence, insert the understood subject *you.*

EXAMPLE
Be good.
(You) Be **good.**

**Reference Note**

For more about **action and linking verbs,** see page 387.

**STYLE TIP**

The use of the nominative-case pronoun, as in the last example of the predicate nominative, is uncommon in everyday speech. You will often hear *It is him,* rather than *It is he.* Remember that in formal English you should use the nominative-case pronoun.

**Reference Note**

For more about the **nominative case**, see page 550.

**(1)** A *predicate nominative* is a word or word group that is in the predicate and that identifies the subject or refers to it.

EXAMPLES    Has she become a **dentist**?

Friendship is **what I value most.**

The new teacher is **he**—the man in the blazer.

**(2)** A *predicate adjective* is an adjective that is in the predicate and that modifies the subject.

EXAMPLES    The soup is **hot.** [hot soup]

That soil seems **dry** and **crumbly.** [dry and crumbly soil]

How **expensive** are those shoes? [expensive shoes]

**Exercise 16  Identifying Subject Complements**

Each of the following sentences has at least one subject complement. For each sentence, give the complement or complements and tell whether each is a *predicate nominative* or a *predicate adjective*.

EXAMPLE    1. Gloria is my favorite character on the show.

1. *character—predicate nominative*

**1.** Does the lemonade taste too sour?
**2.** The chirping of the birds became more and more shrill as the cat approached.
**3.** The window washers on the fifteenth floor appeared tiny.
**4.** Why does he always look so serious?
**5.** Our candidate for the city council was the winner in the primaries.
**6.** You should feel proud of yourself.
**7.** Will the hall monitors for Wednesday be Charlene and LaReina?
**8.** Soft and cool was the grass under the catalpa tree.
**9.** Be a friend to animals.
**10.** The crowd grew quiet when Governor Markham spoke.

**Exercise 17  Writing Subject Complements**

Make complete sentences of the following word groups by adding nouns, pronouns, or adjectives as subject complements. Use five compound complements. Identify each subject complement as a *predicate nominative* or a *predicate adjective.*

EXAMPLE    1. The sky turned

1. *The sky turned cloudy and dark. —predicate adjectives*

1. The artist frequently was
2. Those are
3. Sara Brown became
4. It could be
5. The house looked

6. Are you
7. The weather remained
8. The test seemed
9. Manuel had always felt
10. That recording sounds

## Objects

*Objects* are complements that do not refer to the subject. Objects follow transitive verbs—verbs that express an action directed toward a person, place, or thing.

EXAMPLE    Lee Trevino sank the **putt.** [The object *putt* does not explain or describe the subject *Lee Trevino. Sank* is a transitive verb, not an intransitive verb.]

> NOTE  Transitive verbs may express mental action (for example, *believe, trust, imagine*) as well as physical action (for example, *give, hit, draw*).
>
> EXAMPLE    Now I remember your name. [Remember *what*? Name.]

Reference Note

For more about **transitive and intransitive verbs,** see page 386.

**13j.** A *direct object* is a noun, pronoun, or word group that tells who or what receives the action of a verb or shows the result of the action.

A direct object answers the question "Whom?" or "What?" after a transitive verb.

EXAMPLES
```
S     V    DO
```
Germs cause **illness.** [Germs cause *what*? Germs cause illness. *Illness* shows the result of the action of the verb.]

```
S    V      DO
```
Peter said **Gesundheit.** [Peter said *what*? Peter said *Gesundheit. Gesundheit* receives the action of the verb.]

```
S    V   DO
```
Lucy visited **me.** [Lucy visited *whom*? Lucy visited me. *Me* receives the action of the verb.]

```
             DO    S  V
```
What a scary **movie** we saw! [We saw *what*? We saw a movie. *Movie* receives the action of the verb.]

```
S     V            DO
```
They were taking **whatever was left.** [They were taking *what*? They were taking whatever was left. *Whatever was left* receives the action of the verb.]

Direct objects are generally not found in prepositional phrases.

EXAMPLES  Josh was riding on his bicycle. [*Bicycle* is part of the prepositional phrase *on his bicycle*. The sentence has no direct object.]

Josh was riding his **bicycle.** [*Bicycle* is the direct object.]

### Exercise 18 Identifying Direct Objects

Identify the direct object in each of the following sentences.

EXAMPLE  **1.** I enjoy this magazine very much.

   *1.*  *magazine*

1. This article gives interesting facts about libraries.
2. The city of Alexandria, in Egypt, had the most famous library of ancient times.
3. This library contained the largest collection of plays and works of philosophy in the ancient world.
4. The Roman emperor Augustus founded two public libraries.
5. Fire destroyed all of these libraries.
6. Readers could not borrow books from either the library in Alexandria or the Roman libraries.
7. During the Middle Ages, the monastery libraries introduced a circulating library.
8. By the sixth century, Benedictine monks were borrowing books from their libraries for daily reading.
9. In the United States, we now have thousands of libraries.
10. Readers borrow millions of books from them every year.

┌ H E L P ─

Indirect objects generally precede direct objects.

**13k.** An ***indirect object*** is a noun, pronoun, or word group that often appears in sentences containing direct objects. An indirect object tells *to whom* or *to what* (or *for whom* or *for what*) the action of a transitive verb is done.

|  | S | V | IO | DO |
EXAMPLES  Natalie knitted her **friend** a sweater. [Natalie knitted a sweater for whom? For her *friend*.]

S  V  IO  DO
My little sister sang **me** a song. [My little sister sang a song to whom? To *me*.]

S  V  IO  DO
Uncle Gene sends **whoever requests it** a pamphlet on earthworms. [Uncle Gene sends a pamphlet to whom? To *whoever requests it*.]

**Reference Note**

For information on **transitive verbs,** see page 386.

If the word *to* or *for* is used, the noun or pronoun following it is part of a prepositional phrase and not an indirect object.

OBJECTS OF PREPOSITIONS

My teacher showed the bird's nest to the **class.**

I left some dessert for **you.**

INDIRECT OBJECTS

The teacher showed the **class** the bird's nest.

I left **you** some dessert.

Both direct and indirect objects may be compound.

EXAMPLES

Lydia sold **cookies** and **lemonade.** [compound direct object]

Lydia sold **Geraldo, Freddy,** and **me** lemonade. [compound indirect object]

NOTE Do not mistake an adverb in the predicate for a complement.

ADVERB Go **inside,** Skippy. [*Inside* is an adverb telling *where.*]

COMPLEMENT Tamisha sanded the **inside** of the wooden chest. [*Inside* is a noun used as a direct object.]

**Reference Note**

For information on **prepositional phrases and objects of prepositions,** see page 442.

**Reference Note**

For information on **adverbs,** see page 393.

GRAMMAR

13 k

**Exercise 19** Identifying Direct Objects and Indirect Objects

Identify the direct and indirect objects in the following sentences. Make sure that you give all parts of compound direct and indirect objects.

EXAMPLE

1. Sometimes I read my little brother stories from Greek mythology.

1. *indirect object—brother; direct object—stories*

1. In one myth, the famous artist and inventor Daedalus built the king of Crete a mysterious building known as the Labyrinth.
2. The complicated passageways of this building give us the word *labyrinth,* ("a maze or confusing structure").
3. After the completion of the Labyrinth, the king imprisoned Daedalus and his son, whose name was Icarus.
4. To escape, Daedalus made Icarus and himself wings out of feathers and beeswax.
5. He gave Icarus careful instructions not to fly too near the sun.
6. However, Icarus soon forgot his father's advice.
7. He flew too high, and when the sun melted the wax in the wings, he plunged to his death in the ocean.

**HELP**

Not every sentence in Exercise 19 contains an indirect object.

Link to Literature

8. Though saddened by the death of his son, Daedalus flew on and reached Sicily in safety.

9. Mythology tells us other stories of his fabulous inventions.

10. Even today, the name Daedalus suggests genius and inventiveness.

**Review C** **Identifying Complements**

Identify the complements in the following sentences. Then, tell whether each complement is a *predicate nominative*, a *predicate adjective*, a *direct object*, or an *indirect object*. If a sentence does not contain a complement, write *no complement*.

EXAMPLE    [1] My brother Bill gave Mom a birthday surprise.
1. *Mom—indirect object; surprise—direct object*

[1] My brother made Mom a birthday cake. [2] However, the project soon became a fiasco. [3] First, Bill cracked three eggs into a bowl. [4] Unfortunately, bits of the shells went in, too. [5] Then he added the flour and other dry ingredients. [6] The electric mixer whirled the batter right onto the ceiling. [7] The batter was so sticky that it stayed there and didn't fall off. [8] Bill did not clean the ceiling immediately, and the sticky substance hardened overnight. [9] Mom was not angry, but she did give Bill a suggestion for a gift. [10] "A clean kitchen would be a great birthday present."

**Review D** **Identifying the Parts of a Sentence**

Identify the italicized words in the following passage. Use these abbreviations.

| *s.* | subject | *p.a.* | predicate adjective |
|------|---------|--------|---------------------|
| *v.* | verb | *d.o.* | direct object |
| *p.n.* | predicate nominative | *i.o.* | indirect object |

EXAMPLE    When you draw faces, do they look **[1]** *realistic*?
1. *p.a.*

Before this winter, I couldn't draw a human [1] *face* well. However, our [2] *neighbor*, Mr. Teng, is a portrait [3] *painter*, and he has been giving [4] *me* some instructive [5] *tips*. He says that the most important

**HELP**

Not every sentence in Review C contains a complement; some sentences contain more than one.

**HELP**

Remember that subordinate clauses contain subjects and verbs and may also contain complements.

[6] *thing* is the correct [7] *placement* of the eyes. Apparently, most [8] *people* draw the [9] *eyes* too high. In fact, [10] *they* should be placed halfway down the head. Many people also [11] *make* the ears too small. The [12] *top* of each ear [13] *should align* with the eyebrow, and the [14] *bottom* should align with the tip of the nose. Getting the width of the face right is also [15] *important*. Mr. Teng says, "Use one eye's [16] *width* as a unit of measure and make the head five eye-widths wide." There are many other [17] *guidelines*, but these tips from Mr. Teng are the most [18] *basic*. By following them, I can now draw a human [19] *face* that [20] *looks* realistic.

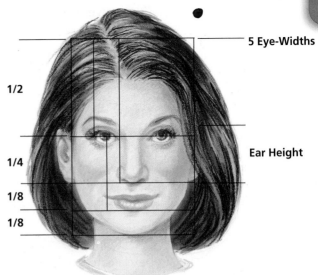

5 Eye-Widths

1/2

Ear Height

1/4

1/8

1/8

# Classifying Sentences by Purpose

**13l.** A sentence may be classified, depending on its purpose, as *declarative, imperative, interrogative,* or *exclamatory.*

**(1)** A *declarative sentence* makes a statement and ends with a period.

EXAMPLES    Jody Williams won the Nobel Peace Prize in 1997.

That one-celled organism is an amoeba.

**(2)** An *imperative sentence* gives a command or makes a request. Most imperative sentences end with a period. A strong command ends with an exclamation point.

EXAMPLES    Please keep to the right. [request]

Take care of your little brother, Rick. [command]

Stop! [strong command]

Notice in these examples that a command or a request has the understood subject *you.*

**Reference Note**

For more information about **understood subjects,** see page 423.

**(3)** An *interrogative sentence* asks a question and ends with a question mark.

EXAMPLES    Can they finish in time**?**

How did she find Yoshi and Sarah**?**

**STYLE          TIP**

Sometimes writers use both a question mark and an exclamation point to express the combined emotions of surprise and disbelief or wonder.

EXAMPLE
Is it really you**?!**

Such usage is appropriate only in informal situations and in dialogue, to convey the speaker's emotions.

**(4)** An *exclamatory sentence* shows excitement or expresses strong feeling and ends with an exclamation point.

EXAMPLES    What a good friend you are**!**

The battery is dead**!**

I can't believe this is happening**!**

**NOTE**    In conversation, any sentence may be spoken so that it becomes exclamatory or interrogative. When you are writing dialogue, use periods, exclamation points, and question marks to show how you intend a sentence to be read.

EXAMPLES    They won**.**   [declarative]
They won**!**   [exclamatory]
They won**?**   [interrogative]

## Exercise 20  Identifying the Four Kinds of Sentences

Punctuate each of the following sentences with an appropriate end mark. Classify each sentence as *imperative, declarative, interrogative,* or *exclamatory.*

EXAMPLE    1.  There are many delicious foods from India

1.  *period—declarative*

**1.** Do you like spicy food
**2.** Some Indian food is hot, and some isn't
**3.** *Sambar* is a soup made with lentils and vegetables
**4.** Save me some of those curried shrimp
**5.** What is that wonderful bread called
**6.** *Palek alu* is a spicy dish of potatoes
**7.** Watch out for the hot chilies
**8.** Isn't this yogurt drink called *lassi* good
**9.** Be sure to add the curry and other spices to the onions
**10.** How tasty this rice-and-banana pudding is

# Chapter Review

## A. Identifying Types of Sentences and Sentence Fragments

Identify each of the following word groups as a *declarative sentence,* an *interrogative sentence,* an *imperative sentence,* an *exclamatory sentence,* or a *sentence fragment.* Supply the appropriate end mark after the last word of each item that is *not* a sentence fragment.

1. Why don't we go to the wildlife park tomorrow
2. What a good time we'll have
3. The big cats especially at feeding time
4. Actually, I enjoy the entire park
5. Meet me at the front gate at ten o' clock
6. We'll first go see the elephants
7. Don't forget the camera
8. My favorite animal is Bonzo the baboon
9. His amazing stunts and antics
10. How graceful the gazelles are

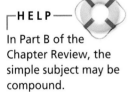

┌─**HELP**─
In Part B of the Chapter Review, the simple subject may be compound.

## B. Identifying the Complete Subject and the Simple Subject

Identify the complete subject in each of the following sentences. Then, underline the simple subject.

11. One of the first advocates of medical hygiene and the use of antiseptics was Ignaz Semmelweis.
12. This German-Hungarian physician was born in 1818.
13. In 1844, he earned a degree from Vienna University.
14. His first position was as an assistant at the obstetric clinic in Vienna.
15. Semmelweis was appalled by the high mortality rate among his patients.
16. He taught medical staff members always to wash their hands in a chlorine solution and by doing so soon reduced the mortality rate.
17. Semmelweis, who was a true pioneer, lobbied the medical establishment to make antiseptic operating conditions a top priority.

18. The medical establishment in many countries remained hostile to Semmelweis for many years.

19. In 1865, the year of Semmelweis's death, a famous British surgeon named Joseph Lister performed his first antiseptic operation.

20. The method introduced by Semmelweis made medicine safer and more humane.

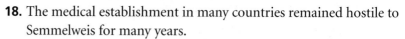

┌HELP┐

In Part C of the Chapter Review, the simple predicate may be compound.

## C. Identifying Complete Predicates and Simple Predicates (Verbs)

Identify the complete predicate in each of the following sentences. Then, underline the simple predicate (or verb).

21. Have you met my brother Lewis?
22. Then listen to this.
23. My brother often dawdles.
24. He chooses odd times for some activities.
25. One day last week, Lewis gathered all of the pencils in the house and sharpened them.
26. Today he woke early and completely rearranged his room.
27. Then my poor little brother was almost late for the school bus.
28. I reminded him, however, of his first-period test.
29. Somehow, Lewis finishes all his chores and assignments.
30. I might buy him a book about time management, though.

## D. Identifying Sentence Parts

Identify each italicized word in the following paragraphs as a *subject*, a *verb*, a *predicate nominative*, a *predicate adjective*, a *direct object*, or an *indirect object*.

    A [31] *carwash* can be a good [32] *fund-raiser*. The freshman class [33] *planned* a carwash for last Saturday. On Saturday morning, the [34] *sky* did not look [35] *good*. In fact, the weather forecast [36] *predicted* thunderstorms. Did [37] *any* of this send [38] *us* a message? Yes, but we had our [39] *carwash* anyway. Our first [40] *customer,* at 9:00 A.M., was a [41] *woman* in a pickup truck. Glancing at the sky, she paid [42] *us* a compliment. "You're really [43] *brave,*" she said. The rain [44] *began* as she was speaking, and our disappointment must have been [45] *obvious.* "Don't worry," she added "there is [46] *nothing* like a rainwater rinse." We [47] *charged* her only one [48] *dollar* because she had cheered us up so much. The morning was intermittently [49] *rainy.* Later, however, the clouds parted and the weather was [50] *perfect.*

# Writing Application
## Using Verbs in a Summary

**Fresh, Lively Verbs**   Your little sister likes you to tell her exciting stories. You have told her so many stories that you have run out of new ones. To get ideas for new stories, you think about events you have read about or seen. Write a summary of an exciting incident from a book, a movie, or a television show. Use action verbs that are fresh and lively. Underline these verbs.

**Prewriting**   Think about books that you have read recently or movies and television shows that you have seen. Choose an exciting incident from one of these works. Freewrite what you remember about that incident.

**Writing**   As you write your first draft, think about how you are presenting the information. When telling a story, you usually should use chronological order (the order in which events occurred). This method would be easiest for your young reader to follow, too. Try to use fresh, lively action verbs.

**Revising**   Imagine that you are a young child hearing the story for the first time. Look over your summary and ask yourself if you could follow this account of the story.

**Publishing**   Read over your summary again, looking for any errors in grammar, usage, and mechanics. You may want to share your story with a younger sibling or with children at a local preschool or kindergarten.

# The Phrase

## Prepositional, Verbal, and Appositive Phrases

# Diagnostic Preview

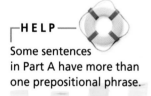

┌─**HELP**─

Some sentences
in Part A have more than
one prepositional phrase.

## A. Identifying and Classifying Prepositional Phrases

Identify each prepositional phrase in the following sentences. After each phrase, write the word(s) it modifies and the type of phrase it is (*adj.* for adjective phrase, *adv.* for adverb phrase).

EXAMPLE   **1.** The museums of different cities are fascinating to tourists.

    *1. of different cities—museums—adj.*
       *to tourists—fascinating—adv.*

1. New York City offers tourists a number of museums.
2. Perhaps the best-known museum is the American Museum of Natural History.
3. This huge museum has exhibits on human history and culture and also shows animals, even dinosaurs, in natural-looking displays, called dioramas.
4. The museum houses the Hayden Planetarium, which teaches visitors about the heavens.
5. Exhibits about earth and space interest young and old alike.
6. The entire complex of exhibits is popular because it offers something for everyone.

7. The city's other museums, which are also fascinating, attract visitors who are interested in specific topics.

8. New York is home to the Museum of Broadcasting, which is filled with old films and radio broadcasts.

9. One of the city's newest museums, Ellis Island Immigration Museum, opened during 1990 and displays many artifacts that had been owned by immigrants who entered the United States through Ellis Island.

10. People who enjoy art can visit museums like the Metropolitan Museum of Art and the Museum of Modern Art.

## B. Identifying Verbals and Appositives

In the following sentences, identify each italicized word or word group as a *participle*, a *gerund*, an *infinitive*, or an *appositive*.

EXAMPLES
1. For some reason, *cleaning* a room, that *dreaded project*, always seems *to create* new projects.

1. cleaning—gerund; dreaded—participle; project—appositive; to create—infinitive

11. John began with every intention of *cleaning* his entire room, the official disaster *area* of his home.

12. He first tackled the pile of CDs *lying* near his *unused* sound system.

13. *Sorting* through them, he found them mostly *outdated*.

14. John decided that his *broken* stereo system, a *gift* from his parents, was the reason.

15. By *repairing* the stereo, he could give himself a reason *to update* his music collection.

16. *Trained* in electronics, John soon saw the problem and began *to work* on it.

17. Some hours later, John had a *working* stereo system but an *uncleaned* room.

18. He had just started *playing* a CD when his sister announced, "Mom's coming *to see* how your room looks!"

19. A tough *taskmaster*, Mom wanted him *to have* it spotless.

20. She applauded his success in *fixing* his stereo but insisted that he clean the room before *doing* anything else.

# What Is a Phrase?

**14a.** A *phrase* is a group of related words that is used as a single part of speech and that does not contain both a verb and its subject.

EXAMPLES     could have been [no subject]

                  instead of Debra and him [no subject or verb]

A group of words that has *both* a verb and its subject is not a phrase.

EXAMPLES     **We found** your pen. [*We* is the subject of *found*.]

                  if **she will go** [*She* is the subject of *will go*.]

NOTE   If a group of words contains both a verb and its subject, it is called a *clause*.

**Reference Note**

For more about **clauses,** see Chapter 15.

### Exercise 1  Identifying Phrases

Identify each of the following groups of words as a *phrase* or *not a phrase*.

EXAMPLES    **1.** with a hammer    **2.** because we agree

                *1. phrase*         *2. not a phrase*

**1.** was hoping
**2.** if she really knows
**3.** with Abdullah and me
**4.** will be writing
**5.** inside the house

**6.** since Mallory wrote
**7.** after they leave
**8.** has been cleaned
**9.** on Miriam's desk
**10.** as the plane lands

# Prepositional Phrases

**Reference Note**

For a list of **commonly used prepositions,** see page 400.

**14b.** A *prepositional phrase* includes a preposition, the object of the preposition, and any modifiers of that object.

EXAMPLES    **to** the pool    **at** the Jacksons' house    **instead of** them

Notice that one or more modifiers may appear in a prepositional phrase. The first example contains *the*; the second contains *the Jacksons'*.

**14c.** The noun or pronoun in a prepositional phrase is called the *object of the preposition*.

EXAMPLE    Clarice went to the **ballet.** [The noun *ballet* is the object of the preposition *to*.]

**NOTE** Do not be misled by a modifier coming after the noun or pronoun in a prepositional phrase. The noun or pronoun is still the object.

EXAMPLE   Heidi and Mrs. Braun worked **at the polls** today. [*Polls* is the object of the preposition *at*. The adverb *today* tells when and modifies the verb *worked*.]

Objects of prepositions may be compound.

EXAMPLES   On the plaza, a guitarist sang for **Victor** and **me**. [The preposition *for* has a compound object: *Victor* and *me*.]

In A.D. 79, the city of Pompeii was buried beneath **lava, rocks,** and **ashes**. [The preposition *beneath* has a compound object: *lava, rocks,* and *ashes*.]

A prepositional phrase can modify the object of another prepositional phrase.

EXAMPLE   Next to the door **of the old barn** stood two horses. [The prepositional phrase *of the old barn* modifies *door*, which is the object of the compound preposition *Next to*.]

A prepositional phrase can contain another prepositional phrase.

EXAMPLE   Meet us **at the Museum of Science and Industry.** [The prepositional phrase *at the Museum of Science and Industry* contains the prepositional phrase *of Science and Industry*.]

**NOTE** Sometimes a prepositional phrase is combined with a noun to form a compound noun.

EXAMPLES   Strait of Hormuz          hole in one

Stratford-on-Avon       University of Pittsburgh

**TIPS & TRICKS**

Be careful not to confuse the preposition *to* with the *to* that is the sign of the verb's infinitive form: *to swim, to know, to see.*

**Reference Note**
For more about **infinitives,** see page 457.

**Reference Note**
For more about **compound no** see page 376.

# The Adjective Phrase

**14d.** A prepositional phrase that modifies a noun or pronoun is called an *adjective phrase.*

EXAMPLE   The members **of the club** want sweatshirts **with the club emblem.** [The prepositional phrase *of the club* is used as an adjective to modify the noun *members. With the club emble* is used as an adjective to modify the noun *sw*

The Phrase

Unlike a one-word adjective, which usually precedes the word it modifies, an adjective phrase almost always follows the noun or pronoun it modifies.

| | |
|---|---|
| ADJECTIVE | Amy closed the **cellar** door. |
| ADJECTIVE PHRASE | Amy closed the door **to the cellar.** |

More than one adjective phrase may modify the same word.

EXAMPLE    Here's a letter **for you from Aunt Martha.** [The prepositional phrases *for you* and *from Aunt Martha* both modify the noun *letter.*]

An adjective phrase may also modify the object of another prepositional phrase.

EXAMPLE    The horse **in the trailer with the rusted latch** broke loose. [The phrase *in the trailer* modifies the noun *horse. Trailer* is the object of the preposition *in.* The phrase *with a rusted latch* modifies *trailer.*]

Often you can convert the objects of adjective phrases into adjectives. Doing so makes your writing less wordy.

| Adjective Phrases | Nouns Used as Adjectives |
|---|---|
| The light **in the kitchen** is on. | The **kitchen** light is on. |
| The airports **in Chicago and New York** are crowded. | The **Chicago** and **New York** airports are crowded. |

However, not all adjective phrases can be changed into one-word modifiers that make sense. Sometimes, changing an adjective phrase makes a sentence awkward and ungrammatical.

| | |
|---|---|
| CLEAR | Please hand me the book on the table. |
| AWKWARD | Please hand me the table book. |

## Exercise 2  Identifying Adjective Phrases

Identify the adjective phrases in the following paragraph, and give the word that each modifies.

EXAMPLE    **[1]** A few years ago our family visited South Dakota and saw a famous monument to great American leaders.

1. *to great American leaders—monument*

[1] My mom took the pictures on the next page when we were visiting this scenic spot at Mount Rushmore National Memorial. [2] As

you can see, the mountainside behind us is a lasting tribute to George Washington, Thomas Jefferson, Theodore Roosevelt, and Abraham Lincoln. [**3**] The figures on the granite cliff were carved under the direction of Gutzon Borglum, an American sculptor. [**4**] Looking at the sculpture, I can certainly believe that this is one of the world's largest. [**5**] The faces are sixty feet high and show a great deal of detail and expression. [**6**] Each president symbolizes a part of United States history. [**7**] Washington represents the founding of the country, and Jefferson signifies the Declaration of Independence. [**8**] Lincoln symbolizes an end to slavery, and Roosevelt stands for expansion and resource conservation. [**9**] Tourists on the viewing terrace must gaze up nearly five hundred feet to see this art. [**10**] As both symbols for the nation and works of art, these massive faces are an inspiration to all who visit Mount Rushmore.

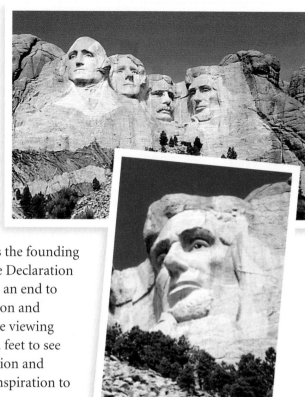

# The Adverb Phrase

**14e.** A prepositional phrase that modifies a verb, an adjective, or an adverb is called an *adverb phrase.*

An adverb phrase tells *how, when, where, why,* or *to what extent.*

EXAMPLES

Britney answered **with a smile.** [The adverb phrase *with a smile* tells *how* Britney answered.]

They sailed **across the lake** yesterday. [The adverb phrase *across the lake* tells *where* they sailed.]

**By Wednesday** Christopher will be finished. [The adverb phrase *By Wednesday* tells *when* Christopher will be finished.]

The calculations erred **by more than two inches.** [*By more than two inches* is an adverb phrase telling *to what extent* the calculations erred.]

In the examples above, the adverb phrases all modify verbs.

An adverb phrase may modify an adjective or an adverb.

EXAMPLES    Melissa is good **at tennis** but better **at volleyball.** [The adverb phrase *at tennis* modifies the adjective *good.* The adverb phrase *at volleyball* modifies the adjective *better.*]

Is the water warm enough **for swimming**? [The adverb phrase *for swimming* modifies the adverb *enough.*]

Adjective phrases almost always follow the words they modify, but an adverb phrase may appear at various places in a sentence.

EXAMPLES    **Before noon** the race started.
The race started **before noon.**

Like adjective phrases, more than one adverb phrase may modify the same word.

EXAMPLE    **During summers,** my older sister works **at the museum.** [The adverb phrases *During summers* and *at the museum* both modify the verb *works.* The first phrase tells *when* my sister works; the second phrase tells *where* she works.]

---

**Exercise 3** **Identifying Adverb Phrases**

Identify the adverb phrases in the following sentences, and give the word or words each phrase modifies.

EXAMPLE    1. The concept of time has inspired many figures of speech over the years.

1. *over the years—has inspired*

1. We use time expressions in everyday speech.
2. In conversation, you may have heard the expression "time out of mind," which means "long ago."
3. When you fall in love, you may feel that "time stands still."
4. Is twenty minutes too long for a "time-out"?
5. If something happens "in no time," it happens very fast.
6. Have you ever noticed that "time flies" when you are chatting with your friends?
7. However, if you are sitting in a waiting room, "time drags."
8. Are you keeping someone's secret "until the end of time"?
9. Do people stop you on the street to ask if you "have the time"?
10. In the meantime, "time marches on" under the steady gaze of "Father Time."

## Review A — Writing Sentences Using Adjective and Adverb Phrases

You are a reporter for your school newspaper. The Young Business Leaders Club has given you an announcement for its upcoming banquet. Write an article about this event, using the information from the announcement below. Use five adjective phrases and five adverb phrases to help you include the necessary information in your article.

**Young Business Leaders Club**

**What?** Annual Banquet
**Where?** Executive Inn Restaurant
North Highway 53
**When?** Friday, May 11, 6:30 to 9:00 P.M.
Tickets are $15.00 per person, available from Alonzo Jackson.

### Program

6:30 **Welcome Address**—Anna Wong, president
6:45 **Introductory Remarks**—J. Zarr, club sponsor
7:00 **Dinner**
8:00 **Speakers' Forum: "Planning Now for Your Future"**—
Rebecca López, nutritionist, Memorial Hospital
John Perri, owner, Computer Solutions
Susanne Drennan, financial planner, United Savings Bank
8:45 **Presentation of Young Business Leader Award**

## Review B — Identifying Adjective and Adverb Phrases

Identify each italicized prepositional phrase in the following paragraph as an *adjective phrase* or as an *adverb phrase*. Then, identify the word or words each phrase modifies.

Link to Literature

EXAMPLE    I enjoy reading all sorts **[1]** *of myths and legends.*
        1. *adjective phrase—sorts*

Have you heard the Greek myth **[1]** *about Narcissus and Echo*? It is a story rich **[2]** *in irony.* Narcissus was a handsome young man **[3]** *with many admirers.* However, he rejected everyone who loved him, including the nymph Echo. As punishment **[4]** *for his arrogant behavior,* the gods sentenced Narcissus to stare forever **[5]** *at his own reflection* **[6]** *in a pond.* **[7]** *For days,* Narcissus gazed adoringly **[8]** *at himself.* Echo the nymph stayed **[9]** *with him* until she wasted away. Finally Narcissus, too, wasted away, and when he died he turned **[10]** *into the narcissus flower.*

## Review C Identifying and Classifying Prepositional Phrases

List all the prepositional phrases in each of the following sentences. Write *adj.* if the phrase is used as an adjective; write *adv.* if the phrase is used as an adverb. Be prepared to identify the word each phrase modifies.

EXAMPLE
1. Theories about the universe have changed over the years.
1. *about the universe—adj.; over the years—adv.*

1. In 1929, Edwin Hubble discovered the existence of galaxies outside the Milky Way.
2. Now we know that perhaps a million galaxies exist inside the bowl of the Big Dipper alone.
3. Astronomers believe that our galaxy is only one among billions throughout the universe.
4. Knowledge has expanded since 500 years ago, when most people believed that the earth was the center of the entire universe.
5. By the 1500s, the Polish astronomer Copernicus suggested that the earth and other planets revolved around the sun.

6. In 1633, the Italian scientist Galileo was tried and convicted for the crime of teaching that the sun is the center of the universe.
7. The Catholic Church condemned Galileo because in his teachings earth and humans were not the center of all things.
8. In Galileo's time, people knew of only five planets besides our own—Mercury, Venus, Mars, Jupiter, and Saturn.
9. Since then we have identified the planets Uranus, Neptune, and Pluto, and we have sent probes into our solar system.
10. Galileo, Copernicus, and other early astronomers would be amazed at the extent of our knowledge of space today.

# Verbals and Verbal Phrases

Verbals are formed from verbs. Like verbs, they may have modifiers and complements. However, verbals are used as nouns, adjectives, or adverbs, not as verbs. The three kinds of verbals are *participles, gerunds,* and *infinitives.*

## The Participle

**14f. A *participle* is a verb form that can be used as an adjective.**

EXAMPLES    We saw the raccoon **escaping** through the back door. [The participle *escaping,* formed from the verb *escape,* modifies the noun *raccoon.*]

             **Waxed** floors can be dangerously slippery. [The participle *Waxed,* formed from the verb *wax,* modifies the noun *floors.*]

Two kinds of participles are *present participles* and *past participles.*

**(1) Present participles end in *–ing.***

EXAMPLES    We ran inside to get out of the **pouring** rain. [The present participle *pouring* modifies the noun *rain.*]

             **Watching** the clock, the coach became worried. [The present participle *watching* modifies the noun *coach.*]

Although participles are forms of verbs, they cannot stand alone as verbs. Participles need to be joined to a helping verb to form a verb phrase. When a participle is used in a verb phrase, it is part of the verb and is not an adjective.

VERB PHRASES    The rain **was pouring.**

             The coach **had been watching** the clock.

**(2) Past participles usually end in *–d* or *–ed.* Other past participles are formed irregularly.**

EXAMPLES    A **peeled** and **sliced** cucumber can be added to a garden salad. [The past participles *peeled* and *sliced* modify the noun *cucumber.*]

             The speaker, **known** for her strong support of recycling, was loudly applauded. [The irregular past participle *known* modifies the noun *speaker.*]

**Reference Note**

For a discussion of **irregular verbs,** see page 519.

Like a present participle, a past participle can also be part of a verb phrase. When a past participle is used in a verb phrase, it is part of the verb and is not an adjective.

VERB PHRASES    I **have peeled** and **sliced** the cucumber.

The speaker **was known** for her strong support of recycling.

**Reference Note**

For more about the **passive voice,** see page 535.

NOTE   Notice in the second example above that a past participle used with a form of the verb *be* creates a *passive-voice* verb. A verb in the passive voice expresses an action done to its subject.

EXAMPLE    The goal **was made** by Josh. [The action of the verb *was made* is done to the subject *goal*.]

### Exercise 4   Identifying Participles and the Words They Modify

Identify the participles used as adjectives in each of the following sentences. After each participle, write the noun or pronoun it modifies.

**HELP**

Some sentences in Exercise 4 contain more than one participle used as an adjective.

EXAMPLES    1.  We searched the island for buried treasure.

1.  *buried—treasure*

2.  The speeding train raced past the platform.

2.  *speeding—train*

1. The prancing horses were loudly applauded by the audience.
2. Colorful flags, waving in the breeze, brightened the gloomy day.
3. Swaggering and boasting, the new varsity quarterback made us extremely angry.
4. The game scheduled for tonight was postponed because of rain.
5. Leaving the field, the happy player rushed to her parents sitting in the bleachers.
6. Branches tapping on the roof and leaves rustling in the wind made an eerie sound.
7. We thought the banging shutter upstairs was someone walking in the attic.
8. Painfully sunburned, I vowed always to use sunscreen and never to be so careless again.
9. Terrified by our dog, the burglar turned and fled across the yard.
10. The platoon of soldiers, marching in step, crossed the field to the stirring music of the military band.

## Exercise 5 Using Appropriate Participles

For each blank in the following sentences, provide a participle that fits the meaning of the sentence.

EXAMPLE    **1.** The _____ tide washed over the beach.

*1. rising*

**1.** Mr. Ortiz explained the effects of pollution and drought on plants _____ in a rain forest.

**2.** _____ from the point of view of a firefighter, the story is full of accurate details.

**3.** The tiger, _____ from the hunters, swam across the river to safety.

**4.** _____ at the traffic light, the driver put on his sunglasses.

**5.** The tourists _____ in the hotel were given a free meal.

**6.** _____ as an excellent place to camp, the park lived up to its reputation.

**7.** _____ by a bee, Steven hurried to the infirmary.

**8.** The poem describes a spider _____ on a thread.

**9.** We stumbled off the racecourse, _____.

**10.** _____, I quickly phoned the hospital.

**Reference Note**

For information on **punctuating participial phrases,** see page 653. The participle as a **dangling modifier** is discussed on page 585. For information on **using participles to combine sentences,** see page 332.

# The Participial Phrase

**14g.** A *participial phrase* is used as an adjective and consists of a participle and any complements or modifiers the participle has.

EXAMPLES    **Seeing the cat,** the dog barked loudly.

The cat hissed at the dog **barking in the yard next door.**

The dog no    barking at the cat had to be brought in.

In each of the following sentences, an arrow points from the participial phrase to the noun or pronoun that the phrase modifies.

EXAMPLES    **Switching its tail,** the mountain lion paced back and forth. [participle with object i

She heard me **sighing lou**    ticiple with the adverb *loudly*]

**Living within his budget,** Adam never needs to borrow money. [participle with adverb phrase *within his budget*]

**Quickly grabbing the keys,** I dashed for the front door. [participle with preceding adverb *Quickly* and object *keys*]

**STYLE** ✏ **TIP**

phrase should
be pl        close to
the word it modifies.
Otherwise, the phrase may
appear to modify another
word, and the sentence
may not make sense.

MISPLACED

He saw a moose riding his motorcycle through the woods. [The placement of the modifier *riding his motorcycle* calls up a silly picture. He, not the moose, is riding the motorcycle.]

IMPROVED

**Riding his motorcycle through the woods,** he saw a moose.

**Exercise 6** **Identifying Participial Phrases**

Identify the participial phrases in the following sentences, and give the word each phrase modifies.

EXAMPLE    1. The sight of skyscrapers towering against the sky always impresses me.

    1. *towering against the sky—skyscrapers*

1. How are skyscrapers created, and what keeps them standing tall?
2. As the drawing shows, columns of steel, or of concrete reinforced with steel, are sunk into bedrock beneath the building.
3. If a layer of rock isn't present, these columns are sunk into a thick concrete pad spread across the bottom of a deep basement.
4. From this foundation rises a steel skeleton, supporting the walls and floors.
5. This cutaway drawing shows how this skeleton, covered with a "skin" of glass and metal, becomes a safe working and living space for people.
6. This method of building, first developed in the United States, is used now in many other places in the world.
7. Chicago, nearly destroyed by fire in 1871, was later rebuilt with innovative designs.
8. The first skyscraper constructed on a metal frame was built there during this period.
9. Architects, using the latest materials, were glad to design in new ways.
10. Chicago, known as the site of the original 10-story skyscraper, now is home to the 110-story Sears Tower.

**Review D** **Identifying Participles and Participial Phrases**

Identify the participial phrases and participles that are used as adjectives in the following sentences. Then, give the words they modify.

EXAMPLE    1. Cats, known for their pride and independence, are supposedly hard to train.

    1. *known for their pride and independence—Cats*

1. One day I was giving Chops, my spoiled cat, treats.
2. Standing on her hind legs, she reached up with her paw.
3. Chops, grabbing for my fingers, tried to bring the tasty morsel closer.

┌HELP─

Some sentences in Review D contain more than one participle or participial phrase.

4. Pulling my hand back a little, I tugged gently on her curved paw, and she stepped forward.

5. Praising my clever cat, I immediately gave her two treats.

6. The next time I held a treat up high, Chops, puzzled but eager, repeated the grab-and-step movement.

7. Soon Chops was taking steps toward treats held out of her reach.

8. I now have an educated cat who can walk on two legs.

9. Grabbing the treats and gobbling them down, she has learned that certain moves always get her a snack.

10. Sometimes after Chops has had her treat, she just sits and looks at me, no doubt thinking that humans are truly a strange bunch!

# The Gerund

**14h.** A *gerund* is a verb form ending in *–ing* that is used as a noun.

Like other nouns, gerunds are used as subjects, predicate nominatives, direct objects, indirect objects, and objects of prepositions.

EXAMPLES     The **dancing** was fun. [subject]

My favorite part of the show was his **juggling.** [predicate nominative]

Shauna tried **climbing** faster. [direct object]

Give **winning** the game your best. [indirect object]

We worked better after **resting.** [object of a preposition]

Like other nouns, gerunds may be modified by adjectives and adjective phrases.

EXAMPLES     We listened to **the beautiful** singing **of the famous soprano.** [The article *the,* the adjective *beautiful,* and the adjective phrase *of the famous soprano* modify the gerund *singing. Singing* is used as the object of the preposition *to.*]

The Mallorys enjoy talking **about their vacation.** [The adjective phrase *about their vacation* modifies the gerund *talking,* which is the direct object of the verb *enjoy.*]

**The harsh** clacking **of the tappets** alerted us to a serious problem in the car's engine. [The article *The,* the adjective *harsh,* and the adjective phrase *of the tappets* modify the gerund *clacking.*]

Like verbs, gerunds may also be modified by adverbs and adverb phrases.

EXAMPLES    Reading **widely** is one way to acquire judgment, maturity, and a good education. [The gerund *Reading* is the subject of the verb *is*. The adverb *widely* modifies the gerund *Reading*.]

Floating **lazily in the pool** is my favorite summer pastime. [The gerund *Floating* is used as the subject of the sentence. It is modified by the adverb *lazily* (telling *how*) and also by the adverb phrase *in the pool* (telling *where*).]

Brandywine likes galloping **briskly on a cold morning.** [The gerund *galloping* is the direct object of the verb *likes*. The adverb *briskly* (telling *how*) and the adverb phrase *on a cold morning* (telling *when*) both modify *galloping*.]

Gerunds, like present participles, end in *–ing*. To be a gerund, a verbal must be used as a noun. In the following sentence, three words end in *–ing*, but only one of them is a gerund.

EXAMPLE    **Circling** the runway, the pilot was **preparing** for **landing.** [*Circling* is a present participle modifying *pilot*. *Preparing* is part of the verb phrase *was preparing*. Only *landing*, used as the object of the preposition *for*, is a gerund.]

### Exercise 7   Identifying and Classifying Gerunds

Identify each gerund in the following sentences. Then, write how each is used: as a *subject*, a *predicate nominative*, a *direct object*, or an *object of a preposition*.

EXAMPLE    **1.** Instead of driving, let's walk.

           *1. driving—object of a preposition*

**1.** Her laughing attracted my attention.
**2.** By studying, you can improve your grades.
**3.** Why did the birds stop chirping?
**4.** Writing in my journal has helped me understand myself better.
**5.** Smiling, Dad said that we would all go to a movie when we had finished the cleaning.
**6.** What Joseph liked best was hiking to the peak.
**7.** Before leaving the beach, we sat and watched the fading light.
**8.** Yesterday, Mrs. Jacobs was discussing having a garage sale.
**9.** One of Alvin's bad habits is boasting.
**10.** Without knocking, the crying child threw open the door.

# The Gerund Phrase

**14i.** A *gerund phrase* consists of a gerund and any modifiers or complements the gerund has. The entire phrase is used as a noun.

EXAMPLES    **The gentle pattering of the rain** was a welcome sound. [The gerund phrase is the subject of the sentence. The gerund *pattering* is modified by the article *The,* the adjective *gentle,* and the prepositional phrase *of the rain.* Notice that the modifiers preceding the gerund are included in the gerund phrase.]

I feared **skiing down the mountain alone.** [The gerund phrase is used as the object of the verb *feared.* The gerund *skiing* is modified by the prepositional phrase *down the mountain* and by the adverb *alone.*]

My dog's favorite game is **bringing me the newspaper.** [The gerund phrase is used as a predicate nominative. The gerund *bringing* has a direct object, *newspaper,* and an indirect object, *me.*]

Evelyn Ashford won a gold medal for **running the 100-meter dash.** [The gerund phrase is the object of the preposition *for.* The gerund *running* has a direct object, *dash.*]

STYLE  TIP

A noun or a pronoun that comes before a gerund should be in the possessive form.

EXAMPLES
**My** playing the radio loudly is a bad habit.

**Ed's** constant TV watching interferes with **our** studying.

**Exercise 8**   **Identifying and Classifying Gerund Phrases**

Find the gerund phrases in the following sentences. Then, tell how each phrase is used: as a *subject,* a *predicate nominative,* a *direct object,* or an *object of a preposition.*

EXAMPLE    1. My favorite hunting trophies are the ones I get by photographing wild animals.
     1. *photographing wild animals—object of a preposition*

1. Exciting and challenging, wildlife photography is surprisingly similar to pursuing prey on a hunt.
2. In both activities, knowing the animals' habits and habitats is vital to success.
3. Scouting out locations is important to both the hunter and the nature photographer.
4. This preparation gives you time for figuring out the best natural light for photography.

**HELP**

Sentences in Exercise 8 may contain more than one gerund phrase.

5. Other important skills are being quiet and keeping your aim very steady.

6. In photography, you must also consider choosing the correct film.

7. Photographers often like taking pictures of animals feeding near ponds and rivers.

8. Setting up a tripod and camera in underbrush nearby is a way to be ready when the animals come.

9. Advance preparation often makes the difference between getting good pictures and getting great ones.

10. Your patience and skill are rewarded when you "capture" a wild creature without killing it.

**Review E** **Identifying and Classifying Gerunds and Gerund Phrases**

Identify the gerunds or gerund phrases in the following sentences. Then, tell how each is used: as a *subject*, a *predicate nominative*, a *direct object*, or an *object of a preposition*.

EXAMPLE     1. Drawing a good caricature is hard to do.

     *1. Drawing a good caricature—subject*

1. A caricature is a picture, usually of a person, that draws attention to key features by emphasizing them.

2. Usually, caricature artists enjoy poking fun at famous people.

3. Looking at caricatures is an entertaining way to capture the "feel" of a historical period.

4. No one looking at this sketch of Teddy Roosevelt can help smiling.

5. The artist began by simplifying the shape of his subject's head.

6. Then he started outlining the temples and round cheeks with bold strokes of his pen.

7. As you probably realize, magnifying reality is very important to good caricature.

8. By enlarging Roosevelt's engaging grin and bristly mustache, the artist emphasizes these features and suggests Roosevelt's energetic, outgoing personality.

9. The artist also uses his subject's narrowed eyes and oval glasses for comic effect by drawing them closer together than they really were.

10. Exaggerating Roosevelt's features has resulted in an amusing but unmistakable likeness.

# The Infinitive

**14j.** An *infinitive* is a verb form that can be used
adjective, or an adverb. Most infinitives begin with

Infinitives can be used as nouns.

EXAMPLES     **To fly** is glorious. [*To fly* is the subject of t

       Brandon wanted **to work** on the play. [*T*
of the verb *wanted*.]

Infinitives can be used as adjectives.

EXAMPLES     The place **to visit** is Williamsburg. [*To v*
noun *place*.]

       That record was the one **to beat**. [*To be*
pronoun *one*.]

Infinitives also can be used as adverbs.

EXAMPLES     Sabina jumped **to shoot**. [*To shoot* modifies the verb *jumped*.]

       Ready **to go,** we soon loaded the car. [*To go* modifies the
adjective *Ready*.]

> **NOTE** *To* plus a noun or a pronoun (*to school, to him, to the beach*) is a
> prepositional phrase, not an infinitive.

## Exercise 9   Identifying and Classifying Infinitives

Identify the infinitives in the following sentences. Then, tell how each
infinitive is used: as a *noun*, an *adjective*, or an *adverb*.

EXAMPLE     **1.** I would like to help you.

       *1. to help—noun*

1. Tamisha's ambition is to teach.
2. To persist can sometimes be a sign of stubbornness.
3. Chen has learned to tap dance.
4. I am happy to oblige.
5. An easy way to win at tennis does not exist.
6. We need to weed the garden soon.
7. The hockey team went to Coach Norton's house to study last night.
8. We met at the lake to swim.
9. That is not the correct amount of paper to order for this project.
10. According to the map, the road to take is the one to the left.

---

**TIPS & TRICKS**

To find out if an infinitive
phrase is being used as a
noun, replace the phrase
with *what*.

EXAMPLES
To fix an air condi
is my next proj
is my next p
an air con
next p
tive

**GRAMMAR**

    suddenly appear from
the shadows.

REVISED
The bear seemed **to
appear** suddenly from
the shadows.

**Reference Note**

For more about
**prepositional phrases,**
see page 442.

**COMPUTER TIP**

Some software programs
can identify and highlight
split infinitives in a document. Using such a feature
will help you eliminate split
infinitives from your formal
writing.

## …nfinitive with *to* Omitted

…etimes the sign of the infinitive, *to,* is omitted in a sentence.

…XAMPLES She's done all her chores except [to] **feed** the cat.

I'll help you [to] **pack.**

The dogs like **to roam** in the field and [to] **chase** rabbits.

Fuel injection helps cars [to] **run** better and [to] **last** longer.

…tioner
…ect. [What
…roject? *To fix*
…ditioner is my
…oject. The infini-
…s a noun.]

…n New York, we went to see Gramercy Park. [We went what? This question makes no sense. The infinitive is not a noun. It is used as an adverb modifying the verb *went.*]

## The Infinitive Phrase

**14k. An *infinitive phrase* consists of an infinitive and any modifiers or complements the infinitive has. The entire phrase can be used as a noun, an adjective, or an adverb.**

EXAMPLES **To make tamales quickly** was hard. [The infinitive phrase is used as a noun, as the subject of the sentence. The infinitive has a direct object, *tamales,* and is modified by the adverb *quickly* and by the predicate adjective *hard.*]

Chris is the player **to watch in the next game.** [The infinitive phrase is used as an adjective modifying the predicate nominative *player.* The infinitive is modified by the adverb phrase *in the next game.*]

We are eager **to finish this project.** [The infinitive phrase is used as an adverb modifying the predicate adjective *eager.* The infinitive has a direct object, *project.*]

NOTE An infinitive may have a subject. An ***infinitive clause*** consists of an infinitive with a subject and any modifiers and complements of the infinitive. The entire infinitive clause functions as a noun.

EXAMPLES I wanted **him to help me with my algebra.** [The entire infinitive clause is the direct object of the verb wanted. *Him* is the subject of the infinitive *to help.* The infinitive *to help* has a direct object, *me,* and is modified by the adverb phrase *with my algebra.*]

Would Uncle Jim like **us to clear the brush in the backyard**? [The entire infinitive clause is the direct object of the verb *Would like. Us* is the subject of the infinitive *to clear.* The infinitive *to clear* has a direct object *brush,* which is modified by the adjective phrase *in the backyard.*]

Notice that a pronoun that functions as the subject of an infinitive clause is in the objective case.

## Exercise 10 Identifying and Classifying Infinitives and Infinitive Phrases

Identify the infinitives and infinitive phrases in the following sentences. After each, tell whether it is used as a *noun*, an *adjective*, or an *adverb*.

EXAMPLE   1.  Scott is the person to elect.

1. *to elect—adjective*

1. To dance gracefully requires coordination.
2. Raymond wanted to join the team.
3. Sandy needs to study.
4. I'm going to the pond to fish.
5. A good way to lose weight is to eat moderately.
6. After our long vacation, we needed to get back in training.
7. The best way to get there is to take the bus.
8. Don't you dare open that present before your birthday.
9. Juanita and Matt tried to find the perfect gift.
10. He lives to swim and water-ski.

┌─HELP─

The sign of the infinitive, *to,* is sometimes omitted. Also, a sentence in Exercise 10 may contain more than one infinitive or infinitive phrase.

## Exercise 11 Identifying and Classifying Infinitive Phrases

Identify the infinitive phrases in the following sentences. Then, tell how each phrase is used: as a *noun*, an *adjective*, or an *adverb*.

EXAMPLE   1.  To create a miracle fabric was the aim of the chemist Joe Shivers.

1. *To create a miracle fabric—noun*

1. He succeeded with spandex, and athletes of all shapes and sizes have learned to appreciate the qualities of his "power cloth."
2. This material has the ability to stretch and snap back into shape.
3. Its sleek fit lessens friction to give the wearer faster movement through air or water.
4. Its slick surface makes an athlete such as a wrestler hard to hold.
5. To say that spandex has athletes covered is not stretching the truth.
6. Spandex is just one of many synthetic fibers to meet today's fashion needs.
7. Nylon was the first synthetic; it originally was made to take the place of silk in women's garments.
8. To replace silk was also the purpose of rayon, another early, low-priced synthetic.

┌─HELP─

In Exercise 11 the sign of the infinitive, *to,* is sometimes omitted.

9. Polyester, developed later, often is combined with natural fibers to reduce wrinkling.

10. To distinguish synthetic fibers (most made from plastic) from natural fibers is not easy.

### Review F  Identifying Infinitives and Infinitive Phrases

Identify the infinitives and infinitive phrases in the following paragraph.

EXAMPLE     **[1]** Laurel and Hardy are a comic team to remember.

    *1.  to remember*

┌HELP┐

In Review F, the sign of the infinitive, *to,* is sometimes omitted.

[1] Together, Stan Laurel and Oliver Hardy have made millions of moviegoers laugh. [2] In their day, to be funny in the movies required the use of body language. [3] Both of them were geniuses in their ability to keep audiences laughing. [4] For his famous head scratch, Stan grew his hair long so that he could scratch and pull it to make a comic mess. [5] Stan also developed a hilarious cry that he used to show his character's childish nature. [6] He would shut his eyes tightly, pinch up his face, and begin to wail. [7] Ollie, too, had an uncanny ability to create his own distinctive mannerisms. [8] For example, he was known for the long-suffering look he used to express frustration. [9] He would also waggle his tie at a person he and Stan had managed to offend and then start giggling nervously. [10] Ollie's intent was to make the person less angry, but his gesture usually had the opposite effect.

### Review G  Identifying and Classifying Verbals and Verbal Phrases

Identify each verbal or verbal phrase in the following paragraph as a *participle, participial phrase, gerund, gerund phrase, infinitive, infinitive phrase,* or as a part of an *infinitive clause.*

EXAMPLE     **[1]** Building the railroad across the United States in the late 1800s required thousands of workers.

    *1.  Building the railroad across the United States in the late 1800s—gerund phrase*

[1] The government commissioned two companies to build railway tracks between Omaha, Nebraska, and Sacramento, California. [2] Building eastward from Sacramento, the Central Pacific Railroad relied on Chinese workers. [3] One-fourth of the Chinese immigrants

in the United States in 1868 helped with laying the track. [4] The terrain was difficult to cover, but the laborers rose to the challenge. [5] Known for their dependability, the Chinese were strong workers. [6] Complaining was a problem with some workers, but seldom with Chinese laborers. [7] It was often necessary to blow up parts of mountains, and the Chinese workers became experts at this task. [8] Chinese and Irish workers set a record on April 28, 1869, by spiking ten miles and fifty-six feet of track in twelve hours. [9] The railroad company divided the Chinese immigrants into working groups, or gangs, each with twelve to twenty men. [10] Keeping many of their traditional ways, Chinese workers ate food that was shipped to them from San Francisco's Chinatown.

# Appositives and Appositive Phrases

**14l.** An *appositive* is a noun or a pronoun placed beside another noun or pronoun to identify or describe it.

EXAMPLES    The sculptor **Isamu Noguchi** has designed sculpture gardens. [The appositive *Isamu Noguchi* identifies the noun *sculptor.*]

Eric, a talented **musician,** plans to study in Europe. [The appositive *musician* describes the noun *Eric.*]

Those, the **ones** on the right, are on sale. [The appositive *ones* identifies the pronoun *Those.*]

**14m.** An *appositive phrase* consists of an appositive and any modifiers it has.

EXAMPLES    Lucy Sánchez, **my longtime friend from my old neighborhood,** has a new Scottish terrier.

Dr. Jackson has a degree in entomology, **the scientific study of insects.**

NOTE    Sometimes, an appositive phrase precedes the noun or pronoun to which it refers.

EXAMPLE    **The terror of our block,** little Anthony was on the warpath.

**Reference Note**

For more about **essential and nonessential phrases,** see page 648.

Appositives and appositive phrases that are not essential to the meaning of the sentence are set off by commas. If the appositive is essential to the meaning, it is generally not set off by commas.

EXAMPLES    My teacher, **Mr. Byrd,** trains parrots. [The writer has only one teacher. The appositive is not necessary to identify the teacher. Because the information is nonessential, it is set off by commas.]

My teacher **Mr. Byrd** trains parrots. [The writer has more than one teacher. The appositive is necessary to tell which teacher is meant. Because this information is essential to the meaning of the sentence, it is not set off by commas.]

NOTE   Commas are generally used with appositives that refer to proper nouns.

EXAMPLE    Linda, **the editor,** assigned the story.

However, a word or phrase that is commonly accepted as part of a person's name or title is not set off by a comma.

EXAMPLE    The Roman Army defeated Attila **the Hun** in A.D. 451.

## Exercise 12 Identifying Appositive Phrases

Identify the appositive phrases in the following sentences. Then, give the noun or pronoun that each appositive phrase identifies or describes.

EXAMPLE    1. I usually write haiku, poems in a traditional Japanese form.

1. *poems in a traditional Japanese form—haiku*

HELP

A sentence in Exercise 12 may contain more than one appositive or appositive phrase.

1. Our community has a new organization, a writers' club called Writers, Inc.
2. Marquita Wiley, a college instructor, started the group at the request of former students.
3. A published author, she conducts the meetings as workshops.
4. The writers meet to read their works in progress, fiction or poetry, and to discuss suggestions for improvement.
5. The members, people from all walks of life, have varied interests.
6. A mechanic by trade, J. D. Ellis writes funny poems about his hobby, bird-watching.
7. My friend Lusita just had a short story about her people, the Zuni, published in a national magazine.

**8.** Next week, we'll meet at our regular time, 3:30 P.M.

**9.** Our guest speaker is Pat Mora, a Mexican American poet whose work emphasizes harmony between cultures.

**10.** Have you read her poem "Bribe"?

**Review H** **Identifying Verbal Phrases and Appositive Phrases**

Find the verbal phrases and appositive phrases in the following sentences. Identify each phrase as a *participial phrase*, a *gerund phrase*, an *infinitive phrase*, or an *appositive phrase*.

┌HELP┐

A sentence in Review H may contain more than one verbal or appositive phrase.

EXAMPLE
   **1.** Automobiles have been partly responsible for drastically changing life in the twentieth century.

   *1. drastically changing life in the twentieth century—gerund phrase*

**1.** Developing the automobile was actually the creative work of many people, but Henry Ford deservedly receives much credit.

**2.** Ford's company, using an assembly line and interchangeable parts, first produced the Model T in 1909.

**3.** Many people in the early 1900s wanted to buy cars because of their low prices and novelty.

**4.** By giving people an alternative to mass transit, automobiles did much to change the social and business scene of the United States.

**5.** No longer dependent on streetcars and trains, the first motorists used automobiles for going on recreational and family trips.

**6.** Clearly overjoyed with their vehicles, many Americans regarded automobiles as necessities by the 1920s.

**7.** One writer, a famous historian, noted that the automobile industry led to such new businesses as gas stations, repair garages, tire companies, and motels.

**8.** To get a clear idea of changes in automobile designs over the years, look at the picture to the right.

**9.** The photo shows Henry Ford, looking contented and proud, in his first car.

**10.** What are some of the main differences between Ford's car, one of the most advanced vehicles of its day, and modern cars?

─HELP─

Although several possible answers are given in the example in Review I, you need to write only one sentence for each item.

**Review I** **Writing Appropriate Phrases**

Rewrite each of the following sentences, supplying an appropriate prepositional, verbal, or appositive phrase to fill in the blank. Use each type of phrase at least twice. Identify each phrase you use as *prepositional, participial, infinitive, gerund,* or *appositive.*

EXAMPLE    1. We have room for only a single passenger _____.

1. We have room for only a single passenger weighing less than one-hundred fifty pounds. — *participial*

or

We have room for only a single passenger in the boat. — *prepositional*

or

We have room for only a single passenger, a small one! — *appositive*

or

We have room for only a single passenger to come aboard. — *infinitive*

1. Only one _____ was left on the plate.
2. Joyfully, she danced _____.
3. Richard, _____, is moving back to the town!
4. During the whole trip to Mexico, her goal was _____.
5. _____, the new computer still sat in boxes on the floor.
6. At the bottom of the river, a huge old catfish lay _____.
7. _____ made them strong enough for the race.
8. Navajo dancers _____ stepped lightly into the open circle.
9. _____ became their goal for the rest of the year.
10. All the clothes _____ had been made in the United States.
11. The lace curtains _____ were not for sale.
12. Are these puppies _____ all yours?
13. What a marvelous aroma is rising _____!
14. _____, the engine finally started.
15. With a glance at the other runners _____, Gretchen pulled ahead.
16. Bill Briggs, _____, greeted the enthusiastic fans.
17. Everyone _____ should move down one seat.
18. _____ was the thought of each student in the class.
19. The children _____ made mud pies.
20. _____ gave them the endurance they needed.

# Chapter Review

## A. Identifying Phrases

In each of the following sentences, identify each italicized phrase as *prepositional, participial, gerund, infinitive,* or *appositive.*

┌HELP┐

In the Chapter Review, if a phrase contains a shorter phrase, identify only the longer phrase.

1. Now I would like *to tell you about my sister Alexandra.*
2. She likes *arriving at school early.*
3. By *doing so,* she can spend extra time preparing for her day.
4. She will resort to anything to get *to school* early, including waking me up, too.
5. For example, when *the beeping of my alarm* woke me yesterday, the sky was as dark as night.
6. I soon realized that Alexandra, *a volunteer crossing guard at school,* had adjusted the alarm.
7. It was, I could see, an occasion for *applying my special technique.*
8. *Called my slow-motion technique,* it always achieves the result I want.
9. I moved *around the house* as if I were underwater; Alexandra watched until she could stand it no longer.
10. Then, I moved faster; I certainly did not want *to be late for school.*

## B. Identifying and Classifying Prepositional Phrases

Identify the prepositional phrases in the following sentences. Identify the word or words modified by each phrase. Then, state whether the prepositional phrase is an *adjective phrase* or an *adverb phrase.*

11. A daily newspaper has something for almost everyone.
12. In addition to news, the paper offers entertainment, classified ads, and much more.
13. Our entire family reads the newspaper in the morning.
14. Dad always begins with the sports pages; Mom prefers the general news.
15. My sister's favorite part of the newspaper is the lifestyle section.
16. She enjoys features like "How-to Hints."
17. I find the editorial and opinion pages interesting, especially when a debate between two sides develops.
18. Sometimes I see the logic behind an argument.

**19.** Other times I wonder why grown people argue about a trivial issue.

**20.** I also like to read news about local events.

## C. Identifying Verbals

Identify each italicized verbal in the following sentences as a *participle*, a *gerund*, or an *infinitive*.

**21.** Many amateur athletes want *to earn* medals for their abilities.

**22.** *Enjoyed* by people throughout history, amateur athletic competitions can be very beneficial.

**23.** *Winning* an event is only part of the reason athletes compete.

**24.** When talented amateurs compete *to test* their skills, they learn a great deal about their sport.

**25.** In addition, the love of a sport, the best reason for *entering* into competition, usually grows as an athlete's performance improves.

**26.** Furthermore, *sharing* hard work with teammates leads a person to appreciate cooperative efforts.

**27.** Competitions *organized* on many levels give amateur athletes a motive for increased practice.

**28.** *Participating* in state, national, and international competitions is important to many amateur athletes.

**29.** *Wanting* to be recognized for their talent, the athletes compete against their peers in such events.

**30.** These competitions also provide athletes with opportunities *to put* their abilities to the test.

## D. Identifying Verbal Phrases

In each of the following sentences, identify the italicized verbal phrase as a *participial phrase*, an *infinitive phrase*, or a *gerund phrase*.

**31.** Maxine gets her exercise by *dancing for at least three hours a week*.

**32.** Eddie likes *to make pizza for his friends*.

**33.** The mother baboon watched her infant *eating a berry*.

**34.** Yolanda went *to get her book*.

**35.** Is the man *pushing the grocery cart* an employee or a customer?

36. *Winning the contest* was a thrill for our cheerleaders.

37. I made a tote bag *to hold my gym clothes.*

38. Richard's summer job is *delivering groceries to the hospital.*

39. Enzo Ferrari became famous by *building fast and stylish cars.*

40. *Preparing for that play* took quite a long time.

41. Samantha overheard Tina and Sue *talking about their vacation plans.*

42. Prepare *to run your fastest.*

43. *Excited by the thought of the trip,* we finished packing early.

44. Koalas get most of their nutrition by *eating eucalyptus leaves.*

45. *Tired of the noise outside,* we closed the window.

# Writing Application
## Using Prepositional Phrases in a Game

**Adjective and Adverb Phrases**   You are planning a treasure hunt for a group of neighborhood children. The treasure hunt will include six stops for clues. For each clue, write a sentence containing at least one prepositional phrase. Use a combination of adjective and adverb phrases.

**Prewriting**   First, think about your neighborhood and pick a good place to hide a treasure. Then, think of six places to hide clues.

**Writing**   Write a sentence giving a clue about each location. The final sentence should lead the children directly to the hidden treasure.

**Revising**   Ask someone who is familiar with the area of the treasure hunt to look over your clues. Revise any clues that are not clear. Be sure that each clue contains at least one prepositional phrase and that you have used both adjective and adverb phrases in your clues.

**Publishing**   Check to be sure that your prepositional phrases are properly placed. An adverb phrase may occur at various places in a sentence. Proofread your sentences for correct capitalization and punctuation. You may want to organize a treasure hunt for younger children in your family or for children that you baby-sit.

# The Clause
## Independent and Subordinate Clauses

# Diagnostic Preview

### A. Identifying and Classifying Subordinate Clauses

Identify the subordinate clause in each of the following sentences. Then, classify each subordinate clause as an adjective clause (*adj.*), an adverb clause (*adv.*), or a noun clause (*n.*). If the clause is used as an adjective or adverb, write the word or phrase it modifies. If the clause is used as a noun, indicate whether it is used as a subject (*subj.*), a direct object (*d.o.*), an indirect object (*i.o.*), a predicate nominative (*p.n.*), or an object of a preposition (*o.p.*).

EXAMPLES  1. After our last class, Elena, Frieda, and I agreed that we would go bicycling in the park.

1. *that we would go bicycling in the park—n.—d.o.*

2. As we set out for the park, we had no idea of the difficulties ahead.

2. *As we set out for the park—adv.—had*

1. Since none of us own bicycles, we decided to rent them there.
2. The man who rented us the bikes was helpful.
3. After we had bicycled six miles, Frieda's bike got a flat tire.
4. What we found was a nail in the tire.
5. We decided to take the bike to whatever bike shop was the nearest.
6. The woman at the bike shop told us that she could fix the tire.
7. After we had paid for the repair and gotten a receipt, we rode back to the park and bicycled for an hour.

8. Our only worry was that the man at the rental shop might not pay us back for the repair.
9. When we returned our bikes, we showed the man the receipt.
10. He refunded the money we had spent to fix the tire.

## B. Classifying Sentences According to Structure

Classify each of the following sentences as *simple, compound, complex,* or *compound-complex.* Be sure that you can identify all subordinate and independent clauses.

EXAMPLES
1. Amanda now plays the violin because of a winter concert that she heard when she was in the third grade.

1. *complex*

2. The concert featured a talented, young violinist from Russia and a famous local pianist.

2. *simple*

11. Amanda loved the sound of the orchestra at her school's winter concert, and she decided then to study the violin.
12. Amanda's first violin was not the standard size, for she was still quite small.
13. When she started the sixth grade, however, Amanda was playing a full-sized violin.
14. She did not always enjoy the many hours of practice, but they were necessary because playing the instrument is complicated.
15. Amanda knew that playing the proper notes could be especially difficult on a violin.
16. On a keyboard instrument, you simply press a key and hear the note for that key.
17. On a violin, however, the placement of a finger on a string can affect the pitch of a note.
18. If the pitch of each note is not exact, even a common tune can be difficult to recognize.
19. Once a student has mastered finger placement to some extent, he or she still has a great deal to think about; posture, hand position, and bowing technique all require great concentration.
20. When students can actually create music with this stubborn instrument, they have reason to be proud.

# What Is a Clause?

**15a.** A *clause* is a word group that contains a verb and its subject and that is used as a sentence or as part of a sentence.

Although every clause contains a subject and a verb, not every clause expresses a complete thought. Clauses that do are called ***independent clauses.*** Clauses that do not express a complete thought are called ***subordinate clauses.***

| | |
|---|---|
| INDEPENDENT CLAUSE | The people left the building |
| SUBORDINATE CLAUSE | when the fire alarm sounded |
| SENTENCE | When the fire alarm sounded, the people left the building. |

┌**HELP**──

A subordinate clause that is capitalized and punctuated as a sentence is a **sentence fragment.**

**Reference Note**

For information about **correcting sentence fragments,** see page 320.

# The Independent Clause

**15b.** An *independent* (or *main*) *clause* expresses a complete thought and can stand by itself as a sentence.

In the following examples, each boldface clause has its own subject and verb and expresses a complete thought.

EXAMPLES **Ms. Santana works in a law office in downtown Concord.**

**Ms. Santana works in a law office** that has a view of downtown Concord.

**Ms. Santana works in a law office in downtown Concord,** and **she has a successful practice.**

In the last example, the independent clauses are joined by a comma and the coordinating conjunction *and.* The clauses also could be written with a semicolon between them:

> Ms. Santana works in a law office in downtown Concord; she has a successful practice.

or with a semicolon, a conjunctive adverb, and a comma:

> Ms. Santana works in a law office in downtown Concord; **indeed,** she has a successful practice.

or as separate sentences:

> Ms. Santana works in a law office in downtown Concord. She has a successful practice.

**Reference Note**

For a list of **coordinating conjunctions,** see page 404. For more about using **semicolons** and **conjunctive adverbs** to join independent clauses, see page 670.

# The Subordinate Clause

**15c.** A *subordinate* (or *dependent*) *clause* does not express a complete thought and cannot stand by itself as a sentence.

Words such as *when, whom, because, which, that, if,* and *until* signal that the clauses following them are likely to be subordinate. *Subordinate* means "lesser in rank or importance." To make a complete sentence, a subordinate clause must be joined to an independent clause. Like phrases, subordinate clauses can be used as adjectives, adverbs, or nouns.

| SUBORDINATE CLAUSES | when you arrive at the airport in Dallas |
| | which grow only locally |
| | that he had granted us an interview |

| SENTENCES | **When you arrive at the airport in Dallas,** call us. |
| | These wildflowers, **which grow only locally,** are of interest to scientists. |
| | Did you know **that he had granted us an interview**? |

As the preceding examples show, subordinate clauses may appear at the beginning, in the middle, or at the end of a sentence. The placement of a subordinate clause depends on how the clause is used in the sentence.

> **NOTE** Many subordinate clauses contain complements (such as predicate nominatives, predicate adjectives, direct objects, or indirect objects), modifiers, or both.
>
> EXAMPLES **what** it is . . . [*What* is a predicate nominative: It is *what*?]
>
> because you look **tired** . . . [*Tired* is a predicate adjective modifying *you*.]
>
> **that** you chose . . . [*That* is the direct object of *chose*.]
>
> before he gave **us** the **quiz** . . . [*Us* is the indirect object of *gave; quiz* is the direct object of *gave*.]
>
> that I bought **yesterday** . . . [*Yesterday* is an adverb modifying *bought*.]
>
> when the coach was calling **to her** . . . [*To her* is an adverb phrase modifying *was calling*.]

**Reference Note**

For more about **sentence complements,** see page 427. For more information on **modifiers,** see Chapter 19.

**STYLE** ✏ **TIP**

Although short, simple sentences can be effective, a variety of sentence structures is usually more effective. To make choppy sentences into smoother writing, combine shorter sentences by changing some into subordinate clauses. Also, avoid unnecessary repetition of subjects, verbs, and pronouns.

CHOPPY
I enjoy feta cheese. It comes from Greece. It is traditionally made from sheep's or goat's milk.

SMOOTH
I enjoy feta cheese, which comes from Greece and is traditionally made from sheep's or goat's milk.

In the example above, two of the short sentences are combined into a single subordinate clause.

**Exercise 1** **Identifying Independent and Subordinate Clauses**

For each of the following sentences, identify the clause in italics as *independent* or *subordinate*.

EXAMPLE    1. *When you think of baseball,* you may think of lightning-fast pitches, bat-splitting home runs, or secret hand signals from coaches and catchers.

1. subordinate

1. *Baseball is a game* that generally depends on good eyesight as well as athletic skill.

2. For this reason, until recently, playing the great American game has been something *that people with visual impairments found virtually impossible.*

3. Only sighted players could participate *until an engineer named Charley Fairbanks invented beep baseball.*

4. *In this version of baseball, the ball beeps and the bases buzz* so that players like the one pictured here can tell when to swing and where to run.

5. Each team has a sighted pitcher and a sighted catcher, *who never get a turn at bat,* and six fielders who wear blindfolds so that they don't have a visual advantage.

6. The pitcher shouts "Ready!" *before the ball is pitched* and "Pitch!" when the ball is released.

7. When the bat strikes the ball, the umpire activates the buzzer in first base, *to which the batter must then run.*

8. When a team is on defense, the pitcher and catcher cannot field the batted ball themselves; *they can only shout directions to the fielders.*

9. *Beep baseball is fun to play,* and its challenges create a bond between sighted players and players with visual impairments.

10. Sighted players *who put on blindfolds and join in* come away from a game with a new respect for the abilities of their visually impaired teammates.

# The Adjective Clause

**15d.** An *adjective clause* is a subordinate clause that modifies a noun or a pronoun.

An adjective clause usually follows the word or words it modifies and tells *what kind* or *which one*. An *essential* (or *restrictive*) clause is necessary to the basic meaning of the sentence; it is not set off by commas. A *nonessential* (or *nonrestrictive*) clause gives only additional information and is not necessary to the meaning of a sentence; it is set off by commas.

EXAMPLES    This is the new music video **that I like best.** [The clause *that I like best* is necessary to tell which video is being mentioned. Because this information is essential to the meaning of the sentence, it is not set off by commas.]

Griffins, **which are mythological beasts,** are included on many coats of arms. [The clause *which are mythological beasts* is not necessary to identify *Griffins.* Because this information is nonessential to the meaning of the sentence, it is set off by commas.]

**Reference Note**

For help in deciding whether a clause is **essential or nonessential,** see page 648.

## Relative Pronouns

Adjective clauses are often introduced by relative pronouns.

| **Common Relative Pronouns** | who, whom, whose, which, that |
|---|---|

These words are called *relative pronouns* because they *relate* an adjective clause to the word that the clause modifies. Besides introducing an adjective clause and relating it to another word in the sentence, the relative pronoun has a grammatical function within the adjective clause.

EXAMPLES    Luís, **who enjoys running,** has decided to enter the marathon. [The relative pronoun *who* relates the adjective clause to *Luís. Who* also functions as the subject of the adjective clause.]

The students questioned the data **on which the theory was based.** [The relative pronoun *which* relates the adjective clause to *data* and functions as the object of the preposition *on.*]

We met the singer **whose new CD was released this week.** [The relative pronoun *whose* relates the adjective clause to *singer. Whose* functions as a possessive pronoun in the adjective clause.]

**Reference Note**

For more information on **using *who* and *whom*** correctly, see page 559. For more about **using *that* and *which*** correctly, see page 607.

Janice, **whom I have known for years,** is my lab partner this semester. [The relative pronoun *whom* relates the adjective clause to *Janice. Whom* functions as the direct object of the verb phrase *have known* in the adjective clause.]

In many cases, the relative pronoun in the clause may be omitted. The pronoun is understood and still has a function in the clause.

EXAMPLES   Here is the salad **you ordered.** [The relative pronoun *that* is understood. The pronoun relates the adjective clause to *salad* and functions as the direct object of the verb *ordered* in the adjective clause.]

He is the one **I met yesterday.** [The relative pronoun *whom* or *that* is understood. The pronoun relates the adjective clause to *one* and functions as the direct object of the verb *met* in the adjective clause.]

Occasionally an adjective clause is introduced by the word *where* or *when.* When used in such a way, these words are called ***relative adverbs.***

EXAMPLES   They showed us the stadium **where the game would be held.**

Saturday is the day **when I mow the lawn.**

## Exercise 2  Identifying Adjective Clauses

Each of the following sentences contains an adjective clause. Write the adjective clause, and underline the relative pronoun or relative adverb that introduces it. If the relative pronoun has been omitted, write it in parentheses and then underline it.

EXAMPLE   1.  Do you know anyone who is familiar with briffits, swalloops, and waftaroms?

        1.  *who is familiar with briffits, swalloops, and waftaroms*

1. Cartoonists use a variety of unusual names for the symbols that commonly appear in comic strips.
2. For example, a *briffit* is the little puff of dust hanging in the spot where a swiftly departing character was previously standing.
3. For times when cartoonists want to make something appear hot or smelly, they use wavy, rising lines called *waftaroms.*
4. *Agitrons* are the wiggly lines around an object that is supposed to be shaking.

5. The limbs of a character who is moving are usually preceded or trailed by a set of curved lines called *blurgits* or *swalloops.*

6. *Plewds,* which look like flying droplets of sweat, are drawn around the head of a worried character.

7. In fact, there are very few motions or emotions for which cartoonists have not invented a clever, expressive symbol.

8. Almost everyone who likes to doodle and draw has used some of these symbols, probably without knowing the names for them.

9. Look at the example cartoon, where you will find the names of other common symbols from the world of cartooning.

10. Now you know a "language" almost nobody outside the cartooning profession knows!

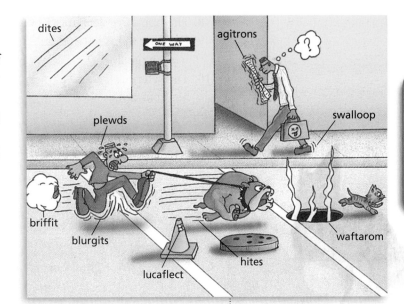

### Exercise 3  Revising Sentences by Supplying Adjective Clauses

Revise the following sentences by substituting an adjective clause for each italicized adjective. Add specific details to make your sentences interesting. Underline the adjective clauses in your sentences.

EXAMPLE  1. The *angry* citizens gathered in front of City Hall.

1. The citizens, <u>who were furious over the recent tax increase</u>, gathered in front of City Hall.

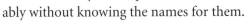

1. As I entered the building, a *colorful* painting caught my eye.
2. The *patient* photographer sat on a small ledge all day.
3. The two attorneys argued all week over the *important* contract.
4. The team of mountain climbers decided to try to reach the top of the *tallest* peak.
5. At the assembly, Ms. León made two *surprising* announcements.
6. Saburo and his friends cautiously entered the *dark* cave.
7. Edna Jackson easily won her *first* political campaign.

**8.** The trainer spoke harshly to the *disobedient* dog.

**9.** Dodging to his left and then to his right, Manuel scored the *winning* goal.

**10.** The veterinarian told Pamela that he was taking good care of her *lame* horse.

## The Adverb Clause

**15e.** An *adverb clause* is a subordinate clause that modifies a verb, an adjective, or an adverb.

An adverb clause generally tells *how, when, where, why, how much, to what extent,* or *under what condition* the action of a verb takes place.

EXAMPLES    **After I had proofread my paper,** I input the corrections. [The adverb clause *After I had proofread my paper* tells *when* I input the corrections.]

**Because crêpes are delicious,** Joy makes them on special occasions. [*Because crêpes are delicious* tells *why* Joy makes them on special occasions.]

You and your brother may come with us **if you want to.** [*If you want to* tells *under what condition* you and your brother may come with us.]

NOTE    As you can see in the first two examples above, introductory adverb clauses are usually set off by commas.

**Reference Note**

For more about using **commas** to set off introductory elements, see page 652.

Like adverbs, adverb clauses may also modify adjectives or adverbs.

EXAMPLES    Have computers made office work easier **than it was before**? [The adverb clause *than it was before* modifies the adjective *easier,* telling *to what extent* work is easier.]

My cousin Adele reads faster **than I do.** [The adverb clause *than I do* modifies the adverb *faster,* telling *how much* faster my cousin Adele reads.]

NOTE    When using adverb clauses to make comparisons, be sure your comparisons are complete.

INCOMPLETE    I like dancing better than you. [Do I like dancing better than I like you? Do I like dancing better than you like dancing?]

COMPLETE    I like dancing better **than you do.**

**Reference Note**

For more about **complete comparisons,** see page 583.

## Subordinating Conjunctions

Adverb clauses are introduced by **subordinating conjunctions**—words that show the relationship between the adverb clause and the word or words that the clause modifies.

| Common Subordinating Conjunctions | | | |
|---|---|---|---|
| after | because | since | when |
| although | before | so that | whenever |
| as | even though | than | where |
| as if | if | though | wherever |
| as long as | in order that | unless | whether |
| as soon as | once | until | while |

Some subordinating conjunctions, such as *after, before, since,* and *until,* may also be used as prepositions.

EXAMPLES    Be sure to hand in your report **before the end** of class today. [prepositional phrase]

Be sure to hand in your report **before class ends today.** [adverb clause]

Exercise 4 **Identifying and Classifying Adverb Clauses**

Identify each adverb clause in the following sentences. Then, write what the clause tells: *when, where, how, why, to what extent,* or *under what condition.* A sentence may have more than one adverb clause.

EXAMPLE    1.  When you see the humble man on the next page, can you believe that he is considered one of the twentieth century's greatest leaders?

    1.  *When you see the humble man on the next page—when*

1. If you look through newspapers from the first half of the twentieth century, you will see many pictures of Mohandas K. Gandhi.
2. This man led India to independence from Britain, and he took his spinning wheel wherever he went.
3. He did so because he viewed spinning as a symbol of the peaceful, traditional Indian lifestyle.
4. He also hoped to encourage the Indian people to make their own clothes so that they would not have to depend on British industry.
5. As a form of protest, he led marches or fasted until the government met his requests.

---

STYLE    TIP

Because a n verb clause does          d location i
must ch
the claus
versions
taining ar
Then, read a.          v
sion to see how i.    p. .ce-
ment of the clause affects flow, rhythm, and overall meaning.

EXAMPLES

After we leave for school, Mom works on her novel.

Mom works on her novel after we leave for school.

COMPUTER TIP

If you use a computer to write compositions, you can easily experiment with the placement of adverb clauses in sentences.

6. Gandhi's nonviolent methods were more powerful than anyone could have predicted.
7. As India's Congress and people increasingly supported Gandhi's nonviolent program, the British government was forced to listen.
8. Gandhi was well qualified to represent India as a diplomat since he had studied law in London before he became involved in India's freedom movement.
9. After independence was assured, Gandhi turned his attention to helping India's many poor people.
10. Because he was loved throughout India and the world, Gandhi was called *Mahatma*, meaning "Great Soul."

## The Noun Clause

**15f.** A **noun clause** is a subordinate clause that is used as a noun.

**Reference Note**

For more information on **subjects, predicate nominatives, direct objects,** and **indirect objects,** see Chapter 13. For more about **objects of prepositions,** see page 442.

A noun clause may be used as a subject, as a complement (such as a predicate nominative, direct object, or indirect object), or as the object of a preposition.

| | |
|---|---|
| SUBJECT | **What Mary Anne did to rescue the injured bird** was brave. |
| PREDICATE NOMINATIVE | The winner of the race will be **whoever runs fastest in the final stretch.** |
| DIRECT OBJECT | She finally discovered **what the answer to her question was.** |
| INDIRECT OBJECT | Give **whatever parts need cleaning** a rinse in detergent. |
| OBJECT OF PREPOSITION | He checks the ID cards of **whoever visits.** |

Noun clauses are usually introduced by

| | | | |
|---|---|---|---|
| that | when | whether | whom |
| what | whenever | who | whomever |
| whatever | where | whoever | why |

Sometimes these words have a grammatical function in the noun clause. Other times they just introduce the clause and have no other function in it.

EXAMPLES  They did not know **who it could be.** [The introductory word *who* is the predicate nominative of the noun clause—*it could be who.* The entire clause is the direct object of the verb *did know.*]

Show us **what you bought.** [The introductory word *what* is the direct object in the noun clause—*you bought what.* The entire clause is the direct object of the verb *show.*]

**What you learn** is your decision. [The introductory word *what* is the direct object in the noun clause—*you learn what.* The entire clause is the subject of the verb *is.*]

She wished **that she were older.** [The introductory word *that* simply introduces the noun clause and has no function within the noun clause. The entire clause is the direct object of the verb *wished.*]

Sometimes the word that introduces a noun clause is omitted. In such cases, the introductory word is understood.

EXAMPLE  Didn't you know **the party was canceled?** [The introductory word *that* is understood.]

### Exercise 5  Identifying and Classifying Noun Clauses

Most of the following sentences contain noun clauses. If a sentence contains a noun clause, identify that clause. Then, tell how the clause is used: as a *subject,* a *predicate nominative,* a *direct object,* an *indirect object,* or an *object of a preposition.* If a sentence does not contain a noun clause, write *no noun clause.*

EXAMPLE  1. We moved to Massachusetts and did not know what we would find there.

1. *what we would find there—direct object*

1. What surprised me first were the yellowish green fire engines.
2. I had thought fire engines were always red.
3. Our neighbors explained that this color keeps the fire engines from being confused with other large red trucks.
4. My sister Michelle made another discovery at the bowling alley.
5. The small grapefruit-sized bowling balls with no holes were not what she was used to!
6. We learned that this sport is called candlepin bowling.

7. Whoever can knock down the pins with one of those bowling balls must be an expert.
8. Later, I was surprised by how delicious the baked beans were.
9. Someone should give whoever invented Boston baked beans an award for this marvelous creation.
10. Now, after we have lived in New England for a year, both Michelle and I are happy in our new home.

### Review A   Identifying Subordinate Clauses

For most of the sentences in the following paragraph, identify the subordinate clause or clauses. Then, tell whether each clause is an *adjective clause,* an *adverb clause,* or a *noun clause.* If a sentence has no subordinate clauses, write *none.*

EXAMPLE    [1] In paintings created before 1880, horses are usually shown in poses that now look quaint and unnatural.

1. *that now look quaint and unnatural—adjective clause*

[1] If you stop to think about it, you can see why painters had a problem. [2] Stop-action photography had not yet been invented, and when painters looked at rapidly moving horses, they could not possibly see where the legs and hooves were at any one instant. [3] Whenever painters wanted to portray a galloping horse, they made up a position they thought suggested speed. [4] The horses in some paintings had both front legs extended far to the front and both hind legs stretched far behind. [5] Today, we know that this is an impossible position for a horse. [6] Stop-action photography was first used in the 1870s by a Californian named Eadweard Muybridge, who took this series of photographs of a galloping horse. [7] Along a racetrack, he set up many cameras whose shutters were controlled by threads stretched across the track. [8] As the horse ran by, it broke the threads and tripped the cameras' shutters one after the other. [9] Painters of the time thought this new technology was truly amazing! [10] They were the first artists in history to know what a horse really looked like at each point in its stride.

# Sentences Classified According to Structure

Sentences may be classified according to purpose as declarative, imperative, interrogative, or exclamatory. Sentences may also be classified according to structure. The term *structure* refers to the number and types of clauses in a sentence.

**15g.** Depending on its structure, a sentence can be classified as simple, compound, complex, or compound-complex.

In the following examples, independent clauses are underlined once. Subordinate clauses are underlined twice.

**(1)** A *simple sentence* contains one independent clause and no subordinate clauses. It may have a compound subject, a compound verb, and any number of phrases.

EXAMPLES
          S     V
The boys wanted to take a vacation last summer.

      S     S     V        V
Ray and Joe worked and saved enough for a trip to Ohio.

**(2)** A *compound sentence* contains two or more independent clauses and no subordinate clauses.

The independent clauses in a compound sentence may be joined by a comma and a coordinating conjunction; by a semicolon; or by a semicolon, a conjunctive adverb, and a comma.

EXAMPLES
          S   V
Originally, they wanted to ride bikes all the way, **but**

   S   V
they decided to take the train instead.

   S  V                  S   V
Ray looked forward to seeing his cousins; Joe was eager to play with his uncle's band.

      S     V
Uncle James played in a country-music band; **however,**

   S   V
Joe preferred rock music.

**Reference Note**

For more on **classifying sentences by purpose,** see page 435.

STYLE TIP

Paragraphs in which all the sentences have the same structure can be monotonous to read. To keep your readers interested in your ideas, evaluate your writing to see whether you've used a variety of sentence structures. Then, use revising techniques—adding, cutting, replacing, and reordering—to enliven your writing by varying the structure of your sentences.

GRAMMAR

**NOTE** Don't confuse a simple sentence that contains a compound predicate with a compound sentence. Compound sentences always have two or more complete clauses.

|  | S | V | | V |
|---|---|---|---|---|
| COMPOUND PREDICATE | **Joe considered** country music corny and **said** so. | | | |

|  | S | V | | S | V |
|---|---|---|---|---|---|
| COMPOUND SENTENCE | **Joe considered** country music corny, and **he said** so. | | | | |

**COMPUTER TIP**

A word processor can help you check for varied sentence structure in your writing. Make a copy of your document to work on. By inserting a return or a page break after every period, you can view the sentences in a vertical list and compare the structures of each sentence in a particular paragraph. Make any revisions on the properly formatted copy of your document.

**(3)** A *complex sentence* contains one independent clause and at least one subordinate clause.

EXAMPLES
$\qquad$ S$\quad$V
Because Joe wanted to keep his guitar with him,

$\qquad$ S$\quad$V
they decided against taking a plane.

$\qquad$ S$\quad$V$\qquad$S$\quad$V
If they took a train, they could see all the sights, too.

**(4)** A *compound-complex sentence* contains two or more independent clauses and at least one subordinate clause.

EXAMPLES
$\qquad$ S$\quad$V$\qquad$S$\quad$V
The band played at a dance, and Ray was pulled into a line

$\qquad$ S$\quad$V
dance that was starting.

$\qquad$ S$\quad$V
To his surprise, he was good at line dancing; afterward,

$\qquad$ S$\quad$V$\qquad$S$\quad$V
he joined in whenever he got the chance.

**Exercise 6** **Classifying Sentences According to Structure**

Classify each of the following sentences as *simple, compound, complex,* or *compound-complex.* Be sure that you can identify all subordinate and independent clauses.

EXAMPLE    **1.** The Iroquois are American Indian peoples originally from New York State.

Link to Literature

   *1. simple*

1. Members of the Iroquois—which include the Mohawk, Oneida, Onondaga, Cayuga, Tuscarora, and Seneca—have an ancient history of storytelling.
2. In the early days, professional storytellers went from house to house, and they were paid for their storytelling with small gifts.
3. Most of what is known today about Iroquois folk tales comes from the Senecas, whose stories have been written down by historians.
4. Some of the most popular stories are about a creature who is hairless except for one strip of fur down his back.
5. He is so huge that his back can be seen above the trees.
6. He eats people; because he cannot be killed in any ordinary way, he is especially frightening.
7. The tales about this creature are even more frightening than are the ones about Stone Coat, who has skin like stone.
8. Fortunately, Stone Coat is not very smart, and many of the folk tales tell of ways that the Iroquois outsmart him.
9. There are also tales about the Whirlwinds, who usually appear as bodiless heads with fiery eyes; in some stories, the Whirlwinds eat sticks and rocks when they cannot catch people.
10. Other Iroquois stories tell about the adventures of Elk, Partridge, Skunk, and Rattlesnake.

## Exercise 7  Classifying Sentences According to Structure

Classify each of the following sentences as *simple, compound, complex,* or *compound-complex.*

EXAMPLE    **1.** In all the world, there is only one art museum for children's art, and it is located in Norway.

   *1. compound*

1. This museum is the International Museum of Children's Art, which occupies a big, old house in Oslo.
2. The walls are covered from top to bottom with brilliantly colored creations by young artists up to age seventeen.

3. Many of the 100,000 works, which come from 150 countries, deal with objects from nature, but a few, like the bicycle sculpture on the previous page, focus on manufactured objects.

4. Of course, a few of the paintings depict troubles or problems, but most of the works express happiness and energy.

5. Rafael Goldin, the museum's director, says a child's first meeting with exhibited art is very important.

6. Children visit the museum, and they "see that a museum can mean joy and color."

7. "If their first visit is to a boring, dusty museum, children will always associate museums with *dusty* and *boring*."

8. Mr. Goldin has even hung some of the paintings at toddlers' eye level to encourage each young visitor's own personal relationship with art.

9. Young visitors are very excited when they learn that all the artwork was created by children, and they are often inspired to start painting.

10. Wouldn't it be great if there were a museum like that here?

**Review B** **Identifying and Classifying Subordinate Clauses**

Identify the subordinate clause or clauses in each of the following sentences. Tell whether each clause is used as an *adjective,* an *adverb,* or a *noun.* If a clause is used as an adjective or an adverb, write the word or words the clause modifies. If a clause is used as a noun, write *subj.* for subject, *d.o.* for direct object, *i.o.* for indirect object, *p.n.* for predicate nominative, or *o.p.* for object of a preposition.

EXAMPLES
1. When our science teacher described insect-eating plants, we listened with amazement.
1. *When our science teacher described insect-eating plants—adverb—listened*

2. What we heard sounded like science fiction.
2. *What we heard—noun—subj.*

1. Plants that eat insects usually live in swampy areas.
2. Because the soil in these regions lacks nutrients, these plants do not get enough nitrogen through their roots.
3. The nitrogen that these plants need comes from the protein in the bodies of insects.
4. How these plants catch their food is interesting.
5. A pitcher plant's sweet scent appeals to whatever insect is nearby.

**6.** The insect thinks that it will find food inside the plant.

**7.** What happens instead is that the insect drowns in the plant's digestive juices.

**8.** The Venus' flytrap shown here has what looks like small bear traps at the ends of its stalks.

**9.** When a trap is open, an insect can wander in and spring the trap.

**10.** The insect is then digested by the plant in a process that can take several days.

**Review C** **Classifying Subordinate Clauses**

Classify each of the following italicized clauses as an *adjective*, an *adverb*, or *a noun clause*. Be prepared to explain your answers.

EXAMPLES    **[1]** *Until our class visited the county courthouse,* we had imagined **[2]** *that most court cases were like the ones on TV.*

    *1.* adverb

    *2.* noun

┌HELP──

In the examples in Review C, the first italicized clause is an adverb clause that modifies the verb phrase *had imagined.* The second italicized clause is a noun clause that acts as a direct object of the verb phrase *had imagined.*

**[1]** *As we left the courtroom,* we thought about the men **[2]** *who had been on trial.* **[3]** *Although they had not committed a serious crime,* they had broken the law. The law says **[4]** *that removing sand from our local beach is illegal.* A police officer caught the men **[5]** *when they could not move their truck,* **[6]** *which had become stuck in the sand.* **[7]** *After the judge had read the law to them,* the men claimed **[8]** *that they had never heard of that law.* The judge, who reminded them **[9]** *that ignorance of the law is no excuse,* fined each man one hundred dollars. The men promised **[10]** *that they would not take any more beach sand.*

**Review D** **Rewriting a Paragraph to Include a Variety of Sentence Structures**

You and a partner are working together on an essay about life in the 1800s. While researching the topic, the two of you discover a diary written by a young woman named Barbara Sneyd. You and your partner have made copies of Sneyd's paintings and have recorded information about her life. Your job is to rewrite the paragraph on the next page to improve its style. You will need to vary the sentence structure, and you may want to add or delete details to improve the organization. Write at least one sentence with each kind of structure: *simple, compound, complex,* and *compound-complex.* Be prepared to identify the structure of each sentence you write.

Barbara Sneyd lived more than one hundred years ago. Her home was in the English countryside. She came from a wealthy family. Her family loved to ride and hunt. Barbara had a governess. The governess kept Barbara very busy studying. Barbara did have time to pursue her greatest passion. Her greatest passion was riding. Her mother encouraged her to keep a diary. The diary would be about Barbara's life. Barbara started the diary. She was fourteen. It took the form of a sketchbook. In it she recorded her family's life. She painted many small pictures of her family's activities. They went fishing, visiting, and picnicking. Barbara was also a keen observer of nature. She drew and painted her family's horses and pets and the flowers from the garden. She painted many small landscapes. The landscapes showed the countryside around her home. Above all, her diary is full of paintings of horses. She loved horses. You may want to see what her paintings look like. Some pictures from her diary are shown on this page.

# Chapter Review

## A. Identifying Clauses

Identify each italicized clause in the following sentences as *independent* or *subordinate*.

1. The fire started *because someone did not smother a campfire.*
2. The family *that bought our house* is moving in next week.
3. Did you know *that Dr. Joel is the new ambassador to Lebanon*?
4. Mr. Kim will buy the store *if the bank lends him the money.*
5. According to Ms. Garza, our math teacher, *the binary system is important to know.*
6. *Wherever Maggie goes,* her poodle Jack follows.
7. *She won the golf match* because she had practiced diligently.
8. *Whatever you decide* is fine with me.
9. *I saw the job advertised in the school paper* and decided to apply for it.
10. We were proud *that you conceded defeat so graciously.*

## B. Identifying and Classifying Subordinate Clauses

Identify the subordinate clause in each of the following sentences. Tell whether each clause is used as an *adjective*, an *adverb*, or a *noun.*

11. Emily Dickinson, who was born in 1830 in Amherst, Massachusetts, was a great American poet.
12. She appeared to lead a fairly normal life until she became a recluse in her family's home.
13. There she wrote poems that literary critics now call "great American poetry."
14. Unfortunately, only a few of Dickinson's poems were published while she was alive.
15. After she died in 1886, her other poems were published.
16. I think everyone should read at least some of Dickinson's poetry.
17. Dickinson is a poet whose work I now read often.
18. The poems I have just finished reading are "A Narrow Fellow in the Grass" and "Apparently with No Surprise."

**19.** The rhythms of Dickinson's poems are best appreciated when you read the poems aloud.

**20.** Whatever I read by Emily Dickinson surprises and inspires me.

### C. Classifying Sentences According to Structure and Identifying Independent and Subordinate Clauses

Classify each of the following sentences as *simple, compound, complex,* or *compound-complex.* Identify all subordinate and independent clauses.

**21.** After eating and drinking, the elephants galloped through the wheat field.

**22.** Mr. Chisholm wanted to go bowling, but Mrs. Chisholm preferred the dinner theater.

**23.** Ten steps up the dark staircase, the twins lost their nerve; dinner at home suddenly seemed much more appealing.

**24.** Kenzuo insisted that the bullet train was the best way to get to Osaka after midnight.

**25.** When the travelers arrived at the inn, the innkeeper greeted them.

**26.** Dr. Bourgeois knew that singing loudly would only irritate others, so he decided to keep his high spirits to himself.

**27.** While preparing to eat, the dog spotted itself in the mirror.

**28.** Mom always wanted to live in New Mexico, but Dad was too used to living in North Carolina to move.

**29.** Before the concert began, the first violinist leaned forward to tie his shoe; this innocent action set off a whole chain of unlikely events.

**30.** Tom Bell is Angela's favorite actor, but Sally likes Ricky Blake.

**31.** While washing the car, Benito paused to admire the vintage biplane flying overhead.

**32.** Joseph had worked hard for straight A's on his exams, and when the results came in, he discovered that his hard work had paid off.

**33.** When the crocodile approached, the heron flew away.

**34.** Arnie carefully lined up the pieces on the chessboard; however, Dario's foot caught the edge of the board, and both board and pieces flew into the air.

**35.** We had hoped that being subtle would be enough, and, indeed, for a while this tactic seemed to be working; but as the day wore on, we slowly realized that a bolder approach was needed.

36. President Kennedy was assassinated while riding through Dallas on November 22, 1963.

37. Charles argued that a picnic lunch was the best idea.

38. Professor Chan showed his class his slides of the Great Wall of China, and he used the slides later as the basis for a lecture on Genghis Khan.

39. After the cyclists rounded the bend, the Swiss champion Michel Neibergall took the lead.

40. When the crows descended on the barren field, the field mice scurried for shelter.

# Writing Application
## Using Sentence Variety in Postcards

**Sentence Structures**   You are writing postcards about your summer activities, such as baseball or soccer camp, computer camp, or cheerleading camp. Write a brief note telling your six-year-old cousin about a few experiences that you think he or she would find interesting. Write another note to an adult friend or relative about your experiences. Use sentence structure and language that are appropriate to each reader.

**Prewriting**   If you have been to a summer camp, make a list of experiences that you could describe. If you haven't been to camp, list activities that you enjoy during the summer.

**Writing**   As you write your first draft, make sure to include details that would interest your different audiences. Show the relationships between your details by using a variety of subordinate adjective, adverb, and noun clauses.

**Revising**   Read your notes to a classmate, without telling which note is to your cousin and which is to your adult friend or relative. If your classmate can't tell which note is to which person, you should revise your language, information, and sentence structures.

**Publishing**   Check to be sure that all your sentences are complete sentences. Pay special attention to the use of commas to separate clauses. You may want to post your notes on a class bulletin board or create a Web page for them.

**Reference Note**

 For more about using **commas,** see page 643.

# Agreement
## Subject and Verb, Pronoun and Antecedent

# Diagnostic Preview

### A. Proofreading Sentences for Subject-Verb and Pronoun-Antecedent Agreement

Each of the following sentences contains an error in agreement. Identify each incorrect verb or pronoun, and supply the correct form.

EXAMPLE    1. Rochelle Richardson, one of our city's former mayors, live next door to me.

       *1. live—lives*

1. When the truck overturned, a herd of cattle were set free on the expressway.
2. The teacher reminded everyone to sharpen their pencil.
3. Not one of our tomato plants are producing any fruit, but the green beans seem to be thriving.
4. Has each of the girls memorized their part?
5. Everybody have been talking about the class picnic ever since you thought of the idea.
6. Both of the finalists played his or her best.
7. Many of their experiments have failed, but neither Dr. Jenkins nor his assistants ever gives up hope.
8. There is a brush, a comb, and a mirror on the dresser top.
9. Many a sailor have perished when his or her ship ran aground on that reef.
10. Read *Little Women* and write a plot summary about them.

## B. Proofreading a Paragraph for Subject-Verb and Pronoun-Antecedent Agreement

Most of the following sentences contain at least one agreement error. For each error, identify the incorrect verb or pronoun and supply the correct form. If the sentence is already correct, write *C*.

EXAMPLE    **1.** Filming an animal in its natural surroundings present many problems.

     *1. present—presents*

**11.** One problem is that the filmmaker, in most cases, have to get quite close to the animal.

**12.** Ten yards often make the difference between a good scene and no scene at all.

**13.** A zoom lens or a telephoto lens are generally used, but even then, getting good photographs can be very difficult.

**14.** Before filming, the crew usually take turns watching the animal for weeks to learn its habits and find good vantage points for taking pictures.

**15.** In addition, the filmmaker and the crew uses every trick of the trade in filming wild animals.

**16.** For example, *Foxes at Night* were almost certainly not filmed at night!

**17.** "Nighttime" films are generally made during daylight hours, when there is plenty of natural light.

**18.** Later, all of the daytime footage are darkened through the use of filters.

**19.** Also, many of the animals used in a nature film has been trained or partially tamed.

**20.** For example, if a filmmaker or a member of the crew take care of a bird from the moment it hatches, it will instinctively follow them.

**21.** The photographer can then easily take close-up pictures of the bird after it matures.

**22.** In many films, scenes of animals giving birth and raising its young are filmed in a studio, not in the wild.

**23.** Photographers get good footage by building a den where he or she can film the baby animals through a window beside the nest.

**24.** This film, along with footage taken in the natural habitat, are then skillfully edited.

**25.** As a result, few of the viewers ever suspect that the film shown to him or her has been shot indoors.

# Number

*Number* is the form a word takes to indicate whether the word is singular or plural.

**16a.** A word that refers to one person, place, thing, or idea is *singular* in number. A word that refers to more than one is *plural* in number.

| Singular | Plural |
|----------|--------|
| student | students |
| princess | princesses |
| child | children |
| tooth | teeth |
| it | they |
| himself | themselves |
| berry | berries |
| deer | deer |

### Exercise 1 Classifying Nouns and Pronouns by Number

Identify each italicized word as either *singular* or *plural*.

EXAMPLE    As a child, the girl in the [1] *photograph* was sure she was not very good at anything.

    1. *singular*

Link to Literature

She was overshadowed by the other [1] *children* in her family, especially by her older sister Madge, who wrote [2] *stories* and plays. Lonely and full of self-doubt, the girl surrounded herself with imaginary [3] *companions*. [4] *Everything* changed, though, when she caught influenza and became restless during her recovery. Her mother brought her a [5] *notebook* and suggested that, like Madge, she might write a story. After practicing on short stories, she decided to tackle a detective [6] *novel*. [7] *"They* are very difficult to do," said Madge. "I don't think you could write one." Madge was wrong: The young author was Agatha Christie, who became the most successful mystery [8] *writer* in history. Her mystery novels and story collections have sold many millions of copies in [9] *English* and in at least sixty other [10] *languages*.

# Agreement of Subject and Verb

**16b.** **A verb should agree in number with its subject.**

**(1) Singular subjects take singular verbs.**

EXAMPLES    **He washes** the dishes. [The singular verb *washes* agrees with the singular subject *He*.]

A **girl** in my neighborhood **plays** in the band. [The singular subject *girl* takes the singular verb *plays*.]

**(2) Plural subjects take plural verbs.**

EXAMPLES    **They wash** the dishes.

Several **girls** in my neighborhood **play** in the band.

In the examples above, the verbs agree in number with their subjects. Like the single-word verbs above, verb phrases also agree with their subjects. However, in a verb phrase, only the first helping (auxiliary) verb changes its form to agree with a singular or plural subject.

EXAMPLES    **He has been washing** the dishes.

**They have been washing** the dishes.

A **girl** in my neighborhood **was playing** in the band.

Several **girls** in my neighborhood **were playing** in the band.

**Reference Note**

For more about **helping verbs,** see page 391.

NOTE   Generally, nouns ending in *–s* are plural (*friends, girls*), but verbs ending in *–s* are generally singular (*sees, hears*).

**Reference Note**

For guidelines on **forming plurals of nouns,** see page 739.

**16c.** **The number of the subject usually is not determined by a word in a phrase or clause following the subject.**

EXAMPLES    The apartments **across the street** do not have balconies. [*Do have* agrees with *apartments*, not *street*.]

The planes **pulling up to the gate** were purchased by a movie company. [*Were purchased* agrees with *planes*, not *gate*.]

Eli, **one of my friends,** was late. [*Was* agrees with *Eli*, not *friends*.]

The movie **that I saw two weeks ago** was reviewed in today's paper. [*Was reviewed* agrees with *movie*, not *weeks*.]

**Reference Note**

For more about **phrases,** see Chapter 14. For more about **clauses,** see Chapter 15. For examples of **subjects whose number is determined by a phrase following the subject,** see page 496.

USAGE

**NOTE** *As well as, along with, together with,* and *in addition to* are compound prepositions. Words in phrases beginning with compound prepositions do not affect the number of the subject or verb.

EXAMPLE **Anne,** together with her cousins, **is** backpacking in Nevada.

### Exercise 2 Identifying Verbs That Agree in Number with Their Subjects

For each of the following sentences, choose the verb in parentheses that agrees with the subject.

EXAMPLE 1. Did you know that people in Japan frequently (*eat, eats*) noodles?

1. *eat*

1. These pictures (*show, shows*) how noodles are prepared.
2. First, the noodle maker (*roll, rolls*) out the dough as thin as possible.
3. Then, the cook (*slice, slices*) the folded layers.
4. Next, the strands of noodles (*is, are*) separated and dusted with flour to prevent sticking.
5. After the noodles have dried a little, they (*go, goes*) into boiling water or broth to cook.
6. The Japanese (*enjoy, enjoys*) noodles made from either wheat flour, called *udon,* or buckwheat flour, called *soba.*
7. A dish of cooked noodles mixed with sauce, broth, fish, or vegetables (*makes, make*) a popular lunch.
8. Noodle shops all over Japan (*serves, serve*) a variety of noodle dishes.
9. These shops often (*resemble, resembles*) fast-food restaurants in the United States.
10. For lunch or a snack, customers at a noodle shop (*order, orders*) noodles with their favorite toppings.

## Exercise 3  Identifying Subjects and Verbs That Agree in Number

Identify the subject of each verb in parentheses in the following paragraph. Then, choose the form of the verb that agrees with the subject.

EXAMPLE    Units of measure sometimes **[1]** (*causes, cause*) confusion.

    *1. Units—cause*

Confusion among shoppers **[1]** (*is, are*) understandable because the traditional system for indicating quantities **[2]** (*makes, make*) shopping a guessing game. For example, the quantity printed on yogurt containers **[3]** (*is, are*) the number of ounces in a container. A shopper on the lookout for bargains **[4]** (*does, do*) not know whether liquid or solid measure is indicated. In addition, different brands of juice **[5]** (*shows, show*) the same quantity in different ways. A can labeled "twenty-four ounces" **[6]** (*contains, contain*) the same quantity as a can labeled "one pint eight ounces." Shoppers' confusion over such labeling, along with rising prices, **[7]** (*is, are*) a matter of concern to consumer groups. These groups believe that the metric system, in use in European countries, **[8]** (*clears, clear*) up most of the confusion. The units in the metric system **[9]** (*has, have*) fixed relationships to one another. As a result, consumer groups in this country **[10]** (*continues, continue*) to advocate our adopting this system of measurement.

## Exercise 4  Choosing Verbs with the Correct Number

Each of the following sentences contains an italicized pair of verbs in parentheses. From each pair, choose the form of the verb that agrees with its subject.

EXAMPLE    **1.** Of all numbers, the number 12 (*is, are*) one of the most versatile.

    *1. is*

**1.** The even division of 12 by 1, 2, 3, 4, and 6 (*is, are*) possible.
**2.** Curiously, the sum of these five divisors (*is, are*) a square, 16; and their product is 144, which is the square of 12 itself.
**3.** When the Greek philosopher Plato devised his ideal state, the system of weights and measures (*were, was*) based on the number 12 because it could be evenly divided in so many ways.
**4.** To this day, many quantities in our lives (*involve, involves*) the number 12.

5. The number of months in a year, inches in a foot, and items in a dozen (*is, are*) 12.

6. In our courts of law, 12 members of a jury (*decides, decide*) a defendant's guilt or innocence.

7. Each player in a game of checkers (*begin, begins*) with 12 pieces.

8. In bowling, 12 consecutive strikes (*give, gives*) you a perfect game.

9. The number of black pentagons on a soccer ball (*equal, equals*) the number of buttons on a push-button telephone—12.

10. Samuel Clemens even used this number as his pen name—the riverboat slang for 2 fathoms, or 12 feet, (*are, is*) *mark twain*!

**16d.** The following indefinite pronouns are singular: *anybody, anyone, anything, each, either, everybody, everyone, everything, neither, nobody, no one, nothing, one, somebody, someone,* and *something.*

EXAMPLES   **Each** of the athletes **runs** effortlessly.

**Neither** of the women **is** ready to start.

**Someone was waving** a large flag.

**Does everyone** who signed up **enjoy** playing tennis?

**16e.** The following indefinite pronouns are plural: *both, few, many,* and *several.*

EXAMPLES   **Were both** of the games **postponed**?

**Few** that I know of **have qualified.**

**Several** of the runners **are exercising.**

**16f.** The indefinite pronouns *all, any, more, most, none,* and *some* may be singular or plural, depending on their meaning in a sentence.

These pronouns are singular when they refer to a singular word and plural when they refer to a plural word.

EXAMPLES   **Some** of the test **is** hard. [*Some* refers to the singular noun *test.*]

**Some** of the questions **are** easy. [*Some* refers to the plural noun *questions.*]

**All** of the exhibit **is** open to the public.

**All** of the paintings **are** on display.

**TIPS & TRICKS**

The words *one, thing,* and *body* are singular and so are the indefinite pronouns that contain these words.

EXAMPLES
**Is** [any]**one** late?

[Every]**body was** welcome.

[No]**thing has** been lost.

USAGE

**Most** of his routine **sounds** familiar.

**Most** of his jokes **sound** familiar.

**Was any** of the feedback positive?

**Were any** of the reviews positive?

The rice was eaten. **None is** left.

The potatoes were eaten. **None are** left.

**More** of the class **is** going to the archaeological dig.

**More** of the students **are** going to the archaeological dig.

**Reference Note**

For more information about **adjectives,** see page 382. For more about **correlative conjunctions,** see page 404.

**Exercise 5** **Identifying Subjects and Verbs That Agree in Number**

Identify the subject of each verb in parentheses. Then, choose the form of the verb that agrees with that subject.

EXAMPLE    1. Several of the kittens (*has, have*) been adopted.

1. *Several—have*

1. Each of the comedians (*tries, try*) to outdo the other.
2. Somebody on the bus (*was, were*) whistling.
3. (*Is, Are*) all of the apples spoiled?
4. Neither of these books (*has, have*) an index.
5. (*Do, Does*) everybody in the class have a pencil?
6. Few of these jobs (*sounds, sound*) challenging.
7. (*Is, Are*) more of the vendors in the market?
8. She said that no one in the office (*leaves, leave*) early.
9. Both of her parents (*has, have*) offered us a ride.
10. (*Do, Does*) most of those CDs belong to her?

**TIPS & TRICKS**

Some of the words listed in **Rule 16d** can also be used as adjectives or as parts of correlative conjunctions: *each, either, neither, one.* Used as these parts of speech, such words cannot function as subjects.

**Review A** **Proofreading a Paragraph for Subject-Verb Agreement**

Identify the agreement errors in the following paragraph. Then, supply the correct form of each incorrect verb.

EXAMPLE    [1] On weekends, I often goes with my mother to antique shops.

1. *goes—go*

[1] Until recently, this hunt for old things were very boring. [2] Then one day I noticed that a dusty shoe box full of antique postcards were sitting near me on a counter. [3] Soon I was flipping through the cards, and before you knows it, I had decided to start a

**Reference Note**

For more information about **indefinite pronouns,** see page 381. For information on distinguishing **indefinite pronouns from adjectives,** see page 382.

USAGE

postcard collection! [4] The cards in my collection is very precious to me. [5] Because I am interested in American history, I has chosen to specialize in cards showing American Indians. [6] On one of my cards, the flames of a campfire glows in front of several Plains Indian tepees under a colorful sunset. [7] Most of the postcards in my collection shows pictures of Native American leaders and warriors. [8] On my favorite card, a Navajo mother wrapped in beautiful blankets are posing with her baby on her back. [9] Collecting postcards are not an expensive hobby either. [10] Many of my cards was priced at a dollar or less.

## The Compound Subject

A ***compound subject*** consists of two or more subjects that are joined by a conjunction and that have the same verb.

**16g.** Subjects joined by *and* generally take a plural verb.

The following compound subjects joined by *and* name more than one person, place, thing, or idea and take plural verbs.

EXAMPLES   **George Lucas** and **Steven Spielberg make** movies. [Two persons make movies.]

**Rhyme, rhythm,** and **imagery help** poets express their feelings. [Three things help.]

Compound subjects that name only one person, thing, place, or idea take a singular verb.

EXAMPLES   My **pen pal and best friend is** my cousin. [One person is my best friend and pen pal.]

**Broccoli and melted cheese makes** a tasty dish. [The one combination makes a dish.]

**16h.** Singular subjects joined by *or* or *nor* take a singular verb. Plural subjects joined by *or* or *nor* take a plural verb.

EXAMPLES   After dinner, either **Anne** or **Tony loads** the dishwasher. [Anne loads the dishwasher *or* Tony loads the dishwasher.]

Neither the **coach** nor the **principal is** happy with the team's performance. [Neither *one* is happy.]

Either the **boys** or their **sisters take** the garbage out.

Neither the **dogs** nor the **cats come** when we call them.

**Reference Note**

For more information about **compound subjects**, see page 424.

**16i.** When a singular subject and a plural subject are joined by *or* or *nor,* the verb agrees with the subject nearer the verb.

ACCEPTABLE    Neither the children nor their **mother was** ready for the trip.

ACCEPTABLE    Neither the mother nor her **children were** ready for the trip.

> **STYLE    TIP**
>
> Constructions like those shown with Rule 16i can sound awkward. Try rephrasing sentences to avoid such awkward constructions.
>
> EXAMPLES
> The **children were** not ready for the trip, and neither **was** their **mother.**
>
> *or*
>
> The **mother was** not ready for the trip, and neither **were** her **children.**

### Oral Practice 1  Using Verbs That Agree in Number with Their Subjects

Read the following sentences aloud, stressing the italicized words.

1. The *books* on that shelf *need* dusting.
2. A *carton* of duck eggs *is* in the refrigerator.
3. *Tina and Betty are* first cousins once removed.
4. *Playing* games *or listening* to old records *is* an enjoyable way to spend a rainy Saturday.
5. *Several* of these insects *eat* through wood.
6. Every *one* of you *has* met my friend Phil.
7. Neither the *twins nor Greg enjoys* listening to that kind of music.
8. Both *Mr. and Mrs. Chen agree* to be chaperons for our spring dance.

### Exercise 6  Choosing Verbs That Agree in Number with Their Subjects

Choose the correct form of the verb in parentheses in each of the following sentences.

EXAMPLE    1. In August, eager players and their fans (*looks, look*) forward to the start of football season.

1. *look*

1. The coach and the player (*was, were*) surprised by the referee's call.
2. (*Is, Are*) Drew or Virgil going out for the pass?
3. Neither the quarterback nor the wide receiver (*hear, hears*) the referee's whistle.
4. The marching band or the pep squad (*has, have*) already performed.
5. (*Do, Does*) Christopher and Alexander enjoy football as much as Rachel does?
6. Either Albert or Selena (*leads, lead*) the student fight song.
7. The drum major and student council president (*is, are*) my older sister Janet.
8. The principal, the band director, and the gymnastics coach (*was, were*) proud of the half-time show.

USAGE

9. Neither the coach nor the players (*has, have*) ever won a state championship game.
10. (*Was, Were*) the announcer or the referees prepared for the triumphant fans to rush the field?

**Review B** **Revising Sentences for Subject-Verb Agreement**

Revise each of the following sentences according to the directions given in parentheses. Change the verb in the sentence to agree with the subject as necessary.

EXAMPLE    **1.** The teachers have finished grading the tests. (Change *The teachers* to *Each of the teachers.*)

    **1.** *Each of the teachers has finished grading the tests.*

1. My aunt is planning a trip to Nairobi National Park in Kenya. (Change *aunt* to *aunts.*)
2. Have Yoko and Juan already seen that movie? (Change *and* to *or.*)
3. Nobody on the team plans to attend the award ceremonies. (Change *Nobody* to *Many.*)
4. My grandmother, as well as my mother and aunts, raises tropical fish to earn extra money. (Change *grandmother* to *grandparents.*)
5. Most of the food for the party is in the refrigerator. (Change *food* to *salads.*)
6. Neither the librarian nor the aides have found the missing book. (Change *Neither the librarian nor the aides* to *Neither the aides nor the librarian.*)
7. Black bean soup and a tossed salad make an inexpensive meal. (Change *Black bean soup and a tossed salad* to *Macaroni and cheese.*)
8. Some of my friends take the bus to school. (Change *Some* to *One.*)
9. Few of the reporter's questions were answered in detail. (Change *Few* to *Neither.*)
10. The puppy playing with my sisters is two months old. (Change *puppy* to *puppies* and *sisters* to *sister.*)

# Other Problems in Agreement

**16j.** The contractions *don't* and *doesn't* should agree with their subjects.

The word *don't* is the contraction of *do not.* Use *don't* with all plural subjects and with the pronouns *I* and *you.*

| EXAMPLES | I **don't** know. | They **don't** give up. |
|---|---|---|
| | You **don't** say. | **Don't** these shrink? |
| | We **don't** want to. | Apathetic people **don't** care. |

The word *doesn't* is the contraction of *does not.* Use *doesn't* with all singular subjects except the pronouns *I* and *you.*

| EXAMPLES | He **doesn't** know. | One **doesn't** give up. |
|---|---|---|
| | She **doesn't** say. | This **doesn't** shrink. |
| | It **doesn't** want to. | **Doesn't** Donna care? |

**STYLE**  **TIP**

Many people consider contractions informal. Therefore, it is generally best not to use contractions in formal speaking and writing.

### Exercise 7 Using *Doesn't* and *Don't* Correctly

Write the correct form (*doesn't* or *don't*) for each of the following sentences.

EXAMPLE    **1.** _____ that bouquet of roses look great?

      *1. Doesn't*

**1.** This apple _____ taste sweet.

**2.** _____ he want to see the game?

**3.** These _____ impress me.

**4.** One of the players _____ plan to go.

**5.** _____ Jason and Tanya like the new band uniforms?

**6.** You and she _____ have time to play computer games now.

**7.** The engine in that old pickup _____ start in winter.

**8.** Tonio asked why we _____ want to go mountain biking.

**9.** _____ several of those in the front window cost more than these in the fruit cart?

**10.** The international children's chorus is so marvelous that their new fans _____ want to leave the theater.

**16k.** A collective noun may be either singular or plural, depending on its meaning in a sentence.

The singular form of a **collective noun** names a group of persons or things.

**Reference Note**

For more information about **collective nouns,** see page 377.

| Collective Nouns | | | | |
|---|---|---|---|---|
| army | class | family | group | public |
| assembly | club | fleet | herd | swarm |
| audience | committee | flock | jury | team |

USAGE

Use a plural verb with a collective noun when the noun refers to the individual parts or members of the group. Use a singular verb when the noun refers to the group as a unit.

EXAMPLES    The class **have completed** their projects. [*Class* is thought of as individuals.]

The class **has elected** its officers. [*Class* is thought of as a unit.]

Notice in the examples above that any pronoun referring to a collective noun has the same number as the noun. In the first example, *their* refers to *class*. In the second example, *its* refers to *class*.

**Reference Note**

See page 511 for more about **pronoun-antecedent agreement** with **collective nouns.**

### Exercise 8  Writing Sentences with Collective Nouns

Select five collective nouns, and write five pairs of sentences that show clearly how the nouns you choose may be singular or plural.

EXAMPLE    1. *The jury is ready.*

*The jury are still arguing among themselves.*

**16l.** A verb agrees with its subject, but not necessarily with a predicate nominative.

|   |   |   |   |
|---|---|---|---|
|   | S |   | PN |

EXAMPLES    The marching **bands are** the main attraction.

|   |   |   |   |
|---|---|---|---|
|   | S |   | PN |

The main **attraction is** the marching bands.

**16m.** When the subject follows the verb, find the subject and make sure that the verb agrees with it.

The subject generally follows the verb in questions and in sentences that begin with *here* and *there*.

EXAMPLES    Here **is** a **list** of addresses.
Here **are** two **lists** of addresses.

There **is** my **notebook.**
There **are** my **notebooks.**

Where **is Heather**? Where **is Chris**?
Where **are Heather** and **Chris**?

**TIPS & TRICKS**

To find the subject in a sentence in which the subject follows the verb, rearrange the sentence.

EXAMPLES
A **list** of addresses **is** here.

My **notebooks are** there.

**Heather** and **Chris are** where?

USAGE

Contractions such as *here's*, *where's*, *how's*, and *what's* include the singular verb *is*. Use these contractions only with singular subjects.

| | |
|---|---|
| NONSTANDARD | There's some facts on that topic in a chart. |
| STANDARD | There **are** some **facts** on that topic in a chart. |
| STANDARD | There**'s** a **chart** with some facts on that topic. |

**Reference Note**

For more on **contractions**, see page 707.

**16n.** An expression of an amount (a measurement, a percentage, or a fraction, for example) may be singular or plural, depending on how it is used.

**Reference Note**

For a discussion of **standard and nonstandard English,** see page 595.

A word or phrase stating an amount is singular when the amount is thought of as a unit.

EXAMPLES    **Thirty dollars is** too much for a concert ticket.

**Two hours is** a long time to wait.

Sometimes, however, the amount is thought of as individual pieces or parts. If so, a plural verb is used.

EXAMPLES    **Five dollars were scattered** on the desk.

**Two hours**—one before school and one after—**are** all I have for practice.

A fraction or a percentage is singular when it refers to a singular word and plural when it refers to a plural word.

EXAMPLES    **Three fourths** of the pizza **is** gone.

Of these songs, **three fourths are** new.

**16o.** Some nouns that are plural in form take singular verbs.

EXAMPLES    **Politics is** a controversial topic.

The **news** of the nominee **was** a surprise.

**Rickets is** a serious health problem in some countries.

NOTE    Some nouns that end in –*s* take a plural verb even when they refer to a single item.

EXAMPLES    The **scissors need** to be sharpened.

**Were** these **pants** on sale?

The **Olympics are** on television.

HELP

If you do not know whether a noun that is plural in form is singular or plural in meaning, look up the word in a dictionary.

**16p.** Even when plural in form, the title of a creative work (such as a book, song, film, or painting), the name of an organization, or the name of a country or city generally takes a singular verb.

EXAMPLES   ***The Souls of Black Folk* is** often **cited** as a classic of African American literature. [one book]

**"Greensleeves" is** an old English folk song. [one piece of music]

**The United Nations was founded** in 1945. [one organization]

**White Plains is** home to several colleges. [one city]

### Review C  Using Titles That Agree with Verbs in Number

Terence and Janeese are at the video rental store deciding what movies they will rent for the weekend. In the following sentences, wherever *TITLE* appears, supply the name of one of the movies shown here or of a movie of your own choice. Then, choose the correct form of the verb to complete each sentence.

EXAMPLE   **1.** Look, Terence. TITLE (*is, are*) supposed to be very funny.

*1.* Horse Feathers—*is*

   **1.** Terence: According to LaShonda, TITLE and TITLE (*is, are*) very exciting.
   **2.** Janeese: Well, TITLE or TITLE (*sounds, sound*) more interesting to me. Let's ask the clerk.
   **3.** Terence: Sir, (*is, are*) TITLE in stock?
   **4.** Clerk:   I'm afraid not, but TITLE (*entertain, entertains*) almost everyone, and you might enjoy it.
   **5.** Terence: Janeese, TITLE (*is, are*) a fairly recent movie, but TITLE (*are, is*) an old-timer.
   **6.** Janeese: Well, I like animated films, and TITLE (*fit, fits*) that category.
   **7.** Clerk:   If you ask me, TITLE (*beat, beats*) every other film we have, but someone just rented my last copy.
   **8.** Janeese: Both TITLE and TITLE (*are, is*) good, but I've seen each of them twice.
   **9.** Terence: (*Isn't, Aren't*) TITLE any good? I'm surprised.
  **10.** Janeese: All right, here's my vote. TITLE (*is, are*) tonight's movie, and either TITLE or TITLE (*is, are*) the movie for Saturday night's party.

**16q.** Subjects preceded by *every* or *many a* take singular verbs.

EXAMPLES    **Every** homeowner and storekeeper **has joined** the cleanup drive sponsored by the town council.

        **Many a** litterbug **was surprised** by the stiff fines.

**16r.** When the relative pronoun *that, which,* or *who* is the subject of an adjective clause, the verb in the adjective clause agrees with the word to which the relative pronoun refers.

**Reference Note**

For more about **relative pronouns,** see page 380. For more about **adjective clauses,** see page 473.

EXAMPLES    This is the store **that has** the discount sale. [*That* refers to the singular noun *store*.]

        London, **which is** the capital of England, is the largest city in Europe. [*Which* refers to the singular noun *London*.]

        The Garcias, **who live** next door, are going with us to the lake. [*Who* refers to the plural noun *Garcias*.]

**Oral Practice 2** **Using Subject-Verb Agreement**

Read each of the following sentences aloud, stressing the italicized words.

**1.** Of the inhabitants, *two thirds are* registered to vote.
**2.** *Many a* writer and scholar *has* puzzled over that problem.
**3.** *Is economics* taught at your high school?
**4.** *Are* there any green *apples* in that basket?
**5.** *Romeo and Juliet has* been made into a ballet, a Broadway musical, and several movies.
**6.** *Two weeks is* more than enough time to write a report.
**7.** My *family is* planning to hold its reunion in October.
**8.** My *family are* planning their schedules now.

**Exercise 9** **Identifying Subjects and Verbs That Agree in Number**

Identify the subject of each verb in parentheses. Then, choose the form of the verb that agrees with the subject.

EXAMPLE    **1.** (*Do, Does*) Meals on Wheels deliver in your neighborhood?

        *1. Meals on Wheels—Does*

**1.** The class (*has, have*) chosen titles for their original plays.
**2.** First prize (*was, were*) two tickets to Hawaii.

USAGE

3. Three quarters of the movie (*was, were*) over when we arrived at the theater.
4. Rattlesnakes (*was, were*) the topic of last week's meeting of the hiking club.
5. (*Has, Have*) every student in the class memorized a poem to present for the oral interpretation contest?
6. *Crime and Punishment* (*is, are*) a world-famous novel.
7. Two thirds of the missing books (*was, were*) returned to the downtown branch of the library.
8. Mathematics (*is, are*) an important part of many everyday activities.
9. Where (*is, are*) the paragraphs you wrote?
10. Four weeks (*is, are*) enough time to rehearse the play.

### Review D  Identifying Verbs That Have the Correct Number

Choose the correct form of the verb in parentheses in each of the following sentences.

EXAMPLE  1. Fifty pesos (*was, were*) a great price for that carving.

1. *was*

1. Mumps (*is, are*) a common childhood disease that causes swelling in glands in the neck.
2. Politics (*is, are*) always a popular subject both to debate and to study at college.
3. Not one of the ushers (*know, knows*) where the lounge is.
4. The team (*is, are*) on a winning streak.
5. Carol, as well as Inés, (*write, writes*) a weekly column for the *East High Record.*
6. "Beauty and the Beast" (*is, are*) a folk tale that exists in many different cultures.
7. Ten pounds (*is, are*) too much weight for a young child to carry in a backpack.
8. It is difficult to concentrate when there (*is, are*) radios and stereos blasting away.
9. (*Has, Have*) either of you read the book or seen the movie version of *To Kill a Mockingbird*?
10. In most situation comedies, there (*is, are*) a very wise character, a very foolish character, and a very lovable character.

# Agreement of Pronoun and Antecedent

A pronoun usually refers to a noun or another pronoun that comes before it. The word that a pronoun refers to is called its **antecedent.**

**Reference Note**

For a further discussion of **antecedents,** see page 378.

**16s. A pronoun should agree in number and gender with its antecedent.**

**(1) A pronoun that refers to a singular antecedent is singular in number.**

EXAMPLES **Daniel Defoe** wrote **his** first book at the age of fifty-nine.

     The **elephant** is a long-lived animal. **It** grows **its** tusks at maturity.

**(2) A pronoun that refers to a plural antecedent is plural in number.**

EXAMPLES Reliable **cars** make **their** owners happy.

     **We** walk **our** dogs daily.

A few singular pronouns have forms that indicate the gender of the antecedent. Masculine pronouns refer to males; feminine pronouns refer to females. Neuter pronouns refer to places, things, ideas, and, often, to animals.

| Masculine | Feminine | Neuter |
|-----------|----------|--------|
| he | she | it |
| him | her | it |
| his | hers | its |
| himself | herself | itself |

Often, when the antecedent of a personal pronoun is another kind of pronoun, a word in a phrase following the antecedent will help to determine gender.

EXAMPLES **One** of the **women** designs **her** own costumes.

     **Each** of the **boys** rode **his** bicycle to school.

     **Neither** of the **kittens** has opened **its** eyes yet.

**STYLE · TIP**

In many cases you can avoid the awkward *his or her* construction by rephrasing the sentence and using the plural form of the pronoun or by substituting an article (*a, an,* or *the*).

EXAMPLES

The **passengers** will be shown where **they** can check in.

A **person** should choose **a** college carefully.

**STYLE · TIP**

In informal conversation, plural personal pronouns are often used to refer to singular antecedents that can be either masculine or feminine. Such usage is becoming increasingly common in writing and may someday become acceptable as standard written English. For now, however, avoid such usage in formal writing and speaking.

INFORMAL
Everybody has packed their lunch in an insulated cooler.

FORMAL
**Everybody** has packed **his or her** lunch in an insulated cooler.

When a singular antecedent may be either masculine or feminine, use both the masculine and the feminine forms, connected by *or.*

EXAMPLES     **Each passenger** will be shown where **he or she** can check in.

A **person** should choose **his or her** college carefully.

If you talk on the phone with **someone** you don't know well, speak clearly to **him or her.**

**16t.** Some indefinite pronouns are singular, and some are plural. Other indefinite pronouns can be either singular or plural, depending on their meaning in a sentence.

**(1)** Use a singular pronoun to refer to *anybody, anyone, anything, each, either, everybody, everyone, everything, neither, nobody, no one, nothing, one, somebody, someone,* or *something.*

EXAMPLES     **Either** of the girls can bring **her** CD player.

**Neither** of the workmen forgot **his** tool belt.

Did **each** of the mares recognize **her** own foal?

**Someone** left **his or her** hat on the field.

**One** of the parakeets escaped from **its** cage.

NOTE    Sometimes the meaning of *everyone* or *everybody* is clearly plural. In informal situations, the plural pronoun should be used.

CONFUSING     Everyone laughed when he or she saw the clowns.

INFORMAL     **Everyone** laughed when **they** saw the clowns.

In formal situations, it is best to revise the sentence so that it is both clear and grammatically correct.

FORMAL     The **audience** laughed when **they** saw the clowns.

**(2)** Use a plural pronoun to refer to *both, few, many,* and *several.*

EXAMPLES     **Both** of the sisters recited **their** lines.

**Few** of the animals willingly leave **their** natural habitat.

**Many** of the volunteers shared **their** coats with the flood victims.

**Several** of the audience were late getting to **their** seats.

**(3)** The indefinite pronouns *all, any, more, most, none,* and *some* may be singular or plural, depending on their meaning in a sentence.

EXAMPLES    **All** of the water has melted; **it** is pooling in the valley.

**All** of the streams are full; **they** are rushing torrents.

**Most** of her cooking tastes good. In fact, **it** is delicious.

**Most** of the dishes she cooks taste good. **They** contain unusual spices.

**16u.** Use a singular pronoun to refer to two or more singular antecedents joined by *or* or *nor.*

EXAMPLES    Neither **Richard nor Bob** distinguished **himself** in the finals.

**Paula or Janet** will present **her** views on the subject.

**16v.** Use a plural pronoun to refer to two or more antecedents joined by *and.*

EXAMPLES    **Mona and Janet** left early because **they** had to be home before ten o'clock.

**Mom and Dad** celebrated **their** twentieth wedding anniversary yesterday.

**16w.** The number of a relative pronoun (such as *who, which,* or *that*) is determined by its antecedent.

EXAMPLES    Aretha is one **friend who** always keeps **her** word. [*Who* refers to the singular noun *friend.* Therefore, the singular form *her* is used to agree with *who.*]

**Many who** volunteer **their** time find **their** experiences rewarding. [*Who* refers to the plural pronoun *Many.* Therefore, the plural form *their* is used to agree with *who.*]

**Review E**    Identifying Antecedents and Writing Pronouns

Each of the sentences on the following page contains a blank where a pronoun should be. Complete each sentence by inserting at least one pronoun that agrees with its antecedent. Identify the antecedent.

EXAMPLE    1. Carmen and Tina said that _____ thought my idea was sensible.

1. *they—Carmen and Tina*

STYLE    TIP

Sentences like those shown under Rule 16u can sound awkward if the antecedents are of different genders. If a sentence sounds awkward, revise it to avoid the problem.

AWKWARD
Ben or Maya will read his or her report.

REVISED
**Ben** will read **his** report, or **Maya** will read **hers.**

**Reference Note**

For more information on **relative pronouns in adjective clauses,** see page 473.

1. Please give me Ronald's address so that I can send _____ a letter.
2. The uniform company finally sent Jerome and Ken the shirts that _____ had ordered.
3. Claire or Ida will go to the nursing home early so that _____ can help the residents into the lounge.
4. Several of the volunteers contributed _____ own money to buy the shelter a new van.
5. Did each of the contestants answer _____ questions correctly?
6. Both of the girls packed _____ suitcases carefully for the trip to Canada and Alaska.
7. Every car at the service center had _____ oil changed.
8. Neither of the women withdrew _____ job application.
9. Anyone can belong to the International Students Association if _____ is interested.
10. Neither the coaches nor the players blamed _____ for the loss.

**Review F** **Proofreading Sentences for Pronoun-Antecedent Agreement**

Many of the following sentences contain errors in agreement between pronouns and their antecedents. Identify each of these errors, and give the form of the pronoun that agrees with its antecedent. If a sentence is already correct, write *C*.

EXAMPLE     1.  All of us need to choose a topic for his or her reports.
             1.  *his or her—our*

1. George has chosen Walt Disney as the subject of his report.
2. Several others in our class have also submitted his or her topics.
3. Dominic, one of the Perrone twins, has chosen Alfred Hitchcock as their subject.
4. Neither George nor Dominic will have difficulty finding material for their report.
5. Each of these moviemakers has left their mark on the world.
6. Either Minnie or Sue offered their help with proofreading.
7. Each of the boys refused politely, saying that they would proofread the report on their own.
8. Does everyone, including George and Dominic, know that they must assemble facts, not opinions?
9. Neither George nor Dominic should forget to include amusing anecdotes about their subject.
10. Nobody likes to discover that they just read a dull report about an interesting subject.

┌HELP┐

Some sentences in Review F may contain more than one error in agreement.

**16x.** A collective noun is singular when it refers to the group as a unit and plural when it refers to the individual members of the group.

EXAMPLES    The **pride** of lions is hunting **its** prey on the savanna. [*Pride* is thought of as a unit.]

               The **pride** of lions are licking **their** chops in anticipation. [*Pride* is thought of as separate individuals.]

NOTE  Sometimes the number of a collective noun depends on the meaning the writer intends.

EXAMPLES    The swim **team** proudly displayed **their** trophies. [The members of the team displayed individual trophies.]

               The swim **team** proudly displayed **its** trophy. [The team as a whole displayed a shared trophy.]

**Reference Note**

For information on **subject-verb agreement** with **collective nouns,** see page 501. For a list of **collective nouns,** see page 377.

USAGE

**16y.** An expression of an amount (a measurement, a percentage, or a fraction, for example) may be singular or plural, depending on how it is used.

A word or phrase stating an amount is singular when the amount is thought of as a unit.

EXAMPLES    **Ten minutes** isn't long; **it** will go by quickly.

               Here is **five dollars.** Is **it** enough?

Sometimes, however, the amount is thought of as individual pieces or parts. If so, a plural verb is used.

EXAMPLES    **Ten** of the twenty minutes were wasted; we spent **them** arguing.

               **Five dollars** were counterfeit, weren't **they**?

A fraction or a percentage is singular when it refers to a singular word and plural when it refers to a plural word.

EXAMPLES    **One third** of the total is yours. Would you like **it** in ones?

               **One third** of the birds have left. Are **they** migrating?

**16z.** Singular pronouns are used to refer to some nouns that are plural in form.

EXAMPLES    Aunt Jean rarely watches the **news** because she finds **it** depressing.

The **United States** celebrated **its** bicentennial in 1976.

After Chad finished reading ***Mules and Men,*** he wrote a report on **it.**

**Future Farmers of America** meets tomorrow to plan **its** convention.

**Marble Falls** is in Texas; **it** is north of San Antonio and Blanco.

NOTE  Plural pronouns are used to refer to some nouns that end in *–s* but that refer to a single item.

EXAMPLES  I'll buy these **pants** because **they** fit better and are a better value than **those.**

If you're looking for the **scissors,** you'll find **them** in the third drawer on the left.

### Review G  Agreement of Pronoun and Antecedent

Some of the following sentences contain errors in pronoun-antecedent agreement. Identify each incorrect pronoun, and give the pronoun that agrees with its antecedent. If a sentence is already correct, write *C*.

EXAMPLE  1. Several people in the neighborhood have expressed his or her views.

1. *his or her—their*

1. The school finally sent Michael and Kathryn the results of the tests he or she had taken.
2. On the Serengeti Plain, a cheetah enjoys its freedom.
3. After World War II, the United States gave most of their foreign aid to help Europe rebuild.
4. Five percent of the profit will be donated, won't they?
5. The U.S. Olympic team won their third gold medal.
6. A person with a health problem should always select the best doctor for their needs.
7. During *ferragosto,* or August holiday, the Italian Parliament takes its recess.
8. Each of the mimes gave their impression of a chimney sweep.
9. I like the way the pants look; also, at that price, it's a great bargain.
10. *War and Peace* are the most famous of Leo Tolstoy's works.

# Chapter Review

## A. Identifying Verbs that Agree in Number with Their Subjects

For each of the following sentences, choose the correct form of the verb in parentheses.

1. (*Doesn't, Don't*) she know when she'll be back?
2. Most of my jewelry (*was, were*) lost in the fire.
3. For better or for worse, politics (*play, plays*) an important part in all our lives.
4. Many ideas in her book (*requires, require*) a great deal of thought.
5. (*Has, Have*) Lisa and Haruo been paid for their work?
6. (*Is, Are*) everybody finished with the project?
7. Neither the president nor the vice-president (*goes, go*) to every meeting.
8. There (*has, have*) been many accidents at that intersection.
9. Three fourths of the apartments (*was, were*) rented before the building was completed.
10. Our class president, with the help of several others, usually (*sets, set*) the agenda for the meeting.
11. Nobody here (*has, have*) the correct time.
12. A herd of cattle (*is, are*) by the river.
13. Some of Pat's nacho recipes (*contains, contain*) very hot spices.
14. One of the owners (*work, works*) at the store on weekends.
15. Physics (*is, are*) a challenging and fascinating subject.
16. Where (*do, does*) the scissors go?
17. The main attraction in the parade (*is, are*) the student floats.
18. Van Gogh's *The Potato Eaters* (*show, shows*) a Dutch farm family at dinner.
19. If two thirds of the people (*vote, votes*) for the measure, it will become law.
20. Here (*is, are*) a new football and a helmet for your birthday.

## B. Proofreading Sentences for Subject-Verb Agreement

Each of the following sentences contains an error in agreement. Identify each incorrect verb, and supply the correct form.

21. Every man and woman were questioned by the police.

USAGE

**22.** The pile of papers were scattered by the wind.

**23.** Each of the girls brought their own tennis balls.

**24.** Some of the sheep from that flock is lost.

**25.** Your explanation don't really help that much.

**26.** Most of the poetry are in English.

**27.** Each of the students were happy the exam was over.

**28.** Many a student have been grateful for being in Ms. Makowski's history class.

**29.** Someone forgot their umbrella.

**30.** Either Bill or his uncles is waiting downstairs.

## C. Identifying Antecedents and Writing Pronouns

Each of the following sentences contains a blank where a pronoun should be. Complete each sentence by writing a pronoun that agrees with its antecedent. Identify the antecedent.

**31.** Uncle Harry and Aunt Nell said that _____ would be happy to contribute to the silent auction.

**32.** Can I have Trevor's phone number, so that I can tell _____ about the ceremony?

**33.** Every horse in the stable had _____ own bucket of oats.

**34.** Louis Pasteur, the great French scientist, made _____ first scientific discovery at the age of 26.

**35.** Teresa or Sandra will go to the airport early so that _____ will be sure to meet Jorge's plane.

**36.** Patsy and Debbie will be late because _____ forgot the appointment.

**37.** Neither of the men changed _____ mind on the issue.

**38.** Because of the strike, several of the drivers had to change _____ own oil.

**39.** Both Henry James and his brother William became famous through _____ writings.

**40.** Neither the film crew nor the writers blamed _____ for the mistake.

## D. Proofreading a Paragraph for Subject-Verb and Pronoun-Antecedent Agreement

For each error in the following paragraph, identify the incorrect verb or pronoun and supply the correct form.

**[41]** CDs of popular music is getting very expensive. **[42]** The economics of this situation have hit young people right in the wallet! **[43]** Few has enough money to buy all the best new songs. **[44]** A teenager will have to use their brains if they want to save money in the music store. **[45]** Several of my friends buy an audiotape instead of a CD if he or she want to save a little money. **[46]** Danny, one of my best friends, take another approach. **[47]** His favorite group are The Avengers, and he tapes every new Avengers song straight off the radio. **[48]** He don't have to pay for anything but the blank tape. **[49]** Copying tapes is perfectly legal if all the music you record are just for your own use. **[50]** Kristi and Selena, two of my friends, save as much as four or five dollars a tape by buying her tapes on sale.

## Writing Application

### Using Agreement in a Paragraph

**Subject-Verb Agreement**    During Career Day, the school counselor asks you to write a paragraph beginning with this statement: "People I know work at a variety of jobs." Using subjects and verbs that agree, describe the jobs of three people you know.

**Prewriting**    Start by listing at least three people you know who have different kinds of jobs. Think of action verbs that describe what these people do. For example, instead of saying "Mrs. Ruíz is a chemistry teacher," say "Mrs. Ruíz teaches chemistry."

**Writing**    As you write your first draft, be sure to include some details that clearly show how the jobs differ from one another.

**Revising**    Check your rough draft to be sure that the examples you have chosen show a variety of jobs. If not, you may want to replace some examples or add new ones. Make sure each job is described vividly.

**Publishing**    Identify the subjects and verbs in each sentence, and be sure that they agree. Read your paragraph aloud to help you recognize any errors in usage, spelling, and punctuation. Be sure that you have capitalized all proper names. Your class might photocopy and display their paragraphs during career day. With the permission of the people you wrote about, your class could also prepare a job information directory.

# Using Verbs Correctly

## Principal Parts, Tense, Voice, Mood

## Diagnostic Preview

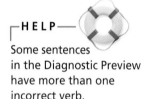
### Proofreading Sentences for Correct Verb Forms

Read the following sentences. If a sentence contains an incorrect or awkward verb form, write the correct form or revise the sentence. If a sentence is already correct, write *C*.

EXAMPLES    **1.** I have always wanted a pet.
       *1.* *C*

       **2.** As a child, I use to dream about having a dog or cat.
       *2.* *used*

**1.** Every time I ask my parents, they said, "No, not in an apartment."
**2.** One day last year, I was setting on the front steps reading the newspaper when I spot an ad for a female ferret.
**3.** Deciding to investigate, I fold the paper, hop on my bike, and rode to the pet shop that had placed the ad.
**4.** When I walked into the store, I seen the ferret right away.
**5.** She was laying in a cardboard box on top of the counter.
**6.** I told the owner I wanted to hold her, and he reaches into the box.
**7.** When he withdrew his hand, the ferret was holding on to his finger with what looked like very sharp teeth.
**8.** I cautiously reached out and taked the ferret's hindquarters in my cupped hands.

9. The rest of her long body poured slowly into my hands until she was sitting on her haunches.

10. She looked up at me and suddenly clamps her teeth on my thumb.

11. The ferret done it to show me who was boss.

12. I should have knowed then that my troubles had just began.

13. I ran all the way home and persuaded my parents to let me keep the ferret on a trial basis.

14. I had already give her a name—Ferris the Ferret—and I lose no time rushing back to the pet shop.

15. When I come home with Ferris, I sit a dish of cat food in front of her.

16. She stuck her snout into the dish and ate greedily.

17. After she had went into each room in the apartment, she choosed the top of the TV as her special place.

18. When my parents objected, I made a cardboard house with two entry holes and set it in a corner of my bedroom.

19. Ferris sniffed around her new home; then she goes in and laid down for a nap.

20. For the next few days, Ferris spent her time either napping or nipping.

21. She always attackted me when I least expected it.

22. Once, as she lies on my desk while I am studying, she suddenly locked her teeth onto my earlobe.

23. I was so startled that I jump up quickly, and Ferris wound up laying on the floor with a look that makes me feel guilty.

24. The next day the bad news was gave to me by my parents: Ferris had to go back to the pet shop.

25. I no longer want a pet ferret, but I have wrote to the local zoo-keeper to ask about snakes.

# The Principal Parts of Verbs

The four basic forms of a verb are called the *principal parts* of the verb.

**17a.** The four principal parts of a verb are the *base form,* the *present participle,* the *past,* and the *past participle.*

The principal parts of the verb *ring,* for example, are *ring* (base form), *ringing* (present participle), *rang* (past), and *rung* (past participle). These principal parts are used to form all of the different verb tenses.

HELP

Some teachers refer to the base form as the *infinitive.* Follow your teacher's directions when labeling this form.

EXAMPLES    The bells **ring** every day.    The bells **rang** at noon.
The bells **are ringing** now.    The bells **have rung** already.

**Reference Note**

For more about how **participles and helping verbs** work together, see page 449.

Notice that the tenses made from the present participle and past participle contain helping verbs, such as *am, is, are, has,* and *have.*

# Regular Verbs

**17b.** A *regular verb* forms its past and past participle by adding –*d* or –*ed* to the base form.

| Base Form | Present Participle | Past | Past Participle |
|-----------|--------------------|------|-----------------|
| ask | [is] asking | asked | [have] asked |
| use | [is] using | used | [have] used |
| suppose | [is] supposing | supposed | [have] supposed |
| risk | [is] risking | risked | [have] risked |

The words *is* and *have* are included in the preceding chart because helping verbs are used with the present participle and past participle to form some tenses.

**NOTE** The present participle of most regular verbs ending in –*e* drops the –*e* before adding –*ing.*

EXAMPLE    smile + ing = smil**ing**

**Reference Note**

See page 735 for more on **spelling words when adding suffixes.**

One common error in the use of the past and the past participle forms is to leave off the –*d* or –*ed* ending.

NONSTANDARD    We use to play soccer.
STANDARD    We **used** to play soccer.

NONSTANDARD    She was suppose to come home early.
STANDARD    She was **supposed** to come home early.

**STYLE    TIP**

A few regular verbs have an alternate past form ending in –*t.* For example, the past form of *burn* is *burned* or *burnt.* Both forms are correct.

Another common error is to misspell or mispronounce verbs.

NONSTANDARD    We were attackted by mosquitoes.
STANDARD    We were **attacked** by mosquitoes.

**Oral Practice 1** **Pronouncing the Past and Past Participle Forms of Regular Verbs Correctly**

Read each sentence aloud, stressing the italicized verb.

1. Aunt Rosie *used* to do needlepoint.
2. What has *happened* to your bicycle?
3. Several people were *drowned* in the flood.
4. The agents *risked* their lives.
5. Aren't you *supposed* to sing?
6. The game was well *advertised*.
7. The critics *praised* Amy Tan's new book.
8. He *carried* the suitcases to the car.

# Irregular Verbs

**17c.** An *irregular verb* forms its past and past participle in some other way than by adding *–d* or *–ed*.

An irregular verb forms its past and past participle in one of these ways:

- changing consonants
- changing vowels
- changing vowels *and* consonants
- making no change at all

| | Base Form | Past | Past Participle |
|---|---|---|---|
| **Consonant Change** | bend | bent | [have] bent |
| | send | sent | [have] sent |
| **Vowel Change** | sing | sang | [have] sung |
| | begin | began | [have] begun |
| **Vowel and Consonant Change** | catch | caught | [have] caught |
| | go | went | [have] gone |
| | fly | flew | [have] flown |
| **No Change** | set | set | [have] set |
| | burst | burst | [have] burst |

"When I say 'runned,' you know I mean 'ran.' Let's not quibble."

© 1998 by Sidney Harris.

┌**HELP**─

If you are not sure about the principal parts of a verb, look in a dictionary, which lists the principal parts of irregular verbs. If no principal parts are listed, the verb is regular.

USAGE

The Principal Parts of Verbs    **519**

**Reference Note**

For more about **standard and nonstandard English,** see page 595.

**NOTE** Since most English verbs are regular, people sometimes try to make irregular verbs follow the regular pattern. However, such words as *throwed, knowed, shrinked,* or *choosed* are considered nonstandard.

| Principal Parts of Common Irregular Verbs | | | |
|---|---|---|---|
| Base Form | Present Participle | Past | Past Participle |
| become | [is] becoming | became | [have] become |
| begin | [is] beginning | began | [have] begun |
| blow | [is] blowing | blew | [have] blown |
| break | [is] breaking | broke | [have] broken |
| bring | [is] bringing | brought | [have] brought |
| build | [is] building | built | [have] built |
| burst | [is] bursting | burst | [have] burst |
| buy | [is] buying | bought | [have] bought |
| choose | [is] choosing | chose | [have] chosen |
| come | [is] coming | came | [have] come |
| cost | [is] costing | cost | [have] cost |
| cut | [is] cutting | cut | [have] cut |
| do | [is] doing | did | [have] done |
| draw | [is] drawing | drew | [have] drawn |
| drink | [is] drinking | drank | [have] drunk |
| drive | [is] driving | drove | [have] driven |
| eat | [is] eating | ate | [have] eaten |
| fall | [is] falling | fell | [have] fallen |
| feel | [is] feeling | felt | [have] felt |
| fight | [is] fighting | fought | [have] fought |
| find | [is] finding | found | [have] found |
| fly | [is] flying | flew | [have] flown |
| freeze | [is] freezing | froze | [have] frozen |
| get | [is] getting | got | [have] gotten *or* got |
| give | [is] giving | gave | [have] given |
| go | [is] going | went | [have] gone |
| grow | [is] growing | grew | [have] grown |

## Principal Parts of Common Irregular Verbs

| Base Form | Present Participle | Past | Past Participle |
|---|---|---|---|
| have | [is] having | had | [have] had |
| hear | [is] hearing | heard | [have] heard |
| hide | [is] hiding | hid | [have] hidden *or* hid |
| hit | [is] hitting | hit | [have] hit |
| hold | [is] holding | held | [have] held |
| keep | [is] keeping | kept | [have] kept |
| know | [is] knowing | knew | [have] known |
| lead | [is] leading | led | [have] led |
| leave | [is] leaving | left | [have] left |
| let | [is] letting | let | [have] let |
| light | [is] lighting | lighted *or* lit | [have] lighted *or* lit |
| lose | [is] losing | lost | [have] lost |
| make | [is] making | made | [have] made |
| put | [is] putting | put | [have] put |
| read | [is] reading | read | [have] read |
| ride | [is] riding | rode | [have] ridden |
| ring | [is] ringing | rang | [have] rung |
| run | [is] running | ran | [have] run |
| say | [is] saying | said | [have] said |
| see | [is] seeing | saw | [have] seen |
| seek | [is] seeking | sought | [have] sought |
| shake | [is] shaking | shook | [have] shaken |
| sing | [is] singing | sang | [have] sung |
| sink | [is] sinking | sank *or* sunk | [have] sunk |
| slide | [is] sliding | slid | [have] slid |
| speak | [is] speaking | spoke | [have] spoken |
| spend | [is] spending | spent | [have] spent |
| stand | [is] standing | stood | [have] stood |
| steal | [is] stealing | stole | [have] stolen |
| sting | [is] stinging | stung | [have] stung |
| strike | [is] striking | struck | [have] struck *or* stricken |

*(continued)*

---

**STYLE TIP**

Some verbs have two correct past or past participle forms. However, these forms are not always interchangeable.

EXAMPLES
I **shone** the flashlight into the woods. [*Shined* would also be correct.]

I **shined** my shoes. [*Shone* would be incorrect in this usage.]

If you are unsure about which past participle form to use, check an up-to-date dictionary.

**USAGE**

| Principal Parts of Common Irregular Verbs | | | |
|---|---|---|---|
| Base Form | Present Participle | Past | Past Participle |
| swim | [is] swimming | swam | [have] swum |
| take | [is] taking | took | [have] taken |
| teach | [is] teaching | taught | [have] taught |
| tear | [is] tearing | tore | [have] torn |
| tell | [is] telling | told | [have] told |
| think | [is] thinking | thought | [have] thought |
| throw | [is] throwing | threw | [have] thrown |
| wear | [is] wearing | wore | [have] worn |
| win | [is] winning | won | [have] won |
| write | [is] writing | wrote | [have] written |

When the present participle and past participle forms are used as verbs in sentences, they require helping verbs.

| Helping Verb | + | Present Participle | = | Verb Phrase |
|---|---|---|---|---|
| forms of *be* | + | taking walking going | = | am taking was walking have been going |

| Helping Verb | + | Past Participle | = | Verb Phrase |
|---|---|---|---|---|
| forms of *have* | + | taken walked gone | = | have taken has walked had gone |

**TIPS & TRICKS**

To avoid nonstandard usage, include a form of *be* with the present participle and a form of *have* with the past participle. Say *do, is doing, did, have done,* for example, or *see, is seeing, saw, have seen.*

NONSTANDARD
  We already seen that program.

STANDARD
  We **have** already **seen** that program.

**Reference Note**

For more about **passive voice,** see page 535.

NOTE Sometimes a past participle is used with a form of *be: was chosen, are known, is seen.* This use of the verb is called the **passive voice.**

USAGE

**Oral Practice 2** **Using the Past and Past Participle Forms of Irregular Verbs Correctly**

Read each of the following sentences aloud, stressing the italicized verbs.

**1.** *Have* you *begun* the research for your report?
**2.** Last week we *saw* a video about Alexander the Great.
**3.** The bell *rang,* and the door *burst* open.
**4.** I *have known* her since the first grade.
**5.** He *brought* his rock collection to school.
**6.** They *fought* to rescue the survivors.
**7.** Elizabeth *has written* a short article for the school newspaper.
**8.** She *has given* us her permission.

**Exercise 1** **Writing the Past and Past Participle Forms of Irregular Verbs**

Change each of the following verb forms. If the base form is given, change it to the past form. If the past form is given, change it to the past participle. Use *have* before the past participle form.

EXAMPLES  **1.** eat  **2.** took
 *1. ate*  *2. have taken*

| | | | | |
|---|---|---|---|---|
| **1.** do | **5.** went | **9.** blew | **13.** drink | **17.** ran |
| **2.** began | **6.** know | **10.** bring | **14.** froze | **18.** ring |
| **3.** see | **7.** spoke | **11.** choose | **15.** drove | **19.** fell |
| **4.** rode | **8.** stole | **12.** broke | **16.** sang | **20.** swim |

**Exercise 2** **Identifying Correct Forms of Irregular Verbs**

Choose the correct form of the verb in parentheses in each of the following sentences.

EXAMPLE  **1.** Mai's parents (*telled, told*) her about their journey in a boat from South Vietnam to Malaysia.
 *1. told*

**1.** They (*rode, rid*) in a crowded boat like the one you see in the picture on the next page.
**2.** Along with many other people, Mai's parents (*chose, choosed*) to make such a journey rather than stay in South Vietnam after the Vietnam War ended.

3. These refugees (*came, come*) to be called "boat people."
4. Mai's parents abandoned their home after the South Vietnamese capital, Saigon, had (*fell, fallen*) to North Vietnamese forces.
5. The people on the boat (*brang, brought*) few possessions or supplies.
6. After they had (*drank, drunk*) what little water was on board, they went thirsty.
7. Mai's father said the people had (*ate, eaten*) all the food in a few days.
8. When another boat of refugees had (*sank, sunk*), its passengers crowded onto Mai's parents' boat.
9. They spent many days and nights on the ocean before they (*saw, seen*) land again.
10. Then it (*took, taked*) months for Mai's parents to be moved from Malaysian refugee camps to the United States.

## Exercise 3 Identifying Correct Forms of Irregular Verbs

For each sentence in the following paragraph, choose the correct form of the verb in parentheses.

EXAMPLE    I just **[1]** (wrote, written) to my Russian pen pal!

1. *wrote*

Joining the Russian-American pen-pal club Druzhba is one of the most interesting things I have ever **[1]** (*did, done*). The founder of the club **[2]** (*chose, chosen*) the name *Druzhba* because it means "friend-ship" in Russian. This club has **[3]** (*given, gave*) American and Russian students the chance to become friends. I **[4]** (*began, begun*) to write to my pen pal Vanya last September. His reply to my first letter **[5]** (*took, taken*) weeks to get to me. I wish it could have **[6]** (*flew, flown*) here faster from the other side of the globe. In his letters, Vanya has often **[7]** (*written, wrote*) about his daily life, his family, and his thoughts and feelings. We have **[8]** (*become, became*) good friends through our letters even though we have never **[9]** (*spoke, spoken*) to each other. Reading each other's essays in the club newsletter has also **[10]** (*brung, brought*) us closer together.

USAGE

## Review A  Writing the Past and Past Participle Forms of Verbs

For each of the following sentences, write the correct past or past participle form of the verb given.

EXAMPLE  **1.** run  Yesterday we _____ around the track twice.

  *1. ran*

**1.** *sing*  Boyz II Men _____ last night.
**2.** *burst*  The car suddenly _____ into flames.
**3.** *drink*  Yesterday they _____ juice with their tossed salads and turkey sandwiches.
**4.** *use*  He _____ to camp out every summer.
**5.** *do*  They _____ their best to repair the damage caused by the very large hail.
**6.** *give*  Grandma has _____ us some old photos.
**7.** *risk*  The detective _____ her life.
**8.** *ring*  My alarm _____ at six o'clock.
**9.** *speak*  Toni has not _____ to me since our argument.
**10.** *fall*  A tree has _____ across the highway.

## Review B  Writing the Past and Past Participle Forms of Verbs

Write the correct past or past participle form of each italicized verb in the following paragraph.

EXAMPLE  All my life I have **[1]** (*know*) that I must make my own choices.

  *1. known*

I have never **[1]** (*choose*) to be on a sports team because I am not a very athletic person. Some people are surprised because my brother and sister have **[2]** (*drive*) themselves very hard and have **[3]** (*become*) excellent athletes. For example, my brother, Emilio, **[4]** (*break*) three swimming records this year alone. He has **[5]** (*swim*) better than anyone else in our school. He also **[6]** (*go*) out for tennis and track this year. My sister, Elena, is only a junior, but she has already **[7]** (*run*) the 100-meter dash faster than any senior girl. I **[8]** (*use*) to think I wanted to follow in my brother's and sister's footsteps, but now I have **[9]** (*take*) a different path in life. My English teacher just **[10]** (*give*) me a chance to lead the debating team, and I am going to grab it!

## Review C Writing the Past and Past Participle Forms of Verbs

Write the correct past or past participle form of the verb given for each of the following sentences.

EXAMPLES
1. *go*    We _____ to the Ozark Mountains.
1. *went*

2. *swim*    I have never _____ in an ocean.
2. *swum*

1. *throw*    Kerry should have _____ the ball to Lee, who could have tagged the runner out.
2. *freeze*    Has the water _____ yet?
3. *write*    Theo has _____ me a long letter.
4. *see*    Have you _____ that actor in person?
5. *sing*    The tenors have _____ in Rome, Paris, and New York.
6. *throw*    I finally _____ my old running shoes away and bought a new pair at the mall.
7. *drown*    Nobody has ever _____ in this lake.
8. *give*    Taro _____ me a bowl of miso soup.
9. *blow*    The strong wind this afternoon _____ down our tree-house in the backyard.
10. *take*    I have already _____ a picture of you, Molly.

## Review D Writing the Past and Past Participle Forms of Verbs

Write the correct past or past participle form of each of the ten italicized verbs in the following paragraph.

EXAMPLE    Have you ever [1] (*take*) a trip to the country?
1. *taken*

We have always [1] (*spend*) summer vacations at Uncle Dan's farm in Vermont. We [2] (*do*) the most relaxing things there last year! We [3] (*swim*) in the millpond and [4] (*eat*) watermelon on the back porch. A few times, we [5] (*ride*) our bikes into town to get groceries. We also [6] (*take*) turns riding Horace, the mule. I have [7] (*fall*) off Horace twice, but I have never [8] (*break*) any bones. Both times, I [9] (*come*) down in a pile of soft hay. Then I dusted myself off and [10] (*climb*) on again.

Proofreading Sentences for Correct
Verb Forms

Some of the following sentences contain an incorrect verb form.
If a verb form is wrong, write the correct form. If the sentence
is already correct, write *C*.

EXAMPLE     1. Marian Anderson sung her way out of poverty.

            1. *sang*

1. She went on to earn fame and the Medal of Freedom.
2. Can you tell from this picture that she use to sing
   classical music?
3. In 1955, Marian Anderson become the first African
   American singer to perform with the Metropolitan
   Opera in New York City.
4. She performed in concerts and operas all over the world,
   but she begun her career as a child singing hymns in
   church.
5. Anderson, who was from a poor Philadelphia family,
   was awarded a scholarship to study music in Europe.
6. European audiences soon taked notice of her.
7. Audiences admired her determination and courage.
8. In 1939, Anderson was not permitted to sing at a hall in
   Washington, D.C., so she give a free concert, attended by
   75,000 people, at the Lincoln Memorial.
9. In the 1950s, the U.S. government choosed her to go on
   a goodwill tour of Asia and to be a United Nations delegate.
10. Anderson writed of her experiences in her autobiography,
    *My Lord, What a Morning.*

Review F  Proofreading a Paragraph for Correct
Verb Forms

The following paragraph contains ten incorrect verb forms. If a verb
form is wrong, write the correct form. If a sentence is already correct,
write *C*.

EXAMPLE     [1] A Confederate search party had went out to get boots
            for their soldiers and saddles for their horses.

            1. *had gone*

   [1] By chance, the search party runned into the Union cavalry.
[2] It is not clear who attackted first, but a battle begun near

Gettysburg, Pennsylvania, on July 1, 1863. [3] The fighting goed on for three days. [4] First one side and then the other got the upper hand. [5] Shells bursted in the air, and cannonballs whistled in all directions. [6] At one point, some Confederate soldiers clumb to the top of Cemetery Ridge, and their flag flown there a brief time. [7] However, the Union army drived them back. [8] By the time the battle had came to an end, 20,000 Union soldiers and 25,000 Confederate soldiers had fell.

# Tense

**17d.** The *tense* of a verb indicates the time of the action or of the state of being expressed by the verb.

The tenses are formed from the verb's principal parts. Verbs in English have the six tenses shown on the following time line:

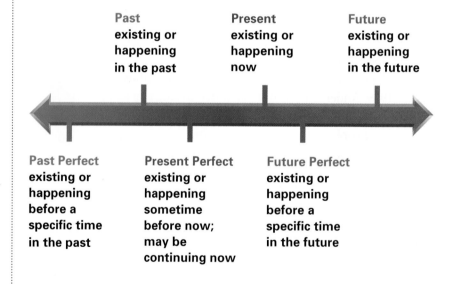

**Past**
existing or
happening
in the past

**Present**
existing or
happening
now

**Future**
existing or
happening
in the future

**Past Perfect**
existing or
happening
before a
specific time
in the past

**Present Perfect**
existing or
happening
sometime
before now;
may be
continuing now

**Future Perfect**
existing or
happening
before a
specific time
in the future

EXAMPLES   Max **has worked** [present perfect] all summer, and now he **has** [present] enough money to buy a bicycle.

The chorus **had practiced** [past perfect] for weeks before they **sang** [past] in public last night.

The surgeon **will have reviewed** [future perfect] the test results by next Friday, and she **will decide** [future] whether or not to operate then.

USAGE

## Conjugation of the Verb *Give* in the Active Voice

### Present Tense

| Singular | Plural |
|----------|--------|
| I give | we give |
| you give | you give |
| he, she, *or* it gives | they give |

### Past Tense

| Singular | Plural |
|----------|--------|
| I gave | we gave |
| you gave | you gave |
| he, she, *or* it gave | they gave |

### Future Tense

| Singular | Plural |
|----------|--------|
| I will (shall) give | we will (shall) give |
| you will (shall) give | you will (shall) give |
| he, she, *or* it will (shall) give | they will (shall) give |

### Present Perfect Tense

| Singular | Plural |
|----------|--------|
| I have given | we have given |
| you have given | you have given |
| he, she, *or* it has given | they have given |

### Past Perfect Tense

| Singular | Plural |
|----------|--------|
| I had given | we had given |
| you had given | you had given |
| he, she, *or* it had given | they had given |

### Future Perfect Tense

| Singular | Plural |
|----------|--------|
| I will (shall) have given | we will (shall) have given |
| you will (shall) have given | you will (shall) have given |
| he, she, *or* it will (shall) have given | they will (shall) have given |

**Reference Note**

See page 536 for a **conjugation of *give* in the passive voice.**

USAGE

S T Y L E    T I P

Traditionally, the helping verbs *shall* and *will* were used differently. Now, however, *shall* can be used almost interchangeably with *will.*

## The Progressive Form

Each of the six tenses has an additional form called the *progressive form,* which expresses continuing action. It consists of a form of the verb *be* plus the present participle of a verb. The progressive is not a separate tense but an additional form of each of the six tenses.

| | |
|---|---|
| PRESENT PROGRESSIVE | am, are, is giving |
| PAST PROGRESSIVE | was, were giving |
| FUTURE PROGRESSIVE | will (shall) be giving |
| PRESENT PERFECT PROGRESSIVE | has, have been giving |
| PAST PERFECT PROGRESSIVE | had been giving |
| FUTURE PERFECT PROGRESSIVE | will (shall) have been giving |

NOTE   The *emphatic form* of a verb is used to show emphasis. The emphatic form consists of the present or past tense of *do* with the base form of the main verb.

| | |
|---|---|
| PRESENT EMPHATIC | Although the grass is green, the lawn **does need** watering. |
| PAST EMPHATIC | The writer endured many setbacks in his career, yet he **did** finally **become** famous. |

─── STYLE ✏ TIP ───

The emphatic form is also used in questions and negative statements. These uses do not place special emphasis on the verb.

QUESTION
Why **do** bears hibernate?

NEGATIVE STATEMENT
If the car **does**n't [does not] start, check the battery.

**17e.** Each of the six tenses has its own special uses.

**(1)** The *present tense* is used mainly to express an action or a state of being that is occurring now.

EXAMPLES   The new jet **has** two engines.

Leotie **belongs** to the Latin Club.

They **are decorating** the gym. [progressive form]

The present tense is also used

- to show a customary or habitual action or state of being
- to express a general truth—something that is always true
- to make historical events seem current (such use is called the *historical present*)
- to discuss a literary work (such use is called the *literary present*)
- to express future time

EXAMPLES    We **recycle** newspapers, glass, and aluminum cans.
[customary actions]

The sun **sets** in the west. [general truth]

In 1905, Albert Einstein **makes** history when he **proposes** his theory of relativity. [historical present]

In *David Copperfield,* Dickens **shows** us the extremes of Victorian life. [literary present]

Finals **begin** next week. [future time]

**(2) The *past tense* is used to express an action or state of being that occurred in the past but that is not occurring now.**

EXAMPLES    They **looked** for seashells.

The manatees **were swimming** in the canal.
[progressive form]

NOTE  A past action or state of being may also be shown with the past form *used*, plus *to,* plus the base form of the main verb.

EXAMPLE    Chicago **used to be** the second-largest U.S. city.

**(3) The *future tense* is used to express an action or a state of being that will occur. It is formed with *will* or *shall* and the main verb's base form.**

EXAMPLES    **Shall** we **set** the table?

The new model cars **will arrive** soon.

They **will be selling** them soon. [progressive form]

NOTE  A future action or state of being may also be shown in other ways.

EXAMPLES    We **are going to make** our own Mardi Gras costumes.

The president **holds** a press conference **next Monday.**

**(4) The *present perfect tense* is used to express an action or a state of being that occurred at some indefinite time in the past. It is formed with the helping verb *have* or *has.***

EXAMPLES    The Mendozas **have invited** us over for a cookout.

The Red Cross **has been delivering** medical supplies.
[progressive form]

USAGE

**NOTE** Do not use the present perfect tense to express a specific time in the past. Instead, use the past tense.

NONSTANDARD    We have seen that movie last Saturday. [*Last Saturday* indicates a specific time in the past.]

STANDARD    We **saw** that movie last Saturday.

The present perfect tense is also used to express an action or a state of being that began in the past and continues into the present.

EXAMPLES    Li Hua **has taken** violin lessons for eight years.

We **have been living** in Amarillo since early 1998. [progressive form]

**(5)** The *past perfect tense* is used to express an action or a state of being that was completed in the past before some other past action or event. It is formed with the helping verb *had.*

EXAMPLES    Once the judges **had viewed** the paintings, they announced the winners. [The viewing occurred before the announcing.]

By the time that the Spanish conquistadors arrived, that redwood **had been growing** for three centuries. [progressive form]

**(6)** The *future perfect tense* is used to express an action or a state of being that will be completed in the future before some other future occurrence. It is formed with the helping verbs *will have* or *shall have.*

EXAMPLES    By the time Mom returns, I **will have done** my chores. [The doing will be completed before the returning.]

In August, Aaron **will have been taking** Hebrew lessons for two years. [progressive form]

### Exercise 4   Explaining the Uses of Tenses in Sentences

Each item on the next page contains two correct sentences. Identify the tense or tenses used in each sentence. Be prepared to explain the meanings of the two sentences in each pair.

EXAMPLE    1.  **a.** For breakfast she eats a bagel and some cereal.
            **b.** For breakfast she is eating a bagel and some cereal.
         1.  a.  *simple present*
             b.  *present progressive*

1. **a.** You will put down your pencils when the bell rings.
   **b.** You will have put down your pencils when the bell rings.
2. **a.** He worked at the gas station in the summertime.
   **b.** He has worked at the gas station in the summertime.
3. **a.** What caused the computer to crash?
   **b.** What has been causing the computer to crash?
4. **a.** When I arrived, Morton left.
   **b.** When I arrived, Morton had left.
5. **a.** Shelley was working on her bicycle.
   **b.** Shelley had been working on her bicycle when we arrived.

**Exercise 5** **Using the Different Tenses of Verbs in Sentences**

Change the tense of the verb in each of the following sentences to the tense indicated in parentheses.

EXAMPLE     **1.** Maria always goes home at five o'clock. (*past*)

          *1. went*

1. The quick, graceful otter swam to the edge of the pool.
   (*present perfect*)
2. Our class will read Shakespeare's *Much Ado About Nothing.*
   (*future progressive*)
3. Before the concert, the orchestra practices the new pieces.
   (*past perfect*)
4. The guests will be arriving at the train station.
   (*present perfect progressive*)
5. By then, I will solve the riddle. (*future perfect*)
6. The three sisters regularly meet for lunch. (*past*)
7. The new computers have been working fine for three weeks.
   (*past perfect progressive*)
8. Wasps were entering the house through the torn screen. (*present*)
9. The lawn mower has started after all! (*past emphatic*)
10. We reset the clocks for daylight saving time. (*future*)

# Consistency of Tense

**17f.** Do not change needlessly from one tense to another.

When describing events that occur at the same time, use verbs in the same tense. When describing events that occur at different times, use different tenses to show the order of events clearly.

| NONSTANDARD | Cara fielded the ball and throws the runner out.<br>[*Fielded* is past tense; *throws* is present tense.] |
| --- | --- |
| STANDARD | Cara **fielded** the ball and **threw** the runner out.<br>[*Fielded* and *threw* are both past tense.] |
| STANDARD | Cara **fields** the ball and **throws** the runner out. [*Fields* and *throws* are both present tense.] |
| | |
| NONSTANDARD | She stands on the mound and will stare at the batter.<br>[*Stands* is present tense; *will stare* is future tense.] |
| STANDARD | She **stands** on the mound and **stares** at the batter.<br>[*Stands* and *stares* are both present tense.] |
| STANDARD | She **will stand** on the mound and **stare** at the batter.<br>[*Will stand* and *stare* are both future tense.] |
| | |
| NONSTANDARD | The batter wished that he practiced more before the game. [Because the action of practicing was completed before the action of wishing, the verb should be *had practiced,* not *practiced.*] |
| STANDARD | The batter **wished** that he **had practiced** more before the game. |

### Exercise 6   Proofreading a Paragraph to Make the Tenses of the Verbs Consistent

Proofread the following paragraph, looking for needless changes of verb tense. Choose whether to rewrite the paragraph in the present or past tense. Then, change the verbs to make the tenses consistent.

**HELP**

For the paragraph in Exercise 6, either the present tense or the past tense can be used correctly.

EXAMPLE    **[1]** It all started as soon as I come home from school.

    1.  *It all started as soon as I came home from school.*

*or*

*It all starts as soon as I come home from school.*

[**1**] I am in my room, and I have planned to study for two hours. [**2**] It was about five o'clock in the afternoon. [**3**] To my surprise, Nancy Chang dropped by. [**4**] She dashes into the house, runs up the stairs, and calls my name. [**5**] What she wanted is a fishing companion. [**6**] All week she has been thinking about going fishing. [**7**] Getting my fishing gear together, I become excited and can almost see the fish fighting over which one is to be my first catch of the day. [**8**] On our way out to the lake, we see clouds beginning to form, and we knew we are in for trouble. [**9**] It rains all right—for the whole weekend. [**10**] The fish were safe for another week.

# Active and Passive Voice

**17g.** A verb in the *active voice* expresses an action done by its subject. A verb in the *passive voice* expresses an action done to its subject.

| | |
|---|---|
| ACTIVE VOICE | The coach **instructed** us. [The subject, *coach*, performs the action.] |
| PASSIVE VOICE | We **were instructed** by the coach. [The subject, *We*, receives the action.] |
| ACTIVE VOICE | **Did** Brandon **score** the winning touchdown? [The subject, *Brandon*, performs the action.] |
| PASSIVE VOICE | **Was** the winning touchdown **scored** by Brandon? [The subject, *touchdown*, receives the action.] |

Compare the following related sentences:

           S                O

ACTIVE    The author **provides** helpful diagrams.

                  S

PASSIVE  Helpful diagrams **are provided** by the author.

In these two sentences, the object of the active sentence is the subject of the passive one. The subject of the active sentence is expressed in a prepositional phrase in the passive sentence. Note that this phrase can be omitted.

PASSIVE  Helpful diagrams **are provided.**

In a passive sentence, the verb phrase includes a form of *be* and the past participle of the main verb. Other helping verbs may also be included.

            S          O

ACTIVE    The tutor **is helping** Sharon.

            S

PASSIVE  Sharon **is being helped** by the tutor.

            S          O

ACTIVE    Someone **has erased** the tapes.

            S

PASSIVE  The tapes **have been erased.**

The chart on the following page shows the conjugation of the verb *give* in the passive voice.

**Reference Note**

For more information on **helping verbs,** see page 391.

**Reference Note**

For the **conjugation of the verb *give* in the active voice,** see page 529.

## Conjugation of the Verb *Give* in the Passive Voice

### Present Tense

| Singular | Plural |
| --- | --- |
| I am given | we are given |
| you are given | you are given |
| he, she, *or* it is given | they are given |

### Past Tense

| Singular | Plural |
| --- | --- |
| I was given | we were given |
| you were given | you were given |
| he, she, *or* it was given | they were given |

### Future Tense

| Singular | Plural |
| --- | --- |
| I will (shall) be given | we will (shall) be given |
| you will (shall) be given | you will (shall) be given |
| he, she, *or* it will (shall) be given | they will (shall) be given |

### Present Perfect Tense

| Singular | Plural |
| --- | --- |
| I have been given | we have been given |
| you have been given | you have been given |
| he, she, *or* it has been given | they have been given |

### Past Perfect Tense

| Singular | Plural |
| --- | --- |
| I had been given | we had been given |
| you had been given | you had been given |
| he, she, *or* it had been given | they had been given |

### Future Perfect Tense

| Singular | Plural |
| --- | --- |
| I will (shall) have been given | we will (shall) have been given |
| you will (shall) have been given | you will (shall) have been given |
| he, she, *or* it will (shall) have been given | they will (shall) have been given |

**NOTE** The progressive forms of the passive voice exist for all six tenses. However, the use of *be* or *been* with *being* is extremely awkward—*give*, for example, in the passive future perfect is *will (shall) have been being given*. Consequently, the progressive form of the passive voice is generally used only in the present and past tenses.

## Using the Passive Voice

Although the passive voice is not any less correct than the active voice, it is less direct, less forceful, and less concise. In general, you should avoid using the passive voice. First, it generally requires more words to express a thought than the active voice does. Consequently, the passive voice can result in awkward writing. Second, the performer of the action in a passive voice construction is revealed indirectly or not at all. As a result, a sentence written in the passive voice can sound weak. Compare the following pairs of sentences.

PASSIVE   The ball **was hit** over the outfield fence by Jody.
ACTIVE    Jody **hit** the ball over the outfield fence.

PASSIVE   The totals for the new budget **were** carefully **checked.**
ACTIVE    The club treasurer carefully **checked** the totals for the new budget.

The passive voice is useful, however, in situations such as the following ones:

**(1)** when you do not know the performer of the action

EXAMPLES   Over three thousand roses **were planted.**

Are the peaches **being harvested** on schedule?

**(2)** when you do not want to reveal the performer of the action

EXAMPLES   Charges **were brought** against the vandals.

Many large donations to the building fund **have been made.**

**(3)** when you want to emphasize the receiver of the action

EXAMPLES   Jacques Chirac **was elected** president of France in 1995.

These remarkable fossils **were found** nearby.

**COMPUTER TIP**

Some software programs can identify and highlight verbs in the passive voice. If you use such a program, keep in mind that it can't tell why you used the passive voice. If you did so for a particular reason, you may want to leave the verb in the passive voice.

### Exercise 7   Identifying Active and Passive Voice

For each of the following sentences, tell whether the verb is in the *active* or *passive* voice.

EXAMPLE   **1.** In the morning, I am awakened by the alarm clock.

*1. passive*

1. The newest CD by my favorite group was not reviewed by most music critics.
2. The student body elects the council president.
3. Angelo's courageous act of putting out the fire in the basement prevented a tragedy.
4. W. C. Handy composed the famous jazz classic "St. Louis Blues."
5. Your generous contribution to help the homeless is greatly appreciated.
6. The half-time show at the state championship was performed by the band from Millersville.
7. This afternoon the baby stood up by himself.
8. Was Mr. Yañez awarded the trophy?
9. I don't understand this math problem.
10. Brian has been appointed captain of the basketball team.

### Exercise 8   Using Verbs in the Active Voice and the Passive Voice

Identify the verb in each of the following sentences as either *active* or *passive*. Then, revise each sentence that is in the passive voice so that it is in active voice.

EXAMPLE   **1.** My 4-H project was just completed.

*1. passive; I just completed my 4-H project.*

1. For my project I grew vegetables in containers.
2. Initially, 4-H clubs were joined only by farm children.
3. Their projects focused on crops and livestock.
4. Later projects, such as personal safety and career studies, interested young people in the city.
5. Projects are often exhibited by members at county fairs.
6. The 4-H club members also learn about good citizenship.
7. Summer camps are attended by many 4-H members.
8. Community projects are planned by our club yearly.
9. The city appreciated our tree-planting project.
10. Many young people are helped by participation in 4-H.

# Six Troublesome Verbs

## *Lie* and *Lay*

**17h.** The verb *lie* means "to rest," "to recline," or "to remain in a lying position." *Lie* does not take an object. The verb *lay* means "to put" or "to place (something somewhere)." *Lay* generally takes an object.

**Reference Note**

For more about **objects of verbs,** see page 431.

| Principal Parts of *Lie* and *Lay* | | | |
|---|---|---|---|
| **Base Form** | **Present Participle** | **Past** | **Past Participle** |
| lie | [is] lying | lay | [have] lain |
| lay | [is] laying | laid | [have] laid |

**S T Y L E     T I P**

The verb *lie* can also mean "to tell an untruth." Used in this way, *lie* still does not take an object. The past and past participle forms of this meaning of *lie* are *lied* and *[have] lied*.

EXAMPLES     **Lie** down if you don't feel well.
                **Lay** those books down.

                Lambert **lay** on the lounge chair.
                Lambert **laid** the towel on the lounge chair.

                He **had lain** on the couch too long.
                He **had laid** the newspaper on the couch.

### Exercise 9   Choosing the Correct Forms of *Lie* and *Lay*

Write the correct form of *lie* or *lay* for the blank in each of the following sentences.

EXAMPLE     **1.** Jennifer _____ the flowers on the table and looked for a vase.

           *1. laid*

**1.** He _____ the report aside and called for order.
**2.** Alma will _____ down for a siesta.
**3.** She has _____ on the couch all morning, watching those silly cartoons and eating cereal.
**4.** The baby was _____ quietly in the nurse's arms.
**5.** Is that today's paper _____ in the mud?
**6.** I have _____ the shoes near the fire to dry, and I hung my wet clothes in the garage.
**7.** _____ down, Spot.
**8.** The lace had _____ in the trunk for years before we explored Grandmother's attic.

USAGE

**9.** Our cat _____ in the sun whenever it can.

**10.** After reading for almost three hours, I _____ back and rested my head on the cushions.

# Sit and Set

**17i.** The verb *sit* means "to rest in an upright, seated position." *Sit* seldom takes an object. The verb *set* means "to put" or "to place (something somewhere)." *Set* generally takes an object.

| Principal Parts of *Sit* and *Set* | | | |
|---|---|---|---|
| **Base Form** | **Present Participle** | **Past** | **Past Participle** |
| sit | [is] sitting | sat | [have] sat |
| set | [is] setting | set | [have] set |

EXAMPLES

Sit down.

Set it down.

The cups **sat** on the tray.

I **set** the cups there.

How long **has** it **sat** on the bench?

She **had set** the picnic basket on the bench.

**Exercise 10** Writing the Forms of *Sit* and *Set*

Write the correct form of *sit* or *set* for the blank in each of the following sentences.

EXAMPLE

**1.** Will you _____ with me, Josh?

*1. sit*

**1.** Please _____ here, Mrs. Brown.

**2.** Have you _____ the seedlings in the sun?

**3.** We were _____ in the park during the Fourth of July fireworks display.

**4.** Someone has already _____ the kettle on the stove.

**5.** Grandpa is busily _____ several varieties of tomato plants in the vegetable garden.

**6.** At the concert, Keith _____ near Isabelle.

**7.** Mrs. Levine _____ the menorah on the mantel and asked Rachel to light the first candle.

---

**USAGE**

STYLE | TIP

You may know that the word *set* has more meanings than the two given here. Check in a dictionary to see if the meaning you intend requires an object.

EXAMPLE

We watched silently as the sun **set.** [Here, *set* does not take an object.]

---

8. They were _____ on the rocks, watching the surfers who were riding the large waves.

9. We had _____ still for almost an hour.

10. Have you ever _____ on the beach at sundown and waited for the stars to come out?

# Rise and Raise

**17j.** The verb *rise* means "to go in an upward direction." *Rise* does not take an object. The verb *raise* means "to move (something) in an upward direction." *Raise* generally takes an object.

| Principal Parts of *Rise* and *Raise* | | | |
|---|---|---|---|
| **Base Form** | **Present Participle** | **Past** | **Past Participle** |
| rise | [is] rising | rose | [have] risen |
| raise | [is] raising | raised | [have] raised |

EXAMPLES   She **rises** early.
She **raises** that question.

The price of cereal **rose.**
The store **raised** prices.

The lakes **have risen** since the spring rains.
The rains **have raised** the water level.

**Exercise 11**  **Writing the Forms of *Rise* and *Raise***

Write the correct form of *rise* or *raise* for the blank in each of the following sentences.

EXAMPLE   **1.** The river has been _____ rapidly since noon.
   *1.  rising*

1. Please _____ and face the audience; then, begin your oral interpretation of the poem.

2. After the speech, the reporters _____ several questions that the senator refused to answer.

3. Will the governor _____ sales tax again this year, or will he wait until after the election?

4. The price of fuel has _____ steadily.

5. Let's get there before the curtain _____.

**STYLE**       **TIP**

The verb *raise* has definitions other than the one given here. Another common definition is "to grow" or "to bring to maturity."

EXAMPLES
They **raise** cotton.
He **raises** cattle.

Notice that both of these uses also take an object.

USAGE

**6.** Jerry and Alexander, two of the stagehands, will _____ the curtain for each act.

**7.** The bread has _____ beautifully.

**8.** The moon _____ and slipped behind a cloud, but there was still plenty of light for us to find our way home.

**9.** The candidate _____ to address her supporters.

**10.** The children _____ their flag for Cinco de Mayo.

---

**Review G** **Identifying the Correct Forms of *Lie* and *Lay*, *Sit* and *Set*, and *Rise* and *Raise***

Choose the correct verb in parentheses in each of the following sentences.

EXAMPLE **1.** The number of immigrants coming to the United States (*rose, raised*) steadily during the late 1800s and early 1900s.

*1. rose*

**1.** The Hungarian mother shown below (*sat, set*) with her children for this picture around 1910.

**2.** They were among thousands of immigrant families who (*sat, set*) their baggage on American soil for the first time at the immigration station on Ellis Island in New York Harbor.

**3.** (*Lying, Laying*) down was often impossible on the crowded ships that brought these immigrants to the United States.

**4.** Most immigrants were thankful to be able to (*lie, lay*) their few belongings on the deck and think of the future.

**5.** Their hopes for new lives must have (*risen, raised*) as they drew closer to the United States.

**6.** The history book (*lying, laying*) on my desk states that eleven million immigrants came to the United States between 1870 and 1899.

**7.** (*Sit, Set*) down and read more about the immigrants who came from Germany, Ireland, Great Britain, Scandinavia, and the Netherlands in the early 1800s.

**8.** After 1890, the number of immigrants from Austria-Hungary, Italy, Russia, Poland, and Greece (*rose, raised*).

**9.** Many United States citizens were (*rising, raising*) concerns that there would not be enough jobs for everyone in the country.

The Granger Collection, New York

USAGE

**10.** However, we know now that immigrant workers helped the country to (*rise, raise*) to new industrial heights.

# Mood

**17k.** *Mood* is the form a verb takes to indicate the attitude of the person using the verb.

**(1)** The *indicative mood* is used to express a fact, an opinion, or a question.

EXAMPLES    Seamus Heaney **is** the Irish poet who **won** the Nobel Prize in literature in 1995.

I **think** he **is** the best of the poets featured in this book.

**Have** you **read** the poem, Anita?

**(2)** The *imperative mood* is used to express a direct command or request.

EXAMPLES    **Halt!** [command]

Please **write** your answers on a separate sheet of paper. [request]

**(3)** The *subjunctive mood* is used to express a suggestion, a necessity, a condition contrary to fact, or a wish.

EXAMPLES    Gerald suggested that we **be** ready to board the train. [suggestion]

It is essential that all of the delegates **be** available for questions. [necessity]

If I **were** you, I would call them immediately. [condition contrary to fact]

Leilani wishes she **were** scuba diving off the Yucatán peninsula. [wish]

PEANUTS reprinted by permission of United Feature Syndicate, Inc.

---

**Review H**  **Identifying the Mood of Verbs**

For each of the sentences on the following page, identify the mood of the italicized verb as *indicative*, *imperative*, or *subjunctive*.

EXAMPLE    **1.** Ferryboats *sail* frequently between Calais, France, and Dover, England.

          *1. indicative*

1. Please *hold* your applause until after all of the presentations.
2. La Paz, in Bolivia, *is* the world's highest capital city.
3. Female marsupials *carry* their young in pouches.
4. Is it necessary that he *rehearse* tonight?
5. *Take* out the trash immediately, Paul!
6. If I *were* you, I would not swim in that lake.
7. How much interest *does* State Bank *pay* on savings accounts and checking accounts?
8. Angela *intends* to continue her work at the humane society after school.
9. Mr. Guzman, please *consider* postponing the practice until next week.
10. For rust to form, it is essential that four atoms of solid iron and three molecules of oxygen *be* present.

## Review I  Identifying Correct Uses of Verbs

From each pair of words in parentheses, choose the correct item.

EXAMPLE    **[1]** Look at this great old photograph that Grandma has just (*gave, given*) me.

    1.  *given*

Grandma told me that the Pop Corn King **[1]** (*been, was*) her grandfather and, consequently, my great-great-grandfather. This warmhearted man **[2]** (*took, taken*) Grandma and her sister into his home after their parents had **[3]** (*drowned, drownded*) in a flood. He would sometimes let the girls **[4]** (*sit, set*) in the driver's seat with him. The photograph was **[5]** (*maked, made*) in 1914 in the resort town of

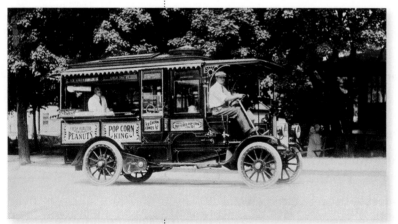

Petoskey, Michigan. During the summer, my great-great-granddad **[6]** (*use, used*) to drive through the streets in the late afternoon. He **[7]** (*rang, rung*) a bell, and children **[8]** (*run, ran*) out to buy treats just as kids do today. Look— the popcorn **[9]** (*cost, costed*) only five cents! The last time I **[10]** (*buyed, bought*) popcorn at the movies, I paid $3.75!

# Chapter Review

## A. Identifying Correct Forms of Verbs

If a sentence contains an incorrect verb form, write the correct form. If a sentence is already correct, write *C*.

1. That car breaked the land speed record.
2. Grandfather walks around the park every morning when he lived in Madrid.
3. The crocodile ran across the marsh and slips into the water.
4. Are the bells of Sant' Angelo rung every day at sunset?
5. After Lourdes had drove two hours, she stopped for a break.
6. Grandpa has swam across Santa Rosa Sound.
7. Our dog Pippa likes to set in the doorway and watch the traffic.
8. Will the bread raise faster in the oven or on the table?
9. Uncle Ben brung us a giant jigsaw puzzle of the Mojave Desert.
10. I could have sworn that the Green Bay Packers won the Super Bowl that year.
11. Carmilla's blouse was stained, but she knowed how to get the stain out.
12. Lilly has drunk two glasses of milk and still wants more.
13. Toucans fly by the window and a cool breeze blew from the gulf.
14. Last night, Dr. Madison talks about the new laser operation.
15. The dogs are laying under the porch.
16. The curtains raised at the beginning of the first act.
17. She has apparently choosed the color blue.
18. The heron waits for the fish before it caught it.
19. We laid the tools down and had lunch.
20. It's a good thing that truck hasn't broke down—it was certainly an expensive investment.

## B. Identifying Active and Passive Voice

For each of the following sentences, tell whether the verb is in the *active* or *passive* voice.

21. The United States president is elected every four years by a majority of popular and electoral votes.

USAGE

22. Yesterday the fawn ate its first full meal.

23. Was Oscar told the news beforehand?

24. The Veterans of Foreign Wars banquet was well attended.

25. Jenny speaks French and Arabic as well as English.

26. Was Ruth Lopez appointed goodwill ambassador by the secretary-general?

27. Most early British racing cars had superchargers.

28. The best songs in the show were performed by a husband-and-wife duet from San Marcos, Texas.

29. Our club sponsors a variety of community projects.

30. Large numbers of elephants are herded into different areas of the park in order to preserve the foliage.

## C. Proofreading a Paragraph for Correct Verb Forms

The following paragraph contains errors in verb usage. If a verb form is wrong, write the correct form. If a sentence is already correct, write *C*.

[31] Last night the wind blowed for hours during the snowstorm. [32] When Libby and I looked outside in the morning, at least a foot of snow had fell. [33] Instead of a brown, lifeless yard, we saw a glittering fantasy world. [34] Never in our lives had we ate our cereal as fast as we did that morning! [35] We quickly put on our parkas and ran out the door to build a snow fort. [36] Mom, smiling, come outside, too. [37] We should have knowed she would start a snowball fight! [38] Before we could get our revenge, mom goes back into the house to warm up. [39] Soon afterward, our feet felt as if they had freezed solid. [40] When we were finally back inside, Mom brung us hot apple cider as a peace offering.

## D. Identifying the Correct Forms of Six Troublesome Verbs

Choose the correct verb in parentheses for each of the following sentences.

41. Their hopes (*raised, rose*) when the sun broke through and shone on the city below.

**42.** Please (*set, sit*) the orchid next to the rhododendron in the greenhouse.

**43.** Tim (*sat, set*) in the old armchair and recalled long summer evenings from his childhood.

**44.** Was that you I saw (*laying, lying*) in the hammock a minute ago?

**45.** (*Lay, Lie*) that magazine down and listen to what I have to say!

**46.** The cadets stood at attention as the color sergeant (*rose, raised*) the flag.

**47.** The mythical phoenix is a bird that (*rises, raises*) from its own ashes.

**48.** He has a cold, so he has (*laid, lain*) on the couch most of the afternoon.

**49.** The seals were (*laying, lying*) on the beach.

**50.** He has (*sat, set*) his tools on the workbench.

 # Writing Application
## Using Verbs in Instructions

**Verb Tense**   You have been asked to teach your eight-year-old brother to make his own after-school snack. Write instructions for making a nutritious treat. Use correct verb tense so that your directions are easy to follow.

**Prewriting**   You will need to choose a snack that a child would be able to make and would enjoy. You may want to list all of the steps first and then go back and number them in order.

**Writing**   As you write your first draft, think about how to define or clarify words that an eight-year-old might not know. Make sure that your verb tenses show the sequence of the steps.

**Revising**   Ask a friend or young child you know to act out your instructions. Revise any steps that confuse your assistant. Add words that indicate chronological order (such as *first, second, then,* and *next*).

**Publishing**   Check to be sure your verb tenses are correct. Use your textbook or a dictionary to check the spelling of the verbs in your instructions. Pay special attention to irregular verbs. Your class may decide to make its own snack cookbook to share with elementary school students or your local parent-teacher organization.

## CHAPTER

# Using Pronouns Correctly
## Nominative and Objective Uses; Clear Reference

## Diagnostic Preview

### A. Correcting Pronoun Forms

Identify each incorrectly used pronoun in the following sentences. Then, write the correct form of that pronoun. If a sentence is already correct, write *C*.

EXAMPLE    **1.** Excuse me, Rhonda, but this arrangement is strictly between Carl and I.

        *1. I—me*

**1.** The author spoke to we history students about Slavic culture in Eastern Europe.
**2.** During the Olympic trials every diver except she received a low score from the judges.
**3.** The instructor, who seemed nervous during the show, was proud of Lani's performance.
**4.** It couldn't have been her.
**5.** Van is more energetic than me.
**6.** Rick couldn't spot Maura and I in the huge crowd at the state fairgrounds.
**7.** Tyrone and he are playing backgammon at Regina's house this afternoon.

8. Laura gave he and Edwin a beautiful poem that she had written about friendship.

9. Angie's neighbors, Mrs. Brandt and he, helped plant the trees for Arbor Day.

10. Whomever can possibly take her place?

## B. Proofreading a Paragraph for Correct Pronoun Forms

Some of the sentences in the following paragraph contain pronouns that have been used incorrectly. Identify each incorrectly used pronoun. Then, write the correct form of that pronoun. If a sentence is already correct, write *C*.

EXAMPLE   **[1]** To Velma and I, Dizzy Dean is one of the greatest baseball players of all time.

    1. *I—me*

[11] We think there never has been another baseball player like him. [12] Fans still talk about he and his teammates. [13] Dean pitched for the St. Louis Cardinals, to who his fastball was a great help, especially in the 1934 World Series. [14] Dean was such a character that his fans never knew what crazy notion might come to he during games. [15] He had a real confidence about him, too. [16] According to one famous story about Dean, whom was also known for his quips, he once said, "Tain't braggin' if you kin really do it!" [17] When Dean became a sportscaster, him and his informal speech appealed to fans. [18] He liked his fans, and they liked him. [19] A big honor for he was being elected to baseball's Hall of Fame. [20] Us fans can go to the Dizzy Dean Museum in Jackson, Mississippi, to find out more about Dean's career.

# Case

**18a.** *Case* is the form that a noun or pronoun takes to show its relationship to other words in a sentence.

In English, there are three cases: *nominative, objective,* and *possessive.* Choosing the correct case form for a noun is usually simple because the form remains the same in the nominative and objective cases.

NOMINATIVE   My **dentist** has opened a new practice in the office building next to the mall.

OBJECTIVE   The receptionist who works for my **dentist** recently graduated from junior college.

Only in the possessive case does a noun change its form, usually by adding an apostrophe and an *s*.

POSSESSIVE    My **dentist's** business is thriving.

Personal pronouns, however, have distinct case forms. In the following example, the pronouns in boldface type all refer to the same person. They have different forms because of their different uses.

EXAMPLE    **I** [nominative] **forgot to bring my** [possessive] **notebook with me** [objective].

## The Case Forms of Personal Pronouns

| Personal Pronouns | | | |
|---|---|---|---|
| | **Nominative Case** | **Objective Case** | **Possessive Case** |
| **Singular** | | | |
| **First Person** | I | me | my, mine |
| **Second Person** | you | you | your, yours |
| **Third Person** | he, she, it | him, her, it | his, her, hers, its |
| **Plural** | | | |
| **First Person** | we | us | our, ours |
| **Second Person** | you | you | your, yours |
| **Third Person** | they | them | their, theirs |

Notice that *you* and *it* have the same form in the nominative and the objective cases. All other personal pronouns have different nominative and objective forms.

## The Nominative Case

Nominative case pronouns—*I, you, he, she, it, we,* and *they*—are used as subjects of verbs and as predicate nominatives.

**18b.** The subject of a verb should be in the nominative case.

EXAMPLES    **I** told Phillip that **we** would win. [*I* is the subject of *told; we* is the subject of *would win.*]

Were **Renata** and **he** on time? [*Renata* and *he* are the compound subject of *were.*]

BORN LOSER reprinted by permission of Newspaper Enterprise Association, Inc.

**Reference Note**

For more about the **subjects of verbs,** see page 416.

## Oral Practice 1  Using Pronouns as Subjects

Read the following sentences aloud, stressing the italicized pronouns.

1. *He* and *I* agree that lacrosse is the most exciting game *we*'ve ever played.
2. *They* and their friends enjoyed the field trip.
3. Will Sue Ann and *she* enter the art contest?
4. Our teacher and *we* are glad that *he* and *she* are returning from their vacation soon.
5. *He* and *she* said that *we* were responsible for counting the ballots and posting the results.
6. Where are *they* and my parents?
7. Will *you* and *he* help us with the book sale?
8. When are *you* and *I* going to Arizona?

┌ T I P S & T R I C K S ┐

To choose the correct pronoun forms in a compound subject, try each pronoun separately with the verb.

EXAMPLE
(*She, Her*) and (*they, them*) answered the ad.
[*She answered* or *Her answered*? *They answered* or *Them answered*?]

**She** and **they** answered the ad.

USAGE

## Exercise 1  Identifying Pronouns Used as Subjects

The following paragraph contains ten pairs of pronouns in parentheses. For each pair, choose the correct pronoun to use as a subject.

EXAMPLE     **[1]** (*They, Them*) may be the most famous husband and wife scientist team ever.

1. *They*

Although Marie and Pierre Curie were both brilliant physicists, **[1]** (*she, her*) is better known than her husband is today. In fact, **[2]** (*I, me*) was genuinely surprised to learn that **[3]** (*them, they*), along with another scientist, shared the Nobel Prize in physics in 1903. **[4]** (*We, Us*) tend to remember only Marie primarily because **[5]** (*her, she*) was the first woman to win a Nobel Prize. During their life together, Marie Curie always felt that **[6]** (*her, she*) and Pierre were a team. Working in a small laboratory in Paris, **[7]** (*they, them*) didn't have room for independent research. Before his death in 1906, **[8]** (*them, they*) collaborated on almost every project. In 1911, **[9]** (*she, her*) was again honored by the Nobel committee when **[10]** (*she, her*) was awarded the prize in chemistry.

**Reference Note**

For more information about **predicate nominatives,** see page 430.

**S T Y L E    T I P**

Widespread usage has made such expressions as *It's me, That's him,* or *Could it have been her?* acceptable in informal conversation and writing. Avoid using them in formal speaking and in your written work unless you are writing notes, informal dialogue, or friendly letters.

**S T Y L E    T I P**

Sometimes pronouns such as *I, he, she, we,* and *they* sound awkward when used as parts of a compound subject. In such cases, it is a good idea to revise the sentence.

AWKWARD
She and we are going to the concert.

BETTER
**We** are going to the concert with **her.**

**18c.** A predicate nominative should be in the nominative case.

A *predicate nominative* is a word or word group in the predicate that identifies the subject or refers to it. A predicate nominative is connected to its subject by a linking verb. A pronoun used as a predicate nominative generally follows a form of the verb *be* or a phrase ending in *be* or *been.*

EXAMPLES    This is **he.**

Did you know that the pitcher was **she**?

**Oral Practice 2** **Using Pronouns as Predicate Nominatives**

Read the following sentences aloud, stressing the italicized pronouns.

**1.** Do you know whether it was *he*?
**2.** I thought it was *they.*
**3.** The winner of the marathon is *she.*
**4.** The ones you saw dancing were not *we.*
**5.** Can the valedictorian be *she*?
**6.** The first ones to arrive were *he* and *she.*
**7.** Do you think it may have been *they*?
**8.** The best speakers are *she* and I.

**Exercise 2** **Identifying Pronouns Used as Subjects and Predicate Nominatives**

Identify the correct pronoun in parentheses for each of the following sentences. Then, give its use in the sentence—as a *subject* or *predicate nominative.*

EXAMPLE    **1.** If the phone rings, it will probably be (*she, her*).

    *1. she—predicate nominative*

**1.** How did you know the guest speakers were (*they, them*)?
**2.** (*She, Her*) and (*he, him*) will move to San Miguel.
**3.** Open the door! It is (*I, me*)!
**4.** You and (*me, I*) are the only candidates left.
**5.** It was wonderful to hear that the winner was (*he, him*).
**6.** (*Us, We*) and (*them, they*) will meet at five o'clock.
**7.** That man looked a little like Harry, but it was not (*he, him*) after all.
**8.** Believe it or not, (*she, her*) was on the radio this morning.
**9.** Yes, the one in costume was really (*she, her*)!
**10.** You and (*we, us*) were the first visitors.

# The Objective Case

Objective case pronouns—*me, you, him, her, it, us,* and *them*—are used as direct objects, indirect objects, and objects of prepositions.

**18d.** A direct object should be in the objective case.

A ***direct object*** is a noun, pronoun, or word group that tells who or what receives the action of the verb or shows the result of the action.

EXAMPLES　　Phil called **her** last night. [*Her* tells *whom* Phil called.]

　　　　　　We still don't know what caused **them**. [*Them* shows the results of the action caused.]

**Oral Practice 3**　**Using Pronouns as Direct Objects**

Read the following sentences aloud, stressing the italicized pronouns.

1. They saw Liang and *me* at the fair.
2. Julia said that she recognized *him* and *me* at once.
3. Has anyone called *her* or *him* lately?
4. They took *us* to the reggae concert.
5. Alicia often visits Charlene and *her*.
6. A dog chased *her* and *me* out of the yard.
7. Within a few hours, the search party found Duane and *him*.
8. Did you ask *them* or *us*?

**Exercise 3**　**Choosing Pronouns Used as Direct Objects**

For each item below, write an appropriate pronoun in the objective case. Use a variety of pronouns. Do not use *you* or *it*.

EXAMPLE　　**1.** Have you told _____ yet?

　　　　　　*1. him*

1. I found Nina and _____ in the library.
2. Will you help _____ or _____ with their homework?
3. Sylvia Chu drove Candy and _____ to the movies.
4. We all watched Aaron and _____ as they ran the marathon.
5. These gloves fit both Carl and _____.
6. Did you tell _____ about the picnic?
7. If you don't call _____, I will.
8. The realtor showed _____ and _____ the apartment.
9. That solution suits _____.
10. The doctor cured _____.

## Reference Note

For more about the different types of **objects,** see page 431.

**S T Y L E　　T I P**

When the object is compound, try each pronoun separately with the verb. All parts of the compound must be correct for the sentence to be correct.

EXAMPLE

Phil's call surprised (*she, her*) and (*I, me*). [*Phil's call surprised she* or *Phil's call surprised her? It surprised I* or *It surprised me?*]

Phil's call surprised **her** and **me.**

USAGE

## TIPS & TRICKS

Generally, the indirect object comes between the verb and the direct object.

EXAMPLES
Grandma knitted **us** sweaters.

We gave **climbing the cliff** our full attention.

**18e.** An indirect object should be in the objective case.

An **indirect object** is a noun, pronoun, or word group that appears in sentences containing direct objects. An indirect object tells *to whom* or *to what* or *for whom* or *for what* the action of the verb is done.

EXAMPLES    Molly made **me** a tape. [*Me* tells *for whom* the tape was made.]

The puppies were muddy, so we gave **them** a bath. [*Them* tells *to what* we gave a bath.]

NOTE  Indirect objects do not follow prepositions. If a preposition such as *to* or *for* precedes an object, the object is an object of a preposition.

### Oral Practice 4  Using Pronouns as Indirect Objects

Read the following sentences aloud, stressing the italicized pronouns.

1. Mrs. Petratos offered *them* delicious moussaka.
2. Show Yolanda and *her* your snapshots of Chicago.
3. Sara made Dad and *me* mittens and matching scarves.
4. Send Tom and *him* your new address.
5. My parents told *her* and *me* the news.
6. Mrs. Morita gave *him* and *her* applications.
7. Tell Willie and *them* the story that you told Erin and *me*.
8. The judges awarded *us* the trophy.

### Exercise 4  Writing Pronouns Used as Indirect Objects

For each item below, write an appropriate pronoun in the objective case. Use a variety of pronouns. Do not use *you* or *it*.

EXAMPLE    **1.** The teacher gave _____ their homework assignments.

1. *them*

1. Hassan asked _____ the most difficult question.
2. Alex baked _____ a loaf of banana bread.
3. The teacher handed _____ and _____ the homework assignments.
4. Linda threw _____ the ball.
5. Mr. Young has never told _____ and _____ the real story.
6. Writing stories gives _____ great pleasure.
7. We brought _____ T-shirts from California.
8. Mr. Cruz sent _____ a pen as a graduation gift.
9. My little sister gave _____ an animal carved out of soap.
10. Lee's cousin knitted _____ a sweater.

**Review A** **Identifying Correct Forms of Pronouns**

Identify the correct pronoun in parentheses for each of the following sentences. Then, give its use in the sentence—as a *subject, predicate nominative, direct object,* or *indirect object.*

EXAMPLE     1. Brian and (*I, me*) visited the computer fair.

1. *I—subject*

1. A guide showed (*we, us*) the latest in technology.
2. She told Brian and (*I, me*) some interesting facts about software.
3. In a short time, we had surprised (*she, her*) and several bystanders with our new computer game.
4. The new computer aces were (*we, us*)!
5. Another guide showed Brian and (*I, me*) all kinds of robotic machines.
6. The guide said that (*he, him*) and his twin sister were going to dance with two robots.
7. The crowd and (*they, them*) seemed to enjoy the performance.
8. One robot reached out and touched (*us, we*) with a metal hand.
9. Brian and (*I, me*) asked our guides how the machines worked.
10. (*They, Them*) patiently explained the control panels.

**18f.** **An object of a preposition should be in the objective case.**

A noun or pronoun that follows a preposition is called the ***object of a preposition.*** Together, a preposition, its object, and any modifiers of that object make up a prepositional phrase.

EXAMPLES     with **me**          before **her**          next to **them**

for **us**          behind **him**          instead of **me**

NOTE   Many people use incorrect pronoun forms with prepositions. You may have heard phrases like *between he and they* and *for you and I.* These phrases are incorrect. The pronouns are objects of a preposition and should be in the objective case: *between him and them, for you and me.*

EXAMPLES     The coaches rode in a bus in front of **us.**

She is always very polite to **him** and **me.**

May I play soccer with **you** and **them**?

Between **you** and **me,** I am worried about **them.**

**Reference Note**

For a **list of common prepositions,** see page 400.

**T I P S** & **T R I C K S**

To determine the correct pronoun form when the object of a preposition is compound, try each pronoun separately in the prepositional phrase.

EXAMPLE

The company sent a letter to (*she, her*) and (*I, me*). [*To she* or *to her*? *To I* or *to me*?]

The company sent a letter to **her** and **me.**

Identify the ten personal pronouns in the following paragraph. If a pronoun is incorrect, write the correct form. If a pronoun is already correct, write *C*.

EXAMPLE **[1]** She thinks all of we should have the experience of working at a store checkout counter.

1. *She—C; we—us*

[1] Mrs. Jenkins, the home economics teacher that Tricia and me admire, told us all about the Universal Product Code (UPC) yesterday. [2] You and us have seen the black-striped UPC symbols on nearly everything that is for sale. [3] Mrs. Jenkins patiently showed the other classes and we how to interpret the twelve-digit number on the UPC. [4] Her explained to we that the first digit identifies the product, the next five digits stand for the manufacturer, the next five digits tell things about the product (such as color and size), and the last digit is a check number that tells the computer if another digit is incorrect. [5] Tricia said that Gregory and her found the lesson especially interesting. [6] The two of they had used the code when they worked as clerks in a store last summer.

# The Possessive Case

**18g.** The personal pronouns in the possessive case—*my, mine, your, yours, his, her, hers, its, our, ours, their, theirs*—are used to show ownership or possession.

**(1)** The possessive pronouns *mine, yours, his, hers, its, ours,* and *theirs* are used as parts of a sentence in the same ways in which the pronouns in the nominative and the objective cases are used.

| | |
|---|---|
| SUBJECT | Your car and **mine** need tune-ups. |
| PREDICATE NOMINATIVE | This backpack is **hers.** |
| DIRECT OBJECT | We finished **ours** yesterday. |
| INDIRECT OBJECT | Ms. Kwan gave **theirs** a quick review. |
| OBJECT OF PREPOSITION | Next to **yours,** my Siamese cat looks puny. |

**(2)** The possessive pronouns *my, your, his, her, its, our,* and *their* are used as adjectives before nouns.

EXAMPLES     **My** alarm clock is broken.

Do you know **their** address?

NOTE  Some authorities prefer to call these possessive forms adjectives. Follow your teacher's instructions regarding these words.

Generally, a noun or pronoun preceding a gerund should be in the possessive case.

**Reference Note**

For more about **gerunds**, see page 453.

EXAMPLES     We were all thrilled by **Ken's** scoring in the top 5 percent.
[*Ken's* modifies the gerund *scoring*. Whose scoring? *Ken's* scoring.]

We were all thrilled by **his** scoring in the top 5 percent.
[Whose scoring? *His* scoring.]

**Review C**  **Identifying Correct Forms of Pronouns**

Choose the correct pronoun from each pair given in parentheses in the following paragraph.

EXAMPLE     My cousin Felicia showed **[1]** (*I, me*) some photographs of buildings designed by I. M. Pei.

1.  *me*

Felicia, who is studying architecture, told **[1]** (*I, me*) a little about Pei. **[2]** (*He, Him*) is a famous American architect who was born in China. In 1935, **[3]** (*him, he*) came to the United States to study, and in 1954, **[4]** the government granted (*he, him*) citizenship. Pei's reputation grew quickly, and by the 1960s many people easily recognized the structures **[5]** (*he, him*) designed. His buildings, such as the East

DRABBLE reprinted by permission of United Feature Syndicate, Inc.

Building of the National Gallery of Art in Washington, D.C., are quite distinctive; consequently, many people greatly admire [6] (*they, them*). [7] (*Him, His*) being in charge of numerous projects in the United States, Europe, and Canada earned Pei an international reputation. Did you know that the architect of the glass pyramids at the Louvre is [8] (*him, he*)? Felicia doesn't like the pyramids because [9] (*they, them*) look so different from the buildings that surround them. However, I think that design of [10] (*him, his*) is a work of art.

**Review D** **Identifying Correct Pronoun Forms**

For each of the following sentences, choose the correct pronoun in parentheses. Then, give its use in the sentence—as a *subject, predicate nominative, direct object, indirect object,* or *object of the preposition.*

EXAMPLE    **1.** Did Alva or (*she, her*) leave a message?

    *1. she—subject*

**1.** The pranksters were (*they, them*).
**2.** (*He, Him*) and (*I, me*) are working on a special science project.
**3.** Is that package for Mom or (*I, me*)?
**4.** No one saw Otis or (*I, me*) behind the door.
**5.** I hope that you and (*she, her*) will be on time.
**6.** The teacher gave Rosa and (*I, me*) extra math homework.
**7.** That's (*he, him*) on the red bicycle.
**8.** Between you and (*I, me*), I like your plan better.
**9.** When are your parents and (*they, them*) coming home?
**10.** Everyone in the class except (*she, her*) and (*I, me*) had read the selection from the *Mahabharata.*

**Review E** **Identifying Correct Pronoun Forms**

For each sentence in the following paragraph, choose the correct pronoun in parentheses. Then, give its use in the sentence—as a *subject, predicate nominative, direct object, indirect object,* or *object of the preposition.*

EXAMPLE    You may not know [1] (*they, them*) by name, but you may remember the actors Ossie Davis and Ruby Dee from movies or television shows.

    *1. them—direct object*

For many years, the actors Ossie Davis and Ruby Dee have entertained [1] (*we, us*) fans of movies and television with their talented performances. My friend Elvin and [2] (*me, I*) really admire both of [3] (*they, them*). Did you know that [4] (*they, them*) have been married since 1948? When Davis worked on Broadway, [5] (*he, him*) wrote and starred in *Purlie Victorious*, and critics gave [6] (*he, him*) great reviews. In addition, [7] (*him, he*) has appeared on the TV show *Evening Shade*. One of the stars of the movie *The Jackie Robinson Story* was [8] (*she, her*). What Elvin and [9] (*me, I*) admire most about Davis and Dee is that [10] (*them, they*) are fine performers who actively support civil rights and other humanitarian causes.

# Special Pronoun Problems

## *Who* and *Whom*

| Nominative Case | | Objective Case | |
|---|---|---|---|
| who | whoever | whom | whomever |

**18h.** The use of *who* or *whom* in a subordinate clause depends on how the pronoun functions in the clause.

When you are choosing between *who* or *whom* in a subordinate clause, follow these steps:

STEP 1    Find the subordinate clause.

STEP 2    Decide how the pronoun is used in the clause—as a subject, a predicate nominative, a direct or indirect object, or an object of a preposition.

STEP 3    Determine the case of the pronoun according to the rules of formal standard English.

STEP 4    Select the correct form of the pronoun.

EXAMPLE    Do you know (*who, whom*) she is?

STEP 1    The subordinate clause is (*who, whom*) *she is.*

STEP 2    The pronoun (*who, whom*) is the predicate nominative: *she is who.*

STEP 3    As a predicate nominative, the pronoun is in the nominative case.

STEP 4    The nominative form is *who.*

ANSWER    Do you know **who** she is?

USAGE

STYLE     TIP

In informal English, the use of *whom* is becoming less common. In fact, when you are in informal situations, you may correctly begin any question with *who* regardless of the grammar of the sentence. In formal English, however, you should distinguish between *who* and *whom*.

**Reference Note**

For information on **subordinate clauses,** see page 471.

STYLE     TIP

Frequently, *whom* in subordinate clauses is omitted, but its use is understood.

EXAMPLE

The people (*whom*) you imitate are your role models.

Leaving out *whom* tends to make writing sound informal. In formal situations, it is generally better to include *whom*.

## TIPS & TRICKS

In the example on the previous page, the entire clause *who she is* is used as a direct object of the verb *do know.* However, the way the pronoun is used within the clause—as a predicate nominative—is what determines the correct case form.

EXAMPLE   Susan B. Anthony, about (who, whom) Sam reported, championed women's right to vote.

STEP 1   The subordinate clause is *about (who, whom) Sam reported.*

STEP 2   The subject is *Sam,* and the verb is *reported.* The pronoun is the object of the preposition *about: Sam reported about (who, whom).*

STEP 3   The objective of a preposition is in the objective case.

STEP 4   The objective form is *whom.*

ANSWER   Susan B. Anthony, about **whom** Sam reported, championed women's right to vote.

### Oral Practice 5   Using the Pronouns *Who* and *Whom* in Subordinate Clauses

Read each of the following sentences aloud, stressing the italicized pronouns.

1. Take this book to Eric, *whom* you met yesterday.
2. Mr. Cohen is the man *who* lives next door to us.
3. Can you tell me *who* they are?
4. Toni Morrison is an author *whom* many readers admire.
5. *Whom* Mona finally voted for is a secret.
6. The coach will penalize anyone *who* misses the bus.
7. *Whoever* wins the race will get a prize.
8. The woman to *whom* I was speaking is conducting a survey of people who ride the bus.

### Exercise 5   Classifying Pronouns Used in Subordinate Clauses and Identifying Correct Forms

For each of the following sentences, choose the correct pronoun in parentheses. Then, give its use in the sentence—as a *subject, predicate nominative, direct object, indirect object,* or *object of a preposition.*

EXAMPLE   1. I know (who, whom) you are.

1. who—predicate nominative

1. Mrs. James, (who, whom) I work for, owns a pet shop in the mall and a feed store in our town.

**2.** Is there anyone here (*who, whom*) needs a bus pass?

**3.** She is the only one (*who, whom*) everybody trusts.

**4.** Both of the women (*who, whom*) ran for seats on the city council were elected.

**5.** I helped Mr. Thompson, (*who, whom*) was painting his garage and shingling his porch roof.

**6.** Eileen couldn't guess (*who, whom*) the secret agent was.

**7.** It was Octavio Paz (*who, whom*) won the Nobel Prize in literature in 1990.

**8.** Her grandmother, to (*who, whom*) she sent the flowers, won the over-fifty division of the marathon.

**9.** The person (*who, whom*) you gave the daisies is none other than my long-lost twin!

**10.** Shirley Chisholm, (*who, whom*) we are studying in history class, was the first African American woman elected to Congress.

# Appositives

**18i. A pronoun used as an appositive is in the same case as the word to which it refers.**

An *appositive* is a noun or pronoun placed next to another noun or pronoun to identify or describe it.

EXAMPLES    The winners—**he, she,** and **I**—thanked the committee. [The pronouns are in the nominative case because they are used as appositives of the subject, *winners*.]

The teacher introduced the speakers, Laura and **me.** [The pronoun is in the objective case because it is used as an appositive of the direct object, *speakers*.]

NOTE  Sometimes a pronoun is followed by an appositive that indentifies or describes the pronoun. The case of the pronoun is not affected by the appositive.

EXAMPLES    **We** soloists will rehearse next week. [The pronoun is in the nominative case because it is the subject of the sentence. The appositive *soloists* identifies *We*.]

Give **us** girls a turn to bat. [The pronoun is in the objective case because it is the indirect object of the verb *Give*. The appositive *girls* identifies *us*.]

**Reference Note**

For more about **appositives,** see page 461.

TIPS & TRICKS

To determine the correct form for a pronoun used with an appositive or as an appositive, read the sentence with only the pronoun.

EXAMPLE
(*We, Us*) scouts offered to help. [*We offered to help* or *Us offered to help*? *We offered to help* is correct.]

**We** scouts offered to help.

**Identifying Correct Pronoun Forms as Appositives and with Appositives**

For each of the following sentences, give the correct form of the pronoun in parentheses.

EXAMPLE    **1.** The principal named the winners, Julia and (*I, me*).

1. *me*

1. The coach showed (*we, us*) girls the new uniforms.
2. Our friends, (*she, her*) and Lucas, made the refreshments.
3. All of the class saw it except three people—Floyd, Ada, and (*I, me*).
4. Mrs. López hired (*we, us*) boys for the summer.
5. (*We, Us*) girls are excellent chess players.
6. Kiole listed her three favorite actors: Leonardo DiCaprio, Cuba Gooding, Jr., and (*he, him*).
7. Come to the game with (*we, us*) hometown fans, and you'll have a better time.
8. The best singers in school may be the quartet, Ellen and (*they, them*).
9. I want to go to the concert with two friends, Iola and (*he, him*).
10. The librarian gave the best readers, Craig and (*I, me*), two books by our favorite authors.

**Review F** **Identifying Correct Pronoun Forms**

For each of the following sentences, choose the correct pronoun in parentheses. Then, give its use in the sentence—as a *subject, predicate nominative, direct object, indirect object, object of a preposition* or an *appositive.*

EXAMPLE    **1.** The cyclist gave (*we, us*) a smile as she rode past.

1. *us—indirect object*

1. Students (*who, whom*) want to help organize the Kamehameha Day celebration should speak to Kai or me.
2. Give these magazines to (*whoever, whomever*) wants them.
3. Don't (*they, them*) know that (*we, us*) students do our best?
4. The candidates, Ralph and (*he, him*), will speak at the rally tomorrow.
5. The Earth Day planners from our community are (*they, them*).
6. Len and (*I, me*) had planned to watch the laser light show together.
7. Will you pass (*I, me*) the dictionary, please?
8. Céline Dion, (*who, whom*) I saw in concert, sings many songs that (*I, me*) like.

9. It would be a great help to (*we, us*) beginners if (*they, them*) would give us more time.

10. Visiting Australia is an exciting opportunity for Clay and (*she, her*).

**Review G** **Identifying Correct Pronoun Forms**

Choose the correct pronoun from each pair in parentheses in the following paragraph.

EXAMPLE     [1] My sister Angela is one of many women in our society (*who, whom*) use makeup.

        1. who

The use of makeup to enhance beauty has a longer history than most of [1] (*we, us*) might imagine. In fact, [2] (*we, us*) cosmetic historians must look back to ancient times for the origins of makeup. For example, heavy, black eye makeup was worn by the ancient Egyptians, [3] (*who, whom*) originally used it as protection from reflected sunlight. It was they [4] (*who, whom*) first lined their eyes with a dark liquid called *kohl,* which [5] (*they, them*) applied with a small wooden or ivory stick. During the reign of Queen Nefertiti, [6] (*she, her*) and her noblewomen used not only *kohl* but other cosmetics as well. To [7] (*they, them*), dark, heavily made-up eyes and red lips were the marks of beauty. European nobles in the Middle Ages and the Renaissance wanted to emphasize their pale skin, so [8] (*them, they*) dusted their faces with chalk-white powder. It was Queen Elizabeth I, an English monarch, [9] (*who, whom*) set this style in her court. Although we might think that [10] (*them, they*) look strange today, both Nefertiti and Queen Elizabeth I were fashionable in their times.

USAGE

# The Pronoun in an Incomplete Construction

**18j.** After *than* and *as* introducing an incomplete construction, use the form of the pronoun that would be correct if the construction were completed.

Notice how pronouns change the meaning of sentences with incomplete constructions.

EXAMPLES    Everyone knows that you like Jolene much better than **I** [like Jolene].

Everyone knows that you like Jolene much better than [you like] **me.**

Did you help Ira as well as **they** [helped Ira]?

Did you help Ira as well as [you helped] **them**?

## Exercise 7  Completing Incomplete Constructions and Classifying Pronoun Forms

Beginning with *than* or *as*, write the understood clause for each sentence, using the correct form of the pronoun. Then, tell whether the pronoun in the completed clause is a *subject* or an *object*.

EXAMPLE    **1.** Did the noise bother you as much as (*she, her*).

    *1.  as the noise bothered her—object*

        *or*

    *as she bothered you—subject*

**1.** Justin throws a football better than (*I, me*).
**2.** The story mystified him as much as (*we, us*).
**3.** Is your sister older than (*he, him*)?
**4.** Have they studied as long as (*we, us*)?
**5.** We have known him longer than (*she, her*).
**6.** Are you more creative than (*he, him*)?
**7.** Did you read as much as (*I, me*)?
**8.** I like René better than (*they, them*).
**9.** Many people are less fortunate than (*we, us*).
**10.** Are you as optimistic as (*she, her*)?
**11.** After winning the city championship, there were no girls happier than (*they, them*).
**12.** When did you become taller than (*I, me*)?
**13.** Mary has collected more coins than (*he, him*).

USAGE

—HELP—
Some items in Exercise 7 may have more than one correct answer.

14. Do you like cantaloupe as much as (*she, her*)?
15. This label says the toy is not safe for a child as young as (*he, him*).
16. When you serve dessert, don't serve yourself more than (*he, him*).
17. Can he really play saxophone as well as (*I, me*)?
18. To win the contest, you must do as many sit-ups as (*she, her*).
19. I'm shocked that you gave her a nicer card than (*I, me*)!
20. Daniel doesn't visit his relatives as often as (*she, her*).

# Clear Pronoun Reference

**18k.** A pronoun should refer clearly to its antecedent.

**(1)** An *ambiguous reference* occurs when any one of two or more words can be a pronoun's antecedent.

| | |
|---|---|
| AMBIGUOUS | My uncle called my brother after he won the marathon. [Who won the marathon, my uncle or my brother?] |
| CLEAR | After my brother won the marathon, my uncle called him. |
| CLEAR | After my uncle won the marathon, he called my brother. |

**(2)** A *general reference* is the use of a pronoun that refers to a general idea rather than to a specific antecedent.

The pronouns commonly found in general-reference errors are *it, that, this, such,* and *which.*

| | |
|---|---|
| GENERAL | The ski jumper faces tough competition and a grueling schedule, but she says that doesn't worry her. |
| CLEAR | The ski jumper faces tough competition and a grueling schedule, but she says these problems don't worry her. |

**(3)** A *weak reference* occurs when a pronoun refers to an antecedent that has been suggested but not expressed.

| | |
|---|---|
| WEAK | Paul likes many of the photographs I have taken; he thinks I should choose this as my profession. |
| CLEAR | Paul likes many of the photographs I have taken; he thinks I should choose photography as my profession. |

**(4)** An *indefinite reference* is the use of a pronoun that refers to no particular person or thing and that is unnecessary to the meaning of the sentence.

| | |
|---|---|
| INDEFINITE | In the book it explains how cells divide. |
| CLEAR | The book explains how cells divide. |

S T Y L E     T I P

Familiar expressions such as *it is raining, it seems as though . . . ,* and *it's early* are correct even though they contain inexact pronoun references.

**Exercise 8** **Correcting Inexact Pronoun References**

Revise each of the following sentences, correcting each inexact pronoun reference.

EXAMPLE    **1.** Have you ever been physically unable to prepare a meal for yourself? That can be a serious problem.

*1. Being physically unable to prepare a meal for yourself can be a serious problem.*

1. Older persons, people with disabilities, and people who are ill sometimes cannot prepare meals for themselves, which is when Meals on Wheels can help.
2. Meals on Wheels is an organization in which they arrange to have meals delivered to people's homes.
3. Because it is a nonprofit organization, Meals on Wheels has a limited budget, which is why it relies on volunteers.
4. Many businesses, churches, clubs, and organizations supply volunteers, and they contribute money.
5. People who receive services provided by Meals on Wheels usually help to pay for these services, but it's voluntary and based on a person's ability to pay.
6. In some Meals on Wheels organizations, they offer clients a variety of other services in addition to delivering meals.
7. Grocery shopping is a service provided to clients by volunteers who purchase and then deliver them.
8. Some clients depend on volunteers for rides when they have appointments and errands to run.
9. To lift their spirits, some volunteers regularly call clients on the phone; other volunteers help clients by performing minor home safety repairs.
10. Volunteers not only provide needed services but also often form personal bonds with their clients; that is why you may want to volunteer at a local Meals on Wheels.

# Chapter Review

## A. Identifying Correct Forms of Pronouns

For each of the following sentences, choose the correct form of the pronoun or pronouns in parentheses.

1. Janell and (*I, me*) painted the room together.
2. Alan, for (*who, whom*) I did the typing, said that he would pay me on Friday.
3. The young Amish couple drove us and (*they, them*) into town in a horse-drawn buggy.
4. Carolyn has been playing the guitar longer than (*she, her*).
5. The last two people to arrive, Tranh and (*me, I*), had trouble finding the skating rink.
6. Hector wrote this song for you and (*I, me*).
7. The winner is (*whoever, whomever*) finishes first.
8. Ellis was worried about his project, but Ms. Atkinson gave (*he, him*) an A.
9. Was the winner of the race (*he, him*) or Aaron?
10. The pictures of the Grand Canyon made a greater impression on the Rileys than on (*we, us*).
11. To (*who, whom*) did you speak?
12. Schuyler and (*she, her*) will lead the group sing-along.
13. Imagine my surprise when I saw Todd Franklin sitting behind Kenan and (*I, me*) in the theater.
14. The most productive employees at the plant were (*they, them*).
15. He was going to have dinner with (*her and me, she and I*), but fog delayed his departure from New York.
16. The prince knew precisely (*who, whom*) to appoint as his chamberlain.
17. Stanislas and Tina were at a Pulaski Day parade in Chicago, and I saw (*they, them*) there on the television news.
18. The ferret, annoyed at being woken up, bit (*she, her*) on the arm.
19. Why don't you come to the play with Carrie and (*I, me*)?
20. The first one to arrive was (*she, her*).

## B. Proofreading a Paragraph for Correct Pronoun Forms

Some of the sentences in the following paragraph contain a pronoun that has been used incorrectly. If a pronoun is incorrect, write the correct form. If the sentence is already correct, write *C*.

[21] Do you grow as many plants as me? [22] Nowadays, scientists are hard at work trying to develop blue roses for us plant enthusiasts. [23] My science teacher, Ms. Phillips, and me wonder whether they can do so. [24] She doubts even more than me that breeding a blue rose is possible. [25] Us modern rose-lovers have never seen a blue rose. [26] However, Ms. Phillips and me learned that an Arab agriculturist in the thirteenth century once grew one. [27] For centuries, rose breeders whom have tried to produce the legendary blue rose have failed. [28] Some genetic engineers that I read about are working on this project now. [29] Scientists aren't sure whom would buy a blue rose. [30] Still, like you and I, they can't resist a challenge.

## C. Identifying Pronouns Used as Subjects and Objects

For each of the following sentences, give the correct form of the pronoun or pronouns in parentheses. Then, tell whether each pronoun is in *nominative* case or *objective* case.

**31.** Dr. Schultz sang to the birthday brothers, Otto and (*I, me*).
**32.** Ms. Vlatkin showed (*we, us*) how to dance a *pas de deux.*
**33.** (*Him and her, He and she*), the brother-and-sister team, were the first archaeologists present at the opening of the royal tomb.
**34.** They went on the trip with their cousins, Jin-Hua and (*he, him*).
**35.** The last remaining contestants—(*she and they, her and them*)— walked in silence to the podium.
**36.** (*We, Us*) students at King High are very proud of our football team.
**37.** The teacher gave the best students, (*her and him, she and he*), a commendation.
**38.** I thought they should give (*we, us*) junior actors a chance to shine.
**39.** Rosa mentioned her favorite Tejano musicians, Emilio, David Lee Garza, and (*he, him*).
**40.** With regard to the Garcia twins, Blair said the best way to tell (*they, them*) apart was to make them laugh.

## D. Correcting Unclear Pronoun Reference

Revise each of the following sentences, correcting each unclear pronoun reference.

**41.** Sally called Carla while she was doing her homework.
**42.** The ship's captain explained to the passenger the meaning of the announcement he had just made.
**43.** Police Sergeant Molloy's daily assignments involve hard work and a certain amount of risk, but he claims that it doesn't bother him.
**44.** Jill is impressed by Jeff's track-and-field records. She thinks he should do it professionally.
**45.** On the radio it said that afternoon thunderstorms were likely.

# Writing Application
## Using Pronouns in a Magazine Article

**Using Correct Case Forms**  You and three of your friends are planetary explorers. Write a magazine article about your exploration of Mars. Use a variety of pronouns as subjects, predicate nominatives, direct objects, indirect objects, and objects of prepositions.

**Prewriting**  To get started, jot down what you know about space travel and astronomy. You could get additional ideas from books and magazine articles about Mars. Think of things that a person might see or do while exploring that planet.

**Writing**  As you write your first draft, be sure to include details that draw your reader into the story.

**Revising**  Ask a classmate to read your story. Should you add or delete any details? Using your classmate's suggestions, revise your story to make it clearer and more entertaining.

**Publishing**  Do your pronouns clearly show who did what? As you check over the grammar, spelling, and punctuation of your story, make sure that all of your pronouns are in the correct case. With your teacher's permission, you may want to post the story on your class bulletin board or create a Web page for it on the Internet.

# Using Modifiers Correctly

## Comparison and Placement

## Diagnostic Preview

### A. Correcting Modifiers

The following sentences contain dangling modifiers, misplaced modifiers, and mistakes in comparisons. Revise each sentence so that it is clear and correct.

┌─HELP─
A sentence in
the Diagnostic Preview
may contain more than
one error.

EXAMPLE 1. When traveling through Scotland, I discovered that stories about monsters were more popular than any kind of story.

1. *When traveling through Scotland, I discovered that stories about monsters were more popular than any other kind of story.*

1. Having received a great deal of publicity, I had already read several articles about the so-called Loch Ness monster.
2. One article described how a young veterinary student spotted the monster who was named Arthur Grant.
3. While cycling on a road near the shore of Loch Ness one day, Grant came upon the most strangest creature he had ever seen.
4. Cycling closer, the monster took a leap and plunged into the lake.
5. Numerous theories have been discussed about the origin and identity of the monster in the local newspapers.

6. Of all the proposed theories, the better and more fascinating one was that the monster must be a freshwater species of sea serpent.

7. Having found a huge, dead creature on the shore of the lake in 1942, the mystery of the monster was thought to be solved finally.

8. One famous photograph of the monster has recently been revealed to be a hoax that seemed to confirm the creature's existence.

9. Skeptical, stories about the Loch Ness monster have always struck some people as unbelievable.

10. However, reported sightings of the monster have continued, perhaps more than of any mysterious creature.

## B. Using Modifiers Correctly in Sentences

Most of the following sentences have mistakes in the use of modifiers. Revise each incorrect sentence to correct these errors. If a sentence is already correct, write *C*.

EXAMPLE    **1.** In the United States, is the use of solar energy more commoner than the use of geothermal energy?

       *1. In the United States, is the use of solar energy more common than the use of geothermal energy?*

11. Kay has a better understanding of both solar and geothermal energy than anyone I know.

12. Yoko isn't sure she agrees with me, but I have talked with Kay more than Yoko.

13. Kay thinks that, of the two, solar energy is the best method for generating power.

14. She claims that the energy from the sun will soon be easier to harness than geothermal energy.

15. Arguing that the sun's energy could also be less expensive to use, Kay says that more research into solar energy is needed.

16. Yoko disagrees and thinks that geothermal energy would provide more cheaper power than solar energy.

17. She told me that for centuries people in other countries have been using geothermal energy, such as Iceland and Japan.

18. However, she added that geothermal energy is less well known than any source of power in our country.

19. Although infrequently used in the United States, Yoko feels that geothermal energy has already proven itself to be safe and efficient.

20. Unconvinced, both points of view seem to me to offer promising new sources of energy.

┌HELP─
Although some sentences in Part B of the Diagnostic Preview can be correctly revised in more than one way, you need to give only one revision.

USAGE

# What Is a Modifier?

A *modifier* is a word or word group that makes the meaning of another word or word group more specific. The two kinds of modifiers are *adjectives* and *adverbs*.

## One-Word Modifiers

### Adjectives

**19a.** An adjective makes the meaning of a noun or pronoun more specific.

**Reference Note**

For more about **adjectives,** see page 382. For more about **adverbs,** see page 393.

EXAMPLES    Samia gave a **broad** smile. [The adjective *broad* makes the meaning of the noun *smile* more specific.]

**Only** she knows the answer. [The adjective *only* makes the meaning of the pronoun *she* more specific.]

The sweater is **soft** and **warm.** [The adjectives *soft* and *warm* make the meaning of the noun *sweater* more specific.]

Isn't he a **well-mannered** boy? [The compound adjective *well-mannered* makes the meaning of the noun *boy* more specific.]

### Adverbs

**19b.** An adverb makes the meaning of a verb, an adjective, or another adverb more specific.

EXAMPLES    Samia grinned **broadly.** [The adverb *broadly* makes the meaning of the verb *grinned* more specific.]

**Sometimes** I wonder about the future. [The adverb *sometimes* makes the meaning of the verb *wonder* more specific.]

The dog is **very** hungry. [The adverb *very* makes the meaning of the adjective *hungry* more specific.]

The alarm rang **surprisingly** loudly. [The adverb *surprisingly* makes the meaning of the adverb *loudly* more specific.]

### Adjective or Adverb?

While many adverbs end in *–ly,* others do not. Furthermore, not all words with the *–ly* ending are adverbs. Some adjectives also end in *–ly.*

Therefore, you can't tell whether a word is an adjective or an adverb simply by looking for the *–ly* ending. To decide whether a word is an adjective or an adverb, determine how the word is used in the sentence.

| Adverbs Not Ending in *–ly* | | |
| --- | --- | --- |
| broadcast **soon** | return **home** | run **loose** |
| **not** sleepy | stand **here** | **very** happy |

| Adjectives Ending in *–ly* | | |
| --- | --- | --- |
| **elderly** people | **only** child | **silly** behavior |
| **curly** hair | **holy** building | **lonely** person |

Some words can be used as either adjectives or adverbs.

| Adjectives | Adverbs |
| --- | --- |
| She is an **only** child. | She has **only** one brother. |
| Tina has a **fast** car. | The car goes **fast.** |
| We caught the **last** train. | We left **last.** |

**19c.** If a word in the predicate modifies the subject of the verb, use the adjective form. If it modifies the verb, use the adverb form.

| | |
| --- | --- |
| ADJECTIVE | The gazelles were **graceful.** [*Graceful* modifies *gazelles.*] |
| ADVERB | The gazelles moved **gracefully.** [*Gracefully* modifies *moved.*] |

| | |
| --- | --- |
| ADJECTIVE | The boy grew **tall.** [*Tall* modifies *boy.*] |
| ADVERB | The boy grew **quickly.** [*Quickly* modifies *grew.*] |

**Reference Note**

For more about **subjects** and **predicates,** see page 414.

# Phrases Used as Modifiers

Like one-word modifiers, phrases can also be used as adjectives and adverbs.

| | |
| --- | --- |
| EXAMPLES | It was time **for celebration.** [The prepositional phrase *for celebration* acts as an adjective that modifies the noun *time.*] |
| | **Uprooting trees and bushes,** the tornado swept across the Panhandle. [The participial phrase *Uprooting trees and bushes* acts as an adjective that modifies the noun *tornado.*] |

**Reference Note**

For more about different **kinds of phrases,** see page 442.

Professor Martinez is the one **to ask.** [The infinitive phrase *to ask* acts as an adjective that modifies the pronoun *one*.]

Ray is becoming quite good **at soccer.** [The prepositional phrase *at soccer* acts as an adverb that modifies the adjective *good.*]

Walk **with care on icy pavements.** [The prepositional phrases *with care* and *on icy pavements* act as adverbs that modify the verb *Walk.*]

The guide spoke slowly enough **to be understood.** [The infinitive phrase *to be understood* acts as an adverb that modifies the adverb *enough.*]

# Clauses Used as Modifiers

Like words and phrases, clauses can also be used as adjectives and adverbs.

EXAMPLES    Vermeer is the painter **that I like best.** [The adjective clause *that I like best* modifies the noun *painter.*]

**Before Toni left for work,** she took the dog for a walk. [The adverb clause *Before Toni left for work* modifies the verb *took.*]

**Reference Note**

For more about **clauses,** see Chapter 15.

USAGE

( Exercise 1 ) **Identifying Modifiers**

Identify the italicized word or word group in each of the following sentences as a *modifier* or *not a modifier.*

EXAMPLES    1. Rudyard Kipling, *who was born in India,* wrote a wonderful story about a brave mongoose.
            1. *modifier*

            2. The mongoose's *name* was Rikki-tikki-tavi.
            2. *not a modifier*

| Link to | Literature |

1. Rikki-tikki was adopted by a *very* kind family.
2. The family fed him meat and bananas and *boiled* eggs.
3. *Like all mongooses,* Rikki-tikki was always curious.
4. While exploring the garden, he *heard* Darzee and his wife, the tailorbirds, crying in their nest.
5. One of their babies had fallen out *of the nest* and been eaten by a cobra.
6. Rikki-tikki had to protect his family and friends *against the snakes.*

7. Mongooses and snakes are *natural* enemies.
8. Rikki-tikki overheard *two* cobras planning to kill the family.
9. He attacked the first cobra *while it was waiting for the father to come into the room.*
10. The second *cobra* dragged Rikki-tikki down a hole in the ground, but Rikki-tikki killed the snake and came out alive.

# Eight Troublesome Modifiers

## *Bad* and *Badly*

*Bad* is an adjective. In most uses, *badly* is an adverb.

ADJECTIVE    The dog was **bad.**
ADVERB    The dog behaved **badly.**

Remember that a word that modifies the subject of a verb should be in adjective form.

NONSTANDARD    The stew tasted badly.
STANDARD    The stew tasted **bad.**

NOTE In informal situations, *bad* or *badly* is acceptable after *feel.*

INFORMAL    He feels **badly** about the incident.
FORMAL    He feels **bad** about the incident.

## *Good* and *Well*

*Good* is an adjective. It should not be used to modify a verb.

NONSTANDARD    He speaks Italian good.
STANDARD    He speaks Italian **well.**
STANDARD    His Italian sounds **good.** [*Good* is an adjective that modifies the noun *Italian.*]

*Well* may be used either as an adjective or as an adverb. As an adjective, *well* has two meanings: "in good health" and "satisfactory."

EXAMPLES    John is **well.** [John is in good health.]

All is **well.** [All is satisfactory.]

As an adverb, *well* means "capably."

EXAMPLE    They did **well** in the tryouts.

# *Slow* and *Slowly*

*Slow* is used as both an adjective and an adverb.

EXAMPLES    We took a **slow** drive through the countryside. [*Slow* is an adjective modifying the noun *drive.*]

Go **slow.** [*Slow* is an adverb modifying the verb *Go.*]

*Slowly* is an adverb. In most adverb uses, it is better to use *slowly* than to use *slow.*

EXAMPLES    The train **slowly** came to a stop.

Drive **slowly** on slippery roads.

# *Real* and *Really*

*Real* is an adjective meaning "actual" or "genuine." *Really* is an adverb meaning "actually" or "truly." Although *real* is commonly used as an adverb meaning "very" in everyday situations, avoid using it as an adverb in formal speaking and writing.

INFORMAL    He batted real well in the game.

FORMAL    He batted **really** well in the game.

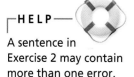

┌─**HELP**─

A sentence in Exercise 2 may contain more than one error.

## Exercise 2    Revising Sentences with Modifier Errors

Most of the following sentences contain at least one error in modifier usage. If a sentence contains an error, revise the sentence with the correct modifier. If a sentence is already correct, write *C.*

EXAMPLE    **1.** The ball was thrown so bad it went over the fence.

    *1. The ball was thrown so badly it went over the fence.*

**1.** You have done very good today, Marcia.
**2.** The nurse shark was moving very slow over the seabed.
**3.** The fireworks exploded with a real loud bang.
**4.** The team did not play badly, but they lost anyway.
**5.** James thinks that Jakob Dylan is a well singer.
**6.** The box was not damaged too bad when it fell.
**7.** The turtle is very slowly on land, but it is much faster underwater.
**8.** Is that really Sammy Sosa's autograph?
**9.** Even if your day is going bad, getting angry at me will not help.
**10.** Slowly but surely, the fawn improved until it could run real good.

USAGE

# Comparison of Modifiers

**19d.** Modifiers change form to show comparison.

There are three degrees of comparison: *positive, comparative,* and *superlative.*

| Positive | Comparative | Superlative |
|---|---|---|
| young | younger | youngest |
| fearful | more fearful | most fearful |
| rapidly | more rapidly | most rapidly |
| good | better | best |

## Regular Comparison

**(1)** Most one-syllable modifiers form the comparative degree by adding *–er* and the superlative degree by adding *–est.*

| Positive | Comparative | Superlative |
|---|---|---|
| large | larger | largest |
| deep | deeper | deepest |

**(2)** Two-syllable modifiers may form the comparative degree by adding *–er* or by using *more.* They may form the superlative degree by adding *–est* or by using *most.*

| Positive | Comparative | Superlative |
|---|---|---|
| wealthy | wealthier | wealthiest |
| lovely | lovelier | loveliest |
| rapid | more rapid | most rapid |
| softly | more softly | most softly |
| common | commoner | commonest |
| | *or* | *or* |
| | more common | most common |

**Reference Note**

For guidelines on **how to spell comparative and superlative forms** correctly, see page 735.

| S T Y L E | T I P |

Most two-syllable modifiers can form their comparative and superlative forms either way. If adding *–er* or *–est* makes a word sound awkward, use *more* or *most* instead.

| AWKWARD | frugaler |
|---|---|
| BETTER | more frugal |
| AWKWARD | rapidest |
| BETTER | most rapid |

USAGE

Write the comparative and superlative forms of the following words.

EXAMPLE    **1.** bright

    *1. brighter, brightest*

**1.** fast      **3.** happy      **5.** simple      **7.** safe      **9.** calm
**2.** soon      **4.** careful    **6.** hazy       **8.** wisely    **10.** pretty

**(3)** Modifiers that have three or more syllables form the comparative degree by using *more* and the superlative degree by using *most*.

| Positive | Comparative | Superlative |
|----------|-------------|-------------|
| energetic | more energetic | most energetic |
| significantly | more significantly | most significantly |

**(4)** To show a decrease in the qualities they express, modifiers
form the comparative degree by using *less* and the superlative
degree by using *least*.

| Positive | Comparative | Superlative |
|----------|-------------|-------------|
| helpful | less helpful | least helpful |
| frequently | less frequently | least frequently |

## Irregular Comparison

The comparative and superlative degrees of some modifiers are irregular in form.

| Positive | Comparative | Superlative |
|----------|-------------|-------------|
| bad | worse | worst |
| good/well | better | best |
| many/much | more | most |
| far | further/farther | furthest/farthest |
| little | less | least |

**STYLE    TIP**

The word *little* also has
regular comparative and
superlative forms: *littler,
littlest.* These forms are
used to describe physical
size (the **littlest** puppy).
The forms *less* and *least* are
used to describe an amount
(**less** homework).

NOTE   Do not add *–er* / *–est* or *more* / *most* to irregularly compared
forms. For example, use *worse,* not *worser* or *more worse.*

## Exercise 4  Using Comparative and Superlative Forms

In the blank in each of the following sentences, write the correct form of the modifier in italics.

EXAMPLE    *little*    **1.** Both pairs of jeans are on sale, but I will buy the _____ expensive pair.

1. *less*

**1.** *well*    I can skate _____ now than I could last year.
**2.** *many*    She caught the _____ fish of anyone in our group that day.
**3.** *bad*    That is the _____ movie I have ever seen.
**4.** *much*    We have _____ homework today than we had all last week.
**5.** *good*    Felicia has the _____ attendance record of anyone.
**6.** *many*    Are there _____ plays than poems in your literature book?
**7.** *good*    Tyrone is the _____ pitcher on our baseball team this year.
**8.** *much*    Of the three groups of volunteers, our group cleaned up the _____ litter.
**9.** *bad*    My notebook looks _____ than Joshua's.
**10.** *little*    I have _____ time to finish than he does.

## Review A  Writing Comparative and Superlative Forms

Write the comparative and superlative forms of the following modifiers. Do not include decreasing comparisons.

EXAMPLE    **1.** meaningful

1. *more meaningful, most meaningful*

| | | | |
|---|---|---|---|
| **1.** bad | **6.** loose | **11.** far | **16.** much |
| **2.** good | **7.** well | **12.** special | **17.** unlikely |
| **3.** early | **8.** noisy | **13.** happily | **18.** elaborate |
| **4.** many | **9.** patiently | **14.** eager | **19.** quiet |
| **5.** fuzzy | **10.** graceful | **15.** sleepy | **20.** rich |

## Exercise 5  Proofreading Sentences for Correct Comparative and Superlative Forms

Identify the comparative and superlative modifiers in the following sentences. If the form of a modifier is incorrect or awkward, write the correct form. If the form is already correct, write *C*.

┌HELP┐

A dictionary will tell you when a word forms its comparative or superlative form in some way other than by adding –er / –est or more / most. Look in a dictionary if you are not sure whether a word has irregular comparative or superlative forms or whether you need to change the spelling of a word before adding –er or –est.

EXAMPLE  1. The Romany make up one of Europe's interestingest cultures.

1. *interestingest—most interesting*

1. The Romany, also known as Gypsies, are commonlier found in Eastern Europe than anywhere else in the world.
2. Although most Romany live in Romania, Hungary, and other European countries, the culture of the Romany suggests that they migrated to Europe from other lands.
3. The bestest theory about the origin of the Romany is that they came from India.
4. As this photograph shows, the Romany wear some of their colorfulest traditional clothing for their celebrations.
5. They also brighten their lives with the most wild violin music they can play.
6. On the move frequentlier than most other Europeans, they used to travel in brightly painted wagons.
7. The Romany usually live in groups, with the largest groups consisting of several hundred families.
8. The most high law in Romany society is the *kris,* a system of rules based on the religious beliefs of the Romany.
9. The Romany generally earn their living as migrant agricultural workers and, less frequently, as entertainers.
10. Although change has come slowlier to these wanderers than to most other ethnic groups in Europe, some Romany now are living in settled communities.

| STYLE | TIP |

In informal situations and in standard expressions, people sometimes use the superlative degree in comparing two things: *Put your best foot forward.* Generally, however, you should use the comparative degree in formal situations when you are comparing two things.

# Use of Comparative and Superlative Forms

**19e.** Use the comparative degree when comparing two things. Use the superlative degree when comparing more than two.

COMPARATIVE  Writing mysteries seems **more challenging** than writing nonfiction.

In my opinion, Dorothy L. Sayers is a **better** writer than Agatha Christie.

| SUPERLATIVE | Writing a mystery story is the **most challenging** assignment I've had so far. |
|---|---|
| | This is the **best** Sherlock Holmes story that I have ever read. |

**Exercise 6** **Identifying Correct Comparative and Superlative Forms**

Identify the comparative and superlative modifiers in the following sentences. If the form of a modifier is incorrect, write the correct form. If the form is correct for the number of items compared, write *C*.

Link to Literature

EXAMPLE 1. Nina's report on American Indian star legends was the more interesting report in the class.

1. *most interesting*

1. Although Nina and I both researched our reports carefully, her report was the most thorough one of the two.
2. The American Indian stories about the stars and the sky are more diverse than the Norse myths, in my opinion.
3. Nina told several stories; I found the myth that she told about the cluster of stars known as the Pleiades to be the more fascinating.
4. The stranger tale, which is from the Monache Indian people of central California, tells how a little girl and six women who wouldn't give up eating onions became the Pleiades.
5. The scariest of the tales is the Skidi Pawnee myth about six brothers and an adopted sister who fight the Rolling Skull.
6. That story was the longer legend that Nina told, and Frank said it was the more interesting.
7. Of all the earthly creatures in the stories Nina told, Coyote is perhaps the more important.
8. In fact, in some stories people often play a least important role than Coyote plays.
9. I told Nina that, compared with my report, hers was the best.
10. She said that telling the stories was easier than finding them.

**19f.** Include the word *other* or *else* when comparing one member of a group with the rest of the group.

| NONSTANDARD | Juan is more considerate than any boy in his school. [Juan is a boy in his school, and he cannot be more considerate than himself. The word *other* should be added.] |
|---|---|
| STANDARD | Juan is more considerate than any **other** boy in his school. |

**Reference Note**
For a discussion of **standard and nonstandard English,** see page 595.

USAGE

| NONSTANDARD | Dana arrived earlier than anyone. [*Anyone* includes all people, and Dana is a person. Since she cannot arrive earlier than herself, *else* should be added.] |
|---|---|
| STANDARD | Dana arrived earlier than anyone **else.** |

### Exercise 7 Revising Faulty Comparisons

Revise each of the following sentences to make the comparisons logical and clear.

EXAMPLE     1. Rodney spells better than anyone in his class.

1. *Rodney spells better than anyone else in his class.*

1. Today has been colder than any day this year.
2. Kumiko eats more slowly than anybody in this cafeteria.
3. Flying is faster than any type of travel.
4. My sunflowers grew taller than any flowers I planted this year.
5. Luís enjoys swimming more than anyone in his family.
6. Dad bought that sedan because it gets better mileage than any car.
7. This hot-and-sour soup is spicier than any soup I've ever tasted.
8. Does Renee study harder than anyone?
9. Whales are bigger than any animals.
10. In my opinion, cycling is more fun than any type of exercise.

**19g.** Avoid using double comparisons.

A **double comparison** is incorrect because it contains both –*er* and *more* (*less*) or –*est* and *most* (*least*).

| NONSTANDARD | She is more funnier than he. |
|---|---|
| STANDARD | She is **funnier** than he. |

| NONSTANDARD | It was the least cloudiest night of the year. |
|---|---|
| STANDARD | It was the **least cloudy** night of the year. |

### Exercise 8 Revising Modifiers to Correct Double Comparisons

Write each incorrect modifier in the following sentences. Then, correct the double comparison by crossing out the unnecessary part.

EXAMPLE     1. Today is more colder than yesterday.

1. ~~more~~ colder

1. That is the most softest sweater I have ever had.
2. You seem to be trying more harder in school this year.

3. Is she the least tiredest runner on the team?

4. Illustrations help make the explanations more clearer to the readers.

5. Georgia is more larger in area than any other state east of the Mississippi.

6. We had the most best basketball team in our division.

7. The first day of winter is the most shortest day of the year.

8. Parrots are more smarter than other birds.

9. Cynthia's room is much less cleaner than John's.

10. Did you know that Rome is one of the most oldest capitals in the world?

**19h.** Be sure your comparisons are clear.

| | |
|---|---|
| UNCLEAR | Weeds in the lawn are harder to get rid of than the garden. |
| | [This sentence incorrectly compares weeds to a garden.] |
| CLEAR | Weeds in the lawn are harder to get rid of than **weeds in** the garden. |

| | |
|---|---|
| UNCLEAR | Is the skin of the rhinoceros harder than the alligator? |
| CLEAR | Is the skin of the rhinoceros harder than **the skin of** the alligator? |

*or*

Is the skin of the rhinoceros harder than the **alligator's?**

Both parts of an incomplete comparison should be stated if there is any chance of misunderstanding.

| | |
|---|---|
| UNCLEAR | Theresa called Greg more than Maria. |
| CLEAR | Theresa called Greg more than Maria **did.** |
| CLEAR | Theresa called Greg more than **she called** Maria. |

**Exercise 9** **Correcting Unclear Comparisons**

Rewrite the following sentences to correct unclear comparisons.

EXAMPLE    1. The annual rainfall in Seattle is higher than London.

1. *The annual rainfall in Seattle is higher than that in London.*

1. A kangaroo's jump is higher than a rabbit.

2. The power of that truck's engine is greater than a sports car.

3. In those days, the Pottstown Panthers' winning streak was longer than the Lindale Lions.

4. Is a baboon's grip stronger than a human?

HELP

Although some sentences in Exercise 9 may be correctly revised in more than one way, you need to give only one revision for each sentence.

5. Tony's bike is as new and gleaming as Juan.
6. The canals in Venice, Italy, are wider than Venice, California.
7. Rome's climate is milder than Houston.
8. Our new windows are bigger than the Costellos' house.
9. The kudu's horns are longer than the ibex.
10. Pat's assignments are usually better written than Jessica.

### Review B  Correcting Modifiers in a Paragraph

Identify and correct the incorrect comparative and superlative forms in each sentence in the following paragraph. Some sentences contain more than one incorrect or unclear comparison. If a sentence is already correct, write *C*.

EXAMPLE     **[1]** Eagles are widely regarded as more majestic than any bird in the world.

1. *Eagles are widely regarded as more majestic than any other bird in the world.*

**[1]** Many cultures have revered the eagle as one of their most strongest symbols of bravery and power. **[2]** In fact, the eagle seems to be the most popular bird used as a national symbol. **[3]** Mexico, Austria, and Egypt are some of the more best-known countries with eagles on their national flags. **[4]** In the United States, early colonial leaders thought that the bald eagle would be a more better symbol for their new country than the turkey. **[5]** Benjamin Franklin had argued that the turkey was the most practical choice of the two birds, but he was outvoted.

**[6]** I think most people would agree that the eagle is the best choice of the two. **[7]** While eagles are not more larger than all birds, they are among the more effective hunters and fliers. **[8]** As you can see from these pictures, the eagle's sharp beak and long claws are more powerful than the turkey. **[9]** The eagle's wings are also more strong and very wide. **[10]** I think the eagle is beauti-fuller, too.

# Dangling Modifiers

**19i.** Avoid using dangling modifiers.

A modifying word, phrase, or clause that does not clearly and sensibly modify a word or a word group in a sentence is a *dangling modifier.*

| DANGLING | Together, the litter along the highway was picked up, bagged, and hauled away. [Was the litter together?] |
| CORRECT | Together, we picked up, bagged, and hauled away the litter along the highway. |

| DANGLING | Time seemed to stand still, watching the sunset and listening to the cicadas. [Was time watching and listening?] |
| CORRECT | Time seemed to stand still as we watched the sunset and listened to the cicadas. |

When a modifying participial or infinitive phrase comes at the beginning of a sentence, the phrase is followed by a comma. Immediately after that comma should come the word or word group that the phrase modifies.

| DANGLING | Jogging in the park, a rabbit peered at me from the underbrush. [Was the rabbit jogging?] |
| CORRECT | Jogging in the park, **I** saw a rabbit peering at me from the underbrush. |

| DANGLING | Listening closely, distant thunder could be detected. [Was the thunder listening?] |
| CORRECT | Listening closely, **she** could detect distant thunder. |

| DANGLING | To master a musical instrument, practice or natural talent is usually needed. [Is practice or talent mastering an instrument?] |
| CORRECT | To master a musical instrument, **a musician** usually needs practice or natural talent. |

| DANGLING | Even when equipped with the best gear, the rock cliff was difficult to climb. [Was the rock cliff equipped?] |
| CORRECT | Even when equipped with the best gear, **the mountaineers** had difficulty climbing the rock cliff. |

A sentence may appear to have a dangling modifier when *you* is the understood subject. In such cases, the modifier is not dangling; instead, it is modifying the understood subject.

EXAMPLE    To find the correct spelling, (you) look up the word.

> **Reference Note**
>
> For more information on **participial phrases,** see page 451. For more information on **infinitive phrases,** see page 458.

> **Reference Note**
>
> For more about the **understood subject,** see page 423.

USAGE

Write complete sentences that begin with the following introductory modifiers.

EXAMPLE   **1.** Having solved one problem,

   *1. Having solved one problem, Joe Harris found that another awaited him.*

 **1.** Leaping from branch to branch,
 **2.** Yawning,
 **3.** While eating our lunch,
 **4.** Surrounded by the cheering crowd,
 **5.** To make sure he wouldn't be late,
 **6.** Alone,
 **7.** Following Leila's example,
 **8.** Not wanting to wake them up,
 **9.** Having filled out the forms,
**10.** To solve this riddle,

# Correcting Dangling Modifiers

To correct a dangling modifier, rearrange the words in the sentence and add or change words to make the meaning logical and clear.

DANGLING   While lighting the birthday candles, the cake started to crumble.

CORRECT   While **I was** lighting the birthday candles, the cake started to crumble.

*or*

While lighting the birthday candles, **I noticed** the cake **starting** to crumble.

DANGLING   To become a physicist, years of study and research are required.

CORRECT   To become a physicist, **you** must spend years studying and doing research.

*or*

**If you want** to become a physicist, **you** must spend years studying and doing research.

*or*

**If a person wants** to become a physicist, **he or she** must spend years studying and doing research.

**Exercise 11** **Correcting Dangling Modifiers**

Most of the following sentences contain dangling modifiers. If a
sentence has a dangling modifier, revise the sentence to correct it.
If a sentence is already correct, write *C*.

EXAMPLE　　**1.** While mopping the kitchen, my baby brother woke up
from his nap.

　　　　　　**1.** *While I was mopping the kitchen, my baby brother woke
up from his nap.*

1. Walking through the gate, the swimming pool is on the right.
2. Lost, the small village was a welcome sight.
3. To earn money, Mom suggested shoveling snow for our neighbors.
4. After studying hard, a long walk can be refreshing.
5. Walking in the woods, listening to the singing birds is enjoyable.
6. To understand a sentence, even little words can be important.
7. To become a great athlete, you need dedication and self-discipline.
8. Standing on the beach, a school of dolphins suddenly appeared.
9. After winning the last game of the season, the celebration lasted
nearly all night.
10. Tired and sore, the job was finally finished.

# Misplaced Modifiers

**19j.** Avoid using misplaced modifiers.

A word, phrase, or clause that seems to modify the wrong word or word
group in a sentence is a *misplaced modifier.* Place modifying words,
phrases, and clauses as near as possible to the words they modify.

MISPLACED　My cousin's dog was chasing the geese, yapping and barking.

CORRECT　**Yapping and barking,** my cousin's dog was chasing the
geese.

MISPLACED　I read about the bank robbers who were captured in this
morning's paper.

CORRECT　I read **in this morning's paper** about the bank robbers
who were captured.

MISPLACED　Blackened beyond recognition, even the birds refused to eat
the toast.

CORRECT　Even the birds refused to eat the toast **blackened beyond
recognition.**

STYLE　　TIP

Be sure to place modifiers
correctly to show clearly
the meaning you intend.
EXAMPLES
**Only** Uncle Jim sells bikes.
[Uncle Jim, not anybody
else, sells bikes.]

Uncle Jim **only** sells bikes.
[Uncle Jim sells bikes; he
does not repair them.]

Uncle Jim sells **only** bikes.
[Uncle Jim does not sell
cars or motorcycles.]

## Exercise 12 Correcting Misplaced Modifiers

Revise the following sentences to correct misplaced modifiers. In revising a sentence, be sure not to misplace another modifier.

EXAMPLE   **1.** The security guard was watching for the arrival of the armored car through the window.

     *1. The security guard was watching through the window for the arrival of the armored car.*

**1.** Michiko went outside to trim the bonsai trees with Uncle Saburo.
**2.** I could see the scouts marching over the hill with my binoculars.
**3.** As a child, my grandfather taught me how to make tortillas.
**4.** One advertiser handed out roses to customers with dollar bills pinned to them.
**5.** I borrowed a radio from my sister with a weather band.
**6.** Did you find any of the hats your mother used to wear in the attic?
**7.** Our cat waited on the porch for us to come home patiently.
**8.** In a tank at the aquarium, we watched the seals play.
**9.** She ate two peaches and a plate of strawberries watching TV.
**10.** We gave the boxes of cereal to the children with prizes inside.

## Review C Correcting Dangling and Misplaced Modifiers

Most of the following sentences contain dangling or misplaced modifiers. If a sentence is incorrect, revise it. If a sentence is already correct, write *C*.

EXAMPLE   **1.** Only the American Falls are slightly higher than the Horseshoe Falls.

     *1. The American Falls are only slightly higher than the Horseshoe Falls.*

**1.** Arriving at Niagara Falls, the sight of nature's tremendous force was awe inspiring.
**2.** When reading about the falls, many facts impressed me.
**3.** Separated by Goat Island, we discovered that the falls are in two principal parts.
**4.** Forming the border between Canada and the United States, most visitors admire both the Horseshoe Falls and the American Falls.
**5.** While climbing the tower, Niagara Falls, shown on the next page, looked magnificent to us.
**6.** Trying to see and do everything around Niagara Falls, the days passed quickly.

7. While riding in a tour boat called the *Maid of the Mist,* the spray from the base of the falls drenched us.
8. Roaring constantly, an awesome amount of power is generated.
9. After walking through Queen Victoria Park, a hearty lunch at the restaurant was refreshing.
10. To see the waterfalls at their most beautiful, a visit at night—when they are illuminated—was recommended by the tour guide.

**Reference Note**

For more information on **adjective clauses,** see page 472.

## Misplaced Clause Modifiers

Adjective clauses should be placed near the words they modify.

MISPLACED   There is a car in the garage that has no windshield.

CORRECT   In the garage, there is a car **that has no windshield.**

MISPLACED   The money and tickets are still in my wallet that I meant to return to you.

CORRECT   The money and tickets **that I meant to return to you** are still in my wallet.

### Exercise 13  Correcting Misplaced Clauses

Revise each of the following sentences by placing the misplaced clause near the word it modifies.

EXAMPLE   1. Alejandro searched the sand dunes for shells, which were deserted.

   1. *Alejandro searched the sand dunes, which were deserted, for shells.*

1. Birds are kept away by scarecrows, many of which eat seeds.
2. The disabled truck is now blocking the overpass that suddenly went out of control.
3. There was a bird in the tree that had a strange-looking beak.
4. A huge dog chased me as I rode my bicycle that was growling and barking loudly.
5. An old log sat in the fireplace that was covered with moss.

6. We thanked the clerk at the post office that had helped us with our overseas packages.

7. There are several books on our shelves that were written by Rolando Hinojosa-Smith.

8. A boy was standing at the bus stop that looked remarkably like my cousin.

9. She crossed the river on a ferry, which was more than a mile wide.

10. There is a flower garden behind the shed that is planted with prize-winning dahlias.

### Review D — Correcting Dangling and Misplaced Modifiers

Revise each of the following sentences by correcting the placement of a modifier or by rephrasing the sentence.

EXAMPLE
1. Feeling nervous about flying, the twin-engine plane looked small but dependable.

1. *Feeling nervous about flying, we thought the twin-engine plane looked small but dependable.*

1. Awakening from a nap, the island of Puerto Rico came into view through my airplane window.

2. Our guide was waiting to take us to our hotel inside the baggage-claim area.

3. To understand the guide's presentation, some knowledge of both Spanish and English proved to be helpful.

4. Driving along the Panoramic Route, the scenery was breathtaking!

5. We stopped for lunch at a stall along the road that was made from palm branches.

6. Hungry, the spicy rice and beans was delicious.

7. We bought a souvenir rock from a young boy that was decorated with island scenes.

8. Look at that strange fish in the water that is puffing up!

9. Anxious to shower and unpack, our hotel room was the next stop.

10. To fully appreciate all the island had to offer, more time was needed.

# Chapter Review

### A. Identifying Modifiers

Identify the italicized word or word group in each of the following sentences as a *modifier* or *not a modifier*.

1. Sammy Sosa is a *natural* baseball talent.
2. The elephant ambled *out of the trees* into the clearing.
3. Two well-known Mexican *authors* are Carlos Fuentes and Octavio Paz.
4. Austin, Texas, is a *pleasant* place to live.
5. As Stan *entered* the house, the cat dashed under the bed.
6. Amrit the waiter is a *very* helpful person, don't you think?
7. Jean-Marc joined the resistance to fight *against the enemy*.
8. The group Los Lobos is *well established* as a major force in the Latino music world.
9. Chi *fed* the three horses in the stables.
10. Gustav Mahler was a *gifted* Austrian composer and conductor.

### B. Correcting Dangling and Misplaced Modifiers

For each of the following sentences, identify the dangling or misplaced modifier and revise the sentence to correct the error.

11. Growing up in a big family, that family movie rings true to me.
12. To paint landscapes, patience and a steady hand are helpful.
13. Almost hidden under the pile of old books, Janelle saw the letter.
14. In different parts of the world I read about unusual customs.
15. A tree was almost destroyed by a bulldozer that was two hundred years old.
16. Jogging in the park, it was a sunny day.
17. The convicts were caught by the police trying to escape from jail.
18. Rushing out the door, Ben's homework was left on the table.
19. When told of the potential threat, nothing was done.
20. The mayor pledged she would build more roads at the political rally.

## C. Identifying Correct Comparative and Superlative Forms and Revising Faulty Comparisons

Identify the comparative and superlative modifiers in the following sentences. If the form of the modifier is incorrect, write the correct form. If the form is already correct, write *C*. Add words to sentences in which a faulty or unclear comparison is made.

**21.** Which plan is more easier to follow, his or hers?

**22.** My bowling was worse than usual last night.

**23.** This paella is more delicious than any dish I've ever eaten.

**24.** His problem is more worse than yours.

**25.** I like both shirts, but I think I like this one the most.

**26.** That was one of the interestingest movies he's seen.

**27.** The tomatoes from our garden taste sweeter than those from the store.

**28.** This is the nicest surprise I've ever had!

**29.** Which route is better—upstream, downstream, or overland?

**30.** The sun is brighter than anything in our solar system.

**31.** The water in the pond was more deep than Nicky expected.

**32.** Arnie is the least helpful of the two brothers.

**33.** Doesn't Granddad feel more better now that he's rested?

**34.** Did you know that the Nile is more longer than any other river in the world?

**35.** When Marcos was five, he was carefuller than he is now.

**36.** Which do you like better—Theseus Flatow's older or more recent music?

**37.** Ken completed the exercise faster than anyone.

**38.** The last problem is the most complicated one in the entire exercise.

**39.** Jesse is feeling more badly about the accident today than he did yesterday.

**40.** The tree in our yard is bigger than our neighbors.

## D. Correcting Misplaced Clause Modifiers

Revise each of the following sentences by placing the misplaced clause near the word it modifies.

**41.** There is a magazine on the table that has no cover.

**42.** The test papers are still in my locker that I want to hand in to Mr. Saenz.

**43.** There is a vase in that display case that was made during the Ming dynasty.

**44.** There was a Dalmatian in the street that had a silver collar.

**45.** The young chestnut mare is drinking water that just won the steeplechase.

**46.** We called the lady at the nursing home that had been so helpful.

**47.** Tom inspected the cars for dents, which were on the dealer's lot.

**48.** A trailer sat in the empty field that was covered with rust.

**49.** There is a mummy in the museum that is five thousand years old.

**50.** A woman was running along the lake that I thought was my friend Fran.

# Writing Application
## Using Modifiers in a Restaurant Review

**Comparative and Superlative Forms**   As the restaurant critic for *Good Food* magazine, you always give a year-end summary of the best restaurants and their foods. Discuss your choices in a paragraph in which you use five comparative and five superlative forms of both adjectives and adverbs.

**Prewriting**   Using either real or imaginary restaurants, make a list of several places and their best dishes. Think of some ways to compare the restaurants (food, atmosphere, service, price).

**Writing**   As you write your first draft, use your list to help you make accurate comparisons.

**Revising**   Read your paragraph to a classmate to see if your comparisons are clearly stated. Revise any comparisons that are confusing.

**Publishing**   As you correct any mistakes in spelling, grammar, and punctuation, pay special attention to the spelling of comparative and superlative forms made by adding *–er* and *–est.* You and your classmates could prepare a *Good Food* newcomer's guide to local restaurants. Decide how you want the guide to look. Then, type the guide and make photocopies or input the guide on a computer and print it out.

**Reference Note**

For information about **spelling words with suffixes,** see page 735.

# A Glossary of Usage
## Common Usage Problems

## Diagnostic Preview

### Correcting Errors in Standard Usage

Each of the sentences in the following passage contains at least one error in formal standard usage. Revise the passage, correcting all such errors.

EXAMPLE    **[1]** Everyone accept him joined this here club.

    *1. Everyone except him joined this club.*

    **[1]** Our school has a hiking club that learns us how to appreciate nature. **[2]** Our club usually goes to parks that we might not of discovered by ourselves. **[3]** We go hiking anywheres that can be reached by bus in a few hours. **[4]** Before we go, we decide what to bring with us. **[5]** The less things that we have to carry, the better off we are. **[6]** Beside water, a hat, and a jacket, little else is needed. **[7]** Those which pack too much soon wish they hadn't of. **[8]** After all, a ten-mile hike effects you differently when you are weighted down then when you are not.

    **[9]** Our adviser, Mr. Graham, he knows where all the best hiking areas are at. **[10]** He always tells us that we won't see nothing interesting without we're willing to exert ourselves. **[11]** We can't hardly keep up with him once he starts walking.

    **[12]** We go on this sorts of walks because we enjoy them. **[13]** Although we sometimes think our lungs will bust, everyone wants to keep up with the others. [14] The real reward is when we see an unusual sight, like a fawn, a family of otters, a panoramic view, and etc. [15] Than we're sure that all of our hiking and time spent outdoors ain't been wasted. [16] We also except nature like it is and do not try to change it none. [17] When we find bottles or cans in the woods, we get upset with people who can't seem to go anywheres without leaving some mark.

[18] Everyone in the club feels the same way, so we're going to start an cleanup campaign. [19] People ought to enjoy being inside of a park without busting or changing anything there. [20] We'd rather have more hikers enjoying the wilderness and less people destroying nature.

# About the Glossary

This chapter provides a compact glossary of common problems in English usage. A *glossary* is an alphabetical list of special terms or expressions with definitions, explanations, and examples. You will notice that some examples in this glossary are labeled *nonstandard, standard, formal,* or *informal*.

The label *nonstandard* identifies usage that is suitable only in the most casual speaking situations and in writing that attempts to re-create casual speech. *Standard* English is language that is grammatically correct and appropriate in formal and informal situations. *Formal* identifies usage that is appropriate in serious speaking and writing situations (such as in speeches and in compositions for school). The label *informal* indicates standard usage common in conversation and in everyday writing such as personal letters. In doing the exercises in this chapter, be sure to use only standard English.

The following are examples of formal and informal English.

**Reference Note**

For a list of **words often confused,** see page 746. Use the **index** at the back of the book to find discussions of other usage problems.

| Formal | Informal |
| --- | --- |
| angry | steamed |
| unpleasant | yucky |
| agreeable | cool |
| very impressive | totally awesome |
| accelerate | step on it |

**USAGE**

**a, an** These *indefinite articles* refer to one of a general group. Use *a* before words beginning with a consonant sound; use *an* before words beginning with a vowel sound.

EXAMPLES    We saw **a** blue jay and **an** owl.

**A** hawk flew over us **an** hour ago. [*An* is used before *hour* because *hour* begins with a vowel sound.]

This is **a** one-way street. [*A* is used before *one-way* because *one-way* begins with a consonant sound.]

**accept, except** *Accept* is a verb that means "to receive." *Except* may be either a verb or a preposition. As a verb, *except* means "to leave out" or "to omit." As a preposition, it means "excluding."

EXAMPLES    I couldn't **accept** such a valuable gift!

Why should they be **excepted** from the test?

No one in my class **except** me has been to Moscow.

**affect, effect** *Affect* is a verb meaning "to influence." *Effect* used as a verb means "to bring about" or "to accomplish." Used as a noun, *effect* means "the result of some action."

EXAMPLES    The bright colors **affect** how the patients feel.

The treatment will **effect** a cure for the disease.

The bright colors have a beneficial **effect** on the patients.

**ain't** Avoid using this word in speaking or in writing; it is non-standard English.

**all the farther, all the faster** This expression is used in some parts of the country to mean "as far as" or "as fast as."

NONSTANDARD    This is all the faster I can go.
STANDARD    This is **as fast as** I can go.

**all right** See page 747.

**a lot** Do not write the expression *a lot* as one word. It should be written as two words.

EXAMPLE    I have **a lot** of homework tonight.

**among** See **between, among.**

**STYLE    TIP**

The expression *a lot* is over-used. Try replacing *a lot* with a more descriptive, specific word or phrase.

EXAMPLES
**mountains** of homework

**four subjects' worth** of homework

**and etc.** *Etc.* is an abbreviation of the Latin phrase *et cetera,* meaning "and other things." Thus, *and etc.* means "and and other things." Do not use *and* with *etc.*

EXAMPLE     We'll need paint, brushes, thinner, some rags, **etc.**
[not *and etc.*]

**anyways, anywheres, everywheres, nowheres, somewheres** Use these words without a final *s.*

EXAMPLE     That bird is described **somewhere** [not *somewheres*] in this book.

**as** See **like, as.**

**as if** See **like, as if.**

**at** Do not use *at* after *where.*

NONSTANDARD     This is where I live at.
STANDARD     This is **where** I live.

**bad, badly** See page 575.

**because** See **reason . . . because.**

**beside, besides** *Beside* is a preposition that means "by the side of" someone or something. *Besides* as a preposition means "in addition to." As an adverb, *besides* means "moreover."

EXAMPLES     Sit **beside** me on the couch.

**Besides** songs and dances, the show featured several comedy sketches.

It's too late to rent a movie. **Besides,** I'm sleepy.

**between, among** Use *between* when you are referring to two things at a time, even if they are part of a group consisting of more than two. Use *among* when you are thinking of a group rather than of separate individuals.

EXAMPLES     Take the seat **between** Alicia and Noreen in the third row.

On the map, the boundaries **between** all seven counties are drawn in red. [Although there are more than two counties, each boundary lies between only two.]

**Among** our graduates are several prominent authors.

There was some confusion **among** the jurors about the defendant's testimony. [The jurors are thought of as a group.]

| COMPUTER TIP

The spellchecker on a computer will usually catch misspelled words such as *anywheres* and *nowheres.* The grammar checker may catch errors such as double negatives. However, in the case of words often confused, such as *than* and *then* and *between* and *among,* a computer program may not be able to help. You will have to check your work yourself for correct usage.

USAGE

**borrow, lend, loan** *Borrow* means "To take [something] temporarily." *Lend* means "to give [something] temporarily." *Loan,* a noun in formal language, is sometimes used in place of *lend* in informal speech.

EXAMPLES    Tadzio **borrowed** a copy of *O Pioneers!* from the library.

I try not to forget to return things people **lend** me.

Could you **loan** me a dollar? [informal]

**bring, take** *Bring* means "to come carrying something." *Take* means "to go carrying something." Think of *bring* as related to *come, take* as related to *go.*

EXAMPLES    **Bring** that box over here.

Now **take** it down to the basement.

**bust, busted** Avoid using these words as verbs. Use a form of either *burst* or *break* or *catch* or *arrest.*

EXAMPLES    Even the hard freeze didn't **burst** [not *bust*] the pipes.

When aircraft **break** [not *bust*] the sound barrier, a sonic boom results.

Molly **caught** [not *busted*] Mr. Whiskers nibbling her tuna sandwich.

Did the police **arrest** [not *bust*] a suspect in the burglary?

### Exercise 1   Solving Common Usage Problems

For each sentence, choose the correct word or words in parentheses, according to standard usage.

EXAMPLE    1. Everyone seemed greatly (*affected, effected*) by her speech on animal rights.

      1. *affected*

1. There was complete agreement (*between, among*) the members of the council.
2. Is that (*all the farther, as far as*) you were able to hike?
3. The (*affects, effects*) of lasers on surgical procedures have been remarkable.
4. My schedule includes English, math, science, (*etc., and etc.*)
5. The boiler (*busted, burst*) and flooded the cellar.

6. Liza promised to (*bring, take*) me the new cassette when she comes to visit.
7. I don't know where it (*is, is at*).
8. Please (*bring, take*) this note to the manager's office when you go.
9. (*Beside, Besides*) my aunts and uncles, all my cousins are coming to our family reunion.
10. Ms. Yu (*accepted, excepted*) my excuse for being late.

### Exercise 2  Proofreading Sentences for Standard Usage

The following sentences contain errors in standard English usage. Identify the error or errors you find in each sentence. Then, write the correct usage. If a sentence is already correct, write *C*.

EXAMPLE    1. It isn't pretty, but the fossilized skull in the picture below has caused alot of talk in the scientific world.

1. *alot—a lot*

1. Discussions between various groups of scholars focus on what killed the dinosaurs.
2. Some scientists believe an asteroid hit earth and wiped out the dinosaurs, but others think there was a severe climate change where the dinosaurs lived at.
3. Even if we don't know why the dinosaurs disappeared, most of us enjoy looking at dinosaur fossils in museums, in exhibitions, on TV, and etc.
4. The San Juan, Argentina, area is one of the best places anywhere to find dinosaur fossils.
5. In 1988, the biologist Paul Sereno's discovery there busted the old record for the most ancient dinosaur remains.
6. On a expedition with some of his students from the University of Chicago, Sereno found the oldest dinosaur fossils unearthed up to that time.
7. Besides being in good shape, Sereno's herrerasaurus fossil doesn't even look its age.
8. In fact, the 230-million-year-old skeleton was amazingly complete accept for the hind limbs.

A Glossary of Usage    **599**

**9.** That quality of find certainly ain't ordinary.

**10.** Sereno and his herrerasaurus have effected the work of biologists and dinosaur-lovers everywhere.

**can, may** Use *can* to express ability. Use *may* to express possibility or permission.

EXAMPLES    **Can** you speak German? [ability]

Pedro **may** join us at the restaurant. [possibility]

**May** I be excused? [permission]

**could of** Do not write *of* with the helping verb *could*. Write *could have*. Also avoid *had of, ought to of, should of, would of, might of,* and *must of*.

EXAMPLE    Diane **could have** [not *could of*] telephoned us.

**discover, invent** *Discover* means "to be the first to find, see, or learn about something that already exists." *Invent* means "to be the first to do or make something."

EXAMPLES    Who **discovered** those fossil dinosaur eggs?

Robert Wilhelm Bunsen, for whom the Bunsen burner is named, **invented** the spectroscope.

**don't, doesn't** *Don't* is the contraction of *do not*. *Doesn't* is the contraction of *does not*. Use *doesn't*, not *don't*, with *he, she, it, this,* and singular nouns.

EXAMPLES    It **doesn't** [not *don't*] matter.

The trains **don't** [not *doesn't*] stop at this station.

**effect** See **affect, effect.**

**everywheres** See **anyways,** etc.

**fewer, less** *Fewer* is used with plural words. *Less* is used with singular words. *Fewer* tells "how many"; *less* tells "how much."

EXAMPLES    **Fewer** students have enrolled this semester.
Therefore, there will be **less** competition.

**good, well** *Good* is an adjective. Do not use *good* to modify a verb; use *well*, an adverb.

NONSTANDARD    Tiger Woods played good.
STANDARD    Tiger Woods played **well.**

While *well* is usually an adverb, it is also used as an adjective to mean "healthy."

EXAMPLE     She does not feel **well.**

NOTE   *Feel good* and *feel well* mean different things. *Feel good* means "to feel happy or pleased." *Feel well* simply means "to feel healthy."

EXAMPLES   Compliments make you feel **good.**

Do dogs and cats really eat grass when they don't feel **well**?

**Reference Note**

For more information about **formal and informal English,** see page 595.

### Exercise 3   Solving Common Usage Problems

For each sentence, choose the correct word in parentheses, according to standard usage.

EXAMPLE     1. Today people are using (*fewer, less*) salt than they did years ago.

    1. *less*

1. You should (*of, have*) written sooner.
2. Who (*discovered, invented*) what makes fireflies glow?
3. (*Don't, Doesn't*) Otis know that we're planning to leave in five minutes?
4. I usually do (*good, well*) on that kind of test.
5. Our doctor advised my uncle to eat (*fewer, less*) eggs.
6. He (*don't, doesn't*) look angry to me.
7. If I had known, I might (*of, have*) helped you with your project.
8. We had (*fewer, less*) snowstorms this year than last.
9. (*Can, May*) I please be excused now?
10. Whoever (*discovered, invented*) the escalator must have been ingenious.

### Review A   Solving Common Usage Problems

Most of the following sentences contain errors in standard usage. If a sentence contains an error in standard usage, write the correct form. If a sentence is already correct, write *C*.

EXAMPLE     1. Don't anyone know when this game will start?

    1. *Doesn't*

1. Perhaps I should of called before visiting you.
2. Who discovered the cellular phone system?

USAGE

**3.** The beautiful weather is effecting my powers of concentration.

**4.** We can't decide between this movie and that one.

**5.** That box contains less cookies than this one.

**6.** We felt good because practice went so well.

**7.** What affect did the quiz have on your grade?

**8.** Why won't you except my help?

**9.** We stood beside the lake and watched the swans.

**10.** Did you bring flowers to your aunt when you went to visit her in her new home?

---

**Review B**  **Solving Common Usage Problems**

Choose the word or expression in parentheses that is correct according to standard usage.

EXAMPLE    Alvin Ailey significantly **[1]** (*affected, effected*) modern dance in America.

1.  *affected*

Alvin Ailey **[1]** (*could of, could have*) just dreamed of being a famous choreographer; instead, he formed **[2]** (*a, an*) interracial dance company that is known all over the world. Ailey started his dance company with **[3]** (*less, fewer*) than ten dancers in New York City in 1958. Today, the Alvin Ailey American Dance Theater has a very **[4]** (*good, well*) reputation **[5]** (*between, among*) modern-dance lovers **[6]** (*everywhere, everywheres*). Ailey also ran a dance

school and **[7]** (*discovered, invented*) many fine young dancers there. **[8]** (*Beside, Besides*) teaching, he choreographed operas, television specials, and numerous ballets. The scene shown to the left is from Ailey's ballet *Revelations*, an energetic and emotional celebration of the cultural heritage of African Americans. During his lifetime, Ailey **[9]** (*accepted, excepted*) much praise, countless compliments, numerous rave reviews, **[10]** (*and etc., etc.*), for his creativity.

**had of**  See **could of.**

**had ought, hadn't ought**  Unlike other verbs, *ought* is not used with *had.*

| NONSTANDARD | Lee had ought to plan better; he hadn't ought to leave his packing until the last minute. |
|---|---|
| STANDARD | Lee **ought** to plan better; he **ought not** to leave his packing until the last minute. |
| STANDARD | Lee **should** plan better; he **shouldn't** leave his packing until the last minute. |

**hardly, scarcely**  See **The Double Negative** (page 609).

**he, she, they**  Do not use an unnecessary pronoun after the subject of a clause or a sentence. This error is called a *double subject.*

| NONSTANDARD | My mother she grows organic vegetables. |
|---|---|
| STANDARD | My mother grows organic vegetables. |

**hisself, theirself, theirselves**  Avoid using these nonstandard forms.

| EXAMPLE | He bought **himself** [not *hisself*] a new notebook. |
|---|---|

**invent**  See **discover, invent.**

**its, it's**  See page 751.

**kind, sort, type**  The words *this, that, these,* and *those* should always agree in number with the words *kind, sort,* and *type.*

| EXAMPLE | **This kind** of wrench is more versatile than **those** other **kinds.** |
|---|---|

**kind of, sort of**  In formal situations, avoid using *kind of* for the adverb *somewhat* or *rather.*

| INFORMAL | We are kind of anxious to know our grades. |
|---|---|
| FORMAL | We are **somewhat** [or **rather**] anxious to know our grades. |

**learn, teach**  *Learn* means "to acquire knowledge." *Teach* means "to instruct" or "to show how."

| EXAMPLE | Some of our coaches **teach** classes in gymnastics, where young gymnasts can **learn** many techniques. |
|---|---|

**leave, let**  *Leave* means "to go away" or "to depart from." *Let* means "to allow" or "to permit."

| NONSTANDARD | Just leave him walk in the rain if he wants. |
|---|---|
| STANDARD | Just **let** him walk in the rain if he wants. |
| STANDARD | **Leave** the dishes for tomorrow, and we'll take a walk. |

**lend, loan**  See **borrow, lend, loan.**

**less**  See **fewer, less.**

**lie, lay**  See page 539.

**like, as**  In informal English, the preposition *like* is often used as a conjunction meaning "as." In formal English, use *like* to introduce a prepositional phrase, and use *as* to introduce a subordinate clause.

EXAMPLES  She looks **like** her sister. [The preposition *like* introduces the phrase *like her sister.*]

We should do **as** our coach recommends. [The clause *our coach recommends* is introduced by the conjunction *as.*]

**Reference Note**

For more information about **prepositional phrases,** see Chapter 14. For more about **subordinate clauses,** see Chapter 15.

**like, as if, as though**  In formal written English, *like* should not be used for the compound conjunctions *as if* or *as though.*

INFORMAL  Scamp looks like he's been in the swamp again.

FORMAL  Scamp looks **as though** he has been in the swamp again.

**may**  See **can, may.**

**might of, must of**  See **could of.**

**no, none, nothing**  See **The Double Negative** (page 609).

**nowheres**  See **anyways,** etc.

**of**  Do not use *of* with prepositions such as *inside, off,* or *outside.*

EXAMPLES  He fell **off** [not *off of*] the ladder **outside** [not *outside of*] the garage.

What's **inside** [not *inside of*] that box?

**ought to of**  See **could of.**

### Exercise 4  Solving Common Usage Problems

For each sentence, choose the correct word or words in parentheses, according to formal, standard usage.

EXAMPLE  **1.** I (*had ought, ought*) to write my report on the Chinese inventions of paper and printing.

*1. ought*

1. The report must be on ancient Chinese history, (*like, as*) my teacher directed.
2. For (*this, these*) kind of report, I should start with the information that the Chinese invented paper as we know it early in the second century A.D.
3. If I (*had of, had*) seen them make paper by soaking, drying, and flattening mulberry bark, I would have been amazed.
4. (*The Chinese they, The Chinese*) didn't have the technology to mass-produce paper for another four hundred years.
5. By A.D. 200, the Chinese were using paper for writing and painting (*like, as if*) they always had done so.
6. I (*hadn't ought, ought not*) to forget that the Chinese also used paper for making umbrellas, fans, and lanterns.
7. In addition to (*this, these*) sorts of uses, the Chinese were using paper money by the seventh century.
8. You could have knocked me (*off of, off*) my chair when I learned that the Chinese were printing by A.D. 600—some eight hundred years before the invention of modern printing in Germany.
9. (*Leave, Let*) me tell you about how they used wooden blocks with characters carved on them for printing.
10. By the tenth century, the Chinese had (*learned, taught*) themselves how to print entire books with wooden blocks and had invented movable type.

**reason . . . because** In formal situations, do not use the construction *reason . . . because*. Instead, use *reason . . . that*.

| INFORMAL | The reason for his victory is because he knew what the voters wanted. |
| FORMAL | The **reason** for his victory is **that** he knew what the voters wanted. |

**rise, raise** See page 541.

**sit, set** See page 540.

**some, somewhat** In formal situations, do not use *some* for the adverb *somewhat*.

| INFORMAL | I've neglected the garden some. |
| FORMAL | I've neglected the garden **somewhat.** |

**sort** See **kind,** etc.

**supposed to, suppose to** Do not leave off the *d* when you write *supposed to*.

EXAMPLE    I am **supposed to** [not *suppose to*] clean my room.

**take** See **bring, take.**

**teach** See **learn, teach.**

**than, then** Do not confuse these words. *Than* is a subordinating conjunction used in comparisons; *then* is an adverb meaning *next* or *at that time*.

EXAMPLES    Algebra is easier **than** I thought it would be.

                    Read the directions; **then,** follow each step.

**their, there, they're** See page 754.

**them** *Them* should not be used as an adjective. Use *those*.

EXAMPLE    I like **those** [not *them*] jeans, don't you?

**this here, that there** The words *here* and *there* are unnecessary after *this* and *that*.

EXAMPLE    I'm buying **this** [not *this here*] cassette instead of **that** [not *that there*] one.

**this kind, sort, type** See **kind,** etc.

**try and, try to** Use *try to*, not *try and*.

EXAMPLE    We will **try to** [not *try and*] be on time.

**type** See **kind,** etc.

**used to, use to** Do not leave off the *d* when you write *used to*.

EXAMPLE    I **used to** [not *use to*] play badminton, but now I don't have time.

**way, ways** Use *way*, not *ways*, in referring to a distance.

EXAMPLE    We hiked a long **way** [not *ways*].

**well** See **good, well.**

**what** Do not use *what* for *that* to introduce an adjective clause.

EXAMPLE    The part of the car **that** [not *what*] lets the wheels turn at different speeds is called the differential gear.

**when, where** In formal situations, do not use *when* or *where* to begin a definition.

INFORMAL  In botany, a "sport" is when a plant is abnormal or has mutated in some way.

FORMAL  In botany, a "sport" is a plant **that is** abnormal or **that has** mutated in some way.

**where** Do not use *where* for *that* to introduce a noun clause.

EXAMPLE  I read in this magazine **that** [not *where*] Carol Clay is a champion parachutist.

**which, that, who** The relative pronoun *who* refers to people only; *which* refers to things only; *that* refers to either people or things.

EXAMPLES  Here is the man **who** will install the new carpet. [person]

We decided to replace our old carpet, **which** we have had for nearly ten years. [thing]

The dealer is a person **that** stands behind all of her products. [person]

It is the kind of carpet **that** will wear well. [thing]

**without, unless** Do not use the preposition *without* in place of the conjunction *unless*.

EXAMPLE  A rattlesnake won't strike you **unless** [not *without*] you surprise or threaten it.

**would of** See **could of.**

**your, you're** *Your* is a possessive form of you. *You're* is the contraction of *you are.*

EXAMPLES  Is that **your** bike?

I hope **you're** going to the party.

### Exercise 5  Solving Common Usage Problems

For each sentence, choose the correct word or words in parentheses, according to formal, standard usage.

EXAMPLE  1. (*That, That there*) motorcycle belongs to my cousin.

1.  *That*

1. Don't use more paper (*than, then*) you need.
2. (*Them, Those*) dogs have impressive pedigrees.

**3.** Manuel prefers (*this, these*) kind of skateboard.

**4.** It is only a short (*way, ways*) to the video store.

**5.** Tricia relaxed (*some, somewhat*) after she began to speak.

**6.** On the news, I heard (*where, that*) the game was called off because of rain.

**7.** Please set the books on (*your, you're*) desk.

**8.** Is she the player (*who, which*) is favored by most to win at Wimbledon this year?

**9.** He would not have released the report (*without, unless*) he had first verified his sources.

**10.** The reason we've requested your help is (*that, because*) you know the grounds better than we do.

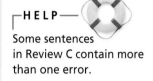

┌HELP┐

Some sentences in Review C contain more than one error.

**Review C** **Correcting Usage Errors**

Identify each usage problem that you find in the sentences in the following paragraph. Then, write the usage that is correct according to formal, standard usage. If a sentence is already correct, write *C*.

EXAMPLE    **[1]** The legendary statue, the Sphinx at Giza in Egypt, would of weathered away completely if it had not been rescued by modern technology.

　　　　　　 1. *would of—would have*

[1] Some famous monuments, such as the Eiffel Tower, don't look like they need any restoration. [2] However, monuments older than the Eiffel Tower, like Egypt's Sphinx, often need alot of care. [3] The Sphinx, who has the head of a human and the body of a lion, was built around 4500 B.C. [4] Some historians think the Sphinx, shown below,

might of been built at the same time as the pyramid of King Khafre, which stands beside it. [5] Those historians they believe the Sphinx's face is a portrait of Khafre. [6] The Sphinx was suffering some from old age, exposure, and bad restoration attempts, so Egyptian museum officials began a major renewal project in 1990. [7] Scientists knew that the world eventually would lose that famous statue without restoration was begun immediately. [8] Workers

USAGE

dismantled many stones, set new ones in their places, and than added natural mortar to let them stones breathe. **[9]** Workers also stabilized the water table under the mammoth Sphinx, which towers sixty-six feet above the desert sands. **[10]** These kind of restorations will help to preserve the Sphinx against the harmful affects of wind, rain, and sand for many years to come.

**Review D** **Correcting Usage Errors**

Revise each of the following sentences, correcting the error or errors in usage.

EXAMPLE  1.  I saw on the news where the mayor doesn't plan to run for re-election.

1.  *I saw on the news that the mayor doesn't plan to run for re-election.*

1.  Optimism is when a person look on the bright side.
2.  Luanne was suppose to buy a birthday card for Jo.
3.  Take this rake and them seedlings to Mae like I asked.
4.  I would of begun my report sooner then I did if I had known it would need this much research.
5.  I heard where people will not be allowed back in the concert hall after intermission without they show their tickets.
6.  The tire came off of the truck and rolled a long ways away.
7.  Heather Ruiz has promised to learn us karate.
8.  The people which witnessed the crime hadn't ought to have left before the police arrived.
9.  Did Thomas Edison discover the lightbulb?
10. Is it safe to leave the dog to run around the park without a leash?

# The Double Negative

In a ***double negative,*** two or more negative words are used when one is sufficient. Do not use double negatives in formal writing and speaking.

**hardly, scarcely** The words *hardly* and *scarcely* convey a negative meaning. They should not be used with another negative word.

EXAMPLES   I **can** [not *can't*] **hardly** turn the key in the lock.

We **have** [not *haven't*] **scarcely** enough time.

"Dropping out of school never done me no harm."

© Jim Unger; distributed by United Media, 1998.

**no, nothing, none** Do not use these words with another negative word.

| NONSTANDARD | That answer doesn't make no sense. |
| STANDARD | That answer **doesn't make any** sense. |
| STANDARD | That answer **makes no** sense. |

| NONSTANDARD | The field trip won't cost us nothing. |
| STANDARD | The field trip **won't cost** us **anything.** |
| STANDARD | The field trip **will cost** us **nothing.** |

| NONSTANDARD | We wanted grapes, but there weren't none. |
| STANDARD | We wanted grapes, but there **weren't any.** |
| STANDARD | We wanted grapes, but there **were none.** |

### Exercise 6  Correcting Double Negatives

Revise each of the following sentences, correcting the usage errors.

EXAMPLE  1.  It doesn't make no difference to me.

1.  *It makes no difference to me.*
            or
*It doesn't make any difference to me.*

1. Rachel didn't say nothing to him.
2. There isn't hardly anything left to eat.
3. I haven't borrowed no books from the library this week.
4. Laura couldn't hardly make herself heard.
5. What you're saying doesn't make no sense to me.
6. By the time we wrote for tickets, there weren't none available.
7. Hasn't no one in the class read *And Now Miguel*?
8. There wasn't scarcely enough water to keep the fish alive.
9. Didn't you never say nothing about the noise?
10. I haven't never told no one about our discovery.

# Nonsexist Language

*Nonsexist language* is language that applies to people in general, both male and female. For example, the nonsexist terms *humanity, human beings,* and *people* can substitute for the gender-specific term *mankind.*

In the past, many skills and occupations were generally closed to either men or women. Expressions like *seamstress, stewardess,* and

USAGE

┌HELP─
Although two revisions are shown for the example in Exercise 6, you need to give only one for each sentence.

*mailman* reflect those limitations. Since most jobs can now be held by both men and women, language is adjusting to reflect this change.

When you are referring generally to people, it is best to use nonsexist expressions rather than gender-specific ones. Below are some widely used nonsexist terms that you can use to replace the gender-specific ones.

| Gender-specific | Nonsexist |
| --- | --- |
| businessman | executive, businessperson |
| chairman | chairperson, chair |
| deliveryman | delivery person |
| fireman | firefighter |
| foreman | supervisor |
| housewife | homemaker |
| mailman | mail carrier |
| man-made | synthetic, manufactured |
| manpower | workers, human resources |
| May the best man win! | May the best person win! |
| policeman | police officer |
| salesman | salesperson, salesclerk |
| seamstress | needleworker |
| steward, stewardess | flight attendant |
| watchman | security guard |

If the antecedent of a pronoun may be either masculine or feminine, use both masculine and feminine pronouns to refer to it.

EXAMPLES    **Anyone** who wants to enter the poster contest should bring **his or her** entry to Room 21 by Friday.

Any student may bring a poster with **him or her** to Room 21.

You can often avoid the awkward *his or her* construction (or the alternative *his/her*) by substituting an article (*a, an,* or *the*) for the construction. You can also rephrase the sentence, using the plural forms of both the pronoun and its antecedent.

EXAMPLES    Any interested **student** may submit **a** poster.

All interested **students** may submit **their** posters.

**STYLE    TIP**

You can make similar revisions to avoid using the awkward expressions *s/he* and *wo/man.*

Rewrite each of the following sentences to avoid using gender-specific terms and awkward expressions.

EXAMPLE   **1.** An airline stewardess works hard to keep her passengers comfortable.

         *1. Flight attendants work hard to keep their passengers comfortable.*

**1.** The project was short of manpower, so the management hired more staff.

**2.** A three-alarm fire broke out in the factory, and the firemen were soon on the scene.

**3.** Whether or not s/he gets a commission depends on how persuasive each salesman is.

**4.** May the best wo/man win!

**5.** Our dog growls when it sees a delivery man and barks loudly at every mailman.

**6.** Being a policeman is a demanding job.

**7.** Did you hear that Susan was elected chairman of the board?

**8.** The foreman of the crew will distribute the helmets.

**9.** When Aunt Tina and Uncle Lewis had a baby, Aunt Tina decided to become a housewife.

**10.** Some man-made medicines are considerably cheaper than natural medicines.

# Chapter Review

## A. Correcting Errors in Standard Usage

For each of the following sentences, identify and correct the error or errors in usage. If a sentence is already correct, write *C*.

1. Why don't Guadalupe try out for the team?
2. Please leave Mike solve the problem by himself.
3. The ball can't go outside of the boundary lines.
4. You are playing good now that you practice every day.
5. We sat beside the lake and fished.
6. Every spring we see less bluebirds than the year before.
7. Tyrone doesn't like this kind of frosting.
8. I read where another royal wedding is taking place.
9. Terry looked like she needed a rest after the relay.
10. They wouldn't of missed going to the mountains.

## B. Proofreading a Paragraph for Standard Usage

For each sentence in the following paragraph, identify and correct the error in standard English usage. If a sentence is already correct, write *C*.

[11] Please bring me a dictionary so that I can look up what *left-handed* means, like I started to do earlier. [12] Left-handedness is where the person uses the left hand more than the right hand. [13] It don't matter which hand a person mainly uses because a left-hander functions just as good as a right-hander does. [14] Being left-handed couldn't hardly be a handicap; alot of clever people have been left-handed. [15] For example, artists like Leonardo da Vinci and Michelangelo Buonarroti were left-handed. [16] Of course, less people are left-handed than right-handed. [17] Many scientists learn their students the theory that left-handedness is determined by which side of the brain is dominant. [18] Some scientists they say that the left side of the brain is more dominant in a right-handed person. [19] They also say that the right side of the brain is more dominant in a left-handed person, but there isn't nobody who knows for sure. [20] Discussions on this subject between various groups of scientists will probably continue into the distant future.

> ⌐**HELP**─
>
> Each sentence in Part B of the Chapter Review may contain more than one error.

**USAGE**

## C. Solving Common Usage Problems

For each sentence, choose the correct word in parentheses, according to formal, standard usage.

**21.** I looked for the library book all over the house, but I couldn't find it (*anywheres, anywhere*).

**22.** The deer searched the ground for food, but there wasn't (*none, any*).

**23.** When the temperature dropped to zero, we worried that the pipes might (*bust, burst*).

**24.** In the 1820s and 30s, the French scientists Louis Daguerre and Nicéphore Niépce (*discovered, invented*) photography.

**25.** That airline's slogan is "We fly (*everywhere, everywheres*)."

**26.** Dr. Mendez advised me to eat (*less, fewer*) sweets.

**27.** What (*affect, effect*) did the good news have on her?

**28.** However much you try to outrun a tornado, it doesn't make (*no, any*) difference; the best idea is to seek shelter immediately.

**29.** Who (*discovered, invented*) what a comet's tail is made of, Kai?

**30.** Nick admitted that he (*should of, should have*) told his family what time he was planning to come home.

**31.** "If you study hard now, you will be more confident later, and you will do (*good, well*) on the final," declared Ms. Echevarria.

**32.** Although it has (*fewer, less*) options than the car advertised, that car on the lot is a better deal, overall.

**33.** From New Orleans to Los Angeles is quite a long (*ways, way*).

**34.** That orchestra has a top-notch reputation (*between, among*) music lovers worldwide.

**35.** The author (*accepted, excepted*) the award with the grace that had long been characteristic of her.

**36.** Mother asked Simon to (*leave, let*) her read her book in peace.

**37.** I heard (*where, that*) today's discounts are the best ever.

**38.** Is Belle the singer (*which, that*) had that TV special last week?

**39.** It's hard to imagine how ice got onto the moon (*without, unless*) there had once been water there.

**40.** (*Their, They're*) comments didn't make sense, but they were funny.

## D. Using Nonsexist Language

Rewrite each of the following sentences to avoid gender-specific terms and awkward expressions.

**41.** The foreman issued her first work order of the day.

**42.** May the best man win!

**43.** Caroline's friend was an airline stewardess.

**44.** Only the very courageous need apply to be firemen.

**45.** Three of the salesmen were under twenty-five.

**46.** The space shuttle is the most useful man-made device ever.

**47.** The deliverymen for that company wear brown shorts.

**48.** My next-door neighbor was a first-rate seamstress.

**49.** Fewer women become housewives these days than in the past.

**50.** The computer plant is advertising for a watchman, I hear.

# Writing Application

## Writing a Business Letter

**Using Formal Standard English**   After reading studies showing the benefits of school uniforms, the school board in your district has proposed requiring students to wear uniforms. One study found that schools that require uniforms experience less violence. Another study concluded that students who wore uniforms made better grades. Write a letter to the school board, telling why your district should or should not require students to wear uniforms.

**Prewriting**   If you already have an opinion about school uniforms, jot down some reasons to support your view. If you are undecided, you may want to make two lists—one pro and one con. Give several reasons to support each position. Then, choose the more persuasive side.

**Writing**   As you write your first draft, keep focused on your topic. Choose only the best reasons from your list and expand on these.

**Revising**   Add, delete, or rearrange details to support your argument. Also, see that the tone and word choice of your letter conform to the standards of a polite business letter.

**Publishing**   Proofread your paper for any errors in spelling and punctuation. Then, use the glossary entries in this chapter to correct common usage errors. You and your classmates may wish to have a debate on the school uniform issue. You might also like to post your letter on the class bulletin board or Web page.

**Reference Note**

For more about **writing business letters,** see "Writing" in the Quick Reference Handbook.

# Capital Letters
## The Rules for Capitalization

## Diagnostic Preview

### A. Correcting Sentences That Contain Errors in Capitalization

Correct the errors in capitalization in the following sentences by capitalizing or lowercasing letters as needed. If a sentence contains no errors, write *C*.

EXAMPLE    **1.** My Aunt and I visited the White house in Washington, D.C.

     *1. aunt, House*

1. Val's new schwinn bike had a flat tire.
2. My father is taking a course in public speaking.
3. The atmosphere on venus is one hundred times denser than the atmosphere on earth.
4. Has your favorite team ever won the rose bowl?
5. The opossum can be found as far south as Argentina and as far north as Canada.
6. For our Spring project, our Club raised money for the American heart association.
7. The maya of the Yucatán peninsula worshiped nature Gods such as chac, a god of rain, and Itzamná, a sky god.
8. My uncle Scott works at Apex hardware store.
9. In drama 2, we staged a production of Denise Chávez's *The flying tortilla Man.*

10. The U.S. senate and the house of representatives may pass a bill into law, but the president can veto it.
11. Mr. Williams is a Reporter for United Press international.
12. We went to Sea World over easter vacation.
13. Both rabbi Frankel and reverend Stone organized aid for the many victims of the fire.
14. The Winter Games of the 1998 olympics were held in Nagano, Japan.
15. Michelangelo's *The creation of the World* and *The Last Judgment* are paintings that depict scenes from the bible.

## B. Correcting Capitalization Errors in a Paragraph

Correct the errors in capitalization in the following paragraph by capitalizing or lowercasing letters as needed. If a sentence contains no errors, write *C*.

EXAMPLE    **[1]** A gentle elephant named jumbo was once the largest, most popular captive animal in the World.

       1. *Jumbo, world*

[**16**] When p. t. barnum bought Jumbo in 1882, the elephant had already become a star with the London royal circus. [**17**] All of england protested the sale when the unhappy elephant refused to board the ship for New York city. [**18**] however, even queen Victoria and the Prince of wales could not prevent Jumbo's going, since the sale had been completed. [**19**] Jumbo's Trainer, Matthew Scott, kept the elephant content on the journey across the atlantic ocean. [**20**] In april, the new addition to the Show arrived in New York, and the 13,500-pound Star marched up broadway to the cheers of a huge crowd. [**21**] Soon Jumbo-mania swept across the United States. [**22**] The elephant was so popular that his name became a common word in the english language—*jumbo*, meaning "extra large." [**23**] He died tragically on September 15, 1885, in the canadian town of St. Thomas, Ontario. [**24**] The big-hearted giant, seeing a train bearing down on a baby elephant, pushed the youngster to safety but could not save himself. [**25**] To keep Jumbo's memory alive, Barnum donated the skeleton of his beloved elephant to the American Museum of natural history.

BORN LOSER reprinted by permission of Newspaper Enterprise Association, Inc.

# Using Capital Letters Correctly

A capital letter at the beginning of a word is an important signal to the reader. A capital letter may indicate the beginning of a sentence and also may mark a significant difference in meaning, such as the difference between *may* (as in *you may*) and *May* (as in *May 3, 1996*).

**21a.** Capitalize the first word in every sentence.

EXAMPLES **T**he world of computers has its own vocabulary. **C**omputer equipment is called *hardware,* and the programs are called *software.*

STYLE  TIP

Some professional writers do not follow the rules shown in this chapter. When you are quoting a person, use capital letters as they are used in the source of the quotation.

MECHANICS

### Exercise 1  Capitalizing Sentences in a Paragraph

Rewrite the following paragraph. Capitalize the ten words that should begin with a capital letter. Add the appropriate punctuation mark to the end of each sentence.

EXAMPLE  **1.** what are some new developments in science

1. *What are some new developments in science?*

work has begun on a new kind of laser radar this instrument would be especially useful for people with visual impairments how does the radar work a laser device that is small enough to fit onto an eyeglass frame emits invisible infrared light beams when the light strikes an object, it bounces back to a receiver placed in the wearer's ear the receiver, in turn, sounds a small tone with this sort of device, the person can "hear" any object nearby the device is very promising in fact, it may one day replace the cane or the guide dog as an aid for people who are blind there are few better examples of how beneficial laser research can be

**21b.** Traditionally, the first word of a line of poetry is capitalized.

EXAMPLES  **A** bird came down the walk:

**H**e did not know I saw;

**H**e bit an angleworm in halves

**A**nd ate the fellow, raw.

Emily Dickinson, "A Bird Came Down the Walk"

**21c.** Capitalize the first word of a directly quoted sentence.

EXAMPLE  Eduardo wondered, "**W**here did I put my backpack?"

Reference Note

For more information on using **capital letters in quotations,** see page 687.

**21d.** Capitalize the first word in both the salutation and the closing of a letter.

EXAMPLES    **D**ear Service Manager:        **S**incerely,

            **D**ear Amy,                    **Y**ours truly,

**21e.** Capitalize the pronoun *I* and the interjection *O*.

Although it is rarely used, *O* is always capitalized. Generally, it is reserved for invocations and is followed by the name of the person or thing being addressed. You will more often use the interjection *oh*, which is generally not capitalized unless it is the first word in a sentence.

EXAMPLES    "Exult **O** shores! and ring **O** bells!" is a line from Walt Whitman's poem "**O** Captain! My Captain!"

            The play was a hit, but **o**h, how nervous I was!

            **O**h, I forgot my book.

### Exercise 2  Correcting Capitalization Errors in Sentences

Correct the errors in capitalization in the following sentences. If a sentence contains no errors, write *C*.

EXAMPLE    1.  in "Jazz Fantasia," the speaker tells the Musicians, "Go to it, o jazzmen."

           1.  *In, musicians, O*

1. yesterday i learned two psalms that begin, "Bless the Lord, o my soul."
2. Ms. Jones asked, "can anyone name the author of that poem?"
3. I haven't decided, but Oh, how I'd like to be an astronaut!
4. "you must be careful of the coral snake," said the guide, "because it is the most poisonous snake in our region."
5. In the poem "The Fool's Prayer," the jester pleads, "O Lord, be merciful to me, a fool!"
6. do you know that the fifth of May is a Mexican American holiday?
7. most trucks have rear-wheel drive.
8. Two days ago—oh, such a short time!—I left without a care.
9. The car stopped suddenly, and Oh, was i glad for my seat belt!
10. My favorite verses from that scene are
       see how she leans her cheek upon her hand!
       oh, that i were a glove upon that hand,
       that i might touch that cheek!

**Reference Note**

For more about **common** and **proper nouns,** see page 375. For a discussion of **proper adjectives,** see page 383.

**STYLE TIP**

Proper nouns and proper adjectives sometimes lose their capitals through frequent usage.

EXAMPLES

**w**att   **t**itanic   **s**andwich

To find out whether a noun should be capitalized, check in a dictionary. The dictionary will tell you whether a word should always be capitalized or whether it should be capitalized only in certain uses.

**21f.** Capitalize proper nouns and proper adjectives.

A **common noun** names any one of a group of persons, places, things, or ideas. A **proper noun** names a particular person, place, thing, or idea. A **proper adjective** is an adjective formed from a proper noun.

Proper nouns are capitalized. Common nouns are generally not capitalized unless they

- begin a sentence

  *or*

- begin a direct quotation

  *or*

- are part of a title

| Common Nouns | Proper Nouns | Proper Adjectives |
|---|---|---|
| a **p**atriot | **T**homas **J**efferson | **J**effersonian ideals |
| a **c**ountry | **T**urkey | **T**urkish border |
| a **q**ueen | **Q**ueen **E**lizabeth | **E**lizabethan drama |
| a **r**eligion | **I**slam | **I**slamic beliefs |
| a **r**egion | the **S**outhwest | **S**outhwestern cooking |

In proper nouns of more than one word, do not capitalize

- short prepositions (generally, ones with fewer than five letters, such as *in*, *on*, and *with*)

- articles (*a, an, the*)

- coordinating conjunctions (*and, but, for, nor, or, so, yet*)

- the sign of the infinitive (*to*)

EXAMPLES    Mary, Queen **o**f Scots

Eric **t**he Red

*Romeo **a**nd Juliet*

"Writing **t**o Persuade"

**(1)** Capitalize the names of persons and animals.

| Given Names | Alana | Mark | LaVerne |
|---|---|---|---|
| Surnames | Diaz | Collins | Williams |
| Animals | Trigger | Socks | Rover |

**COMPUTER TIP**

The spellings of personal names can challenge even the best spellchecking software. However, you may be able to customize your spellchecker. If your software allows, add to it any names that you use frequently but have difficulty spelling or capitalizing.

**MECHANICS**

**NOTE** For names having more than one part, capitalization may vary.

EXAMPLES **De Vere** **de la Garza**

**McGregor** **O'Leary**

**Ibn-Khaldun** **von Braun**

Always check the spelling of such a name with the person who has that name, or look in a reference source.

**(2)** Capitalize initials in names and abbreviations that come before or after names.

EXAMPLES **A. E.** Roosevelt     Lewis **F.** Powell, **Jr.**     **Sr.** Gomez

**Ms.** Sonstein     Sabra Santos, **M.D.**     **Dr.** Alan Berg

**(3)** Capitalize geographical names.

| Type of Name | Examples | |
|---|---|---|
| Towns and Cities | **P**ortland **D**etroit | **M**exico **C**ity **R**io de **J**aneiro |
| Counties, Townships, and Provinces | **K**ane **C**ounty **H**ayes **T**ownship **P**lum **B**orough | East **B**aton **R**ouge **P**arish **Q**uebec **P**rovince **W**illiamson **C**ounty |
| States | **I**owa **M**issouri | **A**laska **N**orth **C**arolina |
| Countries | **E**l **S**alvador **N**ew **Z**ealand | **U**nited **A**rab **E**mirates **S**witzerland |
| Continents | **A**sia | **S**outh **A**merica |
| Islands | **W**ake **I**sland the **W**est **I**ndies | the **I**sle of **P**alms the **F**lorida **K**eys |
| Mountains | **M**ount **A**rarat **H**imalayas | the **A**lps the **M**ount of **O**lives |
| Bodies of Water | **I**ndian **O**cean **A**driatic **S**ea | **R**ed **R**iver **L**ake of the **W**oods |

*(continued)*

**Reference Note**

For more about **capitalizing titles used with names,** see Rule 21h(1). For information on **punctuating abbreviations** that come before or after names, see page 639.

**Reference Note**

**Abbreviations of the names of states are capitalized.** See page 640 for more about **using and punctuating such abbreviations.**

**STYLE TIP**

Words such as *north, west,* and *southeast* are not capitalized when they indicate direction.

EXAMPLES
farther **n**orth
traveling **s**outheast

However, these words are capitalized when they name a particular region.

EXAMPLES
states in the **N**orthwest
driving in the **S**outh

*(continued)*

| Type of Name | Examples | |
|---|---|---|
| Parks and Forests | **C**leburne **S**tate **P**ark | **P**almetto **S**tate **P**ark |
| | the **E**verglades **N**ational **P**ark | **O**uachita **N**ational **F**orest |
| Regions | the **W**est | **G**reat **P**lains |
| | the **S**outheast | **C**orn **B**elt |
| Other Geographical Names | **S**inai **P**eninsula | **H**arding **I**cefield |
| | **C**arlsbad **C**averns | **B**ryce **C**anyon |
| Roads, Streets, and Highways | **S**tate **R**oad 17 | **M**o-**P**ac **E**xpressway |
| | **I**nterstate 787 | **W**est **F**irst **S**treet |

> **NOTE** In a street name that is a hyphenated number, the second word begins with a lowercase letter.
>
> EXAMPLE   Twenty-**s**econd Street

Words like *city, island, river, street,* and *park* are capitalized when they are part of a name. When words like these are not part of a proper name, they are common nouns and are not capitalized.

| Common Nouns | Proper Nouns |
|---|---|
| life in a big **c**ity | life in **N**ew **Y**ork **C**ity |
| the **r**iver | the **S**pokane **R**iver |
| a small **i**sland | **L**iberty **I**sland |
| on a narrow **s**treet | on **S**tate **S**treet |

### Exercise 3   Recognizing the Correct Use of Capital Letters

Write the letter of the correctly capitalized sentence in each of the following pairs.

EXAMPLE   1. a. Drive Northeast until you get to New Haven.
          b. Drive northeast until you get to New Haven.

          1. *b*

**Reference Note**

In addresses, abbreviations such as St., Blvd., Ave., Dr., and Ln. are capitalized. For information about **punctuating abbreviations,** see page 639.

**STYLE TIP**

Since *rio* is Spanish for "river," *Rio de la Plata River* is redundant. Use only *Rio de la Plata.*

Other terms to watch for are

- *sierra,* Spanish for "mountain range" [Use only *Sierra Nevada,* not *Sierra Nevada Mountains.*]

- *yama,* Japanese for "mountain" [Use only *Fujiyama* or *Mount Fuji,* not *Mount Fujiyama.*]

- *sahara,* Arabic for "desert" [Use only *Sahara,* not *Sahara Desert.*]

- *gobi,* Mongolian for "desert" [Use only *Gobi,* not *Gobi Desert.*]

MECHANICS

1. **a.** We went canoeing on the Ohio river.
   **b.** We went canoeing on the Ohio River.
2. **a.** I read the article on south America.
   **b.** I read the article on South America.
3. **a.** Farewell Bend State Park is in Oregon.
   **b.** Farewell Bend State park is in Oregon.
4. **a.** Her address is 1614 Robin Street.
   **b.** Her address is 1614 Robin street.
5. **a.** I will be at Forty-Second Street and Park Avenue.
   **b.** I will be at Forty-second Street and Park Avenue.
6. **a.** The North Sea is east of Great Britain.
   **b.** The North sea is East of great Britain.
7. **a.** Atlanta is a fast-growing City in the south.
   **b.** Atlanta is a fast-growing city in the South.
8. **a.** Pensacola is on the gulf of Mexico.
   **b.** Pensacola is on the Gulf of Mexico.
9. **a.** The Hawaiian Islands are southwest of California.
   **b.** The Hawaiian islands are Southwest of California.
10. **a.** Laredo is on the Mexican Border in Webb county.
    **b.** Laredo is on the Mexican border in Webb County.

**(4)** Capitalize the names of organizations, teams, government bodies, and institutions.

| Type of Name | Examples | |
|---|---|---|
| Organizations | **U**nited **N**ations | **B**oy **S**couts of **A**merica |
| | **N**ational **W**eather **S**ervice | **M**illersville **O**rchid **S**ociety |
| Teams | **G**reen **B**ay **P**ackers | **R**iver **C**ity **A**llstars |
| | **G**olden **S**tate **W**arriors | **L**ady **L**obos |
| | | **P**itt **P**anthers |
| Government Bodies | **C**ongress | **P**eace **C**orps |
| | **F**ederal **T**rade **C**ommission | **S**tate **D**epartment |
| | | **A**ustin **C**ity **C**ouncil |
| Institutions | **S**mithsonian **I**nstitution | **N**ew **C**ollege |
| | | **N**orth **H**igh **S**chool |
| | **S**tanford **U**niversity | **B**ellevue **H**ospital |

STYLE                    TIP

The names of organizations, businesses, and government bodies are often abbreviated to a series of capital letters.

EXAMPLES

| | |
|---|---|
| **N**ational **O**rganization for **W**omen | **NOW** |
| **A**merican **T**elephone & **T**elegraph | **AT&T** |
| **N**ational **S**cience **F**oundation | **NSF** |

Usually the letters in such abbreviations are not followed by periods, but always check an up-to-date dictionary or other reliable source to be sure.

**NOTE** Do not capitalize words such as *democratic, republican,* or *social-ist* when they refer to principles or forms of government. Capitalize these words when they refer to specific political parties.

EXAMPLES  The new regime promises to institute **d**emocratic reforms.

                The **D**emocratic candidate will debate the **R**epublican candidate tonight.

The word *party* in the name of a political party may be capitalized or not; either way is correct. Be consistent in the use of the word throughout a particular piece of writing.

EXAMPLES  Libertarian **p**arty *or* **P**arty

                Federalist **p**arty *or* **P**arty

**(5)** Capitalize the names of historical events and periods, special events, holidays, and other calendar items.

| Type of Name | Examples | |
| --- | --- | --- |
| Historical Events and Periods | **F**rench **R**evolution | **W**orld **W**ar II |
| | **A**ge of **R**eason | **B**attle of **B**ritain |
| Special Events | **S**pecial **O**lympics | **G**ulf **C**oast **T**rack-and-**F**ield **C**hampionship |
| | **P**arents' **D**ay | |
| Holidays and Other Calendar Items | **T**hursday | **V**alentine's **D**ay |
| | **D**ecember | **L**abor **D**ay |
| | **N**ew **Y**ear's **D**ay | **A**ugust |

**NOTE** Do not capitalize the name of a season unless it is personified ("Here is **S**pring in her green dress!") or used in the name of a special event (**F**all **F**estival, **S**pring **J**ubilee).

**Exercise 4**  **Writing Sentences Using Lowercase and Capital Letters**

Correctly use each of the following words in a sentence.

EXAMPLE  **1.** river

             *1.* *The river is rising.*

| | | | | |
| --- | --- | --- | --- | --- |
| **1.** river | **3.** hotel | **5.** street | **7.** march | **9.** west |
| **2.** River | **4.** Hotel | **6.** Street | **8.** March | **10.** West |

MECHANICS

**(6)** Capitalize the names of nationalities, races, and peoples.

EXAMPLES    **C**anadian, **K**orean, **C**aucasian, **A**sian, **K**urds, **Z**ulu, **S**eminole

**(7)** Capitalize the names of religions and their followers, holy days and celebrations, sacred writings, and specific deities.

| Type of Name | Examples | | |
|---|---|---|---|
| Religions and Followers | **J**udaism **B**uddhism | **M**uslim **T**aoist | **B**aptist **Q**uaker |
| Holy Days and Celebrations | **L**ent **D**iwali | **P**assover **E**piphany | **R**amadan **R**osh **H**ashanah |
| Sacred Writings | **B**ible **T**almud | **U**panishads **D**euteronomy | **K**oran **D**ead **S**ea **S**crolls |
| Specific Deities | **A**llah | **B**rahma | **G**od |

NOTE  The words *god* and *goddess* are not capitalized when they refer to the deities of ancient mythology. However, the names of specific mythological gods and goddesses are capitalized.

EXAMPLE    The Greek poet paid tribute to the **g**od **Z**eus.

**(8)** Capitalize the names of businesses and the brand names of business products.

BUSINESSES    **M**otorola, **I**nc., **B**ank of **A**merica, **S**am's **S**hoes

BRAND NAMES    **F**ormica, **C**hevrolet, **A**ce, **K**leenex, **W**hirlpool

NOTE  Do not capitalize a common noun that follows a brand name: Formica **c**ounter **t**op, Chevrolet **v**an, Ace **b**andage.

**(9)** Capitalize the names of planets, stars, constellations, and other heavenly bodies.

| Type of Name | Examples | | |
|---|---|---|---|
| Planets and Other Heavenly Bodies | **S**aturn the **M**ilky **W**ay | **O**rion **V**ega | **J**upiter **P**roxima **C**entauri |

STYLE  TIP

The words *black* and *white* may or may not be capitalized when they refer to races. However, within a particular piece of writing, be consistent in the way you capitalize these words.

STYLE  TIP

In some writings, you may notice that pronouns referring to deities are always capitalized as a sign of respect. In other cases, writers capitalize such pronouns only to prevent confusion.

EXAMPLE
   The Lord called upon Moses to lead **H**is people out of Egypt. [*His* is capitalized to show that it refers to *the Lord*, not *Moses*.]

STYLE  TIP

The word *earth* is not capitalized unless it is used along with the names of other heavenly bodies that are capitalized. The words *sun* and *moon* generally are not capitalized.

MECHANICS

**MECHANICS**

**(10)** Capitalize the names of ships, trains, aircraft, and spacecraft.

| Type of Name | Examples | | |
|---|---|---|---|
| Ships, Trains, Aircraft, and Spacecraft | **A**rgo **S**putnik | **Y**ankee **C**lipper **F**lying **S**cotsman | **C**olumbia **T**hunder **B**ird |

**(11)** Capitalize the names of awards, memorials, and monuments.

| Type of Name | Examples | |
|---|---|---|
| Awards, Memorials, and Monuments | **N**obel Prize **S**ilver **S**tar | Lincoln **M**emorial **T**omb of the **U**nknown **S**oldier |

**(12)** Capitalize the names of particular buildings and other structures.

| Type of Name | Examples | | |
|---|---|---|---|
| Buildings and Other Structures | **T**ower of **L**ondon **G**olden **G**ate **B**ridge | **P**laza **H**otel the **A**lamo **F**ort **K**nox | **S**hasta **D**am **G**reat **W**all of **C**hina |

NOTE Generally, do not capitalize words like *hotel, theater, college, high school,* and *courthouse* unless they are part of a proper name.

EXAMPLES 

Jackson **H**igh **S**chool       a **h**igh **s**chool principal

Copley Square **H**otel       a **h**otel in Boston

Fox **T**heater       a **t**heater in Dallas

Victoria County **C**ourthouse       a **c**ourthouse hallway

### Exercise 5 Correcting the Capitalization of Words and Phrases

Correct the following words and phrases, using capital letters as needed.

EXAMPLE 1. a methodist minister

1. *a Methodist minister*

1. somewhere between mars and jupiter

2. a shopping center on twenty-third street

3. lafayette park in tallahassee, florida
4. some wheaties cereal
5. jefferson racquet club
6. harvard university
7. at the new jewish synagogue
8. on memorial day
9. an african american
10. the sinking of the *lusitania*
11. making easter baskets for the children
12. a visit to the washington monument
13. seeing venus through a telescope
14. reading a passage from the koran
15. flying in the *spruce goose*
16. to the ritz hotel
17. stories about the Egyptian god ra
18. a hammer from Ridgeway hardware store
19. passed by a dodge minivan
20. taking pictures of the eiffel tower

**Review A** **Identifying and Correcting Errors in Capitalization**

Link to Literature

Correct the capitalization errors in each of the following sentences by capitalizing and lowercasing letters as needed.

EXAMPLE    1. The earliest African American Folk tales have their roots in africa.

1. *folk, Africa*

1. Africans who first came to the americas enjoyed folk tales that blended their own african songs with stories they heard here.
2. Before the civil war, African Americans created new tales that reflected their experiences as Slaves and their desire for Freedom.
3. Many of these tales are about Animals, especially the small but clever character named brer rabbit.
4. Zora neale hurston collected a number of these animal stories and published them in *Mules and Men.*
5. Brer rabbit, a character that was especially popular in the south in the 1800s, constantly plays tricks on brer fox and brer wolf.
6. In some later tales, the main Character isn't a rabbit but a slave, john, who outsmarts the slave owner.

THE PEOPLE COULD FLY
American Black Folktales
*told by* VIRGINIA HAMILTON
*Illustrated by* LEO *and* DIANE DILLON

7. The author virginia hamilton, winner of the newbery medal and the national book award, tells other tales in *The People Could Fly: American Black Folktales.*

8. Both the title of that Book and the Painting on its cover refer to another popular kind of black folk tale that developed during the years of slavery.

9. Can you tell that the People on the book's cover are flying above the Earth?

10. "The People Could Fly" is one of many fantasy tales about enslaved people who use Magic Powers to fly away from their troubles.

**21g.** Do not capitalize the names of school subjects, except the names of language classes or course names that contain a number.

EXAMPLES    This year I am taking **g**eometry, **E**nglish, **c**ivics, **D**rafting **I**, and a **f**oreign **l**anguage. Next year I plan to take **A**merican **g**overnment, **E**nglish, **t**rigonometry, **B**iology **I**, and **S**panish.

┌H E L P──
Do not capitalize the class names *freshman, sophomore, junior,* or *senior* unless they are part of a proper noun.

EXAMPLES
All **f**reshmen should meet after school to discuss the **F**reshman-**S**ophomore **B**anquet.

### Review B  Correcting Capitalization Errors in Sentences

Correct the following sentences by changing lowercase letters to capital letters as needed.

EXAMPLE    1.  mi kyung's mother told us that buddhism and confucianism have a long history in korea.

1.  *Mi Kyung's mother told us that Buddhism and Confucianism have a long history in Korea.*

1. in tuesday's class, mrs. garcía explained that the diameter of earth is only 405 miles greater than that of venus.

2. this year's freshmen will be required to take more courses in english, science, and math than prior freshmen at briarwood county high school were.

3. in chicago we visited soldier field and the museum of science and industry, which are known all over the world.

4. Aboard the space shuttle *columbia* in january 1986, franklin Chang-Díaz became the first astronaut to send a message in spanish back to earth.

5. are latin and biology the most helpful courses for someone planning to go into medicine?

6. after i went to the mall and the hardware store, i stopped at quik mart on twenty-second street.

7. we vacationed in the west, stopping to see pikes peak and to go camping and fishing in colorado.

8. in kentucky, one of the border states between the north and the south, you can visit mammoth cave, churchill downs, and the lincoln birthplace national historic site.

9. after labor day last fall, the columbus youth fellowship sponsored a softball tournament at maxwell field.

10. augustus saint-gaudens, a great sculptor who came to the united states from ireland as a child, portrayed abraham lincoln as a tall, serious man standing with his head bowed.

**21h.** Capitalize titles.

**(1)** Capitalize a person's title when the title comes before the person's name.

EXAMPLES  **P**resident Kennedy          **M**r. Nakamura

**D**r. Dooley                         **F**riar Tuck

**P**rofessor Simmons           **P**rincipal Phillips

**M**rs. Robinson                   **L**ady Jane Grey

Generally, a title that is used alone or following a person's name is not capitalized, especially if the title is preceded by *a* or *the*.

EXAMPLES  We saw the **m**ayor at the park.

Daniel Inouye was first elected **s**enator in 1962.

Who was the **q**ueen of England during the Victorian Age?

Titles used alone in direct address, however, generally are capitalized.

EXAMPLES  Well, **D**octor, what is your diagnosis?

There's a message for you, **A**dmiral.

Good morning, **M**a'am [or *ma'am*].

**(2)** Capitalize a word showing a family relationship when the word is used before or in place of a person's name, unless the word follows a possessive noun or pronoun.

EXAMPLES  **U**ncle Jack, **C**ousin Joshua, **G**randfather,
my **u**ncle Jack, your **c**ousin Joshua, Kim's **g**randfather

**Reference Note**

For information about **capitalizing** and **punctuating abbreviations,** see pages 621 and 639.

S T Y L E          T I P

For special emphasis or clarity, writers sometimes capitalize a title used alone or following a person's name.

EXAMPLES

Many young people admire the **M**ayor.

How did the **S**enator vote on this issue?

At the ceremony, the **Q**ueen knighted Paul McCartney.

MECHANICS

Reference Note

For information on using **italics with titles,** see page 684. For information on using **quotation marks with titles,** see page 692.

MECHANICS

┌HELP─

The official title of a book is found on the title page. The official title of a newspaper or other periodical is found on the masthead, which usually appears on the editorial page or the table of contents.

**(3)** Capitalize the first and last words and all important words in titles and subtitles.

Unimportant words in a title include

- articles: *a, an, the*
- short prepositions (fewer than five letters): *of, to, for, from, in, over*
- coordinating conjunctions: *and, but, for, nor, or, so, yet*
- the sign of the infinitive: *to*

NOTE    Capitalize an article (*a, an,* or *the*) at the beginning of a title or subtitle only if it is the first word of the official title or subtitle.

EXAMPLES    "**A**n Ancient Gesture"        **t**he *Saturday Review*

**T**he *Miami Herald*        **t**he *Houston Chronicle*

**A** *Christmas Carol*        **t**he *Odyssey*

| Type of Name | Examples | |
|---|---|---|
| Books | *The Sea Around Us* | *Nisei Daughter* |
| | *Ultimate Visual Dictionary* | *Island of the Blue Dolphins* |
| Chapters and Other Parts of Books | "The Circulatory System" "Lesson 5: Manifest Destiny" | Chapter 11 "Unit 3: Poetry" |
| Periodicals | *The New York Times* | the *Hispanic Review* |
| Poems | "Woman Work" "Mending Wall" | *The Song of Hiawatha* |
| Stories | "The Pit and the Pendulum" | "Raymond's Run" "The Eclipse" |
| Historical Documents | Treaty of Paris The Declaration of Independence | Magna Carta The Emancipation Proclamation |
| Movies and Videos | *It's a Wonderful Life* *Willy Wonka and the Chocolate Factory* | *Fly Away Home* *Yoga: Beginners' Level* |

| Type of Name | Examples | |
| --- | --- | --- |
| Television and Radio Programs | *Ancient Mysteries* | *60 Minutes* |
| | *Meet the Press* | *All Things Considered* |
| | *Law and Order* | *Sesame Street* |
| Plays | *The Three Sisters* | *A Doll's House* |
| Works of Art | *The Rebel Slave* | *La Primavera* |
| Musical Works | "The Flight of the Bumblebee" | *Liverpool Oratorio* |
| | | *Sweeney Todd* |
| Audiotapes and CDs | *Romantic Adagio* | *Blue* |
| | *Left of the Middle* | *This Fire* |
| | *Dos Mundos* | *Ray of Light* |
| Computer Games and Video Games | *Sonic the Hedgehog* | *Sim City* |
| | *Logical Journey* | *Frogger* |
| | *Legend of Zelda* | *X-Men* |
| Cartoons and Comic Strips | *Jump Start* | *Dilbert* |
| | *For Better or Worse* | *Daria* |
| | *Scooby Doo* | *Peanuts* |

**Review C** **Correcting Capitalization Errors**

If the capitalization in a word group below is incorrect, rewrite it correctly. If a word group contains no errors, write *C*.

EXAMPLE
   1. watched the classic movie *casablanca*

   1. *watched the classic movie* Casablanca

1. mayor Cartwright
2. "Home on The Range"
3. the *Reader's Digest*
4. visiting Yosemite national park
5. the president of the United States
6. was a hindu priest
7. saying hello to grandma higgins
8. my Cousin's parents
9. N. Scott Momaday won the Pulitzer Prize.
10. *the Mystery of Edwin Drood*

Correct the sentences in the following paragraphs by capitalizing or lowercasing letters as needed. If a sentence is already correct, write *C*.

EXAMPLE   [1] Louis armstrong was one of america's most gifted Jazz Vocalists and Performers.

1. *Louis Armstrong was one of America's most gifted jazz vocalists and performers.*

[1] In social studies last week, we learned all about Louis Armstrong. [2] Nicknamed "satchmo," Armstrong was born in poverty in new Orleans in august, 1901. [3] He learned to play the Cornet, a kind of small trumpet, while serving a sentence for delinquency. [4] While growing up, he also played the trumpet on the paddleboats that sailed on the Mississippi river.

[5] In 1922, his favorite bandleader, king Oliver, asked him to play second trumpet in a band in chicago. [6] King Oliver's band was called the creole jazz band. [7] While performing with the Creole Jazz band, Armstrong was coached by the band's classically trained pianist, Lil hardin, who became mrs. Armstrong in 1924. [8] Armstrong soon left Oliver and joined the Fletcher henderson band in New York city.

[9] Louis Armstrong soon established himself as a great Trumpeter and Vocalist. [10] One of his innovations was scat, a vocal technique in which a Musician's rhythmic, wordless voice imitates the sound of instruments. [11] This technique first appeared in recordings such as "Heebie jeebies," issued under the band name hot Five. [12] The scat technique was later imitated by other famous african american singers such as ella Fitzgerald and Al jarreau.

[13] As a Composer, Armstrong was known for such classic jazz songs as "dippermouth blues" and "Wild Man Blues." [14] Armstrong's outgoing personality and Style attracted new audiences to jazz. [15] By the Mid-1930's, Armstrong had become a popular entertainer. [16] He retained his brilliance as a jazz trumpeter, however. [17] After world war II, he formed a series of small bands. [18] When the U.S. state department made Armstrong a goodwill ambassador, it honored his worldwide reputation as a generous and well-liked personality. [19] In his capacity as Ambassador, he traveled widely around the world. [20] Louis Armstrong died at his home in queens, New York, in July 1971.

# Chapter Review

## A. Correcting Sentences That Contain Errors in Capitalization

Most of the following sentences contain at least one error in capitalization. Write each sentence, capitalizing or lowercasing letters where necessary. If a sentence is already correct, write *C*.

1. The only U.S. President who was never elected was Gerald Ford.
2. The program was titled *Animals of the serengeti plain.*
3. Would you say that the South and the Northeast are the regions of the United States with the most distinctive accents?
4. Although the wheel was unknown to the inca people, their Empire contained many miles of roads.
5. Students at a yeshiva, or Jewish Seminary, study the torah.
6. The highest peak in the alps is Mont Blanc, on the French-italian border, or so I'm told.
7. I later learned that uncle Steve had been taking three courses in night school.
8. Henri Matisse's early paintings include *A glimpse of Notre Dame in the late afternoon* and *Green stripe.*
9. My aunt Terry is an Editor at a large textbook Publishing Company in Texas.
10. The united nations building is on the east River in New York city.
11. The letter was mistakenly delivered to 1408 West Twenty-third Street instead of 1408 east Twenty-third Street.
12. Uncle Matt served in the Vietnam war before he studied medicine at Iowa state university.
13. While recovering from surgery, Mr. Gomez watched *Good morning, America* every day on television.
14. What is the date of easter Sunday this year?
15. The woman from the U.S. department of labor was sent to our community hospital when she became sick.
16. The *Queen Elizabeth 2* was delayed by serious storms while crossing the Atlantic ocean.
17. Last Thursday, July 4, we Americans celebrated Independence Day.

18. The tenor sang "America the beautiful" at the dedication of the new monument.

19. Did you know, professor, that the *Mona Lisa* will be shown this year at the Metropolitan Museum of Art?

20. On Thanksgiving day, my family thanks god for many blessings.

## B. Correcting Errors in Capitalization

Correct the errors in capitalization in the following paragraph by capitalizing or lowercasing words as needed.

[21] almost everybody has heard of pasteurization, but how many people know what it is, or who originated it? [22] The French Chemist Louis Pasteur developed the process, which involves destroying disease-causing microorganisms by applying heat. [23] That was only one of many accomplishments of this Scientific Genius. [24] Born in 1822 in a small town in Eastern France, he made his first scientific discovery at the age of 26. [25] As his reputation grew, he was elected to the academy of Scientists in Paris and named Director of Scientific studies at one of the Capital City's most prestigious schools. [26] Pasteur's discovery that Microorganisms can cause disease led to recognition of the importance of vaccination. [27] The Great Scientist developed vaccines for rabies, anthrax, and a form of Cholera found in farmyard fowl. [28] Thanks to the support of emperor Napoleon III, a special laboratory was created for Pasteur. [29] In 1874, the French parliament granted him a lifetime stipend, and the Pasteur institute was inaugurated in Paris a few years before he died. [30] His discoveries were crucial, but perhaps Pasteur's greatest contribution to Science was his new way of looking at things.

## C. Proofreading for Correct Capitalization

Correct the following word groups, using capital letters as needed.

31. the cities of san miguel and cuernavaca
32. an irish american
33. the great ship *titanic*
34. at the hotel bristol
35. on christmas day

**36.** a call from uncle Ernesto

**37.** smith and garcia, inc.

**38.** gulf of mexico

**39.** southwest texas state university

**40.** whoever won the nobel prize

**41.** driving a dodge colt

**42.** zilker park in austin, texas

**43.** sarge's deli on third avenue

**44.** on labor day

**45.** the greek god apollo

# Writing Application

## Using Capital Letters Correctly in a Paragraph

**Proper Nouns**   Your school's language club plans to publish a booklet about foreign cities that most interest students. Write a paragraph telling about one city and its major attractions.

**Prewriting**   Choose a foreign city that interests you, and jot down the reasons you find it interesting. You may want to gather some information about it from encyclopedias, travel books or brochures, and magazine or newspaper articles. Make a list of the city's major attractions.

**Writing**   As you write your first draft, be sure to include information about the city's location and historical or cultural importance.

**Revising**   Ask a friend who is unfamiliar with the city to read your paragraph. Does the information you have presented make your friend want to visit the city? Add or delete details to make your writing more interesting and informative.

**Publishing**   Be sure that you have correctly capitalized geographical names and the names of businesses, institutions, places, and events. Pay particular attention to the spelling of foreign words. With your teacher's permission, post your paragraph on the class bulletin board or Web page.

# Punctuation
## End Marks, Abbreviations, and Commas

# Diagnostic Preview

## Correcting Sentences by Adding Periods, Question Marks, Exclamation Points, and Commas

Write the following paragraphs, adding periods, question marks, exclamation points, and commas where necessary.

EXAMPLE    [1] Computers therefore are not my cup of tea

     1. *Computers, therefore, are not my cup of tea.*

[1] Although TV commercials tell you otherwise computers are not for everyone [2] One day in the showroom of a computer store I stared at a personal computer for more than half an hour but I was still unable to locate the on-off switch [3] The demonstrator Pearl Rangely PhD. tried her best to be helpful [4] A computer consultant she quickly explained the functions of various switches buttons and boxes [5] She pressed keys she flashed words on the screen and she pushed around the mouse very quickly [6] I was confused and puzzled and frustrated yet I was also fascinated

[7] Dr Rangely who had often encountered confused consumers before told me that I had a "terminal" phobia [8] With a frown I asked her what that meant [9] She replied grinning broadly that it was the fear that bits and bytes can actually bite [10] What a comedian she was [11] Totally disenchanted I left the store

[12] I headed straight for the library to check out everything that I could find about computers: books magazines catalogs and pamphlets

[13] For example I read *The Soul of a New Machine* a fascinating book written by Tracy Kidder [14] When I had finished the book I knew about input output high-level languages and debugging [15] Armed with this knowledge I confidently returned to the store on Friday March 13 [16] Well the same demonstrator was there smiling like a Cheshire cat [17] I rattled off several technical questions that I think must have surprised her [18] By the end of a single afternoon Dr Rangely had taught me something about every computer in the store [19] I left however without asking one simple embarrassing question [20] Could you please tell me where the on-off switch is

# End Marks

## Sentences

*End marks*—periods, question marks, and exclamation points—are used to indicate the purpose of a sentence.

**22a. A statement (or declarative sentence) is followed by a period.**

EXAMPLES    Nancy López won the golf tournament.

What Balboa saw below was the Pacific Ocean.

Flora wondered who had already gone.

NOTE  Notice in the third example that a declarative sentence containing an indirect question is followed by a period. (An **indirect question** is one that does not use the speaker's exact words.) Be sure to distinguish between a declarative sentence that contains an indirect question and an interrogative sentence, which asks a direct question.

INDIRECT QUESTION   I wondered what makes that sound. [declarative]
DIRECT QUESTION   What makes that sound? [interrogative]

**22b. A question (or interrogative sentence) is followed by a question mark.**

EXAMPLES    Do you know American Sign Language?

Why don't you ask Eileen?

Who wrote this note? Did you?

---

**STYLE TIP**

As you speak, the tone and pitch of your voice, the pauses in your speech, and the gestures and expressions you use all help make your meaning clear. In writing, marks of punctuation, such as end marks and commas, show readers where these verbal and nonverbal cues occur.

Punctuation alone won't clarify the meaning of a confusing sentence, however. If you have trouble punctuating a sentence, check to see whether rewording it would help express your meaning more clearly.

**Reference Note**

For information about how **sentences** are **classified according to purpose,** see Chapter 13.

**MECHANICS**

**S T Y L E     T I P**

Sometimes declarative and interrogative sentences show such strong feeling that they are more like exclamations than like statements or questions. In such cases, an exclamation point should be used instead of a period or a question mark.

EXAMPLES
Here comes the bus**!**
Can't you speak up**!**

**S T Y L E     T I P**

An interjection is generally set off from the rest of the sentence by a comma or an exclamation point.

EXAMPLES
Well**,** I guess so.
Ouch**!** That hurt.

**Reference Note**

For more about **interjections,** see page 405.

**S T Y L E     T I P**

Sometimes a command or request is expressed as if it were a question. The meaning, however, may be imperative, in which case a period or exclamation point is used.

EXAMPLES
May I say a few words now**.**

Will you leave me alone**!**

A direct question may have the same word order as a declarative sentence. Since it is a question, it is followed by a question mark.

EXAMPLES     You know American Sign Language**?**

You're not asking Eileen**?**

**22c.** An exclamation (or exclamatory sentence) is followed by an exclamation point.

EXAMPLES     Hurrah**!** The rain stopped**!**

Ouch**!**

Look out**!**

**22d.** A command or request (or imperative sentence) is followed by either a period or an exclamation point.

When an imperative sentence makes a request, it is generally followed by a period. When an imperative sentence expresses a strong command, an exclamation point is generally used.

EXAMPLES     Please answer my question**.** [request]

Turn off your radio**.** [command]

Answer me right now**!** [strong command]

**Exercise 1**  **Using Periods, Question Marks, and Exclamation Points**

Write the following sentences, adding periods, question marks, and exclamation points where they are needed. Identify each sentence as *declarative, imperative, interrogative,* or *exclamatory.*

EXAMPLE     1. Are you familiar with lacrosse, a field game

1. *Are you familiar with lacrosse, a field game?—interrogative*

1. Do you know how to play lacrosse
2. On TV last night there was a segment on teams playing lacrosse
3. What a rough sport lacrosse must be
4. Did you know that North American Indians developed this game
5. Before Columbus came to the Americas in A.D. 1492, the Iroquois were playing lacrosse in what is now upper New York State and Canada
6. Do you realize that this makes lacrosse the oldest organized sport in America

7. Lacrosse is played by two opposing teams

8. Use a stick to catch, carry, and throw the ball

9. The name of the game comes from *la crosse,* French for a bishop's staff, which the lacrosse stick resembles

10. Lacrosse is especially popular in Canada, the British Isles, and Australia, and it is played in the United States, too

# Abbreviations

**22e.** **Use a period after certain abbreviations.**

An ***abbreviation*** is a shortened form of a word or word group. Notice how periods are used with abbreviations in the examples in this part of the chapter.

## Personal Names

Abbreviate given names only if the person is most commonly known by the abbreviated form of the name.

EXAMPLES    Ida **B.** Wells    **T. H.** White    **M.F.K.** Fisher

## Titles

**(1)** **Abbreviate social titles whether used before the full name or before the last name alone.**

EXAMPLES    **Mr.** Tom Evans    **Ms.** Jody Aiello    **Mrs.** Dupont

             **Sr.** (Señor) Cadenas    **Sra.** (Señora) Garza    **Dr.** O'Nolan

**(2)** **You may abbreviate civil and military titles used before full names or before initials and last names. Spell such titles out before last names used alone.**

EXAMPLES    **Sen.** Kay Bailey Hutchison    **Senator** Hutchison

             **Prof.** E. M. Makowski    **Professor** Makowski

             **Brig. Gen.** Norman Schwarzkopf    **Brigadier General** Schwarzkopf

**(3)** **Abbreviate titles and academic degrees that follow proper names.**

EXAMPLES    Hank Williams, **Jr.**    Peter Garcia, **M.D.**

**STYLE TIP**

Only a few abbreviations are appropriate in the text of a formal paper written for a general audience. In tables, notes, and bibliographies, abbreviations are used more freely in order to save space.

**STYLE TIP**

Leave a space between two initials, but not between three or more.

**MECHANICS**

**HELP**

If a statement ends with an abbreviation, do not use an additional period as an end mark. However, do use a question mark or an exclamation point if one is needed.

EXAMPLES

Mrs. Tavares just received her Ph.D.

When did she receive her Ph.D.?

Abbreviations   **639**

NOTE Do not include the titles *Mr., Mrs., Ms.,* or *Dr.* when you use a
professional title or degree after a name.

EXAMPLE **Dr.** Joan West *or* Joan West, **M.D.** [*not* Dr. Joan West, M.D.]

# Agencies and Organizations

An ***acronym*** is a word formed from the first (or first few) letters of a
series of words. Acronyms are written without periods. After spelling
out the first use of the names of agencies and organizations, abbreviate
these names and other things commonly known by their acronyms.

EXAMPLE My older sister works for the **National Institute of Mental
Health (NIMH).** She is compiling data for one of **NIMH**'s
behavioral studies.

| | |
|---|---|
| **AMA** American Medical Association | **USAF** United States Air Force |
| **HUD** (Department of) Housing and Urban Development | **UN** United Nations |
| **CPU** Central Processing Unit | **NEA** National Endowment for the Arts |
| **RAM** random-access memory | **FM** Frequency Modulation |

NOTE A few acronyms, such as *radar, laser,* and *sonar,* are now considered common nouns. They do not need to be spelled out on first use
and are no longer capitalized. When you're not sure whether an
acronym should be capitalized, look it up in a recent dictionary.

# Geographical Terms

In text, spell out names of states and other political units whether they
stand alone or follow other geographical terms. Abbreviate such names
in tables, notes, and bibliographies.

TEXT On our vacation to Canada, we visited Victoria,
the capital of British Columbia.

CHART

| | |
|---|---|
| London, U.K. | Tucson, Ariz. |
| Victoria, B.C. | Fresno, Calif. |

| | |
|---|---|
| FOOTNOTE | ³The Public Library in Annaville, Mich., has an entire collection of Smyth's folios. |
| BIBLIOGRAPHY ENTRY | "The Last Hurrah." Editorial. *Star-Ledger* [Newark, N.J.] 29 Aug. 1991: 30. |

**NOTE** Include the traditional abbreviation for the District of Columbia, *D.C.*, with the city name *Washington* to distinguish it from the state of Washington.

In text, spell out every word in an address. Such words may be abbreviated in letter and envelope addresses and in tables and notes.

| | |
|---|---|
| TEXT | We live at 413 West Maple Street. |
| ENVELOPE | 413 W. Maple St. |

**NOTE** Two-letter state abbreviations without periods are used only when the ZIP Code is included.

| | |
|---|---|
| EXAMPLE | Cincinnati, **OH** 45233 |

# Time

Abbreviate the frequently used era designations *A.D.* and *B.C.* The abbreviation *A.D.* stands for the Latin phrase *anno Domini*, meaning "in the year of the Lord." It is used with dates in the Christian era. When used with a specific year number, *A.D.* precedes the number. When used with the name of a century, it follows the name.

| | |
|---|---|
| EXAMPLES | In **A.D.** 476, the last Western Roman emperor, Romulus Augustulus, was overthrown by Germanic tribes. |
| | The legends of King Arthur may be based on the life of a real British leader of the sixth century **A.D.** |

The abbreviation *B.C.*, which stands for "before Christ," is used for dates before the Christian era. It follows either a specific year number or the name of a century.

| | |
|---|---|
| EXAMPLES | Homer's epic poem the *Iliad* was probably composed between 800 and 700 **B.C.** |
| | The poem describes battles that probably occurred around the twelfth century **B.C.** |

**MECHANICS**

In regular text, spell out the names of months and days whether they appear alone or in dates. Both types of names may be abbreviated in tables, notes, and bibliographies.

TEXT    Please join us on Thursday, March 21, to celebrate Grandma and Grandpa's anniversary.

NOTE    Thurs., Mar. 21

Abbreviate the designations for the two halves of the day measured by clock time. The abbreviation *A.M.* stands for the Latin phrase *ante meridiem,* meaning "before noon." The abbreviation *P.M.* stands for *post meridiem,* meaning "after noon." Both abbreviations follow the numerals designating the specific time.

EXAMPLE    My mom works four days a week, from 8:00 **A.M.** until 6:00 **P.M.**

## Units of Measurement

Abbreviations for units of measurement are usually written without periods. However, do use a period with the abbreviation for inch (*in.*) to prevent confusing it with the word *in.*

EXAMPLES    mm, kg, ml, tsp, doz, yd, ft, lb

In regular text, spell out the names of units of measurement whether they stand alone or follow a spelled-out number or a numeral. Such names may be abbreviated in tables and notes when they follow a numeral.

TEXT    The speed limit here is fifty-five **miles per hour** [not *mph*].

The cubicle measured ten **feet** [not *ft*] by twelve.

TABLE

| 1 **tsp** pepper | 97° **F** |
|---|---|
| 12 **ft** 6 **in.** | 2 **oz** flour |

### Exercise 2  Using Abbreviations

Rewrite the following sentences, correcting errors in the use of abbreviations.

EXAMPLE    1.  Hillary Clinton was born in Chicago, IL.

1.  *Hillary Clinton was born in Chicago, Illinois.*

**1.** The flight for Montevideo departs at 11:15 A.M. in the morning.

**2.** Julius Caesar was assassinated in the Roman Forum in B.C. 44.

**3.** Harun ar-Rashid, whose reign is associated with the Arabian Nights, ruled as caliph of Baghdad from 786 to 809 A.D.

**4.** The Mississippi River flows from Lake Itasca, MN, all the way to the Gulf of Mexico at Port Eads, LA.

**5.** I will be leaving soon to visit Mr. Nugent on Elm St. in New Paltz, NY.

**6.** The Fbi. is the chief investigative branch of the U.S. Department of Justice.

**7.** The keynote speaker was Dr. Matthew Villareal, Ph.D.

**8.** We will meet at 4:00 P.M..

**9.** I wrote "56 in" in the blank labeled "height."

**10.** G. Washington was the first president of the United States.

**Review A**  **Correcting Sentences by Adding Periods, Question Marks, and Exclamation Points**

Write the following sentences, adding periods, question marks, and exclamation points as needed.

EXAMPLE  **1.** Does Josh come from Chicago

*1. Does Josh come from Chicago?*

**1.** What a great car that is

**2.** Whose car is that

**3.** We asked who owned that car

**4.** Roman troops invaded Britain in 54 BC.

**5.** By AD. 800, Baghdad was already an important city

**6.** Dr Edward Jenner gave the first vaccination against smallpox in 1796

**7.** Why do so many children enjoy using computers

**8.** Please explain why so many children enjoy using computers

**9.** When did Alan Keyes run for president

**10.** Terrific Here's another coin for my collection

# Commas

If you fail to use necessary commas, you may confuse your reader.

CONFUSING  The friends I have invited are Ruth Ann Jerry Lee Derrick Martha and Julie. [How many friends?]

CLEAR  The friends I have invited are Ruth Ann, Jerry Lee, Derrick, Martha, and Julie. [five friends]

# Items in a Series

**22f.** Use commas to separate items in a series.

Notice in the following examples that the number of commas in a series is one fewer than the number of items in the series.

EXAMPLES   All my cousins, aunts, and uncles came to our family reunion. [words in a series]

The children played in the yard, at the playground, and by the pond. [phrases in a series]

Those who had flown to the reunion, who had driven many miles, or who had even taken time off from their jobs were glad that they had made the effort to be there. [subordinate clauses in a series]

| STYLE | TIP |

Because using the final comma is never wrong, some writers prefer always to use the comma before the *and* in a series. Follow your teacher's instructions on this point.

When the last two items in a series are joined by *and*, the comma before the *and* is sometimes omitted if the comma is not necessary to make the meaning clear.

CLEAR WITH COMMA OMITTED   The salad contained lettuce, tomatoes, onions, cucumbers, carrots and radishes.

NOT CLEAR WITH COMMA OMITTED   Our school newspaper has editors for news, sports, humor, features and art. [How many editors are there, four or five? Does one person serve as a features and art editor, or is an editor needed for each job?]

CLEAR WITH COMMA INCLUDED   Our school newspaper has editors for news, sports, humor, features, and art. [five editors]

NOTE   Some words—such as *bread and butter, rod and reel, table and chairs*—are used in pairs and may be considered one item in a series.

EXAMPLE   Our collection includes pop, reggae, mariachi, **rhythm and blues,** and hip-hop music.

**(1)** If all items in a series are joined by *and, or,* or *nor,* do not use commas to separate them.

EXAMPLES   I need tacks **and** nails **and** a hammer.

Sam **or** Carlos **or** Yolanda will be able to baby-sit tomorrow.

Neither horses **nor** elephants **nor** giraffes are carnivorous.

**(2)** Short independent clauses may be separated by commas.

EXAMPLE    The engine roared, the wheels spun, and a cloud of dust swirled behind the sports car.

> NOTE Sentences that contain more than one independent clause are **compound** or **compound-complex sentences.**
>
> COMPOUND    The Wilsons grow organic vegetables, and they sell them at the farmers' market.
>
> COMPOUND-    When the weather is bad, the dog hides under the bed,
> COMPLEX    and the cat retreats to my closet.

**Reference Note**

Independent clauses in a series can be separated by semicolons. For more about this use of **semi-colons,** see page 470.

**(3)** Use commas to separate two or more adjectives preceding a noun.

EXAMPLE    Are you going to that hot, crowded, noisy mall?

When the last adjective in a series is thought of as part of the noun, the comma before the adjective is omitted.

EXAMPLES    I study in our small **dining room.**

Let's have our picnic under that lovely, shady **fruit tree.**

Compound nouns like *dining room* and *fruit tree* are considered single units—the two words act as one part of speech.

> NOTE If one of the words modifies another modifier, do not separate those two words with a comma.
>
> EXAMPLE    Do you like this **dark blue** sweater?

**Reference Note**

For more information about **compound** and **compound-complex sentences,** see page 481.

**Reference Note**

For more information on **compound nouns,** see page 376.

### Exercise 3  Correcting Sentences by Adding Commas

Write each series in the following sentences, adding commas where needed.

EXAMPLE    **1.** Rita plays soccer volleyball and softball.

      *1. soccer, volleyball, and softball*

**1.** Dr. Charles Drew worked as a surgeon developed new ways of storing blood and was the first director of the Red Cross blood bank program.
**2.** I am going to take English science social studies and algebra.
**3.** The loud insistent smoke alarm woke us just before dawn.

When two or more adjectives precede a noun, you can use two tests to determine whether the last adjective and the noun form a unit.

### TEST 1

Insert the word *and* between the adjectives. If *and* fits sensibly between the adjectives, use a comma.

### EXAMPLE

A juicy, tangy apple makes a good snack.
[*Juicy and tangy* makes sense, so the comma is correct.]

### TEST 2

Change the order of the adjectives. If the order of the adjectives can be reversed sensibly, use a comma.

### EXAMPLE

The quiet, polite girl sat next to her mother.
[*Polite, quiet girl* makes sense, so the comma is correct.]

4. Please pass those delicious blueberry pancakes the margarine and the syrup.

5. My twin sister can run faster jump higher and do more push-ups than I can.

6. Where is the nearest store that sells newspapers magazines and paperbacks?

7. Horns tooted tires screeched a whistle blew and sirens wailed.

8. Steel is made from iron other metals and small amounts of carbon.

9. The clown wore a long blue raincoat; big red plastic gloves; and floppy yellow tennis shoes.

10. Robert Browning says that youth is good that middle age is better and that old age is best.

### Exercise 4  Using Commas Correctly in Series

Your school's new counselor wants to get to know the students better. He has developed the following personality questionnaire, and today he has given a copy to all the students in your class. Answer each question by writing a sentence that includes a series of words, phrases, or clauses. Use commas where needed in each series.

EXAMPLE   1.  What do you consider your most outstanding traits?

1.  *I am considerate, thoughtful, and loyal.*

---

```
              Personality Questionnaire

 1. What do you consider your most outstanding
    traits?

 2. What qualities do you admire most in a
    person?

 3. Who are the people who have influenced
    you most?

 4. What are your favorite hobbies?

 5. What famous people would you like to meet?

 6. What countries would you most like to visit?

 7. For what reasons do you attend school?

 8. What are your favorite subjects in school?

 9. What things about the world would you most
    like to change?

10. What goals do you hope to achieve during the
    next ten years?
```

# Independent Clauses

**22g.** Use a comma before *and, but, for, nor, or, so,* or *yet* when it joins independent clauses.

EXAMPLES    Hector pressed the button**,** **and** the engine started up.

She would never argue**,** **nor** would she complain to anyone.

Are you going to the football game**,** **or** do you have other plans for Saturday?

He is an accomplished actor**,** **yet** he's very modest.

Do not be misled by compound verbs, which can make a sentence look like a compound sentence.

SIMPLE SENTENCE    Mara **cleared** the table and **did** the dishes.
[one subject with a compound verb]

COMPOUND SENTENCE    **Mara cleared the table,** and **Roland did the dishes.** [two independent clauses]

> **NOTE** The comma joining two independent clauses is sometimes omitted before *and, but, or,* or *nor* when the independent clauses are very short and when there is no possibility of misunderstanding.
>
> CLEAR    The dog barked and the cat meowed.
> AWKWARD    Bill bathed the dog and the cat hid under the bed.
> [confusing without comma]
> CLEAR    Bill bathed the dog**,** and the cat hid under the bed.

**Reference Note**

For more about **compound sentences,** see page 481. For information on **compound subjects** and **compound verbs,** see page 424.

**STYLE      TIP**

For clarity, some writers prefer always to use the comma before a conjunction joining independent clauses. Follow your teacher's instructions on this point.

**MECHANICS**

### Exercise 5   Correcting Sentences by Adding Commas Between Independent Clauses

Where a comma should be used, write the word preceding the comma, the comma, and the conjunction following it. If a sentence is already correct, write *C.*

EXAMPLE    1. Accident-related injuries are common and many of these injuries can be prevented.

1. *common, and*

1. It is important to know first aid for an accident can happen at almost any time.
2. More than 83,000 people in the United States die in accidents each year and many millions are injured.

3. Many household products can cause illness or even death but are often stored where small children can reach them.

4. Biking accidents are common wherever cars and bicycles use the same road so many communities have provided bicycle lanes.

5. Car accidents are the leading cause of childhood fatalities but seat belts have saved many lives.

6. Everyone should know what to do in case of fire and different escape routes should be tested.

7. If you need to escape a fire, you should stay close to the floor and be very cautious about opening doors.

8. Holding your breath, keep low and protected behind a door when opening it for a blast of superheated air can be fatal.

9. An injured person should not get up nor should liquid be given to someone who is unconscious.

10. Always have someone with you when you swim or you may find yourself without help when you need it.

## Nonessential Clauses and Phrases

**22h.** Use commas to set off nonessential subordinate clauses and nonessential participial phrases.

A *nonessential* (or *nonrestrictive*) clause or participial phrase adds information that is not necessary to the main idea in the sentence.

| | |
|---|---|
| NONESSENTIAL CLAUSES | Eileen Murray, **who is at the top of her class,** wants to go to medical school. |
| | Texas, **which has the most farms of any state in this country,** produces one fourth of our oil. |
| NONESSENTIAL PHRASES | Tim Ricardo, **hoping to make the swim team,** practiced every day. |
| | *The Lord of the Rings,* **written by J.R.R. Tolkien,** has been translated into many languages. |

Omitting each boldface clause or phrase in the preceding examples does not change the main idea of the sentence.

EXAMPLES      Eileen Murray wants to go to medical school.

Texas produces one fourth of our oil.

Tim Ricardo practiced every day.

*The Lord of the Rings* has been translated into many languages.

**Reference Note**

For more information about **subordinate clauses,** see page 471. For more about **participial phrases,** see page 451.

When a clause or phrase is necessary to the meaning of a sentence—that is, when it tells *which one(s)*—the clause or phrase is **essential** (or **restrictive**), and commas are not used.

Notice how the meaning of each of the following sentences changes when the essential clause or phrase is omitted.

"Sure I got all the punctuation: comma, comma, period, period, question mark, comma, semi-colon, comma, exclamation point, period..."

© 1998 by Sidney Harris.

| ESSENTIAL CLAUSE | All students **whose names are on that list** must report to Ms. Washington this afternoon. [All students must report to Ms. Washington this afternoon.] |
|---|---|
| ESSENTIAL PHRASE | A Ming vase **displayed in the museum** was once owned by Chiang Kai-shek. [A Ming vase was once owned by Chiang Kai-shek.] |

Depending on the writer's meaning, a participial phrase or clause may be either essential or nonessential. Including or omitting commas tells the reader how the clause or phrase relates to the main idea of the sentence.

| NONESSENTIAL CLAUSE | LaWanda's brother, who is a senior, works part time at the mall. [LaWanda has only one brother. He works at the mall.] |
|---|---|
| ESSENTIAL CLAUSE | LaWanda's brother who is a senior works part time at the mall. [LaWanda has more than one brother. The one who is a senior works at the mall.] |

NOTE  An adjective clause beginning with *that* is usually essential.

EXAMPLE    Was Hank Aaron the first major league baseball player **that** broke Babe Ruth's home run record?

**Exercise 6** **Correcting Sentences with Essential and Nonessential Clauses by Adding or Deleting Commas**

The following sentences contain essential and nonessential clauses. Add or delete commas as necessary to punctuate each of these clauses correctly. If a sentence is already correct, write *C*.

EXAMPLE    **1.** My mother who is a Celtics fan has season tickets.

   *1. My mother, who is a Celtics fan, has season tickets.*

1. *Jump Start* which is my favorite comic strip makes me think as well as laugh.
2. Ms. Lopez, who teaches social studies and gym will leave at the end of the year.
3. The amusement rides that are the most exciting may be the most dangerous.
4. Many of the first Spanish settlements in California were founded by Father Junípero Serra who liked to take long walks between them.
5. People, who carry credit cards, should keep a record of their account numbers at home.
6. Amy Kwan who is our class president plans to go to Yale after she graduates from high school.
7. A town like Cottonwood which has a population of five thousand seems ideal to me.
8. All dogs that pass the obedience test get a reward; those that don't pass get to take the test again later.
9. Have you tried this pemmican which my mother made from an old Cree recipe?
10. "The Gift of the Magi" is a story, in which the two main characters who are deeply in love make sacrifices in order to buy gifts for each other.

### Exercise 7   Correcting Sentences with Participial Phrases by Adding or Deleting Commas

Add or delete commas as necessary to punctuate the following sentences correctly. If a sentence is already correctly punctuated, write *C*.

EXAMPLE   1.  Our dog startled by the noise began to bark.

1.  *Our dog, startled by the noise, began to bark.*

1. People, visiting the reservation, will be barred from burial sites, which are considered holy by American Indians.
2. Players breaking training will be dismissed from the team.
3. Students, planning to go on the field trip, should bring their lunches.
4. When Tony holding up a parsnip asked whether parsnips are related to carrots, I said, "Well, they certainly look alike."
5. Joe told me that kudzu introduced into the United States in the 1800s now grows in much of the South.
6. Elizabeth Blackwell completing her medical studies in 1849 became the first female doctor in the United States.

7. Pressure and heat acting on the remains of plants and animals turn those remains into gas or oil or coal.

8. Every child, registering for school for the first time, must present evidence of certain vaccinations.

9. The astronauts living in the space station studied the effects of weightlessness.

10. Windsor Castle built during the reigns of Henry III and Edward III stands twenty-one miles west of London.

**Review B** **Correcting Sentences with Nonessential Clauses and Participial Phrases by Adding Commas**

Some of the following sentences contain clauses and phrases that need to be set off by commas. If a sentence is incorrect, add the necessary comma or commas. If a sentence is already correctly punctuated, write *C*.

EXAMPLE    1. Hanukkah which is also called the Feast of Lights is a major Jewish celebration.

1. *Hanukkah, which is also called the Feast of Lights, is a major Jewish celebration.*

1. The picture on this page shows a part of the Hanukkah celebration that is very beautiful.

2. The girl following an ancient custom is lighting the menorah.

3. The menorah which is an eight-branched candlestick symbolizes the original festival.

4. Hanukkah which means "dedication" celebrates the rededication of the Temple of Jerusalem in 165 B.C.

5. This event followed the Jewish people's victory over Syria, which was led by a pagan king.

6. During the first Hanukkah, according to traditional lore, the Jews had a one-day supply of lamp oil that lasted for eight days.

7. Today celebrating the memory of this miraculous event modern Jews light one candle on the menorah each day of the eight-day festival.

8. Hanukkah starts on the twenty-fifth day of the Hebrew month of Kislev which is usually in December on the Gregorian calendar.

9. The festival celebrated all over the world is a time of feasting, gift giving, and happiness.

10. During Hanukkah, children play a game with a dreidel which is a four-sided toy that is like a top.

Add commas where they are needed in the following sentences. If a sentence does not require any commas, write *C*.

EXAMPLE    **1.** The emu is a large flightless bird from Australia.

            *1.* *The emu is a large, flightless bird from Australia.*

**1.** The students sold crafts used books and baked goods at the bazaar.

**2.** John Wayne whose real name was Marion Morrison won an Academy Award for *True Grit.*

**3.** Add flour mix the ingredients and stir the batter.

**4.** People who come to the game early will be allowed to take pictures of the players.

**5.** *Exiles* written by James Joyce will be performed by the Grantville Community Players and will run for three weeks.

**6.** The float in the homecoming parade was covered with large pink rose petals and small silvery spangles.

**7.** Members of the committee met for three hours but they still have not chosen a theme for the dance.

**8.** Helium which is used by balloonists deep-sea divers and welders is an inert gas.

**9.** An eclipse that occurs when the earth prevents the sun's light from reflecting off the moon is called a lunar eclipse.

**10.** In one month our little town was hit by a tornado and a flood and a fire yet we managed to survive.

# Introductory Elements

**22i.** Use commas after certain introductory elements.

**(1)** Use a comma to set off a mild exclamation such as *well, oh,* or *why* at the beginning of a sentence. Other introductory words such as *yes* and *no* are also set off with commas.

EXAMPLES    **Why,** you're Andy's brother, aren't you?

             **Yes,** she's going to the cafeteria.

**(2) Use a comma after an introductory participial phrase.**

EXAMPLES  **Switching on a flashlight,** the ranger led the way down the path to the caves.

**Disappointed by the high prices,** we made up a new gift list.

**Given a choice,** I would rather work in the yard early in the morning.

**(3) Use a comma after two or more introductory prepositional phrases or after a long one.**

EXAMPLES  **Near the door to the garage,** you will find hooks for the car keys.

**Inside the fence at the far end of her property,** she built a potting shed.

**By the time they had finished,** the boys were exhausted.

NOTE  One short introductory prepositional phrase does not require a comma unless the comma is necessary to make the meaning clear.

EXAMPLES  **At our house** we share all the work.

**At our house,** plants grow best in the sunny, bright kitchen. [The comma is necessary to avoid reading *house plants.*]

**(4) Use a comma after an introductory adverb clause.**

EXAMPLES  **After Andrés Segovia had played his last guitar concert,** the audience applauded for more than fifteen minutes.

**If you see smoke,** you know there is a fire.

NOTE  An adverb clause in the middle or at the end of a sentence is generally not set off by a comma.

EXAMPLES  Miranda, please remember to phone me **when you get home this evening.** [No comma is necessary between *me* and *when.*]

We stayed a long time **because we were having fun.** [No comma is necessary between *time* and *because.*]

Reference Note

For information on **participial phrases,** see page 451. For information on **prepositional phrases,** see page 442.

Reference Note

For information on **adverb clauses,** see page 475.

MECHANICS

**Correcting Sentences with Introductory Elements by Adding Commas**

Add commas where they are needed after introductory elements in the following sentences. If a sentence is already correct, write *C*.

EXAMPLE    1. When Marco Polo visited China in the thirteenth century he found an advanced civilization.

         *1. When Marco Polo visited China in the thirteenth century, he found an advanced civilization.*

1. Although there was a great deal of poverty in China the ruling classes lived in splendor.
2. Valuing cleanliness, Chinese rulers took baths every day.
3. Instead of using coins as currency the Chinese used paper money.
4. After marrying a Chinese woman usually lived in her mother-in-law's home.
5. After one Chinese emperor had died he was buried with more than eight thousand statues of servants and horses.
6. Respected by their descendants elderly people were highly honored.
7. Built around 200 B.C. the main part of the Great Wall of China is about four thousand miles long.
8. Why until modern freeways were built, the Great Wall was the world's longest construction.
9. In the painting on this page you can see that Chinese landscapes look different from those created by Western artists.
10. In Chinese art people are very small and are usually shown in harmony with nature.

# Interrupters

**22j.** Use commas to set off elements that interrupt the sentence.

Two commas are used around an interrupting element—one before and one after.

EXAMPLES    His guitar, **according to him,** once belonged to Bo Diddley.

         Mr. Gonzales, **my civics teacher,** encouraged me to enter my essay in the contest.

Sometimes an "interrupter" comes at the beginning or at the end of a sentence. In such cases, only one comma is needed.

EXAMPLES **Nevertheless,** you must go with me.

I need the money, **Josh.**

**(1)** Nonessential appositives and nonessential appositive phrases should be set off with commas.

A *nonessential* (or *nonrestrictive*) *appositive* or *appositive phrase* provides information that is unnecessary to the basic meaning of the sentence.

EXAMPLES Their new parrot, **Mina,** is very gentle. [The sentence means the same thing without the appositive.]

Elizabeth Peña, **my favorite actress,** stars in the movie I rented. [The sentence means the same thing without the appositive phrase.]

An *essential* (or *restrictive*) *appositive* or *appositive phrase* adds information that makes the noun or pronoun it identifies more specific.

EXAMPLES My friend **Tamisha** lost her wallet. [The writer has more than one friend. *Tamisha* identifies which friend. The meaning of the sentence changes without the appositive.]

He recited the second stanza of "Childhood" by the poet **Margaret Walker.** [The appositive *Margaret Walker* identifies which poet.]

We **art club members** made the decorations. [The appositive phrase *art club members* explains who is meant by *We.*]

**Reference Note**

For more information on **appositives** and **appositive phrases,** see page 461.

## Exercise 9 Correcting Sentences with Appositives and Appositive Phrases by Adding Commas

Correctly use commas to punctuate the appositives in the following sentences. If a sentence needs no commas, write *C.*

EXAMPLE 1. My cousin consulted Dr. Moniz an allergy specialist about the harmful effects of pollution.

1. *My cousin consulted Dr. Moniz, an allergy specialist, about the harmful effects of pollution.*

1. *Ecology* an obscure word forty years ago is now a popular term.
2. The word *ecology* comes from *oikos,* the Greek word meaning "house."

3. Ecology is the study of an enormous "house" the world of all living things.
4. Ecologists study the bond of a living organism to its environment the place in which it lives.
5. Humans one kind of living organism affect their environment in both beneficial and harmful ways.
6. My twin sister Margaret Anne is worried about the future of the environment.
7. She and many of her friends attended Earth Day a festival devoted to ecology.
8. An amateur photographer my cousin prepared a slide show on soil erosion in Grant Park.
9. One of many displays at the Earth Day Festival my cousin's presentation attracted wide attention and won a prize.
10. The mayor a member of the audience promised to appoint a committee to study the problem.

**(2) Words used in direct address are set off by commas.**

EXAMPLES **Linda,** you know the rules.

I did that exercise last night **, Ms. Ryan.**

**Sir,** are these your keys?

Your room **, Bernice,** needs cleaning.

**( Exercise 10 ) Correcting Sentences with Words in Direct Address by Adding Commas**

Correct the following sentences by adding commas where they are needed.

EXAMPLE 1. Annabella when will you be at the station?

1. *Annabella, when will you be at the station?*

1. Dad why can't I go to the movies tonight?
2. As soon as you're ready Virginia we'll leave; the car is all packed, and the gas tank is full.
3. Yes Mom I washed the dishes.
4. What we need Mayor Wilson are more playgrounds.
5. Will you answer the last question Jim?
6. Rex fetch the ball!
7. I think ma'am that my piano playing has improved this year.

**8.** We left some for you Bella.

**9.** José how far from here is the teen recreation center that has the heated swimming pool?

**10.** May I help you with the gardening Grandma?

**(3)** Parenthetical expressions are set off by commas.

*Parenthetical expressions* are side remarks that add information or relate ideas.

**Reference Note**

For information on using **parentheses** and **dashes** to set off parenthetical expressions, see Chapter 26.

| Commonly Used Parenthetical Expressions | | |
|---|---|---|
| after all | generally speaking | nevertheless |
| at any rate | however | of course |
| consequently | I believe | on the contrary |
| for example | in the first place | on the other hand |
| for instance | moreover | therefore |

EXAMPLES  **Of course,** I am glad that he called me about the extra movie tickets.

She is, **in fact,** a dentist.

You should try out for quarterback, **in my opinion.**

Some expressions may be used either parenthetically or not parenthetically. Do not set them off with commas unless they're truly parenthetical.

EXAMPLES  Sandra will, **I think,** enjoy the program. [parenthetical]
**I think** Sandra will enjoy the program. [not parenthetical]

**However,** Phuong Vu finished her report on time. [parenthetical]
**However** did Phuong Vu finish her report on time? [not parenthetical—similar to "How did she finish?"]

**To tell the truth,** he tries. [parenthetical]
He tries **to tell the truth.** [not parenthetical]

**After all,** we've been through this situation before. [parenthetical]
**After all** we've been through, we need a vacation. [not parenthetical]

**MECHANICS**

**NOTE** A contrasting expression introduced by *not* is parenthetical and should be set off by commas.

EXAMPLES The divisor**, not the dividend,** is the bottom number of a fraction.

The coach and I believe the winner of the long jump will be Rachel**, not her.**

## Exercise 11 Correcting Sentences with Parenthetical Expressions by Adding Commas

Correctly punctuate the parenthetical expressions in the following sentences.

EXAMPLE 1. In my opinion my little sister Iona has great taste in music.

1. *In my opinion, my little sister Iona has great taste in music.*

1. For instance her favorite collection of songs is called *Gift of the Tortoise.*
2. Performed I believe by Ladysmith Black Mambazo, the lyrics of the songs are a blend of English and Zulu words and phrases.
3. The South African performers in fact sing a cappella (without musical instruments accompanying them).
4. Not surprisingly their powerful style of music is known by millions of people worldwide.
5. Fudugazi by the way is the storytelling tortoise who explains the meaning of the songs.
6. By listening to the song "Finger Dance," Iona has learned believe it or not to count to five in Zulu.
7. She has not yet learned to sing any of her favorite songs in Zulu however.
8. Of course our whole family enjoys listening to these lovely South African songs.
9. The spirited music and moving sound effects moreover seem to transport us to a faraway land and culture.
10. Everyone should I think follow Fudugazi's advice: "There is magic in these songs; close your eyes and listen, and you will feel the magic, too!"

# Conventional Uses of Commas

**22k.** Use commas in certain conventional situations.

**(1)** Use commas to separate items in dates and addresses.

EXAMPLES     After Tuesday, November 23, 2001, address all orders to
Emeryville, CA 94608.

Please send your cards by November 23, 2000, to 7856
Hidalgo Way, Emeryville, CA 94608.

Notice that no comma divides the month and day (November 23) or
the house number and the street name (7856 Hidalgo Way) because
each is considered one item. Also, the ZIP Code is not separated from
the abbreviation of the state by a comma (Emeryville, CA 94608).

> **NOTE** Commas are not needed if the day precedes the month or if only
> the month and year are given.
>
> EXAMPLES    President Bill Clinton took office on **20 January 1993.**
>
> Hurricane Andrew hit southern Florida in **August 1992.**

**(2)** Use a comma after the salutation of a personal letter and after
the closing of any letter.

EXAMPLES     Dear Mr. Arpajian,      Sincerely yours,

My dear Anna,        Yours very truly,

**(3)** Use commas to set off abbreviations such as *Jr., Sr.,* or *M.D.*
when they follow persons' names.

EXAMPLES     Please welcome Allen Davis, Sr.

Carol Ferrara, M.D., is our family physician.

┌─ **HELP** ─
Use a colon
after the salutation of
a business letter.

EXAMPLE
  Dear Service Manager:

**Reference Note**
For more about using
**colons,** see page 675.
For more about writing
**business letters,** see
"Writing" in the Quick
Reference Handbook.

## Review D    Correcting Sentences by Adding Commas

Add commas where they are needed in the following sentences. If a
sentence is already correct, write *C*.

EXAMPLE     **1.** On July 14 1789 the people of Paris stormed the Bastille.

                *1. On July 14, 1789, the people of Paris stormed the Bastille.*

**1.** Please address the envelope to Ms. Marybeth Correio 1255 S.E.
56th Street Bellevue WA 98006.

2. Sources claim that on April 6 1909 Matthew Henson, assistant to Commander Robert E. Peary, reached the North Pole.
3. I glanced quickly at the end of the letter, which read, "Very sincerely yours Alice Ems Ph.D."
4. The Constitution of the United States was signed on September 17 1787 eleven years after the adoption of the Declaration of Independence on July 4 1776.
5. Did you go on a field trip to the desert in March or April of 1999?
6. We used to live in Monterrey but now we live at 100 Robin Road Austin Texas.
7. Tony watch out for that spider.
8. My grandmother a Russian learned English late in life.
9. That man is the governor by the way.
10. The gauchos crossed the hot windy vast expanse of the pampas.

# Unnecessary Commas

**22l.** Do not use unnecessary commas.

Have a reason for every comma and other mark of punctuation that you use. When there is no rule requiring punctuation and when the meaning of the sentence is clear without it, do not insert any punctuation mark.

| INCORRECT | My friend, Jessica, said she would feed my cat, and my dog while I'm away, but now, she tells me, she will be too busy. |
| CORRECT | My friend Jessica said she would feed my cat and my dog while I'm away, but now she tells me she will be too busy. |

### Review E  Correcting Sentences by Adding Commas

For each of the following sentences, write all the words that should be followed by a comma. Place a comma after each of these words.

EXAMPLE
1. Yes Phyllis I know that you want to transfer to Bayside the high school that has the best volleyball team in the city.

1. *Yes, Phyllis, Bayside,*

1. Scuttling across the dirt road the large hairy spider a tarantula terrified Steve Ellen and me.
2. Whitney not Don won first prize.
3. German shepherds are often trained as guide dogs; other breeds that have also been trained include Labrador retrievers golden retrievers and Doberman pinschers.

4. According to her official birth certificate Mary Elizabeth was born September 7 1976 in Juneau Alaska but she does not remember much of the city.

5. Angela and Jennifer are you both planning to write poems to enter in the contest?

6. All entries for the essay-writing competition should be submitted no later than Friday to Essay Contest 716 North Cliff Drive Salt Lake City UT 84103.

7. The best time to plant flower seeds of course is just before a rainy season not in the middle of a hot dry summer.

8. Our next-door neighbor Ms. Allen manages two large apartment buildings downtown.

9. As a matter of fact most horses can run four miles without having to stop.

10. The Comanches like some other nomadic American Indians once traveled throughout the states of Kansas New Mexico Texas and Oklahoma.

11. My favorite story "The Most Dangerous Game" was written back in 1924.

12. Even though I ran quickly around the base of the tree the squirrel always stayed on the opposite side of the tree from me.

13. We planted irises because they are perennials flowers that bloom year after year.

14. One of Cleopatra's Needles famous stone pillars from ancient Egypt stands in Central Park in New York City New York.

15. In April 1976 a fifth-grader in Newburgh New York released a helium balloon; it was found in Strathaven Scotland on the other side of the Atlantic Ocean two days later.

16. Danny's father just bought a 1967 Ford Mustang with green white and red stripes on the sides.

17. Before we begin reading *The Odyssey* we will see a movie about ancient Greece.

18. Mount Waialeale, Hawaii, receives an average of 460 inches of rain each year making it the rainiest place in the world.

19. A light frost was on the ground the leaves were falling the air was cool and the wind was blowing stronger; autumn had arrived overnight.

20. The performance of our school's spring musical has been sold out for weeks but those of us who helped build the set will get free tickets.

MECHANICS

**Adding End Marks and Commas**

Add end marks and commas where they are needed in each sentence in the following paragraph.

EXAMPLE  **[1]** As you can see from the map below Cabeza de Vaca explored areas in North America and South America

1. *As you can see from the map below, Cabeza de Vaca explored areas in North America and South America.*

[1] Did you know that Álvar Núñez Cabeza de Vaca a Spanish explorer participated in two trips to this region [2] To tell the truth neither trip ended successfully [3] In the summer of 1527 he was treasurer of an expedition that was sent to conquer and colonize Florida [4] However the invasion didn't work out as planned and he was one of a handful of survivors [5] These men intended to sail to Mexico but their ship wrecked off the coast of Texas  [6] What an unlucky expedition that was [7] Cabeza de Vaca was captured by a native people but he later escaped and wandered through Texas and Mexico for eight years [8] He tells about his Florida expedition in the book *Naufragios* which has the Spanish word for "shipwrecks" as its title. [9] In 1541 this adventurer led an expedition to South America and he became governor of Paraguay [10] When the colonists revolted Cabeza de Vaca returned to Spain under arrest but he was later pardoned.

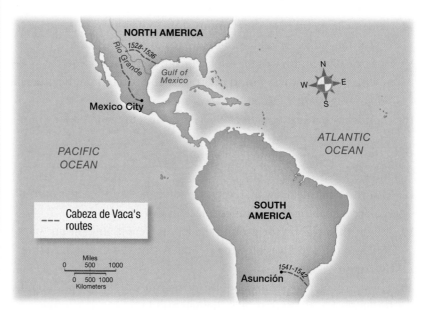

# Chapter Review

## A. Correcting Sentences by Adding End Marks and Commas

Most of the following sentences contain errors in the use of end marks and commas. Write each sentence, adding end marks and commas where needed. If no additional punctuation is needed, write *C*.

1. She says tae kwon do a Korean martial art improves concentration
2. Well that's the last time that I'll ever ride in one of those taxis
3. Is the card addressed to Robert Danieli Jr or to Robert Danieli
4. The batter hoping to advance the runners laid down a perfect bunt
5. Use light colors by the way to make a small room seem larger
6. We used to live in Lansing but now we live at 457 Cleveland Road Huntsville Alabama
7. Did you ask Joe to bring the forks plates and cups to the picnic
8. What an interesting enjoyable book that is
9. When we complained to Mrs Finch about the remark she apologized to us
10. Reva look out for that pothole in the road
11. If the worn tire had not been replaced it could have caused an accident.
12. The green flag the signal to begin the race was seen by thousands
13. Send your application to Box 36 New York NY before June 30 2003
14. Your homework of course must be finished before you go hiking
15. Sitting on their front porch my grandparents talk to the children who pass
16. We looked after our neighbors' dog while they toured Canada for two weeks and they offered to feed our cat next Thanksgiving
17. Wow this movie is exciting
18. People watching the parade were sitting on curbs and standing on sidewalks.
19. At the convenience store on the corner my sister bought juice
20. Désirée I would like to know your secret for a beautiful complexion

## B. Using Periods, Question Marks, and Exclamation Points

Add commas, periods, question marks, and exclamation points where needed in the following sentences. Identify each sentence as *declarative, imperative, interrogative,* or *exclamatory.*

**21.** Did the author Willa Cather write about life on the prairie

**22.** Angelo had cereal a muffin a boiled egg and toast for breakfast

**23.** How long did that project take

**24.** Well, wouldn't hearing Domingo sing be worth the trip

**25.** Oh boy what a great idea

**26.** Students, sign up in the office if you are going on the field trip

**27.** You will find the test on my desk which is near the bookcase

**28.** Rita wants to invite Ingrid Ingrid's cousin and their friend Jamila

**29.** My younger sister who will be twelve wants to have a birthday party

**30.** Turn down the radio

## C. Using Abbreviations

Rewrite the following sentences, correcting errors in the use of abbreviations.

**31.** The guest of honor was Dr. Steve Welch, M. D.

**32.** Maj. Gen. McCambridge, the base commander, was on TV.

**33.** This statue was probably sculpted between B.C. 500 and 400.

**34.** At 9:35 A.M. in the morning, the race started.

**35.** Following family custom, Samuel Brandt, Junior, named his first-born son Samuel Brandt III.

**36.** The interns working in the ER enjoyed the challenges and the unpredictability of life in an emergency room.

**37.** In 1271 A.D., the Italian adventurer Marco Polo left Venice on his long voyage to China.

**38.** My parents spent their early years in Wilmington, DE, and Miami, FL.

**39.** The explorers set up camp in what would later become Seattle, Wash.

**40.** The speeding car was clocked at seventy-five m.p.h.

MECHANICS

## D. Proofreading a Paragraph for End Marks and Commas

In the following paragraph, insert end marks and commas as needed.

[41] As I took photos last Saturday with an instant camera I became increasingly curious about the origin of this type of camera [42] Being the persistent seeker after knowledge that I am how could I not spend time the next day researching the topic [43] The results of my research needless to say were quite interesting [44] Apparently Edwin Land's daughter once asked him why a camera couldn't immediately produce pictures [45] Land who had taught himself physics quickly worked out the basic principles and design of an instant camera [46] What a tremendous achievement that was [47] He became head of Polaroid Corp and that company produced the first Polaroid Land camera in 1948 [48] Did you know that Land later made important contributions to the study of lasers and color vision [49] Land died on March 1 1991 [50] Among his honors were the Presidential Medal of Freedom and of course the National Medal of Science

# Writing Application

## Writing Clear Directions

**Using Commas**   A friend asks you for directions from your school to a particular destination. In your instructions, use commas to separate items in a series, to join independent clauses, to set off an introductory adverb clause, to set off a noun of direct address, and to separate items in an address.

**Prewriting**   Choose a destination (real or imagined), and then outline on paper the way to get there.

**Writing**   As you write your first draft, concentrate on making the directions clear and easy to follow.

**Revising**   Read your directions to be sure they are arranged in a logical order. Check to see that you have used commas in the five ways specified in the instructions for this writing activity.

**Publishing**   Proofread your directions for correct grammar and punctuation. You and your classmates may want to collect your directions into a newcomers' guide for new students at your school.

# Punctuation
## Semicolons and Colons

# Diagnostic Preview

### A. Correcting Sentences by Adding Semicolons and Colons

For the following sentences, write each word or numeral that should be followed by a semicolon or colon, and then insert the missing semicolon or colon. If a sentence is already correct, write *C*.

EXAMPLE   **1.** Someday, robots may do many simple household chores, wash windows, answer the telephone, make repairs, and serve dinner.

    *1.* *chores:*

**1.** I didn't go to the game last night, instead, I took care of my baby brother, Carl.
**2.** The band members will perform at the civic center on Tuesday, January 15, at the Kiwanis Club on Saturday, January 19, and at the Oak Nursing Home on Friday, January 25.
**3.** For the lesson on figures of speech, we had to find examples of similes, metaphors, personification, and hyperbole.
**4.** Dr. Enríquez has traveled to rain forests in many parts of the world, Borneo, Brazil, Costa Rica, and Sri Lanka.
**5.** The first Spaniards who settled in America built forts, missions, and pueblos, evidence of Spanish influence on American architecture can be found throughout the Southwest.

6. The Tower of Babel, as described in Genesis 11 1–9, resembled a ziggurat, or terraced pyramid.

7. Erica seldom misses a football playoff on TV, last Saturday, for example, she watched the NFC championship game from noon to 3 00 P.M.

8. I invited Peggy, Josefina, and Sonya, and Beth, Errol, and Randy are coming too.

9. My brother doesn't like many TV shows; instead of watching TV, he prefers to read books.

10. The events for the annual Ironman Triathlon, which is held in Hawaii and is open to men and to women, are as follows, swimming in the ocean 2.4 miles, bicycling 112 miles, and running 26.2 miles.

## B. Proofreading a Letter for Correct Use of Semicolons and Colons

Find the ten places where a semicolon or a colon should be used in the following letter. Write each word or number that should be followed by a semicolon or a colon; then, add the necessary punctuation mark.

EXAMPLE   **[1]** Last summer we stayed home during summer vacation, this summer we took a trip in the car.

　　　　　　*1. vacation;*

290 Eureka Street
Dallas, TX 76013

August 15, 2001

Director
California Department of Parks and Recreation
Box 2390
Sacramento, CA 95811

**[11]** Dear Sir or Madam,

　　**[12]** While on vacation this summer, my family and I visited the following states Washington, Oregon, and California. **[13]** We wanted you to know that we especially enjoyed our stay in California, we learned a lot and are planning to return soon.

　　**[14]** What we liked best was visiting the Spanish missions in the Los Angeles area they gave us a real sense of history. **[15]** My favorite places were Mission San Fernando Rey de España, located in Mission Hills, Mission San Gabriel Arcangel, located in San Gabriel, and El Pueblo de Los Angeles. **[16]** The Old Plaza Church, Nuestra Señora la

Reina de Los Angeles, which dates from 1822, was especially wonderful, we stayed there from noon to 500 P.M., when the mission closed.

[**17**] Our stay in California was great, we hope to return next summer when we will have more time. [**18**] I would like to visit some of the missions around San Francisco therefore, I would appreciate it if you could send me some information on that area. Thank you very much.

Yours truly,

*Angie Barnes*

Angie Barnes

# Semicolons

| STYLE | | TIP |

Use a semicolon to join independent clauses only if the ideas in the clauses are closely related.

**INCORRECT**
Josh wants to go to Venezuela; Elaine wants to swim.

**CORRECT**
Josh wants to go to Venezuela; Elaine wants to go to Paraguay.

**23a.** Use a semicolon between independent clauses that are closely related in meaning if they are not joined by *and, but, for, nor, or, so,* or *yet.*

Notice in the following pairs of examples that the semicolon takes the place of the comma and the conjunction joining the independent clauses.

EXAMPLES First, I had a sandwich and a glass of milk**, and** then I called you for the homework assignment.
First, I had a sandwich and a glass of milk**;** then I called you for the homework assignment.

Patty likes to act**, but** her sister gets stage fright.
Patty likes to act**;** her sister gets stage fright.

Similarly, a semicolon can take the place of a period to join two or more clauses that are closely related.

EXAMPLES Manuel looked out at the downpour**. T**hen he put on his raincoat and boots. [two simple sentences]
Manuel looked out at the downpour**;** then he put on his raincoat and boots. [one compound sentence]

Rain soaked the earth**. P**lants became green**. F**ragrant flowers bloomed. [three simple sentences]
Rain soaked the earth**;** plants became green**;** fragrant flowers bloomed. [one compound sentence]

**Reference Note**

For information on **simple and compound sentences,** see page 481.

## Exercise 1 Correcting Sentences by Adding Semicolons Between Independent Clauses

Indicate where a semicolon should be placed in each of the following sentences. In some instances, you may prefer to use a period. Be prepared to explain your choice.

┌─HELP─
In the example for Exercise 1, a semicolon is used because the two independent clauses are closely related.

EXAMPLE     1. Great earthquakes usually begin gently only one or two slight shocks move the earth.

            1. *Great earthquakes usually begin gently; only one or two slight shocks move the earth.*

1. Pressure builds along faults, or cracks, in the earth's crust the weight of this pressure causes earthquakes.
2. The San Andreas fault, shown here, extends nearly the entire length of California earthquakes often occur all along this fault.
3. During an earthquake, huge chunks of the earth's crust begin to move the San Francisco earthquake of 1906, pictured here, was one of the most destructive earthquakes recorded in history.
4. Energy released during an earthquake is tremendous it can equal the explosive force of 180 metric tons of TNT.
5. Scientists study the force of earthquakes they measure this force on a scale of numbers called the Richter scale.
6. An earthquake measuring less than 5 on the Richter scale is not serious more than 1,000 earthquakes measuring 2 or less occur daily.
7. In 1906, one of the most powerful earthquakes in history occurred in the Pacific Ocean near Ecuador it measured 8.9 on the Richter scale.
8. Tidal waves are a dangerous result of earthquakes geologists use the Japanese word *tsunami* for these destructive ocean waves.
9. Predicting when earthquakes will occur is not yet possible predicting where they will occur is somewhat more certain.
10. Earthquakes seem to strike in a regular time sequence in California, for example, a major earthquake usually occurs every fifty to one hundred years.

**23b.** Use a semicolon between independent clauses joined by a conjunctive adverb or transitional expression.

EXAMPLES    Emma felt shy; **however,** she soon made some new friends.

My bird does unusual tricks; **for example,** he rings a bell and says "Wow."

| Commonly Used Conjunctive Adverbs | | | |
|---|---|---|---|
| accordingly | furthermore | meanwhile | otherwise |
| also | however | moreover | still |
| besides | indeed | nevertheless | then |
| consequently | instead | next | therefore |

| Commonly Used Transitional Expressions | | | |
|---|---|---|---|
| as a result | for instance | in fact | on the other hand |
| for example | in addition | that is | in other words |

Notice in the examples under Rule 23b that the conjunctive adverb and the transitional expression are preceded by semicolons and followed by commas.

NOTE    When a conjunctive adverb or transitional expression appears within one of the clauses and not between clauses, it is usually punctuated as an interrupter (set off by commas). The two clauses are still separated by a semicolon.

EXAMPLES    Our student council voted to have a Crazy Clothes Day; the principal, **however,** vetoed the idea.

That quilt is quite old; it is, **in fact,** filled with cotton, not polyester, batting.

**23c.** A semicolon (rather than a comma) may be needed to separate independent clauses joined by a coordinating conjunction when the clauses contain commas.

CONFUSING    Alana, Eric, and Kim voted for her, and Scott, Roland, and Vanessa voted for Jason.

CLEAR    Alana, Eric, and Kim voted for her; and Scott, Roland, and Vanessa voted for Jason.

CONFUSING    Scanning the horizon for the source of the whirring sound, Pedro saw a huge, green cloud traveling in his direction, and, suddenly recognizing what it was, he knew that the crops soon would be eaten by a horde of grasshoppers.

CLEAR    Scanning the horizon for the source of the whirring sound, Pedro saw a huge, green cloud traveling in his direction; and, suddenly recognizing what it was, he knew that the crops soon would be eaten by a horde of grasshoppers.

**Exercise 2**   **Correcting Sentences by Adding Semicolons Between Independent Clauses**

Write each word that should be followed by a semicolon in the following sentences and add the semicolon. In some cases, you may prefer to use a period. Be prepared to explain your choice.

EXAMPLE    1. Cape Cod is only one of many attractions in Massachusetts, Boston and the Berkshires are also worth visiting.

        1. *Massachusetts;*

1. My mother and I sometimes go to Massachusetts in late summer, however, last year we went in July.
2. We visit Cape Cod once a year, my grandparents live there, so we always have a place to stay.
3. I miss my friends and sometimes find the yearly trip to Cape Cod boring, besides, my cousins in Massachusetts are all older than I am.
4. To my great surprise, we had a very good time last year, we even did some sightseeing in Boston, Plymouth, and Marblehead.
5. One hot day my mother, my grandparents, and I went to the beach, and my grandfather, the most active man I know, immediately went down to the water for a swim.
6. My grandfather loves the water and is a strong swimmer, nevertheless, because the currents are strong and tricky, we worried when we saw that he was swimming out farther and farther.
7. Grandpa, to our great relief, finally turned around and swam back to shore, he was astonished that we had been worried about him.
8. While he was in the water, Mom had gathered driftwood, dug a shallow pit in the sand, and built a fire in it, and Grandma had put lobster, corn, and potatoes on the coals.
9. By the time we had finished eating, it was quite late, consequently, everyone else on the beach had gone home.
10. We didn't leave for home right away, instead, we spent the evening watching the darkening ocean, listening to the whispering waves, and watching the stars come out.

┌HELP─

In the example for Exercise 2, a semicolon is used because the independent clauses are closely related.

**23d.** Use a semicolon between items in a series if the items contain commas.

EXAMPLES    I would like to introduce Mrs. Boyce, our mayor; Mr. Bell, her secretary; Ms. Lincoln, the editor of our newspaper; and Mr. Quinn, our guest of honor.

The Photography Club will meet on Wednesday, September 12; Wednesday, September 19; and Tuesday, September 25.

( Review A )  **Correcting Sentences by Adding Semicolons**

Write each word or numeral that should be followed by a semicolon in the following sentences and add the semicolon. If a sentence needs no semicolons, write *C*.

EXAMPLE    **1.** Tina likes playing basketball, I prefer hockey.
                   *1. basketball;*

1. The first passenger jet was Britain's *Comet*, first flown in 1949, it had some problems at first but later became a quite popular plane.
2. On our trip to Paris, my sister wanted to visit the Louvre, but I was more interested in the Eiffel Tower.
3. Africa's kingdoms included Mali, on the Niger River, Benin, in what is now Nigeria, and Mwanamutapa, in southern Africa.
4. Formerly, most cars had carburetors, the newer models have fuel injectors.
5. Many words in modern Japanese come from English, for instance, the word *doonatsu* comes from *doughnut.*
6. The Incas planted crops, such as corn, they domesticated animals, such as the llama, and they developed crafts, such as weaving.
7. Many scientists believe that one of the elephant's closest living relatives is not a large animal at all surprisingly, it is a small rodentlike creature called the hyrax.
8. Mrs. Gillis said that we could write about Dekanawidah, the Huron founder of the Iroquois League, Mansa Musa, the Muslim emperor of Mali, or Tamerlane, the Mongol conqueror of the Ottoman Turks.
9. Most of Grandmother's belongings were packed away in the attic, however, Mother discovered another suitcase in the cellar, and there were things locked up in the safe-deposit box, too.
10. In the fifteenth century, the kings of France, England, and Spain grew stronger as they unified their lands.

**Review B** **Correcting Sentences by
Adding Semicolons**

Most of the following sentences contain at least one error in the use of
semicolons. Write the word preceding and following each error, and
add the semicolon. If a sentence is already correct, write *C*.

EXAMPLE    **1.** The largest animal in the world today is the blue whale
the largest blue whale ever caught measured slightly
more than 113.5 feet and weighed about 170 tons.

    *1. whale; the*

**1.** Each of the more than seventy-five species of whales is different
however, all whales migrate with the seasons.
**2.** Whales, which are warmblooded marine mammals, are divided
into two main families, these families are the toothed whales (the
larger family) and the toothless whales.
**3.** The biggest toothed whale, the sperm whale, hunts giant squid
along the bottom of the ocean, like all toothed whales, it uses its
teeth for catching food, not chewing it.
**4.** The sperm whale is a record holder in the animal kingdom; it has
the largest brain and the thickest skin.
**5.** Other species of whales include the gray whale, which is probably
the best-known toothless whale, the Baird's beaked whale, which is
also called the giant bottlenose whale, the bowhead whale, which
is also known as the arctic whale, and the killer whale, which is
also called *orca.*

**MECHANICS**

6. Whales take very full, deep breaths consequently, they can dive almost a mile below the surface of the ocean and remain underwater for more than an hour at a time.

7. Some whale species exhibit remarkable social behavior; for example, members of a group may stay with a wounded animal or even support it in the water.

8. During the past 250 years, whalers have nearly wiped out many species of whales, the whaling industry continues to threaten those species that have managed to survive.

9. Several countries, including the United States, have banned the killing of certain whale species; but the blue whale, which is close to extinction, remains an endangered species.

10. Whale-watching cruises originated with the public's growing concern over the survival of whales today whalewatching attracts as many as 350,000 people a year.

## Review C  Correcting Sentences by Adding Semicolons

Most of the following sentences need at least one semicolon. For each incorrectly punctuated sentence, write the word preceding each missing semicolon, the semicolon, and the word following the semicolon. If a sentence needs no semicolon, write *C*.

EXAMPLE
1. American Indian pottery fascinates me, whenever I can, I watch potters like this woman at the Tigua (pronounced TEE-wah) Indian Reservation and Pueblo in El Paso, Texas.

1. *me; whenever*

1. I could have watched for hours as this artist painted designs on the vases, however, I knew that the rest of my family was eager to see more of the reservation.

2. There is much to see there, and they were determined to see it all!

3. The Tiguas have a large adobe visitors center, where they display their arts and crafts and have dance demonstrations, and my younger brothers, Jaime and Lucas, ran all around it.

4. Of course, we had to sample the Tigua specialties at the restaurant, otherwise, we would have missed a unique experience.

5. I've eaten American Indian dishes in Phoenix, Arizona, Muskogee, Oklahoma, and Taos, New Mexico, but the food at the Tigua Reservation was my favorite.

6. I especially enjoyed the *gorditas,* which are a little like tacos, the bread, which was fresh out of the oven, and the chili, which was very spicy.

7. After lunch, a guide told us that the community was established in 1682 by Tiguas who were displaced from northern New Mexico; he said the reservation is the oldest inhabited community in Texas today.

8. The Tiguas are especially proud of their mission they certainly should be.

9. Now known as the Ysleta Mission, it is a beautiful restored building, we enjoyed seeing it.

10. It is the oldest mission in Texas moreover, it is one of the oldest in all of North America.

# Colons

**23e.** Use a colon to mean "note what follows."

**(1)** Use a colon before a list of items, especially after expressions like *the following* and *as follows.*

EXAMPLES    You will need to bring **the following equipment:** a sleeping bag, a warm sweater, and extra socks.

Additional supplies are **as follows:** a toothbrush, toothpaste, a change of clothes, and a pillow.

Sometimes the items that follow a colon are used as appositives. If a word is followed by a list of appositives, the colon makes the sentence clear.

EXAMPLES    At the air base we saw three signs: To Norway, To Paris, and To Lisbon.

You need to shop for several items: brown shoelaces, a quart of milk, and five or six carrots.

**Reference Note**

For more on **appositives** and **appositive phrases,** see page 461.

**NOTE** Do not use a colon between a verb and its complements or between a preposition and its objects.

INCORRECT    Additional supplies are: a toothbrush and toothpaste, a change of clothes, a towel, a pillow, and an air mattress.

CORRECT    Additional supplies are a toothbrush and toothpaste, a change of clothes, a towel, a pillow, and an air mattress.

INCORRECT    You need to shop for: brown shoelaces, a quart of milk, and five or six carrots.

CORRECT    You need to shop for brown shoelaces, a quart of milk, and five or six carrots.

**Reference Note**

For more about using **long quotations,** see page 690.

**(2) Use a colon before a long, formal statement or a long quotation.**

EXAMPLE    Horace Mann had this to say: "Do not think of knocking out another person's brains because he differs in opinion from you. It would be as rational to knock yourself on the head because you differ from yourself ten years ago."

**(3) Use a colon between independent clauses when the second clause explains or restates the idea of the first.**

EXAMPLE    Thomas Jefferson had many talents: He was a writer, a politician, an architect, and an inventor.

**NOTE** The first word of a sentence following a colon is capitalized.

EXAMPLE    Lois felt that she had done something worthwhile: She had designed and sewn her first quilt.

**HELP**

Use a comma after the salutation of a personal letter.

EXAMPLES
Dear Kim,

Dear Uncle Remy,

**23f.** Use a colon in certain conventional situations.

**(1) Use a colon between the hour and the minute.**

EXAMPLES    10:30 A.M.                    6:30 P.M.

**(2) Use a colon between the chapter and the verse in Biblical references and between titles and subtitles.**

EXAMPLES    Exodus 1:6–14                    *Whales: Giants of the Sea*

**Reference Note**

For more about **writing letters,** see "Writing" in the Quick Reference Handbook.

**(3) Use a colon after the salutation of a business letter.**

EXAMPLES    Dear Ms. González:        Dear Dr. Fenton:

Dear Sir or Madam:        To Whom It May Concern:

## Exercise 3  Correcting Sentences by Adding Colons

Correct the following sentences by adding necessary colons. If a sentence does not need a colon, write *C*.

EXAMPLE
    1. When I came into class at 9 15 A.M., everyone was writing an essay based on this West African proverb "To know nothing is bad; to learn nothing is worse."

    *1. When I came into class at 9:15 A.M., everyone was writing an essay based on this West African proverb: "To know nothing is bad; to learn nothing is worse."*

1. Last summer I read "Choices A Tribute to Dr. Martin Luther King, Jr.," by Alice Walker.
2. Mrs. Hughes named the three students who had completed extra projects Marshall, Helena, and Regina.
3. At the festival we bought tacos and refried beans.
4. The qualities she likes most in a person are as follows reliability, a good sense of humor, and willingness to work.
5. Learn to spell the following new words *aneurysm, fluoroscope, peregrination,* and *serendipity.*
6. An enduring statement of loyalty, found in Ruth 1 16, begins as follows "Entreat me not to leave thee or to return from following after thee, for whither thou goest, I will go."
7. The desk was littered with papers, pencils, paperback books, food wrappers, and dirty socks.
8. From 8 00 A.M. until 6 00 P.M., Mr. Brooks sells brushes, brooms, and cleaning products.
9. Alone in the house at night, I heard some scary sounds the creaking of a board, the scratching of tree branches against a window, and the hissing of steam in the radiator.
10. Tomorrow's test will include the punctuation marks that we have studied so far commas, semicolons, and colons.

MECHANICS

DILBERT reprinted by permission of United Feature Syndicate, Inc.

Correct the following sentences, using semicolons and colons where they are needed.

EXAMPLE
1. We didn't have time to go to Michigan, instead we went to New Mexico.

1. *We didn't have time to go to Michigan; instead, we went to New Mexico.*

1. A small, windowless log cabin stood against the rail fence directly behind it ran a muddy stream.
2. Because the club has run out of funds, the following supplies must be brought from home pencils, erasers, paper, and envelopes.
3. Other jobs take too much time for example, if I worked in a store, I probably would have to work most nights.
4. I enjoy the following hobbies fly-fishing, reading, and riding my bike.
5. American cowhands used the ten-gallon hat as protection from the sun and as a dipper for water the leather chaps they wore served as protection from thorny bushes.
6. A rabbi, a Lutheran minister, and a Catholic priest discussed their interpretations of Isaiah 2 2 and 5 26.
7. In his speech Dr. Fujikawa quoted from several poets Rudyard Kipling, David McCord, and Nikki Giovanni.
8. Sojourner Truth, a former slave, could neither read nor write however, this accomplished woman spoke eloquently against slavery and for women's rights.
9. From 1853 to 1865, the United States had three presidents Franklin Pierce, a Democrat from New Hampshire James Buchanan, a Democrat from Pennsylvania and Abraham Lincoln, a Republican from Illinois.
10. From 12 30 to 1 00 P.M., I was so nervous that I could not sit still I paced up and down, swinging my arms and taking deep breaths, while I rehearsed my lines in my mind.

MECHANICS

# Chapter Review

## A. Correcting Sentences by Adding Semicolons Between Independent Clauses

The following sentences are missing semicolons. Write each sentence, adding semicolons where needed.

─HELP─

In Part A of the Chapter Review, you may need to delete some commas and replace them with semicolons.

1. Irma likes cats, her sister is allergic to them.
2. First I cleaned my room, then I called the movie theater to find out the time of the next show.
3. Two of the world's longest railway tunnels are in Italy, moreover, one of the longest motor-traffic tunnels is also located there.
4. My brother Manuel enjoys cooking, I prefer eating.
5. Marty decided to invite Adam, Oliver, and Dorian, and Don, Guy, and Sarah would be there, too.
6. On our first trip to Houston, I wanted to see the Astrodome, my little brother wanted to visit the Johnson Space Center.
7. Tim and Maria often spend Christmas at home however, this year they are going to visit Maria's family in Guanajuato.
8. The popular names of certain animals are misleading, for example, the koala bear is not really a bear.
9. French and Spanish were Charlotte's most difficult subjects, accordingly, she gave them more time than any of her other subjects at school.
10. The teacher settled the argument, he told us we each had to give a presentation.

## B. Correcting Sentences by Adding Colons

Correct the following sentences by adding necessary colons. If a sentence is already correct, write *C*.

11. You will need to bring the following equipment a hammer, a screwdriver, and safety goggles.
12. At the crossroads we saw three signs To Quebec, To Montreal, and To Ottawa.
13. We need to shop for several items salad greens, milk, and a loaf of bread.

MECHANICS

**14.** Exodus 1 6–14 is my favorite passage in the Old Testament.

**15.** The corner store is open from 6 00 A.M. until 11 00 P.M.

**16.** Last year I read the following novels *David Copperfield,* by Charles Dickens; *The Joy Luck Club,* by Amy Tan; and *Bel-Ami,* by Guy de Maupassant.

**17.** The desert floor was strewn with rocks, pebbles, tumbleweed, and mineral shards.

**18.** This evening's program will focus on what we have discussed so far the changes in the West over the last two centuries.

**19.** Especially challenging were the following spelling words *fluorescent, dissuade, annotate,* and *fortuitous.*

**20.** At 11 45 A.M. the flight to Mexico City, Bogotá, Brasilia, and Buenos Aires will depart from Gate 2.

## C. Proofreading for Correct Use of Semicolons and Colons

The following advertisement contains errors in the use of semicolons and colons. Write the word or number preceding the error, and add the needed punctuation mark.

—H E L P—

In Part C of the Chapter Review, you may need to delete some commas and replace them with semicolons and colons.

[21] Your pet probably loves to watch TV, therefore, it should have the best in quality entertainment. [22] Forcing your dog or cat to watch only what humans watch is not only boring for the pet it is somewhat inconsiderate on your part. [23] Buy your faithful friend the new *Rockin' and Rollin' Pets* video it will change your pet's life. [24] No dog or cat will be bored with this movie on the contrary, Fidos and Tabbies everywhere have been sitting up and taking notice. [25] With this video, your pet will get the exciting, up-to-date entertainment it has been craving, as a concerned owner, you will feel good about what your pet is watching. [26] Science has proven that dogs and cats like the movement and music on television, moreover, they like human contact while watching TV. [27] Ask yourself this question, Are you thinking about your pet's happiness when you turn on the set at 7 00 or 8 00 in the evening? [28] Do you think your pet really likes to watch situation comedies, which are about families it doesn't know, movies, which are too long, and news programs, which are too serious? [29] You already know the answer order your pet a *Rockin' and Rollin' Pets* video today! [30] To place your order, call the following toll-free number 1-000-PET-ROCK.

# Writing Application

## Punctuating a Business Letter

**Semicolons and Colons**   You have volunteered to order the items that the members of your school band will sell to raise money for road trips. Write a short letter to order these items.

**Prewriting**   First, decide what kinds of items to sell (for example, ballpoint pens, dried fruit, candles, or book covers) and how many to order. Also, decide on each item's price and make up a name and address for the company from which you will purchase the items.

**Writing**   As you write your first draft, try to keep the body of your letter short and to the point.

**Revising**   Be sure that you have followed the correct form for a business letter. Make sure that you have included all the information necessary for the order.

**Publishing**   Check that you have used a colon after the salutation and before the list of items that you are ordering. Slowly read your letter, focusing on spelling and punctuation. Have you capitalized all proper names, company names, addresses, and brand names? You may want to put your letter-writing abilities to use for your school band or for another school or community organization that holds fund-raisers.

**Reference Note**

For more about the proper form for **business letters,** see "Writing" in the Quick Reference Handbook.

**MECHANICS**

# Punctuation
## Italics and Quotation Marks

# Diagnostic Preview

### A. Correcting Sentences by Adding Underlining (Italics) and Quotation Marks

Add underlining (italics) and quotation marks where they are needed in each of the following sentences.

EXAMPLE **1.** Don't forget your umbrella, said Jody. I read in the Sun Times that it's going to rain today.

**1.** *"Don't forget your umbrella,"* said Jody. *"I read in the Sun Times that it's going to rain today."*

**1.** My grandmother asked me which one I wanted for my birthday, Laura said, a subscription to Time or one to Popular Mechanics.

**2.** Welcome aboard the Elissa, said the skipper. It was built in the 1800s, but it has been restored and is still a seaworthy ship.

**3.** Emerson once said, The only way to have a friend is to be one; I think he's right.

**4.** In the book The Complete Essays of Mark Twain, you'll find an essay titled Taming the Bicycle.

**5.** Jennifer said, I never can remember how many c's and s's the word necessary has.

**6.** Beth finally figured out that when Tranh used the Vietnamese phrase không biết, he was telling her that he didn't understand.

7. The 18 on her uniform looks like a 13, Earl said.

8. Alexandra replied, I'm surprised you watched Gone with the Wind. Two days ago you said, I don't want to see the movie until I've read the book.

9. Every week the whole family gathered in front of the television to watch 7th Heaven.

10. The Beatles' song Yesterday has been a favorite of several generations.

## B. Correcting Paragraphs of Dialogue by Adding Underlining (Italics) and Quotation Marks

The following dialogue contains errors in the use of underlining (italics) and quotation marks. Correct these errors by adding appropriate marks of punctuation. If a sentence is already correct, write *C*.

EXAMPLES **[1]** I thought the poetry unit in English class would be dull, Ella said, but it's not. **[2]** We're studying Langston Hughes, and he's great!

1. *"I thought the poetry unit in English class would be dull," Ella said, "but it's not. 2. We're studying Langston Hughes, and he's great!"*

─HELP─

In Part B of the Diagnostic Preview, each error in the use of quotation marks involves a pair of single or double quotation marks.

[11] Oh, I've heard of him, Chet said. [12] Didn't he write a poem called The Dream Keeper?

[13] Yes, that's one of my favorites, Ella said. [14] An entire book of his poems is called The Dream Keeper, too. [15] Another one of his best-known poems is called Dreams.

[16] I guess he dreamed a lot, Chet replied.

[17] Ella said, He did much more than that! [18] Mrs. Berry told us that Langston Hughes traveled extensively. [19] For a time, he was on the crew of a steamer that sailed around Africa and Europe. [20] In fact, one of his autobiographies is called The Big Sea.

# Italics

*Italic* letters slant to the right, *like this.* When writing or typing, indicate italics by underlining. If your composition were to be printed, the typesetter would set the underlined words in italics. For example, if you typed the sentence

> Helen Keller wrote <u>The Story of My Life</u>.

it would be printed like this:

> Helen Keller wrote *The Story of My Life.*

## COMPUTER TIP

If you use a personal computer, you can probably set words in italics yourself. Most word-processing software and many printers are capable of producing italic type.

**Reference Note**

For information on **capitalizing titles,** see page 630.

## STYLE  TIP

Chapter headings and titles of magazine articles, short poems, short stories, short musical compositions, and individual episodes of TV shows should be placed in quotation marks, not italicized.

## TIPS & TRICKS

Generally, the title of an entire work (book, magazine, TV series) is italicized, while the title of a part (chapter, article, episode) is enclosed in quotation marks.

**Reference Note**

See page 686 for more about using **quotation marks.**

**24a.** Use italics (underlining) for titles and subtitles of books, periodicals, long poems, plays, films, television series, long musical works and recordings, and works of art.

| Type of Title | Examples |
|---|---|
| Books | *Vanity Fair: A Novel Without a Hero* |
| Periodicals | *Seventeen, The New York Times* |
| Long Poems | *Evangeline, Beowulf* |
| Plays | *The Piano Lesson, King Lear* |
| Films | *Casablanca, Harvey* |
| Television Series | *60 Minutes, Home Improvement* |
| Long Musical Works and Recordings | *The Magic Flute, Sinfonia Antarctica, The Three Tenors, Dos Mundos* |
| Works of Art | *The Thinker, Birth of Venus* |

The words *a, an,* and *the* written before a title are italicized only when they are part of the title. The official title of a book appears on the title page. The official title of a newspaper or other periodical appears on the masthead, which is usually found on the editorial page or the table of contents.

EXAMPLES   I am reading John Knowles's **A** *Separate Peace.*

**An** *Incomplete Education* is a book that tries to summarize everything you should have learned in college.

My parents subscribe to **The** *Wall Street Journal* and **the** *Atlantic.*

NOTE   A long poem is one that is long enough to be published as a separate volume. Such poems are usually divided into titled or numbered sections, such as cantos, parts, or books. Long musical compositions include operas, symphonies, ballets, oratorios, and concertos.

EXAMPLES   In my report on Coleridge, I plan to quote from the seventh stanza of **The Rime of the Ancient Mariner.**

At her recital, she will play a selection from **Swan Lake.**

**24b.** Use underlining (italics) for the names of ships, trains, aircraft, and spacecraft.

| Type of Name | Examples |
|---|---|
| **Ships** | *Titanic, Queen Elizabeth 2* |
| **Trains** | *Orient Express, City of New Orleans* |
| **Aircraft and Spacecraft** | *Spirit of Saint Louis, Apollo 1* |

**24c.** Use italics (underlining) for words, letters, symbols and numerals referred to as such and for foreign words that are not yet a part of the English vocabulary.

EXAMPLES     The word ***Mississippi*** has four ***s***'s and four ***i***'s.

The ***8*** on that license plate looks like an ***&.***

The ***corrido,*** a fast-paced ballad, evolved from a musical form brought to the Americas by early Spanish explorers and settlers.

NOTE   English has borrowed many words from other languages. Once such words are considered a part of the English vocabulary, they are no longer italicized.

EXAMPLES   amoeba (Greek)          judo (Japanese)

boss (Dutch)            kibbutz (Modern Hebrew)

canyon (Spanish)        okra (West African)

chimpanzee (Bantu)      résumé (French)

chipmunk (Algonquian)   vermicelli (Italian)

HELP

If you are not sure whether to italicize a word of foreign origin, look in a recently published dictionary to see if the word is italicized there.

MECHANICS

Rewrite the following sentences. Then, underline all the words and
word groups that should be italicized.

EXAMPLE     1.  We gave Mom a subscription to Working Woman.

            1.  *We gave Mom a subscription to <u>Working Woman</u>.*

1. Jason named his ship Argo because Argos had built it.
2. The motto of the United States Marine Corps is Semper Fidelis,
   which means "always faithful."
3. Have you read the novel Great Expectations by Charles Dickens?
4. When I spelled occurrence with one r, I was eliminated from the
   spelling contest.
5. The Gilbert and Sullivan comic opera The Mikado and the Puccini
   opera Madama Butterfly are both set in Japan.
6. Shari asked if she could borrow my copy of Sports Illustrated.
7. Mrs. Hopkins said that if she had to describe me in one word, the
   word would be loquacious.
8. My grandmother, who grew up in Chicago, still subscribes to the
   Chicago Tribune.
9. My favorite painting is Georgia O'Keeffe's Black Iris; my favorite
   sculpture is Constantin Brancusi's Bird in Space.
10. My parents own a set of the Encyclopaedia Britannica; and my
    aunt, who lives within walking distance of us, just bought a set of
    The World Book Encyclopedia.

# Quotation Marks

**24d.** Use quotation marks to enclose a *direct quotation*—a
person's exact words.

EXAMPLES     Melanie said, "This car is making a very strange noise."
             "Maybe we should pull over," suggested Amy.

Always be sure to place quotation marks at both the beginning and
the end of a direct quotation.

INCORRECT     She shouted, "We can win, team!
CORRECT       She shouted, "We can win, team!"

Do not use quotation marks for an *indirect quotation*—a rewording
of a direct quotation.

| DIRECT QUOTATION | Stephanie said, "I'm going to wash the car." |
|---|---|
| | [the speaker's exact words] |
| INDIRECT QUOTATION | Stephanie said that she was going to wash the car. |
| | [not the speaker's exact words] |

An interrupting expression is not a part of a quotation and therefore should not be inside quotation marks.

| INCORRECT | "Let's sit here, Ann whispered, not way down there." |
|---|---|
| CORRECT | "Let's sit here," Ann whispered, "not way down there." |

When two or more sentences by the same speaker are quoted together, use only one set of quotation marks.

| INCORRECT | Brennan said, "I like to sit close to the screen." "The sound is better there." |
|---|---|
| CORRECT | Brennan said, "I like to sit close to the screen. The sound is better there." |

**24e.** A direct quotation generally begins with a capital letter.

EXAMPLES     Explaining the lever, Archimedes said, "**G**ive me a place to stand, and I can move the world."

Miss Pérez answered, "**T**he rest of the chapter, of course." [Although this quotation is not a sentence, it is Miss Pérez's complete remark.]

> NOTE   If the direct quotation is obviously a fragment of the original quotation, it may begin with a lowercase letter.

EXAMPLE     Are our ideals, as Scott says, mere "**s**tatues of snow" that soon melt? [The quotation is obviously only a part of Scott's remark.]

**24f.** When an interrupting expression divides a quoted sentence into two parts, the second part begins with a lowercase letter.

EXAMPLES     "I wish," she said, "**t**hat we went to the same school."

"I know," I answered, "**b**ut at least we are friends."

If the second part of a quotation is a new sentence, a period (not a comma) follows the interrupting expression, and the second part begins with a capital letter.

EXAMPLE     "I requested an interview," the reporter said. "**S**he told me she was too busy."

**Reference Note**
For more about **capitalizing quotations,** see page 618.

**MECHANICS**

**24g.** A direct quotation can be set off from the rest of a sentence by a comma, a question mark, or an exclamation point, but not by a period.

EXAMPLES    Delores explained, "You know how much I like chicken," as she passed her plate for more.

"When will we be leaving?" asked Tony.

The plumber shouted, "Turn off that faucet!" when the water started gushing out of the pipe.

**24h.** When used with quotation marks, other marks of punctuation are placed according to the following rules:

**(1)** Commas and periods are placed inside closing quotation marks.

EXAMPLES    "I haven't seen the movie," remarked Jeannette, "but I understand that it's excellent."

**(2)** Semicolons and colons are placed outside closing quotation marks.

EXAMPLES    Socrates once said, "As for me, all I know is that I know nothing"; I wonder why everyone thinks he was such a wise man.

The following actresses were nominated for the award for "best performance in a leading role": Helen Hunt, Meryl Streep, Cher, and Jodie Foster.

**(3)** Question marks and exclamation points are placed inside the closing quotation marks if the quotation itself is a question or an exclamation; otherwise, they are placed outside.

EXAMPLES    "Is it too cold in here?" the manager asked as I shivered.

"Yes!" I answered. "Please turn down the air conditioner!"

Can you explain the saying "Penny wise, pound foolish"?

It's not an insult to be called a "bookworm"!

NOTE    When both a sentence and the quotation at the end of that sentence are questions or exclamations, only one question mark or exclamation point is used. It goes inside the closing quotation marks.

EXAMPLE    Did Elizabeth Barrett Browning write the poem that begins with "How do I love thee?"

### Exercise 2 Writing Sentences with Direct and Indirect Quotations

If a sentence contains a direct quotation, change it to an indirect quotation. If a sentence contains an indirect quotation, change it to a direct quotation. Make sure your answers are correctly punctuated.

EXAMPLES   **1.** "Where should we go for vacation?" asked my mother.

      *1. My mother asked where we should go for vacation.*

      **2.** My little brother Jason said that he wanted to see castles like the ones in the brochures.

      *2. My little brother Jason said, "I want to see castles like the ones in the brochures."*

1. When we planned our trip to England, Mom said, "Our stops should include some castles."
2. Our tour book says that Colchester Castle, begun in 1076, is a good place to start.
3. Jason asked whether the castles were haunted.
4. "No," said Mom, "and, besides, we'll stay close together."
5. In England, Jason told Mom that he wanted to swim in a moat.
6. "Warwick Castle," said our guide, "is one of the most beautiful."
7. "One of its towers," he went on to say, "was built in 1066."
8. The guide said that the castle contains many works of art.
9. "I like the collection of suits of armor best," said Jason.
10. "Is it still the home of the Earls of Warwick?" I asked.

**24i.** When you write dialogue (a conversation), begin a new paragraph every time the speaker changes.

EXAMPLE    "What's that?" Sally demanded impatiently.

    Luisa seemed surprised. "What's what?"

    "That thing, what you got in your hand."

    "Oh this . . ." and she held it up for Sally to inspect. "A present."

    "A what?"

    "A present I picked up."

    "Oh." Sally moved her eyes to the house. "Looks like his place burned down. What d'you find inside?"

    "Just this," Luisa said, gazing blankly at the house.

    "What d'you want that for?"

                 Ron Arias, "El Mago"

| STYLE     TIP |

In dialogue, a paragraph may be only one line long and may consist of one or more sentence fragments.

**24j.** When a quoted passage consists of more than one paragraph, put quotation marks at the beginning of each paragraph and at the end of the entire passage. Do not put quotation marks after any paragraph but the last.

EXAMPLE     "At nine o'clock this morning someone entered the Mill Bank by the back entrance, broke through two thick steel doors guarding the bank's vault, and escaped with sixteen bars of gold.

"No arrests have been made, but state police are confident the case will be solved within a few days."

NOTE   A long passage (not dialogue) quoted from a book or another printed source is usually set off from the rest of the text. The entire passage is usually indented and double-spaced. When a quoted passage has been set off in one of these ways, no quotation marks are necessary.

EXAMPLE     In his autobiography The Interesting Narrative of the Life of Olaudah Equiano, or Gustavus Vassa, the African, Olaudah Equiano describes encountering African languages other than his own:

> From the time I left my own nation I always found somebody that understood me till I came to the sea coast. The languages of different nations did not totally differ, nor were they so copious as those of the Europeans, particularly the English. They were therefore easily learned; and while I was journeying thus through Africa, I acquired two or three different tongues.

**24k.** Use single quotation marks to enclose a quotation within a quotation.

EXAMPLES     Annoyed, Becky snapped, "Don't tell me, 'That's not the way to do it.'"

My uncle said, "Remember the words of Chief Joseph: 'I have heard talk and talk, but nothing is done. Good words do not last long unless they amount to something.' This is good advice."

Tiffany exclaimed, "How dare you say, 'Yuck!'"

**Review A** **Correcting Sentences by Adding Quotation Marks for Dialogue**

Correct each of the following passages, adding quotation marks where necessary. Remember to begin a new paragraph each time the speaker changes.

EXAMPLE 1. Is Rio de Janeiro the capital of Brazil, asked Linda, or is Brasília?

1. *"Is Rio de Janeiro the capital of Brazil," asked Linda, "or is Brasília?"*

1. Race-car driver Janet Guthrie, said Chet, reading from his notes, is a trained physicist who has spent many years working at an aircraft corporation.

2. Who shot that ball? Coach Larsen wanted to know. I did, came the reply from the small, frail-looking player. Good shot, said the coach, but always remember to follow your shot to the basket. I tried, but I was screened, the player explained.

3. The *Brownsville Beacon,* the editorial began, will never support a candidate who tells the taxpayers, Vote for me, and I will cut taxes. The reason is simple. Taxes, just like everything else in this inflationary society, must increase. Any candidate who thinks otherwise is either a fool or a liar.

4. In the interview, the candidate said, I am a very hospitable person. Yes, her husband agreed, Ralph Waldo Emerson must have been thinking of you when he said, Happy is the house that shelters a friend.

© Leo Cullum 1998; reprinted by permission.

"WOULD YOU STOP PUTTING QUOTES AROUND EVERYTHING I SAY?!"

**Reference Note**

Remember that the **titles of long poems and long musical works are italicized,** not enclosed in quotation marks. See the examples on page 684.

**MECHANICS**

**24l.** Use quotation marks to enclose titles and subtitles of articles, essays, short stories, poems, songs, individual episodes of TV series, and chapters and other parts of books and periodicals.

| Type of Title | Examples |
|---|---|
| Articles | "What Teenagers Need to Know About Diets" <br> "Satellites That Serve Us" |
| Essays | "Charley in Yellowstone" <br> "An Apartment in Moscow" |
| Short Stories | "The Man to Send Rain Clouds" <br> "The Pit and the Pendulum" |
| Poems | "Fog"  "Incident" <br> "The End of My Journey" |
| Songs | "The Ballad of Gregorio Cortez" <br> "Peace Train" |
| Episodes of TV Series | "The Sure Thing" <br> "Monarch in Waiting" |
| Chapters and Other Parts of Books and Periodicals | "Life in the First Settlements" <br> "The Talk of the Town" |

**NOTE**  For short titles within quotations, use single quotation marks.

EXAMPLE  "Did Thomas Hardy write 'The Dynasts'?" asked Terri.

**Exercise 3**  **Correcting Sentences by Adding Quotation Marks for Titles**

Correct the following sentences by adding quotation marks as needed. If a sentence is already correctly punctuated, write *C*.

EXAMPLE  **1.** Did O. Henry write the story The Last Leaf?

　　　　*1. Did O. Henry write the story "The Last Leaf"?*

**1.** That address to the United Nations can be found in our literature book, in the chapter titled Essays and Speeches.

**2.** One popular Old English riddle song is Scarborough Fair.

3. Have you read the story Split Cherry Tree by Jesse Stuart?

4. Which Eve Merriam poem is that, Cheers or How to Eat a Poem?

5. Have you read Fran Lebowitz's essay Tips for Teens?

6. One of Pat Mora's poems about being bilingual and bicultural is titled Legal Alien.

7. I read Kurt Vonnegut's short story "Harrison Bergeron" last week.

8. In his essay Misspelling, Charles Kuralt examines some of the difficulties people have with spelling.

9. Fiona said, "My favorite Irish ballad is Cliffs of Dooneen."

10. The whole class enjoyed reading Naomi Shihab Nye's poem Daily.

### Review B  Correcting Sentences by Adding Underlining (Italics) and Quotation Marks

Write the following sentences, adding underlining (italics) and quotation marks where needed.

EXAMPLE    1. Please turn to the chapter titled A Walk in the Highlands.

1. *Please turn to the chapter titled "A Walk in the Highlands."*

1. The Bay Area Youth Theater is presenting Bernard Shaw's play Major Barbara.

2. Tyrone announced that he is going to sing Some Enchanted Evening from the musical South Pacific.

3. I have tickets to the opera Carmen, said Karen, and I would like you to be my guest.

4. Does the Swahili word kwa heri mean the same thing that the Spanish word adiós does?

5. My favorite story by Sir Arthur Conan Doyle is The Adventure of the Dying Detective, which is included in the anthology The Complete Sherlock Holmes.

6. Ms. Loudon said, I enjoyed your report on Ernest Hemingway. Remember, however, that the name Ernest is spelled without an a.

7. In her review of The King and I, the drama critic for the Los Angeles Times commented, This production is an excellent revival of a play that never seems to wear thin.

8. In my paper, which I titled The Hispanic Soldier in Vietnam, I cited several passages from Luis Valdez's play The Buck Private.

9. Mrs. Howard asked, In the play Julius Caesar, who said, This was the noblest Roman of them all? Which Roman was being described?

10. Have you read Hannah Armstrong, one of the poems in the Spoon River Anthology by Edgar Lee Masters?

MECHANICS

Correct the following paragraphs by adding underlining (italics) and quotation marks where necessary.

EXAMPLE  **[1]** Are all of these books by or about Benjamin Franklin? asked Bonnie Lou.

1. *"Are all of these books by or about Benjamin Franklin?" asked Bonnie Lou.*

[1] Yes, Bonnie Lou, Mr. Reyes answered. [2] There's even one, Ben and Me by Robert Lawson, that's a biography written from the point of view of Amos, Franklin's pet mouse.

[3] This one, The Many Lives of Benjamin Franklin by Mary Pope Osborne, sounds really interesting, said Jasmine.

[4] It is, Mr. Reyes said. [5] That's exactly what we're going to talk about today—the many lives of this early American genius. [6] Who can tell me about one of them?

[7] He invented electricity, didn't he? asked Liam.

[8] Well, he didn't invent electricity, corrected Mr. Reyes, but his experiments proved that lightning is a form of electricity.

[9] Franklin, he continued, also helped draft some of our important historical documents, and he was a diplomat, a printer, and a publisher. [10] Franklin's writings, especially his Autobiography and Poor Richard's Almanack, have given us many well-known sayings.

# Chapter Review

## A. Correcting Sentences by Adding Underlining (Italics) and Quotation Marks

The following sentences contain errors in the use of underlining (italics) and quotation marks. Write each sentence, adding underlining and quotation marks where needed.

1. The concert ended with a stirring rendition of The Stars and Stripes Forever.

2. There's Still Gold in Them Thar Hills, an article in Discover, describes attempts to mine low-grade gold deposits on Quartz Mountain in California.

3. Mozart's opera The Magic Flute is being performed tonight.

4. The fifth episode in the TV series The African Americans is titled The Harlem Renaissance.

5. I Am Joaquín is an epic poem about Mexican American culture.

6. As a baby sitter I have read the children's book The Pokey Little Puppy at least a dozen times.

7. The journalist Horace Greeley founded the New York Tribune, an influential newspaper.

8. Although the poem When You Are Old has three stanzas, it contains only one sentence.

9. The word recommended has two m's but only one c.

10. Robert Fulton's steamboat, Claremont, was the first one that could be operated without losing money.

11. My father always swore by Newsweek, but Mother preferred U.S. News & World Report.

12. In his novel David Copperfield, Dickens draws a vivid picture of Victorian life.

13. In Spanish, sí means yes; in French, si is also used to mean yes, but only in answer to a negative statement.

14. Tim asked, What time did they say they would be here?

15. Usually, they read the Daily News on Sundays.

16. Those b's look like 6's.

17. I didn't think I would be able to sit through an opera, said Brittany, but I really enjoyed Hansel and Gretel.

**18.** On Mondays during football season, the entire family watches Monday Night Football on television.

**19.** How many m's and t's does the word committee have? asked Betty.

**20.** One of Kathryn's favorite novels is Martin Chuzzlewit by Charles Dickens.

## B. Punctuating Dialogue by Adding Quotation Marks

The following dialogue contains errors in the use of quotation marks. Write each sentence, adding quotation marks where needed.

[**21**] Before our field trip begins, continued Mrs. Garcia, be sure that you have a notebook and a collection kit.

[**22**] Will we need binoculars? asked Melvin.

[**23**] Leave your binoculars at home, answered Mrs. Garcia. Your ears will be more helpful than your eyes on this trip.

[**24**] What will we be able to hear out there? asked Arnold.

[**25**] What a question! exclaimed Felicia. This time of year, you can hear all sorts of sounds.

[**26**] I hope that we hear and see some birds, said Koko. Didn't someone once say, The birds warble sweet in the springtime?

[**27**] When, asked James, do we eat lunch? My mom packed my favorite kinds of sandwiches.

[**28**] Don't worry, said Mrs. Garcia. Most birds are quiet at midday. We can have our lunch then.

[**29**] Ruth Ann said, Mrs. Garcia, would you believe that I don't know one birdcall from another?

[**30**] That's all right, Ruth Ann, laughed Mrs. Garcia. Some birds call out their own names. For example, the bobolink repeats its name: Bob-o-link! Bob-o-link!

## C. Correcting Paragraphs by Adding Underlining (Italics) and Quotation Marks

The following paragraph contains errors in the use of underlining (italics) and quotation marks. Write each sentence, adding underlining and quotation marks where necessary. Be sure to start a new paragraph each time the speaker changes.

[**31**] As most of you probably know, said Mr. Sundaresan, our geography teacher, Everest, on the border of Tibet and Nepal, is the

world's highest mountain; does anyone know the name of the world's second-highest peak? Yes, Elaine? [**32**] It's K2. [**33**] Yes, said Mr. Sundaresan, impressed. How did you know? [**34**] Well, said Elaine, for Christmas my parents gave me a book called K2: Challenging the Sky by Roberto Mantovani. I just finished reading it last night. [**35**] Very good, said Mr. Sundaresan. Now can anyone tell me the name of the highest mountain in Europe? I'll give you a hint: It's not in Switzerland. Elaine's hand shot up again. [**36**] Isn't it Mont Blanc, on the border of France and Italy? she asked. [**37**] Quite right, said Mr. Sundaresan. May I ask how you knew that? [**38**] For my birthday I got a copy of The Alps and Their People by Susan Bullen. It's a really interesting book. [**39**] Well, have you read any books on the Rockies, Elaine? asked Mr. Sundaresan. [**40**] As a matter of fact, I just started reading The Rockies by David Muench, and before you ask, I can tell you that Mount Elbert is the highest peak in the Rockies!

# Writing Application
## Writing a Dialogue

**Using Quotation Marks**   Write a page of dialogue in which characters tell a story, either fact or fiction, through a conversation.

**Prewriting**   Decide on a story and a few characters to tell it. You could retell a favorite anecdote, report the exact words of an amusing conversation, or write an imaginary interview with a famous person.

**Writing**   As you write your first draft, think about making the characters sound different from one another.

**Revising**   First, ask a classmate to read your dialogue. Revise any parts that are unclear or uninteresting to your reader. Be sure that you have begun a new paragraph every time the speaker changes. Also, check that you have followed the rules for punctuating direct quotations and quotations with interrupting expressions.

**Publishing**   Read through your dialogue again, this time concentrating on correcting errors in grammar, spelling, and punctuation. You and your classmates may want to work in small groups to present your dialogues to the class.

# Punctuation
## Apostrophes

# Diagnostic Preview

**Revising Sentences in a Journal Entry by Using Apostrophes Correctly**

In the following journal entry, Josh often incorrectly uses contractions and possessive forms. Write the correct form of each incorrect word or expression used.

EXAMPLE     **[1]** Im still working on todays assignment.

       1. *I'm; today's*

[**1**] Ive just finished tonights homework. [**2**] Writing a composition is usually two hours hard work for me, but Im pleased with this one. [**3**] Ill read it over in the morning to make sure that my handwritings legible. [**4**] My teacher has trouble reading my *d*s, *t*s, and *o*s. [**5**] He also objects to my overuse of *and*s and *so*s. [**6**] If theres an error, Ill have to revise my composition. [**7**] Thats one good reason for being careful, isnt it?

[**8**] My compositions title is "The Reign of Animals." [**9**] Moms friend suggested that I call it "Whose in Charge Here?" [**10**] My familys love for animals is well known in the neighborhood and among our friends'. [**11**] At the moment were owned by two inside cats; three outside cats; our resident dog, Pepper; and a visiting dog we call Hugo.

[**12**] During Peppers walks, Im usually followed by at least one other dog. [**13**] Some owners care of their dogs never seems to go beyond feeding them. [**14**] The city councils decision to fine owners'

who let they're dogs run loose makes sense. [**15**] Hugos a huge dog who's always wandering loose in my neighborhood. [**16**] We took him in several times after hed narrowly escaped being hit by a car. [**17**] In fact, Hugos and Peppers feeding dishes sit side by side in our kitchen.

[**18**] Peter, our senior cat, who was once one of our neighborhoods strays, isnt about to run from anyones dog. [**19**] At times weve seen him safeguarding other cats of ours' by running in front of them and staring down an approaching dog and it's owner. [**20**] Our dogs and cats different personalities never cease to fascinate me.

# Possessive Case

The *possessive case* of a noun or pronoun shows ownership or possession.

EXAMPLES    **Larry's** friend Dana uses a wheelchair.

You need a good **night's** sleep.

Can I count on **their** votes?

I appreciate **your** waiting so long.

**25a.** **To form the possessive case of most singular nouns, add an apostrophe and an *s*.**

EXAMPLES    Yuki**'s** problem    a bus**'s** wheel

the mayor**'s** desk    this evening**'s** paper

Mrs. Ross**'s** job    a dollar**'s** worth

> **NOTE**  For a proper name ending in *s,* add only an apostrophe if the name has two or more syllables and if the addition of *'s* would make the name awkward to pronounce.
>
> EXAMPLES  **Ulysses'** plan        **West Indies'** export
>
>              **Mrs. Rawlings'** car    **Texas'** governor
>
>     For a singular common noun ending in *s,* add both an apostrophe and an *s* if the added *s* is pronounced as a separate syllable.
>
> EXAMPLES  the actress**'s** costumes    the dress**'s** sleeves
>
>              the class**'s** teacher    a platypus**'s** tail

## Exercise 1 Using Apostrophes to Form the Possessive Case of Singular Nouns

Form the possessive case of each of the following nouns. After each possessive word, give an appropriate noun.

EXAMPLE    **1.** Teresa

     *1. Teresa's pencil*

| | | |
|---|---|---|
| **1.** baby | **8.** mouse | **15.** horse |
| **2.** uncle | **9.** Mr. Chan | **16.** Paris |
| **3.** year | **10.** Miss Reynolds | **17.** system |
| **4.** cent | **11.** plane | **18.** judge |
| **5.** class | **12.** boss | **19.** Mr. Jones |
| **6.** Terry | **13.** child | **20.** synagogue |
| **7.** Ellen | **14.** Ms. Sanchez | |

**25b.** To form the possessive case of a plural noun ending in *s*, add only the apostrophe.

EXAMPLES    two bird**s'** feathers      all three cousin**s'** vacation

             the Garza**s'** patio         the Girl Scout**s'** uniforms

      Although most plural nouns end in *s*, some are irregular. To form the possessive case of a plural noun that does not end in *s*, add an apostrophe and *s*.

EXAMPLES    children**'s** shoes      those deer**'s** food

**Reference Note**

For more examples of **irregular plurals,** see page 740.

## Exercise 2 Forming the Possessive Case of Plural Nouns

Form the possessive case of each of the following plural nouns.

EXAMPLE    **1.** knives

     *1. knives'*

| | | |
|---|---|---|
| **1.** men | **8.** cattle | **15.** runners |
| **2.** cats | **9.** mice | **16.** attorneys |
| **3.** teachers | **10.** parents | **17.** allies |
| **4.** enemies | **11.** the Smiths | **18.** friends |
| **5.** princesses | **12.** sheep | **19.** women |
| **6.** dollars | **13.** wives | **20.** bats |
| **7.** elves | **14.** O'Gradys | |

## Exercise 3 Revising Phrases by Forming the Possessive Case of Nouns

Revise the following phrases by using the possessive case.

EXAMPLE      **1.** the parties for seniors

        *1. the seniors' parties*

**1.** prizes for winners             **6.** suits for women

**2.** manners for teenagers      **7.** ideas of inventors

**3.** yokes of oxen                    **8.** medals for veterans

**4.** duties of nurses               **9.** routines for dancers

**5.** names of players             **10.** roles for actresses

NOTE   In general, you should not use an apostrophe to form
the plural of a noun.

INCORRECT   Two player's left their gym suits on the locker
room floor.

CORRECT   Two **players** left their gym suits on the locker
room floor. [plural]

CORRECT   Two **players'** gym suits were left on the locker
room floor. [The apostrophe shows that the
gym suits belong to the two players.]

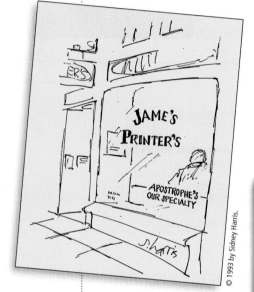

© 1993 by Sidney Harris.

## Review A Recognizing Correct Forms of Nouns

Choose the correct form of each noun in parentheses in the following
paragraph.

EXAMPLES      Several **[1]** (*photographs, photograph's*) taken by *Voyagers
1* and *2* were combined into the illustration on the next
page to show a few of **[2]** (*Saturns, Saturn's*) many satellites.

        *1. photographs*

        *2. Saturn's*

   At least eighteen natural satellites, or celestial **[1]** (*bodies, body's*),
revolve around the planet Saturn. Seven of our solar **[2]** (*systems,
system's*) nine planets have satellites, but Saturn and Jupiter have
the most. **[3]** (*Scientists, Scientists'*) figures on the true number of
**[4]** (*satellites, satellite's*) vary, and new space **[5]** (*probes, probe's*) sometimes reveal more satellites. Two **[6]** (*planets, planets'*), Earth and Pluto,
have only one satellite each. Of course, you are already familiar with our

MECHANICS

own **[7]** (*planets, planet's*) satellite, the moon. As you can see from this illustration, **[8]** (*satellite's, satellites'*) sizes and features vary greatly. Titan, a satellite of Saturn, is the largest of that **[9]** (*planets, planet's*) satellites. Another of **[10]** (*Saturns, Saturn's*) satellites, Mimas, has a crater that covers about one third of its diameter.

**25c.** Possessive personal pronouns do not require an apostrophe.

**Reference Note**

For more about **using pronouns correctly,** see Chapter 18.

| Possessive Personal Pronouns | |
|---|---|
| **Singular** | **Plural** |
| my, mine | our, ours |
| your, yours | your, yours |
| his, her, hers, its | their, theirs |

*My, your, her, its, our,* and *their* are used before nouns or pronouns. *Mine, yours, hers, ours,* and *theirs,* on the other hand, are not used before a noun or pronoun; they are used as subjects, subject complements, or objects in sentences. *His* may be used in either way.

EXAMPLES   Lee has **your** sweater.        Lee has a sweater of **yours.**

That is **your** watch.         That watch is **yours.**

**Her** idea was wonderful.      **Hers** was the best idea.

This is **our** plant.          This plant is **ours.**

There is **his** CD.            There is a CD of **his.**

**Reference Note**

For more about ***whose, its,*** and ***their,*** see pages 756, 603, and 606.

NOTE   The possessive form of *who* is *whose,* not *who's.* Similarly, do not write *it's* for *its,* or *they're* for *their.*

EXAMPLES   **Whose** [not *Who's*] book is this?

**Its** [not *It's*] cover is torn.

Is that **their** [not *they're*] copy?

## Exercise 4 Choosing Correct Forms of Possessive Personal Pronouns

Choose the correct pronoun in parentheses in each of the following sentences.

EXAMPLE　　1. Ralph Ellison, (*who's, whose*) book *Invisible Man* won a National Book Award, studied music at Tuskegee Institute.

　　　　　　　*1. whose*

1. Did you know, Sumi, that two poems of (*yours, yours'*) have been chosen for the literary magazine?
2. When I first read that book, I was surprised by the high quality of (*its, it's*) artwork.
3. (*Hers, Her's*) is the bicycle with the reflectors on (*its, it's*) fenders.
4. Eudora Welty, (*who's, whose*) short stories often involve eccentric characters, is my favorite writer.
5. "The trophy is (*ours, our's*)!" shouted the captain as the *Flying S* crossed the finish line.
6. (*Theirs, Theirs'*) is the only house with blue shutters.
7. Penny and Carla worked as gardeners this summer and saved (*their, they're*) money for a ski trip.
8. The students (*who's, whose*) names are called should report backstage.
9. (*Their, They're*) schedule calls for a test on Tuesday.
10. (*Who's, Whose*) signature is this?

**25d.** Indefinite pronouns in the possessive case require an apostrophe and *s*.

EXAMPLES　　nobody**'s** wishes　　　another**'s** viewpoint

　　　　　　someone**'s** license　　　neither**'s** school

## Exercise 5 Choosing Correct Forms of Possessive Pronouns

Choose the correct pronoun in parentheses in each of the following sentences.

EXAMPLE　　1. That Mozart CD is (*hers, her's*).

　　　　　　　*1. hers*

1. (*No ones, No one's*) guess was correct.
2. (*Ours, Our's*) works better than (*theirs, their's*).
3. (*Who's, Whose*) game is that?

**Reference Note**

For a list of **indefinite pronouns,** see page 381.

┌HELP─

For the expressions *everyone else* and *nobody else,* the correct possessives are *everyone else's* and *nobody else's*.

MECHANICS

4. (*Theirs, Their's*) is the best frozen yogurt in town.
5. Your car needs to have (*its, it's*) oil changed.
6. It wasn't (*anyone's, anyones'*) fault that we missed the bus.
7. (*Her's, Hers*) is the best project in the Science Fair.
8. (*Someones, Someone's, Someones'*) choir robe was left on the bus.
9. (*Everybodys, Everybody's, Everybodys'*) morale suffered.
10. That dog of (*their's, theirs*) should be on a leash.

**Review B** **Writing the Singular, Plural, and Possessive Forms of Nouns**

**Reference Note**

For information on **forming the plurals of nouns,** see Chapter 27.

On a piece of paper, make four columns headed *Singular, Singular Possessive, Plural,* and *Plural Possessive.* Write each of those forms of the following nouns. Add a suitable noun to follow each word in the possessive case. If you do not know how to spell a plural form, use a dictionary.

| EXAMPLE | Singular | Singular Possessive | Plural | Plural Possessive |
|---|---|---|---|---|
| 1. | dog | dog's owner | dogs | dogs' owners |

| | | | |
|---|---|---|---|
| 1. friend | 6. woman | 11. actor | 16. man |
| 2. typist | 7. penny | 12. mechanic | 17. truck |
| 3. bicycle | 8. dress | 13. deer | 18. dish |
| 4. referee | 9. musician | 14. artist | 19. window |
| 5. sheep | 10. lioness | 15. purse | 20. mouse |

**Review C** **Correcting the Forms of Nouns and Pronouns**

Identify and correct the ten incorrect possessive forms in the following paragraph.

EXAMPLE  [1] The women shown in these photographs welcomed us to the Shaker village of Pleasant Hill, Kentucky, during our history class' field trip last spring.

1. class's

[1] As you can see, the style of the womens dresses is quite old. [2] In fact, the villages history goes back to 1806. [3] That was the year that the religious group known as the Shakers founded they're own community. [4] We learned that the Shaker's lively way of dancing gave the group it's name. [5] Everyones life in the Shaker village was supposed to be orderly, simple, and productive. [6] This basic harmony was true of even the childrens' routines. [7] During the days tour of the village, we saw several people practicing Shaker crafts. [8] One guide of our's

told us that the Shakers invented the common clothespin and the flat broom and designed useful furniture and boxes. **[9]** I enjoyed visiting the gardens and the Centre Family House and imagining what a Shakers' life must have been like.

**25e.** Generally, in compound words, names of organizations and businesses, and words showing joint possession, only the last word is possessive in form.

| | |
|---|---|
| COMPOUND WORDS | community **board's** meeting |
| | **vice-president's** contract |
| | her brother-in-**law's** gifts |
| ORGANIZATIONS | the Museum of **Art's** budget |
| | United **Fund's** drive |
| BUSINESSES | Berkeley Milk **Company's** trucks |
| JOINT POSSESSION | Peggy and **Lisa's** tent [The tent belongs to both Peggy and Lisa.] |
| | children and **parents'** concerns [The children and the parents have the same concerns.] |

When one of the words showing joint possession is a pronoun, both words should be possessive in form.

EXAMPLE     **Peggy's** and **my** tent [not *Peggy and my tent*]

25
e

MECHANICS

S T Y L E        T I P

Use a phrase beginning with *of* or *for* to avoid awkward possessive forms.

AWKWARD
  the Society for the Prevention of Cruelty to Animals' advertisement

BETTER
  the advertisement **for** the Society for the Prevention of Cruelty to Animals

**Reference Note**

For more about **acro-
nyms** see page 640.

NOTE The possessive of an acronym (NASA, DOS, CIA, CBS) is formed by adding an apostrophe and *s*.

EXAMPLES    NASA's latest space probe
CBS's hit television series

**25f.** When two or more persons possess something individually, each of their names is possessive in form.

EXAMPLES    **Mrs. Martin's** and **Mrs. Blair's** cars [the cars of two different women]

**Asha's** and **Daniella's** tennis rackets [individual, not joint, possession]

### Exercise 6  Using the Possessive Case

Use the possessive case to rewrite the following word groups.

EXAMPLE    1. the book owned by Natalie and Stan
1. *Natalie and Stan's book*

1. the ticket of Sylvia and the ticket of Eric
2. an investigation by the FBI
3. the duet of Gwen and Carlos
4. a uniform belonging to the master sergeant
5. the history of the Grand Canyon
6. the job shared by Isabel and me
7. an agent for the Acme Life Insurance Company
8. one tractor belonging to my uncle and one to us
9. the award received by the Sales Department
10. the business of her mother-in-law and the business of her cousin

### Review D  Identifying Words That Require Apostrophes

Identify the ten words requiring apostrophes in the following paragraph. Then, write the words, inserting the apostrophes.

EXAMPLE    [1] Have you ever heard of the U.S. Patent Offices Hall of Fame for inventors?
1. *Offices—Office's*

[1] The Hall of Fames members, who are both American and foreign, include many people that you've probably heard of as well as some you haven't. [2] Vladimir Kosma Zworykin's picture tube helped

lead to televisions development. [3] Charles Richard Drew changed peoples lives all over the world with his work on blood plasma in transfusions. [4] Luther Burbanks accomplishment was the development of more than eight hundred new plant varieties. [5] Heart patients pacemakers were invented by Wilson Greatbatch. [6] You'll probably recognize such famous inventors as the Ford Motor Companys founder, Henry Ford. [7] Of course, Thomas Edisons and Alexander Graham Bells achievements assured their enduring fame. [8] No ones pleasure is greater than mine that Orville and Wilbur Wrights invention of the airplane landed them in such good company, too.

# Contractions

**25g.** Use an apostrophe to show where letters, numerals, or words have been omitted in a contraction.

A **contraction** is a shortened form of a word, a group of words, or a numeral. The apostrophes in contractions indicate where letters, numerals, or words have been left out.

| EXAMPLES | | |
|---|---|---|
| | who is . . . who**'s** | I am . . . I**'m** |
| | 1991 . . . **'**91 | you are . . . you**'re** |
| | of the clock . . . **o'**clock | we had . . . we**'d** |
| | let us . . . let**'s** | she has . . . she**'s** |
| | she will . . . she**'ll** | I had . . . I**'d** |
| | Bill is . . . Bill**'s** | we have . . . we**'ve** |

Ordinarily, the word *not* is shortened to *n't* and added to a verb without any change in the spelling of the verb.

| EXAMPLES | | |
|---|---|---|
| | is not . . . is**n't** | were not . . . were**n't** |
| | are not . . . are**n't** | has not . . . has**n't** |
| | does not . . . does**n't** | have not . . . have**n't** |
| | do not . . . do**n't** | had not . . . had**n't** |
| | did not . . . did**n't** | would not . . . would**n't** |
| EXCEPTIONS | will not . . . wo**n't** | cannot . . . ca**n't** |

S T Y L E    T I P

Many people consider contractions informal. Therefore, it is usually best to avoid using them in formal writing and speech.

INFORMAL
The Founding Fathers couldn't foresee the mobility of modern life.

FORMAL
The Founding Fathers **could not** foresee the mobility of modern life.

MECHANICS

Do not confuse contractions with possessive pronouns.

| Contractions | Possessive Pronouns |
|---|---|
| **Who's** at bat? [Who is] | **Whose** bat is that? |
| **It's** roaring. [It is] | Listen to **its** roar. |
| **You're** too busy. [You are] | **Your** friend is busy. |
| **There's** a kite. [There is] | That kite is **theirs**. |
| **They're** tall trees. [They are] | **Their** trees are tall. |

### Exercise 7  Correcting Sentences by Using Apostrophes for Contractions

Write each incorrect contraction in the following sentences, adding an apostrophe as necessary. If a sentence is already correct, write *C*.

EXAMPLE   1. Hes pleased by his promotion.

   1. *He's*

1. "Youve changed," she said.
2. World War II ended in 45.
3. Whos coming to the party?
4. "The stores about to close," said the clerk.
5. Several stores were closed because of the storm.
6. Well have to try to make it there on time.
7. Whose telescope is that, Richard?
8. She gets up at 6 oclock.
9. Im very glad to meet you.
10. Don't you play chess?

### Review E  Recognizing the Correct Use of Apostrophes

Choose the correct word in parentheses in each sentence in the following paragraph.

EXAMPLE   **[1]** (*Your, You're*) likely to see fiesta scenes like the one on the next page in Mexican American communities across the United States each year on September 16.

   1. *You're*

[1] (*It's, Its*) a day of celebration that includes parades, speeches, music, and, as you can see, even colorful folk dances. Of course, [2] (*theirs, there's*) plenty of food, including stacks of tortillas and bowls of beans and soup. [3] (*Who's, Whose*) to say how late the merry-making will last? [4] (*It's, Its*) a joyful holiday of fun, but everyone remembers [5] (*it's, its*) importance, too. Mexican Americans know that

[6] (*they're, their*) celebrating the beginning of Mexico's rebellion to gain independence from Spain. On September 16, 1810, Father Miguel Hidalgo y Costilla gathered his forces for the rebellion and uttered [7] (*it's, its*) first battle cry. Father Hidalgo, [8] (*who's, whose*) parish was in west central Mexico, led an army across the country. If [9] (*your, you're*) in Mexico City on the eve of September 16, you can hear the president of Mexico ring what is believed to be the bell that Hidalgo rang to summon his people for [10] (*they're, their*) historic march.

# Plurals

**25h.** To prevent confusion, use an apostrophe and an *s* to form the plurals of lowercase letters, some capital letters, numerals, symbols, and some words that are referred to as words.

EXAMPLES  Grandma always tells me to mind my *p*'**s** and *q*'**s**.

I got A'**s** on both tests I took last week. [An apostrophe is used because without one the plural spells the word *As*.]

The *1*'**s** in this exercise look like *I*'**s**.

Two different Web site addresses began with ##'**s** and ended with *.com*'**s**.

His *hi*'**s** are always cheerful. [An apostrophe is used because without one the plural spells the word *his*.]

> **Exercise 8** **Forming Plurals by Using Apostrophes**

Use an apostrophe to form the plural of each of the italicized items in the following word groups.

EXAMPLE   **1.** margins filled with *?*

*1.* *?*'s

**1.** *s* that look like *f*
**2.** to put *U* at the end
**3.** two *r* and two *s*
**4.** adding columns of *$* and *%*

MECHANICS

**STYLE** **TIP**

Many writers add only *s* when forming the kinds of plurals listed in Rule 25h. However, using both an apostrophe and *s* is not wrong and may be necessary to make your meaning clear. Therefore, it is a good idea always to include the apostrophe.

**Reference Note**

For more information on **forming these kinds of plurals,** see page 743.

**5.** these *q* or *g*  **8.** too many *her* and *their*

**6.** all *C* and *B*  **9.** your *i* and your *t*

**7.** replace all the *his* with *its*  **10.** two *I* in the sentence

⌐HELP⌐

You may need
to change the spelling of
some words in Review F.

**Review F** **Using Apostrophes Correctly**

Add or delete apostrophes as needed in the following sentences.

EXAMPLE  **1.** Summers here, but because of air conditioning its more bearable than it used to be.

**1.** *Summer's; it's*

**1.** Dont you wonder when people started cooling they're homes with air conditioning?

**2.** Air cooling isnt a new practice; in fact, in ancient Rome, wet grass mat's were hung over window's to cool incoming air by evaporation.

**3.** In the early sixteenth century, one of the greatest Italian artist's and engineer's, Leonardo da Vinci, built historys first mechanical fan.

**4.** The British scientist David B. Reid's air-ventilation system's were installed in the British House of Commons in 1838.

**5.** However, modern technique's of air conditioning werent invented until the early twentieth century in Buffalo, New York.

**6.** One of Buffalos most famous citizen's, Willis Carrier, who's name is still on many air conditioners, invented the first air-conditioning unit in 1902.

**7.** By 1928, the technologys' rapid development had produced the first fully air-conditioned office building, the Milam Building in San Antonio, Texas.

**8.** Wasnt Texas—where in summer the temperature can reach 90 degrees by eleven oclock in the morning—a logical place to have the first air-conditioned office building?

**9.** By the late 1950's, more and more homes' had window air conditioner's, and smaller unit's for motor vehicle's were becoming increasingly common.

**10.** Arent you glad air conditioning is so common nowaday's?

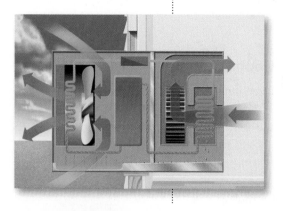

MECHANICS

# Chapter Review

## A. Correcting Sentences by Using Apostrophes Correctly

In the following sentences, apostrophes are either missing or incorrectly used. Write the correct form of each incorrect word. In some cases, an apostrophe must be added or deleted; in others, the spelling of the word also must be changed.

1. Ancient peoples felt that writing had a magic power of it's own.
2. Writing was practiced by the elders' of a tribe to preserve the tribes lore as well as its laws.
3. Were not sure when or how writing began, but we do know that it existed several century's before 3000 B.C.
4. Theres plenty of evidence that people communicated through they're drawings long before they had a system of writing.
5. Spain and France's wonderful cave drawings were painted more than thirty thousand year's ago.
6. The ancient Peruvians message system was a complicated arrangement of knots.
7. Someones research has shown that *W*'s and *J*'s werent used in English writing until the late Middle Ages.
8. In China, ones mastery of basic reading depends on learning one thousand character's.
9. Hardwick Book Stores window display features early system's of writing, such as cuneiform.
10. Bess and Robert, who's reports were on the history of writing, asked one of Mr. Hardwicks clerks for permission to examine the stores display.

## B. Proofreading a Paragraph for Correct Use of Apostrophes

The following paragraph contains errors in the use of apostrophes. For each sentence, write the correct form of each incorrect word.

[11] Despite many years work, scholars were not able to decipher hieroglyphics until the early nineteenth century. [12] In 1799, one of Napoleons soldiers serving in Egypt discovered a stone tablet. [13] The

tablet came to be known as the Rosetta Stone after the town in which it was found: Rashid, which European's called Rosetta. [14] The tablets surface was inscribed in three ancient language's: Greek, Egyptian hieroglyphics, and Coptic, a language derived from ancient Egyptian. [15] The experts translations of the Greek text revealed that the same information had been written in all three languages in 196 B.C. [16] They're next step was to use their knowledge of Greek and Coptic to identify how names' of specific people and places were written in hieroglyphics. [17] It wasnt until 1822, however, that a Frenchman named Jean-François Champollion deciphered the ancient Egyptians' writing. [18] Following another scholars' theory that hieroglyphic symbols represent sounds, Champollion figured out which symbols represent which sounds. [19] He also established that the stones' hieroglyphics were a translation from the Greek—not, as had been thought, the other way around. [20] Though many door's remained to be opened, a key to ancient Egyptian history had been found.

## C. Using Apostrophes to Form Possessive Nouns

Write the possessive form for each of the following nouns. After each possessive word, give an appropriate noun.

21. Humble Oil Company
22. buffalo
23. anything
24. geese
25. Lori

26. Massachusetts
27. Northern Ireland
28. bishops
29. NBC
30. mosque

## D. Using Apostrophes Correctly

The following sentences contain errors in the use of apostrophes. Write each incorrect word or expression, adding or deleting apostrophes where needed. You may need to change the spelling as well.

31. Havent you ever wondered when the first refrigerator's were used?
32. Wealthy Romans main method of refrigeration was to cool food in snow cellars.
33. Snow cellar's were pit's dug in the ground, insulated with straw, and filled with snow and ice.
34. Didnt ancient India and Egypts' cooling techniques include using evaporative cooling to freeze perishable products?

35. Evaporative cooling means placing water in shallow tray's and using the ice thats formed during rapid evaporation.

36. In the sixteenth century, Italians' discovered that a mixture of water and potassium nitrate could be used to cool bottled liquids.

37. During the 1850's, Ferdinand Carré, a French inventor, developed the worlds' first absorption system using ammonia.

38. Absorption system's use the direct application of heat to initiate the refrigeration cycle by changing refrigerant's from liquid to gas and back again.

39. Another system that produces refrigeration is compression, in which compressor's are used to bring about refrigeration cycles.

40. In 1876, the scientific world learned the name of Carl von Linde, a German engineer who's compression system using ammonia was the foundation of modern refrigeration.

# Writing Application
## Using Apostrophes in a Paragraph

**Possessive Case**   Write a paragraph about the musical preferences of one or more family members or friends. Use at least two singular possessive nouns, two plural possessive nouns, and one indefinite pronoun in the possessive case.

**Prewriting**   First, make a list of family members or friends, and beside each name write what you know about that person's musical tastes. If you are not sure about someone's preferences, ask him or her.

**Writing**   As you write your first draft, think about ways of organizing your information by type of music, age of listener, and so on.

**Revising**   Ask a family member or friend to read your paragraph. Is it clear whose preferences are discussed? Are the preferences accurately expressed?

**Publishing**   Check your placement of apostrophes. As you read through your paragraph, correct errors in spelling, grammar, and punctuation. With the permission of the person or persons whose musical tastes you have discussed in your paragraph, post your piece on a class bulletin board, or use it as a basis for a class discussion.

# Punctuation
## Hyphens, Dashes, Parentheses, Brackets, Ellipsis Points

## Diagnostic Preview

### A. Using Hyphens, Dashes, and Parentheses

Use hyphens, dashes, and parentheses to punctuate the following sentences. Do not add commas to these sentences.

EXAMPLE   **1.** Henry Viscardi he founded the National Center for Disability Services dedicated his life to creating opportunities for people who have disabilities.

*1. Henry Viscardi—he founded the National Center for Disability Services—dedicated his life to creating opportunities for people who have disabilities.*

**1.** The soup was three fourths water and one fourth vegetables.
**2.** Twenty six students most of them from the advanced math class represented our school at the all state chess match.
**3.** The Battle of Bunker Hill June 17, 1775 damaged the confidence of the British.
**4.** The ex treasurer of our club he's an extremely self confident person is now running for class president.
**5.** My sister she lives in Boston now is studying pre Columbian art.
**6.** If you have ever dreamed of finding buried treasure and who hasn't? your search could begin on Padre Island.
**7.** George Grinnell was a self taught expert on the American West and helped negotiate treaties with three American Indian peoples the Blackfoot, the Cheyenne, and the Pawnee.
**8.** Aunt Jo murmured, "Please turn out the" and then fell asleep.

9. Rachel Carson was working for the U.S. Fish and Wildlife Service created in 1940 when she first recognized the threat of pesticides.
10. Her book *Silent Spring* copyright 1962 alerted the public to the dangers of environmental pollution.

## B. Using Hyphens, Dashes, Brackets, and Parentheses

Use hyphens, dashes, brackets, and parentheses to punctutate the following sentences. If a sentence is already correct, write *C.* Do not add commas.

EXAMPLE    1. There are several countries Senegal, Gambia, Guinea, Guinea-Bissau, Sierra Leone, and Liberia along the west-central coast of Africa.

1. *There are several countries—Senegal, Gambia, Guinea, Guinea-Bissau, Sierra Leone, and Liberia—along the west-central coast of Africa.*

11. Liberia's history its founding, that is is unique.
12. Liberia was settled in pre Civil War days by freed slaves from the United States.
13. An antislavery group known as the American Colonization Society it was officially chartered by the U.S. Congress started sending freed slaves to a colony in Africa in 1822.
14. Twenty five years later, the colonists how proud they must have been! declared Liberia independent.
15. They named their capital Monrovia in honor of President James Monroe in office 1817–1825.
16. They also modeled their country's constitution and government not surprisingly on those of the United States.
17. The first president of Liberia, Joseph Jenkins Roberts (he originally served for eight years 1848–1856 and again during an economic crisis 1872–1876), was born in Virginia.
18. Roberts began his political career as an aide to the colonial governor, Thomas H. Buchanan a white member of the American Colonization Society.
19. During Liberia's early years, the United States provided aid.
20. However, the U.S. government didn't officially recognize Liberia until President Lincoln's administration 1862.

# Hyphens

## Word Division

**26a.** Use a hyphen to divide a word at the end of a line.

EXAMPLE     The new governor's victory celebration will be organ‑
ized by her campaign committee.

When you divide a word at the end of a line, keep in mind the following rules:

**(1)** Do not divide a one-syllable word.

HELP

If you need to divide a word and are not sure about its syllables, look it up in a dictionary.

INCORRECT     The line of people waiting to buy tickets stret‑
ched halfway down the block.

CORRECT     The line of people waiting to buy tickets stretched
halfway down the block.

CORRECT     The line of people waiting to buy tickets
stretched halfway down the block.

**(2)** Divide a word only between syllables.

INCORRECT     The stars Betelgeuse and Rigel are in the conste‑
llation known as Orion.

CORRECT     The stars Betelgeuse and Rigel are in the constel‑
lation known as Orion.

CORRECT     The stars Betelgeuse and Rigel are in the constella‑
tion known as Orion.

**(3)** A word containing double consonants usually may be divided between those two consonants.

EXAMPLES     con‑nect     drum‑mer

**(4)** Divide a word with a prefix or a suffix between the prefix and the base word (or root) or between the base word and the suffix.

EXAMPLES     pre‑judge     post‑pone     half‑back

    fall‑ing     frag‑ment     con‑fusion

**(5)** Divide an already hyphenated word only at a hyphen.

INCORRECT     The speaker this morning is my moth‑
er-in-law.

CORRECT     The speaker this morning is my mother‑
in-law.

**(6)** **Do not divide a word so that one letter stands alone.**

INCORRECT     The utility company built a new turbine to generate e-
lectricity.

CORRECT     The utility company built a new turbine to generate electricity.

> **Exercise 1**   **Using Hyphens to Divide Words at the Ends of Lines**

Write each of the following words, using hyphens to indicate where
the word may be divided at the end of a line. If a word should not be
divided, write *one-syllable word.*

EXAMPLES    **1.** thoroughly      **2.** cooked

               *1. thor-ough-ly*     *2. one-syllable word*

1. Olympics
2. library
3. fourth
4. unchanged
5. impolite

6. tomorrow
7. breathe
8. corporation
9. through
10. merry-go-round

─HELP─

If necessary,
check a dictionary for the
proper syllabication of the
words in Exercise 1.

# Compound Words

Some compound words are hyphenated (*red-hot*); some are written
as one word (*redhead*); and some are written as two or more words
(*red tape*). Whenever you need to know whether a word is hyphenated,
look it up in a current dictionary.

**26b.** **Use a hyphen with compound numbers from** *twenty-one* **to**
*ninety-nine* **and with fractions used as modifiers.**

EXAMPLES    **seventy-six** trombones

               **three-quarters** cup [but *three quarters* of a cup]

**26c.** **Use a hyphen with the prefixes** *ex–, self–, all–,* **and** *great–;*
**with the suffixes** *–elect* **and** *–free;* **and with all prefixes before a**
**proper noun or proper adjective.**

EXAMPLES    **ex-**coach      **great-**aunt      **mid-**July

               **self-**made     president-**elect**     **pro-**American

               **all-**star        fat-**free**        **pre-**Columbian

**MECHANICS**

**Reference Note**

For more information
on **using a dictionary,**
see "The Dictionary" in
the Quick Reference
Handbook.

| S T Y L E         T I P |

The prefix *half–* often
requires a hyphen, as in
*half-life, half-moon,* and
*half-truth.* However, sometimes *half* is used without a
hyphen, either as a part of
a single word (*halftone,
halfway, halfback*) or as a
separate word (*half shell,
half pint, half note*). If you
are not sure how to spell a
word containing *half,* look
up the word in a dictionary.

**26d.** Hyphenate a compound adjective when it precedes the noun it modifies.

EXAMPLES    a **well-written** book [but *a book that is well written*]

            a **small-town** boy [but *a boy from a small town*]

Do not use a hyphen if one of the modifiers is an adverb that ends in *–ly.*

EXAMPLE    a **bitterly cold** day

─HELP─

If you are unsure about whether a compound adjective is hyphenated, look up the word in a current dictionary.

NOTE  Some compound adjectives are always hyphenated, whether they precede or follow the nouns they modify.

EXAMPLES    a **brand-new** shirt

            a shirt that is **brand-new**

            a **down-to-earth** person

            a person who is **down-to-earth**

### Exercise 2  Hyphenating Words Correctly

Insert hyphens in the words that should be hyphenated in the following sentences. If a sentence is already correct, write *C.*

EXAMPLE    1.  The world famous speaker was very well informed.

            1.  *The world-famous speaker was very well informed.*

1. The exgovernor presented the all American trophy at the competition.
2. Until 1959, the United States flag had forty eight stars.
3. In twenty five days my great grandparents will celebrate their seventy fifth wedding anniversary; about three fourths of the family will attend the celebration.
4. The exambassador's lecture focused on the post Napoleonic era.
5. He added one half teaspoon of sugar free vanilla extract to the mixture and set the timer for thirty five minutes.
6. A documentary called "The Self Improvement Culture" was on TV last night.
7. Herman's new mountain bike was very up to date.
8. Well designed buildings have clearly marked fire escapes.
9. Sally has always been very down-to-earth.
10. The President elect gathered his Cabinet to discuss future policy.

MECHANICS

**Review A** **Identifying the Correct Use of Hyphens**

You have just received the following e-mail message from your friend Eduardo. His computer is acting up again, and it's putting in hyphens that are not supposed to be there. Make a list of words containing incorrectly used hyphens and another list of words containing correctly used ones.

| EXAMPLES | Incorrect | Correct |
|---|---|---|
| | *early-bird* | *brother-in-law* |

Hey there!

[1] So, how have you-been? [2] I can't believe it's mid-April. [3] I've really been running myself ragged with home-work, club-meetings, sports, and ninety-nine other things. [4] You wouldn'-t believe how busy I've been!

[5] I've got a role in our spring-play. [6] It's not a big role, but I'm part of an all-star cast. [7] We're doing *Our Town*. [8] I am managing the props, too.

[9] Enclosed is a good recipe that I used last week to make pop-corn topping. [10] I'm president-elect of the foreign language-club, and it was once again my turn to host the monthly meeting. [11] Thirty-three members came to my house on Friday (we have a total of fifty-one members). [12] Of course, I served refreshments, and every-one loved this topping.

[13] Recipe for Mexican Popcorn Topping: In a small bowl, mix one-fourth cup of chili-powder and one-half teaspoon of salt. Then, add one-teaspoon each of garlic powder, cilantro, and cumin. [14] (Those last two are herbs.) [15] Sprinkle mixture over plain-popcorn.

Take care, and write soon.

Eduardo

# Parentheses

**26e.** **Use parentheses to enclose material that is added to a sentence but is not considered to be of major importance.**

Notice in the following examples that parenthetical material may be omitted without changing the basic meaning and construction of the sentence.

EXAMPLES    During the Middle Ages (from about A.D. 500 to A.D. 1500), both Moors and Vikings invaded parts of Europe.

The music of Liszt (always a favorite of mine) was quite popular in the nineteenth century.

Material enclosed in parentheses may range from a single word to a short sentence. A short sentence in parentheses may stand by itself or be contained within another sentence.

Use punctuation marks within the parentheses when the punctuation belongs to the parenthetical matter. Do not use punctuation within the parentheses if such punctuation belongs to the sentence as a whole.

EXAMPLES    Fill in the application carefully. (Use a pen.)

That old house (it was built at the turn of the century) may soon become a landmark.

After we ate dinner (we had leftovers again), we went to the mall.

## Exercise 3    Using Parentheses Correctly

Use parentheses to set off the parenthetical elements in the following sentences.

EXAMPLE    1.  A fly-specked calendar it was five years out-of-date hung on the kitchen wall.

1.  *A fly-specked calendar (it was five years out-of-date) hung on the kitchen wall.*

**1.** I have read all the *Oz* books that I own a considerable number.

**2.** Edna St. Vincent Millay 1892–1950 began writing poetry as a child.

**3.** In 1850, California entered the Union as a free state read more about free states in Chapter 5.

**4.** Gwendolyn Brooks her first book was *A Street in Bronzeville* has received high praise from critics.

5. Killer whales they're the ones with the black-and-white markings often migrate more than one thousand miles annually.
6. We arrived in Poland through the port city of Gdańsk called Danzig in German.
7. The black rat scientific name *Rattus rattus* is found on every continent.
8. During the French Revolution and the Terror 1789–1793, France underwent dramatic changes.
9. Paulo Coelho born 1947 is a bestselling Brazilian author.
10. The cooking of New Mexico my home state is rich and varied.

# Dashes

Sometimes words, phrases, and sentences are used ***parenthetically;*** that is, they break into the main thought of a sentence.

EXAMPLES    The penguin, **however,** has swum away.

Her worry **(how could she explain the mix-up?)** kept her up all night.

Most parenthetical elements are set off by commas or parentheses. Sometimes, however, parenthetical elements are such an interruption that a stronger mark is needed. In such cases, a dash is used.

**26f.** Use a dash to indicate an abrupt break in thought or speech or an unfinished statement or question.

EXAMPLES    There are a thousand reasons—well, not a thousand, but many—that we should go.

Our dog—he's a long-haired dachshund—is too affectionate to be a good watchdog.

"Why—why can't I come, too?" Janet asked hesitatingly.

"You're being—" Tina began and then stopped.

**26g.** Use a dash to indicate *namely, that is,* or *in other words* or to otherwise introduce an explanation.

EXAMPLES    I know what we could get Mom for her birthday—a new photo album. [namely]

She could put all those loose pictures—the ones she's taken since Christmas—in it. [that is]

**NOTE**  Either a dash or a colon is acceptable in the first example above.

MECHANICS

| S T Y L E      T I P |

Do not overuse dashes. When you evaluate your writing, check to see that you have not used dashes carelessly for commas, semicolons, and end marks. Saving dashes for instances in which they are most appropriate will make them more effective.

| COMPUTER TIP |

When you use a word processor, you can type two hyphens to make a dash. Do not leave a space before, between, or after the hyphens. When you write by hand, use an unbroken line about as long as two hyphens.

**Reference Note**

For information on using **colons,** see page 675.

**Exercise 4** **Inserting Dashes in Sentences**

Insert dashes where they are appropriate in the following sentences.

EXAMPLE  **1.** The winner is but I don't want to give it away yet.

1. *The winner is—but I don't want to give it away yet.*

**2.** It was an exciting game Brazil had taken the lead, but Italy scored in overtime.

2. *It was an exciting game—Brazil had taken the lead, but Italy scored in overtime.*

**1.** Tom said, "I'd like to thank" and then blushed and sat down.
**2.** We were surprised in fact, amazed to learn that the game had been called off.
**3.** The valedictorian that is, the student with the highest average will be given a scholarship.
**4.** She remembered what she wanted to tell them the plane was leaving at seven, not eight.
**5.** My brother's engagement it's been kept a secret till now will be announced Sunday.
**6.** The ancient Mediterranean seafaring cultures the Phoenician, the Greek, and the Roman all used versions of the trireme, a ship driven by three rows of oars.
**7.** The truth is and I'm sure you realize this we have no way of getting to the airport.
**8.** The manager of the restaurant I can't remember his name said he would reserve a table for us.
**9.** Because Maria she's the one who accompanies us will be away next week, choral practice will be postponed until the following week.
**10.** Very few carmakers three, to be precise offer models exclusively with full-time all-wheel drive.

**Review B** **Using Hyphens, Dashes, and Parentheses Correctly**

Rewrite each of the following sentences, inserting hyphens, dashes, and parentheses where they are needed. If a sentence is already correct, write *C*.

EXAMPLE  **1.** State flags you can tell by looking at those shown on the next page are as different as the states themselves.

1. *State flags—you can tell by looking at those shown on the next page—are as different as the states themselves.*

┌H E L P┐
Although some sentences in Review B can be corrected in more than one way, you need to give only one revision for each.

1. I think the shield on the Oklahoma flag reflects that state's pre statehood years as the territorial home of the Osage, the Cherokee, and other American Indian peoples.

2. "What kind of tree is in the center of the South Carolina flag?" Emilio asked. "Is it oh, it's a palmetto."

3. Two goddesses Ceres, or the goddess of agriculture, and Liberty are in the center of New Jersey's flag.

4. On the Colorado flag, one third of the background is white and the rest is blue.

5. Arkansas by the way, a major diamond-producing state has a large diamond on its flag.

6. An ancient Pueblo symbol of the all important sun is on New Mexico's flag.

7. The Union Jack of the United Kingdom look closely is on a corner of the Hawaiian flag.

8. "The Texas flag is red, white, and blue and contains one lone star because" Megan said before she was interrupted.

9. Blue is a dominant color in forty one state flags.

10. Only one state flag Washington's has a green background.

---

**Review C** **Using Hyphens, Dashes, and Parentheses Correctly**

Insert hyphens, dashes, and parentheses where they are needed in the following sentences. Do not add commas. If a sentence is already correct, write *C*.

EXAMPLE
1. You might be able to tell from the photograph on the next page that the Comanche chief Quanah Parker 1845–1911 was a man of strong character.

1. *You might be able to tell from the photograph on the next page that the Comanche chief Quanah Parker (1845–1911) was a man of strong character.*

1. Parker can you tell this from the photograph? was both a great war chief and a great peace chief.
2. He was the son of a Comanche tribal leader and a young woman Cynthia Ann Parker who was captured during a raid on a Texas homestead.
3. In the 1870s, Parker himself led a band of Comanche warriors in the Texas Panhandle.
4. Parker surrendered with his band the Quahadi in 1875; they were the last Comanches on the southern plains to surrender.
5. After surrendering, Parker became a prosperous rancher quite a change of lifestyle and even owned railroad stock.
6. In fact, he embodied the ideal of the self made man.
7. Parker encouraged his people to learn modern ways and to farm.
8. Parker guided the Comanches his title was principal chief during difficult times after the war ended.
9. In later years, he went to Washington, D.C., and this fact may surprise you became a friend of President Theodore Roosevelt.
10. The Texas city called Quanah a Comanche word meaning "sweet smelling" was named after this chief.

# Ellipsis Points

**26h.** Use ellipsis points ( . . . ) to mark omissions from quoted materials and pauses in a written passage.

ORIGINAL      The streetlights along Toole Street, which meandered downhill from the Language Academy to the town, were already lit and twinkled mistily through the trees. Standing at the gates were small groups of students, clustered together according to nationality. As Myles passed by, he could not help overhearing intense conversation in Spanish, German, and Japanese; all of his students had momentarily abandoned English in the urgency of deciding where to go for the weekend and how to get there.

**(1)** When you omit words from the middle of a sentence, use three spaced ellipsis points.

EXAMPLE      The streetlights along Toole Street **. . .** were already lit and twinkled mistily through the trees.

NOTE   Be sure to include a space before the first ellipsis point and after the last one.

**(2)** When you omit words at the beginning of a sentence within a quoted passage, keep the previous sentence's end punctuation and follow it with the ellipsis points.

EXAMPLE    Standing at the gates were small groups of students, clustered together according to nationality. . . . [A]ll of his students had momentarily abandoned English in the urgency of deciding where to go for the weekend and how to get there.

NOTE  Be sure not to begin a quoted passage with ellipsis points.

**(3)** When you omit words at the end of a sentence within a quoted passage, keep the sentence's end punctuation and follow it with the ellipsis points.

EXAMPLE    Standing at the gates were small groups of students. . . . As Myles passed by, he could not help overhearing intense conversation in Spanish, German, and Japanese; all of his students had momentarily abandoned English in the urgency of deciding where to go for the weekend and how to get there.

**(4)** When you omit one or more complete sentences from a quoted passage, keep the previous sentence's end punctuation and follow it with the ellipsis points.

EXAMPLE    The streetlights along Toole Street, which meandered downhill from the Language Academy to the town, were already lit and twinkled mistily through the trees. . . . As Myles passed by, he could not help overhearing intense conversation in Spanish, German, and Japanese; all of his students had momentarily abandoned English in the urgency of deciding where to go for the weekend and how to get there.

**(5)** To show that a full line or more of poetry has been omitted, use an entire line of spaced periods.

ORIGINAL    Half a league, half a league,
Half a league onward,
All in the valley of Death
Rode the six hundred.
"Forward the Light Brigade!
Charge for the guns!" he said.
Into the valley of Death
Rode the six hundred.

                Alfred, Lord Tennyson,
                    "The Charge of the Light Brigade"

─HELP─

Notice in the example to the left that the *a* beginning *all* has been capitalized because it begins the sentence following the ellipsis points. Brackets are used around the *A* to show that it was not capitalized in the original passage.

MECHANICS

|        |                        |
|--------|------------------------|
| WITH   | Half a league, half a league, |
| OMISSION | Half a league onward,        |

• • • • • • • • •

Into the valley of Death
Rode the six hundred.

Notice that the line of periods is as long as the line above it.

**(6)** To indicate a pause in dialogue, use three spaced ellipsis points with a space before the first point and a space after the last point.

EXAMPLE     "Well, I could **. . .** I can't honestly say," he hedged.

# Brackets

**26i.** Use brackets to enclose an explanation within quoted or parenthetical material.

EXAMPLES    In her acceptance speech, the star said: "I am honored by this award **[**the Oscar**]**, and I want to thank my parents and everybody who worked with me." [The words are enclosed in brackets to show that they have been inserted into the quotation and are not the exact words of the speaker.]

The growth of the Irish economy in recent years is a great success story. (See page 15 **[**Graph 1A**]** for a time line.)

**Exercise 5   Using Ellipsis Points and Brackets Correctly**

Revise the following sentences, using ellipsis points and brackets correctly.

EXAMPLE     **1.** Franklin said, "That cat just . . . . . flew up to the top of the refrigerator!"

     *1.* *Franklin said, "That cat just . . . flew up to the top of the refrigerator!"*

**1.** At the committee meeting, Judy said, "We have to make this (the Homecoming Dance) the most memorable event of the year."
**2.** "I . . I can't believe she would have said that!" Aaron exclaimed.
**3.** The levels of photosynthesis activity varied drastically with the different cycles of light and darkness. (See page 347 (Chart 17D) for details.)
**4.** "Do you really believe they have a chance to win the (Stanley) Cup this year?" asked Martin skeptically.
**5.** "But . . . . . then how can we be sure it's true?" Carla asked.

# Chapter Review

## A. Using Hyphens to Divide Words at the Ends of Lines

Write each of the following words, using a hyphen to indicate where the word may be divided at the end of a line. If a word should not be divided, write *do not divide*.

1. baked
2. complete
3. input
4. unexpected
5. yo-yo

6. bagel
7. thorough
8. divide
9. away
10. whale

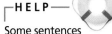

┌HELP┐
Some sentences
in Part B may be
correctly punctuated
in more than one way,
but you need to give
only one answer per item.

## B. Using Hyphens, Dashes, and Parentheses Correctly

Use hyphens, dashes, and parentheses to punctuate the following sentences. Do not add commas to these sentences.

11. Yuri, our Russian exchange student, will be twenty one on the first of September this year.
12. "That sounds like" gasped Jeff as he dashed for the window.
13. A former all state quarterback, our coach insists that there is no such thing as a self made star.
14. A dog I think it was a poodle jumped into the lake.
15. The Historical Society the local members, that is will conduct a tour of the harbor.
16. My sister Patricia she is in college now wants to be a marine biologist.
17. This recipe for savory bread calls for one and one half cups of whole wheat flour.
18. At the auction someone bid one thousand dollars for a pre Revolutionary desk.
19. The Inca empire flourished during the reign of the emperor Pachacuti 1438–1471.
20. Next month of course, I'll write you before then we're going on an overnight trip.

MECHANICS

21. John F. Kennedy 1917–1963 was the first Roman Catholic president of the United States.

22. Four of our former classmates yes, Beth was among them traveled to Australia with the U.S. athletes.

23. My grandparents will celebrate their fiftieth wedding anni versary on the third of October.

24. My friend Juan he went back to Puerto Rico has always wanted to be a veterinarian.

25. Linda Wing she is the ex champion will award the trophies.

26. Doing homework and seeing their improvement raised their self esteem.

27. Add exactly one half tablespoon of sugar to that recipe.

28. Napoleon's reign as emperor of France 1804–1815 was marked by great achievements and great setbacks.

29. "You don't mean to" exclaimed Renata.

30. The Friends of Silesia the Midwestern chapter, of course will have their annual dinner in Chicago this year.

31. Four players have been chosen for the state's all star team.

32. Beth I don't know her last name plays the lead role in the play.

33. She said wearily she often sounded weary "I'll go tomorrow."

34. By mid January twenty four inches of snow had fallen.

35. Mr. Brandt our neighbor of twelve years moved back to Germany after that country's reunification.

36. Franklin D. Roosevelt 1882–1945 was the thirty second president.

37. The ex governor of Kansas will speak at the reception.

38. Blake Ricky Blake, I mean was waiting for me downstairs.

39. Reggae music I heard it in the West Indies is popular here.

40. We all grew up in the same town Boise, Idaho.

## C. Using Hyphens, Dashes, Parentheses, Ellipsis Points, and Brackets Correctly

Correctly use hyphens, dashes, parentheses, ellipsis points, and brackets where needed in the following sentences. If a sentence is already correct, write *C.*

41. The Italian flag red, white, and green is similar in design to the French tricolor flag red, white, and blue.

42. "Well, I'll try . . . . . or maybe not," she stammered.

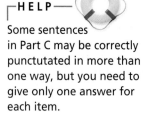

HELP

Some sentences in Part C may be correctly punctutated in more than one way, but you need to give only one answer for each item.

MECHANICS

43. The large building on the corner of Elm Street is the headquarters of the organization.

44. The Battle of Verdun February–July 1916 was a crucial French victory over the Germans in World War I.

45. In Mexico, San Miguel de Allende population approximately 80,000 is a popular destination for American artists and retirees.

46. [See page 100 (Map 2) for a more detailed look at the developing military situation.]

47. "My goodness!" exclaimed Grandpa. "Isn't that the?" and he hurriedly consulted his program.

48. The museum's preColumbian artifacts are well worth seeing.

49. I can think of dozens of people well, maybe not dozens, but quite a few who would agree with me.

50. Lorenzo Da Ponte was the man who wrote the libretto for Mozart's opera *Don Giovanni* and later and this came as a surprise to me taught Italian in New York City.

# Writing Application
## Writing a Report

**Using Punctuation**   Write a short report of no more than three paragraphs on your favorite author. Use at least three of the five elements of punctuation (hyphens, dashes, parentheses, ellipsis points, and brackets) discussed in this chapter.

**Prewriting**   First, gather biographical information on your chosen author. Include any details you find interesting or unusual.

**Writing**   As you write your first draft, think about how you plan to organize your information: by type of writing (fiction, nonfiction, poetry) or chronologically; or you could focus on a particular story, novel, or poem. Compare your draft to other short treatments of the author.

**Revising**   Read through your draft. Is the organization clear? If not, add, cut, or rearrange information to make it clearer.

**Publishing**   Proofread your essay for errors in grammar, spelling, and punctuation. You and your classmates may want to post the finished report on the class bulletin board or on a school Web page.

**Reference Note**

For more about **writing reports and research papers,** see Chapter 6: Investigating a Research Question.

# Spelling
## Improving Your Spelling

## Diagnostic Preview

### A. Choosing Correct Spelling

Choose the correct word from the pair in parentheses.

EXAMPLE  **1.** I was very careful not to (*brake, break*) the vase.

      *1. break*

1. After the Paris-Lyon high-speed train (*past, passed*) the waving onlookers and raced (*threw, through*) the tunnel, it reached a maximum speed of more than 180 miles per hour.
2. When the new (*principle, principal*) talked to her staff, she tried to get (*there, their, they're*) honest opinions.
3. The auctioneer (*led, lead*) the bidding on the original White House (*stationary, stationery*) on which was written President Roosevelt's actual signature.
4. Cuenca, near Madrid, is a lovely old town that is known for its (*piece, peace*) and (*quite, quiet*).
5. My aunt (*who's, whose*) picture appeared in yesterday's paper was (*formerly, formally*) a vice-president at First State Bank.
6. (*Altogether, All together*), the guitar music, the songs, and the aroma of *pan dulce* were a wonderful (*compliment, complement*) to the relaxed atmosphere.
7. Of (*course, coarse*), I found it nearly impossible to (*choose, chose*) between those two movies.

8. I took a (*plain, plane*) to Houston, and I visited family members who live (*there, their, they're*).

9. Although (*its, it's*) smaller than both Geneva and Zurich, Bern is the (*capital, capitol*) of Switzerland.

10. The new British (*council, consul, counsel*) and her husband returned to the embassy after having coffee and (*desert, dessert*) with the emir.

## B. Proofreading a Paragraph for Spelling Errors

Identify any misspelled or misused words in the following paragraph, and then write the words correctly. If all the words in a sentence are already correct, write *C*.

EXAMPLE **[1]** I have read about Santa Fe, but I have never been their.

1. *their—there*

[1] Santa Fe, New Mexico, is an all together charming and unusual city. [2] It is not only the capitol of the state but also a major tourist center. [3] The city lies in the north-central part of New Mexico at a hieght of about 7,000 feet and enjoys outstanding whether year-round. [4] The altitude sometimes has a bad affect on first-time visitors. [5] They are adviced not to exert themselves for the first day or so. [6] Santa Fe is one of the oldest citys in the United States. [7] It was founded in 1610 as the seat of government of the Spanish colony of New Mexico. [8] In 1912, New Mexico joined the United States as the 47th state. [9] I think the food in Santa Fe is awsome. [10] I suggest sampleing Southwestern cuisine, some of which is very spicy.

# Good Spelling Habits

**27a. To learn the spelling of a word, pronounce it, study it, and write it.**

**(1) Pronounce words carefully.**

Mispronunciation can lead to misspelling. For instance, if you say *mis • chē • vē • əs* instead of *mis • chə • vəs*, you will be more likely to spell the word incorrectly.

- First, make sure that you know how to pronounce the word correctly, and then practice saying it.

**HELP**

If you are not sure how to pronounce a word, look in a dictionary. In the dictionary, you will usually find the pronunciation given in parentheses after the word. The information in parentheses will show you the sounds used, the syllable breaks, and any accented syllables. A guide to the pronunciation symbols is usually found at the front of the dictionary.

- Second, study the word. Notice especially any parts that might be hard to remember.
- Third, write the word from memory. Check your spelling.
- If you misspelled the word, repeat the three steps of this process.

**(2) Use a dictionary.**

Whenever you find that you have misspelled a word, look it up in a dictionary. Don't guess about correct spelling.

**(3) Spell by syllables.**

A *syllable* is a word part that is pronounced as one uninterrupted sound.

EXAMPLES    thor • ough [two syllables]

sep • a • rate [three syllables]

Instead of trying to learn how to pronounce a whole word, break it up into its syllables whenever possible. It's easier to learn a few letters at a time than to learn all of them at once.

**Oral Practice**    **Pronouncing Spelling Words Correctly**

Study the correct pronunciations in parentheses after each of the following words. Then, pronounce each word correctly three times.

1. athlete (ăth′ • lēt′)
2. children (chil′ • drən)
3. drowned (drou nd)
4. escape (e • skāp′)
5. library (lī′ • brer • ē)
6. lightning (līt′ • ning)
7. perhaps (pər • haps′)
8. probably (prŏb′ • ə • blē)

**Exercise 1**    **Spelling by Syllables**

Look up the following words in a dictionary, and divide each one into syllables. Pronounce each syllable correctly, and learn to spell the word by syllables.

EXAMPLE    1. possibility

1. pos′ • si • bil′ • i • ty

1. representative
2. awkward
3. candidate
4. temperature
5. apparent
6. similar
7. definition
8. benefit
9. acquaintance
10. fascinate

**(4) Proofread for careless spelling errors.**

Re-read your writing carefully, and correct any mistakes and unclear letters. For example, make sure that your *i*'s are dotted, your *t*'s are crossed, and your *g*'s don't look like *q*'s.

**(5) Keep a spelling notebook.**

Divide each page into four columns:

COLUMN 1    Correctly spell the word you missed. (Never enter a misspelled word.)

COLUMN 2    Write the word again, dividing it into syllables and marking its accents.

COLUMN 3    Write the word once more, circling the letters that give you trouble.

COLUMN 4    Jot down any comments that might help you remember the correct spelling.

Here is an example of how you might make entries for two words that are often misspelled.

| Correct Spelling | Syllables and Accents | Trouble Spot | Comments |
|---|---|---|---|
| probably | prob'•a•bly | prob(ab)ly | Pronounce both b's. |
| usually | u'•su•al•ly | usua(ll)y | usual+ly (Study rule 27f.) |

**COMPUTER TIP**

Spellcheckers can help you proofread your writing. Even the best spellcheckers aren't foolproof, however. Many accept British spellings, obsolete words, archaic spellings, and words that are spelled correctly but used incorrectly (such as *affect* for *effect*). Always double-check your writing to make sure that your spelling is error-free.

**MECHANICS**

**Exercise 2    Spelling Commonly Misspelled Words**

Copy each of the following words or expressions, paying special attention to the italicized letters. Then, without looking at this page or the copy you made of the correctly spelled words, write the words as a friend dictates them to you.

1. answer
2. a*w*kward
3. *wh*ole
4. to*w*ard
5. *kn*ow
6. knowle*dge*
7. *wr*itten
8. of*t*en
9. condem*n*
10. colum*n*
11. r*h*ythm
12. use*d* to
13. inste*a*d
14. me*a*nt
15. *a*isle
16. toni*gh*t
17. su*r*ely
18. tho*ugh*
19. thro*ugh*
20. nin*e*ty

# Spelling Rules

## *ie* and *ei*

| TIPS & TRICKS |

Remember this rhyme:
*I* before *e* except after *c*
or when sounded like *a*
as in *neighbor* and
*weigh*.

**27b.** Write *ie* when the sound is long *e*, except after *c*.

EXAMPLES

| achi**e**ve | chi**e**f | ni**e**ce | shi**e**ld | c**ei**ling |
| beli**e**ve | fi**e**ld | pi**e**ce | thi**e**f | dec**ei**t |
| bri**e**f | gri**e**f | reli**e**f | yi**e**ld | rec**ei**ve |

EXCEPTIONS   **ei**ther, l**ei**sure, n**ei**ther, s**ei**ze, prot**ei**n

**27c.** Write *ei* when the sound is not long *e*.

EXAMPLES

| counterf**ei**t | h**ei**ght | r**ei**gn | forf**ei**t |
| for**ei**gn | h**ei**r | v**ei**l | w**ei**gh |

EXCEPTIONS   fri**e**nd, misch**ie**f, kerch**ie**f

NOTE   Rules 27b and 27c apply only when the *i* and the *e* are in the same syllable.

EXAMPLES   de • **i** • ty      sc**i** • ence

## –*cede*, –*ceed*, and –*sede*

**27d.** Only one English word ends in –*sede: supersede.* Only three words end in –*ceed: exceed, proceed,* and *succeed.* Almost all other words with this sound end in –*cede*.

EXAMPLES

| ac**cede** | inter**cede** | re**cede** |
| con**cede** | pre**cede** | se**cede** |

### Exercise 3   Proofreading Sentences to Correct Spelling Errors

The following sentences contain errors involving the use of *ie, ei,* –*ceed,* –*cede,* and –*sede*. For each sentence, identify the misspelled word or words and then write them correctly. If a sentence has no spelling errors, write *C*.

EXAMPLE   1. On my birthday I recieved a wonderful gift.

1. *recieved—received*

1. My neighbor, who is a good freind of mine, went on a trip out West.
2. He sent me a Dream Catcher like those used by the Sioux to sheild themselves from bad dreams.

3. Charms like this once hung in each tepee, and mine hangs from the cieling near my bed.

4. According to legend, bad dreams get caught in the web and only good ones succede in reaching the sleeper.

5. I do not really believe that my Dream Catcher can interceed on my behalf, but I have not had one bad dream since my birthday!

6. The Plains Indians moved their homes often, so their possessions could be niether bulky nor heavy.

7. Consequently, the Sioux who made the Dream Catcher used common, lightweight materials.

8. The twig bent into a ring is willow wood, and tiny glass beads represent nightmares siezed by the web.

9. Gracefully hanging from either side is a beautiful feather or a horsehair tassel.

10. Wonderful peices of workmanship like this help ensure that the culture of the Sioux will never resede into the past.

# Adding Prefixes

**27e.** When a prefix is added to a word, the spelling of the original word itself remains the same.

EXAMPLES    im + mobile = im**mobile**        mis + spell = mis**spell**

un + certain = un**certain**        over + rule = over**rule**

# Adding Suffixes

**27f.** When the suffix –*ness* or –*ly* is added to a word, the spelling of the original word itself remains the same.

EXAMPLES    time + ly = **time**ly        even + ness = **even**ness

real + ly = **real**ly        late + ness = **late**ness

EXCEPTIONS    1. Words ending in *y* usually change the *y* to *i* before –*ness* and –*ly:* empty—empt**i**ness; easy—eas**i**ly

2. However, most one-syllable adjectives ending in *y* follow Rule 27f: shy—**shy**ly; dry—**dry**ness

3. *True, due,* and *whole* drop the final *e* before –*ly:* truly, duly, wholly.

**Exercise 4** **Spelling Words with Prefixes and Suffixes**

Spell each of the following words, including the prefix or suffix that is given.

EXAMPLE    **1.** un + common

        *1. uncommon*

**1.** un + necessary       **6.** im + moral
**2.** il + legal             **7.** sly + ly
**3.** occasional + ly       **8.** speedy + ly
**4.** cleanly + ness        **9.** same + ness
**5.** mean + ness        **10.** un + usual

**27g.** **Drop the final silent *e* before adding a suffix that begins with a vowel.**

EXAMPLES    tame + ing = **tam**ing     loose + est = **loos**est
              noble + er = **nobl**er      admire + ation = **admir**ation
              tickle + ish = **tickl**ish      move + able = **mov**able

EXCEPTIONS    **1.** Keep the final silent *e* in most words ending in *ce* or *ge* before a suffix that begins with *a* or *o*:

         *knowledg**e**able, courag**e**ous.*

         Sometimes the *e* becomes *i,* as in *gracious* and *spacious.*

      **2.** To avoid confusion with other words, keep the final silent *e* in some words:

         *dy**e**ing* and *dying, sing**e**ing* and *singing*

      **3.** mile + age = mil**e**age

**Exercise 5** **Spelling Words with Suffixes**

Spell each of the following words, including the suffix that is given.

EXAMPLE    **1.** write + ing

        *1. writing*

**1.** become + ing        **6.** sense + ible
**2.** guide + ance        **7.** save + ing
**3.** continue + ous      **8.** advantage + ous
**4.** surprise + ed        **9.** dine + ing
**5.** determine + ation    **10.** hope + ed

**27h.** Keep the final silent *e* when adding a suffix that begins with a consonant.

EXAMPLES    safe + ty = saf**e**ty      large + ly = larg**e**ly

                  hope + ful = hop**e**ful      awe + some = aw**e**some

                  care + less = car**e**less      pave + ment = pav**e**ment

EXCEPTIONS    awe + ful = **aw**ful      true + ly = **tru**ly

                    nine + th = **nin**th      argue + ment = **argu**ment

---

**Review A**   **Spelling Words with Suffixes**

Spell each of the following words, including the suffix that is given.

EXAMPLE     **1.** use + less

              *1. useless*

**1.** announce + ment      **6.** station + ary

**2.** use + age      **7.** hope + less

**3.** imagine + ary      **8.** type + ing

**4.** care + ful      **9.** advertise + ment

**5.** write + ing      **10.** use + ful

**27i.** When a word ends in *y* preceded by a consonant, change the *y* to *i* before any suffix except one beginning with *i*.

EXAMPLES    tidy + er = tid**i**er      glory + ous = glor**i**ous

                  worry + ed = worr**i**ed      terrify + ing = terrif**y**ing

EXCEPTIONS    **1.** Some one-syllable words:

                  shy + ness = sh**y**ness      sky + ward = sk**y**ward

              **2.** *lady* and *baby* with most suffixes:

                  lad**y**like     lad**y**ship     bab**y**hood

**27j.** When a word ends in *y* preceded by a vowel, simply add the suffix.

EXAMPLES    play + ful = **play**ful      boy + hood = **boy**hood

                  array + ed = **array**ed      gray + est = **gray**est

                  pray + ing = **pray**ing      pay + ment = **pay**ment

EXCEPTIONS    day + ly = **dai**ly      pay + ed = **pai**d

                  say + ed = **sai**d      lay + ed = **lai**d

MECHANICS

Spell each of the following words, including the suffix that is given.

EXAMPLE    **1.** ply + able

          *1.* *pliable*

**1.** extraordinary + ly      **6.** baby + ish
**2.** try + ing      **7.** say + ing
**3.** deny + al      **8.** joy + ful
**4.** satisfy + ed      **9.** bray + ing
**5.** rely + able      **10.** fly + ing

## Doubling Final Consonants

**27k.** When a word ends in a consonant, double the final conso-nant before a suffix that begins with a vowel only if the word:

- has only one syllable or is accented on the last syllable

*and*

- ends in a *single* consonant preceded by a *single* vowel

EXAMPLES    dim + est = di**mm**est    red + ish = re**dd**ish
                plan + ed = pla**nn**ed    propel + er = prope**ll**er
                sit + ing = si**tt**ing     refer + ed = refe**rr**ed

Otherwise, simply add the suffix.

EXAMPLES    jump + ed = **jump**ed    tunnel + ing = **tunnel**ing
                sprint + er = **sprint**er    appear + ance = **appear**ance

Exercise **7** **Spelling Words with Suffixes**

Spell each of the following words, including the suffix that is given.

EXAMPLE    **1.** rebel + ed

          *1.* *rebelled*

**1.** swim + er      **6.** prepare + ing
**2.** accept + ance      **7.** control + ed
**3.** number + ing      **8.** slim + er
**4.** excel + ed      **9.** prefer + ing
**5.** riot + ous      **10.** glamor + ous

---

**MECHANICS**

┌HELP┐

The final conso-nant in some words may or may not be doubled. In such cases, both spellings are equally correct.

EXAMPLES
travel + er = trave**ler** *or* trave**ller**

shovel + ed = shove**led** *or* shove**lled**

**Review B** **Spelling Words with Prefixes and Suffixes**

The following paragraph contains spelling errors involving the use of prefixes and suffixes. For each sentence, write the misspelled word or words correctly. If a sentence is already correct, write *C*.

No proper nouns in Review B are misspelled.

EXAMPLE     [1]   Few people know that a teenage boy helped create the awsome Mount Rushmore monument.

    1.   *awesome*

[1] Begining when he was fifteen, Lincoln Borglum helped his famous father, Gutzon Borglum, who planed and made this gigantic sculpture. [2] First, Gutzon Borglum built a plaster model one-twelfth as large as the completted sculpture would be. [3] On top of this model Borglum attached the equipment from which he controlled a plumb line. [4] The plumb line could be dangled in front of each president's likness to record carefuly each feature. [5] Lincoln Borglum helped in making these mea-surments. [6] Then, on top of the cliff, they fastenned an identical machine twelve times as large. [7] Lincoln Borglum was one of the workers who operatted this machine. [8] Using it, he copied the movements of the smaller machine and marked exactly where to cut away the rock. [9] The closer the workers got to finishing the faces, the more carefully the Borglums studied the heads. [10] There were numerous problems, but the monument was finally inaugurated in 1941.

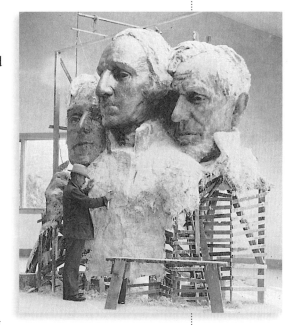

# Forming Plurals of Nouns

**27l.** To form the plurals of most English nouns, simply add *s*.

| SINGULAR | boat | care | storm | radio | Jim |
|---|---|---|---|---|---|
| PLURAL | boat**s** | care**s** | storm**s** | radio**s** | Jim**s** |

**27m.** To form the plurals of other nouns, follow these rules.

**(1)** If the noun ends in *s, x, z, ch,* or *sh*, add *es.*

| SINGULAR | moss | fox | Sanchez | clutch | dish |
|---|---|---|---|---|---|
| PLURAL | moss**es** | fox**es** | Sanchez**es** | clutch**es** | dish**es** |

NOTE Some one-syllable words ending in *z* double the final consonant when forming plurals.

| EXAMPLES | quiz | fez |
|---|---|---|
| | qui**zz**es | fe**zz**es |

---

**Exercise 8** **Spelling the Plurals of Nouns**

Spell the plural of each of the following nouns.

| EXAMPLE | **1.** Evans |
|---|---|
| | *1. Evanses* |

1. guess
2. ax
3. tongue
4. cafeteria
5. wash
6. boss
7. student
8. Owens
9. box
10. ditch

**(2)** If the noun ends in *y* preceded by a consonant, change the *y* to *i* and add *es.*

| SINGULAR | fly | pony | cry | story |
|---|---|---|---|---|
| PLURAL | fl**ies** | pon**ies** | cr**ies** | stor**ies** |

EXCEPTION    plurals of proper nouns: the Hard**ys**, the Car**ys**

TIPS & TRICKS

Noticing how the plural is pronounced will help you remember whether to change the *f* to *v*.

**(3)** For some nouns ending in *f* or *fe*, add *s*. For other nouns ending in *f* or *fe*, change the *f* to *v* and add *s* or *es.*

| EXAMPLES | giraffe | roof | self | life | elf | thief | wolf |
|---|---|---|---|---|---|---|---|
| | giraffe**s** | roof**s** | sel**ves** | li**ves** | el**ves** | thie**ves** | wol**ves** |

NOTE Some nouns can correctly form their plurals either way.

| EXAMPLES | hoof | scarf |
|---|---|---|
| | hoo**ves** | scar**ves** |
| | *or* | *or* |
| | hoof**s** | scarf**s** |

## Exercise 9 Spelling the Plurals of Nouns

Spell the plural of each of the following nouns.

EXAMPLES
1. shelf
1. *shelves*
2. poppy
2. *poppies*

1. thief
2. chef
3. theory
4. gulf
5. ally

6. wife
7. loaf
8. comedy
9. trophy
10. self

**HELP**

To correctly complete Exercise 9, you may wish to refer to a recent dictionary.

**(4) If the noun ends in *o* preceded by a vowel, add *s*.**

| SINGULAR | radio | cameo | kangaroo | Julio |
|---|---|---|---|---|
| PLURAL | radios | cameos | kangaroos | Julios |

**(5) If the noun ends in *o* preceded by a consonant, add *es*.**

| SINGULAR | echo | hero | tomato | veto |
|---|---|---|---|---|
| PLURAL | echoes | heroes | tomatoes | vetoes |

EXCEPTIONS Some common nouns ending in *o* preceded by a consonant (especially musical terms) and proper nouns form the plural by adding only *s*.

| SINGULAR | peso | sombrero | photo | alto |
|---|---|---|---|---|
| | piano | solo | Sotho | Sakamoto |
| PLURAL | pesos | sombreros | photos | altos |
| | pianos | solos | Sothos | Sakamotos |

NOTE A number of nouns that end in *o* preceded by a consonant have two correct plural forms.

| SINGULAR | cargo | grotto | mosquito |
|---|---|---|---|
| PLURAL | cargos | grottos | mosquitos |
| | or | or | or |
| | cargoes | grottoes | mosquitoes |

The best way to determine the plurals of words ending in *o* preceded by a consonant is to check their spellings in a dictionary.

MECHANICS

### Exercise 10  Spelling the Plurals of Nouns

Spell the plural of each of the following nouns.

EXAMPLE    **1.** stereo

*1. stereos*

| | | | |
|---|---|---|---|
| **1.** igloo | | **6.** banjo | |
| **2.** soprano | | **7.** taco | |
| **3.** patio | | **8.** cello | |
| **4.** veto | | **9.** Romeo | |
| **5.** torpedo | | **10.** studio | |

**(6)** The plurals of some nouns are formed in irregular ways.

| SINGULAR | child | foot | goose | man | tooth |
|---|---|---|---|---|---|
| PLURAL | child**ren** | f**ee**t | g**ee**se | m**en** | t**ee**th |

**(7)** Some nouns have the same form in both the singular and the plural.

| SINGULAR and PLURAL | Japanese | spacecraft | sheep |
|---|---|---|---|

## Compound Nouns

**(8)** For most compound nouns, form the plural of only the last word in the compound.

| SINGULAR | spoonbill | smashup | icebox | six-year-old |
|---|---|---|---|---|
| PLURAL | spoonbill**s** | smashup**s** | icebox**es** | six-year-old**s** |

**(9)** For compound nouns in which one of the words is modified by the other word or words, form the plural of the word modified.

| SINGULAR | sister-in-law | notary public | attorney at law |
|---|---|---|---|
| PLURAL | sister**s**-in-law | notar**ies** public | attorney**s** at law |

NOTE  Whenever you are not sure about how to spell the plural form of a compound noun, check a recent dictionary.

### Exercise 11  Spelling the Plurals of Nouns

Spell the plural form of each of the following nouns.

EXAMPLE    **1.** ox

*1. oxen*

1. Vietnamese
2. earmuff
3. mouse
4. cross-reference
5. goose
6. brother-in-law
7. aircraft
8. woman
9. runner-up
10. twenty-year-old

## Latin and Greek Loan Words

**(10)** **Some nouns borrowed from Latin and Greek form the plural as in the original language.**

| SINGULAR | PLURAL |
|---|---|
| alumnus [male] | alumn**i** |
| alumna [female] | alumn**ae** |
| analysis | analys**es** |
| crisis | cris**es** |
| datum | dat**a** |
| phenomenon | phenomen**a** |

**NOTE** A few Latin and Greek loan words have two correct plural forms.

| SINGULAR | appendix | formula |
|---|---|---|
| PLURAL | appendi**ces** *or* appendi**xes** | formul**as** *or* formul**ae** |

Check a dictionary to find the preferred spelling of a plural loan word. The preferred spelling is generally the one listed first.

## Numerals, Letters, Symbols, and Words Used as Words

**(11)** **To form the plurals of numerals, most capital letters, symbols, and words used as words, add either an *s* or an apostrophe and an *s*.**

EXAMPLES
Put the **4'*s*** (*or* **4s**) and the ***T*'s** (*or* **Ts**) in the second column.

Change the **&'*s*** (*or* **&s**) to ***and*'s** (*or* **ands**).

My parents were teenagers during the **'60's** (*or* **'60s**).

Many immigrants came to this country during the **1800's** (*or* **1800s**).

BORN LOSER reprinted by permission of Newspaper Enterprise Association, Inc.

MECHANICS

To prevent confusion, always use an apostrophe and an *s* to form the plurals of lowercase letters, certain capital letters, and some words used as words.

EXAMPLES     What do these **a's** in the margins mean?

Ramon got **A's** last semester.

Her muffled **tee-hee's** did not interrupt the speaker.

**Exercise 12**  **Spelling the Plurals of Nouns, Numerals, Letters, Symbols, and Words Used as Words**

Give the plural form of each of the following words, numerals, symbols, and words used as words.

EXAMPLE     1. *o*
              1. *o's*

1. +
2. parenthesis
3. *so*
4. *9*
5. fulcrum

6. *C*
7. 1840
8. index
9. *!*
10. *ho-ho-ho*

**Review C**  **Spelling the Plurals of Nouns**

Most lines in the following silly poem contain misspelled words. Correct each misspelled word. If a line contains no misspellings, write *C*.

EXAMPLES     1.  A group of mans and womens started up a local zoo.
              1.  *men; women*

              2.  They bought a lot of animales and put them all on view.
              2.  *animals*

1. They caged the oxes with the gooses, the lion with the calfs,
2. The butterflys and mouses with the burroes and giraffs.
3. Armys of people soon arrived. In jalopys they were piled,
4. With wifes and husbands, son-in-laws, and lots of little childs.
5. The boys and girls rode poneys, and they fed the sheeps and deer,
6. And thought their folks were heros to bring them all right here.
7. The mosquitoses had a fine time feasting on the kangarooes;
8. Most of the other animals minded their *p*s and *q*s.
9. The moon shone brightly through the leafs as night began to fall.
10. Why do you think the lion had the nicest day of all?

# Spelling Numbers

**27n.** Spell out a number that begins a sentence.

EXAMPLE    **One thousand five hundred** band members attended this year's State Marching Band Festival.

**27o.** Within a sentence, spell out numbers that can be written in one or two words; use numerals for other numbers.

EXAMPLES    I have only **one** week in which to write **four** reports.

We picked **twenty-one** quarts of peaches.

Agnes has sold **116** magazine subscriptions.

EXCEPTION 1    If you use some numbers that have one or two words and some that have more than two words, use numerals for all of them.

EXAMPLE    Our school had **563** freshmen, **327** sophomores, **143** juniors, and **90** seniors.

EXCEPTION 2    Use numerals for dates when you include the name of the month. Always use numerals for years.

EXAMPLES    School closes on June **6**. [This example could also be correctly written as *the sixth of June,* but not *June 6th.*]

Egypt fell to the Romans in **30** B.C.

**27p.** Spell out numbers used to indicate order.

EXAMPLE    My brother graduated **second** [not *2nd*] in his class.

**Reference Note**

For more about **writing dates,** see page 659.

Write five original sentences, following the directions given below.

EXAMPLE     **1.**   Write a sentence giving the year in which your best friend was born.

      *1.*   *Rudy Garza was born in 1986.*

**1.** Write a sentence beginning with a number.
**2.** Write a sentence containing two numbers, both of which can be written in one or two words.
**3.** Write a sentence containing three numbers, two of them with one or two words and one of them with more than two words.
**4.** Write a sentence using a number to indicate the order in which a person placed in a race.
**5.** Write a sentence giving the month and date of your birthday.

# Words Often Confused

You can prevent many spelling errors by learning the difference between the words grouped together in this section. Some of them are confusing because they are **homonyms**—that is, they are pronounced alike. Others are confusing because they are spelled the same or nearly the same.

| | |
|---|---|
| **advice** | [noun] *counsel*<br>Why don't you ask your father for *advice*? |
| **advise** | [verb] *to give advice*<br>The weather service *advises* boaters. |
| **affect** | [verb] *to influence*<br>Do sunspots *affect* the weather? |
| **effect** | [verb] *to bring about, to accomplish*; [noun] *result, consequence*<br>Our new boss *effected* some startling changes in our use of technology.<br>Name three *effects* of the Industrial Revolution on family life. |
| **all ready** | [adjective] *everyone or everything prepared*<br>We were *all ready* to go. |
| **already** | [adverb] *previously*<br>Sharon has *already* gone. |

MECHANICS

| | |
|---|---|
| **all right** | [This is the only acceptable spelling. Although the spelling *alright* is in some dictionaries, it has not become standard usage.] |
| **all together** | [adjective or adverb] *everyone or everything in the same place*<br>*All together* at last, the travelers relaxed.<br>The band simply must play *all together*. |
| **altogether** | [adverb] *entirely*<br>You're *altogether* mistaken, I fear. |
| **altar** | [noun] *a table used for a religious ceremony*<br>The *altar* was draped with a white cloth. |
| **alter** | [verb] *to change*<br>This actor can *alter* his appearance. |
| **brake** | [noun] *a stopping device*; [verb] *to stop*<br>The *brakes* on our car are good.<br>I *brake* for deer. |
| **break** | [verb] *to shatter, sever*<br>A high-pitched sound can *break* glass. |
| **capital** | [noun] *center of government; money or property used in business*; [adjective] *punishable by death; of major importance; excellent; uppercase*<br>Raleigh is the *capital* of North Carolina.<br>We need more *capital* to buy the factory.<br>Is killing a police officer a *capital* crime?<br>I made a *capital* error in judgment.<br>This is a *capital* detective story.<br>You need a *capital* letter here. |
| **capitol** | [noun] *building, statehouse*<br>The *capitol* is on East Edenton Street. |
| **choose** | [verb, used for present and future tense] *select*<br>You may *choose* your own partner. |
| **chose** | [verb, past tense, rhymes with *nose*] *selected*<br>They *chose* to postpone the meeting. |

*(continued)*

**Reference Note**

In the Glossary of Usage, Chapter 20, you can find many other words that are often confused or misused. You can also look them up in a dictionary.

⎡ TIPS & TRICKS ⎤

To remember the correct spelling of *capitol,* use this memory aid: There is a d**o**me on the capit**o**l.

**MECHANICS**

*(continued)*

| | |
|---|---|
| **coarse** | [adjective] *rough, crude* <br> This *coarse* fabric is very durable. <br> He never uses *coarse* language. |
| **course** | [noun] *path of action or progress; unit of study; track or way; part of a meal;* [also used with *of* to mean *naturally* or *certainly*] <br> The airplane strayed off its *course* in the storm. <br> I'm taking an algebra *course*. <br> She's at the golf *course*. <br> The main *course* at the banquet was roasted turkey with dressing. <br> Cats, of *course*, are predators. |

### Exercise 14 Distinguishing Between Words Often Confused

Choose the correct word or expression from the pair in parentheses.

EXAMPLE    **1.** I was proud to (*accept, except*) the award.

     *1. accept*

**1.** Betty has (*all ready, already*) handed in her paper.
**2.** (*All right, Alright*), I'll wrap the package now.
**3.** The mechanic adjusted the (*brakes, breaks*).
**4.** Do you know which city is the (*capital, capitol*) of your state?
**5.** They were (*all together, altogether*) at dinner.
**6.** The rule goes into (*affect, effect*) today.
**7.** His (*coarse, course*) manners offended everyone.
**8.** A fragile piece of china (*brakes, breaks*) easily.
**9.** Our state (*capital, capitol*) is built of limestone and marble.
**10.** When will they (*choose, chose*) the winners?

### Exercise 15 Proofreading for Words Often Confused

Correct the errors in word choice in the following sentences.

EXAMPLE    **1.** After taking that class, we were already to shoot our own videos.

     *1. all ready*

**1.** The best movie-making advise I ever received came from Ms. Herrera.

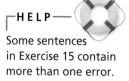

┌HELP─

Some sentences in Exercise 15 contain more than one error.

MECHANICS

2. She taught the video coarse that I choose as an elective last semester.

3. Once we would-be movie makers were altogether, she said simply, "Rule number one: Take the lens cap off."

4. Everyone laughed, but she said, "It's no joke—in every class at least one person brakes this one basic rule."

5. "Of coarse," she added, "forgetting to put a videocassette in the camera has much the same affect."

6. If you chose to make your own home videos, I'd advice you to remember Ms. Herrera's words.

7. They will seriously effect you.

8. I remembered her advice when I went to the steps of the capital for my first shoot.

9. I checked the lighting and angle and chose a subject that was all together satisfactory.

10. When I started to shoot, I realized I had made a capitol error—I had forgotten to take the lens cap off!

| | |
|---|---|
| **complement** | [noun] *something that completes or makes perfect;* [verb] *to complete or make perfect*<br>The office now has a full *complement* of personnel.<br>The rug *complemented* the cozy room. |
| **compliment** | [noun] *a remark that expresses approval, praise, or admiration;* [verb] *to pay a compliment*<br>Ms. Garcia paid me a *compliment*.<br>The review *complimented* Rosemary on her performance. |
| **consul** | [noun] *the representative of a foreign country*<br>Did you meet the Greek *consul* at the reception? |
| **council** | [noun] *a group called together to accomplish a job*<br>Our town *council* meets next Tuesday. |
| **counsel** | [noun] *advice;* [verb] *to give advice*<br>Her *counsel* is invaluable to the president.<br>The engineers *counsel* them to use additional support for the crossbeams. |

*(continued)*

TIPS & TRICKS

To remember the correct spelling of *complement*, use this memory aid: A compl**e**ment compl**e**tes.

MECHANICS

*(continued)*

| | |
|---|---|
| **councilor** | [noun] *a member of a council*<br>At the council meeting, my mother plans to introduce Dr. Watkins, the new *councilor.* |
| **counselor** | [noun] *one who gives advice*<br>I don't think I'm qualified to act as your *counselor.* |
| **desert** | [noun, pronounced des´•ert] *a dry region*<br>The Sahara is the world's largest *desert.* |
| **desert** | [verb, pronounced de•sert´] *to leave*<br>She would never *desert* her comrades. |
| **dessert** | [noun, pronounced des•sert´] *a sweet, final course of a meal*<br>What would you like for dessert tonight? |

**Exercise 16** Distinguishing Between Words Often Confused

Choose the correct word from the choices in parentheses.

EXAMPLE   **1.** The town (*counselor, councilor*) voted on the bill.

   1. *councilor*

   **1.** The funds are for a (*desert, dessert*) irrigation project.
   **2.** The Security (*Consul, Council, Counsel*) of the United Nations consists of fifteen members.
   **3.** The new tie will (*complement, compliment*) my suit.
   **4.** Miss Jee is my guidance (*councilor, counselor*).
   **5.** The house looks (*deserted, desserted*).
   **6.** Listen to your parents' (*consul, council, counsel*).
   **7.** I passed on your charming (*complement, compliment*) to Isabel.
   **8.** All the members of the city (*council, counsel*) agreed.
   **9.** Frozen yogurt is my favorite (*desert, dessert*).
   **10.** The American (*consul, counsel*) in Bahrain announced the recent trade agreement.

| | |
|---|---|
| **formally** | [adverb] *properly, according to strict rules*<br>Should he be *formally* introduced? |
| **formerly** | [adverb] *previously, in the past*<br>The new consul was *formerly* a professor. |

MECHANICS

| | |
|---|---|
| **hear** | [verb] *to receive sounds through the ears*<br>Did you *hear* the president's speech? |
| **here** | [adverb] *at this place*<br>The bus will be *here* soon. |
| **its** | [possessive of *it*] *belonging to it*<br>The lion stopped in *its* tracks. |
| **it's** | [contraction of *it is* or *it has*]<br>*It's* snowing!<br>*It's* started snowing! |
| **lead** | [verb, present tense, rhymes with *deed*] *to go first*<br>I'll *lead* the way. |
| **led** | [verb, past tense of *lead*] *went first*<br>Last week she *led* us to victory. |
| **lead** | [noun, rhymes with *red*] *a heavy metal; graphite in a pencil*<br>We made fishing sinkers out of *lead*.<br>Use a sharp *lead* to draw fine lines. |
| **loose** | [adjective, rhymes with *noose*] *not tight, not securely fastened; not close together*<br>The string on the package is too *loose*. |
| **lose** | [verb, rhymes with *choose*] *to suffer loss*<br>Don't *lose* your ticket. |
| **moral** | [adjective] *having to do with good or right;* [noun] *a lesson in conduct*<br>It's a *moral* question.<br>These fables all have a *moral*. |
| **morale** | [noun] *mental condition, spirit*<br>Letters from home raised our *morale*. |
| **passed** | [verb, past tense of *pass*] *went by*<br>He *passed* us in the corridor. |
| **past** | [noun] *history, what has gone by;* [adjective] *former;* [preposition] *farther than; after*<br>I didn't ask him about his *past*.<br>Her *past* employer recommended her.<br>I went *past* the house.<br>It's ten minutes *past* noon. |

*(continued)*

| peace | [noun] *absence of conflict* |
| | Only after war is *peace* truly appreciated. |
| piece | [noun] *a part of something;* [verb] *to assemble slowly* |
| | Have a *piece* of my homemade bread. |
| | We *pieced* together the puzzle. |

### Exercise 17 Distinguishing Between Words Often Confused

Choose the correct word of the pair in parentheses.

EXAMPLE    1. The two countries settled their dispute and now live in (*piece, peace*).

     1. peace

1. The coach's praise after the game raised the team's (*morale, moral*).
2. It's already (*passed, past*) nine o'clock.
3. The searchers hoped that the search dog would (*lead, led*) them to the missing skier.
4. The two forwards (*led, lead*) the team to victory.
5. I'm more interested in math than I (*formally, formerly*) was.
6. Several children asked what the (*moral, morale*) of the story was.
7. I need a pencil with soft (*led, lead*).
8. Everyone at the dance was dressed (*formally, formerly*).
9. Molly (*past, passed*) the open doorway.
10. Is the bank offering good interest rates on (*it's, its*) savings accounts and loans?

### Exercise 18 Proofreading for Words Often Confused

Correct the errors in word choice in the following sentences.

EXAMPLE    1. My dad's promotion lead to a move for our family.

     1. led

1. Sometimes relocating can feel like abandoning everything and everyone you formally cared about.
2. However, before my family and I moved, one of my friends gave me very good council.
3. "Moving away," she said, "doesn't mean that you are desserting your old friends."

4. After my family moved across the country, I remembered that peace of advice.

5. For the first few months after we moved hear, I felt as though I'd been cut lose from everything I loved.

6. To boost my morale, my parents told me something that I needed to here.

7. If you dwell on the passed, you will loose out on the present.

8. They both moved often when they were young, so I guess they know what its like.

9. Now that a year has past, I understand that every place has it's good points.

10. I've made quite a few new friends, and I'm finally at piece with myself—and with my parents.

| | |
|---|---|
| **plain** | [adjective] *clear, not fancy;* [noun] *a flat area of land*<br>She made her point of view *plain*.<br>Steven wears very *plain* clothes.<br>The storm lashed the open *plain*. |
| **plane** | [noun] *a flat surface; a level; a tool; an airplane*<br>Each *plane* of the granite block was smooth.<br>The debate was conducted on a high *plane*.<br>Chris smoothed the wood with a *plane*.<br>The *plane* arrived on time. |
| **principal** | [noun] *head of a school;* [adjective] *main, most important*<br>Our new *principal* addressed the assembly.<br>Product design is my *principal* responsibility. |
| **principle** | [noun] *a rule of conduct; a law*<br>His *principles* do not allow compromise.<br>Please explain the *principle* of gravity. |
| **quiet** | [adjective] *silent, still*<br>The library is usually fairly *quiet*. |
| **quite** | [adverb] *to a great extent or degree, completely*<br>My little brother is *quite* clever for his age.<br>I'm not *quite* finished. |

**TIPS & TRICKS**

To remember the correct spelling of *principal*, use the following memory aid: The princi**pal** is your **pal**.

*(continued)*

*(continued)*

| | |
|---|---|
| **shone** | [verb, past tense of *shine*] *emitted light*<br>The sun *shone* brightly this morning. |
| **shown** | [verb, past participle of *show*] *revealed, displayed*<br>Li Hua has just *shown* me her scrapbook. |
| **stationary** | [adjective] *in a fixed position*<br>These chairs are *stationary*. |
| **stationery** | [noun] *writing paper*<br>Use white *stationery* for business letters. |
| **than** | [conjunction, used for comparisons]<br>Jimmy enjoys tennis more *than* golfing. |
| **then** | [adverb] *at that time; next*<br>Did you know Bianca *then*?<br>I revised my paper, and *then* I proofread it. |
| **their** | [possessive of *they*] *belonging to them*<br>The girls gave *their* opinions. |
| **there** | [adverb] *at that place;* [also an expletive used to begin a sentence]<br>I'll be *there* on time.<br>*There* isn't any milk left. |
| **they're** | [contraction of *they are*]<br>*They're* at the station now. |

**TIPS & TRICKS**

To remember the correct spelling of *stationery*, use the following memory aid: "You write a lett**er** on station**er**y."

**Reference Note**

For information on **possessive pronouns,** see page 556. For information on **adverbs,** see page 572. For information on **forming contractions,** see page 707.

**Exercise 19  Distinguishing Between Words Often Confused**

Choose the correct word from the pair in parentheses.

EXAMPLE    1. Mrs. Tanaka is our school's (*principal, principle*).

1. *principal*

1. An elephant eats more vegetation (*then, than*) any other animal does.
2. One scene of the movie was not (*shone, shown*) on TV.
3. The deer was (*stationary, stationery*) for a full minute.
4. Gossiping is against his (*principals, principles*).
5. Last night many stars (*shone, shown*) brightly.
6. I wrote the letter on blue (*stationary, stationery*).
7. Rosa learned how to use a (*plain, plane*) in industrial arts class.

**8.** My (*principal, principle*) problem is learning to spell.

**9.** I hope they remembered (*there, their*) homework.

**10.** Is he (*quite, quiet*) sure?

**Review D**    **Proofreading for Words Often Confused**

Correct each error in word choice in the following sentences.

┌**HELP**┐

Some sentences
in Review D contain
more than one error.

EXAMPLE     **1.** Our principle let us out of class early to welcome home
our victorious volleyball team.

     *1. principal*

**1.** King High School won quiet a victory last year—the girls' regional
volleyball championship.

**2.** Everyone wanted to complement the team's abilities.

**3.** The victory had a positive affect on the whole student body.

**4.** Hundreds of students went to the airport to meet the team's plain.

**5.** The flight arrived on time, but than it took more then an hour for
the aircraft to reach the gate.

**6.** Finally someone shouted, "Their they are!"

**7.** "There coming up the ramp!"

**8.** Coach Janos asked for quite and introduced each of the girls.

**9.** They're were loud cheers for each of them, even though quite a few
hadn't played in the final game.

**10.** It was plane that they were quite excited about there success and
were looking forward to the official victory rally the next day.

| | |
|---|---|
| **threw** | [verb] *tossed; pitched*<br>Freddy *threw* three strikes. |
| **through** | [preposition] *in one side and out the*<br>    *opposite side*<br>The firetruck raced *through* the heavy traffic. |
| **to** | [preposition; also used before the infinitive<br>    form of a verb]<br>They've gone *to* the store.<br>She told us *to* wash the windows. |
| **too** | [adverb] *also; excessively*<br>I like soccer, and Ted does, *too.*<br>He was *too* tired to think clearly. |
| **two** | [adjective or noun] *the sum of one + one*<br>I noticed *two* packages on the sofa. |

*(continued)*

*(continued)*

| waist | [noun] *the middle part of the body*<br>This skirt is too big in the *waist*. |
|---|---|
| waste | [noun] *unused material*; [verb] *to squander*<br>*Waste* is a major problem in the United States.<br>Don't *waste* your money on that. |
| weak | [adjective] *feeble, lacking force, not strong*<br>The fawn is still too *weak* to walk. |
| week | [noun] *seven days*<br>Carol has been gone a *week*. |
| weather | [noun] *conditions outdoors*<br>The *weather* suddenly changed. |
| whether | [conjunction indicating alternative or doubt]<br>She wondered *whether* to enter the contest. |
| who's | [contraction of *who is* or *who has*]<br>I can't imagine *who's* at the door now.<br>*Who's* been marking in my book? |
| whose | [possessive of *who*] *belonging to whom*<br>*Whose* bicycle is this? |
| your | [possessive of *you*] *belonging to you*<br>What is *your* idea? |
| you're | [contraction of *you are*]<br>R.S.V.P. so that I'll know whether *you're*<br>planning to be there. |

## Exercise 20 Distinguishing Between Words Often Confused

Choose the correct word from the ones given in parentheses.

EXAMPLE  **1.** Lourdes speaks Portuguese, (*to, two, too*).

  *1. too*

**1.** Next (*weak, week*) the Bearcats will play the Wolverines.
**2.** The ball crashed (*threw, through*) the window.
**3.** (*Your, You're*) up next, Leshe.
**4.** Giving a speech makes me (*weak, week*) in the knees.
**5.** (*Your, You're*) sleeve is torn.
**6.** Each band member wore a gold sash around the (*waist, waste*).
**7.** (*Whose, Who's*) bat is this?

**8.** (*Whose, Who's*) going to be first?

**9.** No, this isn't a (*waist, waste*) of time.

**10.** (*Whose, Who's*) seen my black sweater?

---

**Exercise 21** **Proofreading for Words Often Confused**

Correct the errors in word choice in the following sentences.

EXAMPLE     **1.** Have you ever had the whether ruin you're plans?

        *1.  weather, your*

**1.** Last Labor Day weekend, my brother Jorge and I got up early Saturday morning and rode our bikes four miles too the beach.

**2.** The two of us were to busy talking too notice that the sky was growing darker as we rode along.

**3.** Just as we through our towels on the sand, it started to rain heavily.

**4.** We waisted the next hour huddled under one of the beach shelters, arguing about weather to stay or to go home.

**5.** We also got into an argument about who's fault it was.

**6.** "Your the one who had the bright idea," said Jorge.

**7.** "Whose the one who said it would be sunny?" I retorted.

**8.** Finally, we pedaled back home threw the driving rain.

**9.** It rained all day Sunday and Monday, to.

**10.** We spent the weekend cooped up in the house while whether forecasters predicted sunny skies for the next weak.

---

**Review E** **Identifying Correctly Spelled Words**

Choose the correct word or expression from the pair in parentheses.

EXAMPLE     **1.** a (*stationary, stationery*) exercise bicycle

        *1.  stationary*

**1.** a (*brief, breif*) talk

**2.** (*neither, niether*) one

**3.** (*course, coarse*) cloth

**4.** some good (*advice, advise*)

**5.** fruit for (*desert, dessert*)

**6.** many (*heros, heroes*)

**7.** on the (*cieling, ceiling*)

**8.** two (*copies, copys*)

**9.** looking (*passed, past*) him

**10.** (*weather, whether*) to stay

**11.** the (*altar, alter*) boys

**12.** building (*patioes, patios*)

**13.** recycled (*34, thirty-four*) cans

**14.** we will go (*than, then*)

**15.** a (*mispelled, misspelled*) word

**16.** (*happyly, happily*) ever after

**17.** that's (*awsome, awesome*)

**18.** a (*week, weak*) voice

**19.** this sharp pencil (*led, lead*)

**20.** (*their, they're*) his

# Chapter Review

## A. Proofreading Sentences to Correct Spelling Errors

Most of the following sentences contain spelling errors. Write the misspelled words correctly. If a sentence is already correct, write *C*.

┌HELP┐
Some sentences
in Part A of the Chapter
Review contain more than
one error.

1. Silas has no doubt that his favorite neice will succede in whatever career she chooses to follow.

2. The winter snow and ice damaged the eveness of the road surface.

3. Some critics' reviews were largely favorable; others said the movie was awful.

4. Occasionaly, we stay home on Saturdays to clean the yard.

5. Cousin Mark bought that car because he thinks it is a senseible compromise between style and economy.

6. I read all the recommended books from cover to cover for the finals, and now that exams are over, the books are safely back on the library bookshelfs where they belong.

7. I asked Patrick O'Daniel how long the O'Daniel's had lived in Texas.

8. In his twenties, Grandpa was an awsome swimer.

9. Extraordinaryly quickly, the snake disappeared into the undergrowth.

10. "As you know," said Ms. Garza, "February 15th—that is, tomorrow—is Colleen's birthday."

11. My cheif objection to attending the ceremony was having to listen to all those speech's.

12. "Alright, then," said Mom. "You can go outside, but be careful on those icey sidewalks."

13. How many boxs were stacked near the door?

14. The members of the United Nations Security Counsel are the United States, Russia, China, France, and the United Kingdom.

15. The engineer accidentally shut down the transmitter.

16. Vivian's account of her experiences in New Guinea was breif but vivid.

17. What do you call the passage that preceeds the main body of our Constitution?

18. The paper is delivered dayly, except on Mondays.

MECHANICS

**19.** The elephant was considerring coming into the clearing.

**20.** I'm grumpy because I just had an arguement with a friend.

## B. Distinguishing Between Words Often Confused

Choose the correct word from the pair in parentheses.

**21.** Last night I went (*too, to*) the theater.

**22.** How did the news (*effect, affect*) him?

**23.** We need to order some letterhead (*stationary, stationery*) and paper for the photocopier.

**24.** At the graduation ceremony, Mr. Garcia, the (*principle, principal*), gave a short speech.

**25.** The (*plain, plane*) finally took off after a two-hour delay.

**26.** First we sketched the outline, and (*than, then*) we filled in the features of the house.

**27.** Her duties in her old job were (*quiet, quite*) different from those in the new job.

**28.** "Son," said Dad, "I'd (*advice, advise*) you to keep at it. Quitters never get anywhere."

**29.** For (*desert, dessert*) they had frozen yogurt and shredded pineapple.

**30.** We were all very pleased when we heard that Shawna's dad had been named U.S. (*Counsel, Consul*) in Pretoria, South Africa.

**31.** Please permit me to introduce (*formerly, formally*) Dr. Villanueva, my sponsor.

**32.** When parking on an incline, always remember to set the (*break, brake*).

**33.** I think that tonight's debate is on the subject of (*capital, capitol*) punishment.

**34.** "(*All together, Altogether*) now," said the choir director.

**35.** Going to the Christmas concert with the whole family certainly raised my (*morale, moral*).

**36.** The (*capital, capitol*) of New York State is not New York City, but Albany.

**37.** 1 wonder (*who's, whose*) parka this is.

**38.** From Fran's point of view, volunteering to help clean up the city park was as much a question of (*principal, principle*) as goodwill.

**39.** "Was that really (*you're, your*) best effort?" asked Ms. Yokoyama impatiently.

**40.** He opened his mouth to reply, but Babs had (*all ready, already*) gone.

**41.** Friends never (*dessert, desert*) each other.

**42.** Use a (*led, lead*) pencil to sketch the outlines.

**43.** "How could you (*loose, lose*) an entire bag of groceries?" asked Belinda incredulously.

**44.** The same truck (*past, passed*) us three times on the same stretch of highway.

**45.** Please remember that every journey has (*it's, its*) good and bad points.

**46.** "Improving communication, as many of you will find out, can boost (*moral, morale*)," said Ms. Lockheed.

**47.** The amber harvest moon (*shown, shone*) through the rustling branches and onto the badger's burrow.

**48.** "All the caddies will be paid in full, of (*course, coarse*)," said Mr. Glendinning.

**49.** When the office workers go home, a strange (*quiet, quite*) descends on the downtown business district.

**50.** The tornadoes raced across the barren (*plane, plain*).

# Writing Application
## Using Correct Spelling in a Letter

**Spelling Words Correctly**   The junior varsity volleyball team is having its best season in several years, but no one else in school seems to know about it. Write a letter to the coach explaining the three best things the team can do to raise awareness and interest throughout the school. Use at least five words from the spelling lists and five words from the lists of words that are often confused.

**Prewriting**   Begin by making a list of all the ideas you can think of to promote the team. Look at the other successful sports and activities at your school. What do they do to promote themselves? Narrow your list down to the three ideas that are most likely to work.

**Writing**   Begin your letter by clearly explaining your purpose. Then, list each of your ideas and explain why you think they may help. Include estimates of how much money and time each of the ideas might involve. Conclude by offering to take charge of one part of the effort.

**Revising**   First, read your letter to make sure all of your ideas are clearly and completely explained. Ask yourself if you have thought about all of your ideas thoroughly. Have you considered all the expenses that each plan may involve? Would anyone be offended or hurt by any of your plans? You may want to have an adult friend or family member look at your ideas to see if they are appropriate. Make sure you have used at least five words from the spelling lists and five words from the lists of words that are often confused.

**Publishing**   Check your letter carefully for errors in grammar, usage, and punctuation. Then, think about a sport or other activity at school that does not get the recognition and support you think it deserves. Show your letter to the coach or sponsor of the activity, and offer to help carry out some of the ideas to get the activity more recognition.

MECHANICS

# 75 Commonly Misspelled Words

The following list contains seventy-five words that are often misspelled. To find out which words give you difficulty, ask someone to read you the list in groups of ten. Write down each word, and then check your spelling. In your spelling notebook, make a list of any words you misspelled. Keep reviewing your list until you have mastered the correct spelling.

| | | |
|---|---|---|
| ache | friend | speak |
| across | | speech |
| again | grammar | straight |
| all right | guess | sugar |
| almost | | surely |
| always | half | |
| answer | having | tear |
| | heard | though |
| belief | hour | through |
| built | | tired |
| business | instead | together |
| busy | | tomorrow |
| buy | knew | tonight |
| | know | tough |
| can't | | trouble |
| color | laid | truly |
| coming | likely | Tuesday |
| cough | | |
| could | making | until |
| country | meant | |
| | minute | wear |
| doctor | | Wednesday |
| doesn't | often | where |
| don't | once | which |
| | | whole |
| eager | ready | women |
| easy | really | won't |
| every | | write |
| | safety | |
| February | said | |
| forty | says | |
| | shoes | |
| | since | |

# 300 Spelling Words

Learn to spell the following words this year if you don't already know how.

| | | |
|---|---|---|
| absence | accommodate | accustomed |
| absolutely | accompany | achievement |
| acceptance | accomplish | acquaintance |
| accidentally | accurate | actually |

administration
affectionate
agriculture
amateur
ambassador
analysis
analyze
announcement
anticipate
apology
apparent
appearance
approach
approval
arguing
argument
assurance
attendance
authority
available

basically
beginning
believe
benefit
benefited
boundary

calendar
campaign
capital
category
certificate
characteristic
chief
circuit
circumstance
civilization
column
commissioner
committee
comparison
competent
competition
conceivable

concept
confidential
conscience
conscious
consistency
constitution
continuous
control
cooperate
corporation
correspondence
criticism
criticize
cylinder

debtor
decision
definite
definition
deny
description
despise
diameter
disappearance
disappointment
discipline
disgusted
distinction
distinguished
dominant
duplicate

economic
efficiency
eighth
elaborate
eligible
embarrass
emergency
employee
encouraging
environment
equipped
essential
evidently

exaggerate
exceedingly
excellent
excessive
excitable
exercise
existence
expense
extraordinary

fascinating
fatal
favorably
fictitious
financier
flourish
fraternity
frequent
further

glimpse
glorious
grabbed
gracious
graduating
grammatically
gross
gymnasium

happiness
hasten
heavily
hindrance
humorous
hungrily
hypocrisy
hypocrite

icy
ignorance
incidentally
indicate
imagination
immediately
immense
indispensable

inevitable
innocence
inquiry
insurance
intelligence
interfere
interrupt
interpretation
investigation

jealous

knowledge

leisure
lengthen
lieutenant
likelihood
liveliness
loneliness

magazine
maneuver
marriage
marvelous
mechanical
medieval
merchandise
minimum
mortgage
multitude
muscle
mutual

narrative
naturally
necessary
negligible
niece
noticeable

obligation
obstacle

occasionally
occurrence
offense
official
omit
operation
opportunity
oppose
optimism
orchestra
organization
originally

paid
paradise
parallel
particularly
peasant
peculiar
percentage
performance
personal
personality
perspiration
persuade
petition
philosopher
picnic
planning
pleasant
policies
politician
possess
possibility
practically
precede
precisely
preferred
prejudice
preparation
pressure

primitive
privilege
probably
procedure
proceed
professor
proportion
psychology
publicity
pursuit

qualities
quantities

readily
reasonably
receipt
recognize
recommendation
referring
regretting
reign
relieve
remembrance
removal
renewal
repetition
representative
requirement
residence
resistance
responsibility
restaurant
rhythm
ridiculous

sacrifice
satire
satisfied
scarcely
scheme
scholarship

scissors
senate
sensibility
separate
sergeant
several
shepherd
sheriff
similar
skis
sponsor
solemn
sophomore
source
specific
straighten

substantial
substitute
subtle
succeed
successful
sufficient
summary
superior
suppress
surprise
survey
suspense
suspicion

temperament
tendency

thorough
transferring
tremendous
truly

unanimous
unfortunately
unnecessary
urgent
useful
using

vacancies
vacuum
varies

MECHANICS

# Correcting Common Errors

## Key Language Skills Review

This chapter reviews key skills and concepts that pose special problems for writers.

- **Sentence Fragments and Run-on Sentences**
- **Subject-Verb and Pronoun-Antecedent Agreement**
- **Verb Forms**
- **Clear Pronoun Reference**
- **Comparison of Modifiers**
- **Dangling and Misplaced Modifiers**
- **Standard Usage**
- **Capitalization**
- **Punctuation—End Marks, Commas, Quotation Marks, Apostrophes, Semicolons, and Colons**
- **Spelling**

Most of the exercises in this chapter follow the same format as the exercises found throughout the grammar, usage, and mechanics sections of this textbook. You will notice, however, that two sets of review exercises are presented as standardized tests. These exercises are designed to provide you with practice not only in solving usage and mechanics problems but also in dealing with these kinds of problems on standardized tests.

## Exercise 1   Revising Sentence Fragments

Each of the following word groups is a sentence fragment. Rewrite each fragment to make it a complete sentence. Add whatever words are necessary to make the meaning of the sentence complete.

EXAMPLE    1.  having already read the book

               1.  *Having already read the book, I was not surprised by the film's end.*

1. television, radio, newspapers, billboards, magazines, and now the World Wide Web
2. beside the cold, clear spring tumbling down the rocky slopes
3. when we passed through the turnstile
4. to appreciate adequately the complexity of these drum rhythms
5. according to the most recent experiments
6. exercising regularly for thirty minutes at least three times a week
7. trained as a lab assistant at the local junior college
8. who had once actually stood on the Great Wall of China
9. one of the first women of that rank in the Navy
10. where the laundry had been hung on a line in full sunlight

**Reference Note**

For information on **correcting sentence fragments,** see page 326.

## Exercise 2   Identifying Sentences and Revising Sentence Fragments

Identify each numbered word group in the following paragraph as either a sentence fragment (*F*) or a complete sentence (*S*). Then, make each fragment part of a complete sentence either by adding words to it or by combining it with another fragment or sentence in the paragraph. Change the punctuation and capitalization as necessary.

EXAMPLES    **[1]** I discovered that the jacket was made of linen.

                **[2]** When I got home.

          1.  *S*

          2.  *F—When I got home, I discovered that the jacket was made of linen.*

[1] Before you spend your money on that expensive shirt. [2] Read the label carefully! [3] Because some clothes must be sent to the dry cleaner. [4] They will cost you extra money. [5] A lot of money in the long run. [6] Other clothes must be washed by hand. [7] Requiring extra time and care for their upkeep. [8] If you are looking for quality clothes. [9] That are both attractive and inexpensive to own. [10] It pays to read the label.

**Reference Note**

For information on **correcting run-on sentences,** see page 327.

**Exercise 3** **Revising Run-on Sentences**

Each of the following numbered items is a run-on sentence. Revise each run-on, using the method given in brackets after it. Be sure to change punctuation and capitalization as necessary.

EXAMPLE
1. Today's world offers many kinds of popular entertainment earlier Americans relied mainly on music and dancing. [*Use a comma and coordinating conjunction.*]

1. Today's world offers many kinds of popular entertainment, but earlier Americans relied mainly on music and dancing.

1. Just imagine your life without TV, audio and video recordings, and movies surely you would spend your time quite differently from the way you do now. [*Make two sentences.*]

2. In a world without recorded music, a musician could often attract a crowd even today, good musicians can make a living on the streets of a large city. [*Use a semicolon.*]

3. Music was important to the early settlers they often made their own instruments. [*Use a comma and a coordinating conjunction.*]

4. Many of the settlers owned fiddles, dulcimers, flutes, and guitars music could be a part of everyday life. [*Use a semicolon, a conjunctive adverb, and a comma*]

5. Long before the settlers arrived, there was already plenty of music in North America American Indians prized music and song. [*Use a semicolon.*]

6. The Seneca used rattles similar to the instruments known as maracas Northern Plains Indians used the hand drum. [*Use a comma and a coordinating conjunction.*]

7. The Maidu played flutes and whistles musicians today often incorporate such American Indian instruments into popular music. [*Make two sentences.*]

8. The banjo is widely regarded as a traditional American musical instrument, the banjo originated in Africa. [*Use a semicolon, a conjunctive adverb, and a comma*]

9. West Africans made banjo-like instruments out of gourds for strings, they used dried animal gut. [*Use a semicolon.*]

10. Early banjos had no frets and only four strings frets are the ridges positioned at intervals on the necks of banjos and guitars. [*Make two sentences.*]

**Exercise 4** Revising Sentence Fragments and Run-on Sentences

Most of the following word groups are either run-on sentences or sentence fragments. Identify and correct each sentence fragment and run-on sentence. If a word group is already a complete sentence, write *C.*

EXAMPLE  1. The area where I live used to be a prehistoric sea, some-times my friends and I find fossilized sharks' teeth.

1. *The area where I live used to be a prehistoric sea, and sometimes my friends and I find fossilized sharks' teeth.*

1. Walking slowly over the rocky terrain.
2. A strange rock caught our attention Jackie broke it open.
3. Inside were rows and rows of brilliant quartz crystals, we gasped at our discovery.
4. Gold lies hidden in the West, many people still seek their fortune there.
5. Is one of the best places in the world for prospectors.
6. When rainfall, a landslide, or some other act of nature alters the landscape.
7. Easier to find gold, silver, platinum, and other precious metals.
8. Although most commonly used for jewelry, gold has numerous industrial uses.
9. You can grow your own crystals, some grow quite quickly.
10. With a kit from a hobby shop only two blocks away from my house in Colorado Springs.

**Exercise 5** Choosing Verbs That Agree in Number with Their Subjects

Choose the correct form of the verb in parentheses in each of the following sentences.

EXAMPLE  1. One of the customs most readily shared among cultures (*is, are*) games.

1. *is*

1. Almost everybody (*has, have*) played games that originated in faraway places.
2. Few of these games (*is, are*) difficult to play.

**Reference Note**

For information on **subject-verb agreement,** see page 493.

**COMMON ERRORS**

3. Pictures on ancient Greek pottery (*show, shows*) people playing with yo-yos.

4. (*Was, Were*) the first people who ever played the game lacrosse American Indian?

5. Arctic peoples, Africans, the Maori of New Zealand, and others as well (*plays, play*) cat's cradle.

6. Somewhere, somebody in one of the world's cultures probably (*is, are*) spinning a top right now.

7. Not all card games (*uses, use*) a standard deck of cards.

8. Most of these games (*requires, require*) at least two players, and some require four.

9. Several ancient African games still (*enjoys, enjoy*) popularity among children.

10. None of those colorful Chinese tangrams (*turns, turn*) out to be easy to solve.

Exercise 6 **Proofreading a Paragraph for Subject-Verb Agreement**

Identify the errors in subject-verb agreement in the following paragraph. Then, change each incorrect verb to agree with its subject.

EXAMPLE    **[1]** Many a building design don't meet the needs of people with disabilities.

     1. *don't—doesn't*

[1] Ordinary houses or a public building sometimes present problems for people with disabilities. [2] For example, a person using a wheelchair or crutches often have difficulty maneuvering in narrow halls. [3] Flights of stairs and a front stoop makes access difficult for anyone using a wheelchair or a walker. [4] Moreover, inadequate shower access or high counters needlessly poses problems for people with wheelchairs. [5] One homebuilder and solver of these problems are Craig Johnson. [6] Johnson, with a team of advisors and decorators, seek to make life easier for people with various disabilities. [7] Johnson recognizes that easy access and freedom from barriers is becoming both an issue for our aging population and a growing business opportunity. [8] Creating designs and making modifications for people with disabilities helps others, too. [9] For instance, doesn't most people find that levers are easier to operate than doorknobs are? [10] Also, neither a handrail nor a ramp give anyone any difficulty; in fact, both can come in handy for everyone.

## Exercise 7 — Identifying Antecedents and Writing Pronouns

**Reference Note**

For information on **pronoun-antecedent agreement,** see page 507.

Each of the following sentences contains a blank where a pronoun should be. Identify the antecedent for each missing pronoun. Then, complete the sentence with a pronoun that agrees with that antecedent.

EXAMPLE    1. At about the age of fifteen, Janet Collins followed _____ dream to the Ballet Russe de Monte Carlo.

      1. *Janet Collins—her*

1. Until Janet Collins, nobody of African heritage had ever made _____ debut on the stage of the Metropolitan Opera House.
2. While waiting to audition, she saw other ballerinas on a winding staircase backstage doing _____ warm-up exercises.
3. All of the people who saw Janet at her audition clapped _____ hands.
4. However, because of Collins's color, Mr. Massine, the choreographer, could not hire her for _____ production.
5. Collins continued practicing, and in the end _____ was rewarded.
6. The Metropolitan Opera opened _____ doors to the prima ballerina.
7. Rudolph Bing admired her adagio dancing so much that _____ gave her many opportunities to leap and jump.
8. Two of her roles were in *Carmen* and *Aida,* and _____ helped to make her famous.
9. To be successful, a ballerina must discipline _____.
10. Either Ms. Lawton or Ms. Vicks will show the class _____ autographed picture of Collins.

## Exercise 8 — Proofreading for Pronoun-Antecedent Agreement

Proofread the following sentences, and identify pronouns that do not agree with their antecedents. Give the correct form of each incorrect pronoun. If a sentence is already correct, write *C*.

EXAMPLE    1. From the earliest times, people all over the world have decorated himself or herself.

      1. *himself or herself—themselves*

1. Whether for war, religious rituals, or beauty, cosmetics have always had its place in human society.
2. In ancient Egypt, both men and women used various kinds of cosmetics to make himself or herself more attractive.

COMMON ERRORS

3. In addition, nearly all Egyptians painted their eyelids with green paste to prevent sunburn.
4. One of the Egyptian kings was even buried with rouge and lip color in their tomb.
5. Ancient cosmetics were usually made from natural ingredients, some of which were poisonous to its users.
6. Arsenic and mercury were two of the most dangerous, and it ruined many lives.
7. The Roman man or woman who used cosmetics containing arsenic was slowly killing themselves.
8. Similarly, in Queen Elizabeth I's time, the English girl or woman who used a skin whitener containing mercury risked having their teeth fall out.
9. Since before the time of Cosmis—who sold makeup during the reign of Julius Caesar—to the present, enterprising people have made their fortunes by providing products that help others meet their cultures' standards of beauty.
10. Galen, a man of science in ancient Rome, would be pleased to find that today's cold cream is based on the formula they invented.

### Exercise 9  Revising Sentences for Agreement

Each of the following sentences contains either an error in subject-verb agreement or an error in pronoun-antecedent agreement. Revise the sentences to correct each error in agreement.

EXAMPLE  1. Either Mr. Baker or Mr. Perez have promised to drive his van on the field trip.

1. *Either Mr. Baker or Mr. Perez has promised to drive his van on the field trip.*

1. Many a girl has taken Shirley Chisholm as their model of success.
2. Here, class, is several classic examples of Aztec art.
3. Each member of the cast knows all of their lines for the play.
4. Beautifully illustrated and written, *Saint George and the Dragon* were awarded the Caldecott Medal.
5. Have Ms. Ivy and Mr. Lee played her and his music for the school?
6. Two dollars were once considered generous pay for an hour's work.
7. All of the travelers were surprised when he or she saw the old purple-and-yellow bus.
8. An international team of archaeological researchers is assembling, one by one, at the site of this exciting discovery.

**9.** Do Cindy and Brenda practice her dance routine here every day?

**10.** The two performers has become one of the most popular teams in the history of comedy.

**Reference Note**

For information on **using verbs correctly,** see Chapter 17.

**Exercise 10** **Writing Correct Verb Forms**

Complete each sentence with the correct past or past participle form of the verb in italics.

EXAMPLE     1.  *do*     Have you _____ any research on the Cajun culture?

                  1.  *done*

**1.** *blow*     Yesterday, a hurricane _____ through Louisiana, where most Cajuns live.

**2.** *begin*     The Cajun culture _____ after French immigrants to Acadia, Canada, traveled south.

**3.** *come*     While in Canada, these immigrants _____ to be known as Acadians.

**4.** *take*     In Louisiana, the name Acadian _____ on a different pronunciation—"Cajun."

**5.** *choose*     The Cajuns _____ to befriend the Choctaws, as well as settlers from Germany and Spain.

**6.** *put*     Cajun cooks _____ to their own use what they learned from the Choctaws about native plants and animals.

**7.** *eat*     They _____ seafood seasoned with the Choctaws' filé, which is powdered sassafras leaves.

**8.** *drink*     They _____ coffee flavored with chicory.

**9.** *raise*     German settlers in the bayou country _____ the beef and pork that the Cajuns used in their tasty dishes.

**10.** *bring*     The Cajuns were also delighted with okra, called gumbo by the Bantu, who had _____ it with them from Africa.

**Exercise 11** **Identifying Correct Forms of Irregular Verbs**

Choose the correct form of the verb in parentheses in each of the following sentences.

EXAMPLE     1.  For many years, teams of scientists have (*took, taken*) the opportunity to study the Antarctic Peninsula during the summer.

                  1.  *taken*

**1.** The scientists (*went, gone*) there to study the delicate balance of the ecosystem.

**Reference Note**

For information on **using irregular verbs,** see page 519.

COMMON ERRORS

2. These scientists (*knew, knowed*) that worldwide weather patterns are influenced by events in Antarctica.

3. Before the twentieth century, few people (*choosed, chose*) to brave the frigid voyage to the Antarctic.

4. However, new means of transportation have (*brought, brung*) more people, especially scientists, to Antarctica.

5. Such countries as Chile, Britain, and Russia have (*began, begun*) exploring what's beneath Antarctica's ice and snow.

6. No one knows how long Antarctica's waters have (*ran, run*) red with krill, tiny creatures at the bottom of the food chain.

7. Many times, the Ross Ice Shelf has (*shook, shaken*) as a huge iceberg known as B9 has crashed into it.

8. An oil rig could have (*fallen, fell*) if struck by a roving iceberg.

9. If that had happened, a huge oil spill would likely have (*did, done*) major damage to Antarctica's ecosystem.

10. In Antarctica, the nations of the world have been (*gave, given*) an opportunity to work together in peace.

### Exercise 12  Proofreading for Correct Verb Forms

Most of the following sentences contain incorrect verb forms. If a form of a verb is wrong, write the correct form. If a sentence already is correct, write *C*.

EXAMPLE    **[1]** The brave galleon had rode the waves to an icy grave.

    *1. ridden*

[1] Over thousands of years of seafaring, many a ship has been broke on the rocks or lost in a storm. [2] Thirst for the treasure of these sunken ships has drove opportunists and scholars alike to the dark bottoms of the world's oceans. [3] The invention of scuba equipment in 1943 rung in a new era in underwater exploration. [4] Since then, treasure hunters and scientists have dove into waters all over the world and surfaced with gold and historical artifacts. [5] Expeditions have successfully rose entire ships, such as the *Vasa*, a seventeenth-century Swedish vessel. [6] Astonishingly, divers have swum down and inspected the remains of crafts more than forty centuries old! [7] Not only ships but also towns set on the ocean floor. [8] One such site is the community of Port Royal, which lays near Jamaica. [9] Ironically, although many treasures have been found, the search for treasure has not shrinked. [10] On the contrary, as technology has improved, the number of underwater expeditions has growed.

**Proofreading for Correct Verb Forms**

Most of the following sentences contain an incorrect verb form. If the form of a verb is wrong, write the correct form. If a sentence is already correct, write *C*.

EXAMPLE    **1.** His horse weared a braided bridle.

     *1. wore*

**1.** Luis Ortega has been describe as history's greatest rawhide braider.
**2.** For years, collectors and cowhands alike have spoke of him with respectful awe.
**3.** Ortega was lucky to have had a fine teacher; many braiders do not teach their craft because students have stole their secrets.
**4.** However, even after a generous American Indian taught Ortega to braid, it taked young Luis many years of practice to perfect his skill.
**5.** Ortega has never shrinked from hard work.
**6.** Once a vaquero himself, he throwed many a lasso in his younger days.
**7.** Since the 1930s, Ortega has wore the title of professional braider.
**8.** Ortega not only mastered the traditional craft, but also striked out on his own by adding color to braiding.
**9.** Unlike whips, which have stinged many a runaway steer, a riata is a type of lariat used for roping.
**10.** Pity the cowhand whose heart must have sunk as a steer ran off with his treasured Ortega riata!

Exercise **14**   **Identifying Correct Forms of Pronouns**

Choose the correct pronoun in parentheses in each of the following sentences. Then, tell whether the pronoun is used as a *subject*, a *predicate nominative*, a *direct object*, an *indirect object*, an *object of a preposition*, or an *appositive*.

EXAMPLE    **1.** Mr. Kwan and (*we, us*) members of the recycling club picked up all the litter along the highway last Saturday.

     *1. we—subject*

**1.** Do you know (*who, whom*) safely disposes of old batteries?
**2.** The two Earth Club members who collect items for recycling are James and (*she, her*).
**3.** (*Who, Whom*) threw these cans in the garbage?
**4.** Save all recyclable material for (*we, us*) club members.

**Reference Note**

For information on **using pronouns correctly,** see Chapter 18.

**COMMON ERRORS**

5. Give the co-chairpersons, Lisa and (*she, her*), all of the cans that you have collected.
6. Ask (*whoever, whomever*) you know to save old newspapers for us to collect.
7. (*Who, Whom*) could the next recycling team leader be?
8. To (*whom, who*) do we give this cardboard?
9. The city gave Mr. Kwan, (*who, whom*) everyone in the school respects, an award.
10. Please give Carl and (*he, him*) the maps you three drew yesterday.

### Exercise 15  Correcting Inexact Pronoun References

Correct each inexact pronoun reference in the following sentences. If a sentence is already correct, write *C*.

EXAMPLE    1. When you take medication for your allergies, be sure to read them carefully.

1. *When you take medication for your allergies, be sure to read the directions carefully.*

1. Annie said that she must have sneezed two dozen times today and that it was really bothering her.
2. Annie asked Heather several good questions about her new allergy medication.
3. Everyone knows that Heather has more problems with pollen allergies than I have.
4. Pollen, molds, and animal dander are widespread in our environment; they are three of the most common causes of allergies.
5. Different plants release pollen at different times of the year, which is why people have discomfort at various times.
6. Annie asked Sarah about summer allergies because she is especially uncomfortable during July.
7. To take a pollen count, they place a glass slide coated with oil outside for twenty-four hours.
8. The slide is then placed under a microscope, and the grains of pollen sticking to it are counted.
9. When it rains, the pollen count drops because the rain washes the pollen grains from the air.
10. In the news reports, they often give the pollen count.

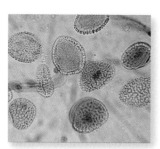

*Pollen Grains*

## Exercise 16 Proofreading for Clear Pronoun Usage

Most of the following sentences contain inexact pronoun references. Revise each incorrect sentence. If a sentence is already correct, write *C*.

**Reference Note**

For information on **using pronouns correctly,** see Chapter 18.

EXAMPLES
1. In India, they belong to laughing clubs.

1. *In India, some people belong to laughing clubs.*

2. These clubs are popular with the people of India because of the conflicts they face every day.

2. *C*

1. Scientists believe that long ago an island slammed into Asia; it created the Himalayas and joined the island to the continent.
2. That landmass is now India, and worlds still collide there, which is seen in the contradictions and conflicts of modern India.
3. India has been independent for more than fifty years, and it has caused many changes in this growing nation.
4. For instance, the famous city of Bombay has been renamed Mumbai, which honors the Hindu goddess Mumba.
5. However, British influences still exist, and that is apparent in English-language street signs.
6. Free-market policies have now been adopted, and many people have taken advantage of that; small, independent businesses are booming.
7. To the refugees who come to Calcutta from Bangladesh, it offers a little hope.
8. There are as many as thirty-seven laughing clubs in Mumbai (members believe it fights stress).
9. At the same time, beside the wall of an alleyway in Calcutta, a woman prepares food for her daughter while she sits in a nearby tree.
10. A country with ample natural resources and millions of highly educated people, India is taking its place on the world stage.

**Reference Note**

For information on **using modifers correctly,** see Chapter 19.

**Exercise 17** Using Comparative and Superlative Forms

Complete each sentence with the correct comparative or superlative form of the word given in italics.

EXAMPLE    1. *well*   Carl can perform CPR _____ than I can.
           1. *better*

1. *few*    Bicyclists who wear helmets have _____ serious injuries from accidents than bicyclists who do not wear helmets.
2. *many*   Our family follows _____ safety procedures than we used to follow in the past.
3. *bad*    Some of the _____ accidents are more likely to happen in the home than anywhere else.
4. *much*   Is it _____ common to have an accident in the kitchen or in the bathroom?
5. *well*   Emergency crews can spot luminous house numbers _____ than numbers that do not glow in the dark.
6. *bad*    A grease fire will become _____ if you put water on it.
7. *good*   Do you know the _____ way to extinguish an electrical fire?
8. *many*   Smoke detectors are found in _____ homes than ever before.
9. *much*   In many small fires, smoke causes _____ of the damage.
10. *good*  Of course, the _____ safety procedure of all is preventing fires from starting in the first place.

**Exercise 18** Proofreading Sentences for Correct Comparative and Superlative Forms

Correct each error in the use of comparative and superlative forms in the following sentences. If no modifiers need to be corrected, write *C*.

EXAMPLE    1. Most oftenest, I plan my day in the morning.
           1. *Most often*

1. One of the importantest skills is the ability to set priorities.
2. You can establish your priorities more easily if you know your goals.
3. Owning a good car, having a rewarding job, and owning a house are three of the most commonest goals people share.
4. You, however, may want a pilot's license, a medical degree, an eighteen-wheeler, or just a comfortabler bed.
5. Whatever your goal, you will be much more likelier to achieve it if you plan your time carefully.

6. Look at even the most small unit of your time.
7. Can you think of ways that you could use your time more better than you do?
8. Try every day to work on your most highest priority.
9. Try more hard to stick to your schedule.
10. With a plan, you can meet your goals quicklier than you could without one.

**Writing Comparative and Superlative Forms**

Write the comparative and superlative forms of the following modifiers.

EXAMPLE      **1.** kind

　　　　　　　　　*1. kinder, kindest; less kind, least kind*

| | | | |
|---|---|---|---|
| **1.** alone | **6.** bad | **11.** natural | **16.** contentedly |
| **2.** loudly | **7.** delightful | **12.** wet | **17.** green |
| **3.** late | **8.** fiercely | **13.** mysterious | **18.** bravely |
| **4.** secretly | **9.** exact | **14.** gleefully | **19.** poor |
| **5.** lucky | **10.** childishly | **15.** timid | **20.** cautiously |

**Exercise 20** **Correcting Double Negatives**

Revise each of the following sentences to correct the double negative that it contains.

EXAMPLE      **1.** The jurors couldn't say nothing about the trial.

　　　　　　　　　*1. The jurors could say nothing about the trial.*

　　　　　　　　　　　　　　　　*or*

　　　　　　　　　*The jurors couldn't say anything about the trial.*

1. Those machines don't take no dollar bills.
2. My grandfather doesn't hardly let anything bother him.
3. Don't never accept a ride from a stranger!
4. Why didn't no one take a message when Mom called?
5. Never use none of those microwave oven pans in a regular oven.
6. The movie hadn't scarcely started when the power went off.
7. I can't see nothing from here.
8. There aren't none of those tamales left now.
9. Don't let nobody tell you that you can't win!
10. Neither cold nor heat nor nothing else discouraged them.

─HELP─

Although two possible answers are shown, you need to give only one answer for each item in Exercise 20.

**Reference Note**

For information on **double negatives,** see page 609.

**COMMON ERRORS**

Revise the following sentences to correct errors in the use of modifiers. You may need to rearrange or add words to make the meaning clear.

EXAMPLE     1. Cold and overcast, the tour group left the city.

          1. *The tour group left the cold and overcast city.*

1. I watched the hawk swoop down and grab its prey with my new pair of binoculars.
2. He is such a hard-working student that he did every bit of his homework when he even got the flu.
3. Running through town, soft moonlight fell on the freight train.
4. You should accept rides from people only you know.
5. A kingfisher sat alertly on the fence post that had been hunting by the creek.
6. I figured out the answer studying the problem.
7. Bulky and dusty, we moved all of the boxes out of the attic.
8. Filled with wildflowers, Amy put that vase on her desk.
9. Suddenly, the bats swarmed out of the cave that we had awakened.
10. A package sat on the doorstep with Michael's name on it.

**Exercise 22** **Correcting Dangling Modifiers**

Most of the following sentences contain a dangling modifier. If a sentence is incorrect, revise it to correct the dangling modifier. If a sentence is already correct, write *C*.

EXAMPLE     1. Following the path, a tiny cottage came into view.

          1. *As we were following the path, a tiny cottage came into view.*

1. Rounding third base, the coach and the fans in the stands cheered and applauded.
2. To manage time better, making a schedule will help.
3. Modified to allow space for an additional bedroom, the floor plan's lack of closets became a problem.
4. While studying for exams, a storm knocked out the electricity.
5. Before beginning your library research, a specific topic or category must be selected.
6. Right in the middle of making a copy of my report, the out-of-paper message flashed.
7. Tired from the long hike, our camp was a welcome sight.

8. After hanging the new plants, the room appeared larger.
9. To save money, a realistic budget is necessary.
10. While we watched the children play, our problems seemed small.

Exercise 23 **Correcting Misplaced and Dangling Modifiers**

The following sentences contain misplaced and dangling modifiers. Revise each sentence to correct the misplaced or dangling modifier.

EXAMPLE    1. Seeing the rescue helicopter, shouts of joy burst out.

       1. *Seeing the rescue helicopter, the crew burst out with shouts of joy.*

1. Customers lined up for copies of the new film about extra-terrestrials in the video store.
2. To save a file, a name must be given to it.
3. The spaceship drifted toward the small moon that had lost its engines.
4. Dozens of white daisies decorated the tables, which had been grown in our own garden.
5. Marked by signs saying "Reserved," we couldn't find anywhere to park.
6. Did George Washington ever meet Robert E. Lee, whose face is on our dollar?
7. Following the trail, camp was quickly found.
8. Having advertised all week, all the tickets had been sold.
9. Patient hawks watched for fish soaring over the lake.
10. Mother packed a picnic lunch humming quietly.

Exercise 24 **Correcting Errors in Standard Usage**

Identify and correct each error in the use of formal, standard English in the following sentences.

EXAMPLE    1. I ain't going to the movies on Saturday.

       1. *ain't—am not*

1. Please bring this note to Ms. Nichols in the gym.
2. Who else was late to the party beside Ronnie and Ed?
3. My science project took alot of time last weekend.
4. Oh, no! I can't find my raincoat anywheres.
5. Common elements include oxygen, hydrogen, iron, and etc.
6. The weather can effect people's moods.
7. Starting next year, each student will wear an uniform.

**Reference Note**

For more on **common usage problems,** see Chapter 20. For information about **formal, standard English,** see page 595.

COMMON ERRORS

**8.** Look out! You almost busted my CD player!

**9.** Gradually, our dog excepted the new kitten.

**10.** The little steam engine pulled all the faster it could.

**Exercise 25** **Correcting Errors in Standard Usage**

Revise the following sentences to correct all errors in the use of formal, standard English.

EXAMPLE 1. Like you would expect, the use of color is very important to artists.

1. *As you would expect, the use of color is very important to artists.*

**1.** Artists which study color know that color, value, and contrast form the foundation of a good painting.

**2.** Many artists would not even begin no painting without they first planned how they would use these elements.

**3.** One of the basics that nearly all artists learn is where color is divided into warm colors and cool colors.

**4.** Like you might of guessed, red is a warmer color then blue, while green is cooler than orange.

**5.** The value, or darkness, of a color can indicate that objects differ some in distance from the viewer.

**6.** For example, a dark color may be used to indicate that something is a long ways off.

**7.** Contrast is when two very different colors are placed besides each other.

**8.** Contrasting values help to show detail, as does the contrast among this here white page and black type.

**9.** For them artists that work only in black and white, contrast and value are major concerns.

**10.** Many people feel that the affect of a painting can depend more on color then on other elements.

# Grammar and Usage Test: Section 1

**DIRECTIONS** Either part or all of each of the following sentences is underlined. Using the rules of formal, standard English, choose the answer that correctly expresses the meaning of the underlined word groups. If there is no error, choose A. Indicate your response by shading in the appropriate oval on your answer sheet.

**EXAMPLE** 1. In 1990, restoration began on the Sphinx, it is an ancient Egyptian statue.

        **(A)** Sphinx, it is an ancient Egyptian statue

        **(B)** Sphinx because it is an ancient Egyptian statue

        **(C)** Sphinx, an ancient Egyptian statue

        **(D)** Sphinx, being an ancient Egyptian statue

        **(E)** Sphinx when it was an ancient Egyptian statue

**ANSWER** 1.

1. The magnificent glass pyramids at the Louvre, which were designed by the American architect I. M. Pei.

    **(A)** The magnificent glass pyramids at the Louvre, which were designed by the American architect I. M. Pei.

    **(B)** Being designed by the American architect I. M. Pei, the magnificent glass pyramids at the Louvre.

    **(C)** The American architect I. M. Pei, who designed the magnificent glass pyramids at the Louvre.

    **(D)** The American architect I. M. Pei designed the magnificent glass pyramids at the Louvre.

    **(E)** I. M. Pei, an American architect, designing the magnificent glass pyramids at the Louvre.

2. Have you read about the tornado that damaged so many homes in today's paper?

    **(A)** about the tornado that damaged so many homes in today's paper

    **(B)** in today's paper about the tornado that damaged so many homes

    **(C)** about the tornado in today's paper that damaged so many homes

    **(D)** about the destructive tornado in today's paper

    **(E)** today about the destructive tornado in the paper

**3.** Most people believe that the Loch Ness monster is just a <u>myth, sightings of the monster continue to be reported</u>.

(A) myth, sightings of the monster continue to be reported

(B) myth, and people report still seeing the monster

(C) myth. Sightings of the monster continue to be reported

(D) myth; sightings of the monster continue to be reported

(E) myth; however, sightings of the monster continue to be reported

**4.** Tamara told Jenny <u>that she probably made an A</u>.

(A) that she probably made an A

(B) that an A was probably what she made

(C) that Jenny probably made an A

(D) about her making an A probably

(E) that her grade was probably an A

**5.** To fully appreciate many of Gary Soto's stories, <u>some knowledge of Mexican American culture is necessary</u>.

(A) some knowledge of Mexican American culture is necessary

(B) the reader needs some knowledge of Mexican American culture

(C) you must learn all about Mexican American culture

(D) knowing something about Mexican American culture

(E) the necessity is to know about Mexican American culture

**6.** <u>In this article, it says that the Chinese were using paper money by the thirteenth century</u>.

(A) In this article, it says that the Chinese were using paper money by the thirteenth century.

(B) According to this article, it says that the Chinese were using paper money by the thirteenth century.

(C) By the thirteenth century, the Chinese in this article were using paper money.

(D) In this article, they say that the Chinese were using paper money by the thirteenth century.

(E) According to this article, the Chinese were using paper money by the thirteenth century.

**7.** <u>The capital of Liberia, Monrovia, which was named by freed slaves in honor of President James Monroe</u>.

(A) The capital of Liberia, Monrovia, which was named by freed slaves in honor of President James Monroe.

(B) Monrovia, the capital of Liberia, named by freed slaves in honor of President James Monroe.

**(C)** Named by freed slaves, Monrovia, the capital of Liberia, in honor of President James Monroe.

**(D)** In honor of President James Monroe, freed slaves named the capital of Liberia Monrovia.

**(E)** In honor of President James Monroe, freed slaves who named Monrovia the capital of Liberia.

8. I bought a collar <u>for my kitten that has a reflective tag and a breakaway buckle</u>.

**(A)** for my kitten that has a reflective tag and a breakaway buckle

**(B)** for my kitten with a reflective tag and a breakaway buckle

**(C)** that has a reflective tag and a breakaway buckle for my kitten

**(D)** for my kitten having a reflective tag and a breakaway buckle

**(E)** for my kitten, and it has a reflective tag and a breakaway buckle

9. Henry Ford wanted to make his cars affordable to everyone; <u>that is why he developed an efficient assembly-line method for manufacturing them.</u>

**(A)** Henry Ford wanted to make his cars affordable to everyone; that is why he developed an efficient assembly-line method for manufacturing them.

**(B)** Henry Ford wanted to make his cars affordable to everyone so that he could develop an efficient assembly-line method for manufacturing them.

**(C)** Henry Ford wanted to make his cars affordable to everyone because he developed an efficient assembly-line method for manufacturing them.

**(D)** Henry Ford developed an efficient assembly-line method for manufacturing his cars because he wanted to make them affordable to everyone.

**(E)** To develop an efficient assembly-line method for manufacturing his cars, Henry Ford wanted to make them affordable to everyone.

10. <u>Having seen that people in some countries were denied basic civil rights, my uncle's appreciation for the Bill of Rights grew.</u>

**(A)** Having seen that people in some countries were denied basic civil rights, my uncle's appreciation for the Bill of Rights grew.

**(B)** My uncle, having seen the Bill of Rights, knew that people in some countries were denied basic civil rights.

**(C)** When basic civil rights are denied people in some countries, my uncle's appreciation for the Bill of Rights grows.

**(D)** My uncle's appreciation for people denied basic civil rights in some countries grew as he read the Bill of Rights.

**(E)** My uncle's appreciation for the Bill of Rights grew after he had seen that people in some countries were denied basic civil rights.

# Grammar and Usage Test: Section 2

**DIRECTIONS**  Read the paragraph below. For each numbered blank, select the word or word group that best completes the sentence. Indicate your response by shading in the appropriate oval on your answer sheet.

**EXAMPLE**  More powerful than optical microscopes, electron microscopes  (1)  researchers to study extremely small objects.

1. **(A)** has enabled
   **(B)** is enabling
   **(C)** enabling
   **(D)** enable
   **(E)** enables

**ANSWER**  1. Ⓐ  Ⓑ  Ⓒ  ⬤D  Ⓔ

---

An electron microscope, using a beam of electrons,  (1)  a magnified image. Unlike an optical microscope,  (2)  instrument does not depend on  (3)  light rays. Instead, an electron lens  (4)  a system of electromagnetic coils that focus the electron beam. The electrons  (5) , of course, aren't visible to the naked eye. Rather,  (6)  are directed at a specimen to form  (7)  image on a photographic plate. The wavelength of an electron beam is  (8)  than the wavelength of light. Therefore,  (9)  magnification is possible with an electron microscope  (10)  optical microscope.

---

1. **(A)** create
   **(B)** is creating
   **(C)** creates
   **(D)** will create
   **(E)** will have created

2. **(A)** this here
   **(B)** this
   **(C)** these
   **(D)** these kind of
   **(E)** that there

3. **(A)** any
   **(B)** not one
   **(C)** no
   **(D)** hardly any
   **(E)** barely some

4. **(A)** use
   **(B)** has used
   **(C)** will use
   **(D)** uses
   **(E)** had been using

5. **(A)** themself
   **(B)** themselves
   **(C)** theirself
   **(D)** theirselves
   **(E)** itself

6. **(A)** them
   **(B)** it
   **(C)** that
   **(D)** this
   **(E)** they

7. **(A)** its
   **(B)** their
   **(C)** they're
   **(D)** its'
   **(E)** it's

8. **(A)** short
   **(B)** shorter
   **(C)** more short
   **(D)** more shorter
   **(E)** shortest

9. **(A)** good
   **(B)** gooder
   **(C)** better
   **(D)** more better
   **(E)** more good

10. **(A)** then with an
    **(B)** then with a
    **(C)** than with an
    **(D)** than with a
    **(E)** then a

COMMON ERRORS

### Exercise 26 Correcting the Capitalization of Words and Phrases

Correct the following words and phrases by either changing lowercase letters to capital letters or changing capital letters to lowercase letters.

EXAMPLE     1. Hank's poem "Waiting for morning in july"

        1. *Hank's poem "Waiting for Morning in July"*

1. geometry I, latin, and civics
2. *national geographic* magazine
3. the god of abraham, isaac, and jacob
4. an Island in the gulf of mexico
5. liberty bell
6. during the great depression
7. readings from "the scarlet ibis"
8. internal revenue service forms
9. mother's day
10. an episode of *party of five*
11. Grandfather Ben and my Cousin
12. Hiroshige's painting *The Moon Beyond The Leaves*
13. an italian custom
14. bill of rights
15. a passage from the koran
16. is that an okidata® printer?
17. dr. and mrs. Dorset
18. a congressional medal of honor recipient
19. chief joseph
20. *King Of The Wind*

### Exercise 27 Proofreading for Correct Capitalization

Each of the following sentences contains at least one capitalization error. Correct each error by changing capital letters to lowercase letters or lowercase letters to capital letters.

EXAMPLE     1. In the barn my Dad is building an ultralight plane that we have named the *hummingbird.*

        1. *dad, Hummingbird*

1. The slave knelt at the feet of the statue and said, "Zeus, o, Zeus, Oh please, help me."
2. long ago, Africans shaped tools from stones; we find these stones wherever they lived.

**3.** My grandma told me that she used to go to Wrigley field with her father and mother.

**4.** This saturday, instead of going to eagle lake, let's go to the Riverdale High School Festival.

**5.** A Yale student laid out the plans for a submarine that was used in the American revolution.

**6.** Fred started sewing kites for himself and his friends and now has a small business known as Fred's fliers.

**7.** "Have you read *Changes in Latitudes*?" i asked.

**8.** Because the Panama Canal is too narrow for some supertankers, they sometimes must pass through the waters of the strait of Magellan at the Southern tip of south america.

**9.** The chess club meets every day after school in the large room East of the auditorium.

**10.** We think our team, the Kennedy middle school bobcats, is the best in Baker county.

## Exercise 28  Proofreading for Correct Capitalization

Each of the following sentences contains errors in capitalization. Correct each error by changing capital letters to lowercase letters or lowercase letters to capital letters.

EXAMPLE     **1.** Often, i feel like a World traveler in my hometown.

      *1. I, world*

**1.** When I ride the bus down central avenue, I can hear people speaking spanish, hindi, japanese, arabic, and some other languages I don't even recognize.

**2.** On independence day, my Mother and I drove our old ford thunderbird to Taylor park.

**3.** Near there we saw mr. Narazaki and Ms. white eagle talking.

**4.** They were in front of the Lincoln building, where the federal bureau of investigation has offices.

**5.** On that same Saturday, we also saw several muslim women wearing long robes and veils in front of hill medical center next to the Park.

**6.** After the band played John philip Sousa's "the Stars And Stripes Forever," people stood beside a statue of the Greek deity Athena and gave readings from the declaration of independence and the bible.

**7.** Later, mayor Mendoza read a telegram from the president of the united states, gave a speech, and awarded Medals to several people for their public service.

8. As soon as the big dipper was clearly visible, the fireworks started, and I thought, "this is definitely the greatest place on Earth!"
9. Next year, I plan to take United States history II at West creek high school.
10. I am going to look in my new history book for a list of all the peoples that make up our country, from the inuits of alaska to the hawaiians of hilo bay.

**Reference Note**

For information on **using commas correctly,** see page 643.

### Exercise 29  Using Commas Correctly

Add and delete commas to punctuate the following sentences correctly.

EXAMPLE
    1. A first-aid kit should contain adhesive tape scissors antiseptic and a variety of bandages.

    1. *A first-aid kit should contain adhesive tape, scissors, antiseptic, and a variety of bandages.*

1. Yes I have a screwdriver and some screws and wood glue.
2. On the balcony of a second-floor apartment a large macaw sat watching us.
3. We moved on October 15; our new address is 5311 East Baker Street, Deerfield Illinois, 60015.
4. All you need to bring are a change of clothes shoes socks a toothbrush and toothpaste.
5. Phobos is I believe one of the moons around Mars Mrs. Farris.
6. Fire damaged a number of houses yet no one was injured not even any pets.
7. Because acrylic a type of water-based paint dries rapidly you must work quickly with it.
8. Birds sang frogs jumped and children played on that hot sunny day.
9. Malfunctioning dangerously the robot moved jerkily toward the table picked up a dish dropped it on the floor and rolled out the door.
10. Easing up on the throttle she coasted in for a smooth landing.

### Exercise 30  Using Commas Correctly

Add and delete commas to punctuate the following sentences correctly.

EXAMPLE
    1. They made beads out of small white seashells Ed.

    1. *They made beads out of small, white seashells, Ed.*

1. Deer thrived sea life flourished and all manner of edible plants grew in the region, that is now California.

COMMON ERRORS

2. Up and down the coastline of California communities of American Indians have lived for centuries.

3. The Karok Pomo Yurok and Modoc are just four of the dozens of peoples living in this area.

4. Skilled in basketwork the Pomo became known for the decoration variety and intricate weaving of their baskets.

5. The Yurok developed an elaborate monetary system which they used in fixing a price on every privilege or offense.

6. While many peoples favored dentalium shells as currency they also exchanged other items in trade.

7. Yurok marriages were arranged with care for marriage was an important public and historic alliance.

8. Yes Helen, the Gabrielino hunted with a stick that is similar to the boomerang the famous Australian weapon.

9. Traditionally, the Coast Miwok peoples were each represented by a male chief, and a female chief and a female ceremonial leader called a *maien*.

10. Kintpuash who was also called Captain Jack was the Modoc leader, who escaped capture on November 29 1872.

### Exercise 31 Proofreading for Correct Use of Semicolons and Colons

Add or delete semicolons and colons to correct the punctuation in the following sentences.

EXAMPLE    1. The party starts at 7 30, we will need to leave our house by 7 00.

        1. *The party starts at 7:30; we will need to leave our house by 7:00.*

1. John is bringing the drinks, ice, and cups, and Wanda is bringing the plates, knives, and forks.

2. Compare these three translations of King David's famous song, Psalm 23 1–6.

3. Don't forget to pick up: Carlos, Kam, Lisa, and Mary at 7 15 sharp.

4. Twin koalas are rare in captivity, consequently, Australia's Yanchep National Park prized Euca and Lyptus, the two born there in 1996.

5. The dance committee still needs to get the following equipment a CD player, outdoor speakers, and a microphone.

6. During our party on the Fourth of July last year, a huge storm forced everyone inside, then lightning knocked the power out.

┌HELP┐

In Exercise 31, you may need to use colons and semicolons to replace incorrectly used commas.

**Reference Note**

For information on **semi-colons and colons,** see Chapter 23.

COMMON ERRORS

7. California's seagulls will eat just about anything clams, chicks, berries, and even the occasional starfish.
8. We have invited exchange students from Dublin, Ireland, Paris, France, and Tokyo, Japan.
9. At 10 30 P.M., he neatly printed the title page, which read "Alfredo in Wonderland A Tale of an Exchange Student in New York."
10. Bamboo is a versatile and flexible building material, in Indonesia, as in many countries, it has a wide variety of uses.

### Exercise 32 Using Punctuation Correctly in Sentences

Add periods, question marks, commas, semicolons, and colons to correct the punctuation in the following sentences.

EXAMPLE    1. In almost every corner of the world dogs do useful work for people

1. *In almost every corner of the world, dogs do useful work for people.*

1. Herding flocks collies and briards and other varieties of sheepdog are on the job wherever there are sheep.
2. Did you know that German shepherds which make good guard dogs can also herd sheep
3. Dogs guard our homes assist people with disabilities herd sheep and hunt game.
4. Sled dogs include the following breeds Samoyeds, huskies, Alaskan malamutes, and a few other strong breeds with thick fur.
5. Partners with police the world over bloodhounds are feared by criminals and praised by the parents of lost children whom these dogs have found.
6. The basenji comes from Africa and is in fact called the Congo dog many people share their homes with these animals whose ancestors date back to 3000 BC
7. Although Mexican Chihuahuas are tiny they fiercely take on any foe they don't back down even when facing a larger dog.
8. Brave little Chihuahuas ignore the good advice given in Ecclesiastes 9 4
9. Those famous lines make an obvious point "A living dog is better than a dead lion."
10. My favorite neighbor Edward Nichols Jr bought his Pekingese on Wednesday January 6 1999.

## Exercise 33 Correcting Errors in the Use of Quotation Marks and Other Punctuation

For each of the following sentences, correct any error in the use of quotation marks, commas, and end marks.

**Reference Note**

For information on **using quotation marks,** see page 686.

EXAMPLE
1. The troop leader said that we should bring the 'barest essentials': a change of clothes, a toothbrush, and a comb.

1. *The troop leader said that we should bring the "barest essentials": a change of clothes, a toothbrush, and a comb.*

1. James seemed excited and said, "Did you see the news last night?
2. "Sorry, Emma" Becky began "but I'm late already."
3. When Coach Myers announced the tryouts this morning, she said, "that anyone could try out."
4. Ms. Waters asked us to read The Tell-Tale Heart and one other short story of our choice this weekend.
5. They are watching reruns of *The Magic School Bus;* this episode is Lost in the Solar System.
6. For tomorrow's assignment, read The Price of Freedom, the next chapter in your textbook.
7. My favorite part of *Reader's Digest* is Humor in Uniform.
8. Why don't you title your poem "Words and Music"? Tom asked
9. The recent article Carbon Monoxide: The Silent Killer details the effects of this deadly gas.
10. Didn't you hear me yell Call 911! asked Erik.

## Exercise 34 Punctuating and Capitalizing Quotations

For each of the following sentences, correct any error in the use of quotation marks, commas, end marks, and capitalization.

EXAMPLE
1. Larry told me that "you were sitting in the library."

1. *Larry told me that you were sitting in the library.*

1. "I can't decide which selection to use for my project" sighed Fran.
2. Mary nodded and said "I haven't made up my mind either." "Are you going to choose a poem or a story"?
3. "I'm going to make a diorama of "Stopping by Woods on a Snowy Evening," interrupted Greg.
4. What if Ms. Hill says 'that you can't'? asked Mary.
5. Didn't she say "anything goes?" Greg answered.
6. "You're right." The instructions say 'write a song, present a play, or draw a picture, added Mary.

7. You play the guitar, Fran pointed out. Maybe you could write a song."

8. Mary smiled and said, "great idea!

9. What I'd really like to do is write extra verses for Woody Guthrie's song This Land Is Your Land, Fran said.

10. Perhaps even," Mary added "make a video of it"!

**Reference Note**

For more information on **using apostrophes,** see Chapter 25.

### Exercise 35 Using Apostrophes Correctly

Add or delete apostrophes to punctuate the following items correctly. If an item is already correct, write *C*.

EXAMPLE
  1. Weve got Matts tickets'.
  1. *We've got Matt's tickets.*

1. Dont use so many *so*s.
2. Its time for Janes report.
3. Ronnies and Eriks desks
4. Mom and Dads only car
5. PBSs most popular show
6. Who's your brother?
7. my sister's-in-laws cars
8. geeses caretaker
9. that baby birds' beak
10. Kerrys and your project
11. anyone's guess
12. Russs' *U*s look like *N*s.
13. Youre right!
14. those foxes dens
15. The blame is theirs'.
16. Lets eat at six oclock.
17. my March of Dimes donation
18. She says that shell bring ours'.
19. There's still time.
20. Bobs dog

### Exercise 36 Proofreading for Spelling Errors

Correct each spelling error in the following sentences.

EXAMPLE
  1. To succede, you must keep triing.
  1. *succeed; trying*

1. I cannot easily make dayly visits, even though I would surly like to.

**Reference Note**

For information on **spelling rules,** see Chapter 27.

2. The judge finaly conceded that the other driver had been exceding the speed limit.
3. The members of the procession carried one hundred twenty-five baskets of beautiful flowers.
4. The desert heat and dryness stoped both armys.
5. My neighbor's childs are always getting into mischeif.
6. A word with two *e*s, such as *deer,* has a long vowel sound.
7. The children truely enjoied hearing thier echoes bounce off the canyon walls.
8. The candidate siezed the opportunity to give a breif statement of his beleifs.
9. Leafs fluttered off the trees and down the desertted beachs during that 1st day of winter.
10. 5 years ago, each of my brother-in-laws was working two jobs.

## Exercise 37 Proofreading for Spelling Errors

For each of the following sentences, write the misspelled word or words correctly.

**Reference Note**
For information on **spelling rules,** see Chapter 27.

EXAMPLE    1.  Six concrete elfs guarded the doorway to my nieghbor's house.

1.  *elves, neighbor's*

1. Leisure activities may be wholely unecessary for survival, but they make life enjoyable.
2. On the way to Japan, his neice met a Chinese man who spoke perfect English.
3. After the clouds receeded, the sun glinted on the wet rooves.
4. Three ranch hands were teaching ropeing to the tourists who had payed for lessons.
5. These attachments are interchangeable, I beleive.
6. While my freinds and I were siting on the porch, we saw a white rabbit hoping across the street.
7. Place two heaping spoonsful of flour in a saucepan; then, slice three small tomatos.
8. Yes, several attorney-at-laws at our offices are alumnuses of the state university.
9. There must have been over one hundred and fifty people standing in line longer than that.
10. Mr. Brady said that suddenly the terrifing possibility of going to school all year had not seemed so bad to the Bradies.

**Reference Note**

For information on **words often confused**, see page 746.

**Exercise 38** Proofreading for Words Often Confused

For each of the following sentences, correct any error in word usage.

EXAMPLE     1.  A camel caravan in the dessert is a noble sight.

              *1.  A camel caravan in the desert is a noble sight.*

1. The roar of the plain's engine broke the quite of the night.
2. Its time to get you're suitcase packed.
3. I put my desert right here on the kitchen table, and now its gone.
4. As the mustangs picked they're way through the canyon, they unknowingly past a cougar hiding in the rocks.
5. Who was the warrior who lead the Zulus in there famous battle against the Boers?
6. Be careful, or you will brake that mirror into a million peaces.
7. Every knight choose his own way threw the forest.
8. First, the pigs got lose; then we spent all day trying too catch them.
9. He couldn't here us; he was too week from the fever.
10. Who's biography did you chose to read?

**Exercise 39** Distinguishing Between Words Often Confused

Choose the correct word in parentheses in each of the following sentences.

EXAMPLE     1.  Is Korean food for dinner (*all right, alright*) with you?

              *1.  all right*

1. I believe that Andrew Young began his political career during the 1960s; (*than, then*) he became a U.S. representative before being named ambassador to the United Nations.
2. Millie, would you care to explain the first (*principle, principal*) of thermodynamics to the class?
3. A (*stationery, stationary*) cold front has been responsible for this week's wonderful weather.
4. Recycling helps cut down on the (*waist, waste*) of resources.
5. Did you (*all ready, already*) qualify for the race?
6. How would you (*council, consul, counsel*) someone in this situation?
7. What (*effects, affects*) will the Internet have on your future career?
8. There's nothing (*plain, plane*) about these stylized medieval reliefs.
9. I think that when it came to scat singing, Sarah Vaughan really was (*all together, altogether*) the best.
10. Designing a golf (*coarse, course*) must be a challenging task.

For each numbered item in the following business letter, correct any errors in mechanics. An item may contain more than one error. If an item is already correct, write *C*.

EXAMPLE       **[1]** 813 E Maple St

              1.  *813 E. Maple St.*

            813 East Maple Street
**[1]** Belleville IL, 62223

**[2]** February 12th, 2001

**[3]** Customer Service
       Super Sport Shoes
       14 Magenta Road
       Woodinville WA, 98072

**[4]** Dear Sir or Madam,

**[5]** Thank you for your prompt response to my
       order (number 51238) for two pairs of
       white jogging shoes. **[6]** These shoe's are
       the most comfortable ones I have ever worn.

**[7]** However, one of the pairs that I
       recieved is the wrong size. **[8]** This pair
       is to small; consequently, I am returning
       these shoes with this letter. **[9]** Please
       exchange them for one pair of white jog-
       gers two sizes larger.

**[10]** Your's truly

        *Neville Walters*

        Neville Walters

# Mechanics Test: Section 1

**DIRECTIONS**   Each of the following sentences contains an underlined word or word group. Choose the answer that shows the correct capitalization, punctuation, and spelling of the underlined part. If there is no error, choose answer E (Correct as is). Indicate your response by shading in the appropriate oval on your answer sheet.

**EXAMPLE**   1. Marla <u>asked, "did you</u> see the meteor shower last night?"

        **(A)** asked, "Did

        **(B)** asked "Did

        **(C)** asked "did

        **(D)** asked did you

        **(E)** Correct as is

**ANSWER**   1.    A    B   C    D    E

1. We keep a variety of emergency equipment in the trunk of our <u>car, a first-aid</u> kit, jumper cables, a blanket, a flashlight, and road flares.

    **(A)** car a first-aid         **(D)** car: a 1st-aid

    **(B)** car: a first-aid        **(E)** Correct as is

    **(C)** car; a first-aid

2. Alvin <u>Ailey, who's choreography</u> thrilled audiences for years, formed the dance company that still bears his name.

    **(A)** Ailey who's choreography     **(D)** Ailey, whose choreography

    **(B)** Ailey whose choreography     **(E)** Correct as is

    **(C)** Ailey who's choreography,

3. Jerome <u>said, "I cant believe</u> that Ben Franklin wanted the turkey to be the symbol for the United States!"

    **(A)** said, "I can't believe      **(D)** said, 'I can't believe

    **(B)** said "I can't believe       **(E)** Correct as is

    **(C)** said, "I can't beleive

4. "Do <u>you," asked Kay 'Know</u> the story of Icarus?"

    **(A)** you, asked Kay, "know      **(D)** you," asked Kay, 'know

    **(B)** you?" asked Kay. "Know     **(E)** Correct as is

    **(C)** you," asked Kay, "know

**5.** I often struggle to open my gym <u>locker; its</u> lock is probably rusty.

(A) locker, its

(B) locker; Its

(C) locker. It's

(D) locker: It's

(E) Correct as is

**6.** Please <u>bring too tomatos,</u> a head of lettuce, and some feta cheese from the market.

(A) bring: two tomatoes,

(B) bring 2 tomatoes

(C) bring two tomatoes,

(D) bring to tomatoes,

(E) Correct as is

**7.** "Did Principal Reeves really say, 'We need *less* <u>discipline?"</u> asked Cassandra.

(A) discipline,'"

(B) discipline'?"

(C) discipline?'

(D) discipline'"?

(E) Correct as is

**8.** Grandfather enjoyed the <u>childrens storys</u> about their visit to the wildlife sanctuary.

(A) childrens story's

(B) childrens' stories

(C) childrens stories

(D) children's stories

(E) Correct as is

**9.** The Leonards <u>visited: Rome, Italy,</u> Athens, Greece; and Istanbul, Turkey, on their vacation.

(A) visited Rome, Italy;

(B) visited: Rome, Italy;

(C) visited, Rome, Italy;

(D) visited Rome; Italy;

(E) Correct as is

**10.** Did <u>aunt Susan,</u> bring the coleslaw?

(A) aunt Susan

(B) aunt, Susan,

(C) Aunt Susan

(D) Aunt, Susan,

(E) Correct as is

# Mechanics Test: Section 2

**DIRECTIONS**  Each numbered item below contains an underlined group of words. Choose the answer that shows the correct capitalization, punctuation, and spelling of the underlined part. If there is no error, choose answer E (Correct as is). Indicate your response by shading in the appropriate oval on your answer sheet.

**EXAMPLE**  **[1]** <u>200 north Vine Street</u>

        **(A)** 200 North Vine street

        **(B)** 200 North Vine Street

        **(C)** Two-Hundred North Vine Street

        **(D)** 200, North Vine Street

        **(E)** Correct as is

**ANSWER**  1.  (A)  (B)  (C)  (D)  (E)

---

200 North Vine Street
Austin, TX  78741

**[1]** <u>May, 5 2001</u>

Athena Wilson
Worldwide Travel, Inc.
4135-A Anderson Avenue
**[2]** <u>San Antonio, Tex. 78249</u>

**[3]** <u>Dear Ms. Wilson:</u>

**[4]** <u>Thank you for you're</u> prompt response to my request for information about traveling to Australia. The color brochures describing the **[5]** <u>different, Australian</u> tours were especially helpful. My family and I are interested in the "Natural Wonders" **[6]** <u>package, that includes</u> day trips to **[7]** <u>the great Barrier reef.</u> **[8]** <u>Well also</u> want to schedule a three-day stay in Sydney. How much will the entire package **[9]** <u>cost, for three</u> adults and one child?

**[10]** <u>Yours truly</u>

*Naomi Baskin*
Naomi Baskin

1. (A) May 5 2001
   (B) May Fifth 2001
   (C) May 5th 2001
   (D) May 5, 2001
   (E) Correct as is

2. (A) San Antonio, Tex 78249
   (B) San Antonio Texas 78249
   (C) San Antonio, TX 78249
   (D) San Antonio TX 78249
   (E) Correct as is

3. (A) Dear Ms. Wilson,
   (B) Dear ms. Wilson:
   (C) Dear Ms Wilson,
   (D) Dear Ms. Wilson;
   (E) Correct as is

4. (A) Thank you for youre
   (B) Thank you for youre'
   (C) Thank you for your
   (D) Thank you for your'
   (E) Correct as is

5. (A) different australian
   (B) different Australian
   (C) different, Australian,
   (D) different, australian,
   (E) Correct as is

6. (A) package that includes
   (B) package that, includes
   (C) package: that includes
   (D) package that includes:
   (E) Correct as is

7. (A) the Great Barrier Reef
   (B) the great Barrier Reef
   (C) the Great Barrier reef
   (D) The great Barrier reef
   (E) Correct as is

8. (A) Well, also
   (B) We'll, also,
   (C) We'll also
   (D) We'll, also
   (E) Correct as is

9. (A) cost for 3
   (B) cost? For three
   (C) cost: for three
   (D) cost for three
   (E) Correct as is

10. (A) Yours' truly,
    (B) Yours truly:
    (C) Your's truly,
    (D) Yours truly,
    (E) Correct as is

# Quick Reference Handbook

# The Dictionary

## Information About Words

**Dictionary Entry** A dictionary entry includes the word and information about it. The following items explain the labels in the sample entry.

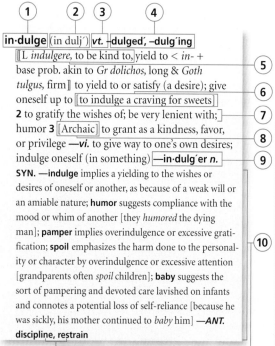

From *Webster's New World Dictionary, Fourth College Edition.* 1999 by Webster's New World Dictionaries, A division of Simon and Schuster, New York. Reprinted by permission of the publisher.

1. **Entry word.** The entry word shows how the word is spelled and how it is divided into syllables. The entry word may also show capitalization and alternate spellings.

2. **Pronunciation.** Pronunciation is shown by the use of phonetic spellings that usually include accent marks and diacritical marks. A pronunciation key explains the meaning of diacritical marks and phonetic symbols.

3. **Part-of-speech labels.** The part-of-speech labels (usually in abbreviated form) indicate how the entry word should be used in a sentence. Some words may be used as more than one part of speech. In this case, a part-of-speech label is given in front of each numbered or lettered series of definitions.

4. **Other forms.** These may show spellings of plural forms of nouns, tenses of verbs, or the comparison forms of adjectives and adverbs.

5. **Etymology.** The etymology is the origin and history of a word. It tells how the word or its parts came into English.

6. **Examples.** Phrases or sentences may demonstrate how the defined word is used.

7. **Definitions.** If a word has more than one meaning, definitions are numbered or lettered.

8. **Special usage labels.** These labels identify words that have special meanings or are used in special ways in certain situations.

9. **Related word forms.** These are various forms of the entry word, usually created by adding suffixes or prefixes.

10. **Synonyms and antonyms.** Synonyms or antonyms appear at the end of some entries.

**Other Parts of a Dictionary**   Most dictionaries also include the following additional information.

- **Abbreviations**   Many dictionaries include a chart of common *abbreviations,* including those for governmental agencies, weights, measurements, and the names of states or geographical regions.

- **Biographical and geographical entries** In some dictionaries, a section identifies famous or influential figures in history, listing their professions and birth and death dates. The geographical section lists populated places in the world and includes pronunciations and population size.

- **Colleges and universities**   School or college dictionaries list all the colleges and universities in the United States and Canada, indicating each school's location, founding date, and student body size.

- **Copyright**   The *copyright* tells you when a dictionary was published. Use the most up-to-date edition; that way, you can be sure that new words and new meanings of old words are included.

- **Guide to the dictionary**   Most dictionaries have a few pages that explain how the material is organized and what the abbreviations and typefaces mean.

- **Index**   An *index* indicates the location of the dictionary features described previously.

- **Pronunciation key**   A *pronunciation key* is provided at the front of any dictionary and also at the bottom of each page or pair of pages within the dictionary.

- **Scholarly essays**   Language experts write *scholarly essays* that provide information about the history and growth of English, how a new edition differs from a previous one, and how the dictionary was researched and prepared.

**Types of Dictionaries**   Since dictionaries differ in the types and amount of information they provide, you should choose a dictionary based on the kind of information you need.

- **Abridged**   An *abridged* dictionary is the most common type of dictionary. (The word *abridged* means shortened or condensed.) It contains most of the words you are likely to use or encounter in your writing or reading. Abridged dictionaries are arranged in alphabetical order and include basic information such as the spelling, definition, pronunciation, part of speech, and source of a word. If you need more detailed information about a word's history or usage, consult an *unabridged* or *specialized* dictionary instead.

- **Specialized**   *Specialized* dictionaries define words or terms that are used in a particular profession, field, or area of interest, such as dictionaries of quotations, synonyms, medical terms, and slang. Specialized dictionaries include information that an abridged dictionary might not have.

- **Unabridged**   An *unabridged* dictionary contains nearly all the words in use in a language. For example, the present edition of the twenty-volume *Oxford English Dictionary* contains over 500,000 entries.

# Document Design

## Manuscript Style

The following chart provides guidelines for preparing handwritten or typed manuscripts. Your teacher may have additional guidelines for you to follow. Remember that these guidelines will help improve the appearance of your papers.

### Guidelines for Handwritten or Typed Manuscripts

1. Use only one side of a sheet of paper.

2. Type or write in blue or black ink.

3. If you write by hand, do not skip lines. If you type, double-space the lines.

4. Leave margins of about one inch at the top, sides, and bottom of each page.

5. Indent the first line of each paragraph.

6. Number all the pages except the first page. Place the number in the upper right-hand corner of the page.

7. All pages should be neat and clean. You may make a few corrections with correction fluid, but they should be barely noticeable.

8. Follow your teacher's instructions for placing your name, the date, your class, and the title of your paper on a cover sheet or on the first page of your paper.

## Desktop Publishing

*Desktop publishing* is the production of professional-looking documents, such as reports or newsletters, on a personal computer. Desktop publishers set text (and sometimes visuals) on a page in such a way that they effectively communicate a message.

### Page Design or Layout

Before the widespread use of computers changed the printing industry, documents were designed by hand. Page designers worked page by page, cutting, arranging, and pasting strips of text, illustrations, headings, and captions. Now almost anyone with a computer can design an entire document. The following section explains some key concepts for designing pages.

**Alignment**   *Alignment* refers to how lines of text are arranged on a page. There are several ways text can be aligned.

- **Left alignment**   Text that is *left aligned* is set so that each line forms a straight edge against the left margin. Most printed documents are set left aligned to aid reading from left to right.

This text is left aligned. Notice how the lines form a straight edge along the left margin.

- **Right alignment**   Text that is *right aligned* is set so that each edge forms a straight line against the right margin. Right-aligned text is not commonly used for large amounts of text because it is difficult to read. Pull-quotes and poetry are occasionally right aligned. (See also **Pull-quote** on page 809.)

EXAMPLE

This text is right aligned.
Notice how the lines
form a straight edge along the
right margin.

- **Center alignment**   Text that is *center aligned,* or *centered,* is set in the middle of the page. Center-aligned text usually appears in invitations, posters, or advertisements.

EXAMPLE

This text is center aligned.
Each line is evenly spaced
on both sides of an invisible, vertical line
running through the center of this column.

- **Justified alignment**   *Justified* means the ends of each line of text form a straight edge against the left and right margins. Extra spaces are added between words to make sure that the lines are even.

EXAMPLE

This sample text is justified. Notice how the lines of text form neat edges along both margins.

- **Ragged alignment**   *Ragged* means that the lines of the text do not create a straight edge

on both sides. Usually the right side of the text is ragged, as in the example of left alignment in the column at the left.

**Bullet**   A *bullet* ( • ) is an icon used to make information in a text stand out. Bullets are often used for lists of parallel items. The bullets attract readers' attention and can make information more accessible to them. Here are some tips for using bullets.

- Always indent a bulleted list from the main body text.
- Use plain bullets in formal documents. Other, decorative icons (such as *, # , or + ) may be used as bullets only in informal writing, such as brainstormed lists.
- Make sure that the items in your list are parallel both in the type of information they contain and in construction. For instance, use all nouns or all imperative sentences, as in this bulleted list.

**Call out**   A *call out* is a line or phrase of text that describes some aspect of a visual, graphic, or illustration. Usually the call out is connected to the visual by an arrow or line. (For examples of call outs, see the labels for **Headings and Subheadings** on page 808.)

**Columns and Blocks of Text**   Text is easier to read when it is contained in rectangular-shaped areas, such as *columns* or *blocks.* The width of a column or block of text varies, depending on the size of the text and the format of the document. The text in posters, advertisements, and fliers, for example, is usually set in blocks so that it may be read quickly. Text in textbooks, reference books, and newspapers, which contain large quantities of information, usually appears in columns. (See also **Line Length** on page 809.)

**Contrast**    *Contrast* refers to the balance of light and dark areas on a page. Dark areas are those that contain blocks of text or visuals. Light areas have little type. A page with high contrast—a balance of light and dark— is easier to read than a page with low contrast—either mostly light or mostly dark. (See also **Contrast** on page 814 and **White Space** on page 810.)

**Emphasis**    *Emphasis* indicates to a reader which information on a page is most important. For example, the front page of a newspaper uses bold or large headlines and photographs to place emphasis on a particular story. Because readers' eyes are drawn naturally to color, large or bold print, and graphics, these elements are commonly used to create emphasis.

**Graphic**    A *graphic* is a picture, chart, illustration, or piece of artwork that is used to convey information visually. Short sections of text, such as headings, subheadings, titles, headers, and footers, may also be considered graphics because they serve a visual function. (See also **Visuals** on page 809.)

**Gray Page**    A *gray page* contains text almost exclusively. It has few or no graphics to indicate visually the organization or structure of the material on the page.

**Grid Lines**    *Grid lines* are vertical and horizontal intersecting lines that provide structure to a page by dividing it into neat sections. Often grid lines are used to plan the layout or final appearance of a page and do not appear in the printed version of the document.

**Gutter**    A *gutter* is the margin of space or crevice between two facing pages in a bound book. For example, the gutter on this page runs between this page and the page on the right.

**Headers and Footers**    *Headers* and *footers* provide information about a printed document. Headers appear in the top margin of a page, and footers appear in the bottom margin. Headers and footers may include

- the name of the author
- the name and date of the publication
- chapter or section titles
- page numbers

**Headings and Subheadings**    *Headings* and *subheadings* (also called *heads* and *subheads*) are used to give readers clues about the content and organization of a document.

- **Headings**    A *heading* gives readers a general idea what a section of text, such as a chapter, will be about. Headings appear at the beginning of a section of text and are usually set in large, bold letters. Often they appear in a typeface different from that of the body of the text.

- **Subheadings**    A *subheading* is more descriptive than a heading and is used to indicate subsections of the text. Several subheadings usually appear under one heading. Like headings, subheadings are also set in large letters, in bold or italic font, or in a different typeface to distinguish them from the headings and the text.

EXAMPLE

## Common Household Pests (heading)
### *What Makes These Pests Tick?* (subheading)

Ants and roaches are common household pests that are difficult to eliminate,    text especially in the warm summer months.

**Indentation**   *Indentation* is the skipping of a few letter spaces to indicate the beginning of a new paragraph in a text. Whether you are using a computer or writing your work by hand, the indentation should be one-half of an inch from the left margin. If you are working on a computer or typewriter, one-half of an inch is equivalent to five letter spaces. Indentation is also used with bulleted lists.

**Line Length**   *Line length* is the number of characters (letters, spaces between words, and punctuation marks) a line contains. (Remember, a line is not a sentence; it is a single line of text that may or may not form a complete thought.) The best line length for a document depends on the size of the type and the format of the document. In general, limit line length to sixty-five characters, or about nine or ten words. This makes the text easier to read. (Remember that one goal of desktop publishing is to design texts that are clear and accessible to readers.)

**Margins**   *Margins* are the spaces that surround the text on a page. Most computer word-processing programs automatically set the side margins at one and one-quarter inches and the top and bottom margins at one inch. Margins are flexible, however. If your teacher recommends different measurements for the margins of your papers, use them instead. (See also **White Space** on page 810 and **Guidelines for Handwritten or Typed Manuscripts** on page 806.)

**Pull-quote**   A *pull-quote* is a quotation from a text, such as a magazine article or story, that has been turned into an eye-catching graphic and set in the margin. The purpose of the pull-quote is to catch the reader's attention. Consequently, pull-quotes should be short but

intriguing "hooks." They should also be quotations that state or suggest an important idea or event in the text.

EXAMPLE

Once upon a time in the middle of winter, when the flakes of snow were falling like feathers from the sky, a Queen sat at a window sewing, and the frame of the window was made of black ebony. And whilst she was sewing and looking out of the window at the snow, she pricked her finger with the needle, and three drops of blood fell upon the snow.

*"Three drops of blood fell upon the snow."*

**Rule Lines**   *Rule lines* are lines used graphically to create visual effects on a page. Rule lines may be thick or thin, vertical or horizontal, and they may separate columns, set text off from a headline or caption, or draw your eye to something on the page. The box around the passage above shows how rule lines may be used.

**Title and Subtitle**   A *title* is the name of an entire document. *Subtitles* are longer and more descriptive than titles. Often a subtitle is separated from a title by a colon and appears in a smaller typeface. In books, titles and subtitles appear alone on a page (the title page) at the very beginning of the book.

EXAMPLE

*The People's Chronology: A Year-by-Year Record of Human Events from Prehistory to the Present*

**Visuals**   *Visuals,* like *graphics,* are pictures, charts, illustrations, or artwork that convey information. (See also **Types of Graphics and**

Visuals on page 815 and the "Graphics and Visuals" section on page 813.)

**White space**   *White space* is any area on a page where there is little or no text, visuals, or graphics. It provides a contrast to the dark ink on a page and helps make the page more readable. Usually, white space is limited to the margins, the gutter, and the spaces between words, lines, and columns. (See also **Contrast** below.)

# Type

*Type* is a particular style of letter and markings used in printing and publishing. When movable type was first introduced, the letters of the type were modeled on handwritten characters or the lettering in manuscript books.

**Capital Letters**   *Capital* (or *uppercase*) *letters* help readers identify the beginning of a new sentence or idea. Capital letters attract readers' attention and may be used in the following ways to create emphasis in a document.

- **Dropped or initial cap**   A *dropped* or *initial cap* is an artistic use of a capital letter in the first word of the first paragraph of a text or a section of a text. Dropped caps imitate medieval illuminated manuscripts in which the first letter of a section or chapter was enlarged and transformed into a colorful drawing.

  EXAMPLE

  Once upon a time in the middle of winter . . .

- **Headings or titles**   Setting a *heading* or *title* in all capital letters helps to create emphasis and contrast in a document such as a newspaper article, especially when the head-

ing or title is in the same typeface as the rest of the text. (See also **Contrast** and **Emphasis** on page 814.)

EXAMPLES

## LOCAL STUDENT TO GO TO NATIONAL SPELLING BEE

## METAPHORS, SIMILES, AND PERSONIFICATION

- **Small caps**   *Small caps* are uppercase letters that are reduced in size and used as lowercase letters. Usually they appear in abbreviations of time, such as *9:00* A.M. and A.D. *1500*. Small caps may also be combined with true capital letters for an artistic effect.

NOTE   Capital letters can be difficult to read. Use capital letters for contrast or emphasis, not for large bodies of text.

**Captions**   *Captions* are lines of text that appear under photographs or illustrations. They explain the meaning or importance of a visual and connect it to the text. Because readers tend to look first at the visuals on a page, captions are often the first text they read. Consequently, captions should be concise, accurate, and interesting. Captions may appear in a smaller size type (usually two point sizes smaller) than the main text or in the same type size but italicized. (See also **Font** and **Font, or Point, Size** on page 811.)

**Contrast**   In terms of typeface, *contrast* refers to the visual effect of using different typefaces in a document. For instance, you might use one typeface for the body of your text and one for the headings and subheadings. Too many different typefaces, however, can create too much contrast, which makes a document difficult to read. (See also **Contrast** on page 814.)

**Font**   A *font* is a complete set of characters of a particular design. In computer software, the word "font" usually stands for a particular typeface which can be manipulated. Size is one of the most common manipulations of font; others are between roman (meaning, in this case, "not slanted") and italic, or between capital letters and lowercase letters. Look at the following examples of fonts. (See also **Fonts, Categories of,** and **Fonts, Styles of** on this page.)

EXAMPLES

ROMAN CAPITALS              *ITALIC CAPITALS*

SMALL CAPITALS              roman lowercase letters

*italic lowercase letters*

**Font, or Point, Size**   The size of the type in a document is called the *font,* or *point, size.* Word-processing software provides many options for sizing text. Many textbooks use type measured at twelve points. Type for headings and headlines may range anywhere from eighteen to forty-eight points. Captions usually appear in nine- to eleven-point type.

**Fonts, Categories of**   The *categories of fonts* refer to a particular style of characters used in print. There are thousands of fonts available, each with its own name and unique appearance. Most typefaces, however, belong to one of the three categories listed below.

■ **Decorative, or script**   *Decorative,* or *script,* typefaces have elaborately designed characters that convey a distinct mood or feeling. They can be used to create an artistic effect; however, they should be used sparingly because they are difficult to read.

EXAMPLES

*This is an example of Zapf Chancery typeface.*

*This is an example of Fresh Script typeface.*

*This is an example of Linoscript typeface.*

■ **Sans serif**   The characters in *sans-serif* typefaces are formed by neat straight lines, with no small strokes at the ends of the letters. (*Sans serif* means "without serifs, or strokes.") Sans-serif typefaces work well as headings and subheadings, pull-quotes, and captions because they have clean edges and are easy to read in small amounts. (See also **Legibility** on page 812.)

EXAMPLES

Gill Sans is a sans-serif typeface.

Helvetica is a sans-serif typeface.

Futura is a sans-serif typeface.

■ **Serif**   The characters in *serif* typefaces have little strokes (*serifs*) attached at each end. Serif typeface was the first style of typeface to be invented and used in printing. The serifs or strokes are believed to be modeled on the connectors between handwritten letters, on which serif type was based. As in handwriting, the little strokes help guide the readers' eyes from letter to letter and word to word. Because of their legibility, serifs are still commonly used to set large bodies of type.

EXAMPLES

Palatino is a serif typeface.

New Century Schoolbook is a serif typeface.

Times is a serif typeface.

NOTE   Mixing decorative, sans-serif, and serif typefaces on a page creates high contrast. However, you should generally not use more than two typefaces on a page because too many can confuse readers.

**Fonts, Styles of**   The *styles of fonts* can provide emphasis and contrast to your regular typeface. For example, titles of books or films and captions are often set in *italics.* **Boldface** or

**boldface italic** can highlight new or important concepts. In addition, computers and desktop publishing software have made fonts from the printing industry available on computers. Look at the following examples of eye-catching fonts. (See also **Fonts, Categories of** on page 811.)

| | |
|---|---|
| **roman boldface** | roman shadow font |
| roman condensed | *italic boldface* |
| roman outline font | roman expanded |
| roman underscored | |

NOTE   Use care in selecting font styles; avoid using too many styles in any one document. Also be consistent in your use of font styles. For example, if you use italic boldface for one heading, use it for all other headings as well. Remember that your reader may be confused if you change font styles frequently or inconsistently.

**Knockout, or Reversed, Type**   *Knockout, or reversed, type* is light type set against a contrasting, dark background for contrast or emphasis. (See also **Contrast** and **Emphasis** on page 814.)

EXAMPLES

Here is dark type set against a light background.
Here is knockout, or reversed, type.

**Leading or Line Spacing**   *Leading* (rhymes with *sledding*), or *line spacing,* is the distance in points between lines of text. Most word processors and typewriters allow you to adjust the amount of line spacing to single-, double-, or even triple-space measurements.

**Legibility**   *Legibility* refers to the ease with which a reader can decipher a short section of text like a headline or cross reference. Clear typefaces and simple fonts in readable sizes make a text more legible.

**Lowercase**   *Lowercase* type consists of lowercase letters, as opposed to capital letters. Lowercase letters are characterized by *ascenders* (rising strokes, as in the letters *b* and *h*) and *descenders* (dropping strokes, as in the letters *g* and *y*). Most text that you read or write will appear in lowercase type because it is more legible than uppercase type. (See also **Legibility** above.)

**Readability**   *Readability* refers to how easily a text can be read. Unlike legibility, readability refers to the ease of reading long sections of text. Documents with high readability often contain text set in a classic serif typeface (like the Minion typeface you are reading at this moment). (See also **Type** on page 810, **Fonts, Categories of** on page 811, **Font, styles of** on page 811, and **Legibility** above.)

# Graphics and Visuals

Graphics and visuals consist of pictures, charts, and other visual representations that are used to

- organize and display data or information
- explain a process or a relationship
- illustrate how something looks, works, or is organized
- show changes over time

It is important to select and develop graphics and visuals carefully. They should convey information clearly and support directly the text that appears on the page. For example, a graph showing the rate of extinction of animal species in the Amazon River Basin would be inappropriate in a text discussing the rate of extinction of animal species in California.

## Arrangement and Design

The challenge of designing a document that contains text and graphics or visuals is to arrange all the parts in a way that communicates information and ideas effectively. When you design a document that includes graphics and visuals, consider the following elements.

**Accessibility** *Accessibility* refers to the ease with which readers can find information in a document. Increase a document's accessibility by labeling any graphics or visuals clearly— their relationship to the text should be immediately clear to readers. (See also **Captions** on page 810 and **Font, Styles of** on page 811.)

**Accuracy** All graphics or visuals must contain *accurate,* or true, information. Be sure that any data included in a graphic is reliable, up-to-date, and completely accurate. Just as readers must be able to trust the information in the text

of your document, they must also be confident of data in graphics and visuals. Never change data in order to better support your argument.

**Color** Color naturally attracts a reader's eye, especially when it contrasts with the black and white of text and white space. Color may be used to

- attract the reader's attention
- highlight a piece of information
- indicate that certain items on a page belong together
- show the organization of the parts of a document or page

When choosing colors for your document, remember the following guidelines.

1. **Use colors for emphasis, not for long sections of text.** Some readers might find color text difficult to read. Color should serve a purpose, not just be decorative.
2. **Use two or more colors, but avoid an overabundance of colors.** Two or more colors provide contrast. A single color, however, will simply look out of place. At the same time, too many colors can confuse your readers. Use a few colors consistently to convey the meaning in a graphic or visual.
3. **Use cool colors, such as blue and green, as background.** These colors have a calming effect.
4. **Use warm colors, such as red and orange, sparingly.** These colors appear to expand or jump off the page.
5. **Choose colors that complement each other.** The colors that appear opposite one another on the color wheel shown on the next page are complementary.

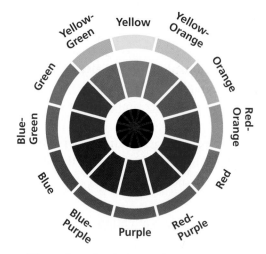

The color wheel above shows how colors relate to one another. The primary colors are yellow, red, and blue; all other colors are the result of combining these colors or mixing them with white or black.

**Contrast**   *Contrast* is the effect of a striking difference between two things. Contrast can attract attention and make it easier for readers to visualize your text and remember its content. To create contrast within graphics and visuals, use different visual cues for different kinds of information. For example, use different colors for each of the wedges of a pie chart. (See also **Contrast** on page 810 and **Fonts, Styles of** on page 811.)

**Emphasis**   You can create emphasis by using visual cues—such as color, capital letters, boldface or italic fonts, and large type size—to draw readers' attention to what you want them to see. Visuals and graphics always provide emphasis because they attract a reader's attention before anything else on the page. (See also **Emphasis** on page 808.)

**Focus**   The content of a visual such as an illustration, photograph, or drawing is its *focus.*

When you choose a visual, always make sure that its focus reinforces the text. Use the following guidelines when choosing visuals to include in your document.

1. Make sure that the subject and its relationship to the text are immediately clear.
2. Crop, or trim, any distracting details.
3. Make sure the subject is shown from an angle that corresponds with the reference to it in the text. For example, if the text refers to an aerial view of Mount Fuji, be sure that the visual shows an aerial view.
4. Make sure the visual includes everything you want to show the reader about the subject. For example, a map of Africa that omits places discussed in the document should be replaced with a map that includes those places.
5. Add any captions or labels that readers will need in order to understand a visual. However, be careful not to add so many labels that the visual becomes cluttered or unclear.
6. Choose visuals that have a tone similar to the tone of the text. For instance, if the text discusses a comical topic, then the visuals and graphics should be equally funny or playful, rather than formal and serious.

**Integration**   *Integration* refers to the way visuals and text fit together on a page. Visuals and text that are related or cover the same material should be placed close together. In addition, the text should direct the reader's attention to the visual and explain its content.

EXAMPLE

The data in the bar graph below shows that freshmen and juniors are more likely to vote in student elections than sophomores and seniors.

**Labels and Captions**   To help readers understand them, many graphics and visuals need *labels, captions,* or both. Labels can be used to identify the contents of charts, tables, and diagrams. Usually they appear within the body of the graphic or visual, but sometimes they are linked to the visual or graphic by thin rule lines. As a rule, avoid using more than five labels per visual. Captions are usually full sentences that describe a visual such as a photograph or illustration. They appear directly under, beside, or above the visual. (For examples of labels and captions, see page 817.)

**Organization**   *Organization* refers to the arrangement of text and graphics or visuals on a page. All the elements that deal with a similar subject should be grouped or "chunked" together. Use visual cues such as headings and subheadings, similar typefaces, color, and rule lines to show that certain text and visual elements are related. (See also **Integration** on page 814.)

**Type Size and Font**   Text that appears in visuals and graphics should be obviously different from the main text. The type may appear in the same font as the main text, but should be one to two and one-half points smaller, or in italics. You can also provide a visual contrast by setting all labels and captions in a contrasting typeface. (See also **Labels and Captions** on page 814 and **Fonts, Styles of** on page 811.)

# Types of Graphics and Visuals

Graphics and visuals can add to the effectiveness and appeal of a document, but how do you decide which kind to use? Here are some of the different types of graphics and visuals from which you can choose.

**Charts**   *Charts* show relationships among ideas or data. Two types of charts you are likely to use are flowcharts and pie charts.

■ **Flowcharts**   A *flowchart* uses geometric shapes linked by arrows to show the sequence of events in a process. Labels are placed inside the shapes, and the direction of the flow is from left to right and from top to bottom.

EXAMPLE

**Writing the First Draft of a Research Paper**

■ **Pie charts**   A *pie chart* is a circle that is divided into wedges. Each wedge represents a certain percentage of the total.

EXAMPLE

Career Goals of Seniors at Felicity High School

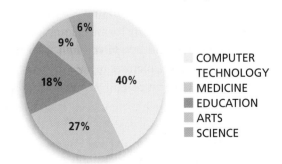

**Diagrams**   *Diagrams* are simple line drawings that can be used to show what something looks like, how something works, or how to do something. Some diagrams are realistic, while

QUICK REFERENCE HANDBOOK

others are more abstract, using shapes or symbols to represent things. Diagrams can be drawn by hand or generated by a computer, and they are almost always spare, showing only important details. The diagram below shows how to measure an angle with a protractor.

EXAMPLE

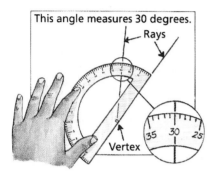

This angle measures 30 degrees.
Rays
Vertex

**Graphs** *Graphs* use numbers to present facts and figures. There are two types of *graphs,* both used to show how one thing changes in relation to another. For instance, a graph might show how the time a person spends watching television changes in relation to the person's age.

■ **Bar graphs** A *bar graph* can be used to compare quantities at a glance, to show trends or changes over time, or to indicate the parts of a whole. Bar graphs are formed along a vertical and horizontal axis. In a *pictograph,* a special kind of bar graph, pictures replace the bars. The example in the next column shows a bar graph.

EXAMPLE

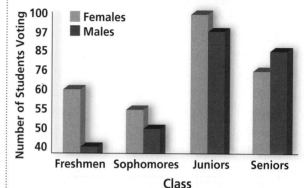

Number of Students Voting in
School Elections by Class

■ **Line graphs** A *line graph* can be used to show changes or trends over time, to compare trends, or to show how two or more variables interact.

EXAMPLE

Number of Students Voting in School Elections

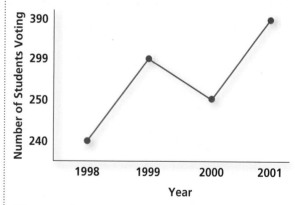

**Illustrations** *Illustrations,* such as drawings, photographs, and other artwork, may be used to show readers

■ something new, unfamiliar, or indescribable

■ how something works

■ what something or someone looks like

The photograph on the next page illustrates the powerful but graceful swing of baseball player Joe DiMaggio during his record hitting streak in 1941.

**Storyboards** *Storyboards* depict the scenes of a narrative and can be used to plan a video or to map out the events in a story. They usually consist of boxes containing drawings and text, although sometimes the text appears outside or under the boxes, called *panels*. The following example shows two of the panels that a student created while making a documentary film about school elections.

**Tables** Using rows and columns, *tables* provide detailed information arranged in an accessible, organized way. In the following examples, notice that information is logically organized and clearly labeled.

EXAMPLES

Two-Column Table

| Numbers of Students Voting in School Elections | |
|---|---|
| Year | Numbers of Students Voting |
| 1998 | 240 |
| 1999 | 299 |
| 2000 | 250 |
| 2001 | 390 |

Three-column Table

| Numbers of Students Voting in School Elections by Class and Gender | | |
|---|---|---|
| Class | Numbers of Females Voting | Numbers of Males Voting |
| Freshmen | 60 | 40 |
| Sophomores | 55 | 50 |
| Juniors | 100 | 97 |
| Seniors | 76 | 85 |

Allison Gomez giving her campaign speech

Gomez answering students' questions

**Time Lines**  *Time lines* identify the events that have taken place over a given period of time. Usually, events are identified or described above the time line and the time demarcations are indicated below it. Some time lines are illustrated.

EXAMPLE

### Events in the History of the City of London

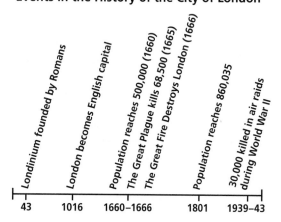

Time lines are sometimes used to present the main events in the life of a famous person. In this case, the time line is often arranged vertically in two columns, with the dates in the left column and the corresponding events in the right.

EXAMPLE

### Events in the Life of Mark Twain

| | |
|---|---|
| 1835 | Born Samuel Langhorne Clemens in Florida, Missouri. |
| 1853 | Began traveling and working as a journeyman printer in St. Louis, Cincinnati, Philadelphia, and New York |
| 1856 | Became a river pilot, navigating steamboats on the Mississippi River |
| 1862 | Took a job for the *Virginia City Territorial Enterprise* and began writing articles and stories for the paper under the pseudonym Mark Twain |
| 1867 | Published *Innocents Abroad* |
| 1870 | Married Olivia Langdon |
| 1876 | Published *Tom Sawyer* |
| 1883 | Published *Life on the Mississippi* |
| 1884 | Published *The Adventures of Huckleberry Finn* |
| 1894 | Traveled abroad giving lectures to pay for increasing debts |
| 1904 | Suffered the death of his wife Livy |
| 1910 | Died of angina and heart disease |

# The History of English: Origins and Uses

## History of English

The English language was first written about 1,300 years ago, but was spoken long before that. Over the centuries, English has grown and changed to become the rich, expressive language we use today. The history of this development is a story of people, places, and times.

**Beginnings of English**   Many of the world's languages come from an early language called *Proto-Indo-European.* We have no records of this parent language, but it was probably spoken by Eastern Europeans six or seven thousand years ago. Tribes of these people slowly migrated across Europe and to India. As they wandered in different directions, each tribe developed its own *dialect,* or distinct version of the language. The dialects eventually developed into separate languages. The map on this page shows how the Indo-European root word *mater* (mother) developed in some of these languages. The arrows indicate directions of migration.

**Old English**   Around A.D. 450, tribes known as the Angles and the Saxons invaded Britain. They took over land that had been settled earlier by the Celts. The separate dialects these tribes spoke eventually blended into one language—*Old English,* sometimes called Anglo-Saxon. Modern English still bears traces of its Anglo-Saxon roots. For example, the words *eat, drink,* and *sleep* come from the Old English words *etan, drincan,* and *slæp.* The Anglo-Saxons used an –s to form the plurals of many nouns, just as we do. We also have Old English to thank for irregular verb forms such as *swim, swam,* and *swum.*

**Middle English**   In 1066, the Normans from France seized control of England. For the next 150 years, French was the official language of government, business, and law. Because of this,

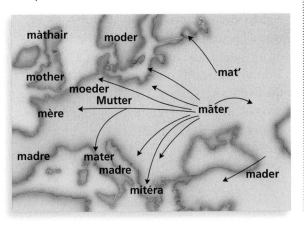

màthair

moder

mother

mat'

moeder
Mutter

mère

māter

madre

mater
madre

mader

mitéra

many English words that are connected with wealth and power come from the French, such as *governor, attorney,* and *fashion.* The common people of England, however, still spoke English—a changing form of the language we call **Middle English.** The grammar of English was becoming simpler as many of the complicated word endings disappeared.

The following lines are matching excerpts from the Lord's Prayer (Matthew 6:9–13) in Old English and Middle English. As you can see, Middle English looks much more like the English you know.

**Old English:** Fæder ure þu þe eart on heofonum, si þin nama gehalgod.

**Middle English:** Fader oure þat art in hevene, i-halwed bee þi name.

## Modern English

Before 1476, speakers and writers in different parts of England used different versions of the language, and therefore they often had trouble understanding each other. When William Caxton set up the first printing press in England around 1476, all of this changed. Early printers standardized spelling, and since London was the center of English trade and culture, they printed all books in London English. London English soon became the standard throughout England. Once standards were set, people wanted to learn the proper way to speak and write their language. Soon, grammar and usage handbooks sprang up, along with the first English dictionaries.

Two other factors influenced Modern English. One factor was its expansion into an international language through the discovery of new lands. From the sixteenth century through the nineteenth century, English merchants, explorers, and settlers spread English to other parts of the globe. They also learned new words from other languages, enriching English with international imports.

**EXAMPLES**

| | |
|---|---|
| **Japanese:** soy | **Dutch:** cruise |
| **Turkish:** yogurt | **Spanish:** siesta |

The language was also affected by the scientific revolution of this time. Words had to be created to name the new discoveries being made.

**EXAMPLES**

atmosphere     pneumonia     skeleton

## American English

Immigration to the American colonies brought about a new version of the language—**American English.** Like the United States itself, American English represents a variety of cultures and peoples. Native Americans, Africans, and immigrants from most countries around the world have enriched the language with words from their native tongues. For example, Native Americans gave us *coyote* and *squash; jazz* and *gumbo* came from Africa; and Italian immigrants added *spaghetti* and *ravioli* to the menu.

## English in the Twenty-first Century

English has become the most widely used language in the history of the world, with over 750 million users. It is an official language in eighty-seven nations and territories. It is the world language of diplomacy, science, technology, aviation, and international trade. As people around the world contribute to the language, the word count grows. The last count was over 600,000 words. The count grows so quickly that dictionary makers cannot keep up with the growth of English vocabulary.

# Varieties of English

English is a rich and flexible language that offers many choices. To speak and write effectively—at home, at school, and on the job—you need to know what the varieties of English are and how to choose among them.

**Dialects of American English**   Like all languages, American English has many distinct versions, called *dialects.* Everyone uses a dialect, and no dialect is better or worse than another. Each has unique features of grammar, vocabulary, and pronunciation.

■ **Regional dialects**   The United States has four major regional dialects: the *Northern,* the *Midland,* the *Southern,* and the *Western.* Pronunciations of words often vary from one dialect region to another. For example, some Southerners pronounce the words *ten* and *tin* the same way—as "tin." Similarly, regions differ in grammar and vocabulary. For example, you may say "sick *to* my stomach" if you come from New York but "sick *at* my stomach" if you come from Georgia. You may drink *soda, tonic,* or *pop* depending on what part of the country you come from.

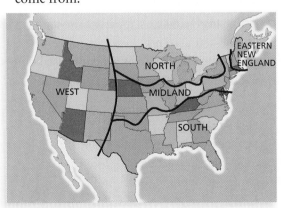

■ **Ethnic dialects**   An ethnic dialect is used by people who share the same cultural heritage. Because Americans come from many different cultures, American English includes many different ethnic dialects. The most widely used ethnic dialects are African American Vernacular English and the Hispanic English of many people from Cuba, Mexico, Central America, and Puerto Rico. Many everyday words began as ethnic dialect words but then became part of the general English vocabulary. For example, *tote* and *chigger* came into English through Black dialect, and *avocado* and *taco* were added to English by Hispanic Americans.

**Standard American English**   Every variety of English has its own set of rules and guidelines. No variety is the best or the most correct. However, ***Standard American English*** (SAE) is the one variety of English that is more widely used and accepted than others in the United States. Because it is commonly understood, SAE allows people from many different regions and cultures to communicate with one another clearly. It is the variety of English you read and hear most often in books and magazines, on radio and television. It is the kind of English that people are expected to use in most school and business situations. This textbook presents many of the rules and guidelines for using standard American English. To identify the differences between standard American English and other varieties of English, this book uses the labels *standard* and *nonstandard.* Nonstandard does not mean wrong language. It means language that is inappropriate in situations where standard English is expected.

## Standard English—Formal to Informal

Depending on your audience, purpose, and occasion, the language you use can be formal, informal, or somewhere in between. The following chart shows some of the appropriate uses of very formal and very informal English.

### Uses of Formal and Informal English

**Formal**

**Speaking:** formal, dignified occasions, such as banquets and dedication ceremonies

**Writing:** serious papers and reports, tests, business letters

**Informal**

**Speaking:** everyday conversation at home, school, work, and recreation

**Writing:** personal letters, journal entries, and many newspaper and magazine articles

You can say the same thing in many different ways. For example, *chow down* and *dine* both mean "eat," but one is much more formal than the other. The main differences between formal and informal English are in sentence structure, word choice, and tone.

### Features of Formal and Informal English

**Formal**

**Sentence Structure:** longer and more complex

**Word Choice:** precise, often technical or scientific

**Tone:** serious and dignified

**Informal**

**Sentence Structure:** shorter and simpler

**Word Choice:** simple and ordinary; often includes contractions, colloquialisms, and slang

**Tone:** conversational

**Uses of Informal English**   In informal speaking and writing, people constantly make up new words and give new uses to old ones. This makes informal English flexible. Dictionaries help you to see this flexibility by giving labels to different informal uses of words. The two most commonly listed usage labels are **colloquialisms** and **slang.**

- **Colloquialisms**   *Colloquialisms* are the informal words and phrases of conversational language. They bring flavor and color to everyday speech and a friendly, conversational tone to writing. Many are figures of speech that aren't meant to be taken literally.

   EXAMPLES

   I may have made a mistake, but you don't have to **fly off the handle** about it.

   Today, many young couples **foot the bill** for their weddings rather than having their parents pay for them.

   My mother told us to quit **making such a racket.**

- **Slang**   *Slang* is made up of newly coined words or of old words used in unconventional ways. It is usually clever and colorful. It is often a special language for specific groups of people, such as students and military personnel. Some people use slang to be up-to-date. Sometimes a slang word becomes a lasting and widely used part of the language. More often than not, however, it lives a short and limited life. Slang is generally used only in the most informal speaking situations.

   EXAMPLES

   *beat*—tired
   *bummer*—a depressing experience
   *cool*—pleasing, excellent
   *hassle*—to annoy, harass
   *kooky*—strange

# The Library/ Media Center

## Using Print and Electronic Sources

The library/media center in your school or community provides you with a range of print and electronic sources of information. *Print sources* include books, periodicals (magazines, newspapers, and journals), and specialized forms (such as microforms or vertical files). *Electronic sources* include CD-ROMs, the Internet, DVDs, and online databases. To determine whether a particular source suits your specific purpose, use the features discussed in this section.

> **TIP**  Do not limit your searches for information to the library. Real-world documents—schedules, directories, maps, technical directions, user manuals, warranties, product information, and government records—can be excellent sources for specific purposes.

**Call Number**  A *call number* is a unique code assigned to a book in a library. The call number indicates how a book is classified and where it is shelved in the library. The two systems of classification are the Dewey decimal system and the Library of Congress system.

- **Dewey decimal system**  The *Dewey decimal system* assigns numbers to nonfiction books according to ten general subject areas.
- **Library of Congress system**  *The Library of Congress system* uses call numbers that include code letters to identify subject categories. The first code letter identifies a book's general category (such as history) and the second letter identifies the subcategory (such as the Middle Ages). Numbers also identify specific books within a category.

**Card Catalog**  A *card catalog* is a collection of index cards that contains important information about the books in a library. For each book, there are at least two cards, a *title card* and an *author card.* If the book is nonfiction, there is also a third card, a *subject card.* The cards are arranged in alphabetical order and contain the following information:

- The **call number** assigned by the Library of Congress or Dewey decimal system
- The **author's full name,** last name first

- The full **title** and **subtitle** of a book
- The place and date of **publication**
- The general **subject** of a book; a subject card may show specific headings
- A **description** of the book, such as its size and number of pages, and whether it is illustrated
- **Cross-references** to other headings or related topics under which a book is listed

As libraries acquire computer technology, however, card catalogs in drawers are being converted to electronic or online formats. (See also **Online Card Catalog** on this page.)

**CD-ROMs**   A *CD-ROM* (*C*ompact *D*isc-*R*ead *O*nly *M*emory) is a compact disc that is designed to hold visual as well as audio information. The data is encoded digitally and can be accessed only by a computer with a CD-ROM drive. A single CD-ROM may contain the equivalent of 250,000 pages of printed text. Many reference tools, such as encyclopedias, dictionaries, and indexes, are now available on CD-ROMs. CD-ROMs contain the same text as the printed versions but have the added attractions of searching capabilities, interactive graphics, and audio. (See also the **Reference Sources chart** on page 826.)

**Internet**   The *Internet* is a global network of computers. With the Internet, a computer user may access information from another computer or network of computers anywhere in the world. Created in the late 1960s, the Internet was originally used by research scientists to share data electronically with each other. The content exchanged on the Internet has since expanded beyond scientific matters to include almost any topic. The Internet may be used by almost anyone who has a computer equipped with a modem. There are many ways to view material on the Internet, including FTP (File Transfer Protocol), Gopher, and Telnet; as well as *World Wide Web browsers,*

which provide access to files and documents, news and discussion groups, bulletin boards, e-mail, and the *World Wide Web* (see page 827). The World Wide Web is the place on the Internet you are most likely to go for your research. (See also the **Evaluating Web Sites chart** on page 831.)

**Microforms**   *Microforms,* photographically reduced articles from newspapers and magazines, can be either *microfilm* or *microfiche.* Special machines are needed to enlarge microfilm and microfiche images and project them onto a screen for viewing or reading.

**Online Card Catalog**   An *online card catalog* is an electronic or computerized version of the card catalog. Instead of searching through individual cards, you may find a book by typing in a book's *title, author,* or *subject.* (If you don't have a specific book in mind, you may type in *key words* that may appear in the title or description of the book.) The computer retrieves information based on your request.

**Online**

**Search Results of Online Catalog**

FULL RECORD
CALL NUMBER: 932.014/Weeks
AUTHOR: Weeks, Kent R.
TITLE: The lost tomb
EDITION: 1st ed.
PUBLISHER: New York : William Morrow, 1988.
DESCRIPTION: xv, 330 p., [24] p. of plates : ill. (some col.)
NOTES 1: Includes bibliographical references and index. "In 1995, an American Egyptologist discovered the burial site of the sons of Ramses II: this is his incredible story of KV 5 and its excavation."
Maps on end papers.
SUBJECT 1: Ramses II, King of Egypt.
SUBJECT 2: Weeks, Kent R.

**Online Databases**   An *online database* is a contained system of electronic information that may be accessed only by computer. In most cases, organizations such as universities, libraries, or businesses create or subscribe to databases that are of specific interest to people in the organizations. LEXIS/NEXIS is an example of a subscription-only database. Some databases are public and may be accessed through the World Wide Web.

**Online Sources**   Information that is *online* is information that may be located and accessed by using computers. Computers that are online are able to communicate with each other over telecommunication lines, such as telephone lines and fiber-optic cables, and via satellite. When computers are linked, they form a *network.* Computer networks are what make the Internet and the World Wide Web possible.

**Radio, Television, and Film**   *Radio* and *television* are important sources of news and information. Newscasts, newsmagazines, and documentaries are regular features on radio and television. Documentaries and educational materials are also produced on *film* or *video.* Descriptive listings of radio and television programs appear in newspapers and, in some cases, on the Internet. Indexes of educational films and videos, such as *The Video Source Book* (Gale, 1998) are available at libraries and bookstores. Be sure to check the ratings provided for the films and videos before viewing them.

**Readers' Guide to Periodical Literature**
The *Readers' Guide to Periodical Literature* is an index of articles from more than two hundred fifty magazines and journals (periodicals). As the sample entry on this page shows, the articles are listed alphabetically by author and by subject; the

---

### Printed *Readers' Guide*

**CROWN BOOKS CORPORATION**
(2) Independent snatches up closing Crown store [Chester County Book Company expansion ] K. Howell, *Publishers Weekly* v245 no48 p20 N 20 '98
(4) Independents feel little effect from Crown closings. J. High. *Publishers Weekly* v245 no37 p25 S 14 '98
(3) **CROWN CENTRAL PETROLEUM CORP.**
Strikes
Oil workers call a boycott J. Slaughter. il *The Progressive* v62 no10 p16 O '98
(5)

**CROWN MOLDINGS (ARCHITECTURE)** *See* Moldings (Architecture)

(1) CROWS
Caw of the wild [increase of crows in Los Angeles] D. J. Hotaling. il *Los Angeles* v43 no12 p44 D '98

(6) CROZIER, LORNA, 1918
(7) The apocrypha of light [poem] *The Canadian Forum* v76 no866 p36 Ja/F '98
The blues [poem] *The Canadian Forum* v76 no866 p37 Ja/F '98
Inventions of the lesser gods [poem] *The Canadian Forum* v76 no866 p37 Ja/F '98
The origin of the species [poem] *The Canadian Forum* v76 no866 p36 Ja/F '98
(8) Tower of Babel [poem] *The Canadian Forum* v76 no866 p37 Ja/F '98
What Adam meant when he named it grass [poem] *The Canadian Forum* v76 no866 p37 Ja/F '98

(9) **CRT DISPLAY TERMINALS** *See* Video display terminals

**1** Subject entry

**2** Title of article

**3** Date of periodical

**4** Author of article

**5** Page reference

**6** Author entry

**7** Name of periodical

**8** Volume number of periodical

**9** Subject cross-reference

headings are set in boldface type. A key located in the front of the *Readers' Guide* explains the meanings of the abbreviations used in the entries.

**Reference Books**   Reference books are books of specialized information. Examples include encyclopedias, dictionaries, thesauri, indexes, books of quotations, atlases, and almanacs. Reference books focus on one particular topic or kind of information. The information is organized in a logical way,

such as alphabetical or chronological order or by category. (See also the **Reference Sources chart** below.)

**Reference Sources**   There are many different kinds of reference sources that you can use to find specific kinds of information. The chart below identifies and describes common reference sources and provides examples of print and electronic reference sources.

| Reference Sources | | |
|---|---|---|
| **Types** | **Description** | **Examples** |
| ALMANACS | Information about current events, facts, statistics, and dates | • *Information Please Almanac*<br>• *The 20th Century Video Almanac* CD-ROM |
| ATLASES | Maps and geographical information | • *Hammond Atlas of the World*<br>• *Microsoft Encarta World Atlas* CD-ROM |
| BIOGRAPHICAL REFERENCES (GENERAL) | Information about birth, nationality, and major accomplishments of prominent people | • *Who's Who in America*<br>• *Who's Who 1897–1996: One Hundred Years of Biography* CD-ROM |
| BIOGRAPHICAL REFERENCES (SPECIALIZED) | Information about people noted for accomplishments in a field or for membership in a group | • *Who's Who Among African Americans*<br>• *Dictionary of Women Artists*<br>• *American Indian: A Multimedia* CD-ROM |
| BOOKS OF QUOTATIONS | Famous quotations indexed or grouped together by subject | • *The Oxford Dictionary of Quotations*<br>• *Bartlett's Familiar Quotations* CD-ROM |
| BOOKS OF SYNONYMS | Lists of exact or more interesting words to express ideas | • *Roget's International Thesaurus*<br>• *Oxford Thesaurus on* CD-ROM |
| ENCYCLOPEDIAS | Articles of general information arranged alphabetically by subject in several volumes | • *The World Book Multimedia Encyclopedia*™<br>• *Compton's Interactive Encyclopedia* CD-ROM |
| LITERARY REFERENCES | Information about various works of literature and authors | • *Contemporary Literary Criticism*<br>• *Gale's Literary Index* CD-ROM |
| STYLE AND WRITING MANUALS | Information about proper writing style and preparation of research papers | • *The Chicago Manual of Style*<br>• *Harbrace College Handbook* CD-ROM<br>• *MLA Style Manual and Guide to Scholarly Publishing* |

**Vertical File**   A *vertical file* is a set of file drawers containing up-to-date materials that are not likely to be cataloged anywhere else, such as pamphlets, newspaper clippings, and photographs. As the use of electronic resources such as the Internet increases, vertical files are less likely to be maintained by libraries in the future.

## World Wide Web (*WWW* or the *Web*)

The *World Wide Web* is one part of the Internet. The Web is an enormous system of connected, or linked, documents that contain text, graphics and visuals, sounds, and even video. Documents (*Web sites* or *Web pages*) on the World Wide Web are connected by *hyperlinks.* Clicking on a hyperlink quickly brings up a new site on your screen. To navigate or view the World Wide Web, you must have *browser* software installed on your computer.

**World Wide Web, Key Terms**   The following terms will help you understand the workings of the World Wide Web.

- **Browser**   A *browser* is a software application that allows you to find and access information on the Web. It allows you to explore, read, save, and download documents, images, sounds, and videos that you may find there. Using a browser to locate and read documents is called *browsing.* (See also **Web Site** on the next page.)

- **Domain**   A *domain* is the name of a computer or server on the Internet from which you may access information. Every Web address specifies a domain, or particular computer. (See also **URL** in the next column.)

- **Home page**   A *home page* is the first screen or page of a Web site. Usually, it identifies the person or organization that sponsored or created the site, provides an index or table of contents for the site, and often includes hyperlinks to related sites on the Web. (See also **Web Site** on the next page.)

- **Hyperlink**   A *hyperlink* is a "button" or code word that allows a user to move from one place or page on the World Wide Web to another. On-screen, hyperlinks usually appear in a contrasting color and are underlined. (See also **HyperText Markup Language** below.)

- **Hypertext**   A *hypertext* program allows a user to find and open related files and documents on the Web without having to quit or close the original file. It allows a user to move to and from one document to another via hyperlinks.

- **Hypertext Markup Language** (HTML) *Hypertext Markup Language* is the language used to create documents on the World Wide Web.

- **Hypertext Transfer Protocol** (HTTP) *Hypertext Transfer Protocol* is the language used by browser software to connect to different sites or documents on the World Wide Web.

- **Search engine**   A *search engine* is a tool for finding specific information on the Web. (See also **World Wide Web, Searching** on page 829.)

- **URL** (*U*niform *R*esource *L*ocator)   A *URL* is the address of a specific document on the Web. A typical URL includes words, abbreviations, numbers, and punctuation. The URL shown below would connect you to the listings of science programs that are broadcast on National Public Radio. The parts of the address are explained below.

  1           2         3
  http://www.npr.org/programs/science
  1. The *protocol,* or how the site is formatted.
  2. The *domain name.* Domain names have at least two parts. The part on the left is the name of the company, institution, or other organization. The part on the right is the

general domain. A list of the most common general domain abbreviations follows. (See also *domain* on the previous page.)

| Common Domains on the World Wide Web | |
|---|---|
| **com** | commercial |
| **edu** | educational |
| **gov** | governmental |
| **net** | administrative |
| **org** | nonprofit organization |

3. The **subdirectory name** that shows where the specific piece of information you want is stored. (Each word following a slash requests a more specific search into the site.) Not all addresses will have this part.

■ **Web Site (or Web Page)**   A *Web site* or *Web page* is a document or location on the Web that is linked to other locations on the Web. Below is a typical example of what you would see if you had located a Web site with a typical browser.

1. **Toolbar**   The buttons on the toolbar allow you to complete different functions, such as moving to different pages, printing out information, searching, and seeing or hiding images.

2. **Location indicator**   This box shows you the URL, or address, of the site you are seeing before you.

3. **Content area**   This is the area of the screen where the text, images, hyperlinks, and other parts of a Web page appear.

4. **Icon**   By clicking on an icon, you can move to a different page that contains information about the topic listed next to the icon.

5. **Hyperlink**   Hyperlinks are words or phrases that are underlined or are a different color than the rest of the text. Clicking on a hyperlink will take you to another page that contains more information about the word or phrase.

6. **Scroll Bar**   Clicking the arrows at the end of this bar scrolls the page horizontally. There is also a vertical scroll bar on the right side.

**World Wide Web, Plagiarism**   To take another person's idea or work and present it as your own is called *plagiarism.* Because the World Wide Web is such a vast source of information and because it is easy to download or copy information, plagiarism of electronic material has become a serious concern. Plagiarism is highly unethical. It is very important, therefore, for you to treat any information you find on the World Wide Web as if it were from a printed or published source. **Make sure that you cite the source of your information.** (See page 227 for examples of **citations of online sources.**)

**World Wide Web, Searching**    There are three ways to search for information on the World Wide Web: *direct address, search engines,* and *subject catalogs.* Each type of search has benefits and drawbacks, which are described below. In general, unless you know exactly what you are looking for on the Web, a combination of all three types of searches works best. Most search services on the Web allow you to use all three.

- **Direct address**    The most direct way to find a Web site is to type in the Web site's address or URL in the Location box. The address must be typed exactly, using the proper case (upper or lower) and punctuation. This strategy does not work, of course, if you do not have the site's address.

- **Search engines**    *Search engines* allow you to search databases that contain information about the millions of sites on the Web. These databases are compiled automatically by computer programs called robots. *Search engines* are the tools that allow you to search the indexes' databases for specific information. (For more on how to use a search engine, see *World Wide Web, Using Search Engines* in the next column.)

- **Subject catalogs**    A *subject catalog* provides an extensively organized table of contents of the World Wide Web. Information from Web sites is organized in broad categories, such as *Education* and *Entertainment.* (Unlike search engines, subject catalogs are organized by humans, not by machines.) Each category in the catalog contains many specific subcategories, which in turn break down into even more specific sub-subcategories. A subject catalog or Internet guide is searched by starting with a general topic and narrowing down to a specific one.

**World Wide Web, Using Search Engines** Unlike subject catalogs, *search engines* allow you to search for Web sites that contain key words or phrases. These search tools also allow you to refine your searches.

- **Key word search**    A *key word search* lets you look for sites that contain specific words or phrases. Type key words in the space provided on the search engine screen and press the Return key or the Search or Find button. The search engine analyzes the Web sites indexed in its database for the words you requested. The results appear in the form of a list. The sites that contain all your key words should appear at the top of the list, and the list continues in descending order of relevant matches. Most search engines assign the items on the list a percentage or rank number to indicate how well the site matched your request. The key word search works best when you have a very clear and specific topic to research.

- **Refining a Key Word Search** Because search engines may identify hundreds or thousands of Web sites—or none at all—that contain your key words, you should consider *refining*, or focusing, your search. Below are some strategies that may help you. Keep in mind, however, that different search engines may require slightly different commands than those listed here. (The ones here are recommended by the search engine Webcrawler.) Consult the Help section of your search engine for specific commands.

| Refining a Key Word Search | |
| --- | --- |
| **Tip** | **How It Works** |
| Replace general terms with more specific ones. | A key word that is common or used in ways you do not expect can result in irrelevant matches. |
| | EXAMPLE   If you are interested in long-distance running races, enter *marathon* instead of *race*. |
| Use quotation marks. | By placing your key words or phrases in quotation marks, you instruct the search engine to find sites that use the words exactly as you have typed them. |
| | EXAMPLE   Enter "sled dog races" to find sites about the Iditarod. If you enter *sled dog races* without the quotation marks, the search engine may turn up sites about bobsledding or dog grooming. |
| Use *and* and *not*. | Narrow your search by putting the word *and* between your key words. The search engine will find only Web sites that contain all words connected by *and*. |
| | EXAMPLE   For sites that mention both the New York and the Boston marathons, enter *New York and Boston and marathon*. |
| | Use *not* between key words to make sure that the search engine does not pull up sites that deal with topics that are similar but unrelated. |
| | EXAMPLE   Enter *marathon not Greece* to avoid Web sites about the Greek city of Marathon. |
| Use *or*. | To broaden your search, use *or* to let the search engine know that you would accept sites that contain any of your key words. |
| | EXAMPLE   If you want sites that discuss either the New York or the Boston marathon, enter *New York or Boston marathon*. |

## World Wide Web, Web Site Evaluation

Because the content of the World Wide Web is not monitored for accuracy in the way most newspapers, books, or television programs are, you must be critical of the information you find there. For questions to help you to *evaluate* a Web site's value as a source of information, see the following chart.

| Evaluating Web Sites | |
|---|---|
| **Questions to Ask** | **Why You Should Ask** |
| Who created or sponsored the Web site? | The kind of information on a Web site is determined by the site's creator or sponsor. The Web site's home page should identify who this is. Use only Web sites that are affiliated with reputable organizations, such as government agencies, universities, museums, and national news organizations. The Web sites for these organizations will usually belong in the *edu, gov,* or *org* domains. Reputable Web sites tend to give the names of authors or contributors to the site. |
| When was the page first posted and is it frequently updated? | This information usually appears at the end of a home page. Most often, it includes a copyright notice, the date of the most recent update, and a link to the creator's e-mail address. As with any reference source, you want the information you obtain from a Web site to be up-to-date. |
| What other Web pages is the site linked to? | Looking at the links provided in a Web site can help you determine how legitimate it is. If a site is a source of accurate information, it will have links to other reputable Web sites. |
| Does the Web site present information objectively? | Look for signs of bias, such as strong language or statements of opinion. If the site is trying to be objective, it will present ideas from both sides of an issue or debate. |
| Is the Web site well designed? | A well-designed Web site has legible type, clear graphics, and working links; it is also easily searched or navigated. The written content of the site should be well organized and well written, with proper spelling, punctuation, and grammar. |

# Reading and Vocabulary

## Reading

### Skills and Strategies

You can use the following skills and strategies to become a more effective reader.

**Author's Purpose and Point of View, Determining**    An author's main *purpose* for writing a selection may be to inform, to persuade, to express, or to entertain. To help you identify purpose, look at the form a piece takes. For example, business writing and user manuals are usually written to inform, while policy statements and letters to the editor are often written to persuade. Other forms, such as Web sites, can suit multiple purposes. In addition, authors have opinions or attitudes about their subjects called *point of view.* Determining the author's purpose and point of view will help you to get more meaning from the text and can help you detect bias. If you suspect an author is biased, examine the clarity and accuracy of the information. (See also page 251.)

> EXAMPLE    Volunteering at the hospital is rewarding. Teenage volunteers deliver meals, visit patients, and run errands. Benefit your community and yourself by volunteering today.

Author's purpose:  To persuade teenagers to volunteer at the hospital

Author's point of view:  Volunteering benefits both the individual and the community.

### Cause-effect Relationships, Analyzing

A *cause* makes something happen. An *effect* is what happens as a result of that cause. Ask "Why?" and "What are the effects?" as you read to examine causes and effects. (See also page 837.)

> EXAMPLE    Exercising regularly has changed my life! Since I began walking or jogging for thirty minutes four times a week, the results are amazing. Besides feeling better about the way I look, I have more energy and feel happier.

Analysis:  Regular exercise is the *cause* of these *effects*: better appearance, increased energy, and improved mood.

**Clue Words, Using**    Depending on the text structure, writers use certain *clue words* to connect ideas or to show relationships between ideas. You can use these clue words—such as those listed on the next page—to identify the organizational pattern a writer has used. (See also **Text Structures, Analyzing** on page 836.)

| Clue Words | | | | |
|---|---|---|---|---|
| **Cause-effect** | **Chronological Order** | **Comparison-contrast** | **Listing** | **Problem-solution** |
| as a result | after | although | also | as a result |
| because | as | as well as | finally | consequently |
| consequently | before | but | for example | furthermore |
| if . . . then | finally | either . . . or | in fact | indeed |
| nevertheless | first | however | in the first place | nevertheless |
| since | not long after | not only . . . but also | most important | otherwise |
| so that | now | on the other hand | such as | therefore |
| therefore | second | similarly | to begin with | this led to |
| this led to | then | unless | | thus |
| thus | when | yet | | |

**Conclusions, Drawing**   A *conclusion* is a statement you make by combining information in a text with information you already know. As you read, you gather information, connect it to your experiences, and then draw conclusions that are logical yet specific to the text.

EXAMPLE   Jacob looked around in awe and nervously reached for his mother's hand. The desks looked so big! The water fountain looked so tall! There were so many new faces!

Conclusion: Jacob is a small child experiencing his first day of school.

**Fact and Opinion, Distinguishing**   A *fact* is something that can be proven true by concrete information. An *opinion* expresses a personal belief or attitude, so it cannot be proven true or false. Facts are often used to support opinions. A reader who can distinguish between a fact and an opinion will not be easily misled. (See also page 287.)

EXAMPLE

Fact: In 1992, Mae C. Jemison became the first African American woman in space. [Reference works support this as a true statement.]

Opinion: The space program needs more female astronauts. [This is what one writer thinks or believes; the statement cannot be proven to be true or false.]

**Generalizations, Forming**   A reader forms a *generalization* by combining information in a text with personal experience to make a judgment or statement that goes beyond the text to the general world.

EXAMPLE   The city of Davis is taking on a clean, new look. Over the past few months, the streets and sidewalks seem less littered. Residents see almost no drink cans, food wrappers, or plastic containers. City officials report that they have issued no littering citations in the last year. The people of Davis have "cleaned up their act."

Generalization: People are becoming more aware of the need to protect the environment and are taking responsibility for cleaning up after themselves.

**Implied Main Idea, Identifying**   Some writers do not directly state the main idea; instead, they choose to *imply* or suggest it. In this case, you, the reader, have to analyze the meaning of the details in the text and decide what overall meaning these details combine to express. (See **Conclusions, Drawing** on page 833 and **Stated Main Idea and Supporting Details, Identifying** on page 836.)

EXAMPLE  Training for a marathon should begin at least six months before the actual marathon. Injuries occur when runners add too many miles too quickly, but taking it slow is often hard for enthusiastic runners. The body needs time to adjust to the increased workload, so runners should add only one mile a week to their long weekly run.

Implied main idea: Patience is extremely important in marathon training.

## Inferences, Making   An *inference* is an educated guess based on information in the text and on the reader's prior knowledge and experience. As you read, you make decisions about ideas and details that writers do not directly reveal. (See also page 162.)

EXAMPLE  "It's snowing! I can't believe it's snowing!" exclaimed Tara. As she stood with her face pressed to the window, she watched her excited neighbors filter outside. The Smiths were holding hands and dancing around their yard. Little Bart had found a cardboard box and was sliding down the driveway. Tara ran to get her coat.

Inference: Seeing snow was an unusual experience for Tara and her neighbors.

## Paraphrasing   A *paraphrase* is a type of summary in which you restate an author's ideas in your own words. Paraphrasing is a good way to check your understanding of the original text. (See also **Paraphrasing** on page 863.)

EXAMPLE  The world's top athletes with disabilities compete at the Paralympic Games, which are held just after the Olympics and at the same location. Competing at the international level requires the same dedication and skill of athletes with disabilities as are required of all athletes. Besides offering the participants entertainment and social contact, the Paralympic Games help its competing athletes to improve their physical strength, muscular coordination, and self-confidence.

Paraphrase: Top athletes with disabilities from around the world can compete on an international level at the Paralympic Games, which follow the Olympic Games. With the same determination and skill required of all athletes, the disabled athletes gather to compete and socialize. Many find that the experience increases their strength, coordination, and self-esteem.

## Persuasive Techniques, Analyzing   An author uses *persuasive techniques* to convince readers to think or act in a certain way. As you read persuasive writing, look for logical reasoning and facts; don't be misled by an overemphasis on emotional appeals or faulty reasoning. (See also page 253.)

EXAMPLE  We need a stoplight at the corner next to the high school. Each school day, 150 vehicles and 350 pedestrians go through the intersection between the hours of 7:00 and 8:00 A.M. and 2:00 and 3:00 P.M. Three students have been hit by cars in the last two years. Every other high school in the state uses stoplights for traffic control. Installing one at our high school will make us an accident-free school.

Analysis: The second and third sentences use facts to support the opinion in the first sentence. The fourth sentence contains an emotional appeal. The final sentence contains faulty reasoning: There is no guarantee that installing a traffic light will make the school accident-free.

## Predicting   *Predicting* is deciding what will happen next. To make predictions, you use information from the text plus your own knowledge and experience.

EXAMPLE  One by one the campers crawled out of their makeshift tents to check the weather. Dark clouds blocked out the sun, and thunder rumbled in the distance. Suddenly, lightning flashed!

Prediction: The campers will be caught in a rainstorm. Because their tents are makeshift, the campers will probably have to break down camp quickly and run for shelter.

## Problem-Solution Relationships, Analyzing

A *problem* is an unanswered question. A *solution* is an attempt to answer the question. When authors write about a problem, they usually suggest at least one solution and explain the outcomes and final results of the solution. As a reader, you can analyze a problem by asking three questions: *What is the problem? Who has the problem? Why is it a problem?* Then, you can analyze and evaluate the solution by asking: *What is the outcome of each solution?* (In other words, did the solution work, or did it cause other problems?) *What is the final result of the solution?* (Was the problem solved?)

EXAMPLE   Two years ago, Gramercy High School had budgeted enough money to install a computer lab but not enough to hire someone to maintain it. A parent who worked with computers volunteered her time, but she could work only on weekends when students were not in school. Another solution was offered by students—to use student volunteers who could work in the computer lab during lunch or study breaks. The use of student volunteers has been so successful that other schools in the area are trying the idea.

Analysis: *What is the problem?* The problem is that the school did not budget enough money to pay someone to run the computer lab. *Who has the problem?* Students have a problem if the computers in the lab do not work properly. *Why is it a problem?* Without computers, students do not benefit from having the technology available in the school. *What is the outcome of each solution?* One solution, using a parent volunteer, did not work. A second solution, allowing student volunteers to run the lab, did work. *What is the final result?* The final result is that other schools are now using student volunteers.

## Reading Log, Using

A *reading log* is simply writing about reading. As you read, write down your honest reactions to the text: Ask questions, make associations, and note especially important passages. You can also use a Reading Log to record any prereading or postreading ideas. Because readers have different experiences, interests, beliefs, and opinions, no two Reading Logs will be alike.

## Reading Rate, Adjusting

*Reading rate* is the speed at which you read a text, as shown in the chart below. How quickly or how slowly you read depends on three factors: why you are

### Reading Rates According to Purpose

| Reading Rate | Purpose | Example |
| --- | --- | --- |
| Scanning | Reading for specific details | Hunting for the name of the town that is used as the setting for a short story |
| Skimming | Reading for main points | Reviewing chapter headings, subheadings, and time lines in your history textbook the night before a test |
| Reading for mastery | Reading to understand and remember | Taking notes and outlining a section in your science textbook before you begin your homework |
| Reading for enjoyment | Reading at the speed you find most comfortable | Reading a magazine article about an interest or hobby |

reading—your purpose; the difficulty of the text you are reading; and your background knowledge and experience with the material in the text. Adjusting your reading rate to suit your purpose, the text, and your background knowledge helps you to read more efficiently.

**SQ3R**    *SQ3R* is a popular reading-study strategy. SQ3R stands for the five steps in the reading process:

**S**  *Survey* the entire text. Look briefly at each page—the headings, titles, illustrations, charts, and the material in boldface and italics.

**Q**  *Question* yourself as you do your survey. What should you know after completing your reading? Make a list of questions to be answered.

**R**  *Read* the entire selection. Think of answers to your questions as you read.

**R**  *Recite* in your own words answers to each question.

**R**  *Review* the material by re-reading quickly, looking over the questions, and recalling the answers.

Remember: By responding actively to what you are reading, you are more likely to recall what you have read.

### Stated Main Idea and Supporting Details, Identifying

A *main idea* is the focus or key idea in a piece of writing. Main ideas often appear as topic sentences of paragraphs or in an introductory or concluding paragraph in a longer piece of writing. *Supporting details* support or explain the main idea.

NOTE    A stated main idea is also called an *explicit* main idea. (See also page 91 and **Implied Main Idea, Identifying** on page 833.)

EXAMPLE    Traditional Japanese houses blend with their surroundings. Most are simple, wooden buildings within walled gardens. Rooms are separated by sliding paper screens, which can be removed to allow breezes to blow through the house.

Stated main idea:  Traditional Japanese houses blend with their surroundings.

Supporting details:  They are usually simple wooden buildings with walled gardens. Paper screens are used to separate rooms.

**Summarizing**    A *summary* is a short restatement of the main points of a selection. When you *summarize,* you try to present a complete picture of a text by using as few words as possible. (See also **Summarizing** on page 864.)

EXAMPLE    Between December 26 and January 1, African Americans around the world celebrate Kwanzaa. Friends and families gather together to honor the past and to commit to a positive future. The focus of Kwanzaa is centered around seven principles with particular emphasis on family unity. The celebration has many aspects but usually includes rituals, narratives, poetry, singing, dancing, and feasting.

Summary:  Kwanzaa is a seven-day African American spiritual holiday celebrating family, community, and culture.

**Text Structures, Analyzing**    A *text structure* is the pattern a writer uses to organize ideas or events. Writers commonly use five major patterns of organization: *cause-effect, chronological order, comparison-contrast, listing* and *problem-solution.* Being able to recognize how ideas are related will help you to understand a text. Use the guidelines on the next page to analyze a text structure.

1. **Search the text for the main idea.** Look for clue words that signal a specific pattern of organization. (See also the **Clue Words** chart on page 833.)

2. **Study the text for other important ideas.** Think about how the ideas connect, and look for an obvious pattern.

3. **Remember that a writer might use one organizational pattern throughout an entire text or might combine patterns.** (Professional writers often combine patterns.)

4. **Use a graphic organizer to map the relationships among the ideas.** The five common text structures, or organizational patterns, are illustrated below.

- **Cause-effect pattern** shows the relationship between results and the ideas or events that made the results happen. (See also page 129.) The following example shows how heavy rains (cause) led to damaged crops, lost livestock, lost homes, and casualties (effects).

### Causal Chain

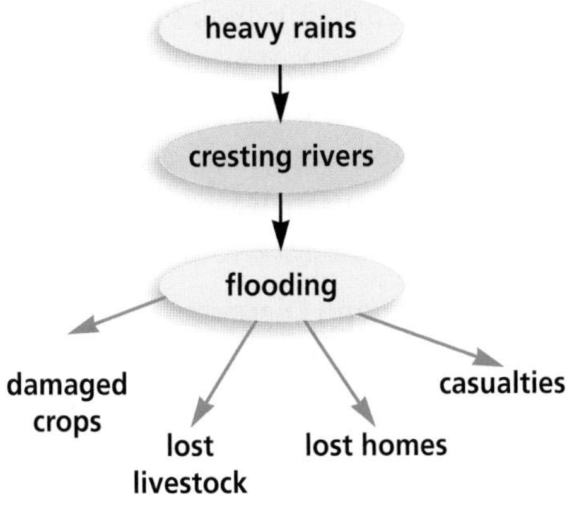

- **Chronological pattern** shows events or ideas happening in sequence. (See also page 359.) The example in the next column shows the sequence for making a smoothie.

### Sequence Chain

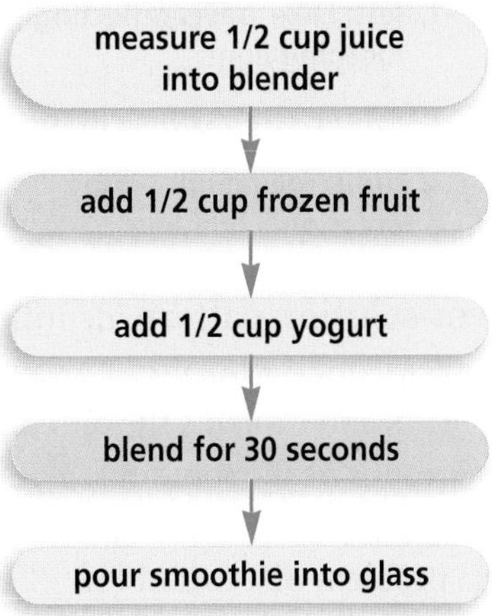

- **Comparison-contrast pattern** points out likenesses and/or differences. (See also page 93.) The following example compares baseball and the British sport of cricket.

### Venn Diagram

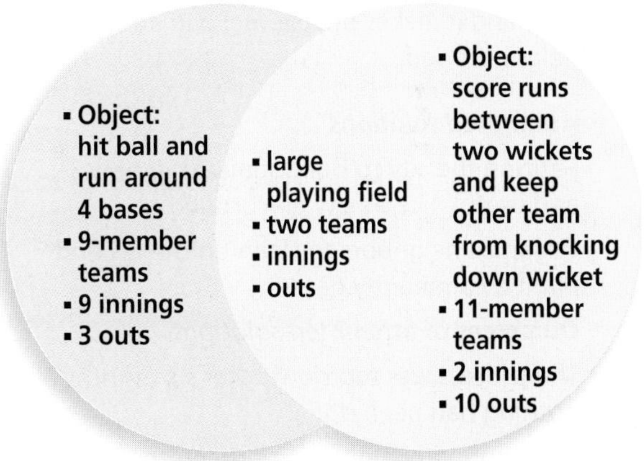

- **Listing pattern** presents material according to certain criteria such as size, location, or importance. The example on the next page lists details according to their location.

## List

1. left: Lake Travis reflecting morning light
2. center: city's skyline in fog
3. right: rolling hills with occasional building

- **Problem-solution pattern** identifies at least one problem, offers one or more solutions to the problem, and explains the outcomes and the final results of the solutions. The following example shows how a neighborhood dealt with the problem of a vacant lot.

### Problem-Solution Analysis

**What is the problem?**

A vacant neighborhood lot is filled with trash and overgrown with weeds.

**Who has the problem?**

The people who live in the neighborhood

**Why is it a problem?**

The lot is a dangerous place for children to play, and it makes people feel bad about the neighborhood.

**Attempted solutions**

Petition the city to build something new and useful, like a new playground

Organize neighbors to clean up the lot and plant a community garden

**Outcomes of attempted solutions**

The process was too slow; after six months nothing had been done.

Once enough neighbors were interested, the lot was cleaned up within a few weeks and then divided into garden plots.

**Final results**

The neighbors eventually turned the lot into a safe, enjoyable place where they could grow flowers and vegetables and meet friends.

## Transitional Words and Phrases, Using

*Transitions* are words and phrases writers use to connect ideas and create coherence. As a reader, your ability to recognize transitions will help you to understand how all the ideas in a selection fit together. (See page 365 for a chart of transitional words and phrases.)

## Visuals and Graphics, Interpreting

*Visuals* and *graphics* convey complex information in a simple, visual format by using pictures or symbols. Well-designed visuals and graphics draw readers to the important information on a page and help them to understand it. Most often, they provide a clear comparison of different but related points of information. As a reader, your task is to interpret the information presented in a visual or graphic and to draw your own conclusions. The most common forms of visuals and graphics are **charts, diagrams, graphs, tables,** and **time lines.**

- **Diagrams** use symbols (such as circles or arrows) or pictures to compare ideas, show a process, or provide instruction. A **Venn diagram** uses intersecting circles to compare two ideas or things. Keep in mind that diagrams should not be used to present numerical data. The shapes and forms used in diagrams are generally not accurate ways to represent amounts.

### Venn Diagram

A   B

Differences   Similarities   Differences

Diagram

**Layers of Soil**

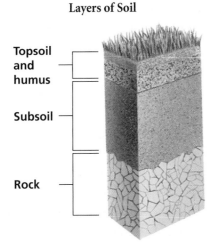

Topsoil and humus

Subsoil

Rock

■ **Line and bar graphs** show changes or trends over time. The horizontal axis in a line or bar graph indicates points in time, and the vertical axis shows quantities. In the following examples, notice how the vertical axis on each graph begins at zero. Having a vertical axis start with zero ensures that the data will be plotted accurately. Check for this when reading line or bar graphs.

Line Graph

**Comparison of Two Students' Study Schedules**

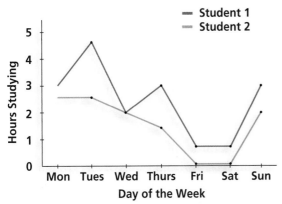

Bar Graph

**Comparison of Two Students' Study Schedules**

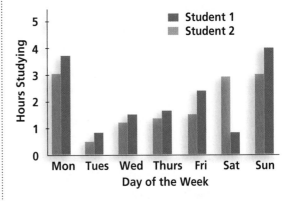

Be wary of any graph that switches the vertical and horizontal axes. If the vertical axis indicates time passing, the resulting peaks and valleys shown on the graph may be misleading.

Reversed Axis Line Graph

**Comparison of Two Students' Study Schedules**

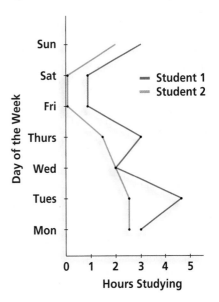

■ **Pie graphs** show the relationships of the parts of a whole to each other. In the following example, notice how the segments of the pie chart are identified as percentages, not as hours. The emphasis in a pie chart is always on the proportions of the sections, not on the specific amounts of each section nor on the value of the whole pie.

**How an Average Student's Day Is Spent**

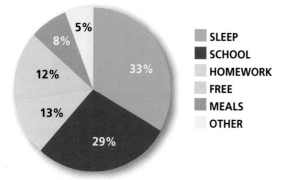

- SLEEP
- SCHOOL
- HOMEWORK
- FREE
- MEALS
- OTHER

■ **Tables** provide information in its least processed form. They do not show trends and patterns in data. Readers must draw their own conclusions about any relationships in the data.

| Number of hours used for study and grade-point averages of students in Language Arts III | | |
|---|---|---|
| Student | Study hours per week | GPA at the end of 1st semester |
| 1 | 15 | 2.8 |
| 2 | 18 | 3.6 |
| 3 | 16 | 3.2 |

■ **Time lines** identify events that take place over the course of time. A time line is basically the horizontal axis of a graph. Events are identified above the time line, and the time periods are indicated below it.

Event 1    Event 2    Event 3    Event 4

Time period   Time period   Time period   Time period

Effective visuals and graphics contain the following elements.

- The **body** presents information in the form of a graph, chart, time line, diagram, or table.
- **Labels** identify and give meaning to the information shown in the graphic.
- A **legend,** or **key,** identifies special symbols, color coding, scales, or other features readers need to know in order to read the graphic; it appears as a small box placed near the body.
- The **source** is where the information contained in the graphic was found.
- A **title** identifies the subject or main idea of the graphic.

As a reader, you should always read graphics or visuals carefully and critically. Keep in mind the following tips:

- **Always read the title, labels, and legend** of any visual or graphic before analyzing the data in a visual or graphic.
- **Draw your own conclusions,** and compare them to those of the writer.
- **Think about the information that is *not* included** in the graphic. Often, important information is left out because it does not match the author's conclusions.
- **Watch out for optical illusions in graphs.** For example, bar graphs and pie charts that are shown in three dimensions are easily misread because some sections look more dense than others.
- **Look for manipulated data** by making sure that the horizontal axis of any graph indicates time, not amount. Also, make sure that the axes of a graph or sections of a pie chart are clearly labeled.

# Vocabulary

**Context Clues**    To find clues to the meaning of an unfamiliar word, you can examine its *context,* the group of words or sentences surrounding the unfamiliar word. The following chart shows examples of the common context clues. (See also pages 27, 96, and 132.)

| How To Use Context Clues |
|---|
| **Type of Clue** |
| **Definitions and Restatements:** Look for words that define the term or restate it in other words. *The judge seemed **impartial**, not favoring one side in the case over the other.* |
| **Examples:** Look for examples used in context that reveal the meaning of an unfamiliar word. *Many **sovereigns** attended the exhibit, including the queen of England and the king of Denmark.* |
| **Synonyms:** Look for clues that indicate an unfamiliar word is similar in meaning to a familiar word or phrase. *Rico, like his overjoyed teammates, was **exultant** about the team's victory.* |
| **Antonyms:** Look for clues that indicate an unfamiliar word is opposite in meaning to a familiar word or phrase. *Instead of being stormy, the weather turned **balmy** in the afternoon.* |
| **Cause and Effect:** Look for clues that show an unfamiliar word is related to the cause or is the result of an action, feeling, or idea. *Because his pet lizard was lost, Mark felt **dejected**.* |

**Word Bank**    A *word bank* is a list of words that you create from your reading, listening, and viewing. Storing new words in a word bank is a good way to increase your vocabulary. Check your dictionary for the meaning of each new word. You may want to compile your personal word bank in a notebook or on a computer file.

**Word Meanings**    Words have many layers of meanings. Their messages can change depending on the time, the place, and the situation in which they are used. Use the following definitions and examples to help you make sure that your words say what you want them to.

- **Analogies**    In an *analogy,* you are asked to analyze the relationship between two words and then identify another pair of words that has the same relationship. Analogy questions often appear on standardized tests because they measure your knowledge of vocabulary as well as your ability to identify relationships and patterns between words.

  EXAMPLE
  1. COOKING : CHEF ::    *C*
  **A.** snow : cold          **C.** shaving : barber
  **B.** drinking : water     **D.** running : jumping

- **Clichés**    A *cliché* is a tired expression. Its overuse has made its message weak and boring. You can use a thesaurus or a dictionary of synonyms to find livelier, more precise words.

  EXAMPLES    busy as a bee, quick as a flash, accidents will happen, last but not least

- **Denotation and connotation**    The *denotation* of a word is its direct, plainly expressed meaning—the meaning a dictionary lists. The *connotation* is the meaning suggested by or associated with the word. Because connotations often stir people's feelings, they can have powerful effects on the listener or reader.

EXAMPLE   The words *proud* and *arrogant* have similar denotations, but they suggest different ideas. *Proud* can suggest self-respect and a sense of accomplishment. *Arrogant,* on the other hand, has negative connotations of snobbishness or a kind of superior attitude.

■ **Euphemisms**   A *euphemism* is an agreeable-sounding term that is substituted for a more direct, less pleasant-sounding one. Some euphemisms are used as a courtesy to avoid offending people; however, others are used to mislead people—to hide unpleasant truths or misrepresent the facts.

| Euphemism | More Direct Term |
|---|---|
| passed away | died |
| underprivileged | poor |
| sanitation engineer | garbage collector |

■ **Figurative language**   *Figurative language* goes beyond the literal meaning of the words to create a special effect or feeling. The following chart shows the most common types of figurative language.

| Type of Figurative Language | Example |
|---|---|
| A **metaphor** says that something *is* something else. | *The night is a dark cloak.* |
| **Personification** gives human characteristics to nonhuman things. | *With open arms, the cozy chair beckoned me.* |
| A **simile** compares two basically unlike things, using the words *like* or *as*. | *Jumping the hurdle, she looked like a graceful deer.* |

■ **Idioms**   *Idioms* are phrases that mean something different from the literal meanings of the words. Idioms often can't be explained grammatically, and they make no sense if translated word-for-word into another language.

EXAMPLES
I tried to call you, but you were *on the phone.*
We *talked out* the problem.
Suzanne really *gets into* soccer.

■ **Jargon**   *Jargon* is a special language used by groups of people who share the same profession, occupation, hobby, or field of study. Jargon is effective only if the reader or listener is familiar with its special meaning. Note in the following example how the word *lead* can mean different things to different groups.

EXAMPLE   *lead*
Card players—the act of playing first
Electricians—a wire that carries current
Journalists—the opening paragraph of a news story
Musicians—the main melody in a musical composition

■ **Loaded words**   Words that are intended to provoke strong feeling, either positive or negative, are called **loaded words.** A writer or speaker who wants to prejudice you for or against something may appeal to your emotions with loaded words.

EXAMPLE
After suffering *defeat* in last week's election, Senator Blank addressed a *mere handful of people* last night at the Civic Center.
After suffering a *setback* in last week's election, Senator Blank addressed a *small but spirited audience* last night at the Civic Center.

- **Multiple meanings** Many English words have more than one meaning. When you use a dictionary to find a word's meaning, look at all the definitions given. Keep in mind the context in which you read or heard the word. Then, try the various definitions in that context until you find the one that fits.

EXAMPLE

My cousin has a *berth* as a summer lifeguard. (The third definition best fits the meaning in context.)
**berth** (burth) *n.* **1.** the space necessary for safety between a ship and another object **2.** a ship's place at anchor **3.** a position or job **4.** a place to sleep on a ship, train, or airplane

- **Tired words** A *tired word* is one that has lost its freshness and force. It has been used so often and so carelessly that it has become worn-out and almost meaningless. (See also **Clichés** on page 841.)

EXAMPLES nice, fine, pretty, wonderful, terrific, great

**Word Origins** The *origin* of a word is its coming into existence. The origin and history of a word—its etymology—often appear in brackets along with its dictionary definition. The following etymology indicates that the word *victory* came to Middle English (ME) from Old French (OFr) and Latin (L).

EXAMPLE: **victory** [ME < OFr *victorie* < L *victoria* < *victor*]

**Word Parts** Most English words are made up of smaller units called *word parts.* The three types of word parts are *roots, prefixes,* and *suffixes.* Knowing the meanings of these word parts can help you determine the meanings of many unfamiliar words.

- **Roots** The *root* is the foundation on which a word is built. It carries the word's core meaning, and it is the part to which prefixes and suffixes are added.

## Commonly Used Roots

| Roots | Meanings | Examples |
|---|---|---|
| *Greek* | | |
| –bibli–, –biblio– | book | bibliography, bibliophile |
| –chron– | time | chronological, synchronize |
| –dem– | people | democracy, epidemic |
| –graph– | write, writing | autograph, geography |
| –log(ue)–, –logy– | study, word | logic, mythology |
| –micro– | small | microbe, microscope |
| –phil– | love | audiophile, philharmonic |
| –phon– | sound | phonograph, euphony |
| –sym–, –syn– | with, together | symphony, synchronize |
| *Latin* | | |
| –aud–, –audit– | hear | audible, auditorium |
| –bene– | well, good | benefit, benevolent |
| –cis– | cut | incision, concise |
| –cogn– | know | recognize, cognition |
| –duc–, –duct– | lead | educate, conductor |
| –fid– | belief, faith | fidelity, infidel |

*(continued)*

| Roots | Meanings | Examples |
|---|---|---|
| –gen– | birth, kind, origin | generate, generic, generous |
| –ject– | throw | projectile, reject |
| –loqu–, –loc– | talk, speech | eloquent, locution |
| –magn– | large | magnitude, magnify |
| –mal– | bad | malady, dismal |
| –mit–, –miss– | send | remit, emissary |
| –ped– | foot | pedal, quadruped |
| –pend–, –pens– | hang, weigh | pendant, suspense |
| –port– | carry, bear | export, important |
| –tract– | pull, draw | tractor, extract |
| –vis–, –vid– | see | visible, videotape |

■ **Prefixes**   A *prefix* is a word part that is added before a root. The word that is created from a prefix and a root combines the meanings of both its parts.

| Prefixes | Meanings | Examples |
|---|---|---|
| **Commonly Used Prefixes** | | |
| *Greek* | | |
| anti– | against, opposing | antipathy, antithesis |
| dia– | through, across, between | diagonal, diameter |
| hemi– | half | hemisphere, hemitrophic |
| syn–, sym–, syl–, sys– | together, with | synchronize, sympathy, syllable, system |
| *Latin* | | |
| bi– | two | bimonthly, bisect |
| co–, col–, com–, con–, cor– | with, together | coexist, collide, compare, convene, correspond |
| de– | away, from, off, down | defect, desert, decline |
| in–, im– | in, into, within | induct, impose |
| inter– | between, among | intercede, international |
| non– | not | nonsense, non-cooperative |
| post– | after, following | postpone, postscript |
| pre– | before | prevent, predisposed |
| re– | back, backward, again | revoke, recede, recur |
| sub–, suf–, sum–, sup–, sus– | under, beneath | subjugate, suffuse, summon, suppose, suspect |
| trans– | across, beyond | transmission, transfer |

QUICK REFERENCE HANDBOOK

## Commonly Used Prefixes

| Prefixes | Meanings | Examples |
|---|---|---|
| *Old English* | | |
| mis– | badly, not, wrongly | misfire, misspell |
| over– | above, excessive | oversee, overdo |
| un– | not, reverse of | untrue, unfold |

■ **Suffixes**   A *suffix* is a word part that is added after a root. Often, adding or changing a suffix will change both a word's meaning and its part of speech, as in *please/pleasure. Please* is a verb; *pleasure* is a noun.

## Commonly Used Suffixes

| Suffixes | Meanings | Examples |
|---|---|---|
| *Greek, Latin, and French* | | |
| *Nouns* | | |
| –ance, –ancy | act, quality | acceptance, hesitancy |
| –ity | state, condition | possibility, ability |
| –ment | result, action | disappointment |
| –tion | action, condition | selection, relation |
| *Adjectives* | | |
| –able | able, likely | capable, changeable |
| –ible | able, likely | flexible, possible |
| –ous | characterized by | religious, furious |
| *Adjectives or Nouns* | | |
| –ant, –ent | actor, showing | servant, confident |
| –ite | formed, showing | composite, favorite |
| *Verbs* | | |
| –ate | become, cause | populate, activate |
| –fy | make, cause | identify, glorify |
| –ize | make, cause to be | sterilize, idealize |
| *Old English* | | |
| *Nouns* | | |
| –dom | state, condition | freedom, wisdom |
| –hood | state, condition | childhood, falsehood |
| –ness | quality, state | softness, shortness |
| *Adjectives* | | |
| –en | made of, like | wooden, golden |
| –ish | suggesting, like | foolish, childish |
| *Verbs* | | |
| –en | cause to be | deepen, darken |

**Words to Learn** The 300 words in the list below may be used as the basis of your vocabulary study this year. Make it a habit to learn unfamiliar words from this list regularly.

abhor
abrasive
acclaim
acknowledge
adage
addicted
adversary
advocate
affected
affirmation
agility
agitation
alleged
allusion
aloof
alteration
amends
amity
animated
annals
apathy
apparition
applicable
arrogance
assess
asterisk
attribute
authenticity
autonomous

belligerent
benefactor
benign
bibliography
bilingual
biographical
bizarre
bland
brochure

buoyant

cadence
carnivorous
cascade
centrifugal
chivalry
chronic
chronological
circumscribe
citadel
clamber
collaborate
collateral
collective
comply
condolence
congeniality
congruent
connive
conspiracy
contaminate
contemptible
convey
cope
credentials
culmination
cumbersome
cynic

deficient
defile
defraud
demoralize
denote
denounce
depict
depreciate
devout
dexterity

diligent
discredit
discreet
discretion
disperse
disrupt
dissuade
docile
drastic
dubious
dupe
dwindle

elapse
elude
emerge
emissary
encore
entice
epic
equation
eradicate
essence
evict
exasperate
expend
exploit
extremely
extrovert

fallacy
fauna
fervent
figurative
flora
fluent
formidable
frenzied
frivolous
functional

galvanize
garb
gaudy
genealogy

genial
granular
grueling

haphazard
havoc
hectic
herald
hereditary
hideous
hindrance
hoax
homage
horde
humanitarian
humanoid
hypothetical

ideally
ideology
immaterial
immunity
impertinent
implement
inaudible
incalculable
incandescent
incessant
incompatible
incomprehensible
inconspicuous
inconvenient
indivisible
induction
infamous
infest
inflammation
influential
ingenuous
initiative
instigate
intact
intensive
intervention
intimate

intimidate
intonation
inventory
inverse
invigorating
irony
irreducible
irretrievable

jaunt
jovial
jurisdiction

kindle

landlocked
larceny
lavish
lax
lethal
liability

maintenance
malicious
manifest
manipulate
meander
medieval
meditate
medley
metamorphosis
metaphor
mimic
misconstrue
moor
morbid
murky

necessitate
negotiate

nimble
nominal
nonchalant

objective
obsession
obtuse
omen
ominous
opaque
oppressive
optimistic
oratory
orthodox
ostracize
ovation

palatial
panorama
paramount
passive
perceptible
perennial
perspective
pessimistic
plaintiff
plaintive
ponderous
potency
potion
precedent
predatory
predominant
premature
preposterous
priority
promenade
prominence

prospective
prowess
pungent

quest
quorum
quota

radical
raucous
ravenous
recede
recession
reconcile
relevant
reluctant
repast
replenish
replica
reprimand
resourceful
retract
retrieve
rostrum

sage
satirical
sector
seethe
simile
sinister
skeptical
smug
soliloquy
solvent
somber
sovereign
sparse

spurn
stagnant
statute
subsequent
superfluous
surmount
surpass
susceptible

tantalizing
tentative
thesis
tolerate
transcribe
transpire
tripod
trivial
turbulent
tycoon

ultimate
uncanny
undergo
unkempt
unscrupulous
upheaval

vanity
veneer
venerable
virtual
volatile

wary
wrangle
wry

yearn

# Speaking and Listening

## Speaking

Casual conversations with family and friends account for most of the occasions upon which you speak. There are times, however, when you will be required to speak in situations that are not so casual. For every speaking occasion there are certain **conventions of oral language** you should observe. These conventions are the generally agreed upon rules and regulations of oral communication—the proper grammar, vocabulary, and style to use for different audiences, occasions, and purposes. For example, you would not use the same grammar, vocabulary, and style to respond to questions during a job interview that you would to recount an anecdote to a group of friends. No matter what the situation, you can use certain strategies and techniques to become a better speaker.

### Debate

A *debate* involves two groups or teams who publicly discuss a controversial topic in a systematic way. The topic under discussion is called the *proposition*. One team, the *affirmative team,* argues that the proposition should be accepted. The other side, the *negative team,* argues that the proposition should be rejected.

**Features of a Debate**    While there are different formats for debates, some features are common to all of them.

- **Debate proposition**    The issue in a debate is a proposition that is phrased as a resolution and limited to a specific idea. The proposition should be an issue that gives each side an equal chance to build a reasonable case. The proposition should be clearly stated so that debaters and the audience can easily understand it. An example of a clear and debatable proposition is "Resolved: That research on alternatives to fossil fuels should be substantially increased."

- **Debate etiquette**    Proper etiquette, or manners, is required of debaters. Ridicule, sarcasm, and personal attacks are not acceptable. A debate should be won or lost only on the basis of a well-prepared case convincingly delivered. Also, it is customary to refer to debaters with polite terms such as "the first affirmative speaker," "my worthy opponent," "my colleagues," or "my teammates."

- **Debate officials**    A chairperson often rules over a debate. A debater may appeal to the chairperson if he or she believes that any debating rules have been broken by the opposing team. The most common method of determining the winner of a debate is by the decision of three appointed judges. Occasionally, an audience may vote to determine the winning team.

**Formats of Debate**   Most debates are divided into two parts. In the first part, both sides make constructive speeches, attempting to build their cases by presenting their arguments for or against the proposition and anticipating and attempting to disprove the points of the opposing side. Then, after an intermission, both sides make rebuttal speeches, trying to reply to the other side's best arguments. Specific time limits are assigned for each speech, although these limits vary depending on the type of debate.

- **Traditional, or formal, debate**   This debate format has two speakers on a team. Each member of each team speaks twice within set time limits.

- **Cross-examination debate**   This type of debate also features two affirmative and two negative speakers. In this debate format, participants are allowed to question opponents. During this cross-examination period, a speaker can clarify issues and point out weaknesses in an opponent's position.

- **Lincoln-Douglas debate**   This type of debate commemorates the famous debates between two candidates for senator from Illinois in 1858—Abraham Lincoln and Stephen A. Douglas. This format features one affirmative speaker and one negative speaker debating a proposition.

**Preparing for Debate**   To be an effective debater, you must prepare carefully by researching the proposition thoroughly, just as you would if you were writing a research paper. You also must identify the *issues,* or main differences, between your position and the position of the opposing team. You must organize support for your arguments in the form of examples, expert testimony, statistics, and logical reasons. You must also organize all your arguments and supporting evidence into a *brief,* an outline of your team's position in the debate. A brief is like a detailed sentence outline of an argumentative essay. Next, you must be prepared to *refute,* or disprove, your opponents' arguments with the same sort of evidence you used to build your own case—logical reasons, facts, statistics, and the like. Last, you must anticipate your opponents' refutations so that you can prepare a *rebuttal,* a rebuilding of your case in which you repair the damage that was done to your arguments when your opponents refuted them.

## Formal Speaking Occasions

Formal speaking is done at a specific time and place and for a specific reason. There are steps you can take to prepare for every formal speaking occasion.

**Formal Speeches**   Formal speeches do not simply happen; like book reports or research papers, they require time and thoughtful preparation. The process of preparing a formal speech is similar to the process of writing a paper. To prepare a formal speech, follow the steps explained below.

1. **Identify your purpose**   Begin the process of preparing a speech by identifying the purpose for your speech. Your general *purpose* is the overall reason you are giving your speech. Most often the purpose of a speech is to inform or to persuade an audience. Common purposes for giving speeches are described in the chart on the next page.

| General Types of Speeches | | |
| --- | --- | --- |
| **Type of Speech** | **Purpose** | **Examples** |
| Informative Speech | To present new information to an audience or to provide a new view of old information | <ul><li>Lecture</li><li>News broadcast</li><li>Orientation</li><li>Instruction</li></ul> |
| Persuasive Speech | To change an attitude or belief or to move an audience to action | <ul><li>Campaign speech</li><li>Advertisement</li><li>Debate</li></ul> |
| Special Occasion Speech | To entertain or amuse an audience or to acknowledge a special reason for the audience's presence | <ul><li>After-dinner speech</li><li>Anecdote</li><li>Oral interpretation of a piece of literature</li><li>Speech honoring a retiring teacher</li></ul> |

2. **Select a topic** If you may choose the topic of your speech instead of speaking on an assigned topic, be sure to pick a topic in which you are interested. If you are not enthusiastic about your topic, you cannot expect your audience to be enthusiastic. Consider the answers to the following questions in selecting your topic.

- *What is the occasion of your speech?* What, in other words, prompts you to speak? For example, have you been asked to speak on behalf of your scout troop to a group of veterans on Memorial Day? Your topic should fit the occasion.
- *How much time will you have to deliver your speech?* You have to limit the scope of your speech to fit the time you are given.

3. **Analyze the audience** Once you select your topic, you must think about how to tailor your speech to your audience's needs or interests. Use the following questions for adapting material to a particular audience.

- *What does the audience already know about the topic?* Provide enough back-

ground for your audience to understand your speech. Some audiences might need extensive background information. Others might need none.

- *How interested will the audience be in your topic?* The degree of the audience's interest in your topic should influence the content of your speech. An uninterested audience needs to be convinced that the topic is worthwhile. An interested audience needs to hear information that will justify and maintain their interest.

4. **Gather material and organize content** The next step in preparing a speech is to research the topic you have selected. (For more on the **library or media center,** see "The Library/Media Center" section of the Quick Reference Handbook. For more on **taking notes and preparing outlines,** refer to the "Study Skills" and "Writing" sections of the Quick Reference Handbook.)

5. **Write the speech** In writing your speech, you must think about three things: the structure of your speech, the language you use,

## Features of a Formal Speech

### Structure

The speech should be composed of three parts:

- an *introduction* with a thesis statement or main idea
- a *body*
- a *conclusion*

### Language

The language you use should be appropriate for your audience. Keep in mind the following points.

- Use formal, standard English.
- Use technical terms sparingly and be sure to define them.
- Avoid slang and jargon.

### Audience Involvement

It is important to remember that written English sounds different when it is delivered orally. Make your speech more "listener-friendly" by doing the following:

- Use personal pronouns. For example, say "you may think" or "we believe" instead of "one may think" or "people believe."
- Ask questions instead of making statements. For example, instead of telling the audience a fact or statistic, ask them "Did you know that . . . ?" A question like this, which is not meant to be answered but is asked only for effect, is called a *rhetorical question.*

and the way you involve your audience in your material. The chart above shows you the basic features of a formal speech.

6. **Determine method of delivery**   Now you need to decide how you will deliver your speech. There are several methods, each of which has advantages and disadvantages.

- The *manuscript speech* is read word-for-word from your written manuscript. This method allows little chance for mistakes, but it does not permit you to respond to audience feedback and often sounds dull and lifeless.

- The *memorized speech* is memorized word-for-word from your written manuscript. This method does give you the freedom to move around and to maintain eye contact with the audience, but it may sound stiff and unnatural. With this method, you also run the risk of forgetting parts of the speech.

- The *extemporaneous speech* is carefully outlined and rehearsed but not memorized. This method sounds natural and allows you to respond to the audience, but requires much rehearsal time. When you organize your materials for an extemporaneous speech, first write out a complete outline. Then, using the guidelines below, prepare note cards that you may refer to as you present your speech.

## Guidelines for Extemporaneous Speech Note Cards

1. Put only one key idea, possibly accompanied by a brief example or detail, on each card.

2. Make a special note card for material that you plan to read word-for-word, such as a quotation, a series of dates, or a list of statistics.

3. Make a special note card to indicate when you should pause to show a graphic, such as a chart, diagram, graph, picture, or model.

4. Number your completed cards to keep them in order.

7. **Rehearse the speech** You will give a better and more convincing presentation if you rehearse. One of the ways an audience will judge your presentation is by your use of **nonverbal** and **verbal signals.** You use these signals any time you speak, but they are especially noticeable in a formal speech.

- *Nonverbal Signals* In addition to communicating with words, you can communicate with nonverbal signals, like those described in the following chart.

### Communicating with Nonverbal Signals

| Nonverbal signals | Tips and Effects |
| --- | --- |
| **Eye contact** | Look directly into the eyes of as many members of the audience as you can. Eye contact communicates honesty and sincerity. It makes the audience feel as if you are speaking *with* them rather than *to* them. |
| **Facial expression** | Facial expressions—smiling, frowning, raising an eyebrow, and so on—can reveal your feelings and add to or even take the place of a verbal message. |
| **Gesture** | Making relaxed and natural gestures with your head, hands, or arms as you speak emphasizes verbal messages. Nodding the head for "yes" or shaking it for "no" or pointing with the index finger can effectively punctuate your speech. |
| **Posture** | Stand up straight and look alert to communicate an air of confidence to your audience. |

- *Verbal Signals* Use your voice expressively when you deliver a speech. The following verbal signals will help you communicate your message to an audience.

### Communicating with Verbal Signals

| Verbal signals | Tips |
| --- | --- |
| **Diction** (the clarity of your pronunciation) | Always speak clearly and carefully so that your listeners can understand you. |
| **Emphasis** (the stress put on a word or phrase) | Emphasize key ideas or points in your speech by saying those words with a little more volume than you have been using. |
| **Pause** (small silences in your speech) | Use pauses to help listeners catch up or to suggest that what you have said or are about to say is important. |
| **Pitch** (the highness or lowness of your voice) | A nervous speaker's pitch tends to be high. Take a deep breath and relax before you speak to keep your pitch natural. |
| **Rate** (the speed at which you talk) | Normal speed is about 120 to 160 words per minute. When delivering a speech, speak at a slower-than-normal rate. |
| **Volume** (the level of sound you create) | Although you might not be used to speaking loudly, your audience appreciates the extra volume. Be sure to ask listeners if they can hear you before you begin your speech. |

**8. Deliver the speech** Most amateur speakers are nervous before delivering a speech. Here are some suggestions for keeping nervousness from interfering with your speech.

- *Be prepared.* Avoid excessive nervousness by organizing and being familiar with your speech notes and any audiovisual devices you plan to use.
- *Practice your speech.* Rehearse as if you are actually delivering your speech.
- *Focus on your purpose for speaking.* Think about what you want your listeners to do, believe, or feel as a result of your speech.
- *Pay attention to audience feedback.* Different audiences will react differently to your speech. Pay attention to the messages the audience sends you. Are people in the audience alert or are they yawning? Are they shaking their heads in disagreement or nodding in agreement? Depending upon the feedback you receive from the audience, you might need to adjust your pace, use more gestures, or speak more loudly to keep their attention.

**9. Use audiovisual devices (if appropriate)** Audiovisual devices are resources that you use to clarify or add to your presentation. Some audiovisual devices that are often used in multimedia presentations are listed below.

- audio recordings (such as cassettes or compact discs)
- images, audio files, and text stored and presented on a computer
- videotapes or videodiscs
- short films
- slides or filmstrips
- graphics such as charts, graphs, illustrations, and diagrams

Use the following questions to determine whether your presentation will benefit from the use of audiovisual devices.

- *Will audiovisual devices help you clarify a point?* Some ideas are easily explained, but others need a visual to help clarify them. Using a chart or a poster will save you time and keep the audience on track.
- *Will the audiovisual devices help the audience remember a point?* Not every point in your speech is equally important. Decide which points will benefit from the emphasis given by the audiovisual.
- *Will the audiovisual devices distract the audience while you are speaking?* Make sure that the audiovisual devices are essential to your talk and can be displayed without distracting the audience.

NOTE Make certain your audience can see or hear the audiovisual device you have chosen. Audio materials should be cued up. Graphics should be large and clear enough to be seen from the back of the audience. (See also **Graphics and Visuals** on page 813.)

**Group Discussion** A *formal group discussion* occurs when clubs, organizations, and other groups meet to discuss issues of importance. Formal groups often follow an established set of rules known as *parliamentary procedure.* The basic principles of parliamentary procedure, listed below, protect the rights of the individual members of the group while providing a system for dealing with issues that come before the group.

- The majority decides.
- The minority has the right to be heard.
- Decisions are made by voting.
- Only one issue is decided at a time.
- Everyone has the right to be heard and to vote.
- All votes are counted as equal.
- All sides of an issue are debated openly.

# Interviewing

An *interview* is a communication situation in which one person, the *interviewer*, gathers ideas or firsthand information from another person, the *interviewee*.

■ **Conducting an interview** Successful interviews require careful planning. The following chart provides useful suggestions for planning and conducting an interview.

### Conducting an Interview

**Preparing for the Interview**
- Make arrangements well in advance. Set up a time that is convenient for the other person to meet with you.
- Make a list of questions to ask. Make sure the questions are arranged in a logical order and require more than yes or no answers.

**Participating in the Interview**
- Arrive on time; be polite and patient.
- Ask the other person's permission to take notes or use a tape recorder.
- Avoid argument. Be tactful and courteous. Remember the interview was granted at your request.
- Listen carefully, and ask follow-up questions if you do not understand an answer or if you think you need more information.

**Following up on the Interview**
- Review your notes to refresh your memory, and then make a summary of the material you have gathered.
- Send a note expressing your appreciation for the interview.

■ **Interviewing for a job** A job interview can be a nerve-racking situation; being thoroughly prepared to be interviewed can relieve some of the anxiety. The following chart tells you how to be a successful interviewee.

### How to Interview for a Position

1. **Arrange an appointment.** Write a business letter of application in which you request an interview for a job. If you are granted an interview, be prompt for your appointment.

2. **Bring a résumé.** If you have not already submitted a résumé, take one to the interview and give it to the interviewer. (See also **Résumés** on page 900.)

3. **Be neat and well groomed.** It is important to look your best when you are interviewing for any type of job.

4. **Answer questions clearly and honestly.** Answer the questions the interviewer asks, adding any additional information that might inform the employer that you are the right person for the job.

5. **Ask questions.** Questions that job applicants usually ask include requests for information about work hours, salary, or chances for advancement. By your questions, show that you know something about the company or business.

6. **Be prepared to be tested.** The employer may require you to take tests that demonstrate your skills, intelligence, or personality.

7. **Follow up the interview.** After the interview, write a short thank-you note. Tell the interviewer that you appreciated the opportunity for the interview and that you look forward to hearing from the company in the near future.

# Informal Speaking Occasions

Informal communication involves sharing information in casual situations. Unlike formal speaking situations, in which you are usually at a distance from your audience, informal speaking situations are more personal. The chart below describes some common informal speaking situations and some strategies for dealing with them.

**Informal Group Discussion** *Informal group discussion* takes place when a small group of people meets for a particular purpose. The following section explains two elements of group discussion.

- **Identifying a purpose** When the group has a specific purpose or goal, the point of the discussion is how to achieve that purpose or goal. Every group discussion should begin

| Informal Speaking Situations | | |
|---|---|---|
| **Situation** | **Purpose** | **Preparation and Presentation** |
| Directions | To explain how to get to a particular place (Informational situation) | • Choose easiest route.<br>• Divide the route into logical steps.<br>• Use terms that are accurate or visual. If necessary, draw a map. |
| Impromptu speech | To speak on the spur of the moment, without any preparation (Informational or persuasive situation) | • If you choose the topic, think of one that is appropriate for your audience.<br>• Think of a main idea, an interesting beginning, and some supporting ideas.<br>• Speak clearly and in a confident voice.<br>• Use a tone that is appropriate to the topic. |
| Instructions | To give information on how to do a particular task (Informational situation) | • Divide the information into clear, logical steps.<br>• Give the steps in order.<br>• Make sure your listener understands. |
| Introductions | To introduce yourself or another person to a person or group (Social situation) | • Take the initiative and introduce yourself if no one else does.<br>• When introducing another person, identify the person by name.<br>• When introducing another person, it is customary to address first<br>  • a person of higher status<br>  • an older person before a younger one<br>  • the person you know better. |
| Telephone conversations | To communicate via telephone (Social situation) | • Call people at appropriate times of day.<br>• Identify yourself and state the reason for your call.<br>• Be polite and patient.<br>• Keep your call to an appropriate length. |

with the announcement of the purpose of the discussion. Below are typical purposes for group discussion.

### Purposes for Discussion

- to brainstorm ideas
- to learn cooperatively
- to make a decision, evaluation, or recommendation
- to make plans
- to negotiate agreements
- to solve a problem
- to resolve conflicts

■ **Participating in Discussion**    Each member of a group discussion has certain responsibilities.

**All group members:** All members of a group discussion are responsible for paying attention to the discussion, respecting all group members' opinions, and offering thoughtful comments.

**Chairperson:** If a group has chosen a discussion leader or chairperson, he or she is responsible for introducing, guiding, moderating, and closing the discussion. The chairperson helps resolve any conflicts between members and makes sure that the group stays focused on its purpose or goal.

**Group Secretary or Recorder:** One person from the group usually is asked to take notes on important points or decisions made during a discussion. The group secretary or recorder is responsible for these notes and for reading them aloud at the beginning of the next group discussion.

## Oral Interpretation

In an *oral interpretation,* you present your ideas about the meaning of a work of literature by reading the work aloud. You use speaking and acting skills—vocal techniques, facial expression, body language, and gestures—to express your interpretation of the literary work. The following steps help in preparing an oral interpretation.

1. **Find and cut material**    When you look for material for an oral interpretation, you usually have a specific purpose,  audience, and occasion in mind. As a general rule, no props or costumes are required for oral interpretation. For your oral interpretation, you will need to make an abbreviated version, or *cutting,* of a work of fiction or nonfiction, poetry, or drama. Use the following guidelines:
   - Follow the story line of the literary work in time order.
   - Delete tag lines, such as "she replied sadly." Instead, use these clues to tell you how to interpret the character's words as you express them.
   - Delete passages that do not contribute to the overall effect or impression you intend to create with your oral interpretation.

2. **Prepare the reading script**    A reading script is usually typed (double-spaced) and can be marked to assist you in your interpretive reading. For example, you might underline words to remind you to use special emphasis or make a slash (/) to indicate where you would like a dramatic pause.

3. **Rehearse your interpretation**    Once you have developed a reading script, rehearse different interpretations. Pronounce words carefully. Use body language and gestures to emphasize the meaning or to reveal traits of the major characters in the story as you narrate and act out what they say and do.

4. **Deliver your presentation**    To begin your presentation, introduce the piece of literature you are interpreting. Give your audience information that sets the scene, tells something about the author, or gives some necessary details about what has already taken place in the story. Then, deliver your interpretation.

# Listening

Active listening involves more than hearing a speaker's words. When you listen actively, you receive verbal and nonverbal messages and construct meanings for and respond to those messages.

## Basics of the Listening Process

Listening is an indispensable part of the communication process. The stages in the listening process are explained in the following chart.

---

### The Three Stages of the Listening Process

**Before you listen**

**Be physically and mentally prepared to listen.** To be an effective listener, you should be physically comfortable and free of distractions that interfere with your ability to focus.

**Determine your reason for listening.** Are you listening to be entertained? to be informed? to provide support or understanding? to receive instructions or directions? Identifying a reason for listening sets you up as an active listener.

**Decide what you already know about the speaker and the subject.** Bringing your prior knowledge of a subject or of a speaker to the

surface can make your listening experience more productive.

**Add to your prior knowledge of the speaker and the subject.** Brainstorming with others or doing individual research to increase your knowledge of the speaker and subject will improve your ability to understand and evaluate both.

**Keep an open mind.** Set aside any biases, prejudices, or preconceived notions you might have concerning the speaker or the topic of the speech. Make your judgments after listening to what the speaker has to say.

---

**As you listen**

**Make connections to prior knowledge and experience.** Try to relate what the speaker is saying to what you know from other sources—experience, books and magazines, television, school, and so on.

**Think of questions you would like to ask the speaker.** You may or may not have an opportunity to ask the speaker to clarify a point or expand upon an idea, but making

yourself think of questions helps you to focus on the speaker's meaning.

**Make educated guesses about what a speaker will say next.** If you are wrong, try to determine what misled you.

**Find meaning behind what the speaker says directly.** Make inferences about a speaker's attitudes or opinions by paying attention to what he or she does not say.

---

**After you listen**

**Discuss the speaker and his or her message with others.** Exchange ideas, agree or disagree with the speaker's opinions, and relate the speaker's words to your experience.

**Write a summary and evaluation of the speaker and the presentation.** Writing about a presentation clarifies and solidifies your thoughts and opinions.

## Evaluating Yourself as a Listener

For oral communication to be effective, you must be a good listener. In fact, the listener carries as much of the responsibility for clear communication as the speaker does. Therefore, it is important for you to be able to evaluate yourself as a listener. The following chart gives several of the points you should look for when you are evaluating yourself as a listener.

| Evaluating Yourself as a Listener |
|---|
| *A good listener should* <br><br> • be mentally and physically prepared to listen <br> • be able to ignore distracting behavior by the speaker and members of the audience <br> • focus on the speaker throughout the presentation <br> • follow the organization of the speaker's presentation <br> • distinguish between facts and opinions <br> • think of questions to ask the speaker <br> • determine the speaker's main idea and primary supporting details <br> • withhold judgment until the presentation is over <br> • listen for and detect bias or prejudice on the speaker's part <br> • reflect upon the presentation after it is over <br> • ask questions of the speaker if given the opportunity <br> • discuss the presentation with others <br> • write a summary or evaluation of the presentation |

## Four Types of Listening

There are four basic types of listening and a number of purposes associated with each type.

### Appreciative (or Aesthetic) Listening

The purpose of this type of listening is enjoyment. When you listen to someone read a story or a poem, you are engaged in appreciative listening. There are certain strategies that can make this type of listening experience more rewarding.

■ **Before you listen, activate what you know about the literary work you will hear presented.** What do you know about the work, the author, or other works by the same author? To what literary *genre,* or type, does the work belong? What literary elements—conflict, imagery, character, figurative language, climax, rhyme—are important in this type of literature? Make predictions about what you might hear.

■ **While you listen, make connections to other literary works and to your personal experiences.** Does the presentation remind you of something else you have read, seen, or heard? Do any of the descriptions remind you of places you have been, people you have known, or feelings you have had? Try to visualize—see in your mind's eye—what you are hearing.

■ **After you listen, discuss the presentation with others and evaluate it.** Were your predictions correct or incorrect? Can you determine the reason for any incorrect predictions? What literary and artistic qualities did you find as you listened? Was the speaker's presentation clear? Did the speaker use the appropriate body language? Did the speaker speak effectively? Write what you liked and did not like about the presentation and why.

**Critical Listening** In this type of listening, you attempt to understand, analyze, and evaluate the speaker's points and the value of the ideas. Critical listening should be applied to messages heard in school, in the workplace, or in the media. You can use the strategies in the following chart to analyze and evaluate media presentations as well as live presentations.

| How to Listen Critically | |
|---|---|
| **What to do** | **What to listen for** |
| Identify the speaker's purpose. | Does the speaker make clear why he or she is giving the speech? |
| Distinguish between facts and opinions. | Does the speaker make statements with which you agree or disagree? Ask yourself why you disagree. (Such statements are opinions. An opinion is a belief or a judgment about something that cannot be proved. A fact is a statement that can be proved true.) |
| Identify main ideas. | What are the most important points? (Listen for clue words or phrases, such as *major, main,* and *most important.*) |
| Identify significant or supporting details. | What dates, names, or facts does the speaker use to support the main points of the speech? What kinds of examples or explanations are used to support the main ideas? |
| Identify the order of organization. | What kind of order does the speaker use to present the information—time sequence, spatial order, order of importance, logical order? |
| Listen to detect bias. | Is the speaker biased, or prejudiced, toward one point of view? Does the speaker use extreme or all-inclusive words such as *never* or *always*? Does the speaker acknowledge other points of view? |
| Evaluate the speaker's credibility. | Does the speaker refer to sources of information? Are the sources respectable or credible, such as newspaper and journal articles or reference materials? |
| Note comparisons and contrasts. | Are some details compared or contrasted with others? |
| Predict outcomes and draw conclusions. | What can you reasonably conclude from the facts and evidence presented in the speech? |
| Look for logic. | Does the speaker build arguments in a logical way? Does the speaker use false logic, such as hasty generalization, false cause and effect, or circular reasoning? |
| Look for emotional appeals. | Does the speaker use the bandwagon appeal? the glittering generality? snob appeal? plain folks appeal? the veiled threat? |
| Understand cause and effect. | Do some events described by the speaker relate to or affect others? Does the speaker make the logical connections between cause and effect? |

**Comprehensive Listening**  When you listen for the content of a message, you are engaged in *comprehensive listening.* Some people call this type of listening *informational listening.* Much of the listening you do in school is of this type. Listening for information and listening to instructions are examples of comprehensive listening.

- **Listening for information**  You are often in situations where you listen to acquire information. When a teacher describes a certain chemical reaction, for example, he or she is delivering information you need to understand, not attempting to be persuasive or entertaining. The following strategies are helpful in these situations.

  1. **The LQ2R Method** helps you when you listen for information from a speaker.

     **L**  Listen carefully to material as it is being presented.

     **Q**  Question yourself as you listen. Mentally, or in your notes, make a list of questions as they occur to you.

     **R**  Recite in your own words the information as it is being presented. Summarize the material in your mind.

     **R**  Review the whole presentation. You should restate or reemphasize major points.

  2. **Note Taking**  One way to keep track of a speaker's ideas is to take notes. Of course, you cannot possibly write down every word the speaker says. Develop an effective way to jot down the speaker's main points and supporting details as well as your own thoughts, questions, or comments. For example, you could use split-page notes—divide your paper so that forty percent of

the page lies to the left and sixty percent lies to the right. Take brief notes on the left-hand side only, leaving the right-hand side for reorganizing and expanding your notes after listening. (See also **Notes on Reading or Lectures** on page 863.)

- **Listening to instructions**  Because instructions are usually made up of a series of steps, you can easily misunderstand them. The following steps can help you make sense of instructions.

  1. **Listen for the order of the steps.** Listen for words such as *first, second, next, then,* and *last* to tell you when one step ends and the next one begins.

  2. **Identify the number of steps in the process.** Take notes if the instructions are long or complicated. Do not hesitate to ask for clarification or for the speaker to slow down as you take notes.

  3. **Visualize each step.** Imagine yourself actually performing each step. Try to get a mental image of what you should be doing at every step in the process.

  4. **Review the steps.** When the speaker is finished, be sure you understand the process from beginning to end. Ask questions if you are unsure.

NOTE  When you take a message on the telephone, you are listening for information that answers the basic *5W-How?* questions—*Who? What? When? Where? Why?* and *How?* For example, you should take down details that answer questions such as *Who is calling? What is the message or purpose for the call? Where can the caller be reached? When can the caller be reached?* and *How may you help the caller?*

### Empathic (or Reflective) Listening

When you want to help a friend understand a difficult problem or when you want to show someone your understanding and acceptance, you use **empathic listening.** To show empathic listening through your facial expressions and body language and through your responses to the speaker, use the following strategies.

- Do much more listening than talking.
- Show genuine warmth and concern.
- Paraphrase what the speaker says to show your understanding.
- Respond to the speaker's feelings rather than analyze the facts.
- Keep your opinions to yourself.

## Special Listening Situations

Some situations—**group discussions** and **interviews**, for example—require that you participate not only as a careful listener, but also as a speaker.

### Listening in a Group Discussion

Listening as a member of a group discussion is different from listening as a member of a large audience because you participate as both a listener and a speaker. The following tips should help you participate effectively in a group discussion.

- Sit up, look at each speaker, and nod to show agreement or understanding.
- Demonstrate respect for the other group members by paying attention and not making comments while they are speaking.
- Take notes on each speaker's points and list your questions or comments.
- When you are ready to speak, raise your hand and be recognized.
- Concentrate on what the speaker is saying, not on what you intend to say when it is your turn to speak.

### Listening in an Interview
An interview is a unique listening situation that usually takes place between two people: the interviewer and the interviewee. In addition to the strategies recommended in "Conducting an interview" and "Interviewing for a job" on page 854, use the following special listening techniques to make the most of an interview.

- As interviewer
  1. **When you ask a question, listen to the complete answer.** Be courteous and patient; think of related follow-up questions as your interviewee responds.
  2. **Respect the interviewee's opinions, even if you do not agree with him or her.** You may state your disagreement politely only if your comment will serve to prompt the interviewee to clarify, expand, or provide support for a statement or claim. Avoid disagreeing if you are likely to upset your interviewee and disrupt the interview.
  3. **Monitor your nonverbal communication.** Make sure that your nonverbal reactions, such as your facial expressions and gestures, reflect a respectful tone. Maintain good eye contact, nod to show understanding, and smile to indicate your interest.
  4. **Always thank the interviewee at the end of your interview.**

- As interviewee
  1. **Listen to the interviewer's complete question before answering.** If you start answering the question before the interviewer finishes asking it, you might answer the wrong question.
  2. **Answer the question.** Stick to the point the interviewer is addressing. Do not simply ignore the question and respond with something totally off track.

# Studying and Test Taking

## Study Skills and Strategies

### Why Study?

The purpose of studying is not just to do well on tests and get good grades. It is also to help you understand and remember information you may need later. (See also **Test-Taking Skills** on page 865 and **Reading and Vocabulary** on page 832.)

**Making a Study Plan**   The following suggestions may help you use your study time effectively.

1. **Know what's expected of you before you study.** Record your assignments and the dates they are due on a calendar or planner. Know what your teacher expects you to do or know.
2. **Manage your time.** Divide larger assignments into smaller units. For example, study one section of a chapter, take a break, then study the next section. Schedule time to complete each of the smaller units.
3. **Focus your mind on your studies.** Plan where and when you will study. Have a regular time to study and a place that is strictly for studying. Be realistic about what things distract you. If the television will distract you, turn it off or study where it won't be a problem.

### Organizing and Remembering Information

The strategies listed below can help you organize and remember information as you study.

**Classifying**   *Classification* is a method of organizing items into categories. When you make an outline, for example, you use classification to decide which ideas fit together under a certain heading. When you group things, you identify relationships among them.

> EXAMPLE   What do the following cities have in common: London, Paris, Warsaw, Prague, Rome?
>
> Answer   They are all European capitals.

You also classify when you identify patterns. For example, look at the following number sequence.

| What is the next number in the series? |
| --- |
| 8   11   15   20   26   <u>33</u> |

Answer   *3* is added to the first number to produce the second number. *4* is added to the second number to produce the third number; *5* is added to the third number; and *6* to the fourth number. Therefore, *7* should be added to the fifth number (26) to produce the answer, which should be *33*.

**Graphic Organizers**  You may find it helpful to reorganize information from a reading passage or from class notes into a chart, map, or diagram. Graphic organizers work by translating information into a visual form. (See also **Graphic Organizers** on page 815.)

**Memorization**  To memorize and remember what you have learned, you should practice in frequent, short, focused sessions. Try playing memory games such as making a word out of the first letters of key terms or ideas.

**Notes on Reading or Lectures**  Taking careful *notes* while reading or listening to a lecture will help you organize and remember information later when you study for tests or write research papers. The steps below explain how to take study notes.

---

### How to Take Notes

**1. Recognize and record main points.**  In a lecture, listen for **key words** and **phrases** used by the speaker, such as *major* or *most important.* Key words like these indicate points that you should remember. In a textbook, pay attention to chapter headings, subheadings, lists, charts, time lines, or illustrations.

**2. Summarize what you hear or read.** Don't record every detail. Summarize and abbreviate information about key ideas. Indent supporting points to distinguish them from the main points.

**3. Note important examples.**  Make note of important examples that illustrate the main points of the lecture or lesson. Just jotting the phrase *Boston Tea Party* or sketching a divided cell in your notes may jog your memory later.

---

Look at the following student notes. The student who made these notes arranged details in groups beneath headings (underlined) that indicate the key ideas from the passage.

Jade Snow Wong

Biography
- Chinese American
- born in 1922 in San Francisco
- graduated from Mills College in 1942
- began pottery business in 1946

Early Disappointment
- pottery not accepted at first
- considered too crude, like peasant pots

Perseverance
- received good advice
- continued producing pottery

Success
- pottery sold outside her native community
- people loved simplicity, understated beauty
- business soon thriving, work highly regarded
- awarded regional and national prizes
- pottery placed in museums

**Outlines**  When you write an *outline,* you record important ideas and information, then group them into an organized pattern that shows their order and their relationship to one another. (See also **Formal** and **Informal Outlines** on page 895.)

**Paraphrasing**  A *paraphrase* is a restatement of someone else's ideas in your own words. When you restate an idea in your own words, you are not just switching around words, but actually concentrating on the concept expressed in those words. By considering the concept carefully through paraphrasing, you are often more likely to understand and remember the ideas. A paraphrase is approximately the same length as the original. (See also **Paraphrasing** on page 834.)

**SQ3R**    *SQ3R* stands for *Survey, Question, Read, Recite,* and *Review.* This strategy involves you in actively responding to any text that you are reading. (See also **SQ3R** on page 836.)

**Summarizing**    A *summary* is a restatement in condensed form of the main points of a pas-

sage. When you summarize, you must decide which ideas and details in a passage are important enough to include. Making these decisions helps you remember the information in a passage. (See also **Summarizing** on page 836.)

**Writing to Learn**    Writing is a valuable study tool. By writing, you may focus your thoughts, respond to ideas, record your observations, plan your work, and restate ideas in your own words. Use the different forms of writing described below as you study.

| Type of Writing | How It Helps | Guidelines and Examples |
| --- | --- | --- |
| **Diary** | helps you recall your impressions and express your feelings | • Diary writing is often more personal than other writing, so you will want to be sure to keep your diary in a safe place. Try to write in your diary regularly.<br>• Write about your reactions to issues raised during a lecture or in a chapter you read for class. |
| **Freewriting** | helps you focus your thoughts | • When freewriting, don't censor your thoughts. Try to get down everything that comes into your mind about your topic.<br>• Write for three minutes after class or after reviewing your notes in order to focus on the most important points. |
| **Journal** | helps you record your observations, descriptions, solutions, and questions | • Like diary writing, journal writing is best if you make entries on a regular basis. Remember that you should not worry about making mistakes; you should include observations, reflections, or even inquiries. Also, remember to date all your entries.<br>• Write about problems or successes you had in solving word problems in math. |
| **Learning Log** | helps you present a problem, analyze it, and propose a solution | • As you write about your learning process and about the material you are covering in class, make connections between this new information and what you have learned before. You could also create your own vocabulary list of words that are important to remember for a certain unit or class.<br>• Write about the way you will incorporate a source or piece of information into a research paper for your social studies class. |

# Test-Taking Skills and Strategies

You are likely to take two types of tests in school—**classroom tests** and **standardized tests.** Different kinds of tests will ask different questions; you will need to consider different strategies to approach each.

## Classroom Tests

The typical *classroom test* measures how well you use the skills you have learned or whether you have learned certain required information about a subject. You will usually find a combination of many kinds of test questions in a classroom test. For example, a test in a science class might begin with objective multiple-choice questions, and then conclude with an essay question that tests for deeper understanding of a concept. To prepare for a classroom test, familiarize yourself with the material that will be covered, or practice the skill you must demonstrate at the time of testing. Also make sure you are aware of the different kinds of questions that are asked on classroom tests.

**Essay Questions**  In answering an *essay question* you must demonstrate a critical understanding of the material you have learned. More than just knowing details such as dates and definitions, you must often know how these details relate to each other—for example by showing how one event influenced another or by showing how one item compares to another. You will need to be sure to cover all the major points mentioned in the question. Essay questions also test your ability to express your understanding in a well-written, well-organized composition. There is never just one correct answer to any essay question; each student has different ways of thinking and writing about a topic. Nonetheless, these steps should help you prepare for any essay question:

- Review your textbook and lecture notes carefully.
- Make an outline of your study materials by identifying key ideas and supporting details.
- Create a set of possible questions and practice writing out answers for each.
- Check your answers for accuracy by using your textbook and notes. Revise your answers and use them to spin off new study questions.

### How to Answer Essay Questions

**1. Preview the test.** How many questions does the test ask? Budget your time between preparing and writing each answer.

**2. Carefully read all the questions.** Note the key terms in each question to be sure what the question is asking. If there are several parts to each question, be sure you cover all parts in your answer.

**3. Note key verbs in each question.** Every essay question asks you to perform a specific task that is expressed with a verb. Learn to recognize the key verbs that commonly appear on essay tests. (See also the **Key Verbs That Appear in Essay Questions** chart on page 866.)

**4. Plan your answer by using prewriting strategies.** Make notes or an outline to help you decide what you want to say. Write notes or a rough outline on scratch paper. (See also **Prewriting Techniques** on page 897.)

**5. Evaluate and revise as you write.** You will rarely have time to redraft your whole essay, so be sure that your main points are strong and well written. Leave time to re-read your answer and to correct any spelling, punctuation, or grammatical errors.

## Key Verbs That Appear in Essay Questions

| Key Verb | Task | Sample Question |
|---|---|---|
| **Analyze** | Look carefully at the parts of something to see how each part works. | **Analyze** the relationship between water quality and aquatic life in local streams. |
| **Argue** | Take a stand on an issue and give reasons to support your viewpoint or opinion. | **Argue** whether or not the school year should be twelve months long. |
| **Compare** or **Contrast** | Point out the similarities or differences between things, people, or ideas. | **Contrast** the most recent national election with the national election of 1996. |
| **Define** | Give specific details that make something or some idea unique. | **Define** the term *federalism* as it applies to the foundations of the United States Constitution. |
| **Demonstrate** | Provide examples to support a point. | **Demonstrate** how the use of car seat belts has reduced the number of traffic fatalities across the United States. |
| **Describe** | Give a picture in words. | **Describe** the behavior of an Asian elephant when it feels threatened. |
| **Discuss** | Examine in detail. | **Discuss** the term *planned obsolescence.* |
| **Explain** | Give reasons or make the meaning clear. | **Explain** the development of the American two-party political system. |
| **Summarize** | Give a brief overview of the main points. | **Summarize** the *Emancipation Proclamation.* |

Each essay question requires you to perform a specific task, expressed with a verb. You can prepare yourself for creating a specific response to these tasks by familiarizing yourself with the key terms and the kinds of information called for in essay questions. Each essay question response is as unique as the person who writes it. Still, a well-written essay meets all of the following guidelines:

- The essay answers the question, including all parts.
- The essay has an introduction, a body, and a conclusion.
- The main ideas and supporting points are clearly presented in the body.
- All the sentences are complete and well written.
- The essay has no errors in spelling, punctuation, or grammar.

**Matching Questions**   In matching questions, you need to match the items on two lists.

**Directions:** Write the letter of each state (from the right column) next to its capital (in the left column).

| | | |
|---|---|---|
| C | **1.** Trenton | **A.** Montana |
| A | **2.** Helena | **B.** New Hampshire |
| B | **3.** Concord | **C.** New Jersey |

**How to Answer Matching Questions**

**1. Read the directions carefully.** Sometimes answers may be used more than once.

**2. Scan the columns and match items you know first.** That way, you can gain some time for evaluating other answers.

**3. Complete the matching process.** On any remaining items, make an educated guess.

**Multiple-Choice Questions**   The *multiple-choice question* asks you to select a correct answer from among a number of choices.

EXAMPLE

**1.** Which of the following items is *not* a characteristic of the manatee, or sea cow?

   **A.** It can remain underwater for thirty minutes.

   **B.** It is usually found in small groups.

   **C.** It is a coldblooded animal.

   **D.** It prefers water temperatures above 46°C.

**How to Answer Multiple-Choice Questions**

**1. Read the initial statement carefully.** Make sure you understand the statement completely before looking at your choices. Always look for qualifiers, such as *not, always,* or *never,* because these words limit or affect the answer. In the example above,

you must choose the quality that a manatee does *not* have.

**2. Read all the answers before making a choice.** Sometimes the answer includes two or more choices, such as "Both **A** and **B**" or "All of the above." Remember, in the example, you are looking for the quality that a manatee does *not* have, so you must consider the possible answers carefully.

**3. Narrow your choices by eliminating the answers you know are incorrect.** Some answers are clearly wrong, while others are somewhat related to the correct answer. You may know that manatees can easily stay underwater for thirty minutes. Since you are looking for qualities a manatee does *not* have, you can easily rule out **A**.

**4. From the remaining choices, select the answer that makes the most sense.** The answer is **C**.

**Short-Answer Questions**   *Short-answer questions* ask you to explain what you know about a subject in a brief, written reply. In general, short-answer questions require a specific answer of one or two sentences. (Some short-answer questions, such as maps or diagrams that you are supposed to label, or fill-in-the-blank questions, can be answered with one or a few words.)

EXAMPLE

**1.** Why do insects shed their outer shells?

**1.** An insect's outer shell does not grow. As the insect grows, it must shed the old shell and grow a new one that fits.

**True/False Questions**   *True/false questions* ask you to determine whether a given statement is true or false.

EXAMPLE

**1.** T  F   All spiders build webs to catch prey for food.

## How to Answer True/False Questions

**1. Read the statement carefully.**

**2. Check for qualifiers.** Words such as *always* or *never* qualify or limit a statement's meaning. The example above is false because many spiders hunt their prey without the use of web snares. The word *all* limits the statement and makes it false.

**3. Choose an answer based on two following principles:** One, if any part of the statement is false, the entire statement is false; and two, a statement is true only if it is entirely and always true.

# Standardized Tests

*Standardized tests* measure the skills you've learned in school. Your scores on these tests are evaluated in comparison to a standard or norm compiled from the scores of other students who have taken the same test. Two tests of this type, the *Scholastic Aptitude Test* (SAT) and the *American College Testing Program* (ACT), are given to students across the entire United States. To help you prepare for standardized tests, keep in mind the three tips in the following chart.

## How to Prepare for Standardized Tests

**1. Learn what will be tested.** Information booklets may be provided. Practice with these or with published study guides.

**2. Know what materials you will need.** On the day of the test, you may need to bring specific materials, such as your official test registration card, number-two pencils, or lined paper for writing an essay.

**3. Determine how the test is evaluated.** If there is no penalty for wrong answers, make your best guess on every question. If wrong answers are penalized, however, make guesses only if you are fairly sure of the correct answer.

The following information describes and explains the types of questions and writing prompts you may encounter on standardized tests and provides some strategies for answering them.

**Analogy Questions**    *Analogy questions* ask you to analyze the relationship between a pair of words and to identify a second pair of words that has the same relationship. Analogy questions usually appear on standardized tests in multiple-choice form.

EXAMPLE

Directions: Select the appropriate pair of words to complete the analogy.

TOE : FOOT :: _____

    **A.** hand : glove     **C.** trumpet : piano
    **B.** bowl : spoon     **D.** sleeve : jacket

Sometimes, however, analogies are written as fill-in-the-blank questions, and you may need to fill in the missing item.

EXAMPLE

WILD CAT : LION :: tool : _*hammer*_

## How to Answer Analogy Questions

**1. Analyze the first pair of words and identify the relationship between them.** In the first example above, the relationship of *toe* to *foot* is that of a part to its whole. (See also **Types of Analogies** chart on page 869.)

**2. Express the analogy in sentence or question form.** The example would be expressed as, "A *toe* is a part of a *foot,* just as a _____ is a part of a _____." Fill the blanks with the possible answers and see which makes sense. For example, does answer **A** work? Let's check: A *toe* is a part of a *foot,* just as a _hand_ is a part of a _glove_." That answer doesn't make sense.

Since a spoon is not a part of a bowl and a trumpet is not a part of a piano, **D** must be the correct answer. "A _toe_ is a part of a _foot_, just as a _sleeve_ is a part of a _jacket_."

**3. Find the best available choice to complete the analogy.** If multiple choice answers are provided, select the pair of words that shares the same relationship as the first pair of words. If you must fill in a word, look closely at the first pair and then select a word that has a similar relationship to the single given word.

In addition to these guidelines, remember the following helpful tips for solving analogies.

- **Consider the parts of speech.** Some words may be used as more than one part of speech. If you cannot unlock the relationship in the analogy, it may help to determine if one of the words can be another part of speech.

- **Familiarize yourself with the types of analogy relationships.** Become familiar with the types of analogies typically found on standardized tests. (For more on **identifying analogy relationships,** see the **Types of Analogies** chart below.)

- **Remember: The relationship between the words is important, not the meanings of the individual words.** Look again at the second example on page 868. A _lion_ and a _hammer_ have nothing in common; but the relationship a _wild cat_ has to a _lion_ is the same as the one a _tool_ has to a _hammer_: classification. A lion is a kind of wild cat and a hammer is a kind of tool.

Although there are many different relationships that can be represented in analogies, a smaller number of specific relationships are fairly common. Examples of these common types are shown in the following chart.

## Types of Analogies

| Type | Example | Solution |
|------|---------|----------|
| **Action to Performer** or **Performer to Action** | PLOWING : FARMER : : sewing : tailor | _Plowing_ is performed by a _farmer_, just as _sewing_ is performed by a _tailor_. |
| **Antonyms** | ETHICAL : IMMORAL : : compassionate : cruel | _Ethical_ behavior is the opposite of _immoral_ behavior, just as _compassionate_ is the opposite of _cruel_ behavior. |
| **Cause** or **Effect** | ACCIDENT : SADNESS : : gift : joy | An _accident_ causes _sadness_, just as a _gift_ causes _joy_. |
| **Characteristic** | LIONS : CARNIVOROUS : : cows : herbivorous | _Lions_ are always _carnivorous_ (meat eaters), just as _cows_ are always _herbivorous_ (plant eaters). |
| **Classification** | SPIDER : ARACHNID : : frog : amphibian | A _spider_ is a kind of _arachnid_, just as a _frog_ is a kind of _amphibian_. |
| **Degree** | CHUCKLE : LAUGH : : whimper : cry | A _chuckle_ is a little _laugh_, just as a _whimper_ is a little _cry_. |

_(continued )_

| Type | Example | Solution |
|---|---|---|
| **Measure** | THERMOMETER : TEMPERATURE : : clock : time | A *thermometer* is used to measure *temperature,* just as a *clock* is used to measure *time.* |
| **Part to Whole** or **Whole to Part** | CHAPTER : BOOK : : act : play | A *chapter* is a part of a *book,* just as an *act* is a part of a *play.* |
| **Place** | BATON ROUGE : LOUISIANA : : Paris : France | *Baton Rouge* is the capital of *Louisiana,* just as *Paris* is the capital of *France.* |
| **Synonyms** | DRY : ARID : : horrid : ghastly | *Dry* is similar in meaning to *arid,* just as *horrid* is similar in meaning to *ghastly.* |
| **Use** | BOW : VIOLIN : : keyboard : computer | A *bow* is used to play the *violin,* just as a *keyboard* is used to operate a *computer.* |

**Critical-Reading Questions**  Standardized tests ask questions that test your ability to examine a piece of writing in detail and show your understanding of it. These ***critical-reading questions*** (sometimes called ***on-demand reading questions***) require that you look closely at a particular text to determine its organizational structure, meaning, and purpose. These questions may also require you to decide whether the passage is effective in conveying the writer's intended meaning. Critical-reading questions focus on either a specific element of a passage or on how the writer created his or her work. The following chart shows the usual kind of critical-reading questions and how you should approach answering them. For more information and practice with any of the bulleted items indicated, see the pages referred to in parentheses.

### Critical-Reading Test Questions

**Rhetorical strategy questions,** or **evaluation questions,** ask you to decide how effective a writer's techniques are. These test items have you identify and analyze

- the author's intended audience
- the author's purpose (page 257)
- the author's opinions (page 257)
- the author's tone or point of view (page 257)

**Inference questions,** or **interpretation questions,** ask you to draw conclusions or make inferences about the information given in a passage. You will often be asked to identify

- unclear information (page 339)
- specific conclusions or inferences that can be drawn about the author or the topic of a passage (page 833)
- conclusions or inferences based on given material (page 158)

(See also **Inference Questions** on page 167.)

## Critical-Reading Test Questions

**Organization questions,** or **main idea** or **detail questions,** ask you to identify how the writer organized the passage. These test items often ask you to find

- the main idea of a passage (page 347)
- arrangement of supporting details (page 359)
- the author's use of particular writing strategies (page 133)
- techniques used to conclude the passage
- transitional devices that make the passage coherent (page 363)

(See also **Main Idea and Detail Questions** on page 28.)

**Style questions,** or **tone questions,** ask you to look closely at a passage to evaluate the author's use of style. You will often be asked to identify

- the author's intended audience
- the author's style
- the author's voice and tone

**Synthesis questions** ask you to demonstrate your knowledge of how parts of a passage fit together into a whole. You will be asked to interpret

- the cumulative meaning of details in a passage (page 355)
- techniques used to unify details (page 355)

**Vocabulary-in-context questions** ask you to infer the meaning of a word from its context in a passage. (page 841)

Here is a typical **reading passage** followed by sample test questions based on this passage.

In our world of microwave ovens and supersonic jets, waiting on a computer seems to be the most tedious of things. Why do these so-called "electronic brains" take so long at times? Probably because they are speaking another language. Computer language is based on the binary number system—that is, all words, images, and sounds are transmitted through an alphabet made up of only two digits: 0 and 1. For example, if we convert our twenty-six-letter alphabet into numbers using only 0 or 1, then A could be 0, B could be 1, C could be 10, D could be 11, and so on. Using this system, the binary code representing the word *dog* could be a long number like 000110111000110.

Can you imagine sending an e-mail message this way, or downloading your favorite song off the Internet? Without a shortcut, one second of a high-definition video would take more than seven hours to reach your home across the average modem.

Mathematics not only helped create this system—a language that machines can understand—but also created means of making it work more efficiently—binary data compression. Systems have been developed that compress data into a form that not only can be transmitted across the Internet in less time, but also can be decompressed without losing any significant amount of the original data. In this way, computer compressors significantly reduce the size of any file for easy transmission across cyberspace.

## Sample Critical-Reading Questions

1. What is the main idea of this passage?

   **A.** Computers use an alphabet of 0's and 1's.

   **B.** Computers are slower than users expect them to be.

   **C.** Binary data compression helps speed information exchange over the Internet.

   **D.** E-mail messages contain huge amounts of information.

   [This organization question requires you to identify the paragraph's main idea.]

2. The word *binary* in this passage means

   **A.** electronic

   **B.** expressed by two digits

   **C.** tied together

   **D.** mechanically complex

   [This vocabulary-in-context question requires you to examine the word's context to determine its meaning.]

3. In which of the following sources was the passage most likely originally found?

   **A.** a computer manual

   **B.** a Web site introducing readers to the Internet

   **C.** an introductory mathematics textbook

   **D.** a scientific journal

[This rhetorical strategy question requires you to identify the author's intended audience.]

4. Microwave ovens and supersonic jets are referred to because

   **A.** Microwave ovens and supersonic jets both use computers.

   **B.** The author thinks these two items are more advanced than computers.

   **C.** Modern people are used to fast technology.

   **D.** Like the computer, they are twentieth century inventions.

[This inference question requires you to examine the context of these two details to explain their purpose in the passage.]

5. The author of this passage wants to explain

   **A.** that computers are actually faster than you might think

   **B.** the binary number system

   **C.** the mathematical principles behind the Internet

   **D.** that computers are slow because they use a complex language

[This synthesis question requires you to read the passage as a whole to make a generalization about the passage from the details.]

---

**NOTE** Sometimes it helps to compare the wording of the prompt to the wording in the reading passage. Finding the same or similar language may lead you to the place in the passage where the answer can be found. For example, question two in the chart above cites a word (*digit*) that is clearly present in the second paragraph of the reading passage. However, if the same or similar words from the prompt cannot be found within the reading passage, you will have to come up with your own examples or draw your own conclusions.

**Multiple-Choice Questions** *Multiple-choice questions,* similar to those found on classroom tests, are commonly found in many standardized tests. The multiple-choice questions on standardized tests will generally begin with simpler questions, then become harder the farther you get into the test. Start by answering all the questions you can easily answer before attempting the more difficult ones, because each question, whether easy or difficult, is worth the same amount. Budget your time by not spending too much time on any single question. (See also **Multiple-Choice Questions** on page 866.)

## On-Demand Writing Prompts

*On-demand writing prompts* are the core of many state writing tests. They are similar to essay questions because they require you to write several paragraphs on a broad topic in a limited amount of time. The key difference is that you will not know in advance what the topic of an on-demand writing prompt will be. The compositions that you write will usually be either persuasive, informative, or descriptive.

EXAMPLE

Many states are now requiring all bicyclists under the age of eighteen to wear a helmet when they ride. Write a persuasive essay in which you argue whether or not such helmet laws are a good idea.

Another variation of the on-demand writing prompt is found in proficiency tests that ask a general question that must be answered with specific details pulled from your knowledge of a specific subject area.

EXAMPLE

In many literary works, the setting plays a major part in conveying the author's message. In a well-organized essay, describe how the author manages to strengthen the message of his or her work through the setting. Avoid plot summary.

---

### How to Respond to an On-Demand Writing Prompt

**1. Read the prompt and determine what it is telling you to do.** Look for key verbs to indicate whether your answer should be persuasive, informative, or descriptive. (See also the **Key Verbs That Appear in Essay Questions** chart on page 866.)

**2. Plan your response using prewriting techniques such as freewriting and clustering.** (See also **Prewriting Techniques** on page 897.)

**3. Evaluate and revise your response as you write.** Make sure that your answer has a topic sentence, supporting details, transitions between ideas, and a clear conclusion.

---

Although you cannot study for the content of an on-demand writing test, you can still prepare yourself by following these steps:

- *Become familiar with the kinds of writing on-demand writing tests often require.* Read and learn to recognize the key qualities of persuasive, informative, and descriptive essays.

- *Practice writing answers to on-demand writing prompts.* If possible, practice with questions that have appeared on standardized tests administered at your school in the past—usually available through your school counselors or library. Use a timer to simulate the time limits of an actual test.

- *Revise and proofread your answers.* If possible, share and discuss your answers with classmates. Talk about the aspects of your answer that show that it is persuasive, informative, or descriptive.

## Reasoning or Logic Questions

Some questions may test your reasoning abilities more than your knowledge of a specific subject.

*Reasoning* or *logic questions* (sometimes called *sentence completion questions*) are multiple-choice questions that measure your ability to recognize certain kinds of relationships. These questions may ask you to analyze a sentence or brief passage and to fill in one or more blanks with the most appropriate word or words given.

### EXAMPLE

Considering the vast amounts of information that are _____ through cyberspace, it is a wonder that data compression systems work so _____.

A. exchanged . . . efficiently
B. deciphered . . . technologically
C. busy . . . expensive
D. flying . . . unsuccessfully

### How to Answer Reasoning or Logic Questions

**1. Be sure that you understand the instructions.** Reasoning or logic questions are usually multiple-choice questions.

**2. Analyze the relationship implied in the question.** Look carefully at the question to gather information about the relationship shared by the items. The example question suggests a cause-and-effect relationship between the amount of information in cyberspace and how data compression systems work.

**3. Insert each word or pair of words to see if the sentence makes sense with the insertion.** Remember that if a pair of words is asked for, the first word in the suggested pairs may make perfect sense, but the second may not. For example, the first word in answer **D**, *flying*, seems like a possibility but the second word, *unsuccessfully*, makes little sense in the context of the sentence.

## Verbal-Expression Questions

Standardized tests often assess how well you understand written expression and grammatical correctness. The following chart shows the four standard types of verbal-expression questions. (For more information and practice on the **grammar, usage, and mechanics elements,** refer to the pages in parentheses.)

### Verbal-Expression Questions

*Grammar Questions*

You identify the correct answer, using standard grammar and usage rules. These test items often cover use of
- principal parts of verbs (page 517)
- pronouns (page 378)
- subject-verb agreement (page 493)

*Punctuation Questions*

You identify use of correct punctuation. These test items often cover correct use of
- apostrophes and hyphens (pages 698 and 714)
- end marks and commas (page 636)
- parentheses and quotation marks (pages 720 and 793)
- semicolons, colons, and dashes (pages 666 and 714)

*Sentence Structure Questions*

You show knowledge of what makes a complete sentence. These test items often cover
- combining sentences (page 330)
- fragments and run-ons (pages 320 and 327)
- parallel structure (page 339)
- transitional words (page 364)
- verb usage (page 516)

*Revision-in-Context Questions*

You show appropriate revision to a composition. These test items often cover
- arranging ideas (page 359)
- composition structure (page 369)
- tone
- unity and coherence (pages 355 and 359)

Standardized tests usually do not ask verbal-expression questions by themselves. Instead, you find them within the context of a reading passage. A sample passage, usually a paragraph, includes several words and phrases that are underlined and numbered. You then choose the answer that best expresses the meaning, is grammatically correct, or is consistent with the style and tone of the passage. Here is a typical verbal-expression test passage followed by sample questions:

Although the Yamal peninsula of northern Siberia sits atop the world's largest untapped natural gas reserves nearly<sub>(1)</sub> one third of the Nanet people living there still live as nomadic reindeer herders. Each family of Nanet herders lives<sub>(2)</sub> in transportable, tepee-like "chooms." The children of the Nanet<sub>(3)</sub> attend boarding school in Yar Sale, the region's only town. They commute to school by helicopter. They commute by flying in and out of town at the beginning and end of each school year.

There are two basic types of test items used to test verbal expression on national tests.

### Most Common Types of Verbal-Expression Test Items

**"NO CHANGE" Items**

- give a list of suggested revisions of underlined, numbered portions of passage
- always contain one "NO CHANGE" choice if the indicated part is correct as is

**Critical Thinking Items**

- ask you to analyze and evaluate the passage as a whole
- ask you to make inferences about portions of a passage as related to the whole

### Sample Verbal-Expression Questions

**1. A.** NO CHANGE
   **B.** reserves; nearly
   **C.** reserves. Nearly,
   **D.** reserves, nearly (circled)

[This question about punctuation requires that you know appropriate punctuation.]

**2. A.** NO CHANGE (circled)
   **B.** live
   **C.** are living
   **D.** living

[This question about grammar requires that you know correct subject-verb agreement.]

**3.** Which is the best revision of this portion of the passage?
   **A.** NO CHANGE
   **B.** They attend
   **C.** Their children attend (circled)
   **D.** The children who are Nanet attend

[This revision-in-context question requires that you use revision skills to express best the ideas in the passage.]

**4.** How should the final two sentences be combined?
   **A.** The children commute to school by flying in and out of town at the beginning and end of each school year by helicopter.
   **B.** The children commute to school by helicopter, flying in and out of town at the beginning and end of each school year. (circled)
   **C.** The children commute to school by helicopter; and they commute by flying in and out of town at the beginning and end of each school year.
   **D.** Because the children commute to school by helicopter, they commute by flying in and out of town at the beginning and end of each school year.

[This question about sentence structure requires you to combine sentences.]

# Viewing and Representing

## Media Terms

Because media messages, such as advertisements, television programs, music videos, and movies, are a constant part of life, it is important to be able to understand, interpret, analyze, evaluate, and create media messages. The terms defined below refer to many different areas of media communication, including television and film production, advertising, and journalism. The terms are grouped into three lists: **electronic media terms** (below), **general media terms** (page 880), and **print media terms** (page 883). (Terms relating to the Internet and the World Wide Web can be found in the **Library/Media Center** section on page 823; terms relating to use of type and graphics can be found in **Document Design** on page 806.)

### Electronic Media Terms

**Advertising**    (See **Advertising** on page 883.)

**Affiliate**    An *affiliate* is a privately owned, local television or radio station that presents the programming of a national network. (See also **Network** on page 879.)

**Animation**    *Animation* is the film art of making drawings appear to move. An animated film may combine drawing, painting, sculpture, or other visual arts. Animators take film or video pictures of a scene at a rate of twenty-four frames per second, making small changes as they go. When viewed, the frames create the illusion of movement. Animation is used in many different types of media messages, including advertising and cartoons. (See also **Advertising** on page 883.)

**Broadcasting**    *Broadcasting* means using airwaves to send television or radio content over a wide area of potential viewers or listeners. **Commercial broadcasting** is for profit. Advertisers pay broadcasters for airtime in which to persuade the audience to buy their products or services. **Public broadcasting** is not-for-profit. In the United States, the Public Broadcasting Service (PBS) has more than three hundred affiliates, or member stations. The service is funded mostly by the federal government, corporations, and individual viewers and listeners. (See also **Affiliate** on this page.)

**Byline**    (See **Byline** on page 884.)

**Cable Television**  *Cable television* is a method of distributing TV signals using cables and wiring instead of airwaves to bring messages into people's homes. There are two principal types of cable TV companies. Some companies *create* original programming in the form of channels or networks, such as all-news networks or all-music channels. Other companies *distribute* packages, or groups, of many different channels into homes.

**Camera Angle**  The *camera angle* refers to the angle at which a camera is set when it is pointed at its subject. The angle may be low, high, or tilted. The effect of a low angle is to make the subject look tall and powerful. The high angle makes the subject look small. The tilted angle suggests that the subject is not balanced.

**Camera Shots**  A *camera shot* is what the viewer sees in a movie or video. Just as a story needs many words, a film or video needs many shots in order to create a scene or story. Below are the most common shots used in film production.

- **Close-up shot**  A *close-up shot* is a shot of only the subject, usually a person's face.
- **Extreme close-up shot**  An *extreme close-up shot* is a very close shot, usually of only part of a person's face or part of the subject.
- **Long shot**  A *long shot* is a shot that shows a scene from far away, usually to show a place or setting of a scene.
- **Medium shot**  A *medium shot* is a shot that shows the subject, usually a person from the waist up, and perhaps some of the background.
- **Reverse angle shot**  A *reverse angle shot* is a view of the opposite side of a subject or of another person in the scene.

**Channel**  In general communication, a *channel* is the means by which a message is communicated. For example, if you are communicating verbally (such as by talking or singing), the channel is sound waves. If you communicate nonverbally (for instance, by gestures, expressions, handshakes, or sounds such as laughter or clapping), the channel is waves of light, sound waves, or the sense of touch. In television and radio, a channel is a fixed band of frequencies used for the transmitting of television or radio broadcasts. (See also **Medium** and **Message** on page 885.)

**Copy**  (See also **Copy** on page 884.)

**Credits**  *Credits* refer to the list of names of people who worked to produce a program. This list usually appears at the end of a television program, film, or video or on the back of a compact disc case.

**Demographics**  (See **Demographics** on page 884.)

**Digital Editing**  (See **Digital Editing** on page 884.)

**Docudrama**  *Docudrama* is a type of documentary that blends elements of both documentary and drama to explore an actual historical, political, or social event. For example, docudramas may use actors and scripted dialogue to re-create historical events.

**Documentary**  *Documentary* is a genre of film and television programming which uses language, sounds, and imagery to provide an interpretation of real-life events. Although documentaries attempt to relate factual information, they may only show one producer's perceptions or point of view. Documentaries often have informative, persuasive, and artistic purposes.

**Drama**   *Drama* is an art form that tells a story through the speech and actions of the characters in the story. Most dramas use actors who impersonate the characters. Some dramas are performed in a theater, while others are presented on film.

**Editor**   (See **Editor** on page 884.)

**Electronic Media**   The term *electronic media* refers to the forms of mass media products that are available to consumers through some type of electronic technology such as a computer or a television. Electronic media products can be found on the Internet, on the radio, and on television.

**Feature News**   (See **Feature News** on page 884.)

**Hard News**   (See **Hard News** on page 885.)

**In-Camera Editing**   *In-camera editing* refers to any editing that is performed through the operation of a video or film camera and not by the cutting and shaping of an editor. The sequence of shots and scenes remains exactly as they were gathered by the camera operator. In-camera editing is an effective method of creating video when editing is time-consuming or equipment is unavailable. To create an effective work using in-camera editing, a great deal of pre-production planning is required, including a complete shot list and storyboards. In most cameras, sound can be added after the images have been shot.

**Internet**   The *Internet* is a global network of computers. With the Internet, a computer user may access information from another computer or a network of computers anywhere in the world. The Internet may be used by almost anyone who has a computer equipped with a modem.

**Lead**   (See **Lead** on page 885.)

**Marketing**   (See **Marketing** on page 885.)

**Medium**   (See **Medium** on page 885.)

**Message**   (See **Message** on page 885.)

**Multimedia Presentation**   A *multimedia presentation* is any presentation that involves two or more forms of media. For example, when you give an oral presentation including visuals (such as slides, transparencies, or posters), you are giving a multimedia presentation, one medium being your voice, the other being the visuals you use to support your presentation. A multimedia presentation that involves the use of presentation software or Web sites is sometimes called a **technology presentation.**

**Nielsen Rating**   *Nielsen rating* refers to the ratings system invented by the A. C. Nielsen Company, one of the largest marketing research companies in the United States. Nielsen ratings gather information about household television viewing choices from a sample of five thousand households selected to represent the population as a whole. Using a device called a peoplemeter, the firm gathers and later distributes information including the program watched, who was watching it, and the amount of time each viewer spent watching. Nielsen ratings are used to measure a program's popularity and to pinpoint target audiences for shows. Advertisers make decisions about buying airtime for their commercials during specific shows based in part on Nielsen ratings.

**Network**    A *network* is a company that obtains and distributes programming to affiliated local stations or cable systems. Networks are not TV stations, but nearly 85 percent of all TV stations are affiliated with a network. Examples of networks include CBS, ABC, NBC, FOX, and WB. Each local station is responsible for its own programming, but a station that is affiliated with a network receives morning news programs, talk shows, soap operas, national news programs, situation comedies, dramas, and late-night programming. The networks provide the programs free to stations in exchange for the right to sell advertising. (See also **Affiliate** on page 876.)

**News**    (See **News** on page 886.)

**Newsmagazine**    (See **Newsmagazine** on page 885.)

**Photography**    (See **Photography** on page 885.)

**Political Advertising**    (See **Political Advertising** on page 886.)

**Producer**    A *producer* is the person responsible for overseeing the creation of a movie or television or radio program. He or she is responsible for the following tasks.

- developing the overall message
- finding appropriate materials
- organizing a crew or staff
- finding and budgeting funding
- keeping the production on a timetable

**Public Access**    *Public access* refers to the channels on a cable television system that are set aside specifically for use by the public to create a variety of programs. These channels are often controlled by education officials or government leaders.

**Ratings**    *Ratings* are the system of categorizing films, TV programs, or video games by considering whether the content is appropriate for people of different ages. Ratings help adults and children evaluate the content of a message before viewing. (See also **Nielsen Ratings** on page 878.)

**Reality TV**    *Reality television* is the presentation of actual video footage taken by amateurs with police monitors and by surveillance cameras. Usually the footage is highly edited; but because reality TV is presented as an eyewitness account, people tend to find it believable.

**Reporter**    (See **Reporter** on page 886.)

**Script**    A *script* is the text or words of a film, play, or television or radio show. The format for film and TV scripts often includes information about the images to be shown. The script for news broadcasts is called *copy*. (See also **Copy** on page 884.)

**Sequencing**    *Sequencing* is the order in which scenes or images appear in a narrative. In television, film, and video, sequencing is enhanced in the editing process, in which scenes, usually filmed separately and in different locations, are spliced or joined together to create a sense of flow or sequence.

**Situation Comedy**    A *situation comedy* is a television format that involves stories about a regular set of characters in either a home or work setting. Situation comedies involve humor and focus on life's ordinary problems and solutions. (See also **Genre** on page 882.)

**Soft News**   (See **Soft News** on page 886.)

**Source**   (See **Source** on page 886.)

**Sponsorship**   A *sponsorship* takes place when a business gives money to support a particular TV or radio program in return for commercial airtime. Sponsorship is different from advertising because in sponsorship, a company's name is acknowledged but usually the product is not promoted. Even though public broadcasting does not include commercials, it may include sponsors' names and slogans. (See also **Broadcasting** on page 876.)

**Storyboard**   A *storyboard* is a visual script, or series of drawings, that indicates the appearance and order of shots and scenes in a script as well as audio and visual cues. (See **Storyboards** on page 817.)

**Target Audience**   (See also **Target Audience** on page 886.)

**Text**   (See also **Text** on page 886.)

## General Media Terms

**Audience**   An *audience* is a group of receivers of a media message. Audiences may receive a message by listening, reading, or viewing. The audience is important to understanding the economics of the mass media business, since advertisers pay to reach specific audiences when they place ads in newspapers, magazines, radio, television, or the Internet. Audiences are often identified by specific characteristics, or demographics. (See also **Demographics** on page 884.)

**Authority**   *Authority* refers to a quality of a message. When a message seems believable because it comes from a trustworthy and knowledgeable individual, the message has authority. For example, we would say a message about the health of a panda would have more authority coming from a zookeeper than from a spectator at the zoo. (See also **Credibility** on this page and **Source** on page 886.)

**Bias**   A *bias* is a negative connotation or point of view. An editorial writer with a bias may present only one side of an issue or ignore information that does not support his or her position. (See also **Point of View** on page 883.)

**Communicator**   A *communicator* is a person involved in the act of communicating or sharing messages with another person or persons. The communicator is the person who sends the message to the audience. The receiver takes on the role of communicator when he or she returns the message.

**Credibility**   *Credibility* is the willingness to believe in a person or to trust what a person says and does. Credibility is not a characteristic of a speaker. It is a perception that exists in the minds of a listener or viewer. (See also **Authority** on this page.)

**Critical Viewing**   *Critical viewing* is the ability to use critical thinking skills to view, question, analyze, and understand issues presented in visual media, including photography, film, television, and other mass media. Critical viewers use **media literacy** concepts to access, analyze, evaluate, and communicate media messages. On the next page are five key concepts of media literacy and some questions to help you evaluate media messages.

| Media Concepts | Evaluation Questions |
|---|---|

**1. All messages are made by someone.**

Every media message is written, edited, selected, illustrated, or composed by one or more individuals. Writers, photographers, artists, illustrators, and TV and radio producers all decide which elements (words, images, sounds) to include in a media message, which ones to leave out, and how to arrange and sequence the chosen elements. Knowing how media messages are constructed will help you better interpret the meaning of a message.

Ask yourself:
"What words, images, or sounds are used to create the message?" and "What words, images, or sounds may have been left out of the message?"

**2. Media messages are not reality, but *representations* of reality that in turn shape people's ideas of the world.**

Fictional stories in the media can seem realistic if characters act in ways that seem authentic, but, of course, the stories are not real. An eyewitness news account of a fire can seem real, but it usually reflects only one person's point of view, filtered through a TV camera and edited down to a few images and words. Media messages can never match the complexity of the real world. Every media message also affects the way you think about the world. It is important that you judge the accuracy of media messages and whether or not you think the messages reflect reality.

Ask yourself:
"What is the point of view or experience of the message maker?" and "How does this message affect the way I think about a particular topic or idea?"

**3. Each person interprets media messages differently.**

Your interpretation of a media message is based on your knowledge and experience. You can use your prior knowledge and experience to examine the many different stylistic features of a message and to evaluate the message within its context.

Ask yourself:
"How does the message make me feel?" or "Of what does the message make me think?"

**4. People have a wide range of purposes for creating media messages.**

People create and share messages for many reasons; in modern culture making money is one of the most important. When people have political purposes, they use messages to gain power or authority over others. Understanding how messages operate in terms of their economic, political, social, and aesthetic purposes will help you better understand the context of a work.

Ask yourself:
"Who created the message and why?" or "Is the producer's purpose to inform, to influence, to present ideas, to make money, to gain power, or to express ideas?"

**5. Each mass medium—from TV to the newspaper to the Internet—has unique characteristics.**

A media producer makes choices about which forms and techniques are most appropriate to convey a particular message to a particular audience. For example, TV news favors messages that are immediate and visual to appeal to an audience that needs information quickly. Print news stories may provide in-depth analysis for an audience interested in the big picture. Knowing how the medium shapes the message will help you understand why certain techniques were used and what effect the story has on you.

Ask yourself:
"Through what medium is the message delivered?" and "How does the form affect the message?" or "How might the techniques used affect various audiences?"

QUICK REFERENCE HANDBOOK

**Decoding**   *Decoding* is the making of meaning from verbal and nonverbal signals. For example, audiences decode symbols, such as words and pictures, when they watch TV or read a newspaper.

**Deconstruction**   *Deconstruction* is the process of analyzing, or taking apart, the pieces of a media message to understand its meaning. The process of deconstruction involves looking at both what is stated, such as the words printed on a newspaper page, and what is not directly stated, including elements of the historical, economic, and political context in which the newspaper was created.

**Feedback**   *Feedback* is a response from an audience to the sender of a message. It can be immediate or delayed. Applause, booing, and asking questions are typical forms of immediate feedback from an audience. Writing a letter to the editor to respond to a newspaper editorial and filling out a questionnaire on a Web page are forms of **delayed feedback.**

**Genre**   A *genre* is a category of artistic forms or media products that shares **conventions,** or commonly accepted ways of presenting messages. For example, prime-time TV programs usually begin with a short, attention-grabbing segment before the opening credits and commercials. Each genre has a particular audience and conventions. Examples of genres within television include documentary, drama, game show, infomercial, music video, news broadcast, sitcom (situation comedy), soap opera, and talk show.

**Interpretation**   *Interpretation* is the process of creating meaning from exposure to a message through reading, viewing, or listening.

People's interpretations of messages differ, depending on their life experiences, backgrounds, and points of view.

**Media Law**   Various government structures, laws, and policies regulate access, content, delivery, and use of the mass media. For example, the *First Amendment* to the Constitution forbids Congress to set up or in any way pass laws limiting speech or the press. *Copyright law* protects the rights of authors and other media owners against the unauthorized publishing, reproduction, and selling of their works. *Censorship* is any governmental attempt to suppress or control people's access to media messages. Some censorship, however, may be used to protect citizens against damage to their reputations (*libel*) or against invasions of their privacy.

**News Values**   *News values* are the set of criteria journalists use to determine whether information is newsworthy. News values include

- **timeliness**   events or issues that are happening now
- **conflict**   unresolved events or issues that are interesting to the public
- **novelty**   stories that contain unique, interesting elements
- **relevance**   stories that are of interest to local readers
- **human interest**   stories that touch people's emotions
- **prominence**   stories about celebrities, politicians, or other noteworthy people
- **impact**   stories that make a difference in people's lives

If a news event has these features, it is more likely to be covered by the news media.

**Newsworthiness**    *Newsworthiness* is the quality of an event that is worthy of being reported in a newspaper or news broadcast. An event must be of interest or importance to the public in order to be considered newsworthy. (See also **News Values** on page 882.)

**Omission**    An *omission* is what is left out of a media message. All messages are selective and incomplete. For example, some advertisements omit information about the cost or the negative side effects of their products. Some editorials present only one side of an issue, omitting facts and opinions that are contrary to the writer's opinion. Noticing what is not included in a message helps to identify the author's point of view. (See also **Point of View** below.)

**Point of View**    *Point of view* can refer to the position or view of the person reporting a story or telling a tale in the mass media. Point of view is also a literary concept which can be used to interpret mass media texts ranging from docu-dramas to feature news stories. In the electronic media, point of view can be indicated by the type of narration used or by the type of camera shot used. There are many possible points of view.

**Propaganda**    *Propaganda* is any form of communication that uses persuasive techniques to reach a mass audience. Propaganda was originally defined as the spreading of biased ideas and opinions through lies and deception. This definition gave the concept of propaganda a negative connotation. However, as scholars began to study the topic in the 1940s, they came to realize that propaganda was everywhere. Over time, the concept of propaganda has lost some of its negative connotation. Propaganda is now thought of as the communication of a point of view with the goal of having audience

members come to voluntarily accept this position as one of their beliefs. Advertising is one of the major forms of propaganda. (See also **Advertising** below.)

**Purpose**    The *purpose* of a media message is what its sender or creator intends to achieve. Usually, the purpose of a message is to inform, to educate, to persuade, to entertain, to express oneself, or to make money. A message may have a primary and a secondary purpose at the same time.

**Sensationalism**    *Sensationalism* is the media's use or portrayal of material that is intended to generate curiosity, fear, or other strong responses. The material can be exaggerated or shocking in content. Content that refers to romance, death, children, or animals is often sensational. (See also **Reality TV** on page 879 and **Tabloid** on page 886.)

**Stereotypes**    *Stereotypes* are generalized beliefs based on misinformation or insufficient evidence about an entire group of individuals. A stereotype about teenagers, for example, would be that all teenagers sleep late. (See **Stereotypes** on page 153.)

**Visual Literacy**    *Visual literacy* is a person's awareness of how meaning is communicated through visual media, including the use of color, line, shape, and texture.

## Print Media Terms

**Advertising**    *Advertising* is the use of images or text to promote or sell a product, service, image, or idea to a wide audience. Advertising is a marketing technique that is designed to persuade an audience. Typical advertising formats include print advertisements in newspapers and magazines, billboards, radio and television commercials, and electronic billboards on the World Wide Web. (See also **Marketing** on page 885 and **Sponsorship** on page 880.)

**Byline**   A *byline* is the name of the reporter or writer of a report published in a newspaper or magazine or presented on television or radio.

**Circulation**   *Circulation* is a measurement of the size of the audience for print media. It includes the total number of copies of a publication, such as a newspaper or magazine, that is delivered to subscribers, newsstands, and vendors.

**Copy**   *Copy* is the text in a media message.

**Demographics**   *Demographics* are the characteristics that define a particular audience. They include gender, age, educational background, cultural heritage, and income. Advertisers use demographics to target certain audiences. For example, advertisers know that many children watch Saturday morning cartoons, so they will advertise toys during Saturday morning commercial breaks.

**Digital Editing**   *Digital editing* is the use of computer technology to alter or change an image before it is presented to an audience. Photo editors often edit out distracting elements—such as telephone wires or shadows—from photo illustrations. However, large-scale digital editing of hard-news photographs is thought to be an unethical practice.

**Editor**   An *editor* supervises reporters. Editors decide what news stories will appear in print media or in broadcasting. They also check facts for accuracy and correct errors. (See also **News Values** on page 882.)

**Elements of Design**   *Elements of Design* are the parts of an idea's visual representation—such as *color, line, shape* and *texture*—that give meaning to the visual representation. The following list explains how each element communicates meaning. (See also **Document Design** on page 806.)

- *Color* creates mood and adds realism with its visual appeal. Color designates areas of space by separating and emphasizing parts of a visual. Viewers also associate certain items with particular colors. For example, usually oranges and tangerines are associated with the color orange. (See also **Color** on page 813.)
- *Line* determines the direction and speed of the viewer's eye movement. For example, straight lines suggest decisiveness, while curvy lines indicate gracefulness. Lines also communicate factual information in graphic organizers. (See also **Types of Graphics** on page 815).
- *Shape* emphasizes elements in the visual and adds interest. Often, shapes evoke emotional responses. For example, a square represents solidarity, while a circle indicates completeness.
- *Texture* is the manner in which the visual representation appeals to a viewer's sense of touch. Sometimes superficial texture in a visual may be created by cross-hatching, diagonal lines, or stippling.

**Feature News**   *Feature news,* also called soft news, refers to news stories whose primary purpose is to entertain. Feature stories usually are not timely. Stories about celebrities and ordinary people, places, animals, events, and products are considered feature news because they generate sympathy, curiosity, or amazement in viewers, readers, or listeners. An example of feature news would be a profile of a chef who works in the White House. (See also **Hard News** and **Soft News** on pages 885 and 886.)

**Font**   A *font* is a style of lettering used for printing text. (See also **Fonts** on page 811.)

**Hard News**   *Hard news* refers to fact-based reporting of breaking news stories. Hard news answers the basic *5W-How?* questions about timely subjects, such as national and international politics, economics, social issues, the environment, and scientific discoveries. An example of hard news would be a story reporting results the day after a presidential election. (See also **Feature News** on page 884 and **Soft News** on page 886.)

**Headline**   A *headline* is the title of a newspaper or magazine article, usually set in large or bold type. It has two purposes: to inform the reader of the content of the article and to get the reader's attention.

EXAMPLE

# Stock Market Hits Historic High

**Lead**   A *lead* is the introduction to a newspaper article or a broadcast report. It ranges from one sentence to several paragraphs in length and contains information that motivates a reader or viewer to continue with the story. A lead usually contains the major facts of a story and may also describe a curious or unusual situation to attract reader or viewer attention.

EXAMPLE

CAPE CANAVERAL, July 23—After two postponements this week, space shuttle *Columbia* blasted off early today with the world's most powerful X-ray telescope and Eileen Collins, the first woman to command a U.S. spaceflight.

**Marketing**   *Marketing* is the process of moving goods or services from the producer to the consumer. It includes identifying consumer wants or needs; designing, packaging, and pricing the product; and arranging for locations where the product will be sold. Marketing also includes promoting the product to a target audience through advertising or other means. (See also **Advertising** on page 883.)

**Medium**   The *medium* of a message is the form in which it is presented or distributed, including film, video, radio, television, the Internet, and print.

**Message**   A *message* is a combination of symbols that is communicated to one or more people. Messages are created by people who use symbols, including language, gesture, images, sounds, and electronic forms. Media messages are communicated through various mass media. (See also **Medium** above.)

**News**   *News* is the presentation of current and interesting information that will interest or affect an audience. Local news is produced by local newspapers and radio and TV stations, which use their own equipment, reporters, and resources. The focus of local news is information that affects a small audience with regional interests. National news is produced by large newspapers and radio and TV stations. Because their resources are greater, national news organizations may cover more national and world issues or events.

**Newsmagazine**   A *newsmagazine* is a weekly, biweekly, monthly, or bimonthly printed journal that focuses on news issues. On TV, a newsmagazine is a news program divided into several news segments or stories.

**Photography**   *Photography* is a process of making pictures by using cameras to record patterns of light and images on film or on computer disks. Photography is both an art form and a major component of the mass media; it is used in making still photographs and motion pictures. People sometimes think that "a photograph never lies," but a photograph, like all media messages, is selective and incomplete. Photographers use a wide range of techniques to communicate their points of view, including the framing and composition of an image, the use of filters or digital editing, and the selection of what to include in the frame. (See also **Digital Editing** on page 884 and **Point of View** on page 883.)

**Political Advertising**   *Political advertising* is the use of the mass media to persuade listeners and viewers about a political candidate's ideas or opinions. Political candidates who use advertising must use techniques similar to those used to sell products. Their messages must be simple and attention-getting. (See also **Advertising** on page 883.)

**Print Media**   *Print media* refers to the hard copies of mass media products that are printed on paper to be read or looked at by consumers. Examples of print media are newspapers, magazines, pamphlets, and flyers.

**Reporter**   A *reporter* is a journalist who is responsible for information gathering.

Reporters gather information and work with editors to create TV and print news. (See also **Editor** on page 884.)

**Soft News**   *Soft news,* or feature news, is the presentation of general interest material, such as celebrities and sports, in a news format. Soft news is designed to entertain readers or viewers. (See also **Feature News** on page 884 and **Hard News** on page 885.)

**Source**   A *source* is the person who first supplies information or ideas that are then shared with others. Journalists rely on sources for the information they report, and select individuals that they believe are credible and have authority. (See also **Authority** on page 880.)

**Tabloid**   A *tabloid* is a publication with a newspaper format that provides sensational news items and photographs. Tabloids are highly dependent on stories and photographs of media celebrities. Tabloid producers often admit that the stories they report are either false or exaggerations of the truth.

**Target Audience**   A *target audience* is a segment of the population for which a product or presentation is designed. (See also **Demographics** on page 884.)

**Text**   *Text* refers to the symbols used to create a message, such as a book, a magazine article, or a TV show.

# Writing

## Skills, Structures, and Techniques

You can use the following ideas and information to become a more effective writer.

**Business Letters**   Use a *business letter* for business-related matters, such as applying for a job or requesting goods or services. A business letter must look and sound professional.

| Guidelines for Business Letters |
|---|
| Use plain, unlined $8\frac{1}{2}$" × 11" paper. |
| Type (single-spaced) or neatly write the letter, using black or blue ink. Avoid typing errors, misspellings, cross-outs, and all smudges. |
| Use equal margins on all sides. |
| Use only one side of the paper. Carry over at least two lines onto the second page, if necessary. |
| Use a polite, respectful, professional tone. |
| Use formal, standard English. Avoid slang, contractions, and most abbreviations. |
| Include all necessary information, but get to the point quickly. Be sure your reader knows why you wrote and what you are asking. |

■ **Parts**   There are six parts of a business letter, usually arranged on the page in one of two styles. In **block form,** all six parts begin at the left margin. In **modified block form,** the heading, the closing, and your signature are aligned on the right-hand side of the page. All the other parts begin at the left margin, and paragraphs are indented.

1. The *heading* usually has three lines:
   - your street address
   - your city, state, and ZIP Code
   - the date the letter was written
2. The *inside address* gives the name and address of the person to whom you are writing. Use a courtesy title (such as *Mr.* or *Miss*) or a professional title (such as *Dr.* or *Professor*) in front of the person's name. Include the person's business title after the name.
3. The *salutation* is your greeting. Use *Dear,* a courtesy title or professional title, and the person's name. End with a colon. If you don't have the name of a specific person, use a general salutation such as *Dear Sir or Madam:,* or you can use a department or a position title.

4. The **body,** or main part of your letter, contains the message. If you include more than one paragraph, leave a blank line between paragraphs.

5. The **closing** is your ending. Appropriate closings are *Yours truly, Sincerely,* or *Sincerely yours.* End the closing with a comma.

6. Your **signature** should be handwritten in ink, directly below the closing and above your typed or printed name. Always sign your full name with no titles.

**Block Style**

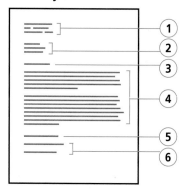

**Modified Block Style**

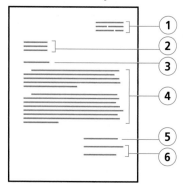

■ **Types** There are three types of business letters.

1. **Request or order letters** In a *request letter,* you are asking for information about a product or asking for someone's time or

services. Enclose a self-addressed, stamped envelope if you're asking someone to send information. Make requests of individuals well in advance. An **order letter** requests something specific, such as a free brochure. Here is a sample request letter.

Bethlehem High School
700 Delaware Avenue
Delmar, NY 12054
October 12, 2001

Ms. Ellen Phillips, Staff Writer
The Albany Times Mirror
News Plaza 1000
Albany, NY 12212

Dear Ms. Phillips:

    I would like to invite you to be one of our speakers at the Bethlehem High School Career Day. This year's event will be December 16, from 9:00 A.M. to 4:00 P.M.

    Please let me know if you would be interested in speaking to an audience of about fifty students for a fifteen-minute talk about your career in journalism. We can schedule your talk at your convenience.

    I look forward to your reply.

       Yours truly,

       *Jennifer Savage*

       Jennifer Savage,
       Student Coordinator
       Career Day 2001

2. **Complaint or adjustment letters** The purpose of a **complaint** or **adjustment letter** is to report an error or to state that you have not received services or products that you have reason to expect. In a calm, courteous

tone, tell why you are displeased. Tell what solution you want to correct the problem. Here is the body of a sample letter.

```
    On January 2, 2000, I ordered
a plaid shirt from your catalog:
Item # 3121HH, size 38 medium,
described as "a washable
wool/polyester blend." The shirt
cost $27, plus $1.50 shipping and
handling, for a total of $28.50.

    The first time I washed the
shirt, the side seam split apart.
I followed the washing directions
on the label carefully.

    I am returning the shirt.
Please send a replacement shirt
or a refund. Thank you for your
attention to this matter.
```

3. **Appreciation or commendation letters** In an *appreciation* or *commendation letter,* you express your appreciation for a person, a group, an organization, or a product or service. Be specific about why you are pleased. Here is the body of a sample.

```
    I am writing to let you know
how much I enjoyed your museum's
recent exhibition on contemporary
African American artists. My high
school's art class was impressed
and inspired by what we saw. I
particularly enjoyed the paint-
ings by Lawrence and Bearden.
```

**Compositions**    A *composition* is a longer piece of writing consisting of paragraphs. A composition usually has three main parts: *introduction, body,* and *conclusion.* Each of these has a function, yet they all work together to communicate the writer's main idea.

■ **Introduction**    Your composition's *intro-duction* should do three things.

1. **Catch readers' attention.** Your introduction should make your readers want to read on.
2. **Set the tone.** Your **tone** can be formal, informal, humorous, or serious. The tone you adopt depends upon the **occasion,** or what prompts you to write on a particular topic, and the makeup of your **audience,** the people who will read your composition.
3. **Present the thesis.** A *thesis statement* is a sentence or two that announces your topic and your main idea about it. A thesis statement works in a composition like a topic sentence works in a paragraph. Your thesis statement can guide you as you plan, write, and revise your paper. Here are some strategies for writing a thesis statement.

## Strategy & Example

**1.** Review the facts and details in your prewriting notes and begin thinking about how they fit together.
*Much of the information in my notes on recycling is about the amount of usable and reusable materials we throw away.*

**2.** Ask yourself the following questions: *What is my topic? What do I want to say about my topic?*
Topic: *recycling*
My idea about my topic: *We throw away far too much usable and reusable material.*

**3.** Sharpen your focus and present a defi-nite, focused idea—a thesis statement.
*We would use the earth's limited resources more wisely if we recycled as much as possible.*

**4.** Ask yourself whether your audience will care about your topic. *My audience consists of classmates, most of whom are concerned about the environment. They would be interested in recycling.*

Often, an introduction begins with general information and moves to the specific with the thesis as the final statement. The following graphic may help you to visualize the organization.

**Introduction**

**General**

**Specific
(Thesis)**

To write an effective introduction, try one of the following techniques. The examples show how you might introduce a composition about recycling.

■ **Body**   The *body* states and develops the composition's main points. Together, all the paragraphs in the body support one main idea—the thesis statement. When writing the body of your composition, keep in mind the following guidelines.

1. Arrange your information in a way that makes sense to your readers. This gives your composition *coherence.*

2. Eliminate any details that do not support your thesis. This gives your paper *unity.*

3. Show how your ideas are connected by using direct references and transitional expressions. (See page 364.)

| Technique | Example |
|---|---|
| Begin with an anecdote or example. | Last weekend when I was baby-sitting a five year-old neighbor, I had an eye-opening experience. I was about to throw away the trash from our snack, when little Ana yelled, "Wait! Aren't you going to recycle that bottle? Don't you care about the earth?" She's right. Recycling is everyone's responsibility. |
| Begin with a startling fact or by adopting an unusual position. | Our earth is not very pleased with us Americans. Every year we throw away enough office paper to build a twelve-foot-high wall. We dispose of enough diapers to stretch from the earth to the moon seven times. The list goes on. |
| Use an appropriate quotation. | In her acceptance speech Mayor Cosby said, "Recycling must become the norm—a way of life. With a few minor changes and minimal effort, we can reap great rewards." |
| Start with background information. | Recycling is the collecting, processing, and reusing of materials. Throughout history people have recycled. For example, metal tools and weapons have been melted and reused for thousands of years. |
| Begin with a simple statement of your thesis. | With an increase in population and a decrease in natural resources, people around the world are viewing recycling as the way of the future. |

■ **Conclusion**　As the final part of your paper, the *conclusion* should do two things:

1. **Leave the reader with a sense of completeness.** Most readers don't like to be left hanging or to feel that they have been abruptly dismissed.
2. **Reinforce the main idea.** The conclusion should bring your readers back to the main idea. Often a conclusion begins with a specific statement, such as a restatement of the thesis, and moves to general information.

The following graphic may help you to visualize the organization.

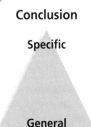

**Conclusion**

**Specific**

**General**

To write an effective conclusion, try one of the techniques in the following chart:

| Technique | Example |
|---|---|
| Restate your main idea. | Our world is changing: The population is increasing and the natural resources are decreasing. To offset this change, many people are committing to recycling. |
| Summarize your major points. | With an increase in population comes an increase in trash. Landfills are overflowing, so the solution is to produce less trash. Materials ranging from old newspapers to precious metals can be recycled. The recycling process reclaims original materials and uses them in new products. |
| Close with a final idea or example. | Last year the freshman class initiated a month-long "Recycle Today!" campaign. Throughout the community, the freshmen distributed educational pamphlets. Within the school, they set up recycling containers in the cafeteria and in the courtyard. The response was telling: With a little guidance, people are willing to make recycling a part of their lives. |
| End with a comment on the topic (a thoughtful reaction or observation, a personal look to the future). | The idea of recycling is catching on. More and more people in my neighborhood are setting out their recycling bins on collection day. The cafeteria's recycling containers are overflowing at lunch. People are showing that they do care about the future of our planet. Maybe it's not too late. |
| Call on your readers to take action. | Of the 160 million tons of trash we produce each year in the United States, 80 percent is used in landfill, 10 percent is burned, and only 10 percent is recycled. We can change those percentages. Start recycling today. |
| Refer to your introduction. | The next time you start to throw away a recyclable article, think of Our Earth. Make her smile. |

**E-mail**   Electronic mail, or *e-mail,* is correspondence sent via the computer rather than through your local post office. E-mail can be used to write personal, informal letters or to send business messages. Because e-mails are easy to write, send, and receive, many e-mail users ignore the guidelines associated with writing letters. Informal content and format are often acceptable when you write to someone you know well or send comments to a newsgroup or chat group where the discussions are clearly relaxed. However, if you are writing to someone you do not know well for business or research purposes, you should use the following guidelines. Remember: Online etiquette, or "Netiquette," stresses the importance of good manners and common sense in cyberspace, just as etiquette does in the real world.

**Envelopes**   For a letter to arrive promptly at its destination, it must be addressed correctly. Place your complete return address in the top left-hand corner of the envelope. Center on the envelope the name and address of the person to whom you are writing. For a business letter, the addressee's name and address should exactly match the inside address. Use the two-letter state code on the envelope rather than writing out the state name.

## E-mail Guidelines

- Keep your message concise and to the point. Limit yourself to one full screen or less of text. Scrolling through long e-mail messages can be tedious.

- Use bulleted lists and indentations to make the document easy for your readers to read on-screen. Bulleted lists are especially helpful if you are raising more than one question or point.

- Always make sure that your spelling, grammar, and punctuation are correct, and use standard English.

- Include salutations, such as "Dear Dr. Brunelli," if you are writing for the first time to someone you do not know. Also, a closing, such as "Sincerely" or "Thank you," followed by your full name is always considered polite.

- Always be polite in your messages—even if you know the person to whom you are writing. Being rude to someone in an e-mail is called *flaming.* Flaming often backfires because there is always the chance that your angry message could be forwarded and read by someone you didn't intend to see it.

- Avoid using capital letters in your messages. CAPITALS CONVEY SHOUTING. No one wants to be shouted at in cyberspace. (If you want to show emphasis, place asterisks [*] on either side of the important word or term instead—for example, "What do you think about the *metaphor* in Chapter 2?"

- Use *emoticons* sparingly and never use them in formal e-mails. *Emoticons* are combinations of symbols that, when you tilt your head to the left, look like faces and suggest feelings. For example, the emoticon :-) suggests laughter or "I'm just kidding." Use them in informal e-mails only.

- Always pay attention to the addresses entered in your address line. Make sure that you are sending appropriate messages to the right people.

- Always fill in the subject line before you send a message. Providing a subject will help your readers prioritize your message, which could be one of many they receive.

- Avoid forwarding e-mail without asking the permission of the original sender. Private e-mails are usually intended for your eyes only.

**Forms**   Printed forms vary, but the following techniques will help you fill out any form—from a job application to a contest entry—accurately and completely.

- Read all of the instructions carefully.
- Type or write neatly. Type, or print your information in either blue or black ink, unless pencil is specified.
- Proofread your completed form and correct errors neatly. Be sure you have given all information requested on the form.

**Graphic Organizers**   A *graphic organizer* is a visual that helps you "see" what you are thinking. You can use graphic organizers to find a subject to write about, to gather information, and to organize your information.

- **Charts**   By dividing a subject into its logical parts, you can analyze and organize the details you have gathered. A *chart* helps you to arrange information into categories. The following chart describes scientific research in space with the three branches of science as categories.

| Scientific Research in Space | |
| --- | --- |
| Branch of Science | Type of Experiment |
| biology | experiments on how zero gravity affects the biological rhythms of living things such as fish and plants |
| physics | experiments on how zero gravity affects the development or manufacture of crystals |
| astronomy | studies of the universe, using X-ray astronomy, without the distorting effects of the earth's atmosphere |

- **Clustering**   (See **Prewriting Techniques** on page 897.)
- **Mapping**   (See **Prewriting Techniques** on page 897.)
- **Sequence chain**   A *sequence chain* helps you see how one event leads to another. They work well when you are narrating or explaining a process. The following sequence chain organizes notes about tie-dyeing a shirt.

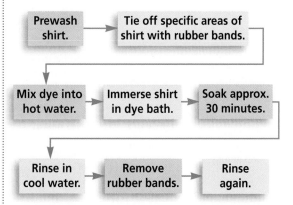

- **Time line**   A *time line* organizes information chronologically along a horizontal line from left to right, and from the earliest events to the most recent events. The following example traces civil rights events.

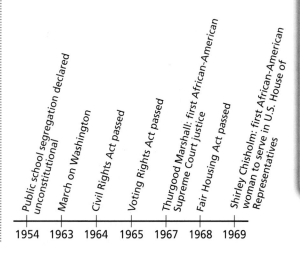

Skills, Structures, and Techniques   **893**

■ **Venn diagram**   A *Venn diagram* uses intersecting circles to show the similarities and differences between two subjects. The area of overlap between the two circles shows how two subjects are similar; the remaining areas show how they are different. In the following Venn diagram, the writer compares and contrasts visiting his two uncles.

| Differences | Similarities | Differences |
|---|---|---|
| Uncle in Florida | | Uncle in Maine |

- can drive to his house
- Uncle Max golfs
- friends in the neighborhood
- weather hot and muggy

- good food
- my own room
- lots of activities
- family dogs

- too far to drive; must fly
- Uncle Ben fishes
- no one my age lives nearby
- weather cool and refreshing

**Informal or Personal Letters**   The content and appearance of a personal letter is less formal than a business letter. Personal letters are usually handwritten rather than typed. Use the modified block form, but do not include an inside address. (See **Business Letters** on page 887.) There are three common types of informal or personal letters.

■ **Thank-you letters**   A *thank-you letter* tells someone that you appreciate his or her taking time, trouble, or expense on your behalf.

■ **Invitations**   An informal *invitation* should contain specific information about the occasion, the time and place, and other details your guest might need to know.

■ **Letters of regret**   Send a *letter of regret* if you have been invited somewhere and are unable to go. A written reply is especially appropriate if you were sent a written invitation with the letters *R.S.V.P.* (in French, an abbreviation for "please reply").

**Manuscript Form**   When you formally share your composition with others, its appearance is important. These guidelines will help improve the appearance of your paper.

| Guidelines for Manuscript Form |
|---|
| Use only one side of a sheet of paper. |
| Write in blue or black ink, or type. |
| If you write by hand, don't skip lines. If you type, double-space the lines. |
| Leave margins of about one inch at the top, sides, and bottom of a page. |
| Indent the first line of each paragraph. |
| Number all pages except the first page. Place the number in the upper right-hand corner. |
| All pages should be neat and clean. You may make a few corrections with correction fluid. |
| Follow your teacher's instructions for placing your name, the date, your class, and the title of your paper. |

**Memos**   A memorandum, or *memo,* is a written message for conducting business within an organization. For example, an individual might send a memo to co-workers to remind them about a meeting, or all employees might receive a memo describing a new policy. An organization or department often has a set format for memos.

**Messages**   Writing a *message* requires listening to information, usually by telephone, and then communicating that information to someone else. Think of the five *W* questions when writing a message.

*Who* is the message from and for *whom*?
*What* is the message?
*When* was the message written (date and time)?
*Where* can the sender be reached, if necessary?
*Why* is the message important?

**Outlines**    An *outline* is a plan—a way of grouping and organizing information to show the relationships among ideas. An outline can guide writers to present ideas clearly and can help readers perceive the relationships among ideas.

■ **Formal outlines**    A *formal outline* is a highly structured, clearly labeled writing plan. It uses letters and numbers to label main headings and subheadings. An outline can use either words and phrases or complete sentences for each item. Here is an example of a formal outline about preseason athletic training.

**Title:** Is Preseason Training Necessary?
**Thesis statement:** A preseason training program that includes lifting weights, stretching, and living a healthy lifestyle will greatly improve an athlete's performance.

I. Lifting weights
  A. Increased power
  B. Injury prevention
II. Stretching
  A. Increased flexibility
  B. Injury prevention
III. Living a healthy lifestyle
  A. Good nutrition
  B. Adequate sleep
  C. Hydration
    1. At least eight glasses of water daily
    2. No dehydrating drinks
      a. beverages with caffeine
      b. beverages high in sugar
      c. carbonated beverages

■ **Informal outlines or early plans**    An *early plan* doesn't have a set form. You simply sort your ideas or facts into groups and arrange the groups in order. To sort your information into groups, ask yourself, *Which items belong together? What do they have in common? Which items don't fit anywhere?* Then, give each group a heading that shows how the items in it are related. Next, order, or arrange, your information in a way that will make sense to your readers: chronological order, spatial order, logical order, or order of importance.  Some papers will suggest a natural order; however, more than one order may be possible. Ask yourself, *Is the purpose and the order of each grouping of details understandable?* (See also page 359.)

**Paragraphs**    A *paragraph* is a group of sentences that present and support a main idea; it is also the primary building block in a composition. Although most of the paragraphs in a single composition will often be one of the following major types, many compositions contain more than one type of paragraph. The four types of paragraphs vary by their purpose.

■ **Descriptive paragraphs**    A *descriptive paragraph* lets your readers truly see your subject, whether it is a person, an object, or a scene. Descriptive paragraphs often use spatial order and usually contain sensory details.

> The golf bag was enormous. It seemed a dull conservative color when I saw it in the late afternoon gloom of a Florida golf shop. But when I took it out on a practice round the next day, it glowed a rich oxblood color, like a vast sausage. It was very heavy with a metal bottom with brass

**Sensory detail 1**

*(continued)*

Sensory detail 2

Sensory detail 3

studs around it, and when I first went out, I felt guilty for seeing it on a caddy's back. But the clubs let off a fine chinking sound as the bag was carried, as expensive and exclusive as the sound of a Cadillac door shutting to, and the fact that the porters, caddies, and I myself, whoever carried it, were bent nearly double by its weight only seemed to add to its stature.

George Plimpton, "Golf"

■ **Expository paragraphs** An *expository paragraph* is used to explain and inform. Because explanations are clarified by organizing information into categories, expository paragraphs frequently use logical order. The following paragraph explains what makes the ladies' "long program" in ice-skating unique for both spectators and athletes.

The ladies' "free skate," or long [four-minute] program, is by far the most popular activity in women's sports—the only sports event in which the women's version is more popular than the men's. These four minutes are as pure a dose of live performance as the media offer. For the athletes, they are also among the most pitiless and harrowing four minutes in sports. Although the long program is an endurance event—within a minute and a half the exercise becomes anaerobic—the skater has to continue to look as if she were enjoying herself. The smile at the end of the routine is of the utmost importance: skaters practice many hours in front of the mirror to get it right.

John Seabrook, *The New Yorker*

■ **Narrative paragraphs** A *narrative paragraph* is used to tell a story or to illustrate an event or a series of events, usually in chronological order.

Event 1

Event 2

Event 3

Event 4

Down the stretch, the game belonged to William. With the lead cut to three in the final minutes, William drove, stopped suddenly, pivoted towards the basket, and drew a foul. His knee was aching, but he blocked the pain, as well as the sound of the crowd and Proviso's players telling him not to choke. He allowed himself to see only the basket, as though to make the free throw were as simple as dropping a ball in a bucket that lay at his feet. The ball fluttered from his fingertips and slipped through the net. He hit both free throws and two others to ice the win.

Ben Joravsky, *Hoop Dreams*

■ **Persuasive paragraphs** A *persuasive paragraph* is used to express a writer's opinion about a particular subject, for the purpose of convincing others to share the opinion or to take action. Writers of persuasive paragraphs usually use order of importance or logical order to organize their ideas.

Am I saying that anything goes in sports—as long as you don't get caught? Of course not. Deliberate low blows are wrong in boxing, even when the referee is shielded from the action. Kicking a downed player is wrong on the football field, whether an official sees it or not. Spitballs are wrong in baseball and, while I couldn't swear to it, surely there must be some behavior on a hockey rink that is considered unethical. Dirty play is wrong, and its encouragement—by coaches or fans—can have implications well beyond the playing field.

William Raspberry, *The Washington Post*

**Prewriting Techniques**   You can use the following techniques to find a subject to write about and to gather information about a subject. Although the prewriting techniques are presented separately, you may often use more than one technique at a time. You may also prefer to use some techniques more than others.

- **Asking the *5W-How?* questions**   Ask yourself the reporter's questions—*Who? What? When? Where? Why?* and *How?*—to find ideas to write about.

  EXAMPLE

  *Who* are some local people who go fly fishing?
  *What* equipment do you need for fly fishing?
  *When* is the best time of day to fish?
  *Where* are some good local fishing spots?
  *Why* do some people tie their own flies?
  *How* do you tie a fly?

- **Asking "What if?" questions**   To stimulate your creative thinking, ask a variety of "What if?" questions about a subject. Imagine everyday situations that are different, and see where these ideas take you.

  EXAMPLE

  What if there were no sunlight?
  What if everyone spoke the same language?
  What if I could travel to another time?
  What if our school had no rules?

- **Brainstorming**   Write down a subject, and then list all your ideas about that subject that come into your mind as quickly as you can. Resist the urge to evaluate your ideas; remember that you are trying to come up with as many ideas as possible. Keep going until you run out of ideas. Brainstorming is a good group activity.

  EXAMPLE

  **Movies**

  | expensive to make | ticket prices | movie stars |
  |---|---|---|
  | costumes | popcorn | special effects |
  | cold theaters | soundtracks | bad movies |

- **Clustering**   Like brainstorming, clustering (also called *webbing* or *making connections*) is useful for spurring creative ideas. First, write a subject in the middle of your paper. Circle the subject. Then, in the space around the subject, write whatever related ideas occur to you. Circle the new ideas and draw lines to connect the new ideas with the original subject. Continue to branch off as necessary. Let your mind wander, and continue to draw circles and lines to show connections among ideas.

  EXAMPLE

■ **Cubing** Investigate a subject by imagining a cube that has one of the following suggestions on each of its six sides: *Describe it. Compare it. Associate it. Analyze it. Apply it. Argue for or against it.* Write for three minutes about each side of the cube.

EXAMPLE

**Masks**

*Apply it.* **(Tell how it can be used or what you can do with it.)**

**People throughout the ages have worn masks for various reasons. When used in rituals, masks are believed to have great power. In some cultures, masks are used to frighten away evil spirits. Festival and theatrical masks are used for masquerade, entertainment, and storytelling. War masks are worn in battle. Some sports require protective masks.**

■ **Freewriting** When you freewrite, you write whatever pops into your head. Think of a word or topic that interests you, and write about it for three to five minutes. Don't worry about complete sentences or proper punctuation. Just write as much as you can. If you cannot think of anything new to write, copy the same word or phrase until something comes to mind.

EXAMPLE

*SUMMER: Hot, lazy days. Going to the lake with family and to the community pool with friends.*

*Television in the mornings. Movies late at night. Lots of good books. Will we visit my cousins? Helping out around the house—mow the grass, baby-sit.*

■ **Listening with a focus** You can gather ideas for writing by listening to radio and television programs, audiotapes, and experts in personal or telephone interviews. Write down your topic, and then brainstorm what you already know about it. Make a list of questions that you would like to have answered as you listen. This list of questions should help guide and focus your listening. Listen carefully with your questions in front of you. Take careful notes and pay close attention.

■ **Looping** Looping will help you generate ideas that can be developed into an essay.

1. In this prewriting activity, you start with a topic and freewrite about the topic for a set period of time. The topic may be assigned or may be one of your own choosing. For example, you may be asked to write on the characters in a certain novel.

2. Include anything that comes into your mind on the topic. Even if you cannot think of anything to say, continue writing for the specified period of time. You may write, "I can't think of anything to say," until eventually you do think of something. The important thing is to keep your pen or pencil moving.

3. After the time limit is up, read what you have written and pick out what seems to be most important or "weighty" in the loop. This is the center of gravity for that loop. You may have stated this center of gravity, or you may have to figure it out. For example, you may have written a number of things about a certain character in a novel, and that character would be your center of gravity for the first loop.

4. Finally, write your center of gravity sentence and begin the process again for two more loops. For example, you may turn your attention to other characters in the novel and begin writing. You will discover in the two additional loops two other centers of gravity. These three centers of gravity may then be turned into the three main points of your essay.

■ **Mapping**   Mapping resembles clustering in form but is used to organize ideas. It is a helpful graphic for determining whether you have enough support for each main idea. Notice how the following map groups main ideas and supporting ideas.

creating the treats
original recipe
healthy
tasty
various shapes
natural ingredients
my dogs love them

profit
costs
investment capital

starting my own business—homemade dog treats

market
local sites?
pet stores?
mail order?

packaging
inexpensive
flashy
preserve freshness
recyclable?

■ **Pentad**   Investigate a subject by imagining a five-pointed star. Each of its points has one of the following questions: *What is happening? Who is causing it to happen? How is it being done? Where and when is it being done? Why is it happening?* After answering each question, determine a focus: Which points did you write the most about, and is there an interaction between those points? This focus will probably be your thesis statement. A pentad is a good prewriting technique to use when you are writing about literature.

**What is happening?**
Roger tries to steal Mrs. Jones's purse. She catches him, drags him home, gives him food and money, and talks to him.

**How is it being done?** Roger instigates the attack. Then, Mrs. Jones is in control. At the apartment, Roger does have choices.

**When and where is it happening?** Mostly in Mrs. Jones's apartment.

**Story: "Thank You, M'am" by Langston Hughes**

**Who is causing it to happen?** Roger Mrs. Jones

**Why is it happening?** Mrs. Jones wants Roger to see that people can change.

■ **Reading with a focus**   You can get ideas for writing by reading books, newspapers, or magazines. When you read to find information, don't read everything. Use the index and table of contents to narrow your search. Skim the material, searching only for information about your topic. When you find relevant information, read carefully and take notes.

■ **Track Switching**   Start by freewriting along a familiar track of thinking, and then switch to another track of thinking about a topic. This technique often leads to fresh ideas. The following steps will help you.

1. Start by creating a statement about your topic, and freewrite about that statement for five minutes. For example, you may begin with a statement such as, "My favorite character in the novel made good choices."

2. Switch tracks by creating a second statement about your topic. Your second statement should be as different as possible from the first statement you made. Write on this track for five minutes. For example, you may write, "Every character in the novel made poor choices."

3. Repeat this back-and-forth writing process for five tracks, letting your words flow along your different tracks of thinking.

■ **Using your five senses**   Observe your topic through all five senses: sight, hearing, smell, taste, and touch. If you stop to focus on all the sensory details around you, you will have an endless supply of specific details for your writing.

EXAMPLE   Chinese New Year's festival

**touch:**   damp, chilly morning; cool breeze; crisp, crunchy fried wontons

**sound:**   cymbals and drums as parade goes by, cheering of spectators, chatter of street vendors and their customers, gong of passing streetcar

**smell:**   garlic and ginger cooking in hot oil, egg rolls frying, dumplings cooking in bamboo steamers

**taste:**   tangy, hot tea; salty soy sauce on steamed dumpling; spicy hot mustard and sweet plum sauce on egg roll

**sight:**   dazzling light, colorful merchandise, red and gold decorations on dragon in parade, banners with Chinese characters

■ **Visualizing**   Visualizing means making mental images of something in your mind's eye. As you "see" your scene, try to use your other senses as well.

EXAMPLE I'm riding down a country road at sunrise on my bicycle. The sunrise's brilliant orange lights up the eastern sky. A few birds chirp noisily and the smell of morning dew and budding blossoms fills the cool, crisp air.

■ **Writer's notebook or journal**   Use a special notebook or file folder to record your experiences and observations, feelings and opinions, brilliant ideas and questions. You can also collect print material that has special meaning to you, such as poems, songs, cartoons, and newspaper articles. Try to write in your notebook daily, and date your entries. Soon your journal will be a sourcebook full of ideas for you to write about.

**Résumés**   A *résumé* is a one-page summary of your skills, education, accomplishments, and experience. When applying for a job or seeking admission to a college, you will probably be asked for a résumé. The following sample résumé is for a summer job applicant. Notice that the work experience supports the job objective.

```
                  Amanda Vinh
               1056 Cape Coral Way
               Wilsonville, NC 54321
                  (555) 328-9087
Objective
    Summer position as a cashier in
    a bookstore
Qualifications
    Familiarity with and a love for
    books
    Excellent people skills
    Experience with cash registers
    and computers
Work Experience
    June, 1998, to present—
    volunteer at local library
    September, 2000—organized
    middle school book fair
    June-August, 2000—cashier at
    Big Brother's Books
Education
    Mountaineer High School,
    Wilsonville, North Carolina
    Presently in ninth grade;
    3.8 grade-point average
Extracurricular
    Math Club, Yearbook Staff
Achievements
    Good Citizen Award—2000
References
    Available on request
```

## Revising and Proofreading Symbols

When you are revising and proofreading, indicate any changes by using the symbols shown in the chart below.

**Technical Documents**   Use the following strategies to help you write technical documents, such as minutes of a meeting, procedures for conducting a meeting, or a manual of rules for conflict resolution.

1. Report information and convey ideas logically and correctly.
2. Offer detailed and accurate specifications.
3. Include scenarios, definitions, and examples to aid comprehension.
4. Anticipate readers' problems, mistakes, and misunderstandings.

**Transitions**   Transitions, or *transitional expressions,* are words and phrases that show readers how ideas and details fit together. (See page 365 for a chart of transitional expressions.)

**Voice**   The way a piece of writing "sounds," or its *voice,* is determined by sentence structure, word choice, and tone. Although audience and purpose influence your writing voice, always try to sound honest and natural.

| Symbols For Revising And Proofreading | | |
|---|---|---|
| **Symbol** | **Example** | **Meaning Of Symbol** |
| ≡ | Fifty-first street | Capitalize a lowercase letter. |
| / | Jerry's Aunt | Lowercase a capital letter. |
| ∧ | differant | Change a letter. |
| ∧ | the capital Ohio | Insert a missing word, letter, or punctuation mark. |
| ⌐‾ | beside the river | Replace a word. |
| ℓ | Where's the the key? | Leave out a word, letter, or punctuation mark. |
| ℒ | an invisibile guest | Leave out and close up. |
| ⌣ | a close friend ship | Close up space. |
| ∿ | thier | Change the order of letters. |
| (tr) | Avoid having too many corrections (of your paper) in the final version. | Transfer the circled words. (Write *tr* in nearby margin.) |
| ¶ | ¶ "Hi," he smiled. | Begin a new paragraph. |
| ⊙ | Stay well | Add a period. |
| ∧ | Of course you may be wrong. | Add a comma. |
| # | icehockey | Add a space. |
| ⊙ | one of the following | Add a colon. |
| ∧ | Maria Simmons, M.D. Jim Fiorello, Ph.D. | Add a semicolon. |
| = | a great grandmother | Add a hyphen. |
| ∨ | Pauls car | Add an apostrophe. |
| (stet) | On the fifteenth of July | Keep the crossed-out material. (Write *stet* in nearby margin.) |

# Grammar at a Glance

┌HELP┐

**Grammar at a Glance** is an alphabetical list of special terms and expressions with examples and references to further information. When you encounter a grammar or usage problem in the revising or proofreading stage of your writing, look for help in this section first. You may find all you need to know right here. If you need more information, **Grammar at a Glance** will show you where in the book to turn for a more complete explanation. If you do not find what you are looking for in **Grammar at a Glance,** turn to the index on page 942.

**abbreviation** An abbreviation is a shortened form of a word or a phrase.

■ **capitalization of**

| | | | | |
|---|---|---|---|---|
| TITLES USED WITH NAMES | **M**r. | **D**r. | **J**r. | **Ph.D.** |
| KINDS OF ORGANIZATIONS | **A**ssn. | **I**nc. | **D**ept. | **C**orp. |
| PARTS OF ADDRESSES | **A**ve. | **S**t. | **B**lvd. | **P.O. B**ox |
| NAMES OF STATES | [without ZIP Codes] | | **K**y. | **T**ex. |
| | | | **T**enn. | **N. D**ak. |
| | [with ZIP Codes] | | **KY** | **TX** |
| | | | **TN** | **ND** |
| TIMES | **A.M.** | **P.M.** | **B.C.** | **A.D.** |

■ **punctuation of** (See page 639.)

| | |
|---|---|
| WITH PERIODS | (See preceding examples.) |
| WITHOUT PERIODS | VCR  ESPN  NAACP  FCC |
| | DC [D.C. without ZIP Code] |
| | kg  lb  tsp  km  ft |
| | [Exception: inch = in.] |

**action verb** An action verb expresses physical or mental activity. (See page 387.)

EXAMPLES  Kurt **ran** toward the ledge.

Owen correctly **guessed** the number of jelly beans in the jar.

**active voice** Active voice is the voice a verb is in when it expresses an action done by its subject. (See page 535. See also **voice.**)

EXAMPLE  Napoleon's armies **conquered** most of western Europe.

**adjective** An adjective modifies a noun or a pronoun. (See page 382.)

EXAMPLE   **The** peninsula has **high** mountains and **winding** roads.

**adjective clause** An adjective clause is a subordinate clause that modifies a noun or a pronoun. (See page 473.)

EXAMPLE   The man **who disappeared** was soon found again.

**adjective phrase** A prepositional phrase that modifies a noun or a pronoun is called an adjective phrase. (See page 443.)

EXAMPLE   We approached the highest peak **in the Alps.**

**adverb** An adverb modifies a verb, an adjective, or another adverb. (See page 393.)

EXAMPLE   Helen **rarely** loses her temper.

**adverb clause** An adverb clause is a subordinate clause that modifies a verb, an adjective, or an adverb. (See page 476.)

EXAMPLE   We will try to get indoors **before the storm arrives.**

**adverb phrase** A prepositional phrase that modifies a verb, an adjective, or an adverb is called an adverb phrase. (See page 445.)

EXAMPLE   Terry cleaned his room **in a few minutes.**

**agreement** Agreement is the correspondence, or match, between grammatical forms. Grammatical forms agree when they have the same number and gender.

■ **of pronouns and antecedents** (See page 507.)

SINGULAR   **Ethan** politely asked for an increase in **his** allowance.
PLURAL   Ethan's **brothers** politely asked for an increase in **their** allowances.

SINGULAR   **Everyone** in the play made **his or her** own costumes.
PLURAL   **All** of the performers made **their** own costumes.

SINGULAR   Is **Matthew or Terence** looking forward to reciting **his** poem in front of **his** classmates?
PLURAL   **Matthew and Terence** are looking forward to reciting **their** poems in front of **their** classmates.

■ **of subjects and verbs** (See page 493.)

SINGULAR The art **teacher has painted** a mural on a wall of the cafeteria.

The art **teacher,** with the help of her students, **has painted** a mural on a wall of the cafeteria.

PLURAL The art **students have painted** a mural on a wall of the cafeteria.

PLURAL The art **students,** with the help of their teacher, **have painted** a mural on the wall of the cafeteria.

SINGULAR **Everyone** in this class **is learning** sign language.

PLURAL **All** of the students **are learning** sign language.

SINGULAR **Neither Diego nor I was** ready to compete in the battle of the bands.

PLURAL **Salsa, reggae, and zydeco were** among the kinds of music played at the band competition.

SINGULAR Here **is** your book **bag.**

PLURAL Here **are** your **books.**

SINGULAR **Ten dollars is** the cost of the ticket.

PLURAL In this stack of bills, ten **dollars are** torn.

SINGULAR **Two thirds** of the freshman class **has voted.**

PLURAL **Two thirds** of the freshmen **have voted.**

SINGULAR *Symphonies of Wind Instruments* **was composed** by Igor Stravinsky.

PLURAL Stravinsky's other **symphonies were** also well **received.**

SINGULAR **Is mathematics** your favorite school subject?

PLURAL **Are** my **binoculars** in your locker?

**ambiguous reference** Ambiguous reference occurs when a pronoun incorrectly refers to either of two antecedents. (See page 565.)

AMBIGUOUS Martina is supposed to meet Jada at the library after she practices her cello lesson.

CLEAR After **Martina** practices **her** cello lesson, **she** is supposed to meet Jada at the library.

CLEAR After **Jada** practices **her** cello lesson, **she** is supposed to meet Martina at the library.

**antecedent** An antecedent is the word or words that a pronoun stands for. (See page 378.)

EXAMPLE **Alfred** sent **Julie** and **Dave** the money **he** owed **them.**
[*Alfred* is the antecedent of *he. Julie* and *Dave* are the antecedents of *them.*]

## apostrophe

■ **to form contractions** (See page 707.)

EXAMPLES couldn*'*t let*'*s o*'*clock *'*99

■ **to form plurals of letters, numerals, symbols, and words used as words** (See page 709.)

EXAMPLES *p*'s and *q*'s *A*'s and *I*'s

10*'*s and 20*'*s $*'*s and ¢*'*s

■ **to show possession** (See page 699.)

EXAMPLES gymnast*'*s routine

gymnasts*'* routines

children*'*s toys

everyone*'*s opinion

Whitney Houston*'*s and Denzel Washington*'*s performances

a year*'*s [or twelve months*'*] leave of absence

**appositive** An appositive is a noun or a pronoun placed beside another noun or pronoun to identify or describe it. (See page 461.)

EXAMPLE My great-aunt **Rina** was born in Poland.

**appositive phrase** An appositive phrase consists of an appositive and its modifiers. (See page 461.)

EXAMPLE Kublai Khan, **the first emperor of the Yuan dynasty,** united China under his rule.

**article** The articles, *a, an,* and *the,* are the most frequently used adjectives. (See page 384.)

EXAMPLE On **an** overpass south of **the** city, **an** incident occurred that convinced John that he needed **a** new car.

**B**

## *bad, badly* (See page 575.)

NONSTANDARD   Do you think these leftovers smell badly?

STANDARD   Do you think these leftovers smell **bad**?

## base form The base form, or infinitive, is one of the four principal parts of a verb. (See page 517.)

EXAMPLE   This computer program has helped me [to] **learn** Spanish.

## brackets (See page 726.)

EXAMPLE   The history book points out that "the name Hundred Years' War is a misnomer **[**a wrong name**]**, for the name refers to a series of wars that lasted 116 years **[**1337–1453**]**."

**C**

## capitalization

- **of abbreviations and acronyms** (See **abbreviations.**)

- **of first words** (See page 618.)

  EXAMPLES   **M**y sister writes in her journal every night.

  **O**mar asked, "**W**ould you like to play on my soccer team?"

  **D**ear Ms. Reuben:

  **S**incerely yours,

- **of proper nouns and proper adjectives** (See page 620.)

| Proper Noun | Common Noun |
|---|---|
| **J**ames **L**ovell, **J**r. | astronaut |
| **A**lexander the **G**reat | leader |
| **S**outh **A**merica | continent |
| **A**ppalachian **M**ountains | mountain chain |
| **M**innesota **V**ikings | team |
| **D**emocratic **P**arty (or **p**arty) | political party |
| **F**rench and **I**ndian **W**ar | historical event |
| **J**urassic **P**eriod | historical period |
| **M**other's **D**ay | holiday |
| **G**eneral **M**otors **C**orporation | business |

■ **of titles** (See page 629.)

**G**overnor **P**ataki [preceding a name]

Pataki, the **g**overnor of New York [following a name]

Thank you, **G**overnor. [direct address]

**A**unt Ramona [*but* our **a**unt Ramona]

*Dust **T**racks **o**n a **R**oad* [novel]

*The **L**ion **K**ing* [movie or play]

*Nova* [TV program]

*Mona Lisa* [work of art]

"**T**he **S**tar-**S**pangled **B**anner" [song]

"**A**migo **B**rothers" [short story]

"**N**othing **G**old **C**an **S**tay" [poem]

**case of pronouns** Case is the form a pronoun takes to show how it is used in a sentence. (See page 549.)

NOMINATIVE   **He** and **I** are making vegetable quesadillas.
Two of the class officers are Eric and **she.**
Either player, Cheryl or **she,** can play shortstop.
**We** volunteers have worked very hard on the recycling campaign.
Is Ernesto Galarza the author **who** wrote *Barrio Boy*?
Do you know **who** they are?
I helped Ms. Wong as much as **he.** [meaning "as much as he helped Ms. Wong"]

OBJECTIVE   This jacket will not fit Yolanda or **her.**
Aunt Calista brought **him** and **me** souvenirs of her trip to the Philippines.
Were you three cheering for **us** or **them**?
The mayor thanked **us** volunteers for our contributions.
Maya Angelou, **whom** many readers admire, is certainly my favorite author.
One of the candidates for **whom** I will vote is Tamisha.
I helped Ms. Wong as much as **him.** [meaning "as much as I helped him"]

POSSESSIVE   **Your** interpretation of **her** poem was different from **mine.**

**clause** A clause is a group of words that contains a verb and its subject and is used as part of a sentence. (See page 470.)

INDEPENDENT CLAUSE    Theo installed the blinds

SUBORDINATE CLAUSE    while Dorothy worked on the wiring

**colon** (See page 675.)

■ **before lists**

EXAMPLES    The recipe calls for the following herbs: thyme, basil, cilantro, and oregano.

The documentary profiled three women artists of the twentieth century: Audrey Flack, a painter; Louise Nevelson, a sculptor; and Margaret Bourke-White, a photographer.

■ **in conventional situations**

EXAMPLES    6:30 A.M.

Ecclesiastes 11:7–10

*Computers and You: A Video Guide*

Dear Sir or Madam:

**comma** (See page 643.)

■ **in a series**

EXAMPLES    Tony, Julian, and Katie helped me make the fruit salad by cutting up the oranges, bananas, grapes, and papayas.

We rode our bicycles to the park, bought snacks at the juice bar, found a picnic table, and then played chess for an hour.

The silly cat had run through the living room, over the sofa, between my feet, through the door, across the hall, and up the stairs.

■ **in compound sentences**

EXAMPLES    I like all kinds of music, but jazz is my favorite.

The students listened to each candidate's speech, and then they left the auditorium to cast their votes.

■ **with nonessential phrases and clauses**

EXAMPLES    Didn't Mount Etna, Europe's largest volcano, erupt a few years ago?

In the mid-1900s, the Inuit, whose ancestors had led nomadic lives of hunting and fishing, began settling in urban areas of the Arctic region.

David will be bringing fresh salsa, which his father makes from tomatoes and herbs that they grow in their garden.

■ **with introductory elements**

EXAMPLES   In the first match of the tennis tournament, Pablo competed against the player who was ranked first in the state.

When the exciting game was over, many of the fans raced onto the field to praise and congratulate the winning player.

■ **with interrupters**

EXAMPLES   The most memorable part of our vacation, however, was our visit to the Smithsonian Institution.

You might consider making a mobile, for example, or some other simple present.

The most demanding role, I believe, is that of King Lear in Shakespeare's tragedy of the same name.

■ **in conventional situations**

EXAMPLES   On Monday, June 5, 2000, the Walkers flew from Detroit, Michigan, to San Juan, Puerto Rico, to attend their family reunion.

I mailed the package to 1620 Palmetto Drive, Tampa, FL 33637, on 15 September 2000.

**comma splice** A comma splice is a run-on sentence in which two sentences have been joined with only a comma between them. (See page 327. See also **fused sentence** and **run-on sentence.**)

COMMA SPLICE   My sister Eileen has a paper route, I help her sometimes, especially when the weather is bad.

REVISED   My sister Eileen has a paper route, **and** I help her sometimes, especially when the weather is bad.

REVISED   My sister Eileen has a paper route; I help her sometimes, especially when the weather is bad.

REVISED   My sister Eileen has a paper route. I help her sometimes, especially when the weather is bad.

### comparison of modifiers (See page 577.)

- comparison of adjectives and adverbs

| Positive | Comparative | Superlative |
|----------|-------------|-------------|
| strong | stronger | strongest |
| happy | happier | happiest |
| ambitious | more ambitious | most ambitious |
| quietly | less quietly | least quietly |
| well/good | better | best |

- comparing two

EXAMPLES   Which is **longer,** the Nile River or the Amazon River?

Of the cheetah and the gazelle, which animal can run **more swiftly**?

Mount Everest is **higher** than **any other** mountain peak in the world.

- comparing more than two

EXAMPLES   Of all of the lakes of the world, the Caspian Sea is the **largest.**

In the school's walkathon, one of the freshmen walked the **farthest.**

### complement A complement is a word or word group that completes the meaning of a verb. (See page 427.)

EXAMPLES   I gave **Sally** that **picture.**

This is an old **sofa,** but it's very **comfortable.**

### complex sentence A complex sentence has one independent clause and at least one subordinate clause. (See page 482.)

EXAMPLE   Beethoven, who had a hearing impairment most of his adult life, wrote his ninth symphony after he had become deaf.

### compound-complex sentence A compound-complex sentence has two or more independent clauses and at least one subordinate clause. (See page 482.)

EXAMPLES  While Arianna was at the shopping mall, she checked both bookstores for Barbara Kingsolver's latest novel, but neither store had a copy in stock.

At the cookout on Saturday, we served yakitori; it is a Japanese dish of bite-sized pieces of meat and vegetables that are placed on skewers and grilled.

**compound sentence** A compound sentence has two or more independent clauses and no subordinate clauses. (See page 481.)

EXAMPLES  My family and I recently moved into a new house, and now I have a room of my own.

By area, New York City is the largest city in the world; however, by population, Tokyo-Yokohama is the world's largest urban area.

**conjunction** A conjunction joins words or groups of words. (See page 403.)

EXAMPLES  **Both** Robin **and** Michelle arrived early, **but** all the good seats were taken.

**While** you were sleeping, I worked out.

**contraction** A contraction is a shortened form of a word, a numeral, or a group of words. Apostrophes in contractions show where letters or numerals have been omitted. (See page 707. See also **apostrophe.**)

EXAMPLES  you're [you are]                    there's [there is or there has]

who's [who is or who has]          they're [they are]

weren't [were not]                    it's [it is or it has]

'91–'94 model [1991–1994 model]    o'clock [of the clock]

**dangling modifier** A dangling modifier is a modifying word, phrase, or clause that does not clearly and sensibly modify a word or a word group in a sentence. (See page 585.)

DANGLING  Riding the Ferris wheel, most of the park's other attractions could be seen.

REVISED  **Riding the Ferris wheel, we** could see most of the park's other attractions.

**dash** (See page 721.)

EXAMPLE  One of the substitute teachers—Ms. Narazaki, I believe—will accompany us on the field trip.

**declarative sentence** A declarative sentence makes a statement and is followed by a period. (See page 435.)

EXAMPLE  People still enjoy going to movies, despite the popularity of videos**.**

**direct object** A direct object is a word or word group that receives the action of the verb or shows the result of the action. A direct object answers the question *Whom?* or *What?* after a transitive verb. (See page 431.)

EXAMPLE  They gave the **oats** to the horse.

**double comparison** A double comparison is the nonstandard use of two comparative forms (usually *more* and *–er*) or two superlative forms (usually *most* and *–est*) to express comparison. In standard usage, the single comparative form is correct. (See page 582.)

NONSTANDARD  These small boxes are much more heavier than they appear.

STANDARD  These small boxes are much **heavier** than they appear.

**double negative** A double negative is the nonstandard use of two or more negative words to express a single negative idea. (See page 609.)

NONSTANDARD  The annual sports banquet doesn't cost the athletes nothing.

STANDARD  The annual sports banquet **doesn't** cost the athletes **anything.**

STANDARD  The annual sports banquet costs the athletes **nothing.**

NONSTANDARD  Yesterday, my throat was so sore that I couldn't hardly eat no solid food.

STANDARD  Yesterday, my throat was so sore that I could **hardly** eat **any** solid food.

**double subject** A double subject occurs when an unnecessary pronoun is used after the subject of a sentence. (See page 603.)

| NONSTANDARD | Laura and her sister they have a large aquarium of tropical fish. |
|---|---|
| STANDARD | **Laura and her sister have** a large aquarium of tropical fish. |

**end marks** (See page 637.)

■ **with sentences**

EXAMPLES   Tiger Woods has won the golf tournament. [declarative sentence]

How long has Tiger Woods been playing professional golf? [interrogative sentence]

Oh! [interjection]

What a remarkable golfer Tiger Woods is! [exclamatory sentence]

Imagine how you would feel if you were playing in a tournament with Tiger Woods. [imperative sentence]

Don't talk while someone is hitting the ball! [strong imperative sentence]

■ **with abbreviations** (See **abbreviations.**)

EXAMPLES   We are planning to go to Washington, D.C.

When are you going to Washington, D.C.?

**essential clause/essential phrase** An essential, or restrictive, clause or phrase is necessary to the meaning of a sentence and is not set off by commas. (See page 649.)

EXAMPLES   The man **whose sudden appearance caused the uproar** rose to identify himself. [essential clause]

Students **going on the field trip** should meet in the gym. [essential phrase]

**exclamation point** (See **end marks.**)

**exclamatory sentence** An exclamatory sentence expresses strong feeling and is followed by an exclamation point. (See page 436.)

EXAMPLE   That's absolutely incredible!

**fragment** (See **sentence fragment.**)

**fused sentence** A fused sentence is a run-on sentence in which sentences have been joined together with no punctuation between them. (See page 327. See also **comma splice** and **run-on sentence.**)

FUSED    According to my research, the Dome of the Rock was built in Jerusalem during the seventh century it is the oldest existing Muslim shrine.

REVISED    According to my research, the Dome of the Rock was built in Jerusalem during the seventh century**. It** is the oldest existing Muslim shrine.

REVISED    According to my research, the Dome of the Rock was built in Jerusalem during the seventh century**; it** is the oldest existing Muslim shrine.

**general reference** A general reference is the incorrect use of a pronoun to refer to a general idea rather than to a specific noun. (See page 565.)

GENERAL    The illusionist escaped from a locked trunk, made various fruits and vegetables dance in the air, and levitated. This thrilled her audience.

REVISED    The illusionist thrilled her audience by escaping from a locked trunk, making various fruits and vegetables dance in the air, and levitating.

REVISED    The illusionist escaped from a locked trunk, made various fruits and vegetables dance in the air, and levitated. These illusions thrilled her audience.

**gerund** A gerund is a verb form ending in *–ing* that is used as a noun. (See page 453.)

EXAMPLE    **Fishing** for blue crabs is especially popular in the Gulf Coast states.

**gerund phrase** A gerund phrase consists of a gerund and its modifiers and complements. (See page 455.)

EXAMPLE    **Photographing old stone bridges** is one of Tracy's hobbies.

***good, well*** (See page 575.)

EXAMPLES    Benita is a **good** saxophone player.

Benita played extremely **well** [not *good*] at the tryouts for the school orchestra.

**hyphen** (See page 716.)

- **to divide words**

    EXAMPLE    In their flower garden, they planted zinnias, mari-
    golds, and dahlias.

- **in compound numbers**

    EXAMPLE    They planted twenty-three varieties of those kinds of
    flowers.

- **with prefixes and suffixes**

    EXAMPLES    All of the flowers were in full bloom by mid-July.

    Our garden is pesticide-free.

**imperative mood** The imperative mood is used to express a direct command or request. (See page 543.)

EXAMPLES    **Sit** down! [command]

Please **read** the minutes of our last meeting. [request]

**imperative sentence** An imperative sentence gives a command or makes a request and is followed by either a period or an exclamation point. (See page 435.)

EXAMPLES    Please return this to the display case. [request]

Clean this room now! [command]

**incomplete construction** An incomplete construction is a clause or phrase from which words have been omitted. (See page 564.)

EXAMPLE    I like cheddar cheese more **than he [likes cheddar cheese].**

**indefinite reference** An indefinite reference is the incorrect use of the pronoun *you, it,* or *they* to refer to no particular person or thing. (See page 565.)

INDEFINITE    In the first issue of the school newspaper, it shows a calendar of the school's major events.

REVISED    The first issue of the school newspaper shows a calendar of the school's major events.

REVISED    In the first issue of the school newspaper is a calendar of the school's major events.

**independent clause** An independent clause (also called a *main clause*) expresses a complete thought and can stand by itself as a sentence. (See page 470.)

EXAMPLE  **Shawna planted the sunflower seeds and tried to imagine** what the flowers would look like.

**indicative mood** The indicative mood is used to express a fact, an opinion, or a question. (See page 543.)

EXAMPLES  Georgia O'Keeffe **is** famous for her abstract paintings. [fact]

Georgia O'Keeffe, in my opinion, **was** the most talented American artist of the twentieth century. [opinion]

**Did**n't O'Keeffe **paint** *Cow's Skull: Red, White, and Blue*? [question]

**indirect object** An indirect object is a noun, pronoun, or word group that often appears in sentences containing direct objects. An indirect object tells *to whom* or *to what* (or *for whom* or *for what*) the action of a transitive verb is done. Indirect objects generally precede direct objects. (See page 432.)

EXAMPLE  Sandy gave **Grandma** the watch.

**infinitive** An infinitive is a verb form, usually preceded by *to,* used as a noun, an adjective, or an adverb. (See page 457.)

EXAMPLE  Patty tried **to play** the trumpet but decided she preferred **to learn** the clarinet.

**infinitive phrase** An infinitive phrase consists of an infinitive and its modifiers and complements. (See page 458.)

EXAMPLE  Ms. Snyder tried **to explain the meaning of the phrase,** but we still found it hard to understand.

**interjection** An interjection expresses emotion and has no grammatical relation to the rest of the sentence. (See page 405.)

EXAMPLE  **Oh no!** I completely forgot!

**interrogative sentence** An interrogative sentence asks a question and is followed by a question mark. (See page 436.)

EXAMPLE  Did you visit Las Cruces when you were in New Mexico**?**

**intransitive verb** An intransitive verb is a verb that does not take an object. (See page 386.)

EXAMPLE    The queen **waved** good-naturedly.

**irregular verb** An irregular verb is a verb that forms its past and past participle in some way other than by adding *–d* or *–ed* to the base form. (See page 519. See also **regular verb.**)

| Base Form | Present Participle | Past | Past Participle |
|-----------|--------------------|------|-----------------|
| be | [is] being | was, were | [have] been |
| drive | [is] driving | drove | [have] driven |
| fall | [is] falling | fell | [have] fallen |
| go | [is] going | went | [have] gone |
| run | [is] running | ran | [have] run |
| sing | [is] singing | sang | [have] sung |
| speak | [is] speaking | spoke | [have] spoken |
| think | [is] thinking | thought | [have] thought |
| write | [is] writing | wrote | [have] written |

**italics** (See page 683.)

■ **for titles**

EXAMPLES    *Their Eyes Were Watching God* [book]

*U.S. News & World Report* [periodical]

*The Ascent of Ethiopia* [work of art]

*Mozart Portraits* [long musical recording]

■ **for words, letters, and symbols used as such and for foreign words**

EXAMPLES    Notice that the word *Tennessee* has four *e*'s, two *n*'s, and two *s*'s.

A *jeu de mots* is a pun or a play on words.

***its, it's*** (See page 751.)

EXAMPLES    **Its** [The coyote's] howling frightened the young campers.

**It's** [It is] six o'clock.

**It's** [It has] been raining all day.

**lie, lay** (See page 539.)

EXAMPLES   I think I will **lie** down and take a short nap before dinner.

               I think I will **lay** this quilt over me.

**linking verb** A linking verb connects the subject with a word that identifies or describes the subject. (See page 388.)

EXAMPLE   Renata's grandma **looked** great at the party.

**misplaced modifier** A misplaced modifier is a word, phrase, or clause that seems to modify the wrong word or words in a sentence. (See page 587.)

MISPLACED   Standing in line behind us, we thought we saw the great baseball player José Canseco.

REVISED   We thought we saw the great baseball player **José Canseco standing in line behind us.**

**modifier** A modifier is a word, phrase, or clause that makes the meaning of another word more specific. (See page 572.)

EXAMPLE   We **closely** watched him apply the finish **during his demonstration.**

**mood** Mood is the form a verb takes to indicate the attitude of the person using the verb. (See page 543. See also **imperative mood, indicative mood,** and **subjunctive mood.**)

**nonessential clause/nonessential phrase** A nonessential, or nonrestrictive, clause or phrase adds information not necessary to the main idea in the sentence and is set off by commas. (See page 648.)

EXAMPLE   Granddad's Hudson convertible, **which he bought new in 1951,** was the next item up for auction.

**noun** A noun names a person, place, thing, or idea. (See page 375.)

EXAMPLE   Before the **war,** most **people** I know never gave the **Balkans** a **thought.**

**noun clause** A noun clause is a subordinate clause used as a noun. (See page 478.)

EXAMPLE **What's really going to amaze you** is how much I paid for it!

**number** Number is the form a word takes to indicate whether the word is singular or plural. (See page 492.)

| SINGULAR | bird | I | foot | woman |
|---|---|---|---|---|
| PLURAL | birds | we | feet | women |

**object of a preposition** An object of a preposition is the noun or pronoun that ends a prepositional phrase. (See page 400.)

EXAMPLE Faced with a huge **pile** of **papers** when she arrived, she took a deep breath and plunged in. [*With a huge pile* and *of papers* are prepositional phrases.]

**parallel structure** Parallel structure is the use of the same grammatical forms or structures to balance related ideas in a sentence. (See page 339.)

NONPARALLEL My parents promised to buy a video camera and that they would let me take it on my school trip.

PARALLEL My parents promised **to buy a video camera** and **to let me take it on my school trip.** [two infinitive phrases]

**parentheses** (See page 720.)

EXAMPLES Ganymede **(**see the chart on page 322**)** is our solar system's largest satellite.

Ganymede is our solar system's largest satellite. **(**See the chart on page 322.**)**

**participial phrase** A participial phrase consists of a participle and its complements and modifiers. (See page 451.)

EXAMPLE At the wildlife park, we were startled by the gibbons **swinging through the trees.**

**participle** A participle is a verb form that can be used as an adjective. (See page 449.)

EXAMPLE The **exhausted** hikers headed for home.

**passive voice** The passive voice is the voice a verb is in when it expresses an action done to its subject. (See page 535. See also **voice.**)

EXAMPLE The posters on the bulletin board outside the principal's office **were changed** once a week.

**period** (See **end marks.**)

**phrase** A phrase is a group of related words that does not contain both a verb and its subject and is used as a single part of speech. (See page 442.)

EXAMPLES **A man of elegance and style,** Uncle Jesse lives **in Georgia.** [*A man of elegance and style* is an appositive phrase. *Of elegance and style* and *in Georgia* are prepositional phrases.]

Press this lever **to open the cage door.** [*To open the cage door* is an infinitive phrase.]

**Smiling at her fans,** the actress signed autographs. [*Smiling at her fans* is a participial phrase. *At her fans* is a prepositional phrase.]

**Being on time for appointments** is courteous. [*Being on time for appointments* is a gerund phrase. *On time* and *for appointments* are prepositional phrases.]

**predicate** The predicate is the part of a sentence that says something about the subject. (See page 414.)

EXAMPLE They **had been living in California for twenty years.**

**predicate adjective** A predicate adjective is an adjective that is in the predicate and that modifies the subject of a sentence or a clause. (See page 429.)

EXAMPLE Does the garage smell **strange**?

**predicate nominative** A predicate nominative is a word or word group that is in the predicate and that identifies the subject or refers to it. (See page 429.)

EXAMPLE Federico Fellini was a famous **filmmaker.**

**prefix** A prefix is a word part that is added before a base word or root. (See page 735.)

EXAMPLES    un + known = **un**known    il + legible = **il**legible

re + write = **re**write    pre + school = **pre**school

self + confidence
   = **self**-confidence

trans + Siberian =
   **trans**-Siberian

mid + August =
   **mid**-August

ex + president =
   **ex**-president

**preposition** A preposition shows the relationship of a noun or a pronoun to some other word in a sentence. (See page 400.)

EXAMPLE    He came **from** Mexico and settled **near** Houston to find jobs **for** his family.

**prepositional phrase** A prepositional phrase is a group of words that includes a preposition, the object of the preposition (a noun or a pronoun), and any modifiers of that object. (See page 442.)

EXAMPLE    Having breakfast **on the Bar X Ranch** was a real treat **for all of us.**

**pronoun** A pronoun is used in place of one or more nouns or pronouns. (See page 378.)

EXAMPLES    Colin thinks **he** might be moving upstate.

Did **you** paint **your** room by **yourself?**

**Some** of the puppies look like **their** mother.

**question mark** (See **end marks.**)

**quotation marks** (See page 686.)

- **for direct quotations**

EXAMPLE    **"**Before the secretary of state returns to Washington, D.C.,**"** said the reporter, **"**she will visit Dar es Salaam, Tanzania, and Nairobi, Kenya.**"**

- **with other marks of punctuation** (See also preceding example.)

EXAMPLES    **"**In which South American country is the Atacama Desert**?"** asked Geraldo.

Which poem by Edgar Allan Poe begins with the line "Once upon a midnight dreary, while I pondered weak and weary"?

Carlotta asked, "Did Langston Hughes write a poem titled 'A Dream Deferred'?"

■ **for titles**

EXAMPLES "The Rockpile" [short story]

"Muddy Kid Comes Home" [short poem]

"River Deep, Mountain High" [song]

**regular verb** A regular verb is a verb that forms its past and past participle by adding *–d* or *–ed* to the base form. (See page 518. See also **irregular verb.**)

| Base Form | Present Participle | Past | Past Participle |
|---|---|---|---|
| ask | [is] asking | asked | [have] asked |
| drown | [is] drowning | drowned | [have] drowned |
| suppose | [is] supposing | supposed | [have] supposed |
| use | [is] using | used | [have] used |

*rise, raise* (See page 541.)

EXAMPLES The hot-air balloon is **rising.**

She is **raising** the windows to let in some fresh air.

**run-on sentence** A run-on sentence is two or more complete sentences run together as one. (See page 327. See also **comma splice** and **fused sentence.**)

RUN-ON In 1903, Marie Curie and her husband, Pierre, won the Nobel Prize in physics in 1911 she alone won the Nobel Prize in chemistry.

REVISED In 1903, Marie Curie and her husband, Pierre, won the Nobel Prize in physics. In 1911, she alone won the Nobel Prize in chemistry.

REVISED In 1903, Marie Curie and her husband, Pierre, won the Nobel Prize in physics; in 1911, she alone won the Nobel Prize in chemistry.

**semicolon** (See page 668.)

- **in compound sentences with no conjunction**

  EXAMPLE    Salma decided to read Amy Tan's *The Joy Luck Club*; her English teacher recommended it.

- **in compound sentences with conjunctive adverbs**

  EXAMPLE    Elizabeth went to the library to check out Carson McCullers's *The Member of the Wedding*; **however,** another reader had already checked out the library's only copy.

- **between items in a series when the items contain commas**

  EXAMPLE    This summer I read three great books: *The House on Mango Street,* a collection of short stories by Sandra Cisneros; *Pacific Crossing,* a novel by Gary Soto; and *The Piano Lesson,* a play by August Wilson.

**sentence** A sentence is a group of words that contains a subject and a verb and expresses a complete thought. (See page 413.)

                      **S**     **V**

EXAMPLE    The leaves scattered on the autumn wind.

**sentence fragment** A sentence fragment is a group of words that is punctuated as if it were a complete sentence but that does not contain both a subject and a verb or that does not express a complete thought. (See page 320.)

FRAGMENT    The spider monkey, found chiefly in Costa Rica and Nicaragua.

SENTENCE    The spider monkey, found chiefly in Costa Rica and Nicaragua, is an endangered species.

**simple sentence** A simple sentence has one independent clause and no subordinate clauses. (See page 481.)

EXAMPLES    Dr. Mae C. Jemison is an astronaut.

                  Who first walked in space?

*sit, set* (See page 540.)

EXAMPLES    The music students **sat** quietly, enjoying a sonata by Frédéric Chopin. [past tense of *sit*]

                  The music director **set** the sheet music on each student's desk. [past tense of *set*]

***slow, slowly*** (See page 576.)

EXAMPLE    Proceeding **slowly** [not *slow*] through the food court, the mariachi band played festive music to entertain the diners.

**stringy sentence** A stringy sentence is a sentence that has too many independent clauses. Usually, the clauses are strung together with coordinating conjunctions like *and* or *but*. (See page 340.)

STRINGY    Yesterday afternoon, my friends and I were playing kickball in my backyard, and when Rahm kicked the ball to the fence, we spotted a wren, and it was hobbling on one leg, so I gently picked up the bird and carried it inside to my mother, and she tried hard to make a splint for the injured leg, but she was unsuccessful, so finally she and I decided to take the wren to our veterinarian.

REVISED    Yesterday afternoon, my friends and I were playing kickball in my backyard. When Rahm kicked the ball to the fence, we spotted a wren hobbling on one leg. I gently picked up the bird and carried it inside to my mother. Although she tried hard to make a splint for the injured leg, she was unsuccessful. Finally, she and I decided to take the wren to our veterinarian.

**subject** The subject tells whom or what a sentence is about. (See page 414.)

EXAMPLE    Isn't the **mayor** going to be there?

**subject complement** A subject complement is a word or word group that completes the meaning of a linking verb and identifies or modifies the subject. (See page 429.)

EXAMPLE    My grandfather, who is usually **cheerful,** is an **optimist.**

**subjunctive mood** The subjunctive mood is used to express a suggestion, a necessity, a condition contrary to fact, or a wish. (See page 543.)

EXAMPLES    It is essential that Luisa **attend** the meeting on Monday. [necessity]

If I **were** you, I would apply for the scholarship. [condition contrary to fact]

Ashley wishes she **were** able to go with you to the Juneteenth picnic. [wish]

**subordinate clause** A subordinate clause (also called a *dependent clause*) has a subject and a verb but does not express a complete thought and cannot stand alone as a sentence. (See page 471. See also **adjective clause, adverb clause,** and **noun clause.**)

EXAMPLE    **After they had dinner,** they sat on the porch and remembered old times.

**suffix** A suffix is a word part that is added after a base word or root. (See page 735.)

EXAMPLES    brave + ly = brave**ly**          kind + ness = kind**ness**

happy + ness = happi**ness**          obey + ing = obey**ing**

drop + ed = dropp**ed**          dream + er = dream**er**

**tense of verbs** The tense of verbs indicates the time of the action or the state of being expressed by a verb. (See page 528.)

**Present Tense**

| I give | we give |
| you give | you give |
| he, she, it gives | they give |

**Past Tense**

| I gave | we gave |
| you gave | you gave |
| he, she, it gave | they gave |

**Future Tense**

| I will (shall) give | we will (shall) give |
| you will (shall) give | you will (shall) give |
| he, she, it will (shall) give | they will (shall) give |

**Present Perfect Tense**

| I have given | we have given |
| you have given | you have given |
| he, she, it has given | they have given |

*(continued)*

*(continued)*

**Past Perfect Tense**

| | |
|---|---|
| I had given | we had given |
| you had given | you had given |
| he, she, it had given | they had given |

**Future Perfect Tense**

| | |
|---|---|
| I will (shall) have given | we will (shall) have given |
| you will (shall) have given | you will (shall) have given |
| he, she, it will (shall) have given | they will (shall) have given |

**transitive verb** A transitive verb is an action verb that takes an object. (See page 386.)

EXAMPLE    Ms. Southall **excused** me when I **explained** the situation.

**underlining** (See **Italics**.)

**verb** A verb expresses an action or a state of being. (See page 386.)

EXAMPLES    The waters of the Brahmaputra River **flow** from the Himalayan snows.

He **is** happy.

**verbal** A verbal is a verb form used as an adjective, a noun, or an adverb. (See page 449.)

EXAMPLES    **Chattering** and **screaming,** the monkeys disappeared into the treetops.

I especially enjoyed the **dancing.**

Is that hard **to see?**

**verbal phrase** A verbal phrase consists of a verbal and its modifiers and complements. (See page 449. See also **participial phrase, gerund phrase,** and **infinitive phrase.**)

EXAMPLES    **Pleased to see his master,** Alf the dachshund wagged his tail vigorously.

**Studying together** helps me.

He'd like **to give Ella a gift.**

**U**
**V**

**verb phrase** A verb phrase consists of a main verb and at least one helping verb. (See page 391.)

EXAMPLE     Strange as it **may seem, I have** never **eaten** an avocado.

**voice** Voice is the form a transitive verb takes to indicate whether the subject of the verb performs or receives the action. (See pages 535.)

ACTIVE VOICE     Steven Spielberg **directed** the movie.
PASSIVE VOICE     The movie **was directed** by Steven Spielberg.

**weak reference** A weak reference is the incorrect use of a pronoun to refer to an antecedent that has not been expressed. (See page 565.)

WEAK     I was surprised to learn that my aunt Frances, who is a programmer for a computer company, does not have one in her home.

REVISED     I was surprised to learn that my aunt Frances, who is a programmer for a computer company, does not have a computer in her home.

**well** (See *good, well.*)

**who, whom** (See page 559.)

EXAMPLES     Enrique, **who** had applied for a part-time job at the animal clinic, asked me to write a letter of recommendation.

Enrique, **whom** I had recommended for a part-time job at the animal clinic, learned today that he will start working this weekend.

**wordiness** Wordiness is the use of more words than necessary or the use of fancy words where simple ones will do. (See page 341.)

WORDY     In spite of the fact that my friend Akira, who is my best friend, is moving to another state, we think that, in our opinion, we will continue to remain good friends due to the fact that we have so much in common.

REVISED     Although Akira, my best friend, is moving to another state, we think we will remain good friends because we have so much in common.

# Diagramming Appendix

## Diagramming Sentences

A ***sentence diagram*** is a picture of how the parts of a sentence fit together and how the words in a sentence are related.

### Subjects and Verbs

**Reference Note**

For more about **subjects** and **verbs,** see page 414.

The sentence diagram begins with a horizontal line intersected by a short vertical line that divides the complete subject from the complete predicate.

EXAMPLE    Fish swim.

| Fish | swim |
|------|------|

┌─**H E L P**─

Notice that a sentence diagram shows the capitalization but not the punctuation of a sentence.

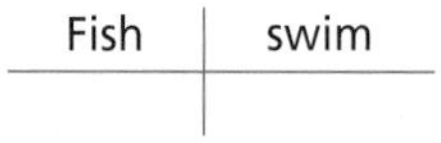

### Understood Subjects

EXAMPLE    Wait!

| (you) | Wait |
|-------|------|

**Reference Note**

For information about **understood subjects,** see page 423.

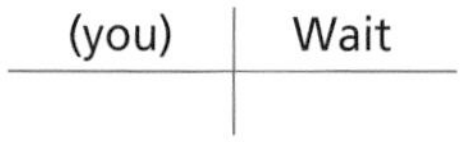

## Nouns of Direct Address

EXAMPLE    Sit, **Fido.**

```
                    Fido
         ┌──────────────────────┐
         │ (you)  │  Sit
         └────────┴─────────────
```

**Reference Note**

For information about **nouns of direct address,** see page 656.

## Sentences Beginning with *There*

EXAMPLE    **There** is hope.

```
                    There
         ┌──────────────────────┐
         │  hope  │  is
         └────────┴─────────────
```

**Reference Note**

For information about **sentences beginning with *there*,** see page 422.

## Compound Subjects

EXAMPLE    **Carmen** and **Basil** were fishing.

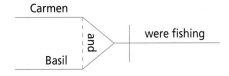

## Compound Verbs

EXAMPLE    They **stopped** and **ate.**

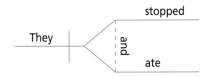

**Reference Note**

For more about **compound subjects,** see page 424. For more about **compound verbs,** see page 425.

The following diagram shows how a compound verb is diagrammed when the helping verb is not repeated.

EXAMPLE    They are **sitting** and **reading.**

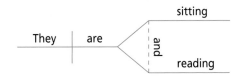

## Compound Subjects and Compound Verbs

EXAMPLE **Coaches** and **players jumped** and **cheered.**

Sometimes the parts of a compound subject or a compound verb are joined by correlative conjunctions. Correlatives are diagrammed like this:

EXAMPLE **Both** Bob **and** Teri can **not only** draw **but also** paint.

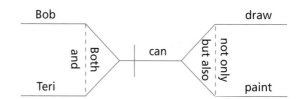

# Adjectives and Adverbs

**Reference Note**

For more about **adjectives,** see page 382. For more about **adverbs,** see page 393.

Both adjectives and adverbs are written on slanted lines connected to the words they modify.

EXAMPLE **That old** clock has **never** worked.

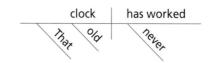

When an adverb modifies an adjective or an adverb, it is placed on a line connected to the word it modifies.

EXAMPLE This **very** beautiful glass **almost** never breaks.

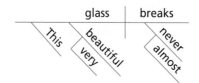

Notice the position of the modifiers in the following example:

EXAMPLE    **Soon** Anne and **her** sister will graduate and will move.

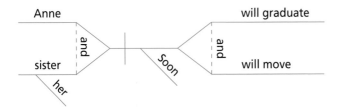

Above, *her* modifies only one part of the compound subject: *sister*. *Soon* modifies both parts of the compound verb: *will graduate* and *will move*.

When a conjunction joins two modifiers, it is diagrammed like this:

EXAMPLE    The **English** and **Australian** athletes worked **long** and **very hard**.

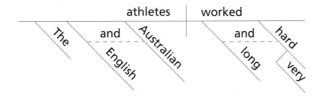

# Subject Complements

The subject complement is placed on the horizontal line with the subject and verb. It comes after the verb. A slanted line separates the subject complement from the linking verb.

## Predicate Nominatives

EXAMPLE    Cathedrals are large **churches.**

**Reference Note**

For more about **predicate nominatives,** see page 430.

## Predicate Adjectives

**Reference Note**

For more about **predicate adjectives,** see page 430.

EXAMPLE    Cathedrals are **large.**

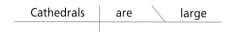

## Compound Subject Complements

EXAMPLE    My friend is **small** and **quiet.**

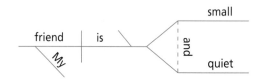

# Objects

## Direct Objects

**Reference Note**

For more about **direct objects,** see page 431.

A vertical line separates a direct object from the verb.

EXAMPLE    We like **music.**

## Compound Direct Objects

EXAMPLE    We like **plays** and **movies.**

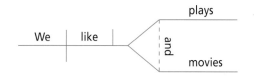

## Indirect Objects

**Reference Note**

For more about **indirect objects,** see page 432.

The indirect object is diagrammed on a horizontal line beneath the verb.

EXAMPLE    Pete bought **Mario** a sandwich.

## Compound Indirect Objects

EXAMPLE    Latoya gave her **family** and **friends** free tickets.

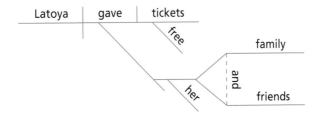

# Phrases

## Prepositional Phrases

**Reference Note**

For more information about **prepositional phrases,** see page 442.

The preposition is placed on a line slanting down from the word the phrase modifies. The object of the preposition is placed on a horizontal line connected to the slanting line.

EXAMPLES    **By chance,** a peasant uncovered a wall **of ancient Pompeii.** [*By chance* is an adverb phrase modifying the verb; *of ancient Pompeii* is an adjective phrase modifying the direct object.]

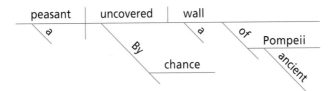

Our team practices late **in the afternoon.** [adverb phrase modifying an adverb]

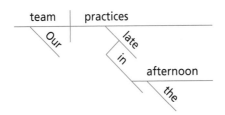

They drove **through the Maine woods** and **into southern Canada.** [two phrases modifying the same word]

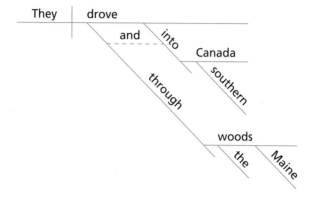

Mom taught the game **to my father, my uncles, and me.** [compound object of preposition]

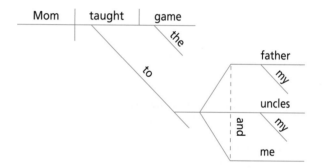

Follow the signs **to Highway 3 in Laconia.** [*In Laconia* is a prepositional phrase modifying the object of another preposition.]

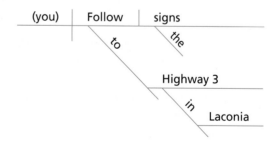

## Participles and Participial Phrases

EXAMPLES    I found him **crying.**

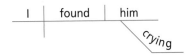

**Reference Note**

For more information about **participles** and **participial phrases,** see page 449.

**Wagging its tail,** the large dog leaped at me.

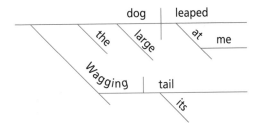

Notice that *tail,* the direct object of the participle *Wagging,* is diagrammed like any other complement.

## Gerunds and Gerund Phrases

EXAMPLES    **Walking** is healthful exercise. [gerund used as subject]

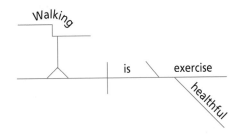

**Reference Note**

For more about **gerunds** and **gerund phrases,** see page 453.

**The constant cold** is a good reason for **taking a vacation in the winter.** [gerund phrase used as an object of preposition]

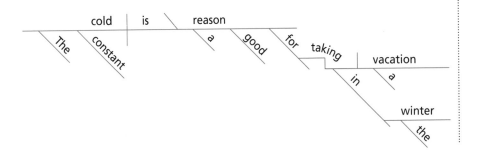

Reference Note

For more information about **infinitives** and **infinitive phrases,** see page 457.

## Infinitives and Infinitive Phrases

EXAMPLES    **To leave** would be rude. [infinitive used as subject]

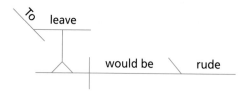

**To join the Air Force** is her longtime ambition.
[infinitive phrase used as subject]

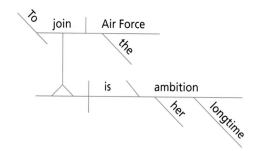

Infinitives and infinitive phrases used as modifiers are diagrammed much as prepositional phrases are.

EXAMPLES    I am happy **to help.**

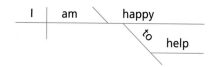

I am leaving early **to get the tickets.** [infinitive phrase used as adverb]

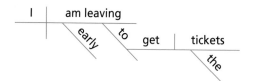

## Appositives and Appositive Phrases

Place the appositive in parentheses after the word it identifies or explains.

EXAMPLES    My brother **Josh** is a drummer in the band.

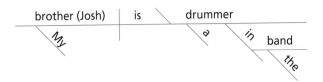

**Reference Note**

For more information about **appositives** and **appositive phrases,** see page 461.

The next show, **a musical comedy,** was written by Mike Williams, **a talented young playwright.**

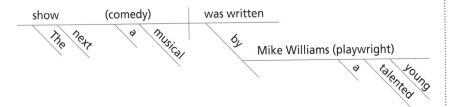

# Subordinate Clauses

## Adjective Clauses

An adjective clause is joined to the word it modifies by a broken line leading from the relative pronoun to the modified word.

**Reference Note**

For more about **adjective clauses,** see page 473.

EXAMPLES    The restaurant **that we like best** serves excellent seafood.

He is the teacher **from whom I take lessons.**

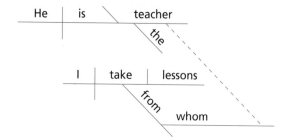

**Reference Note**

For more about **adverb clauses,** see page 476.

## Adverb Clauses

Place the subordinating conjunction that introduces the adverb clause on a broken line leading from the verb in the adverb clause to the word the clause modifies.

EXAMPLE  **If you visit Texas,** you should see the Alamo.

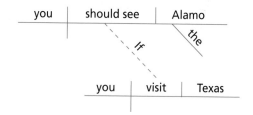

**Reference Note**

For more about **noun clauses,** see page 478.

## Noun Clauses

Noun clauses often begin with introductory words such as *that, what, who,* or *which.* These introductory words may have a function within the subordinate clause, or they may simply connect the clause to the rest of the sentence. How a noun clause is diagrammed depends upon its use in the sentence. It also depends on whether or not the introductory word has a grammatical function in the noun clause.

EXAMPLES  **What you eat** affects your health. [The noun clause is used as the subject of the independent clause. The introductory word *What* functions as the direct object of the noun clause.]

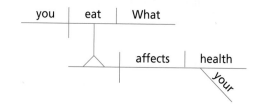

We strongly suspected **that the cat was the thief.** [The noun clause is the direct object of the independent clause. The introductory word *that* does not have a grammatical function within the noun clause.]

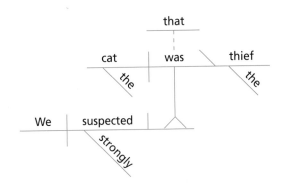

Sometimes the introductory word in a subordinate clause may be omitted. In the example above, the word *that* can be left out: *We strongly suspected the cat was the thief.* To diagram this new sentence, simply omit the word *that* and the solid and broken lines under it from the diagram above. The rest of the diagram stays the same.

# Sentences Classified According to Structure

## Simple Sentences

EXAMPLES    George Vancouver was exploring the Northwest.

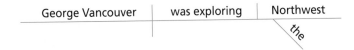

Cities in Washington and British Columbia are named for him.

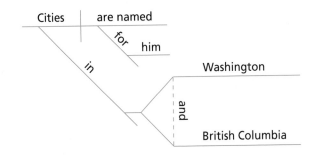

**Reference Note**

For more about **simple sentences,** see page 481.

**Reference Note**

For more information about **compound sentences,** see page 481.

## Compound Sentences

EXAMPLE    James Baldwin wrote many essays, but he is probably more famous for his novels.

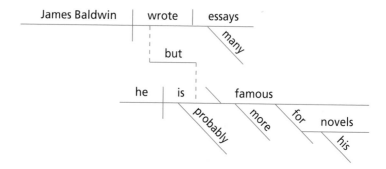

If the compound sentence has a semicolon and no conjunction, place a straight broken line between the two verbs.

EXAMPLE    Baldwin was a distinguished essayist; his nonfiction works include *Notes of a Native Son.*

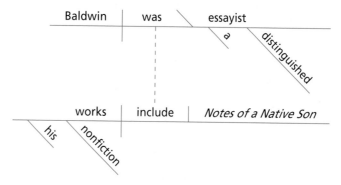

If the clauses of a compound sentence are joined by a semicolon and a conjunctive adverb, place the conjunctive adverb on a slanting line below the verb it modifies.

EXAMPLE    Baldwin was born in New York; however, he lived in France for nearly ten years.

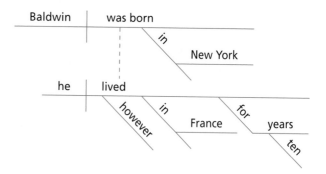

## Complex Sentences

EXAMPLE    Jaime Escalante always believed that his students could do well in math.

**Reference Note**

For more about **complex sentences,** see page 482.

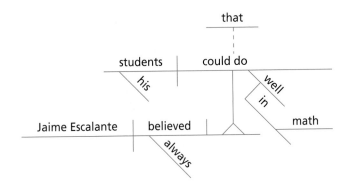

## Compound-Complex Sentences

EXAMPLE    Before her plane mysteriously disappeared in 1937, Amelia Earhart had already forged the way for women in aviation, and she was later recognized for her achievements.

**Reference Note**

For more about **compound-complex sentences,** see page 482.

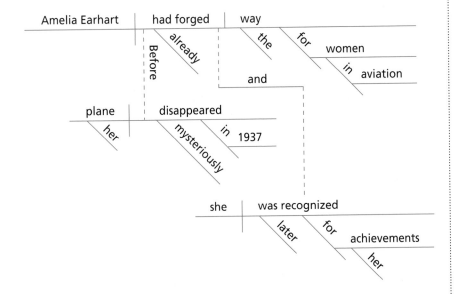

**B**

*Bad, badly,* 575, 906
**Bar graphs, definition of,** 816, 839
**Base form,** 517–18, 906
*Be,* **forms of,** 388
*Because, reason,* 605
*Become,* **principal parts of,** 520
*Begin,* **principal parts of,** 520
**Believability.** *See also* **Credibility**
　　persuasive speaking and, 279
*Beside, besides,* 597
*Between, among,* 597
**Bias**
　　definition of, 880
　　gender bias in advertisements, 277
**Billboard, designing of,** 281
**Biographical and geographical entries, in dictionaries,**
　　805
*Bird Feeder Book, The* (Stokes & Stokes), 353
**"Birds, The"** (du Maurier), 356
**Block method of ordering comparison/contrast article,**
　　88, 104–105
*Blow,* **principal parts of,** 520
*Borrow, lend, loan,* 598
**Brackets,** 726, 906
**Brainstorming**
　　causes and effects, 123
　　guidelines for, 897
*Brake, break,* 747
*Break,* **principal parts of,** 520
*Bring,* **principal parts of,** 520
*Bring, take,* 598
**Broadcasting, definition of,** 876
**Brooks, Gwendolyn,** 79–80, 173
*Build,* **principal parts of,** 520
**Bulletin boards, on Internet,** 117
**Bullets, definition of,** 807
*Burst,* **principal parts of,** 520
**Business letters.** *See also* **Letters** (correspondence)
　　formal Standard English in, 615
　　parts of, 887–89
　　punctuation in, 676, 681
　　types of, 888–89
**Business texts.** *See also* **Business letters**
　　field notes, 45
*Bust, busted,* 598
*Buy,* **principal parts of,** 520
**Byline, definition of,** 115, 884

**C**

**Cable television,** 877
**Call numbers, definition of,** 823
**Call outs, definition of,** 807
**Camera angles**
　　definition of, 877
　　for videotaping, 48
*Can, may,* 600
*Capital, capitol,* 747
**Capitalization**
　　of abbreviations, 621, 906
　　of awards, 626
　　of brand names, 625
　　of businesses, 625
　　of calendar items, 624
　　common nouns and, 620
　　in direct quotations, 687
　　family relationship words and, 629
　　of first words, 618, 906
　　of geographical names, 621–22
　　of government bodies, 623
　　of historical events and periods, 624
　　of holidays, 624
　　of hyphenated numbers, 622
　　of initials after names, 621
　　of institutions, 623
　　of interjection *O,* 619
　　in letter writing, 619
　　of manuscript titles and subtitles, 630–31
　　of monuments, 626
　　of names consisting of more than one word, 621
　　of names of holy celebrations, sacred writings, 625
　　of names of people, 620–21
　　of names of religions and their followers, 625
　　of nationalities, races, peoples, 625
　　of organizations, 623
　　of planets and heavenly bodies, 625
　　in poetry, 618
　　of pronoun *I,* 619
　　of proper adjectives, 620–26, 620
　　of proper nouns, 620–26, 620, 906
　　rules for, 616–31
　　of school subjects, 628
　　in sentences, 618
　　of ships, 626
　　of special events, 624
　　of specific deities, 625
　　of teams, 623
　　of titles, 629, 907
**Capital letters, in document design,** 810
**Captions, definition of,** 810
**Card catalog, definition of,** 212, 823

**The New York Times Company:** From "Topics: The Sounds of Manhattan" (retitled "The Sounds of the City") by James Tuite from *The New York Times,* August 6, 1966. Copyright © 1966 by The New York Times Company. From "Bananas for Rent" by Michiko Kakutani from *New York Times Magazine,* November 9, 1997. Copyright © 1997 by The New York Times Company.

**Random House, Inc.:** From *Extinction: The Causes and Consequences of the Disappearance of Species* by Paul and Anne Ehrlich. Copyright © 1981 by Paul R. Ehrlich and Anne H. Ehrlich.

**John Seabrook:** From "Born Slippy" by John Seabrook from *The New Yorker,* January 12, 1998. Copyright © 1998 by John Seabrook.

**Kathy Svitil:** "Hot times in the operating room" by Kathy Svitil from *Discover,* vol. 17, no. 11, November 1996. Copyright © 1996 by Kathy A. Svitil.

**Tribune Media Services International:** From "Time Out! Is Baseball Finnished?" by Bob Secter from *The Miami Herald,* August 3, 1990. Copyright © 1990 by Los Angeles Times Syndicate.

**University of Connecticut as Executor of the Estate of Edwin Way Teale:** From "The Death of a Tree" from *Dune Boy* by Edwin Way Teale. Copyright 1943, © 1971 by Edwin Way Teale.

**Viking Penguin, a division of Penguin Putnam Inc.:** From *Rebound: The Odyssey of Michael Jordan* by Bob Greene. Copyright © 1995 by John Deadline Enterprises, Inc.

**The Washington Post Writers Group:** From "Dirty play is wrong, but, hey, let 'em play" by William Raspberry from *The Washington Post,* June 22, 1998, p. A21. Copyright © 1998 by The Washington Post Writers Group.

**Nancy Willard:** From "Ding-Dong Bell: 'Ariel's Song' from *The Tempest* by William Shakespeare" by Nancy Willard from *Touchstones: American Poets on a Favorite Poem,* edited by Robert Pack and Jay Parini. Copyright © 1996 by Nancy Willard.

**The H. W. Wilson Company:** Entries from "Crown Books Corporation" to "Crude Oil" from *Readers' Guide to Periodical Literature,* February 1999. Copyright © 1999 by the H. W. Wilson Company.

## SOURCES CITED:

From "Peak Flow Meters" and from "85% of Americans Don't Know the Air in Their Homes May Be Hazardous to Their Health" from *The American Lung Association* Web site, accessed March 24, 1999, at http://www.lungusa.org.

From *Hoop Dreams: A True Story of Hardship and Triumph* by Ben Joravsky. Published by Kartemquin Educational Films, Inc., Chicago, 1995.

From entry "Emoticon" from *New Words in English* by Suzanne Kemmer. Published on *Rice University* Web site, at http://www.owlnet.rice.edu/ling215/NewWords/index.html, 1999.

From "The Granddaddy of the Nation's Trails Began in Mexico" by Douglas Preston from *Smithsonian,* vol. 26, no. 8, November 1995. Published by Smithsonian Institution, Washington, D.C., 1995.

From "What is a mummy?" from *Mummies, Myth and Magic in Ancient Egypt* by Christine El Mahdy. Published by Thames & Hudson Ltd., 1989.

# PHOTO CREDITS

Abbreviations used: (tl)top left, (tc)top center, (tr)top right, (l)left, (cl)center left, (c)center, (cr)center right, (r)right, (bl)bottom left, (bc)bottom center, (br)bottom right.

**COVER:** Scott Van Osdol/HRW Photo.

**TABLE OF CONTENTS:** Page viii, Eric Meola/Getty Images/The Image Bank; ix, Joel Nakamura/ The Stock Illustration Source, Inc.; x, John Lawrence/Getty Images/Stone; xiii, Todd Davidson/Getty Images/The Image Bank; xiv, EDF/Ad Council; xv, John Langford/HRW Photo; xvi, Peter Steiner/Corbis Stock Market; xvii, K.G. Vock/Okapia, 1989/Photo Researchers, Inc.; xviii, Scala/Art Resource, NY; xix, Pat Street; xx, Jerez/Viesti Collection; xxi, Image Copyright ©2001 Photodisc, Inc.; xxii, Image Copyright ©2001 Photodisc, Inc.; xxiii, Shaker Village of Pleasant Hill; xxiv, Pete Saloutos/Corbis Stock Market; xxv, The Granger Collection, New York; xxvi, Louis Psihoyos/Matrix International; xxvii, Jerome Wexler/Photo Researchers, Inc.; xxviii, Image Copyright ©2001 Photodisc, Inc.

**PART OPENERS:** Page xxxiv, 1, 318, 319, 372, 373, 802, 803, ©Dave Cutler/The Stock Illustration Source, Inc.

**TAKING TESTS:** Page 2, Digital Image copyright ©2004 EyeWire; 4, Brandon D. Cole/CORBIS; 7, Amos Nachoum/CORBIS.

**CHAPTER 1:** Page 16, Eric Meola/Getty Images/The Image Bank; 20, Joseph Pobereskin/Getty Images/Stone.

**CHAPTER 2:** Page 50, ©Joel Nakamura/ The Stock Illustration Source, Inc; 53, Image Copyright ©2001 PhotoDisc, Inc.; 55, Bob Krist/Black Star; 70, Phillip Colla/Peter Arnold, Inc.; 82, (cl) (c) (cr), Randal Alhadeff/HRW Photo.

**CHAPTER 3:** Page 86, John Lawrence/Getty Images/Stone; 90, CORBIS/Philip Gould; 115, Pittsburgh Tribune-Review.

**CHAPTER 4:** Page 126 (bl), Larry Mulvehill/Photo Researchers, Inc.; 126 (br), Augustine Medical, Inc.; 149, S.S. Archives/Shooting Star International.

**CHAPTER 5:** Page 161, Ferdinand Lured by Ariel, 1849 (panel) by Sir John Everett Millais (1829-96)/The Makins Collection/Bridgeman Art Library, London/New York.

**CHAPTER 6:** Page 194, Todd Davidson/Image Bank; 199, (t) (br), UPI/Corbis-Bettmann; 226, (tl), AFP/CORBIS; 226 (tr), Reuters/Tom Szlukovenyi/Archive Photos.

**CHAPTER 7:** Page 246, EDF/Ad Council; 249, Eric Brissaud/Gamma Liason.

**CHAPTER 8:** Page 282, John Langford/HRW Photo.

**CHAPTER 9:** Page 321, Culver Pictures, Inc.; 323, Archive Photos; 328, HRW Photo Research Library; 329, Bettmann/CORBIS.

**CHAPTER 10:** Page 332, Fotos International/Hulton Archive/Getty Images; 333 (cr), Ted Horowitz/The Stock Market; 333 (tr), Seidman/HRW Photo Library; 334, Michael Krasowitz/Getty Images/FPG; 336, Ray Manley/SuperStock; 338, James D. Watt/ Mo Yung Productions/Norbert Wu; 339, SuperStock; 341, Doug Armand/Getty Images/Stone; 344, K.G. Vock/Okapia, 1989/Photo Researchers, Inc.; 345, Zandria Muench/Getty Images/Stone.

**CHAPTER 11:** Page 349, Joe McDonald/Animals Animals/Earth Scenes; 350, David R. Frazier Photo Library; 354, Andrew D. Bernstein/Allsport; 356, Phillip Colla; 358, Hulton Archive/Getty Images; 362, British Museum, London; 364, Peter Steiner/The Stock Market; 367, Waterford.

**CHAPTER 12:** Page 378, Walter Choroszewski; 381, Culver Pictures Inc./SuperStock; 395, John Lemker/Earth Scenes; 399, SuperStock.

**CHAPTER 13:** Page 415, Fairfield Processing Corp.; 428, 432, 436, Image Copyright ©2001 Photodisc, Inc.

**CHAPTER 14:** Page 445 (tr) (br), John Harrison; 448 (cr) (br), Hulton Archive/Getty Images; 456, *Cartooning Fundamentals,* Al Ross, Stravon; 460, HRW Photo Research Library; 461, Southern Pacific Photo; 463, Culver Pictures, Inc.

**CHAPTER 15:** Page 472, Robert E. Daemmrich/Getty Images/Stone; 478; Hulton Archive/Getty Images; 480, Eadweard Muybridge/Culver Pictures, Inc.; 483, International Museum of Children's Art, Oslo, Norway; 484, Jerome Wexler/Photo Researchers, Inc.; 486 (bl) (br), Courtesy of Ursula Gibson.

**CHAPTER 16:** Page 492, Torquay Natural History Society; 494, (cl) (l) (bl) (bc), Kodansha International Ltd.; 498, Copyright 1905 Fred Harvey; 504, Eric Beggs/HRW Photo; 510, Image Copyright ©2001 Photodisc, Inc.

**CHAPTER 17:** Page 524, Richard Tomkins/Liaison International; 527, Marian Anderson/Culver Pictures, Inc.; 534, Image Copyright ©2001 Photodisc, Inc.; 538, Image Copyright ©2001 Photodisc, Inc.; 542, The Granger Collection, New York; 544, Prairie Fires and Paper Moons: The American Photographic Postcard:1900-1920, Hal Morgan and Andreas Brown, David R. Godine (Publisher), Boston, 1981.

**CHAPTER 18:** Page 551, Brown Brothers; 556, 557, David R. Frazier Photolibrary; 563 (tr), Scala/Art Resource, NY; 563 (br), National Portrait Gallery, London/SuperStock; 566, Image Copyright ©2001 Photodisc, Inc.

**CHAPTER 19:** Page 575, Image Copyright ©2001 Photodisc, Inc.; 580, Jerez/Viesti Collection; 584 (cl), Gary Griffen/Animals Animals/Earth Scenes; 584 (bl), Pete Saloutos/The Stock Market; 589, Cosmo Condina/Getty Images/Stone.

**CHAPTER 20:** Page 599, Louis Psihoyos/Matrix International; 602, Andrew Eccles/Alvin Ailey American Dance Theater; 605, Corbis Images; 608, Eric Brissaud/Gamma Liaison.

**CHAPTER 21:** Page 627, Random House, Inc.

**CHAPTER 22:** Page 651, Gutzon Borglum/Getty Images/FPG; 654, The Newark Museum/Art Resource, NY; 658, Image Copyright ©2001 Photodisc, Inc.

**CHAPTER 23:** Page 669 (cr), CORBIS/Philip Gould; 669 (br), Library of Congress/HRW; 671, Image Copyright ©2001 Photodisc, Inc.; 673, Doug Perrine/Innerspace Visions Photography; 675, Texas Department of Transportaion.

**CHAPTER 24:** Page 689, Christie's Images, London, UK/Bridgeman Art Library, London/New York; 694, Image Copyright ©2001 Photodisc, Inc.

**CHAPTER 25:** Page 702, The Stock Market; 704, 705, Shaker Village of Pleasant Hill, KY; 709, Joe Viesti/Viesti Associates, Inc.

**CHAPTER 26:** Page 723, One Mile Up, Inc.; 724, HRW Photo Library/courtesy Gibbs Memorial Library, Mexia, Texas.

**CHAPTER 27:** Page 735, Pat Street; 739, Gutzon Borglum/Getty Images/FPG; 749, Image Copyright ©2001 Photodisc, Inc.

**CHAPTER 28:** Page 769, 773, Image Copyright ©2001 Photodisc, Inc.; 774, ©1997 Radlund & Associates for Artville; 776, Image Copyright ©2001 Photodisc, Inc.; 777, Mary Miller/HRW Photo; 789, 792, Image Copyright ©2001 Photodisc, Inc.

**QUICK REFERENCE HANDBOOK:** 817 (tl), CORBIS.

## ILLUSTRATION CREDITS

**TABLE OF CONTENTS:** Page xi (cl), Franklin Hammond; xii (tl), HRW.

**CHAPTER 1:** Page 47 (b), HRW.

**CHAPTER 2:** Page 57 (br), Leslie Kell.

**CHAPTER 4:** Page 122 (all), Franklin Hammond.

**CHAPTER 5:** Page 156 (all), HRW; 162 (b), Leslie Kell.

**CHAPTER 6:** Page 215 (all), 216 (c), 217 (all), Leslie Kell; 236 (c), HRW.

**CHAPTER 11:** Page 360 (cl), Ortelius Design.

**CHAPTER 12:** Page 408 (c), Leslie Kell; 408 (c), Dory Grace.

**CHAPTER 13:** Page 435 (tr), Joann Daley.

**CHAPTER 14:** Page 452 (cl), Uhl Studios, Inc.

**CHAPTER 15:** Page 475 (tr), Keith Bowden.

**CHAPTER 22:** Page 662 (b), Ortelius Design.

**CHAPTER 25:** Page 710 (bl), Uhl Studios, Inc.

**CHAPTER 27:** Page 733 (c), Leslie Kell; 745 (t), Steve Shock.

**QRH:** Page 832 (cl), David Griffin; 833 (b), HRW; 835 (bl), Keith Bowden; 837 (bl), MapQuest.com, Inc.; 844 (cr), Leslie Kell; 855 (tl), George Kelvin; 914 (cl), HRW.